A Human Venture

A Human Venture

*To Establish A Purely Human
Spirituality And A Way To The
Mysterious More For Our Times*

V. Virom Coppola

To order additional copies of this book, contact:
Xlibris Corporation
1-888-795-4274
www.Xlibris.com
Orders@Xlibris.com
68747

Contents

Dedicated to Joan, Mom, Dad, Jimmy, and all our shaggy
"wolves" and chirping "dinosaurs" down the years.

Introduction

Halfway into life's allotted time for us, I found myself
in a dark mass, a place far from the light, a light that I
sought in vein. It's hard to speak of, what it was like, that
obscure oblique place, so brutal that even to think about
it now grips me with unfocused dread. So bitter, it was
like chilled extinction itself. Yet, still, I want to tell you the
truth I discovered there; and to do so I am forced to tell
you everything I experienced in that visible darkness.

> Dante, *Inferno*, my translation.

The world I have come to realize is a very odd place, certainly an uncertain
place. In point of fact, this whole venture might be a cerebral aberration. Perhaps
consciousness itself is an aberration in the cosmos. Perhaps wisdom after the big
bang is as impossible to get to as before it. Since we do not see the world as it is
in and of itself, but build a mental model on our axons and dendrites, we have
to wonder about our epistemology, about our ethics, about everything really. Yes,
we, you and I, and all of us are alive to the world of our time, and the Principle of
Uncertainty, capitalized or not, is our compass, so we hesitate as if at the edge of
some black hole when it comes to any certainties about heady stuff, and words like
undecidability, anonymity, deconstruction, and the like become all the rage. But
can we, my fellow voyagers in this venture, first and foremost, still dare to reach
a purely human spirituality as mentioned in the title of this work, and, via that,
dare on to make some minuscule sense of . . . call it what you will, the mystery
that surrounds us, the impossible, what some call God, and I merely call more,
or when the wind blows southerly even More, the Mysterious More?

A contemporary venture into Whatever-That-Is seems the last thing we are capable of doing, let alone find a purely human spirituality applicable to all humans at all times, especially ours, when deep reality itself is still a scientific and philosophic riddle for us, and what holds a person together in a person's innermost is more than ever a battleground of paradigms. Am I setting the reader up for inevitable disappointment and this author for utter failure and ridicule? How could we reach a grounding for a universal spirituality without knowing deep reality, let alone what each of us is in our innermost being?

When we consider the vastness of our universe, the billions of island galaxies far too far to travel to, the unknown vistas and possibles, the non-space-time dimension before our own, the mathematical megabrane universes and speculated strumming strings as a starting point of it all, not to mention the labyrinthine journey to find out about our own planet, we must consider the possibility that we do not know the real nature of much of anything, let alone ourselves. We were not easy to produce, after all, we humans. We came out of a misty evolutionary process ending up as conscious matter, conscious matter that was so dependent on so much that was precarious, from a totally chancy beginning to historical constraints at every turn along the way, all of which, as a dead scientist put it, could be so different if we were to roll back the tape and let it evolve all over again. Who knows what creatures still more strange would wiggle in the silence of enormous swamps only to have crawled out as our replacements? Who knows what channelized instincts they would have had? What lurking brains within their heads? As it is, we are a venture within our own heads, a super-organic marvel within each solitary skull that voyaged through billions of genetic filaments to become an "eye-brain" where each of us hangs out and says in a litany of languages, *je suis, io sono, I am*. As I write that and you read it, the human mind that allows for this has now become the uncertain and even precarious means for carrying on its own evolutionary pathway. Such is the next shaky step in evolution. But even before we put our evolutionary foot forward in such a step, there is a shaky one here and now we must take. Although there are those, caught in some cerebral hubris, who pontificate that we are here merely to procreate, one has to ask—to procreate what? There is a part of our humanness that is not fixed instinctually and irrevocably but subject to change, chance, choice, and even the unknown. In everyday life even as we all imagine that we can figure out how to get up in the morning and make it through the day and back to bed again, as we stand before the whole of spacetime and existence itself we have to realize in our most honest moments our fundamental ignorance about so much. And isn't it ironic, the more we get to find out the more we realize we know so little, as if some joke on us. So what do we do—stop this venture? Can we? Or in all this is there something deeper still in us that has come with us from the beginning, through the reptilian stem and mammalian middle and frontal leaps that has to be sought and fought for? Something more? And we are restless until we find it, whatever it is.

Yes, there is so much in the great venture of being we know so little about, including ourselves. Even more so the mystery that made us, no not mom and dad, I am talking about the ultimate Mystery, call it what you will. Yet, like with ourselves, that quest has been with us since the caves. Maybe before. Is there a built-in biological urge in us to mount the stars, whether manifested in Mayan mathematicians or modern Magi and their megabranes, and all this because we are looking for the Mystery that made us? But I have to ask; in trying to find a way to this Mystery, the second part of our endeavor, am I or any of you who come along on this whale of a hunt as mad as Ahab? For in order to venture to the Mystery that made us wouldn't we have to journey past the stars to before the big bang, to a nowhere out of which a somewhere came, a nothing out of which a something came? One has to admit that might be a bit much; certainly at least bordering on the insane to even attempt it, for it is an impossible feat to know what is incomprehensible, to talk about a Mystery which is beyond us, of an Enigma which conjures up only linguistic annihilation, of a Secret which resists our mortal towers of science and telescopes and leaves us looking up at the night sky in a desperate encounter between our human effort and non-space-time's Anonymous Silence.

How can we, who are something and somewhere, venture to nowhere and nothing? We can't even conjure up a notion of nowhere and nothing! We can only think as space-time creatures and merely apply those words, *nowhere* and *nothing*, to we know not what. You can't expect us to know a nothing and nowhere any more than you can a fish in the Hudson to imagine Manhattan, though you say the word over and over and over again to the Striped Bass avoiding his weekend killer from Manhattan. One can only rationally conclude that the author is, as many scholars, saints, and scoundrels have whispered with wry smiles and sophisticated smirks, a complete clown, and this work a worthless tower of babble and not wisdom after the big bang at all.

Give up all hope those who enter here? Is that the fate of not only the author, but also humanity itself grappling and galumphing for a God, especially an understandable one? Even if we say there must be a Source behind it all, what could it possibly (or impossibly) be? Really, does any talk of God become the Jabberwocky, *ou le Jasseroque, oder der Jammerwoch*? Is any real theology, any real talk of God, dead, and God with it? Does such a Mystery merely become the complete Other, period? No more to be said?

That does indeed leave our view on God nowhere, and indeed nothing more can be said.

And yet, our view is not from nowhere. A view from nowhere would require us to have an unbirthday; but unless I am mistaken you have one, and me, too, and everyone who ever was or is, and so just maybe something more can be said out of this somewhere. Granted it has all the comic agony of Luigi's silly six creatures in search of an Author, or, indeed, Alice falling through the hole in her head, and that has to keep us hermeneutically humble with regards the text and subtext of existence, especially as we venture to understand the Unseen, Unoriginated, Uncreated, Unborn, Unformed, Uneverything! But existence is all we have. So, in the riverrun we call life, in the uncertainty of it all, in this perilous perhaps of breathing and the dark swamps that still swim within us, can contemporary humanity come up with *one minimal certainty*, and, if we can, can we finally in that, despite the swarming multiplicity of religions and ethics, moralities and baffling bushidos, not to mention string, balloon, and megabrane theories, discover the grounding for a purely human spirituality, one which, besides showing us how to truly act as humans, can dare to venture into sensing something of the Mystery that made us, dare to make the impossible possible? That is the double-helix question and quest before us; using the only thing we have, our existence. Existence alone! My somewhat sort of postmodern mind tells me to be careful here. It plagues me with questions that holler throughout the hallways of my head. "Why can I think up better worlds than exist?" the right hemisphere of my brain yells out. "And since I can, will I do the same here with regards a More?" the left yells back. "Think up a better one than could ever possibly be?" a holistic hundred billion neurons respond in an interconnection of brain cells greater in number than the number of atoms in the universe. No I am not swellheaded; all our heads have as much. And like every other head as well I am caught in contradictions and contradictions of those contradictions.

Let me catch my cerebral breath here and state what I honestly feel. I have an expectation without knowing what I expect. The revelation of something! A message that will arrive, or one that doesn't, but is still meaningful. I have seen beauty, witnessed goodness, and known love. And in it all, I have sensed something mysteriously more about my life, the undertones in me of something numinous, of something strange and queer to it all, if the truth be known, something like a sensed providence; and with all that still, a somewhat sort of Presence. And yet, the opposite is true as well, for I cannot deny the undertones of something cosmological that threatens, something missing, without being able to say what it is, sometimes only a fear of futility and at others a melancholy in matter itself. One that tells me I am such stuff as dreams are made on, and my little life is to be rounded with a little death, unnoticed in the cosmos. One that tells me that I am nothing more than a psychic crystallization around an abyss, alive to a universe, a world, an existence without ultimate grounding—afloat in the face of just what happens, at the mercy of chance, chaos, or the universal contingency, alone alas along the riverrun. Perhaps, we conscious creatures cannot face that, because it is too awful.

Of course, the opposite might be true, that we cannot accept such an awful actuality because it is not actually so, and a wordless wisdom tells us so. Half my mind says one thing, the other half another, and a third half says carry on "as if!" Life leaves us in such a strange place.

So can we *through existence alone,* and by the skin of our truth, without being crazy or on Clown Alley, but with a certain madness still and seeming clownbursts because of it, with all our baggage on board, establish a purely human spirituality applicable to all humans and thus honestly know how to act in the face and fact of the cosmos? And accomplishing that first impossible, can we, using it as our grounding, climb the other helix and authentically know the Impossible? As humans uncomfortable with the answers of the past, and with those of our own age as well, that is the venture before us.

And yet . . . and yet I hesitate . . . yet again.

"Why this time?" I hear somewhere in my head complain. I hesitate—not because I think for a moment that the butterfly I dream of is the really real and me the dream. I know I bleed and those I love die for real. I know children starve to death and creatures of all sorts suffer for real! No, we are not here to play word games, like that old butterfly bon mot. We are here to face existence, head on. Existence alone! And that is the problem. Doesn't the fact of children starving to death and creatures of all sorts suffering tell us from existence alone—already—that we are alone, alone in this cosmos! It is a moment of shivering thought, to be alone in this cosmos. We need whatever bit of broken shelter we can find as we face this winter gripping at the marrow of our bones, this abyss in our stomachs. It is why I hesitate, hesitate to trust in any transcendence or trance thereof that is devoid of life and living, or hesitate to spend time on what seems a waste of it. I remember an event in my twenties, when alone with my thoughts on a winter walk, I came upon a stray dog couched behind an old gravestone in a graveyard that went back to the Revolutionary War, a bitter temperature falling towards death for the old furry canine. I wanted to save him with everything in me, but when I got to the suffering creature, he just looked up at me and my heart broke for I knew it was too late. In that moment I saw the snow turn yellow with urine and the shaking creature gasp a long shocked instant and then defecate. There had been no caring God for him. He had survived alone and now died alone, and I was expected to go back to Saint Andrew's and pray. Where is the wisdom in that? Aren't we all that animal in truth? The Mystery that made us is not the Good Samaritan. Wasn't that what existence was saying, showing in that graveyard? Isn't all my writing, my philosophizing, my theologizing, my praying merely a piece of music in the winter wind? My computer has to glitch with what it is typing out across my I-Mac screen . . . Is all that is left for us merely to live as if it made a difference . . . when in truth it doesn't? A sense of loss lingers with that thought. "Would I be a savior of a world where no salvation exists?" Isn't that Christ's real prayer—and mine? Socrates' search finally realized as meaningless? Γνωθι σεαυτον (*know thyself*) a bad joke? Yes, isn't it all merely music in the winter wind?

My computer pauses and I with it. "Isn't that what this venture will tell us, one way or another?" a billion brain cells blast out in my head. "What it is about? To see what it is all about? See why you and I and everyone with us are filled with a sense of incompleteness, with only a winter wind, and want some meaning to this journey in spacetime? Something more?" *Yes, sane, si, oui*—the task before us, my fellow humans, is the clear and present danger of finding out who we really are and what's what with all this. No matter the outcome! As such it is only for those who would dare to venture into the domain of bold breathing! As such, only for you who would write with your own blood as the man from Rocken so ingeniously put it. Our venture cannot abstract itself out of existence, the flesh and blood of it, and ever hope to know it or grasp the creature behind the eyes looking out at it. Each of us and existence—that is all we have to go on.

Whatever existence is, madness or meaningful, a dream or divine comedy, I am witness to it, you are witness to it. The one constant in my life, in your life, in every life is this starting point for each and every one of us. Each of us is witness to whatever existence is and the overwhelming double-helix quest that comes calling out of it—everything ultimately depending on that outcry and its response. There is no asylum from it. Consciousness worked its way up, up through the material of reptilian stem and mammalian middle, through frontal leaps, to a brain and more, itself. As such, we all are unsure and wide-eyed creatures in a world where we are in point of existential fact looking for the point to it all and us in it. I sip at my glass of deep rich burgundy, all the while looking at the wine dark sea that is my mind, in search of a way, an authentic way to face the cosmos. "If there is a point to our existing, it can only be found in us, in our own actuality, the everyday of it, because that's where we are everyday," somewhere calls out to me from those cerebral contortions in this hard head of mine. Yes, it is here, in existence alone, that the answer has to be found, whatever it is to be. It is all we have and we can't really step out of it, not really.

So *is there* a meaning to it all, a more *and* a More? Or when all the cerebral dust settles is our outcry all we have?

Each of us is awakened to a life filled with this same trenchant search; it is reflected in our eyes, whether we admit it or not. Those eyes are witness to what I say, and an honest look into the mirror of life will tell you so. It will leave you asking about yourself as you look into your own countenance, and about the life you are alive to, whether it is, as it seems, a madhouse? But, one, in which we must find a sane answer to our existence nonetheless! Our human eyes turn pale with the prospects, leaving us asking if we are alive to an odyssey between our entrance and exit filled with laughter and love, suffering and loss, until we still into that forever requiem, nothing more for me and you and the dog and everyone else than the journey? And shouldn't that be enough, to just have existed, to have been? Merely for me to say I have taken place? Or is that a preposterous proposal? Of course it is, for as long as we are not brain dead we have to answer the outcry inside of us! What's the meaning in and to all this, and me in it? In truth, in that you and I and every one of us have come alive to the human venture! Been born into the thick of it! The flesh and blood of it! The incarnation of it! No matter how we might try to put it out of our minds, perhaps even going out of our minds because of it, the event we call life forces each of us to face the human outcry and the human venture it calls out for. Starting where each and every one of us starts, as a witness to existence, every human that ever was, is, or will be is forced to ask that most basic of all questions as he or she sets out on this odyssey, the first and foremost question of existence whether in the ice age or the space age: but who am I in all this?! It is both a question and an exclamation. Who really am I and what am I doing here?! And how do I act unless I know that?!

Though it is an odd mix, grating grammatically—exclamation and question mark together—it is what we have been born to, our presence in the cosmos leaving us staring at a situation demanding that we find out something essential to us that we may not be able to find out, yet imperative that we do! "This is another fine mess you got me into," my inners complain a la Fatty to Shinny, that shaking in my stomach trying to pass for a joke as I fiddle with what's really real and lose my Derby in a swirl of wind and worry and wounds.

Achieving wisdom after the big bang takes a human venture for each of us, and it is hard, especially when faced with suffering, the primary problem of existence, no matter how it comes into our lives. Does each in truth end up like the dog in the graveyard, alone in a silent outcry; all the while expected to pray to we know not what? Is there a wisdom in the waste? Is there a meaning to it all, a more *and* a More? I have to confess, I am moved greatly by the suffering on this planet, our own human vulnerability and that of the animals. Like Darwin's forever love of dogs and all animals, I love those wonderful innocent creatures we give the name animal to, and for many moons now, I have chosen to realize that love by respecting their right to live without me turning them into my menu. Even if the whole world goose-steps down *Les Champs Elysee* to nature's drum, I don't have to. Even if the whole world says whatever it does about whatever it does, I must be honest to what I see and synthesize. But what I see and synthesize is often in conflict with the deepest experience in me, my love. I see a cosmos that is indifferent, a nature although beautiful brutal, and a humanity that comes out of both, acting accordingly. What I see is that the arguments against a caring divinity that shapes our ends outnumber the lonely one for it, my own human love. Can I really dare to disturb the universe with such a lonely love? Is that wisdom after the big bang, each of us left lovingly hopeless, hopelessly loving? It does seem so! Yet on a golden afternoon or a rainy one when the wind is southerly and I know a hawk from a handsaw, and get a glimpse into my own innermost and sense more and perhaps More with it, what can I do but wonder? Aristotle said all philosophy begins with wonder. This book is a venture into that wondering. Love striving to understand.

One Minimal Certainty, Please!

I sit with my cup of coffee, at a midnight diner wondering, pondering, pursuing. It's raining outside the large Deco window as I manage a creased-lipped smile across to the bag lady in from the night. I can only wish that the Mystery that made us cares for her, for me, for the stray dog outside in the drizzle. Or is that trying to domestic the wind? Is what we call God just different and we alone with our kindness? Just the bag lady and me against the whole of everywhere, is that the way it is, just me sending a bowl of soup over to this hungry stranger?

I think this little encounter brings home the situation we are all in, one way or another, at a café at the edge of whatever with a choice as how to act in the face of it, even as we still don't know the whole of it, let alone if there is any holy of holies hidden in its make up, or our own. We may be stammering postmoderns stumbling over a globe of guesswork, applying words to something unknown that is doing we know not what, and in our confusion taking care of the sounds and allowing the sense to take care of itself, but even as witness to such a gyre and gimble we are witnesses who must respond, one way or another. The anthropic principal ironically may not be applicable to science or life with it, but the third question of philosophy is more than applicable, it is the very sojourn of life, and so we must be able to answer it. *How do I act in the face of existence?* Whether existence be madness, sanity, a mistaken dendrite, a dream or divine comedy, I am witness to it and must act in the face of it. Witness to the bag lady starving across the counter of life from me, and me looking across the caffeine at her presence out of my own, and what is called for out of that!

I have to ask again, as I did in the outset of this venture of ours, after consciousness has looked across time to the beginning of time itself, can we at least dare to disturb the universe with some minimal certainty? If nothing else, we must reach a *minimal certainty* in this desperate encounter between ourselves and the silence of the universe, some *minimal certainty* in all this chaos and chaord of being—some grounding to ourselves, from which we can know how to act. Even as our cerebral compass reacts first one way and then another we must keep trying to find that one minimal certainty. It is the foremost necessity as we set out on our venture, surrounded as we are by a sea of uncertainty as far as the mind can see. It is absolutely the *sine qua non* if we are to proceed.

"But we already know what it is!" I hear myself shout out to my computer, my Old English cocking his shaggy head at my wide-eyed eureka, always ready to join in the fun. "Yes," I tell him, "I know how Archimedes felt when he found a fulcrum to move the world!" He barks at my behavior, not quite sure about this game. "You know what it is, too," I insist his way. "You and me and everyone with us! Not just the two others who might be reading this book."

So what is it—this one minimal certainty? I hear you.

The answer is to be found in our café encounter. One we would reach, as well, in every other encounter in existence. In a word *presence*! It is what allows us to be the witness and the witnessed, and to act out of that.

The one constant in my life, in your life, in every life is this starting point for each and every one of us, what makes each of us as a witness possible. Each of us is *a presence* witnessing whatever existence is—and the overwhelming outcry that comes calling out of it! Everything ultimately depends on that outcry and its response, and there is no asylum from it. No matter how we might try to put it out of our minds, perhaps even going out of our minds because of it, as I said and might already be, the event we call life forces each of us to face the quintessential query of life, that outcry and its response. Starting where each and every one of us starts, as *a presence witnessing existence*, every human that ever was, is, or will be is forced to ask and must somehow answer, before any choice can rightly be made on how to act, that most basic of all questions, what *really* is this witness, this factuality, *my presence?*

Lilly Tomlin, a comedienne, just in case you are an intelligent life form from outer space and don't have a ringy dingy who she is, in one of her skits of yesteryear, said that reality is the hunch we all take, and I like to quote her, because in a very real sense it is true. Sir Popper, title and all, agrees, "We do not know; we can only guess."[1] Yet, in that hunching and guessing there is something each of us definitely knows that is not a hunch or a guess, something that grounds existence for each of us. That is what I want to focus in on more closely, because it gives us our *only grounding* in the drifts and fog, the tears and prayers, the hunches and honeybunches. For as we stand, kneel, or lie supine looking out at spinning space and fleeting time, each of us still knows something we don't argue to—*a presence! A presence no one can deny—no matter what one might say about it!* And no matter what they might say about it, it is a presence that gives forth to a narration as it travels the odyssey of life, or perhaps more accurately put, the *odd*-yssey of life. Looking out at the *odd*-yssey, this presence, when all is said and done, is all each of us has to make our way; all each of us is as we make our way.

Before anything then, I want to dwell on this presence that each of us is, because you cannot turn the page without it, silly as that sounds. Even if it turns out that each of us is merely a psychic crystallization around an abyss, as long as we are such, each is still a presence. From bambino to our last breath! When a baby is forming in the womb, and then comes out of the womb, it doesn't remember being in the womb or its birth. Yet, there is still a presence that seeks its mama's breast to survive—from nature—and also, as well, after the baby has dinned, at its baby leisure, a presence that looks inquisitively at its own hand, extending it out and back again. There are levels of being in this presence and the baby is becoming aware of it; growing in wisdom and age, as the hand it was looking at grows in use and entropy. That presence grows shouldn't surprise us, nor that there are levels of being in each presence. Or that it knows it will end sometime somewhere, and knows it all the more so as it comes closer and closer to that ending. As the madman warned in my play: "If humanity doesn't get you, nature will!" Yet in and through it all is this presence; yes, mortal and maybe only a psychic crystallization around that abyss, but it is present no matter.

The root-reality for each of us is this, this presence! It is each of us! And for each of us it *is fundamentally present to us.* My immediate experience is that I exist and I act accordingly, yours that you exist and you act accordingly, and so on for each and everyone on planet earth. *So it is a presence that is conscious of its own presence.* This is our self-being calling out to us and claiming its place in the tide of time, in this riverrun of existence, in the cortical and contextual sea of postmodernism, no matter how it got here, how it came to be. But even as it claims its place in existence it is faced with the very riddle of itself. Even its origin, as I said. Something we shall tackle later. But no matter, so far we can say, whether this self is there before, originating an unreal amount of time ago, or at our baby beginnings, or even brain-made after, whether "mind first/brain second," or "brain first/ mind second," or yet to be found in Da Vinci's insight about it, it does not take away from the authenticity of its presence. Such a conscious presence is *the* necessary ingredient for living no matter what!

Once it comes into being, no matter how, it is real, in point of fact, for each of us, as stated, our root-reality. *I have taken place!* What this comes down to is that you really exist as you, and me as me, again, no matter how this came about. Whether you are at the moment reading this book or not, and if you are, reading it with a winter giggle on a rainy night alone with it and yourself, or reading it on a sunny day with a summer giggle sharing a hammock with your dog, your essence is your existence, your existence your essence, *all in one presence having many levels of being within it,* some of which you are aware of and some not, from invisible quanta that are the basic material that makes you up, through the raw elemental energies of evolution we call nature and instinct, biology and the brain, to the phenomenon of a consciousness in the cosmos, and on finally, coming out of all this, to the narration we call a person's life story or odyssey. *Presence itself is precisely presence!* That is to say, what is present in its many levels of being is so as the whole of each of us, and it remains so, remains one, even as we specifically speak about this level or that within it, and even as awareness is its sine qua non. There are those who would limit deconstruction just to a presence's narration, maintaining that when they deconstruct or peal way our culture there is nothing left of us. In our own deconstruction in this our human venture we take in the whole human, from the start of an individual existence all the way to the atoms-that-make-an-individual-up finally breaking asunder in the "eye-opener" we call dying, from the quanta, through the instincts coming out of the raw elemental energies of evolution, to the phenomenon of consciousness, and then the story each one lives as his or her life, all of it constituting the acting, aware, presence each of us is in its many levels of being. Each of us is a single helix of presence, one pervasive presence.

This is often where some people go astray—they think in terms of a duality instead of levels of being; or, in an attempt to do away with a duality, they throw the baby out with the basket and say there is no real self, only as it were the basket. As I said, we shall get into that controversy more deeply later on. For now, we can at least say that there is a root-reality, which is the basis or source out of which a narration grows, and however the self is created, it does not change the result; namely, *a presence in the world.* One can argue that the self has to be conscious of itself to be called self and is created after birth by the brain, in other words the "brain first, mind second" hypothesis, or one can argue the opposite, or even a simultaneity in evolution for consciousness and consciousness aware of itself—but, again, at this point in our sojourn let's not get *ourselves* involved in that argument; rather merely repeat that, no matter, the end result is *a presence in the world as witness to it and out of which we face the world.* Once it comes to that—however it does—it is an actuality, a factuality, I have taken place! Or to continue in plain American, you are really reading this book and I really wrote it—you are a real presence and I am a real presence, too!

"Io sol uno," Dante said, and he was right![2] *"I myself alone!"* It is the first affirmation of self three times over in any writing anywhere, and I think this outcry from the hook-nosed Poet speaks for all of us, giving each an aloneness in the journey of breathing, yet in that very fact, a universality. Each of us is truly

this presence—a presence alone, together like every other—as we pass through the hell, purgatory, and paradise we call life. Dante called it a divine comedy; I prefer to call our sojourn on planet stress a comic-agony, merely a comic-agony, not knowing if there is a divine to blame it on. Yet, even as I grandiloquently hold the mask of laughter and the mask of tears in each hand morphing them into one, I must sidestep defending my preference for them being hyphenated into one telling truth, because something deeper still is demanding to be heard. It seems we must do this before we do anything or *can do* anything further—before we can even examine the myriad levels of existence in you or me, before we can morph a smiling and weeping mask into an honest representation of breathing, before we can even began to talk about Dante's divine or anyone else's!

By now you see that when I speak of *io solo uno, me, myself, and I* as applicable to each one of us, I am not talking of it in an amorphous, nebulous, abstract way, nor as some aggregate or appendix, nor as a substance separate and dualistic, but true to our most immediate experience and existence; namely, *a very real presence with an integrity of being conscious of its own presence*, each of us true individuals and encountering the world as such; each of us this presence, this conscious matter.

Conscious matter! That is rather amazing in and of itself.

Let's stop right there. Look into a mirror; that is consciousness looking in, but not looking back. One is conscious matter; one is not. It is a marvel to behold when you think about it—and this marvel, whose make-up has come down the long labyrinth of life with no direct traces as to its misty beginnings, today still remains embedded in mystery. The mystery looking into your mirror! We know it is here, de facto, but what it is remains to be determined, or better yet, discovered, even as it is looking back at us out of reflective eyes.

Yes out of reflective eyes, the real ones doing the reflecting and what is behind them, you. I must say here that consciousness is not something floating around out there, but individualized in the person of you and me and each of us; it is conscious matter, yes, yet conscious matter aware of itself, aware of itself without any mirror, there is a chaordinator in it all called the self, so each of us can and do say, *io sol uno*.

The contemporary human respects science, so let's be as contemporary as can be and start the approach to the discovery of presence, this conscious matter of ours, via science, specifically with inferences from studies of the brain, studies ranging from the sophisticated network of speech to those activities that lie below that threshold, as in painstaking endeavors like the Blue Brain Project. Studying the brain certainly can be a stop along the way, for it seems somehow consciousness worked its way up, up through the reptilian stem and mammalian middle through frontal leaps to a material brain and more, itself, *conscious* matter. One can argue to a different journey of course, but no matter, the roots of consciousness were either there before, parallel with, or the last to come along in the instinctive brain. We simply don't know. What we do know is that it is an existing phenomenon, present in your presence as the highest level of your being. If the roots of our consciousness travel back deep into earth's past or only as deep as our own brain's history, it is still embedded in the encephalon, in part constructed of or at least in a symbiosis with the chemicals and pathways which are in a strange simultaneity with it, becoming conscious how, yet again we have no idea. If that sounds like a confusing vicious circle, it is because it is. *Conscious matter is still a mystery.* Somehow we have awareness, can look out at the cosmos and be aware of it and ourselves. At times it seems to have its own evolution within the whole process, from plants with their own type of awareness as Kirlian photographs try to establish, on through the different qualities of awareness different animals display, headlong all the way to us, we conscious creatures that act at different levels of being, from the Serengeti to the spiritual. On the other hand maybe it comes after the fact of established evolutionary encephala and maybe that is the way evolution brought this next level about. Just as the brain expands with the advent of our network of language, whether innate as Chomsky might say or not, as such it is still an integral part of our humanness, so, too, with regards consciousness, if perchance it is produced by the brain, whether innately there and enhanced, or after the fact solely; still it is necessary as a root-reality to our humanness, no matter how it comes about—and once it does is really there! There will be those, of course, who will take a Cyclops approach to that, and pontificate as fact without a scientific basis that it is *only and simply* in the neurological pathways, in this or that slice of the brain, overlooking the synaptic gap in their spin, as well as missing the fact of the quality of consciousness. The paradox is that the brain and consciousness seem the same and different at the same time. With the advent of quantum mechanics that shouldn't surprise us. There are models, surprises, and suggestions that might help us in this phenomenon, namely, the particle and the wave, the neutrino, even the entanglement in the EPR experiment, and heaven knows what else in that wonderful world of quanta. It is my own sense, sans as yet the verification required, in science or anywhere else, so sans teeth, sans eyes, sans taste, sans everything else, it is my sense allow me to say, since this is still a free country relatively speaking, and to say without I hope frightening you, since it can hardly be called the acceptable position of anyone anywhere but Leonardo and me, and maybe Mad Mildred, that in time consciousness will show itself to be throughout our form, as Da Vinci suggested; but for the time being I shall leave it at that because I must, except to say that although it sounds farfetched, it is not as farfetched as it sounds, as we shall venture to see. For now, however, let us stay with the brain, which offers something we can at least wrestle with when it comes to this mystery of conscious matter presented to us.

Neuroscience, so far at least, looks at the brain from outside in, without, at the same time, being able to look from the inside out. Science can't *experience* the brain. Presence, from that inside, is more than the sum of its sliced up parts whatever those parts are, from their individual axo-dendritic patterns through the whole of the neo-cerebral cortex making up 80% of the human brain, to the encephalon intoto. Although there is an on-going search to discover the genetic code of consciousness, so far that has proved as futile as the search for the Holy Grail. The daunting fact that each consciousness is unique and invisible, only seeing the world through its own I, presents a problem in and of itself, even before you get to the plasticity of the brain per se dynamically adjusting and readjusting to the experience of living. Take a "peculiar" perception as in the case of someone with synesthesia where one hears color, sees sounds, and tastes a touch. Notwithstanding, an individual presence is still there. "We've got all these tools for studying the cortex," Henry Markram, the Director of the Blue Brain Project admits openly, "but none of these methods allow us to see what makes the cortex so interesting, which is that it generates worlds. No matter how much I know about your brain, I still won't be able to see what you see."[3] Your presence is your own, his his own, and so on with everyone of us, and this for each of us is our root-reality, our presence, our very self-being.

Before I am misunderstood I want to mention something here that I will elaborate on later. Let me say so no one misunderstands where I am, as awe-inspiring as the brain is, as elegant as DNA and messenger RNA is, as exciting as the current happenings in paleontology, molecular studies and the human genome, *all of which I hold to dearly*, there is still *more* to us. Of course I find it fascinating to be shown the DNA molecule. Traveling through the outer backbone of ribboned phosphates and into the inner sanctum of the blueprint of life with its rungs of laddered chemical components in A, C, G, and T, each in a particular shape, has to make one giddy, and giddier still as the messenger RNA moves on in an inner $\pi\alpha\nu\tau\alpha\ \rho\epsilon\iota$ into a place called ribosome and converts into an amino acid. I would be dead not to appreciate that! That will be spelled out, further, but for now, I had to make mention of it here, so as not to mislead you as I fight for more.

One can say, to play in Wild Will's word box, that there truly is more in heaven and earth than is dreamt of in and about human heads. The Bard himself plays with the dialogue in the original, and in his whimsy with words underlines this for us, for the full quote uses the code name Ho-ratio, which I remind the reader is a play on *ratio,* the Latin for *reason*. "There are more things in heaven and earth, Ho-ratio, than are dreamt of in your philosophy."[4] How clever that Shakespeare was. Following his clever lead then, we can go on to say, consciousness, which gives us the very ability to philosophize, is more than reason, philosophy, science, poetry or pasta can at present say it is, more than we know it is, perhaps even more than we can know. Who knows? That's what we are about here, penetrating into this presence. There is a blind painter in Turkey who is redefining what it means to see. Esref Armagan drew the Baptistery in Florence in three dimensions, what Filippo Brunelleschi a sighted genius did when he invented perspective in painting centuries earlier. In his research with Esref, according to Doctor John Kennedy, the Director of Life Sciences at the University of Toronto, the blind artist's visual cortex lit up as he painted as if he was seeing. No doubt someday we might know why, and on that day, if Esref Armagan is still alive, he will still be a presence both painting and knowing how as a blind man he is "seeing" in that endeavor. In that sense we are like Esref, trying to find out how we "see," our consciousness in a strange symbiosis with the brain anatomy, not another yet not the same, in a simultaneity even as it is something more, not the same yet not another. It sounds like a koan given to us by a drunken Zen master, but it isn't; it's a koan right out of existence itself, the way it appears awareness works with matter, leaving us . . . well, where we are. There are miles and miles to go before we sleep, so let us be on our way and dare to go where angles and sheepdogs dare not venture, deeper still into our conscious state of being.

Since we really don't know, my fellow venturer and ventured one, how the hell, heaven, and earth our conscious state of being came about, we have our pick of possibles. We could take the mind first/brain second path, or the brain first/mind second position just as well, arguing that just as the organic arose out of the inorganic, the seemingly "non-material" phenomenon consciousness could have arisen out of the very material brain. We don't know what it really is or how it got here is what I am underlining for one and all, and this is so even as the mystery of consciousness is "married" to the brain as it were, joined at the synaptic gap, even as it is simultaneous with, the same yet different, and cannot exist in spacetime as far as we know without the brain. For that reason, to discover the neurological underpinnings for awareness, although a staggering undertaking, is a necessary pursuit and must continue, to see first and foremost if they are such underpinnings, and if so what they are, and how much they contribute to the mystery of awareness, and if truly it was part of evolution's next step and therefore more in that way as well, as the brain is more than the tide pools out of which it evolved. No matter where one is coming from in his or her choice of possibles, a thoughtful person realizes the mind/brain problem is fundamental to our quest for self-knowledge and that first question of life, "who am I?"—and thus this neurological inquiry is a natural outcome, along with all our ways of knowing. Yet within that context and confusion both, one must still be aware and realize that although the brain is a sine qua non of consciousness in spacetime, consciousness can supersede the brain and does with a bowl of soup, and that can never be dismissed. Again, be patience, for as sure as my Old English has hair you shall see what I mean by that and how within that situation consciousness is more than the brain, for as long as it lasts, even if it turns out it came from the brain, is dependent on the brain, and dies in spacetime with the brain, no matter, it is more than the brain as the brain is more than the tide pools that gave forth to it.

Within the process of evolution came forth all this wonder: matter, life, brain, consciousness . . . from the inorganic to organic aware matter, in point of fact, this irreplaceable individual presence with many levels of being, whose brain is as unique as its fingerprints and whose consciousness can say *io sol uno* because it is so. In the whole of space and time, no matter what else is contained in spacetime, there is not another like you. You are unique and irreplaceable. That has to give you pause.

With that said, we can now take up those that would deny this to you. I thought I could pass over in silence—at least for a while—the nonsense of you not having a real self, of me not having a real self, of any and all of us not having a real self. But it is vital that I address that head on, face to face as it were.

Of late it has been the vogue, the rage, and the rant to deny one's self as real; not merely those traveling all the way from either side of the Himalayas to tell us we have no real self-being, but some homegrown negation as well. We read such silliness printed in books and magazines, see it on so-called "in-depth" television shows, and hear lecturers on tour proclaim to their audiences that they really don't exist, not really. I myself remember arguing with Krishnamurti over this years ago, and although he insisted that he didn't have a real self he became really angry. Of course, the famous man had a real self, made up of all the levels of being within him—like each of us does, whether famous or not. So, first and foremost, let me state: no one, but no how, can deny each of us our self-presence in the world. That is fundamentally present to each of us; it is our birth right and right of passage. *Basically what those who deny the self are really doing is saying that what is fundamentally present to you is a lie.*

Of course, right from the start, any student in logic 101 would see that if what is fundamentally present to you is a lie, how could you be sure of anything, including and especially the denial of what is fundamentally present to you, that root-reality! The truth is, each of us has a self-presence; it is our root-reality and each of us functions out of it, whether smiling or weeping, or getting really angry. Those that deny this still have it; but what they don't have is a leg to stand on. I am talking about the evidence for their conclusion whether Buddhists or biologists; the Buddhists relying on a faith to hold their position, namely a religious history that says so; the biologists *who do so* relying on a spin to hold their position, namely, lame pronouncements not worthy of being called scientific, for none of them are grounded in what is demonstrable.

The proponents of denying our most fundamental reality and accepting theirs instead all end up in an untenable position. For no matter, as I stated, how the self came to be, *it is*, and each of us acts accordingly, despite what one might say, be he Buddhist or biologists or boogieman. Here we enter into a comedy worthy of Aristophanes, with characters making themselves disappear before our very eyes. We see the Buddhist choosing to be a Buddhist while saying he has no real self to choose. Poof! End of play and path as well, eightfold or otherwise! On to the stage comes the biologist who says that there is no real self in a more modern refrain, sounding like something out of a lighthearted Broadway show as he slices a brain a la baloney and calls his overly thin results the truth of life, the mind, and everything else in a ringing rendition of *Biology uber alles!* It makes *Springtime for Hitler* look serious in comparison. By the time the boogieman enters with his attempts to spook us out of ourselves, we are doubling over in laughter. Oh why not have fun with such people pretending to be Buddhists and biologists and boogiemen! According to them they're not there anyway. Well, not all there to be sure. *The truth is, they are present, and they are present no matter how they got so.* Although they protest with a spin worthy of a politician that there is no there there, there they stand shouting out of the there that isn't supposed to be there, and doing so as if they really are there, highly protective of their position. Yes, Santa Claus, there is a Virginia. Life is not a *bonbonniere* to be sure, but it is real, and so are you! *You are present and you are present no matter how you got to be so.* "I have taken place," to quote myself. Here I am.

What I would like to do, therefore, since it is the core reality of everything for each and every one of us, is to continue to give evidence for and of the fact that each of us is real, and therefore so is our life experience as well. That latter is equal in importance as the former. And we shall see why. But first, again, in plain American, let me assure you that you and I really and truly do exist, and exist as you and I—*as the self-presence each is, with its many levels of being.* One can say each is a non-self-source out of which a someone comes, as I said we might do without damage to self-being as real; or one can argue that self-being is there already as the basis or sourceforce or innermost of each of us out of which the narration I mentioned grows. In other words, even if the self grows out of the brain or body-makeup, or is simultaneously already there in our evolutionary make up, again, either way, self-being is a factuality and our root-reality, either post or simultaneous to brain/body/baby in the womb, and it is exactly how we act in the world, whether we write books, magazine articles, appear on TV talk shows, lecture to audiences on tour, sit on a zafu empting our mind in meditation, or slice and dish out baloney for a living.

Lest you misunderstand my point, I do know the brain is the door to speech and seeing if I might put it that way, and that a microscopic vessel can change a person's whole voyage by diseasing the brain or a part of it. We have forward facing eyes that see the world in 3 D and have evolved from *a nail not a claw* as the fossils show. I know that these nail-not-claw primates are said to be Plesiadspeforms who came onto the evolutionary scene 56 million years old, and that our scientific scent for the roots of the primate tree doesn't stop there. I know that the nail is not the oldest part of us, for the most primitive primate skeleton found to date is the Dryomomys, which shows our oldest signs are in our mouth. How appropriate. I know there was as well the Ignacius clarkforkensis close behind, but not number one in our primate tree. Interesting also, at least to me, I love this sort of stuff, there was a co-evolution taking place; namely, the flowers and fruit were happening along with the earliest primates, and those earliest of our family tree became flower and fruit eating creatures. So don't misunderstand what I am saying; the raw elemental energies are us! But, also, a presence is here as well, a level in us, something deeper still, something that happened as well in the evolution to you who are reading this masterpiece and me who along with the Muses is writing it.

It was Christof Koch, the supreme materialist, who said in the flesh as I listened to his charming Teutonic accent, "Subjectivity is the most important thing we have." How could it be otherwise for a you, and a you, and a you . . .[5]

Each of us is a presence that is conscious of its own presence; conscious matter conscious of itself as a uniquely individual and irreplaceable *io sol uno*. Yes, each of us can *really* say, I am! *Je suis! Io sono!* And this is fundamentally present to each of us. My immediate experience, my primary intuition, is that I exist and I act accordingly, yours that you exist and you act accordingly, and so on for each and everyone on planet earth; it is our birth right and right of passage, I have indeed taken place.

Here I am reminded of three men and a boy that will definitely confuse the issue at hand, but perhaps at the same time give us a handle on it. I want to take you to a hell more horrible than Dante's—the world of the 'de-souled,' where any bridge between the physical and the personal has to be the single most terrifying question facing the person observing such a nightmare. In such 'lost souls' all inner narrative seems gone and one's organic mooring of identity with it.

First let's look at a person who was brought to Doctor Viktor Frankl. The doctor said he was facing a ruined personality, a man who had been so over many decades. The poor man came to be regarded as an idiot. In frustrated moments of great outbursts or excitement he managed, however, to regain his self-control. Frankl asked him how he did that. There was a pause of some seconds, and then the man answered that he did it for God's sake. "At this moment," Frankl says, "the depth of his personality revealed itself, and at the bottom of this depth, irrespective of the poverty of his intellectual endowment, an authentic religious life was disclosed.[6] Why do I bring this up—not because of any bias for religion on my part, that is for certain, but because there was still something deeper still there, a presence; one acting out of love, irrespective of where he placed his love. Both the presence and the act of love showed itself; even in such a person, suffering such a challenge in his existence because of chemistry and circumstances, and chance maybe as well.

Doctor Oliver Sacks spoke of a similar experience, of a man who had 'gone to pieces' and could not make one sentence follow another in any meaningful order. One tended to speak of him, Sacks tell us, as a 'lost soul': "Was it possible that he had really been 'de-souled' by a disease? 'Do you think he *has* a soul?' I once asked the Sisters. 'Watch Jimmie in chapel when he receives communion,' they said, 'and judge for yourself.'[7] Sacks did of course. The man was wholly held, absorbed. There was no forgetting, no Korsakov's disease then, he was no longer at the mercy of a faulty and fallible mechanism—that of meaningless sequences and memory traces—but was absorbed in an act, an act of his whole being, which carried feeling and meaning in an organic continuity and unity, a continuity and unity so seamless it could not permit any break. "Jimmie, who was so lost in extensional 'spatial' time, was perfectly organized in Bergsonian 'intentional' time . . . there was something that endured and survived." Sacks goes on: "I had wondered, when I first met him, if he were not condemned to a sort of 'Humean' froth, a meaningless fluttering on the surface of life, and whether there was any way of transcending the incoherence of his Humean disease. Empirical science told me there was not—but empirical science, empiricism, takes no account of the soul, no account of what constitutes and determines personal being." The Doctor concludes: "however great the organic damage and Humean dissolution, there remains the undiminished possibility of reintegration . . . by touching the human spirit: and this can be preserved in what seems at first a hopeless state of neurological devastation."[8]

Sacks just after that speaks of a man devoid of even the look of sadness and resignation that Jimmie's face wore outside his chapel, a man called William, whose world disquieted the Doctor and everyone else with its delirium without depth. There was activity without anyone behind it. What came out of him in his torrential, ceaseless confabulation, Sacks tells us almost in a written whisper, was a peculiar quality of comic indifference, as if nothing really mattered because there was nothing there. All efforts to reconnect William failed, all except when the doctors and nuns abdicated their efforts and William wandered into the quiet garden, and there, in his quietness, recovered his own quiet, as Sacks relates, the presents of the plants allowing his identity-delirium to relax and a rare self-sufficiency in him to breathe again, as if in a deep wordless communion with the plants, a love or a trust rustled in the silence of the man who wasn't there, yet most definitely was.

Does the brain make us who we are or is there something deeper still? Or if the brain, does it make something deeper still? Of course, the brain like our body has its obviousness in our make-up, but the question goes beyond that for true detectives and witnesses to being. After all, we don't know what consciousness really is, what the deep reality of our own being is. And if we are to be honest detectives, we must take in all the evidence.

In all three case studies, broken men—where it counts most physically, one's brain—showed somehow there was something more to them that acted out of something deeper still than the tragedy of their neurological devastation as so reported by two trained professionals in their fields; one a psychiatrist, neurologist, and psychotherapist and the other a clinical neurologist and researcher in neurophysiology and neurochemistry.

Questions about the very nature of knowing are raised in the case studies of those suffering neurological devastations. Jimmie in the chapel and Frankl's 'idiot' are pointed out, as is William perhaps the most remote from us of the three, but there are so many others.[9] "What mediates this, we wonder? What sort of cerebral organization could allow this to happen? Our current concepts of cerebral processing and representation are all essentially computational. But could the computational alone provide for us the richly visionary, dramatic and musical quality of experience—that vivid personal quality which *makes* it 'experience'? The answer is clearly, even passionately, 'No!' Computational representations—even of the exquisite sophistication envisaged by Marr and Bernstein—could never, of themselves, constitute 'iconic' representations, those representations which are the very thread and stuff of life."[10] Pythagoras might approach it with a deep almost mystical innate arithmetic, and modern algorithm worshipers with trying to trace the intricate meandering of innate wiring via a mechanistic-materialistic paradigm, but there seems to be something deeper still. Rough-hew it how life will.

I am not arguing how it got there or why, only that there it is. I am not even saying that there are those who don't show this something deeper still in their devastation and that is what freezes us in our cerebral tracks—the possibility of disappearing altogether.

What I am saying is that even though there are those who may correctly suggest that the brain is the device that communicates and transmits information and in doing so not only orientates behavior but also assembles meaning, we see the phenomenon of a root-reality showing itself there even when the brain is broken. In fragmented moments to be sure, but displayed nonetheless, even as was said, with a broken brain. Though all of us may be brain broken on one level or another, most who are not glaringly so act out of a sense of conscious connection to an inner core of meaning, an identity. Our choardinator is functioning full force, full sourceforce. Yet, what we have seen—in those who suffer a rupture in their lives to such an extent that they do not function at our level—is, notwithstanding, an existential situation wherein some such afflicted people still act with a meaning in their existence *at certain times*, as if done at a deeper level still. I said *some* and underline it, for we don't know what goes on in the silence of others. And I don't pretend to know. It may be that the person has been destroyed and what is there is a hollow shell worse than death itself. *Io non mori' e non rimasi vivo; pensa oggimai per te, s'hai fior d'ingegno, qual io divenni, d'uno e d' altro privo. I did not die, and I am not alive; think for yourself, if you have any wit, what I have become, deprived of life.* Yes, it is the Ninth Circle of Hell in such a state of being. It may be that if the brain is that-out-of-which the self arose, the self subsides as the brain breaks down, that this simultaneity, this symbiosis, this spacetime soul-like quality, like life itself, depends upon the brain, and when the brain is "dead" to functioning, it is crippled and dies its own "death" as described so well in the above Italian, until both it and the brain do finally go out like a flickering flame. I don't pretend to know at this time, *nor does anyone else*. What we do know is at least those we have looked at touch upon a very deep and personal meaning despite their cerebral nightmare. *They still have a presence hiding in the horror.*

I am not saying, again so that you do not misunderstand me, that the presence is not tied into the brain and its synaptic gaps, nor the chemistry of the body either, of course not; what I am saying is that once the self or presence is present, even if scarred and scared by a malfunctioning brain and body, it is still there, no matter how it came into being, even as it might be dying a slow death within, bleeding psychic blood and in a Swan song as it were before it disappears altogether and is buried beyond any ability on our part to comprehend. It would be like looking into the eyes of someone alive and then dies while you still hold on those eyes, knowing they are the same eyes, but with something gone forever in them; only slowly here, and thus more horrifying. Although they had a presence before, it is now gone, a death has taken place in both cases.

We have seen three case studies that display both the 'something deeper still' and a love coming out of that presence that was hiding in a horror. Here is yet another, one that has to do with an autistic boy from India. I saw this in a report, as I recall on *60 Minutes,* and took notes on it. Tito, a severely autistic child, was 'freed' from his 'captivity' because of his mother's incredible love. She persisted in breaking all the basic training techniques as to how to handle the autistic; she ignored the erratic movements and wandering eyes, and focused, instead, on the person inside. She fed him music, Shakespeare, geometry . . . When Tito was asked some years later what was the hardest thing for people like himself, he said that people think that they are not really there. Another autistic child, helped by this same method, echoed that same astonishing insight; that he was listening to everything around him, even though the people around him thought he wasn't, wasn't there behind his disease. *We have so much to learn about our own depth of being.* "Never fall victim to the tyranny of thought of your own age," I must caution, and we definitely are trying not to, attempting instead to honesty venture into what appears a depth of being each of us has.

We function in spacetime and of course are subject to its laws of physics and psyche both—I can crush your body under a truck—likewise, if you give me a bunch of chemicals it is of course going to have its impact on me. That doesn't mean I don't exist as me, it means I am subject to the laws of spacetime. Somehow that confuses some. They would relegate us to the 'truck' or 'the chemicals' or 'the autistic nightmare' or to 'the synaptic gaps' in our brains. That should be a caveat to us as sleuths and humans both. Brain-snatching or self-seizing by any means, chemical or a catechism of any sort, is out there in wait, yet even so, there is an intrinsic root-reality to it all we can rely on as well, our very presence in it all. Viktor Frankl mentions how those who ran the concentration camps tried not just to break one physically, but take away one's innermost identity and meaning, one's very self. Those who do that in today's world, outside of concentration camps, each in their own way, are committing the same 'unforgivable sin'—but only if we let them, as Frankl himself brought out so forcefully in relating his life in Hitler's hell. The fight for self-preservation is more than for a physical preservation. That presence, that intrinsic root-reality, that something deeper still, is the core of everyone alive, call it what you will, the stuff of Jimmie in the chapel if you so choose. It is our deepest identity of being, and we suffer when it is scarred and suffocated by and in any situation. It is what being is in its very depth of being for each of us, our innermost. In worse case scenarios, even as we seem swallowed up by disease, this truth about ourselves can at times still be displayed. Somehow even then, that inner grasp of our identity, our source, our self, our presence shines through in particular situations, though through a glass darkly, in some tragic cases a very dark glass indeed.

"When you meet such patients," Steven Hyman, a prominent figure in modern biological psychiatry, said, "you are driven by compassion to want to do everything you can."[11] *"Was mich nicht umbringt, macht mich starker,"* Nietzsche said. I would change only the word *starker (stronger)* . . . that which does not kill me, makes me *mitleidig, compassionate*. Steven Hyman's account of his experience with such profound suffering is right-on—as is the follow-up to do something. I want to underline that for further recall. Meanwhile, Hyman cautions that bad models of how the brain works or is to be cured, whether they are Freudian or pharmacological reductionism, should not be followed. He admits they are not the answer. Howard Gardner, a psychologist and professor of education at Harvard University, has expressed a similar view when he says that none of these fields come close to solving the riddle of the human mind. Gardner's main complaint about a strictly biological approach to the mind is that it has not advanced our understanding of the core topic. That doesn't mean that either he or I are against the continued study of the biological make up of the brain—hardly! What he cautions is that our cores "seem particularly resistant to decomposition, elementarism or other forms of reductionism."[12] It appears even Freud agrees with that, when he writes just before his death: "We know two kinds of things about what we call our psyche (or mental life): first, its bodily organs and scene of action, the brain (or nervous system) and, on the on the other hand, our acts of consciousness, which are immediate data and cannot be further explained by any sort of description. Everything that lies in between is unknown to us, and the data do not include any direct relation between these two terminal points of our knowledge."[13]

That is one of the main problems at hand. How do we explain consciousness and the results that come out of it, pain, joy, laughter, love? But we will come to that, for now let us stick with presence per se, remembering we have to dig up the dirt before we can get the garden, ever since that first one that is. That is what we have been doing and continue to now, doing this necessary groundwork, so bear with me. The mystery of conscious matter, call it self-being or a conscious self, or simply the self, this deep reality is still a scientific and philosophic riddle for us, and what holds a person together in a person's innermost is more than ever a battleground of paradigms.

If in the process of evolution, as the tide pools gave forth to life and then life to a body, and a body to a brain, why would I have an objection to the brain giving forth to the self—I don't. If that is the way it happened and can be shown as such, so it is. The self is still real. Also I have no objection if consciousness evolved in a parallel evolution to the brain, if that is the way it happened and is. The self is still real that way as well. As it is, either way, we finish ourselves, ending up on our deathbed with the person each created by his or her choices. So, if the brain creates the self, fine. It could have been part of the evolutionary process, as we finishing ourselves by our choices is part of that process. Someday, I have no doubt, if we don't destroy ourselves first, as we now add to the body with devices, we will implant aids in the brain itself. Further extensions of the very creature we are creating. Certainly the gadgets being concocted by students at MIT and Stanford attest to this. All I am asking, as a good philosopher must, as well as a lover of science and wisdom both, not to mention pasta and poetry, plays and Puccini, all I am asking with regards to what we are discussing here—is that it be scientifically proven that the brain creates the self; not as some modern day warmed-over neurobabble, little more than phrenology reincarnated, as Toga was honest enough to point out about his and Mazziotta's pretty pictures at UCLA, but as scientific fact, which so far it has not![14] A faith-based science is not *scientia*, so please don't drag me or science into saying someday you *believe* it will be. Your belief is merely that, not science. Nor is a poll of scientists any stronger, as we shall see when it comes to the big bang and what all but a handful thought before that famous singularity. In our venture we are interested in what can legitimately be grounded in existence, as good detectives, scientist, and philosophers would and should be.

Again, do not misunderstand me. Will we understand so much more about the brain? Of course. Not only will, but should! Must! As I already made clear and do again, for myself if no one else. With the help of MRI's, fMRI's, positron emission tomography scanners, and optical and electromagnetic signal imagers, and stranger machinery yet in experimental stages, the terrain of the brain is being mapped out as I write. Computerized arrays of electrode trace magnetic and electrical signals associated with encephalon processes, complex neuron patters for emotional responses within the encephalon, perhaps an integrated view of the brain itself—that organ of billions of neurons and trillions of synapses communicating through an elaborate system of electrical and chemical signals—all of this is on the way, and I hope the litany will be long and impressive, without, I hope, yielding to the temptation of spin science; but rather, keeping in mind, I would always hope, the difference between science and spin.

Many new findings within the biological structure of our species—the mapping of the human genome, genetic engineering and cell research, advances in psychiatric and other drugs, brain SPECTing, advancements in computers and the boundary between the animate and inanimate, to mention only a few—will and should continue, but the depths of our being still has to give us pause. Those in science must realize that science is a process. In physics alone not too long ago, as I already indicated, it was conventional (if not absolute) wisdom to pronounce the universe eternal, and then a big bang happened and changed that. Now a beautiful theory is stating that strings in vibration are at the bottom of everything and everywhere. Or is it to be the membrane theory? I think you get the point. One paradigm is not enough to answer the question of who we are, especially a paradigm that is in process itself. A scientific absolute about the root-reality of each of us is something beyond even hubris. Dr. Frankl told us what Dr. Frankenstein couldn't—we cannot explain everything in terms of matter and the measurable; most especially what it really means to be this creature called human. We exist at many levels of being as I keep saying.

Of course, Niels Bohr said something very similar to what Frankl did, and maybe even myself and my levels of being, when he contended that just as physics had to cope with an uncertainty principle in its attempt to understand our little friend and fiend, the electron and its behavior, so, too, the hubris of the biologists would face a fundamental limitation when they in turn tried to dig into the depths of living organism. That is certainly true when it comes to consciousness. There is vast knowledge held in reserve within the mystery we call consciousness that will not go away, despite the panderers to biological fashion. Stephen Gould, I believe, was a biologist who did not fall into this panderer category, as his work with Niles Eldredge attests. He was far too good a scientist and realized that maybe, as he himself once put it, there are ways in which this universe is structured that we just can't rationalize about. This is true, even as we come "to greater empirical adequacy," to use Gould's own words. Gould and Bohr with him appear to realize this. This humble witness to being agrees. Of course, those who have made science their faith can no more be convinced of that than a fundamentalist Muslim could be that he is wrong about women, the world, and what Allah wants. Or a fundamentalist Christian or Jew for that matter, not to mention those 'true believers' in politics who have shouted at us because we dared not accept their candidate as the second coming. *I am a conscious presence* whereby spacetime is made open to thinking about or theologizing concerning—and any science, philosophy, religion or politics that denies that most fundamental fact of facts is denying the most basic actuality for each and every one of us in existence. Evolution gave us a body that is functional, and we can add to that—add to it not merely for those who have lost bodily functions, but we can enhance other functions in all of us as well. But like anything humans do, it will be important how we do it and what conclusion we draw about it—most especially conclusions about who we really are. A science of the brain, like one of the body, and also those extensions, is part of the process in the spacetime situation we find ourselves in and should not shock anyone; nor should a 'theology' of the foresaid either when parts are added to us, even to our brain. The point to be made here is that the presence continues on with whatever 'garment' or 'gadget' or 'get up' is added to the brain or body. The body is still the best interface with the outside world; but the body can change, get fat or skinny, so, too, with regards parts, mechanical parts, expansion parts added to it—or to the brain. That doesn't do away with who we are—*that root-reality*—it only adds another level of experience. We are still something deeper still, with all our different levels of being, and now with something added to the strange symbiosis within spacetime between our mind and brain and by extension body and additions to both body and brain. It is a fascinating phenomenon that can never be simplified to merely one field of inquiry. But there is a synthesis—and that is the self itself, this presence in the world—out of which each of us functions on our many levels of being. Yes, mine is a holistic approach! But so is life's.

Again, either way, that the self is created by the brain post birth, or there already, no matter how, it remains *a real presence in the world*. The riddle that I am has entered existence, and as Cicero once said, "It's a problem for Archimedes." Of course he was talking about the political state of Rome at the time, but I think I can put the phrase to better use here, as I have, facing the riddle of consciousness in the cosmos. It is a presence that can be damaged in it, even done away with by death, but once it has entered existence it is a presence that is very real indeed, however it arrived, via material evolution or another evolutionary process. When someone denies or ignores that very real presence (as for example what they did to the Indian boy I spoke of who was treated as if he wasn't there) such people are not only insensitive, but also insensate, without sense or reason. The depth of a person's self-being can't be ignored without profound damage to one's own self-being, not to mention one's intellectual life. We see this in doctors who treat patients as objects as Oliver Sacks so succinctly put it in talking about his own profession.[15] A person must have the honesty to admit we don't know where self-being comes from, but we do at least know of our self-being, a presence that interacts with the existence all around, whether that presence is scarred in whatever way or made happy as it both bares and bears witness to breathing. "I am world-weary, mirror shy," I might protest because of it, echoing a character in my play—or with Capra shout out that 'it's a wonderful life!' But no matter what I say, I am present in the face of it all.

The way to face it all and the way to it all is through us. Max Planck pointed this out as well: "Science cannot solve the ultimate mystery of nature. And it is because, in the last analysis, we ourselves are part of the mystery we are trying to solve."[16] This is Planck's second wall as I like to call it, and the one we must penetrate if we are ever to find what we are looking for. The purpose of this chapter has been and continues to be exactly that, to establish presence and then to penetrate into it, with profundity. Not only that it is here, but then to discover what it is, in its innermost integrity of being. Only then can we venture to establish a purely human spirituality; only then dare to venture into the other part of our incredible feat as well.

I mentioned the three men and a boy precisely to pursue our presence and penetrate into it, but also to give us pause at the same time! Continuing in that endeavor I would like to tell you about an encounter of my own, one I hope in particular expands our appreciation of the phenomenon of consciousness, now revealing not only it as conscious of itself and uniquely individual, but something else so very important about it. It was an unusually overcast day on which an unusual thing happened, I was privileged to get familiar with a rat. I had been looking out of my back window telling myself perhaps I had grown too old for truths, when I saw this little rat struggling down the telephone wire to my house with his prize and his survival held firmly in his mouth, a large piece of bread, bigger than he was. I tapped at the window, telling him my house was a no no. He looked up frightened, and I saw a face. It was amazing actually, how much was there, especially in those eyes. For a freeze frame moment or more I recognized the 'primitive' dialogue in all of us, even in those strange yellow orbs holding on me. He, too, was preoccupied with living, and thinking about it. After a balancing act of arduous concentration he dropped the piece of bread he had struggle so mightily with and turned and ran back up the telephone wire. No, the moment could not be held in the magic of actuality, but I hold it still in my memory. How much alike all consciousness is across the constriction and contradiction of form.

What had been our chance meeting, ironically, on a telephone wire, let me know that you are never too old for truths. Yes, I realized yet again what consciousness was in this place and that the phenomenon crosses form, but also yet again what consciousness was in me, too, as it stirred up a feeling for a rat. It was well before cocktail time, so I can't blame that. For that freeze frame moment, though I recognized how alone in a dread-filled universe all consciousness is, I also realized there was something more as well, maybe out of that fact, namely, another fact, the fact of compassion. Within this conscious presence of ours is something *more* we call compassion. In Latin it is called *misericorida, a suffering of the heart*, or before that possibly rooted in the Greek πασχω, *to undergo suffering with,* and in Latin again least likely but with *cum*, a *cum passus sum* perhaps. But no matter the Latin or the Greek, we know it from life, at least from the life of those who are sensitive to something more in breathing.

Consciousness runs up and down the ugly food chain, and yet it gives us, we who call ourselves humans, a way out of nature's way of doing things, by means of something we have called compassion. We have reached something rather profound; even as it is stands against the whole of everything and everyday life on planet earth, from nature and its food chain to humanity and its own rendition of that. Even the man dubbed the father of nihilism, the great Nietzsche, revealed something inside of him that wouldn't go away when he embraced the suffering horse in la Piazza Carlo Alberto, this great philosopher sobbing in Turin's rainy night. It had to be tied into what he deep down thought *der ubermensch* should be, had to be, was when all was said and written, sad and done. It was his last sane act, embracing another suffering creature, another sentient being. So conscious matter is not only conscious of itself, and conscious of itself as a uniquely individual and irreplaceable, but also as conscious matter that can have compassion! That has to give us pause, even as it penetrates into our presence with profundity.

The purpose of this chapter again is exactly that, to establish presence and then to penetrate into it, with profundity. Let me repeat that, for no other reason than to make sure I know what I am doing here: to establish presence and then to penetrate into it, with profundity. But have I, and you with me, been going about this correctly? Especially since we ended up with something contrary to the cosmos itself? Consciousness and compassion both!

We can see, as obvious and evident in nature, the elemental forces out of which we emerged, call them what you will. They are part of all matter, each creature carrying them within its very make up. One has only to view the late Hugo van Lawich's revealing documentary on the wild dogs of the Serengeti to witness this graphically displayed. Yet, something else is displayed besides the raw elementary energies of evolution and nature's brutality, or at best its indifference. *Consciousness is not at home on the Serengeti.* Ultimately, Hugo has to, *chooses to*, intervene to help a little dog Solo left to die by nature and her pack. And when he does choose to help the unfortunate pup, consciousness is displayed facing the jungle, confronting it with compassion. There is no continuation of one's species here, as there isn't in Nietzsche's embrace of the suffering horse as well. Simpatico, compassion, love is present in our presence, and it is a simpatico, compassion, love not for just forms as our own, but can and does pass beyond to other forms life takes, challenging nature itself in this. I honestly love my dog. Loren Eiseley obviously loved his Wolf. We humans can give of ourselves in different ways to help the other creatures on the planet. A garden is different than the Serengeti; a garden has been humanized, humanized by a consciousness not at home on the Serengeti, by a consciousness that can care, can have compassion, that can give of itself. Yes, love is the flower of this garden—after all of consciousness's evolutionary journey and our own groundwork, we reach and realize the phenomenon of love.

I have called love *a mysticism without ecstasy* in other works because it is so everyday, yet with its own kind of mysterious quality. You can see it in a hospital waiting room, in *all* the quiet sacrifices of people who love: a father, mother, son, daughter, sister, brother, friend, child, a stranger for a stranger on a rainy night. You can see it in the waiting room of a veterinarian as well, even in that creature with a different form than your own looking up at you. You can see it at a graveside, a bedside, in the conviviality of family and friends at feast and fun, feel it in the soft hand of a child or the winkled hand of someone coming to the end of her day in the sun. You know it in the smile of someone you love and who loves you. Oh yes, it comes with a sacred sense sometimes, too.

In a very real way, I think we all know what I itemized in the above paragraph, *or at least could*; and it is within this realization—and I mean realization in the full sense of the word, not only to understand but to real-ize, bring about, do—that one gets a sense of something more in us to us within us, a deep-rooted reality that is us, though ironically out of step with nature and too often much of humankind as well. Yet, when displayed by that humankind it brings us to tears; you certainly have had such experiences in your private lives. But so that we are not alone in this, on the same page as it were, let's use an experience of it we all shared. You all remember that day in September, a September to remember. Did those firemen finding their way into that inferno of Gemini giants merely act in and out of a vacuum? Though the air around them might indeed become such as it was being sucked up by the fire, were they themselves acting in a vacuum, out of a vacuum? Of course not, they were acting out of themselves, the love in them. Learned, yes, in the sense that we do, we creatures called human, have to have influences that make us sensitive to such an inner and so profound insight. Like our ability to learn a language is innate, so, too, is our ability to answer the invitation within each of us to be sensitive to the deepest part of our being, the call in our very consciousness to reach its deepest sense of being, its highest evolution. We are creatures of space and time, and each and all have a history on planet earth called experience, and as such, from bambino on need others to help open the door to so much in life, on the natural level like a child being fed, to social behavior, as well as being sensitive to the deepest part of being. Is that so shocking—that we are alive to spacetime, creatures all, creatures who need other creatures, from bambino to burial? Of course nurturing is necessary; but in a strange way love is already in us to be nurtured. In the most basic of human tensions, these firefighters were addressing our sense of more as well as our mortal coil—facing the fire, the fact of the fire, with the instinct to run away, but also with the fact of something deep within their being as well, the giving of themselves, no matter what the influences in their lives that opened that for each of them.

Sartre might rightly or wrongly say 'hell is other people,' but for sure love is. That is nothing new to us, the oldest piece of literature known to our species talks of love, of love and loss, of love and loss and confusion over that suffering, of love as somehow nonetheless saying what it's all about even as we are dumbfounded by all of it. But we never have to turn a page of literature to know that; or ever read a newspaper about others display of it, as if studying some aliens and their acts. It is part of our own story, yours and mine and everyone who as flesh and blood actually experience this mysticism without ecstasy and what it means. We are interested in that—pursuing that! Pursuing that in the real world! Pursuing it *as something grounded in life and living!* Paul Feyerabend, the philosopher of the conquest of abundance, on the final page of his autobiography, written in his final days, concluded that love is all that matters in life. He ends his autobiography with the word—*love.* Camus, in his *The Rebel*, opted for a rebellion that could not exist without a strange form of love, an insane generosity. Viktor Frankl based his psychiatric credo on a supra-meaning, a light shining in the darkness as he put it, at one's innermost core, telling us the greatest secret and salvation itself is through love and in love.[17] He went on to say how strong this love was: *Was Du erlebt, kann keine Macht der Welt Dir rauben. What you have experienced, no power on earth can take from you.*[18] Loren Eiseley ends the compilation of his work with the following: "It was here that I came to the final phase of love in the mind of man—the phase beyond the evolutionists' meager concentration upon survival. Here I no longer cared about survival—I merely loved."[19] Again I must make mention that even the so-called father of nihilism, the great Nietzsche, revealed something inside of him that wouldn't go away when he embraced the suffering horse in the Pizza Carlo Alberto.

So maybe there is something in this thing we call love. It's been with us since Gilgamesh and before, no doubt since the dawn of consciousness. Maybe *it can* lead us to what we are looking for. Can it be that we *really* have an answer of how to act in the face of the swarming multiplicity all around us, in the face of the suffering, in the face of the uncertainty, in the face of what we call spacetime, in the face of being itself that confuses us so—do we have a way from life itself to live and breathe? We have to honestly ask ourselves that—*honestly,* for it may not be the way. It might be a pipe dream, and love a mistake in evolution, an aberration in actuality.

Yes, perhaps it is an aberration in actuality. Truly there—but an aberration! For it appears invisible to the razor of rational reductionism or the slicing cold cut machine of brain researchers. It defies rules and regulations, is without dogma or canons, without eightfold pathways or nine either. In truth, it is anti-religious as well as anti-rational—Camus even calls it an insane generosity. Insanity after all is often defined as not facing reality. Is love insane then? Wrong-headed? Have we been? History and humans have not changed generally speaking. "Look back over the past, with its changing empires that rose and fell, and you can foresee the future, too." Marcus Aurelius is said to have written the statement, and although unsourced textually, it is nonetheless true. Politics really hasn't changed over the centuries, *panem et circis* is still the order of the day, the will to power the real driving force behind all the rhetoric and reform, Caesar replacing Caesar, the right the left, the left the right, in an on-going madness that makes *Marat/Sade* look like it is telling the truth with its absence of love throughout. Love is alien to politics and economy and almost everything groups of humans undertake; it seems such an enormous struggle, without and within, and all around, not to mention above and below as well. All of it has to give us pause, make us wonder, when all is said and done, if a loving life has to be a hopeless loving one, loving hopelessly? Even if a person fights off goose-stepping down the *Les Champs Elysee* to nature's drum, isn't there still a part of us that thrills to the band, forgetting what brought it out? So is it sane to give of ourselves, to give of ourselves to make the world better, knowing as we do what it is, as well as what we are? Do I save little Solo or drive on? Share my soup or not? And when I do, I still have to know that all and every act of compassion or rebellious love will make very little difference in the tide of time. In Book VII of his *Meditations*, number 59, Marcus Aurelius says in a most sourced way, "Look within. Within is the fountain of good, and it will ever bubble up, if you will but continue to dig." In other words, it takes continued effort, the battle is never over; the tension within our very make up doesn't end with us merely knowing about it, a person has to *realize* it; which will often require overcoming the realizations mentioned above. It is on-going, with slips and slides, stumbles and out and out stupidities on the way, not to mention slumps in our spirit because of the world we live in and the nature of nature itself. Yes, insanity is often defined as not facing reality, as I mentioned, but we *are* facing it, never denying the harsh reality of the world as a whole and nature as well—and yet simultaneous to that we also have to know and accept another reality, namely, that—no, I want to stop there. We are on the cusp of something very important, but let's stop and catch our breath. I feel uncomfortable with the quickness of our venture to this point. It will take a longer development, a deeper digging, a slower more methodic process to come to this cusp I spoke of, not to mention what awaits us after. It is much too important to rush. It is the foundation of each of us we are dealing with, as well as to everything to follow in this book.

Whether I learned it in my mother's wonderful kitchen or whether it just popped up in my devious mind along the way, I cannot say, but it has become the very mantra of my philosophy: *the proof of the pasta is always in the tasting*. Or to put it in more philosophical terms, the evidence of and for anything is and must always be rooted in existence, in an existence lived with awareness to it; it is the only thing we really have or have to go by. Whatever the results, that has to be our approach in this venture. Even if it tells us the universe is not eternal and consciousness an aberration in it, not to mention compassion as well. Existence is all we really have to work with. There is no other way to approach anything but through existence. So, although not completed yet, at least in that regards, our venture has started off correctly. "Yes," I sing out with a shout, my Old English up on all fours. "This may be a bold assertion," I put it to him in dulcet tones, "but it has to be said. Pasta is our salvation. Our souls have to be fed. So start the water boiling, get out the olive oil. Stir that sauce and cut that bread—it's not over, folks, till we're dead!" By this time he is out of the room. He does this when I sneeze, too. Anyway, I'll spare you the rest of the song and leave it for the play. I know you'll love it! Unlike you know who.

Meanwhile, allow me, and you with me, to continue to see *from existence alone* what's here and there, up and down, far and wide, and where it all leads, and at greater length this time, and deeper yet—just to make sure we've got it right, to make sure all the things I have said thus far are not "epistles of delusion" from me and about me, but rather written in my own blood as the man from Rocken so ingeniously put it. In other words, because it is all-important, like good detectives and philosophers both, let's again start *ab ovo,* and as with any experiment or gathered evidence *repeat the procedure* to see where indeed the sweep of spacetime leads and if we can & have indeed, truly, in fact, in reality, precisely, exactly, and verily come out of our cosmic evolution with this essential grounding we so desperately need to accomplish our Archimedean task of having a place to stand that is our root-reality, namely, a *presence* we are certain of as we are of nothing else, a you and me, a you and me as really real, despite the un-decidability of deconstruction, despite the doctrine of the day that says it's all relative, despite the danger of the ever-present abyss and the imagined devil, too.

Play it again, Sam!

Of course, a problem immediately arises that might confound our ability to prove ourselves really real—one outside of Buddhism and biology and things that go bump in the night. We are aware from mathematics that Kurt Godel's incompleteness theorem denies us the possibility of construction of a complete, consistent mathematical description of reality[20]; and we have the same result from modern physics, where deep reality and the connection of it all into one grandness escapes us.[21] But one needn't be a Godel or the happy couple of Hawking & Penrose to know that; life shows it to us in our everyday breathing. Life is a labyrinth of twist and turns, and we know not what around the next corner. It is *knowingly uncertain* if you have even half a brain, and we are going to grant ourselves at least that. So, how then can I talk of this one minimal certainty in such a sea of mental mimsy? "Get real," you might complaint—get real and accept that you can't prove yourself real! Or even that you aren't! What I have to do then, as I see it, is to take all this, you and me, Luigi and Alice, the comedienne and fellow fallibilosopher, along with the whole of postmodernism, be it that litany out of the Derridan desert with his inherited historical faith, or a tangle of deconstruction that leaves the Principle of Uncertainty itself uncertain, not to mention but I will, a use of Plato's Khora or non-use of Kierkegaardian leaps, and maybe even Caputo's alleged prayers and real tears—and without recasting the desert or the darkness, the suffering or the shadows, the myths or the math, center it in the truest moment of our being as breathing humans, and show that as such.

How? How do I show the truest moment of our being as breathing humans? If I can't do that I am a failed philosopher and each of us a failed person. So I better be able to do this—for your sake as well as mine! But, again, how? Especially since I am no Hamlet—make that Heidegger—nor was meant to be. First and foremost, with the anthropic principal, *at least my version*, firmly in my entropic hand, by going to the deepest kind of knowing we have!

I think it might be interesting to anticipate what I am going to go into at greater length later and say here that when philosophy first burst unto the human stage, at least our Greek version of it, it centered on what today is called reason, but reasoning was thought of in a much broader sense than what we have come to categorize it today with the limited notion of logic as we know it, or rationality as we connote it. The Greeks had a freshness, dare I say wholeness to thinking. Going back to those very beginnings of Greek thought, let's look at Parmenides' famous phrase, Χρη το λεγειν τε νοειν τε εον εμμεναι. Heidegger is correct when he says 'the making-to-appear' and 'letting-lie-before-us' is, in Greek thought, the essence of λεγειν and λογος, and 'take-to-heart' the essence of νοειν, and thus the beginning of Western thought and thinking rooted in Parmenides famous phrase, Χρη το λεγειν τε νοειν τε should be understood thusly; namely, 'Useful is the letting to lie-before-us also taking to heart too . . .'[22] For now I'll just stay with that from the phrase and point out how the Greeks used thinking in a much wider way than we have come to define it. True later on λεγειν/λογος comes to be understood in the sense of proposition and νοειν understood in the sense of apprehension, with the Romans later centering into it as *ratio*, what is rational, the coupling of λεγειν and νοειν as one, and *ratio* (Ho-ratio) has stayed with us through the Scholastics and Shakespeare, Aristotelianism (not Aristotle) and everyone in line, all the way to today with so many in contemporary philosophy limiting it further and sacrificing human thinking on the altar of an analytical approach solely. So the original way of approaching existence, εον εμμεναι, disappears and analysis as we know it assumes dominion. But that limitation on knowing and thinking limits rather than enlightens, leaving us with a rigid definition of thinking and thus actually blocking our way to actuality, that very existence that is what philosophy is thinking about. All that was to say again that we have many ways of knowing.

It is said that Einstein confessed that he first grasped his theory of e=mc2 *intuitively*, before he came up with any expression of it in formula form. There is a quote of his that touches upon intuition: "The intellect has little to do on the road to discovery. There comes a leap in consciousness, call it Intuition or what you will, the solution comes to you and you don't know how or why." Penrose, who gave us the singularity theorem, also attests to the fact that his best work arose from intuitions.[23] Even so, what I am talking about is not an eureka, as in those two cases or any other, for you and I don't come to our existence as a flash of insight, *it is a deeper grasping still*, something that can never really be properly put into words, one which each of us knows as we know nothing else. It is absolutely our most basic grasp of reality; each person's *primary* intuition of one's being, what is innermost to each of us and *fundamentally present to us*. We don't argue to it. We could argue to it like Descartes and say *je pense, donc je suis*. But that is ass-backwards, turning the subject into an object. Rather, it is I-am, with everything following from that. I-am and I can . . . How ironic it is that what is most fundamentally present to this presence in the universe is its own presence, not as a presence arguing to itself, but as the presence itself *grasping without object, directly, sans separation, its very being*. That, without a doubt, is a hard concept to grasp—because it is not a concept. It is rather our root-reality, what is fundamentally familiar, existentially instinctual, directly grasped, innermost, and, in truth, the most certain thing each of us knows.

So let's at least admit to the fact—our most basic fact—you simply know you are present. It is known to you as you know nothing else on this road of relative relativity Lilly and I, and you as well, are all hazarding a hunch about. No you can't objectify it, as you can't touch the end of your forefinger with that very forefinger, but I will explain that later. Meanwhile, though the cosmos around us might spin in a merry-go-round of apparent madness, if not real madness itself, there is this starting point for each and every one of us in it all, I exist, you exist, Lilly, the bag lady, too—and each of us knows that as we know nothing else—*as our one minimal certainty.*

Even to deny you exist needs you to exist to deny it. And if what is fundamentally present to you is not true, as already underlined, everything that follows has to be more than suspect. Including your denial of it. "Stop the world I want to get off," you might rightly yell, but it is a real world with a real scream and a real you screaming. Borges, the Argentine writer, though his works were often in the nebulous orb, says toward the end of the beautiful book, *Labyrinths*, "The world, unfortunately, is real; I, unfortunately, am Borges."[23] Although we might not be as unfortunate as this wonderful writer for whom the world began to dim due to his approaching blindness, you and I know suffering is real—and laughter, too—and love—and the presence of all that and in all that, oh yes you and I are real! Anything else is "a hideous hypothesis." A hilarious one, too. I quote Hume's phrase in satire. However, although "Humean" or "humean" is often used to denote a lack of core or self, even Hume talked of a "uniting principle" "which I pretend not to explain" and takes it as something given.[24]

Suffering the loss of that presence, as we saw in the three men and a boy, is the greatest of nightmares. That is true for us witnessing it, as it was for those behind that silencing horror. It may be the farthest point from life. I am reminded of that "creature who was once a handsome presence," as Dante pens it, and then goes on to have it say as already put forth, *"Io non mori' . . . I did not die, and I was not alive; think for yourself, if you have any wit, what I became, deprived of life and death.* You can see why William James shuttered one cloudy day when he saw such a creature. While visiting an insane asylum James recounted a "black-haired youth with greenish skin, entirely idiotic . . . moving nothing but his black eyes and looking absolutely non-human. That shape am I, I felt, potentially." James said he was left with a "horrible dread at the pit of my stomach, and with a sense of insecurity of life that I never knew before, and that I have never felt since."[25] All of this—Dante's description of the depths of hell, and James' of the depths of human dread—is because each of us knows we are our presence and the loss of it *is* dreaded; and should be, because it is life itself for us. We will again return to both James and the biggest problem in existence; but for now let us continue with our immediate pursuit, this presence we all so cherish.

I could go into a scientific sojourn here as already suggested and take the model of the neutrino and apply it to the mind/matter problem that haunts the halls of higher learning and drives philosophers to drink, stating how neutrino mass can, in principle, turn matter into antimatter and back again, and change the balance between them. Why would I do that? To show that something can be one thing and another, even matter and antimatter, and *apply that type of thinking* to the mind/matter or consciousness/brain problem. Since we really don't know what causes the mind or consciousness, yet it exists simultaneous to our brain mass, with suffering and self and love and laughter, and a sense of more somehow coming out of it all, we certainly can use such models from science to try to show that such a thing as the neutrino puts forth is at least possible and can be useful in trying to get a handle on the machinations of the mind with/in matter. It provides a way of thinking, opening the situation up as quantum mechanics has done in and to science. I could even use the "together in separation" of the particle/wave within quantum mechanics, or the scientific dimensionality of space-time and non-spacetime the big bang offers, all of which I have done in a labyrinthine book before this one; but I shall forego all that here and merely send a bowl of soup over to a hungry stranger, or with Frankl and Sacks, Hyman and Gardner, have compassion for our three men and a boy, or this author for a rat; and in that come to the point of that long book in one sentence: *I am and I can . . .*[26]

But allow me to play my own Devil's Advocate and interrupt our minimal certainty with a return to biology, and perhaps to subliminal meanderings out of the lengthy book I mentioned as well. For the sake of more confusion permit Dr. Llimas, a neuroscientist at NYU his say, that the "self" is merely the interaction of the thalamus and cortex. Although he has *not* scientifically proved this, let us again for confusion's sake say it is so, that his leap of thalamic-cortical faith is fact. No matter, even if the self is created by the brain after we are born, it is not the same yet not another thereafter. In other words, something has happened which changes everything, including the brain. That said, I should like to go on to mention the fact that consciousness precedes birth, the baby is conscious in the womb. Yes, you might say, but not as a self! *Au contraire!* Give me consciousness and you give me the self. For my point has been all along, consciousness involves a level of presence. True, it is not at the level the baby will be conscious after living in the world outside the womb. But once consciousness is present inside the womb, at the level it is at that time—whether reacting to Mozart or to the voice of its mother—it follows that with the fact of pre-natal consciousness, no matter how it came about, we must accept the self in its root-reality of being before the trauma of birth and the beginning of its journey on planet stress. Of course, once out of the womb that presence is enhanced by more experience, the extended experience of life and living in which the baby, like you or I, grows in self-awareness as well as entropy, as well as language and the towers of babble coming out of it called books.

Obviously, by now you are aware that I am enthralled with true science. In fact, let me add, my own philosophical method is like true science's, in that it always has to go back to my mantra or motto as you recall, back to and be shown in the real world as the final proof. Like pasta the truth *is* in the tasting. Da Vinci's motto was not about pasta, though it may have come out of his diet. No matter, it was about truth, which is our concern as well. *Virtutem forma decorat,* he writes (*the form embellishes, adorns, beautifies, decorates the truth*). Not bad for a genius, for each of us has a form, and each of us has a truth which decodes it, decorates it, defines it, does almost everything for it, namely consciousness, *our most basic truth as humans.* There truth speaks to us most intimately. We don't exist without consciousness; it is the sine qua non of being human, of being us—even if it is reduced to the stem of our brain and the reptilian trance of a coma. The fact or truth of conscious existence is at the core of our existence. We have no other way to proceed. However we come by it, it is the most important level of being within us, the tool for our functioning as human beings and not functioning merely as our toiletry. It is our way to the world, to being the witness we spoke of—the very self we spoke of. We really can't proceed as humans without it, whether being a Buddhists, biologist, or the human version of Beelzebub. How thrilling and terrifying both! How thrilling that you and I, and every man and woman with us, are both the witness and way to the truth of actuality, at least our own, and more still if it or any part of it can be known by humans. And this is so because we *are* conscious creatures. But how terrifying at the same time, because consciousness itself is vulnerable, vulnerable to a fate worse than death as both Dante and James reminded us. Without it we seem gone, crippled to carry on, except, at best, momentarily, when we find an instant of love in a chapel or find a moment of silent strange peace surrounded by plants. This terror and thrill both points out rather graphically that each of us is a conscious creature, and consciousness is our self-being at root-reality, growing as we go. Yet, I am stuttering . . . fishing for words . . . because . . . well think about it . . . how can I say what consciousness is? "We have no accepted theory of consciousness," says even Christof Koch.[27] That does indeed leave us splashing about between Scylla and Charybdis, a rock and whirlpool, a particle and a wave, a thalamus and a cortex. Should we laugh at our predicament? It does sound more like the stuff of Aristophanes than Sophocles, and I am willing to forgive a lot for a good laugh. And it is a good one! For what we have here is something that is the measure of all things even as it is un-measurable. As I mentally roll on the floor in jocular abandon, quixotically fighting off all hundred and thirty five pounds of my concerned Old English, I hear myself mockingly ask the mirror across the room if this is supposed to be like some Delphic riddle or other? The face I am looking into becomes serious. I get up off my imagined floor and my fingers begin typing away. It is precisely *the* Delphic riddle, the most famous of all—γνωθι σεαυτον! As each of us listens with a hushed inner attentiveness, the words become the call from life itself—*know thyself!* The enigma of life is that the enigma of life, life itself as *consciousness in the cosmos* affords us access into the mysteries of being otherwise unfathomed and unfathomable without it, and this includes life itself as consciousness in the cosmos even as we really don't know what consciousness is in and of itself.

Even as we have not yet fully realized the depths of that mystery and therefore the depths of ourselves, have we at least realized Archimedes' one request here? *Give me a place to stand, and I will move the world. Δος μοι του στω και ταν γαν κινασω.* Yes! And I put it in the original, because it is so important. Whether playwright or physicist, clown in a traveling circus or gravedigger for a madhouse, we have realized Archimedes' one request and our own, we have one minimal certainty in it all, a place to stand from which we can move the world—it is our presence, this consciousness in the cosmos. "This secret must be hugged," Aeschylus calls out from the wings. But it is no secret—everyone knows it, dear Aeschylus! Everyone alive on planet stress, including that isle you died on so comically! It is the very presence you lost that day, and the one I have today! The one my two readers as well as everyone else alive have!

Because consciousness is at the depth of our presence, I should make mention and it should be understood that when I say presence I always include consciousness. So presence or words like you and me, or self-being, always include consciousness as understood—they are synonymous existentially with consciousness or awareness. This is so even though each presence takes in the whole of a human and has many levels of being within it, and should be understood as such, going as I said from the elemental to the evolutionary to this phenomenon of awareness; but *consciousness is the sine qua non for the completion of one's presence.*

As it is I might interject, for evolution, the highest rung on that great push from tide pools to paws to people. No doubt, in time, science can come up with alternative accounts of the material world than it has at present, and models and abstract structures might change in philosophy, but not the essential reaching through them or in life itself; namely, what is essential in us, *a consciousness in the cosmos.*

What is essential in us then becomes essential to our continued pursuit. It is something we must penetrate further, of course—to go from the elemental particles in evolution to the elemental us—and this can be seen as I mentioned in the rich history of our own universe from the beginning, as elementary particles form into atoms and atoms into molecules and molecules into gases, liquids, and solids that, in turn, form galaxies and our planet and ultimately the brains in our heads, which are in concert with this thing we call awareness, the apex of evolution—however the hell it got here and no matter what happens to it once it exists.

Eventually, we shall address, at length, *the deepest experience* in our conscious presence, but for the present let's continue with just this conscious presence. Physically we know we are carbon-based creatures who have a genetic history as well as a nurturing, notional, and nutritional one—all coming together as our experience of existence; namely, as a consciousness in the cosmos. There does, I must state, slither through our primal beginnings a joyless force of anonymous and relentless darkness that primitive humankind sensed and responded to. It seems loveless and removed, so removed from us, and yet is the raw nature out of which we came. But there is more to us than the raw elemental energies of evolution and we live with it everyday. What slouched out of that tide pool to be born is more than mud and carries a mystery within it called awareness. We cannot abstract ourselves out of that reality—it is where we are and what we are—made up of the raw elemental energies of evolution and this phenomenon called consciousness that gives our presence its very definition.

Though a blood-blameless tide was let loose and our river of life run red with it, still within this thing we call evolution, something wide-eyed with being itself was also called forth, at wits end to find its own and everything else's meaning, including what might be called the mysteries that made it.

It's way before dawn and the den seems hung in a film noir of mental whispers as a slow rain murmurs in the wind outside. I suppose it's the perfect time, in such a milieu, to make mention that I do indeed hold for a "liberty proper to the human mind."[28] And at such a time as now I feel drawn to it. Perhaps it is here where true thinking takes place and Heidegger is right when he says thinking is to be drawn to what withdraws, and humans thus the pointer. Maybe, maybe not, but Descartes is right when he talks about a liberty proper to the human mind, even as he ended up closing it down. No matter about his finale, it is a freedom that can take us where no one has gone before, one that can go from the somber to the scherzo, from the antediluvian inside our heads to the anticipated. Such a freedom applied to the mystery of ourselves allows for the possibility that consciousness may be more than we imagine, since by that very consciousness we have fathomed so deeply as to come up with the beginning of the universe itself, and so a meta-physical before it.

That being the case, as it is, this is not a question about whether there is a *meta*physical, *μετα τα θυσικα*, *meta* meaning more than, for we do indeed have such a non-spacetime dimension as we see with regards the big bang which began spacetime and our physical universe. Of course, we don't know what happened before the singularity we call the big bang, no matter what poetry and philosophy scientists write about it; but we do know that as the pasta goes, matter and time begins with that primal explosion, and in there is consciousness in the cosmos. The question is then whether anything meta-physical manifests itself in the physical reality called spacetime. From what we have from existence, of course. We must stay true to the chapter. Here, because it opened the metaphysical to us, nebulous and mystifying as it sounds, I can speculate, with a liberty proper to the human mind, that the enigma of consciousness itself appears as though it might hint at an answer to that question, even as consciousness itself stymies us, and maybe does so because of this quality it possesses. So when I speak of our presence, while I realize that each of us can act only on the options presented to us in this journey called life, I am aware that that horizon can be greater by far than we might imagine. We could mirror actuality itself, combining in that very consciousness all the dimensionalities, each of us made in the image and likeness of it, each of us living in a more within, even as we are most definitely vulnerable to a truck, a virus, or the economy we are alive to. While we recall Shakespeare's warning to reason that there are things beyond it, it is reason itself, the liberty of it, that tells us such a mirroring of the meta could be so and has reason to be so. The proof the pasta is in tasting I have said from the start, and such is the situation even here, in that it was consciousness that brought us to the multi-dimensional, to the meta-physical, and so could as well possess such a quality itself. *Quidquid recipitur, secundum modum recipientis recipitur;* *"Whatever is received is received according to the manner/capacity of the one receiving."* I have been so level headed up to now, but there is a sudden surge of electricity inside my skull, a freedom that wants to fly freer yet, like a butterfly that would escape its cranial cocoon. Allow me this! A moment to fly, even if it is only with Peter Pan to Neverneverland, or with Nietzsche to something greater than *der untermensch*, that "last man" he mocks so, the one who blinked at the things he talked about and would no doubt at what I am about to. Is consciousness in the cosmos the rarest thing in spacetime, because it—how should or could I say this—because it does indeed incorporate both what is measurable and what is not measurable in us, what is physical and what is metaphysical, somehow stretching beyond our pedestrian notion of it and ourselves, the true nature of which we don't know and yet maybe do through this rarity in spacetime called conscious matter, you and me?

The smell of sheepdog just entered the room interrupting my mental labyrinth in search of myself. How beautiful he is. How beautiful awareness is—to allow me to realize that. To realize everything I do! Yes, Albert, the moon is there whether you look at it or not. And maybe more, too! No, not to do with the moon, but behind those eyes looking out at it, for the cosmos without consciousness is only solar wind and silence, a vastness without vision. And what are we without it? And what is conscious doing in a place like this? And what is it really? What are we really—this presence in all this? Are we more than the matter that surrounds us and makes us up? Is part of us indeed a strangeness in space, and we strangers because of it? Because we hold inside ourselves this awareness that stretches across actuality?

"More questions about yourself?" my Old English asks as he flops his overweight body onto the rug. "I am more than the cosmos," I inform him. He says nothing, closing his eyes and leaving me to myself.

The grandfather clock has struck the hour. It is four in the morning and I find myself impatient with language. I hear the haunting sound of a train in the distance. Maybe it is merely a reflection of the night, but I have to stop and ask, past the rhapsody of words, am I in my somewhat-peculiar-sort-of postmodern philosophy trying to break out of the grip of myth into the world of reality beyond it and merely constructing my own myth in its place? Are we merely selected objects in space and nothing more? What is this liberty proper to the human mind? "Not to understand, to be stupefied—this is the closest one can come to understanding the un-understandable," a round faced, round nosed, round-eyed man once rounded it off. I think such a statement could be my own.[29] It is the reason I am a philosopher, unfit for anything else, perhaps a failed philosopher, one that is exceedingly silly, constructing a wisdom of bon mots, using language that is inconsequential and even banal, posturing with the air of sequiturs that more than often turn out to be non sequiturs. Yes, of course, I am a failed philosopher. As everyone is a philosopher, everyone is a failed one. I should stop trying to explain the human condition and its origins and simply live with it; swallow it all with a desperate courage, keeping a baby dinosaur and mammoth as my household pets. But I digress—or do I? Is listening to the music in my make up a digression? Or is it somehow touching and hearing the strings that started us and everything with us? "I swim in darker waters than I want," I tell the Doppler sounding train, "because for me the world should be glad, happy, laughing and love, but it is not." Where does that leave me, even as I would change it all if I could? I am a stranger in a strange land, a consciousness that cares in a cosmos that can't, and me thinking thoughts beyond it. Does this liberty proper to the human mind make us reconnoiter for that which isn't or can even be? Or is the listening to the music in my make up somehow the way to what is more than this place and somehow I know that? This driven passion to understand is our hallmark as humans, our heaven and our hell. "Thoughts against thoughts in groans grind." Am I in a Hopkins-like mood because of the hour, and like him realize caring is wasted on the world, and should let the world go where the world will. Is this the vineyard's fire that speaks? Or blind blood brooding? Maybe an ancient anguish? Or merely a nostalgic heart? This would-be wise man is in so many ways so different from his world and would be satisfied with nothing less than a new one, a world constructed, of course, on his own terms, as I suppose all of us would. Only I am mad enough to actually attempt it! "By writing a mere book?" I hear my cockatiel laugh out and my shaggy wolf concur with a suppressed howl. "Isn't it rather venturesome to think that a combination of words, a la philosophy, a la theology, can tell us about being, can tell us about the secrets of the soul, can make humans better animals?" I hear my wall ask joining in the guffaw. "Isn't it as ridiculous as keeping a baby rhinoceros for you to think that your particular babble can tell us a bit *more* than any other?" the ceiling concurs overhead, trying to prompt a yes from me. "Dinosaur, baby dinosaur," I correct and turn my attention back to my computer. "So you intend to keep this venturesome nonsense going then," the floor counters underfoot. I can sense the room ganging up on me, even my mirror wants out, and my Old English has abandoned me, his swift departure a demonstration that discretion is indeed the better part of valor. No matter, I venture on, bad hair day or not! Let's finish this book and write poetry thereafter . . . no better yet, comedy . . . no still better, comic-agony.

The artist in me and the philosopher there as well often argue, but it is the clown who always wins out, a clown too childish-foolish for this world. My autobiography in a sentence! I honestly hold life should be happy. What a child. What a fool. What a disappointment. A laugh, a laugh, my dingdom for a laugh! Yes, let's finish this book and write poetry thereafter . . . no better yet, comedy . . . no still better, comic-agony.

But I digress—or do I? No, I will not leave it to others to distill the human venture into dry theories devoid of all that we are or might be.

After a break for some required food, required both by my body and my prescribed Glucophage, I sit for a while in the quite of my living room before I return to the I-Mac and begin anew my involvement in this liberty proper to the human mind, sugar level in tack. However, my thinking is not in tack or tow, for that wonderful wanderer would still create better worlds than exist. That gives me pause. I tell myself that we can do that, cerebrally create better worlds than exist, only because we know this one, the everyday of it, including the more in us, the more that makes us want to make a better world than exists. What is that based on? No, not the thought per se, nor even the ability to know a better from what we know, but the more itself, the want of a better? What is this want, this will for more within me? Again, what am I really? What are you? We know, like an inner stalking all the way back to the savannahs or was it the sea, that matter is our inheritance, those raw elemental energies of evolution and what awaits each of us in that, the dreaded curtain. But with this, in this, is a marvel called awareness, that still unspoken gathering and gatherer both that I am! I have taken place and I am aware of all this! You, too! I am conscious matter! Matter has given forth to life, and life to this equally astonishing phenomenon, awareness, and not only that, but an awareness that can want, wish for, will better worlds than exist. Awareness, know thyself! Isn't that what we are about here—wanting to know what we are really, we conscious creatures that can want, wish for, will? Will for more than our daily bread and butter, but for whole new universes and the mystery of everything and being itself with it—what is this creature really, what are we really?

It is a question that can leave us shivering! Shivering with the clear and present danger of finding out what we really are—finding out if it is true, as each of us sometimes feels on cold nights, that every psyche is merely an amalgam of myth, each a reflection of its dreams and its nightmares, left with nothing but mirrors and other mirrors after that and no source for the image itself. You and me, really a *reductio ad absurdum*! *But are we* comes back a whisper within, for even in such a winter of discontent, when the wind blows out of a bitter northerly nothing, hissing we are nothing, tempting us to agree, our presence still senses more about itself. Our challenge is the same as the sentry on that crisp cold night in Denmark, in my den, and everywhere else, "Who's there?" It leads us expectantly forward, like a great drama, each of us living on two planks and a passion, vital data always being peeled away, level by level, as we look for, well ourselves. And maybe Godot on the way. Prayer and plays always have a fascinating ambiguity about them. Perhaps the playwright, more than philosopher or priest, scientist or sage, is the only one who has it right, telling us we hardly know what's up or down, or worse, who the hell we really are, and yet daring to say we do . . . in the busy murmur of stage wind, in the rapidity of fake rain, in a lonely and silly soliloquy. The dramatist of the human condition knows that although on cold nights we might write beautiful words saying, "it's all a threnody being intoned by a melancholy spirit" there is still more in each presence, or why is the word said, the work written, the cry raised, the quest started, the love given? We respond to such a dramatic poet, because like the playwright, every human within themselves is in this same tug-a-war between a call to nothing and the response of consciousness, each of us trying to answer that question about ourselves which has been with us from the dawn of our species. "Who's there?" And so it goes, I can't stop, my shaggy dog would think it queer without a farmhouse near. I must answer the sentry!

Stephen Gould shortly before his death, pointed out that even his hero the great Galileo made a mistake—he didn't, Gould says of Galileo, have the theoretical space to conceptualize that Saturn could have rings.[30] Of course, he didn't have a good telescope either. Our analytical age doesn't have the theoretical space to grasp *a presence in all its levels of being*, and that is not because it does not have the telescope, but because of an analytical arrogance that refuses to use it, to us all our ways of knowing. We have to open ourselves up in our attempt to see being for what it is, and that requires using the whole of our own being. We are our own best telescope. That is why we can answer the sentry! Though fractal and through a glass darkly, the fact that we have being can lead us to the insight we need to understand what is most important about being. Not just any old kind of being, but conscious being.

Is that too optimistic? Too much in favor of liberty, too much in favor of the human mind's ability to venture for this our postmodern age?

In this year of Darwin's bicentennial perhaps a greater insight into evolution can be fostered by looking within. Yet, despite the absolute necessity of knowing ourselves, knowing ourselves as we really are, I dare say what is most important about being for us, the very core of our being human, is a missing link not only in the science of evolution, but in the love of wisdom as well. We must make it central, our very launching pad for any philosophical sojourn. Because it is such! Everything each of us is in existence is rooted in this *unifying identity*, and it cannot be dismissed by philosophy, or anything else for that matter. In this *presence* is the answer, in this consciousness in the cosmos that can have an experience that the cosmos itself cannot have, in this awareness from which we can wonder why and even dare to disturb the universe. With this root-reality we have our fulcrum and can cry out *eureka*, naked to the elements though we might be, like Archimedes himself in the streets of Syracuse when he, too, cried out his famous find with the word *"ευρηκα!"*

I think you are beginning to realize I am approaching this quite differently than does 'traditional' philosophy, let alone postmodernism: for I hold that not only is it through *all our ways of knowing* that we must philosophize, but that we actually can come to a certainty when we do, minimal true—if you call your very presence such—but there nonetheless. I think you are beginning to realize I am looking at this in and of itself quite differently as well.

The self is not a ghost in a machine, nor is it a Sartrean reflective nothing. It is more than Husserl's functional description or Hume's foam, more than Heidegger's "ecstatic pro-ject," Dennett's concocted "I", Wilson's hum of an anthill, or the silly half-truth within a cutesy one, "we don't know who we are and that's who we are." The most basic truth of being for us is that we are not a foam, a mere functional description or a pro-ject, merely the hum or hill of our parts, totally anonymous to ourselves and at bottom an empty desert abyss, a no-place leaving us nowhere and so having to cling to a Caputonian faith of undecidability. You love your children, John, not on faith, but on what you know as you know nothing else, build on that. Undecidability ends there and real freedom begins; begins with a flesh and blood root-reality so different than Caputo's credo of cerebral circumcision. But these men of renown are speaking out of a mindset subject to either analytical abstraction or Derridan deconstructionism, and insist it is the way to the truth of being and ourselves, even as they repudiate the self or ever being able to know it. However, they might on a passionate night with Madame de Beauvoir or Madame de Bovey or even Kathy C know better; and maybe, God help them, even go beyond the raw elemental energy of evolution's evening of safe sex and know the intimacy of love, a very real experience in each of their very real selves.

No, we are not looking at a grin without a cat, but what each of us knows first and foremost, in the deepest way we can know: *je-suis, io-sono, I-am!* I am and I can!

This is essential, not only because life would be literally and matter-of-factly, accurately and honestly, objectively and subjectively, strictly speaking and existentially different than it is, but because it is the way it is![31] How did instinctive urges become a conscious creature? When did creature grunts become the spoken word and the drive to procreate first become love, a phenomenon that could even challenge the survival drive in nature itself? When did the mind dive into the depths of its own inner world and know it was unique in the universe, something so dramatically different as to dare to have to disturb the universe itself? We humans are sleuths by birth, but we may never know the answers to those questions. However, we do know what the end result of all that is, *a conscious creature that can . . .* This is so not because of our culture, strong as it is in our make up, but because it is our root-realty, universal to every human, from before Sumer to the Space Age and on into whatever comes after it, that creature that slouches towards the future to be born. Just as Noam Chomsky talks of an innate/ pre-condition in us that takes on the particular language of our particular location, all of us have a presence/pre-fulfilled, that completes itself by its choices, and this is universal to our species, both the presence and the choosing.

From bambino to burial, just being alive makes us the conscious creatures that can . . . Life is a continual unfolding of this presence for each of us, a journey of choosing that creates the finished presence that then meets the confusion of death, an echoless place in our consciousness. Consider again for a moment the historical and pre-historical fact that since the dawn of human consciousness we have been grappling with the situation we found ourselves in, left wondering about that very consciousness itself as it wandered across the landscape of life in this desperate encounter between itself and the unconscious cosmos. Wondering about its end. This has been so since our species first put flowers on the grave of someone loved and lost to death; a loving remembrance some say the species before us did as well, those strange Neanderthals with their oval-shaped graves, or the *Homo heidelbergenis* did before them, one strange day 350,000 years ago, when these humanoid ancestors laid a single pristine rose-colored quartz ax among their dead, 100,000 years before the mastery of fire. Even on the far off landscapes across space-time itself, we will carry what we are with us, each of us a conscious creature; and in that, challenging the very loveless cosmos we find ourselves in. Each of us is this presence in the face of it all, each of us the center of the perspective of his or her own observation. Inner fragmentation does not reach down to a person at his or her root-reality, even as postmodernism accepts that it does and calls that our only reality. But it isn't! We do know more; we do know who we are! This is not a know-it-all presumption; it is our minimal certainty in breathing, still allowing for so much still unknown, about ourselves and so much more, but with that *unifying identity* there. When all is said and done, we cannot really function without it, or in the fullness of reality in a fragmentation of it. Be advised that fragmentation is not the same as levels of being, or the reality of a frayed and even frightened creature.

Perhaps we postmodern humans have too often confined ourselves to Derrida's desert, each a creature left abandoned to the future, waiting as it were for a messiah. But I am proposing another and different image, one truer to what we are, not a creature abandoned to the future, but one alive to the present. You and me here and now—and finding our way, not in and through any future or faith, forgotten or otherwise, but as each of us is, a real presence and the center of the perspective of his or her own observation here and now; this despite our past baggage and all our vulnerability and vicissitudes, caught as we are "in a knowledge of critical guesswork, in a net of hypotheses, a web of surmises," as our knighted philosopher so aptly puts it. Yes, we are all still "siblings of the same dark night," but not devoid of life's deepest utterance.[32]

This is what it means to truly think for yourself, out of the root-reality of yourself, where awareness is the essence of idea-forming, idea itself coming from the Greek root 'to be face to face,' and here what-you-are face to face with yourself and everything else. One can say it is where thinking itself reigns and not afterthoughts, where presence at its depths hangs out, that quality of being so integral to our humanness that it has to be approached with all our ways of knowing as a human, realizing as we do that we are more than the particles that make us up, more than the neurons, too, even as the brain is where this awareness comes to be. Listen to the nearness of its appeal; it is you yourself, not as what is spoken, but speaker. "If a fish is deprived of the fullness of its element, if it is dragged onto the dry sand, then it can only wiggle, twitch, and die," Heidegger wrote when talking about what thinking was and means to us.[33] I can easily apply this to awareness. We are like the fish without it. Only solar wind and silence, a vastness without vision . . . I have not taken place. Deprived of the depth of our very being as humans, our deepest utterance, we disappear—and since, in the perilous perhaps of our odyssey, you can do this to yourself, can I at least scream for you not to!

Of course whether we scream or whisper, when we talk of that deepest utterance we can only use an accumulation of adjectives—the self is formed by an accumulation of adjectives and can only be, not because the self is not there, but because we can't honestly and accurately put our finger on it, since it is non-conceptual; that is, it could never be made into an object and thus objectified as we do everything else. At times it is determined by mere simultaneity with the brain, at others by contrast with the world around it, while at others still *via vino* and verisimilitudes, or poetry, or all too often, incorrectly, with psychobabble or merely the association of afterthoughts. The paradoxical truth is that, in conjunction with all its levels of being, of course, it is the self doing all this, life's deepest utterance! And that is the point I am making! Of course words fall off the page when we attempt to give verbal expression to it, for we are trying once again to describe what really is essentially indescribable, our being-ness at its root-reality, life's deepest utterance which cannot be uttered. However, since it's there, or as I prefer to say, here, here we are trying to describe it, trying to answer the sentry and ourselves. And I am saying, daring to say, contrary to what I just said, that, from existence and existence alone, which is all we have anyway, we can answer the sentry and ourselves. For the world is fortunately or unfortunately real, I, fortunately or unfortunately, am as well. You, too!

Is it my blasphemous intention then to attribute being to what is?

Yes! And in doing so come to know myself!

This is not some happy conjecture on my part, it can be affirmed by you yourself without me. How fortunate for me . . . and you!

As enticing as it might be to say this is all an illusion, the world and us in it, it isn't. The lady chewing at her lip because of the pain in her cancerous stomach is real, so is the lady laughing at the antics of her chubby cherub of a bambino. Life is real and you in it. When you abstract yourself out of it, you can never know either it or yourself—you can never answer the sentry! But I am saying because of the fact that you are real and present you can answer the sentry, as long as you stay focused on that real presence.

It will become evident how this is applicable to our pursuit of a purely human spirituality as we go, but first let me continue with what we have been doing so far, establishing our presence; except now dwell on its interiority and develop that further. It is impossible to deny that *an interior* appears at the very core of our lives. There are many ways to show this, each of them rooted in being witnesses to being, and a being with many levels of being I must always add; however, I think the best way to bring out this interiority, "out it" if you will, is to demonstrate the realization of ourselves in *contrast to* the cosmos. Let's do just that, and to help us do it, reduce the cosmos down to our more immediate encounter with it; namely, our earth and this thing we call nature. Such a focus will bring home the point I want to make all the more clearly. Nature sometimes appears as warm and inviting, restful as a field of flowers at sunset or birds chirping away on a golden afternoon as we picnic with Alice. We even feel something behind it all, maybe even a sense of something sacred. Yet, we also know that it is a deadly beauty, one that is brutal and indifferent and without one ounce of compassion. "Nasty, brutish, and short," as a nasty, brutish, and short man once said. It is more than Thoreau's "prairie for outlaws" or a Taoist "miracle to contemplate." In truth, it is more like a vortex of savage energies. In fact, nature becomes part of *an otherness* for us when we *consciously* examine it. Yes, we evolved out of it and are in its grasp, but it is so different than something deep within us, that we, as conscious creatures, ceaselessly are looking behind nature, toward something invisible to any eye but our own human one, *something closer to our consciousness, to our own interiority.* Of course, that is arguably something we are never sure about—what it is or that it is. It is the second topic of this endeavor—can we know God, can we know what is essentially unknowable? But, putting that aside for the time being, we do at least sense a difference between our consciousness and this indifferent and too often brutal nature, between our consciousness and this vast impersonal and cold cosmos. We are in the midst of it all, yet in contrast to it—and we know it, know it as we look out at the universe around us.

Here let's pause, and give 'flesh and blood' expression to the example of contrast I gave, and do that by a look at what I have found to be so well suited for this; namely, Candide Savoy, the sane man in my novel, *Wisdom After The Big Bang*, who saw driving along a jungle road in Amazonia with his mad sidekick Zero riding shotgun, the contrasts between nature and a presence looking out at it . . . articulating so demonstrably this interiority in the face of it all, in near opposition to it all.

>Candide could barely make out the rusted sign at the fork in the road, but a chancy three hours later, they reached the river's edge. The Amazon flowed along under the translucent mist waiting for the descending darkness, its flat waters extending out over its banks into the twilit rainforest covering its floor a foot deep or so as far as the eye could see. It made the trees look like they were lonely bathers watching the Rover riding the river, the water licking its rushing wheels as it traveled along on the unseen road underneath. The air was thick and pungent with jungle smells. It was all so tropical—where only a day or so before they were battling the sleet.
>
>Fireflies began to show themselves in the setting sky, the thoughtful driver watching them challenging the sinking sun. Or was it the riotous growth beneath them they were challenging with their fiery flight? It all depends on how you see it he told himself. Seen from below in their gawking Rover, the forest canopy was all a roof of leaves, with tunnels of light between the silhouettes of branches and their bromeliads. But the observing driver knew that each of us prunes existence to a single perception in order to perceive at all; otherwise it's all too much. We are, despite heart pumps and very real blood, when all is said and done, nothing more than creatures of our own distilled perception. Creatures locked into what we are. A tiger by any other name is still a tiger. A horse by any other color still a horse. None of us can help it. It's what we are. He

pondered over the possibility of it being otherwise. Of seeing it all from a different perspective than what we are. A different life form than our own. Not as a man, but as creatures of a jungle only a tree top away. He tried to put aside that flight of fancy, but found himself holding on the jungle they were traveling through, his pondering mind lifting upward.

Suppose, he thought, we *could* see the arboreal gardens *from above*. Not as me and my passenger anymore, but now merely as outside looking in—or down in this case study. He could only imagine how it would be. How it would be to see nature's way of going about the business of existence untouched by human hope and human pain. Of going about it in a world devoid of any and all anthropic horse coloring . . . where the woven moss and air plants at the top of each tree formed minute galaxies, in which living forms as different as poison dart frogs, ferocious ant colonies and mosquito larva, tree snakes and mouse opossum, butterflies, crabs, beetles, and yet unnamed species, all lived out their own kind of existence . . . each creature clambering around the spiny growths of the tree-dwelling succulents and competing for space within a tight world of rosette leaves and lilliputian lakes. Without a thought in the world? Silence could only wonder as it watched each creature struggling just to stay alive and make it to the next day. With nothing else to do but that? It seemed so. For there, in those aquatic nurseries, each and every form of life which inhabited that upper strata of the jungle's canopy had to forever fight off the plethora of predators coming to eat them and their young—as they themselves sought out, picked at, and fed on another's hatch and brood. It all made for an odd and desperate existence, filled as it is with decaying tiny corpses and the excrement of what was eaten of them. Silence blinked. It couldn't conceive of life without thought. And thought without a meaning to it all.

Can the human mind reconcile itself to such a garden? The silent driver drove on; the man riding shotgun holding on his own mind's two-eyed perception.

Up and down the road it was the same. As up and down the tall jungle trees, the driver cautioned from his blindside; letting his silence surmise what was really taking place out there . . . away from humanity's coloring book. Beneath the succulent array of star-shaped silhouettes that festooned the top of the trees, through the porous shield of broad-leaved fissures and clefts, emerged a sort of middle kingdom . . . like some *awakening* in this primeval myriad of swarming multiplicity. For in this profusion of flora and fauna were stranger creatures still, monkeys as varied as the foliage and birds as varied as life itself—*conscious* creatures. Consciously conscious creatures? He could verify it to be so! He had seen the monkeys at play and the birds dance before an audience of their peers. He had documented it through his father's lens. A picture is worth a thousand words and he had thousands of pictures of how they daily ventured out to fly and swing between the branches and entanglement of their own quantum coherence. But thinking what? Seeing what? Feeling what in their locked-in world of monkey thoughts and bird perceptions? He knew one at least that had loved.

They drove on alone along alas; the driver pondering in his next cerebral breath what existence held in store on the forest floor beneath that profusion of life and loss and love he had just wondered about. More consciousness? Or just a different menu? He looked out of their speeding machine and realized as he did, giant carnivores were roaming about, feeding off of what they could corner and kill. Heaven only knew what went through *those* brain structures. Or for that matter, those of their victims as well . . . darting deer or squealing boar . . . as chance and contingency caught them in their killers' brutal jaws struggling to survive. The driver paused a thoughtful moment . . . only to succumb to his thought.

No, he couldn't just watch without drawing a conclusion. Without judging. Without deciding what was good and what wasn't. Without thinking. It was impossible. He might as well not be there. He nodded a cerebral nod. Yes, he was back where he started . . . full circle after his vertical jungle run, the observing driver conceded. From the top of the trees to the top of the food chain! Back to seeing the world the only way we can see it: hopelessly human. Such a trapped truth. He could almost hear his mind moaning. It wanted to know the really real—beyond the confines of its head. Beyond the glittering guilt and glory we concoct and call the truth. Or by any other name—science included. Yes, our supposedly most objective of views is only human. Another coloring book. Like my own. Or the secret thoughts of Leonardo. The noblest of calculations just one more version of the anthropic principle. As bold and bad and bleary as the observer. The driver fell off with one thought and returned with another. And yet this feeling still! Through it all. Behind it all. Especially in the loneliest of moments. That there is more. And that I must find it. Is that only part of being human as well? Like the roar of a lion in *its* loneliness, or the eerie trumpet call of an elephant at *its* burial grounds? Merely part of *our* make up? *Thought's reflex at the unthinkable?*

A slight shrug of irony followed, the road widening to a stretch of expressway; smack in the middle of the jungle. He expected to see billboards advertising software appear at any minute. One actually did—sort of. It was a large sign telling everyone who passed along the slightly elevated highway that the dry facility they were driving along was provided by the Peruvian government: to enjoy and travel at a reasonable speed.

The driver had to laugh. It was funny . . . in a funny sort of way. They always are—humans. Even as the most dangerous of all animals—funny. They started out as weak creatures evolving multi-regionally across the continents, only to end up as the stalking species itself! The whole wide world their feeding grounds. Finally, the world itself. Nature's karma . . . come home to devour nature itself. He had to laugh. It was funny . . . in a funny sort of way. Nature's final spread—itself! The creator of everything-eating-everything-else finally being eaten up itself. Talk about the consequence of one's act! Now that *is* comic relief. Biting the hand that feeds you . . . no, actually eating it! Eating it off and swallowing it up. And everything else, too. Gone, not with a bang, but a swallow! Consummate karma!

The driver grimaced, his pale eyes holding on his thought. Of course, the world would go on, he told himself in a dismissive rebuttal of such melodrama . . . and to recall what had been, there would be underground libraries, at the heart of every secured survival center, and a plethora of laser discs for all the children in breathing suits to play with, all full of pictures and prose about the planet above them and the creatures who used to inhabited it. Lions, and tigers, and bears, he almost whispered aloud. So nothing would *really* be lost. Besides, it might be what evolution wanted. "If evolution had a point that is."

The gentle singing of birds mixed with the buzz of *cicadae*. Monkeys hollered and jaguars roamed. In the hanging gardens above, as well as the on the ground below, through twilight's music, the creatures of each perception were either closing down for the night or waking to the bewildering ritual of survival, everything intricately entwined and as baffling to the human eye as the light coming from 10214+4724 far off in the furthest reaches of our macrocosm. If evolution had a point that is, someone repeated in silence. Snaky vines entangled themselves around everything on either side of the fast-moving machine as it sped its way down the odd stretch of expressway in the middle of nowhere, through the fiery fog at dusk.

"This place is one of the most remote," his passenger offered towards the staring driver.

The sinking sky and mist circled around them. They passed yard-wide lilies and heard the growingly familiar caws of macaws coming out of the thickening fog. The howls of howler monkeys, too. A beautiful egret with long white plumes landed on the roof of the Rover and stayed with them for nearly half a mile, when, for no apparent reason, it flapped its farewell and flew off into the formless mist.

Each face is its own inscape. There is more to us than meets the eye, something deeper still, something within us, at our very core of being, which we are constantly in search of, constantly trying to uncover to the full light of the sun, a sun and an universe that is unconscious, different, in contrast to this phenomenon we call our conscious presence, what makes each of us able to say *io sol uno, I myself alone!* This unique awareness looking out at what is not aware does indeed seem almost too strange for the space-time it finds itself in.

Even if it began as a nothing out of which a someone came or if it was a hunk of matter three pounds in weight out of which a me came, self-being is my root-reality, is your root-reality, whether it came forth from nowhere and nothing or the thalamus and cortex having cerebral intercourse. It is the basic fact of life for each of us and everyone acts accordingly. Once again, even if the self is assembled neurologically, once it is, it is something more than whence it came and even different than the nature it came out of. It can be called the mysterious more—small letters to be sure—but still more and still mysterious. To say otherwise is the great blindness of whoever says it, be it out of biology, or anything else. What is this thing called mind that some would have matter or meditation destroy? No—mind is more than either and still more.

However, our interiority and the set of data most immediately available to each of us, I must again underline, get left behind in too much of present day philosophy and science, many in their lectures and literature stating when talking about us that there is no there there, no *real* there there, even as they, like myself, are sounding off from there. Or as I like to say, from here, our hereness, or *haecceittas, this unique here that each is.*[34] Yes, although it might touch our funny bone in a funny sort of way being told we are not really here, many, in each of these fields, approach human existence as if you and I are *not really here.* Yet the truest reality is that you and I are here, we do indeed exist, no matter how we got here. For some to deny the subjective—under the guise of being objective—becomes ludicrous. Such a silly stricture does not banish the fact of subjectivity from the universe. Not even if they invoke the divine right of kings to do so. And yes their position is as comical and outmoded!

Those who say we can do away with our core reality by saying we are merely matter, like the mirror they are looking at, or that meditation will empty us of this self, or any other such nonsense are all forgers of folly. They have no grounding, are groundless. I say this not to be mean, but the climate of opinion under which we conduct our lives is important, especially as it relates our very selves.

You know how in all the gangster novels or movies before they killed anyone they would say 'this isn't personal'—well this is! It gets very personal when someone tries to do you in, and saying you don't exist, not really, is a form of doing you in. The self is under attack as never before, and even the very interiority we all experience as part of that presence is made to sound unreal. I already told you the Latin expression from my early college days: *Quidquid recipitur . . .* Is this applicable to x-ray machines, too? What do I mean by my snippy question? I mean that it is not nice for certain radiologists to jump to conclusions denying you as really real because of snapshots of the brain by their x-ray devices, it is not within the device's *recipitur* to do so. Although I will address a parade of follyforgers at length in a future section of this masterpiece, I am going to give a foreshadow of that here and discuss an individual who has sunk to such a degree of folly that he must now be singled out for abuse, prior to all the serious fun we are going to have with the other forgers of folly later. We need a little comic relief right now I feel—weren't those the very words of Wild Will when he wrote the gravedigger's scene in Hamlet? Enter Andrew and his x-ray machine! In his rush to spin his snapshots, the radiologist Andrew Newberg would go so far as to talk in terms of advancing a notion of my eclipse, saying there is no real me, and this without ever having met yours truly. Or himself it would seem. Then he goes on to say that he has taken a cerebral snapshot of God; God as in a certain part of your brain he could photograph with his device. That is warmed over Feuerbach talking neurobabble, although I could use another more scatological sounding word. What Newberg is saying is little more than phrenology reincarnated, as I already pointed out with Toga's statement about his and Mazziotta's own pretty pictures. The self is not going to show up in an x-ray of your arm or leg or brain. Nor is the Mystery we call God going to show up in an x-ray of your hypothalamus—any more than a hippopotamus would!

Of course there are legitimate questions one can put forth about both these topics of self and God and we shall pursue them further, but not as merry Andrew does. He waves his pictures around proclaiming his find with the self-gratification of a schoolboy boasting about a premature ejaculation with Fatty Patty his blow up doll. Unfortunately, one of the editors at *America* magazine did not pick up on this when he went gaga over Newberg's find. We appreciate that the Polish Pope pretty much lobotomized the Jesuits, so forgiveness is in order for the Order here. But I am not in a forgiving mood with those who say I don't exist, or would reach before the big bang itself and tell us *the truth* about God himself—simply because of picture taking of parts of the brain. The area said to be responsible for defining the limits of the physical self, and generating the perceptions of space in which the self can be orientated and where God hangs out, is, after the hype and headline appeal, really only Newberg's legless opinion, or premature ejaculation with Fatty Patty if you prefer. Of course when he speaks in scientific terms people freeze like deer in front of headlights on a dark night. The truth is, the entire brain is a limiting device and the reduction of neural impulses to the parietal lobe is merely that. One could take peyote and know that it would generate a sense of a limitless awareness melting into infinite space. The brain will, of course, behave as a brain. To jump from that to talking about a snapshot of God, no self, and reality as nothing more than a feeling or perception is neither science nor theology; it's sensationalism. Then to build an epistemology on all that is to say the least very bad philosophy. But not bad press apparently. It's locker room enhancement of the facts and should be treated as such.

The sky outside my window is in concert with the Gregorian chant coming from the outer room, it is *valde mane* and although always good for a laugh I am tired of these types telling us we don't really exist or defining us merely as dendrites, so I am tempted to continue my Jon-Stewart-like rant, but I will put that pleasure aside for the follyforger section, and, instead, continue to pursue the primary purpose of this chapter, namely, establishing presence and penetrating further into it with the statement that *once consciousness came along, existence changed and had to.*

If perchance the self is produced by the brain, whether innately there and enhanced, or after the fact solely, still once consciousness came along, existence changed and had to. Yes, once consciousness came along, existence changed and had to. For once consciousness came into the process the purely natural laws of evolution no longer stood alone. *Consciousness began to pull in its own direction and continues to pull in its own direction.* This shows in all that is human, in general as well as in particular, from laughter to loneliness, and certainly in our spiritual, moral, and ethical aspirations. People question: should it be the law of the jungle or the law of reason? Social Darwinism or social awareness? Survival of the fittest or something more? The will to power or the will to love? Each of those questions is really asking the same thing: should we act above nature? Bertrand Russell says in *Religion and Science* that the amoral world in which we find ourselves is not worthy of us. No, nature is not worthy of us. Instead of that amoral world of nature, here I would like to mention what Bertrand Russell said governed his own life, "three passions, simple but overwhelmingly strong: the longing for love, the search for knowledge, and unbearable pity for the suffering of mankind."[35] Even the consummate naturalist Thoreau said man "consists not in his obedience, but his opposition to his instincts." Camus and Christ, too, would have us rebel against amoral nature with what each called love; Buddha, as well, called for an all-embracing compassion, Lao Tzu kindness above all, and both India's Jainism and its Hinduism the absence of all harmful intent. Even Darwin suffered this divide and struggled against what he discovered in natural selection, opting to live a life of caring despite what selfish genes and the like intended. Yes, Russell, Camus, Christ, Buddha, Lao Tzu, Charles D, and little ol'me with them, all want to make us better animals, by acting above the nature out of which we came—more than it! That seems to be a strange invitation on their part and mine included. We are animals, so how could we be more than what we are?

The answer is that we aren't, the more is in each of us. *Even if I am wrong about everything else in this venture, I can still choose to be compassionate and that makes me more than the universe that surrounds me.* That is amazing in and of itself. The amoral world in which we find ourselves is not worthy of us, and I think somehow we know it. Yes, the amoral world in which we find ourselves is not worthy of us and somehow we know it.

Yet, despite that, more or less *semper et ubique*, Brutus chooses to betray Caesar and Judas chooses to betray Jesus. For Judas-Brutus is there too in the human make-up, as much a part of us as our reptilian brain stem. Old Cicero, witnessing the actual betrayal of Brutus, not to mention life at the crossroads of the world, certainly knew the human beast and maybe subliminally about evolution as well when he proclaimed, *"Simia quam isimilis, turpissiums bestia, nobis!"*[36] *What an ugly beast the monkey, and how like us!* Now I think on a sunny day in the ruins of the Forum I could defend both the looks and behavior of the monkey, but not the ugly and beastly choices of so many humans down the centuries and well into our own. Some people of course will say we can no more help ourselves than the monkey who's DNA we share so abundantly or the snake who's at the stem of our brain.

As I type away, the face of the actor in *The Lives Of Others* comes to mind, those haunting eyes of his as he throughout views his world, a world where practically everyone acts out of the will to power or the will to survive, and he, this lone figure, calling up something inside of him acts out of a giving of himself that expects nothing in return.

Perhaps in this sense we see how far into the depths of ourselves we must go in order to vanquish that serpent which, projected into biblical mythology is, in fang, venom, and scale, a considerable part of our long evolutionary heritage, and, perhaps, our nemesis.[37] Francis Bacon saw this even before Darwin pined over his discovery, and in a remarkably positive way. "By reason whereof," he says, "there is agreeable to the spirit of man, a more ample greatness, a more exact goodness, and a more absolute variety, than can be found in the nature of things."[38] Therein is the fundamental spiritual tension in all of us, *consciousness in some sort of evolutionary tug of war with what nature would dictate.* Perhaps we could even elaborate here and say it is consciousness in some sort of evolutionary tug of war with matter itself. Not abstractly, but within our very own make up. Consciousness would have us be more—more than the very fabric that allows it to stretch out to take in all of actuality, even as it still is swimming away for dear life in Heraclites' on-going river. What that means and *is* is what we are trying to get at. "There is strong archaeological evidence to show that with the birth of human consciousness there was born, like a twin, the impulse to transcend it," Loren Eiseley states, quoting an unknown source at the beginning his essay on *The Inner Galaxy*.[39] He underlines this yet again in yet another of his wonderfully written works, it seems so important to him. "There is another aspect of man's mental life which demands the utmost attention, even though it is manifest in different degrees in different times and places and among different individuals; this is the desire for transcendence—a peculiarly human trait."[40] Zbigniew Brzezinski refers to this as well, when, in a documentary, he talks of "the transcendental mystery of the human being." Camus posts it too, when in his book on rebellion he tells us, "There is a living transcendence."[41] As Wilde Oscar put it, "We are all in the gutter, but some of us are looking up at the stars."[42] I am glad the clever man said some of us, for it is a choice, even though that transcendent urge is there.

There, true, but who knows what that transcend urge is in us—evolution's pull to the next stage, Chardin's *Omega*, Nietzsche's *uberwunden,* a call back to the stars from which we came, or the Mystery that made us inviting each to the depth of one's own being? What we do know, at least so far in this venture, is that it is part of our self-being, the level within our presence where consciousness challenges the rainforest it finds itself in. And to the degree that we let others project on us their erroneous and limiting conceptions of our presence being less than that, less than it is, we will, consciously or not, reshape ourselves to less, and thus to less of a performance sadly. I already mentioned my madman's caveat, now listen to his reversal of it: *if nature doesn't get you, humanity will.* Consciousness is in a challenge with the rainforest within and without and that is something we must further develop, for sure, and will, but for the present with regards our presence, let us continue with consciousness's battle with nature itself, and center in on one particular that has haunted conscious creatures even before our own species walked upon the earth, as it still does, for it is consciousness's final battle with nature, when the eyes lose awareness and stare out of emptiness. *Dies irae! Dies illa!* All that was gathered in the walk through life finished—and I bring this in, not only as a discussion of consciousness' demise, but also and more to our point, because consciousness cannot conceive of it itself as not being there! Even as we see it gone in the eyes of the dead. It seems so impossible to consciousness to be no more. It seems brutal. And is. There is nothing pretty about that day consciousness ends and leaves empty eyes.

If I might allow myself a personal insertion here concerning those physical laws we do battle with and that particular which has haunted consciousness since the caves and before, I would like to mention the death of my father. My mother, sister, and myself had returned from a breakfast he had passed on and sat a while on one of the benches along the boardwalk looking out at the Pacific.

As we walked back to the house, one of the men who ran the parking lot said he thought he saw my dad come out looking for us. When we got back to the house, he was lying on the couch, and so we didn't bother him. We stood in the living room all talking, until I noticed his eyes. They were the eyes of the dead. Ever since I was a youngster, I always had to fight those who would rob me of my enthusiasm, and at least some of that spirit in me came from Ignatius Francis whom the Second Law of Thermodynamics caught up with thirty years ago today. Today is the thirtieth anniversary of his death and it brings with it rush of remembrance.

The Stoics and sages suggest we accept death with a silent peace. Maybe we can with regards to our own death, but the death of someone you love is not easy to live through. Nature they say abhors a vacuum, but nature leaves a vacuum in you when anyone you love dies. And yet . . . and yet, there is a certain, sense of, for want of a better word, quieting that accompanies the surreal sleeplessness and sorrow you go through, and somehow your love is enhanced, even as it is hopeless and you will never see the loved-one again.

My father used to say ever morning that "life is sweet" and talk about sorrows in a person's life as a "tough break"—and he had a lot of them. When he died, I put on his tombstone: *if such things are possible let's all meet again, love, the family.* I had thought the same when my noble and wonderful first Old English Sheep Dog Sperabamus died and broke my heart only six months before the profound sorrow of my father's own death. There is a beautiful song written by the Irish singer Phil Coulter about the death of his father that comes to mind once again as I write. Also a *haiku* poem I love by Issa.

> *Visiting the graves,*
> *The old dog*
> *Leads the way.*

And my old shaggy did. I have seen so much death since that year he and my father died, felt so much loss. My mother, my sister, friends, my beautiful birds and high-spirited dogs . . . yes, life can try to steal your enthusiasm and steel your heart as it does. But love is as much a reality check as death. And, ironically, the 'gift' death gives is that it teaches us that love is the most important thing in life. I give my heart to my dead loved one, to more in life, *the* more in life, despite the suffering and emptiness it leaves.

I said as you recall that I would change only one word in Nietzsche's famous cry, *"Was mich nicht umbringt, macht mich starker."* "That which does not kill me makes me stronger," I changed to that which does not kill me makes me compassionate, makes me give my heart to. Ironically, by giving one's heart to, one does become stronger, a different kind of stronger. I don't think he had that in mind when he said *starker,* but he would have I believe years later when he hugged a horse in a silent simpatico, even as he fell under the weight of sanity. The Chinese have an expression "to eat bitterness"—it is about those who suffer in silence. Nietzsche ate bitterness that rainy day in la Piazza Carlo Alberto, but not with a steel heart. The old horse had led the way.

Yes, there is a living transcendence, a living more, in our human sojourn, even as it might dissipate into thin air as we might ourselves when the Second Law of Thermodynamics catches us one rainy night, alone with our last breath.

By now, you realize that I am a person who must ground things in existence and existence alone, in what is very down to earth, not only the sorrow of death, but our daily living and life, our daily bread and breath, our very real everyday human love, so when I bring up transcendence I am not flying off to Arcturus with David Lindsay or anyone else, but still looking for and finding that in existence itself, whether a piazza on a rainy day or a place in the sun. In this sleuthing sojourn of ours what we have found is that it is not death, struggle, and survival alone that have marked existence, there is also beauty and goodness, laughter and love, all which give existence an exuberance and expanse that is contrasting and confusing within the same presence.

We are told there exists a fish in the Brazilian waters, one of the cyprinodonts, "which sees with a two-lensed eye, a kind of bifocal adjustment that permits the creature to examine the upper world of sunlight and air, while with the lower half of the lens he can survey the watery depths in which he lives."[43] In this, our fish resembles ourselves—he is a physical metaphor of we who came after him on the evolutionary scale—no, we don't have bifocalled eyes, but a bifocalled be-ing so to speak. We live in a simultaneous situation, an awareness in spacetime of more, something which goes to the very core of our being in a way which we are struggling with, for it seems so in contrast to the rainforest, as we saw with Candide, or on a rainy day with our own drive through life. It is a contrast we will carry with us across the length of living, one that burdens us in this segment of our venture and will all the way into the species-specific problem of the Mystery we call God. But, my fellow bipeds who laugh, we are not there yet, in what we might accurately call postmodernism's forbidden zone.

Leaving behind postmodernism's forbidden zone and any further talk of our own, those empty eyes that await even yours truly, let's continue as it were on our drive through the rainforest with Candide, shamelessly sounding off with a statement that just happens to be true, subjectivity is an objective fact of existence! We live inside out. In an inside that is often in conflict and contrast to the outside; consciousness in it a tug-a-war with nature as it were. Those magnificent eyes in each head looking out at nature know this. This is so in each of us; it stems from the intrinsic root-reality we call self-being, and it has a quality of more in it, something that would transcend the brutality of nature, something in contrast to nature, even as it is part of nature. That is as much an objective fact as the world is round, spins around the sun, in a universe that had a beginning. Maybe even more so! For when all is said and done, the human mind is capable of incredible inward expansion. I can create better worlds than exist! Within ourselves we can travel faster than light—I could think about Mars long before light physically gets there from where I am sitting thinking about it. Yes, I already told you all this, told you that thinking is the fastest way to travel in spacetime, not to mention the place to come up with intuitions and then formulae about spacetime itself. It is all part of that statement by Descartes, a major figure in rationalism, who nonetheless realized, perhaps on a lonely windy morning, this ability within us, writing, as you know, about a "liberty proper to the human mind." Do taste the words; realize what they mean. When all is said and done, repeated and reminded, *the inscape of our being* is where reside ways to think not yet concocted, in languages not yet conceived. This phenomenon, this conscious matter thing, is almost impossible when you think about it, yet it is true. As it is true that there are monsters in the rainforest and the rainforest in them, as in us, and it is to the rainforest in us they make their appeal, these learned learned men, with degrees on their walls, who would abstract you out of yourself, cut your cerebral wings, and dry you to dust. Such men would swallow you up as much as any predator, as any man-eating tiger or cannibal. They would stop you and me, all and each, at a boarder they have contrived, demanding that we keep within their assigned thinking and definition and cut the more out of us, trying to convince us we are less than we are, that we are merely and only the rainforest in us. "Never fall victim to the tyranny of thought of your own age," I warned as you remember.[44] Such a warning comes with an understandable authority, existence itself! Understandable because it is our own very existence! Our own very existence that warns of the rainforest within ourselves, as it should about it in them as well! Do we bringing our life down to a primitive level, or do we follow our innermost certainty in being and very birthright in answer, a conscious creature that can choose to be more than nature?

So far then in our venture, we as conscious matter, we as conscious matter conscious of itself, we as conscious matter that can be compassionate, we as conscious matter in conflict with the raw elemental energies of evolution out which we came because of that conscious compassion, that giving of ourselves, that love, now know that each of us as human beings can emerge from our lowest level to our highest by means of his or her own doing, his or her own inner decision, and that struggle is the sojourn of breathing, the very souljourn of it.

So where does this leave us?

In the toilet!

Let me explain. Or better yet, let a former gravedigger J C explain it for me, in a play within a play taking place in a madhouse. "To life," J C toasts out to the audience sitting on his toilet seat, "and what it sends along the cholingergic pathways and synaptic gaps in our heads!" He smiles some. "You really shouldn't be here. It's not part of the play. Funny things can happen to you in here. Here where evolution proves its point every single day of one's life. Reminding us who we are. What we are. Then confuses us with . . . with what I feel. I feel, I feel sitting in this confusing toilet . . . on a cold wooden toilet seat with stale wine on my breath and my own waste filling my nostrils . . . I feel . . ." He stops as if he could barely say it. "Love. A love that's the final phase of love in the mind of a person. Maybe all humankind! Maybe everything! That's what it feels like. Merely love. Empty of return. Flimsy or even flimflam perhaps . . . almost beside myself and this funny body. As if the whole world were alive with it."

"Holy shit!" Zero responds.

"The perfect definition of humanity," the chorus of Lunatics chimes in. "Even as our sitting gravedigger can't put the two together—what's in one part of him with what's in another!"

We have been trying to do just that—since the start—put together the raw elemental energies of evolution with the mystery of consciousness in the cosmos; and not only with that mystery of consciousness but then with that mystery's deepest phenomenon, love, and thus answer the question of how to act in the face of the world. Perhaps we are in the toilet in all this, as mad as all those lunatics at Saint HaHa's, but we have come up with an inner decision, a way to face actuality that might do just that, by allowing us to act out of that consciousness, out of the deepest experience in that consciousness, in spite of our toiletry.

We can never stop our toiletry as long as we are alive. So we will always have the problem of the raw elemental energies of evolution as defining us in a tug of war with what J C speaks of with such amazement. In a very real way, we are creatures complicated and confounded both by this intermix of the primordial forces within organisms as necessary urges, and this phenomenon of consciousness with its mysterious call of love.

Consciousness in the cosmos adds a level that is not there without it—and so most definitely does love. Love—our tainted humanity's solitary boast.

There does slither through our primal beginnings a force of anonymous and relentless darkness that primitive humankind sensed—and we do, too. It seems loveless and removed, so removed from our conscious life. It gives rise to what is loveless in us. Yet, despite that call out of the tide pools, we can still choose another call, a phenomenon we have given the name love. "The world is the will to power—and nothing more. And you yourselves are also this will to power—and nothing more," Nietzsche tells us and in a very real sense he is right.[45] But so is J C in his toilet, for we are indeed our dump and our depths both, and in this we humans come to *the fundamental tension that is in our make up; a will to power and a will to love both within us.* Such is the choice conscious matter opens up for us—and that is in essence our odyssey of being.

Let's make that even more explicit. To act out of our consciousness, in spite of our toiletry, requires *an inner decision,* an inner decision based on this profound realization J C speaks of, and that inner decision is *the will to love.* The pull of naked nature and the forces out of which we emerged and uncoiled will always be there, pulling us—but so will something more in us, calling us to be sensitive to the deepest part of life and living and the giving of ourselves, something more than the fearful symmetry or the rainforest it came out of. The 'holy' part of us will always require acting out of what is more in us.

It is very difficult for anyone to pass on such an inner sense of being—*love can only be understood directly.* To make people understand what could only be understood directly is an admittedly difficult task I have given myself; but it is a necessity if one is to achieve an honest venture into our humanness. It starts with *I am* . . . each of us finishing the sentence for one's self, either out of the deepest experience in existence one can have as the way to live, or out of something less than that prowling in the rainforest within each of us. That is the fundamental tension and choice of human existence.

As we creatures look up at the night sky wondering, in a desperate encounter between ourselves and the silence of the universe, occasionally we must with great sadness and a hole in our heart turn back to lay a flower on the grave of someone we loved and lost to death. The hand here is the same as Gilgamesh's or that of some Neanderthal of old before our species even was. At such times a person opens his mouth to escape suffocation. No matter if we come out of a Cambrian explosion as confusing surely as any Wonderland Alice was subjected to, we know, like she did, that "if I wasn't real, I shouldn't be able to cry." My gravedigger, looking over at us sitting on his toilet seat, nods, and nods again, knowing full well that both yours and mine, and his tears, too, are indeed real, as is the cause of them, our love. We already have the self as one of two necessary ingredients for any hope we might have of attaining what's really real, so what is the other I speak of? In a very real sense it is what caused those tears to be real, as real as me shedding them, as real as you shedding them.

One of Eugenio Montale's beautiful poems, *Monologo,* states, *"qualcosa sta accadendo ne'll Universo, una ricerca di se stesso."* "Something is happening in the Universe, a search for the self." Something else is happening as well. Something that comes out of the depths of that self. "The tragedy is that what we refuse to attend to cannot reach us," I hear somewhere in my memory whisper. If that is allowed to happen we would be a presence that has estranged ourselves to our own depths. But the opposite is true as well, for love makes a person harken to the innermost of his existence, of her existence, to the outermost as well.

People talk of a root image of existence. How it affects our lives. A root image is a fundamental image of how a person thinks reality is, a person's most basic picture of reality; it is that person's ultimate concern. People call it a root image—but we want more than that. We want root actuality—that is what we have been driving so hard for, you and I getting at actuality, an ultimate concern for what's real, to be alive to what is *really real*. We have the first *human* ingredient to that, now we have the second; *existence and the deepest experience in existence*. Our venture, our very human venture, has taken us from the tide pools to conscious matter and conscious matter to this. Being sensitive to the deepest part of life and living, and thus the giving of ourselves, is something open to each human being; it is acting out of what is more in us, more than the raw elemental energies of evolution. Love can be elevated to the unconditional validity of our human existence, because it is, no matter that we end and suffer before we do. Yes, our human venture has taken us literally from the big bang and the beginning of spacetime, to this phenomenon in spacetime called love, the highest expression of consciousness.

I know what your devious mind is thinking—is love merely an instinct? How do we know love is not just a biological or chemical happening? Isn't it instinctive for a mother to care for her offspring? Unfortunately, not always, but let's say it is always and everywhere instinctual for a mammalian mother and any in the class Aves, too, to care for her off-spring. So how then can we prove love is not just a biological need for the continuation of our own human species? Right at the start, let me say, of course, biology and chemistry take place in us when we perform any action, and again that shouldn't shock us. But with regards to love we shall also see more is required. We do indeed find a realization of what we call love expressed in all conscious creatures, from those that seem less aware and more instinctual to those we marvel at because of their actions of care, so similar to our own. As everything else presents itself in levels of being, so does love, making its way through higher and higher realization, just as with presence itself.

Let's do just that, make our way through instinct to love, and start by looking at this from two of the most basic natural drives in us, first and foremost survival, then sex. For the moment let's look at the latter, before we look at survival itself. Summer giggles aside, you have to admit that in sex you can realize the difference between instinct and love. You know that love is not an erection. Healthy as it may be, an erection is instinct, whether this is so with you in your prime at eighteen or taking Viagra at eighty. For the time being let's put victorious Viagra and those silly seniors taking it aside; and merely look at male as well as female arousal. If

I show a room full of young men a picture of the reigning female sex celebrity, they will respond accordingly. If I show a room full of young women a picture of the reigning male sex celebrity, they will respond accordingly. And maybe the young men with them, and it would be OK, as with the young women with the female sexpot. All of that is built into the brain, one way or other. Despite the homophobic culture that we are part of, we do not have to share in that prejudice; or the mean-spiritedness religious-based bigotry promotes. But I digress. There is a sexual drive in humans in which even smell plays a part, and all of that is fine and dandy, as it is as natural as eating, or going to the toilet for other reasons than experiencing love.

This is so across the animal experience. Victor Schaffer, in *The Year of the Whale*, described sex with regards the largest living mammals as follows. "Hour after hour the pair swim side by side, keeping in touch by flippers and flukes, or simply rubbing sides . . . Presently the male moves to a position above the female, gently stroking her back . . . the cow turns responsively upside-down, and the bull swims across her inflamed belly . . . At last the pair rise high from the sea, black snouts against the sky, belly to belly, flippers touching, water draining from the warm, clean flanks. They copulate in seconds, then fall heavily into the sea with a resounding splash."

Although it is not 'slam, bam, thank you mam,' it is sex; the bull afterwards going after the two tons of food he has to eat daily to survive, no doubt really really hungry now.

That said, I must mention that there is also an attraction that involves sexual union which is *more* than that of instinct, one hopefully everyone gets to experience in their lives. No, you don't find this in a bordello or at any modern version of a Chippendales' male revue; you're there to satisfy instinct. Nor, in truth, am I merely talking about coupling. There may be all sorts of reasons for coupling that are not what we are discussing here. I am talking about you looking at the other in a very personal encounter, in an I-I relationship.

Human sexuality is "not confined to periods of being in heat, nor does it merely serve the continuation of the species. It is not limited to the specific genital activity of procreation but *encompasses the entire person* in an act of complete concentration on and attention to the sexual partner," writes the psychotherapist John Mc Neill.[46]

Such an attraction can be said to have sex mixed *with something more*, the giving of one's self to the other person. Sex without that is like eating, but with it, well something more in life, nourishing of a different kind. One that still exists, I might add, after sexual satisfaction. One that involves something deeper than the self-gratification in a sexual act, something more than the biology and natural selection in us, something we might honestly call self-giving, a mutual self-giving.

So, of course, when I talk of love, as I said, there are levels of realization within it, and we will come to that in more detail, but for now we are discussing it as it blends on the level of sex. And as it does, even there it shows what it is, and how it is more than instinct. *As we are conscious matter, our expressions of love, too, involve us acting as such, but at a higher level of being than mere instinct, rather in an intimacy of breathing.*

The partners in a sexual act that is more than the raw elemental energies of evolution see one another as of equal value. "The essential immorality of prostitution is not that it involves sex outside of marriage, but that it involves one person using another as an object and that object allowing him or herself to be used."[47] In love, no one is reduced to merely a sexual object. "Recent psychodynamic theory recognizes that the basic drive of the human psyche is not toward pleasure (as Freud believed) but toward intimacy."[48]

Intimacy requires individuality, and individuality an interiority that can have *this intimacy* with the other. It is not an impersonal sexual encounter, but a personal communion, integrating our nature into the will to love—a very human love. Intimacy never makes the person an object, but the exact opposite of object, namely, a very special individual, wrapped in an embrace that takes in the whole body and being.

In our presence we see levels of being from the invisible quanta all the way to the highest realization of awareness. Remember how I said *even if* the self were formed out of the brain, it still becomes more than merely three pounds of muscle in our skulls, and we can see this in that it can choose contrary to the brain's natural drives. Now, just as the tide pool gave forth to brains, something more than the tide pool, brains give forth to something more, presence; and just as the brain is as real as the tide pool, so is the evolved presence as real as what it emerged from. So too with love! Of course it has a bearing in matter, but also a *realization* that can supersede that very matter. Love always entails the giving of one's self, and so too in sex. A relationship involving sex can have this or the opposite, the will to power, the use and even abuse of the other for self-gratification. So even in sex we see the will to power or its complete opposite. Also, there is merely sex, wherein two consenting adults merely seek sexual gratification, but again that is not love. And to be truthful it too has a touch of the other as object in it, but at a level above the mere will to power, and since I am not a puritan such mutual consent is fine, only not fulfilling. Unlike Marcus Aurelius one needn't describe it as the mere "release of slime by rubbing a woman's innards," or in any other derogatory way.[49] I must make mention here, that when one is having sex with someone whom one loves, it is wonderful to enjoy the sexuality; like eating together, it becomes a conviviality—from the Latin, *convivo, convivere, to live together, to feast with*—to be alive with each other. Thinking in the evolutionary horizon I have proposed makes one get a handle on this way of perceiving love as well as sex.

Love is more than the sum of all its parts I might playfully put forth—and we know it is. Again, the proof of the pasta is in the tasting—a realization one can see on one's own; one where the act can and does supersede natural instincts, even as it might be blended with instinct and express itself biologically. The smell of one's hair, the touch of one's body, the memory of crossing the street together on a windy autumn day, our full incarnation is part of it. The self is where all the elements of one's being are gathered and the source out of which one loves. Love is being ultimately concerned, and this involves the one concerned and the one concerned about. So the determining factors are always the things I mentioned: an intimacy that never makes the person an object but rather the exact opposite of object; namely, a very special individual, wrapped in an embrace that takes in the whole body and being; in a mutual giving of one's selves. "A mutual giving in a mutual clinging to" one might say, thus bringing out both the love and the instinctual in the one act. Like everything we do it involves us acting out of and in our levels of being, and I mention it again so one knows what I am talking about and what I am not. There is in each of us the ability to be more than the tide pools and terrible Serengeti, more than the drive to procreate or the three pounds of assembled neurons and synaptic gaps in each cranium, even in a *contra natura* way.

And so we come to the other drive from nature within us, one stronger than the instinctual sexual drive, the one of survival. It too will demonstrate the difference between instinct and love. I will elaborate on this more fully later when we come to Frankl and Freud and behavior in a concentration camp, but for now I can at least say the following. Sharing one's soup in a concentration camp defied the instinctually drive for survival, superseding it with one of the giving of one's self, love. No, I am not proposing that you go to a concentration camp and share your soup with someone else who is starving in order to prove this to yourself, but at least know and appreciate the fact that came out of such a place, and that Frankl was right and Freud was wrong about the sharing of one's soup as it were, and what this demonstrates in real time and space, flesh and blood. When you read how the first thing to go in the horror of Hitler's hell was any sexual drive, and that *meaning* became Frankl's search and *love* his salvation, one begins to see in the most extreme of experiments, courtesy of laboratories provided, ironically, by those who held for the will to power, that there is more, more than instinct, whether sexual and even survival itself. This is not some dry theory purported in the comfort of a ivy tower or in some pretty psyche lab on a sunny campus, this is experimentation at its most real, with human beings stripped down to survival of the fittest in a place where only power counted; and in those conditions, contrary to the consensus of the comfortable, a will to love emerges, and "it became clear that the sort of person the prisoner became was the result of an inner decision." "The experiences of camp life show that man does have a choice of action." Even as some chose cannibalism and betrayal, others chose sharing and love. For some, "staying alive forced the prisoner's inner life down to a primitive level," while others heard, Frankl goes on to say, "a victorious 'Yes' in answer to the question of ultimate purpose." As I said, we shall see this more in detail as we proceed, but for the present let's state here what Frankl did about his wife. "Love goes very far beyond the physical person of the beloved. It finds its deepest meaning in one's spiritual being, one's inner self."[50] That underlines and even pinpoints what I have being saying about the difference between instinct and love, and the levels therein.

Thinking in terms of our flesh and blood reality, within the evolutionary horizon I have proposed, gives us the answer to the question of whether love is merely instinctual, showing us love is not only more than instinct, but that it finds realization within a person's inner being at the highest level of one's humanness, at the highest level of evolution itself—even at the lowest place in that evolution, a place like Dachau.

> Men have died from time to time,
> And worms have eaten them,
> But not for love.
>   Shakespeare *As You Like It*

Let's not mix up love with instinct. Each of us will die in time as is our nature as mortal creatures, and worms will eat us, or the pyre's fire, or whatever way a people put aside their dead, but before that empty day, each can experience the deepest experience in breathing, and that is more than your toiletry—it is what makes death so very painful for anyone who has lost someone. Yet as painful as it is, it is better to have loved that person and lost him or her than never to have loved them at all, and no one who has would ever say otherwise.

Such is consciousness's journey at its deepest level of being. My deconstruction has led us past sexual instinct, both as silly as Fatty Patty or serious as a bull whale wallowing in procreating waters, all the way to love, our deepest experience in existence and tainted humanity's solitary boast, our last best hope or hopelessness. And even if hopeless on the slopes of breathing . . . left hanging on the crooked cross of existence, abandoned to the elements and the indifferent cosmos as it were . . . it finds realization within our flesh and blood at the highest level of our humanness, at the highest level of evolution itself. Yes, even if existential deconstruction would lead us there, still in such a state of being, love is still our ultimate concern and ultimate purpose when all is said and done, if we would be honest to our humanness.

I mentioned deconstruction and so I suppose should address what the number one and number two in using that postmodern philosophical device have to say about love. Since we are still on the subject of love, especially as expressed in our postmodern world, I ask you to bear with this dramatic urgency in defense of it. Jacques Derrida says that, "deconstruction never proceeds without love."[51] If that is all he said about it how could I disagree? But it isn't, he tells us what he means by both, and therein is the problem. His American disciple, John Caputo, thinking he is praising Derrida, instead, brings out the fundamental problem Derrida and his deconstruction have with love, and life as well. "The affirmation for the unconditional, the experience of the impossible, is what deconstruction is all about, its least bad definition, as Derrida says. The love of the impossible goes hand in hand with, in fact depends upon and is nourished by the impossibility of love, so that 'deconstruction never proceeds without love.'"[52]

The impossibility of love—the phrase sticks out. Really what does that mean in flesh and blood, real tears and Derridan prayer, for love is real in the flesh and blood and that is how we know it and the only way we can. It is not impossible. Perhaps hopeless, given out situation, but real nonetheless. Although both men would lose us in a labyrinth of encrypted writing, here is where there is a clear chasm between these two and what existence shows us. Though I might share their melancholy about it, I don't run away from it. In the end, they end up as groundless as their deconstruction, even making love possess the quality of deceit.

When they talk of love in that way, it seems they are talking about the relationships of bad coupling—but we are not interested in their memoirs. For such a love isn't love, but just the opposite, and usually rooted in the will to power. Derrida and Caputo with him go on to say love has to be narcissistic, which of course proves my point about them not knowing or at least not talking about love. He confuses considering one's self and the other as precious with being narcissistic. Caputo calls love "a paralyzing impossibility"—but, John, to get up in the night to take care of someone you love is not a paralyzing impossibility, it is love in action, the giving of one's self. Caputo then goes on to call love a non-event, but again getting your ass up in the morning to take care of someone is not a non-event, but very much a real happening.[53]

Both men talk as if disconnected from everyday existence, and because of that both men say love is the shore one can never reach. But it is reached everyday on planet earth! It is the giving of one's self in the everyday of being, the flesh and blood of it; and that is done hopefully with a mutual 'embrace,' but even that is not necessary. For love seeks only to give and will do so even if no love is being giving back. It is not at root-reality a quid pro quo—a measure for measure, which Caputo says it is. "To love someone is to demand that one be loved in return," in his own words.[54] No, it is an *invitation* to love in return. I am sure if his children ever stopped loving him, he would still go on loving them no matter, of course, hoping in that they are invited to love in return, but never stopping in his love, no matter if they didn't take up the invitation.

"Beware of deconstructionists bearing gifts," is what I warn from all they put forth. Definitely do not go along with their definition of the impossibility of love, saying the other is irreducibly other—*tout autre*. Yes, they say that too. And, of course with that, love *would be* impossible. You block any love with such a mindset. In positing their position of *tout autre, totally other*, the word *haecceitas* is used, a word I myself use; but they twist that unique and singular form of *this-ness* against itself. They misunderstand the beauty of *haecceittas* and make it a barrier rather than the root-reality of the person and communion it can be—both for the one loving and the one loved, the intimacy involved—for love is always personal, the giving of one's self, that very unique *haecceittas* you are. Sadly, in their philosophy love is lost in the labyrinth of a life-negating deconstructionism.

Caputo says that he has been perfectly clear and decisive about the undecidability by which all things are beset—except of course when it comes to his own decidability and clarification. Love is not something unknown to us poor humans, no matter how much he might decide and protest that it is. It is known in our very humanness and human condition. It is not something unreal yet-to-come, some ideal, so removed from flesh and blood as to be unknown and impossible. It seems the pair are on the cusp of a new version of nihilism—at present nothing, *nihil*, but always in wait—for Godot or democracy or the Messiah, love, or whatever. Of course everything is in process, but that doesn't mean it's not real now. Gilgamesh's love for his friend was real way back then, as Caputo's is for his children now.

They do not give a credible critique of consciousness when it comes to love. In fact, *everything* is groundless for them, only (con)text as Caputo admits. And finally he even says we are "severed from truth."[55] Of course we are beset with ignorance about so much, more perhaps then is comfortable to say, but we do know something, and love is one of the very real things we know, even as we do not know the theory of everything. If they were right, and we were severed from truth, then whether they want to admit it or not, anything goes would have to be the conclusion, which is another way of saying nihilism prevails.

Of course, Derrida and Caputo try to save themselves from such a fate by faith. An *il faut croire* as Derrida says is deconstruction itself, even though we know "this faith of deconstruction" is groundless, all the way to the vacuum we are. Yet he still says "there is no excuse for inaction or indecision or lack of faith, but rather that they supply the very conditions of the 'urgency' of the faith and decision. Undecidability is the condition of possibility of a decision, one with real teeth in it."[56] Let's stop there. How does it have real teeth in it—based on what—since its very grounding is denied. Even my loving hopelessly, hopelessly loving, is grounded in the reality of love. There is no faith involved in that, especially in a faith in something groundless, although I suppose that is what faith is, and why I put both it and Derrida aside in answering how to meet life. You can't build on what there is no evidence of or for, which is the very definition of faith, you have to build on what is real, and love is real, found in existence itself. The most sincere thing I can say about Caputo and the now deceased Derrida is that even as they deny dogma, they have made deconstruction into a dogma, their religion as it were, even as they mean and meant well, and I believe they did and do; but in doing what they have, they were and are left crawling, with tears and prayers both, towards the abyss of nihilism, even if they themselves were and are not nihilists. But like some others waving the banner of postmodernism they come close. In general there is a certain abstraction in all postmodern philosophers. The tyranny of thought of our own age, which they have taken up, makes us in essence the narratives they speak of, but without a foundation, without a root-reality. I should say something about the claim that truth can only be found in the particular, at least as they speak of it in their postmodern relativism. I myself advocate the concrete, the pasta as you recall, but this should not be confused with saying truth is merely particular, as if it never goes beyond a particular narrative or is absolutely bound to a certain time and place, wallowing in a forever relativism unable to answer who I am or how to act in the face of existence. There is a universal grounding in the face of the relativism of postmodernism and its allegiance to the notion that the narrative is somehow without a grounding of at least minimal certainty. Isn't that what we have been about in this chapter for God's sake, well at least for our own sake.

Since I mentioned other postmodern philosophers above, and since Caputo shared a book with one of them, *After the Death of God*, I should say something about Gianni Vattimo here. Vattimo differs with his co-author on God as *tout autre*; his God doesn't die as totally other, and in point of fact only dies by half. Vattimo's notion that transcendence disappears with the incarnation and replaced with an abstract and formal *caritas* is his form of deicide. I must make mention that even as he might use the word *caritas,* this is very different than what I am saying about what love is and does. Here the name Slavoj Zizek comes to mind. Why do I bring up Zizek in this context? Because, although he is different in other ways, he also does away with all transcendence and uses or should I say abuses the word love, both men displaying a radical materialism that even throws out the dimensionality of science along with an dimensional Mysterious More.

For Zizek the notion of a God beyond is merely a projection a la Feuerbach, and 'love' becomes violence, which is the will to power in verbal abuse.

I could be late-night comedy here and say when one reads either of these men, one gets a sense of very stale bread warmed over; warmed over Marxism and God is dead stuff, even as they now use ecclesiastical terminology to try to resurrect these passé agendas. But instead I shall pass over in silence Zizek's tower of Lucanian psychobabble and Vattimo's *il pensiero debole* or criterion of *thinking weakly,* by which he dissolves everything into a thoroughly contingent, historical, and material mix as though he himself were a mix of Marx and Monk Joachim of Fiore reincarnated in postmodern garb. I will pass over in silence the one's making love a call to violence and the other's so-called *caritas* as a sort of cold categorical imperative. I will pass over in silence that in doing what they do they misunderstand the flesh and blood of being human, and in my flesh an blood opinion, the sound of pasta slurping in my mouth, I will only say that although both continue to use the incarnation as their be all and end all, I think they miss out on it and us, ending up in a place apart from the deepest experience in that flesh and blood, still interpreting even the use of the word love in overtones of Marxism.

If I might give a personal experience here, when I was Venice Beach chair of a make-shift town council, back when Venice Beach was wonderful and our town hall meetings would make *Marat/Sade* look tame, it came to our attention that one of our older folk was being evicted from her long-lived-in apartment by the owner so he could make more money. Ironically, he was a survivor of the camps, but I have to tell you, I often thought as a Commandant rather than a camp prisoner the way he acted towards Sadie and the other old Jews he was evicting. Anyway, not only did we get Sadie legal help, but picketed the Kemper Apartments. In that picket line were myself and others, some of whom were Marxists; all of us there to supposedly help Sadie by keeping shelter over her gray hair. As we were picketing, the media arrived, Venice always a good place for the news cameras—and here is my point—one of the Marxists turned to me and said it was wonderful, Sadie would be evicted and the news coverage could be used for the cause. He said this as the other Marxists nodded in agreement. Do you see the difference between what I talk about when I say love and what Zizek does, or Vattimo as well. I was there for this flesh and blood alive and breathing old lady, to keep her in her apartment; the Marxists' motivation was ideological, not unlike this violent "love" Zizek advocates, which isn't love at all, but the will to power using and abusing the word love. Gianni's categorical *caritas*, again, is not the root-reality I am speaking of either. You love Sadie the person and wish her well, not some abstraction in whatever format, Zizek's or Vattimo's or the pious legalism of so much of religion around the world as well. Zizek's and Vattimo's approach, each in their own way, ultimately are apart from being in the midst of our humanness, even as I applaud each man's attempt to correct the world, which, despite my words about them and my mock Ciceronian humor, I honestly appreciate, seeing as they do that the octopus of global corporatism is destroying our world, that Goldman Sachs is not the answer, that the so-called growth economy is the out-growth of the underbelly in our evolution, as is, I must add, the dictatorship of the proletariat. I have to remind both men and everyone else that the third question of philosophy has to be answered by correctly answering the first.

Although we are locked into patterns and orientations, "even floating adrift on an endless sea of unknowing," there still is something, universal over ages and cultures, a glimpse into which, an experience of which, makes all the difference and defiance in the world, all the difference and defiance in our existence, and hopefully in any understanding of one another as well.[57] Derrida and Caputo, if we might return to the main billing, try to tangle one up in their talking points, but a person must cut through the Derridan knot with existence itself—cut through *all* the encrypted thinkers who would abstract you out of yourself and breathing and make you merely talking outside of yourself, or from your underbelly as the case may be. There *is* a living definition for being fully human and a grounding for how to act in the face of existence. And we find it in existence itself. Does our find take the mystery out of breathing? *Mais non!* But it does shed light in the darkness. It is not necessary to have faith—*il faut croire*—in the future or in a materialistic construct either, for as I mentioned, in the face of what they all purport we stand on the side of existence itself, honestly looking at the subject of this venture, *moi et toi*. In that most immediate of all actualities to us we have evidence of and for what we say, found in that very existence itself and deepest experience in it, and in that how to act in the face of the world.

There is much in deconstruction that I agree with, I have used it in my own way, but *to get to* something, something past the mental mist, battle scarred and scared as we are, and that something is the root-reality in life, existence and the deepest experience in existence. I am and I can love . . . even if it turns out to be hopeless and I never know the answer to theory of everything and on a rainy day of the soul pen my poems in psychic blood.

> Clear-eyed/not clean-eyed
> Forces me to see
> People are what they are
> Biology and brain
> Thorn thoughts and sullen rage
> Cheerless in the rain
> Robbed of what never was theirs
> And I alone stand sinking

But I still know I can love and that I do. Ultimately, without saying it or even knowing it perhaps, at least articulating it as such, both Derrida and Caputo with him are calling upon *the giving in existence* when they touch upon it with regards to Socrates and Kierkegaard, "as having kept up the watch in the name of what they loved, even if it is a nameless name." Why can Socrates and Soren do this? They can do it because love is real and the call to it is real, real in their very human existence, no matter if nameless or not, or hopeless or not.

Caputo, disappointingly, after mentioning Socrates and Kierkegaard as having kept the watch in the name of what they loved, and after, what seems to me at least, his affirmation of them, then goes on to say we are in a game in which we do not know what the stakes are or who we are ourselves. Again, John P. C, yes and no! Still, no matter, you can't make the affirmation you do about Socrates and Soren that I mentioned above without some grounding in life and living. Taste the pasta, Giovanni.

What is true has to be in the tasting of existence itself, not in what the two *faithfully* put forth. It is from a love that is experienced, no matter how badly it has been bruised, that the affirmation, the yes, the will to keep up the watch, comes and shows us how to act in the face of planet stress.

Caputo emphatically states that from the point of view of what is now called the postmodern, affection for system is a fatal flaw.[58] Yet, doesn't he and Derrida with him fall into their own fatal flaw with their proclamation that deconstruction is the only way when all is said and done, that there is no way to escape it or get to any root-reality? Then, adding inaccuracy to insult, he goes on to make the *absolute* statement that there is no inner soliloquy of the soul with itself, a solitary, world-less, naked and prelinguistic contact of the soul with itself. First of all, how does he prove this except to say it? He has set up his own system, even as, in a Derridan duplicity, the dynamic duo deny it to others. Again, of course, we can approach words and the world through deconstruction, but that doesn't preclude root-realities, root-realities that one can get to across the ages and different constructions, or their deconstructions.

Using the old Scholastic adage I myself have Caputo states the obvious . . . "we are constantly receiving impute from the world, but whatever we received is received in a manner that is suitable for the receiver who must make ready for the reception."[59] Yes, he states the obvious, but he wrongly thinks it backs up his deconstruction position. I want to touch upon three things here, first, the adage says what I have been saying one way or another all along; namely, *in the midst of our humanness* is where we must go *and can only go*. And second, for him to make such a statement he has to know who and what the receiver is, and remember he says we don't. Finally, it has to be said that reducing us to a mere construct to be deconstructed is not getting to the whole of the receiver he is talking about. *We are not merely a mass of deconstructions ending in a vacuum,* and though we do not know what to expect next, we do know that love is real, and life is more than a secret that is withheld from us. It is laughter and the faces we love looking back at us, it is beauty and goodness when and where we find it, it is the actuality of breathing, despite not knowing the theory of everything or even everything about ourselves.

As already mentioned, John Paul Caputo calls it all a game, one way or another, that we are in a game in which we do not know what the stakes are or who we are ourselves, that everything is a game of words. In many cases that may be so, but not the whole of everything, otherwise all of us would be alive to the very cynicism he denounces. There is a certain smirk involved in his "truth-telling," and I say fine, that may be his way of getting to a postmodern pose as adopted in postmodern architecture. I do it myself as a devotee of the whimsical. But here is where we part company, or comic agony as the case may be—I know there is more involved. Even Nietzsche showed as much in his madhouse pronouncement. *"Siamo contenti? Son dio ho fatto questa caricatura." "Are you content? I am the god who made this joke."* Whimsical, oh yes, but much more, a statement of human suffering, our sufferer in a broken embrace of a horse half-forgotten, of a mind half-forgotten, and a hopeless love in it all left to his broken brain, broken heart, and bitter humor acting out in a question of true comic agony. Of course I had to use it in my own madhouse play as a memento to him, only I put it in the mouth of god. No, we are not merely a mass of deconstructions ending in a vacuum, and though we do not know what to expect next, we do know that love is real, even as it may be hopeless and we whimsically portraying our human condition in such a painful knowing. It goes without saying that much—*de trop—too much*—is withheld from us about being as we travel through it; but neither I in my toilet love, nor Friedrich in his hopeless one, nor Socrates and Soren keeping up the watch in the name of what they loved, nor someone somewhere clutching this ramshackle of a work knowing such love as well, *no one but no how can wash his or her hands of his or her presence and the grounding that gives to us, no one can deny his or her existence and the deepest experience in that existence.*

That is what a true deconstruction gets us to.

Without that grounding there is no way to make our way, and despite Caputo's denial of relativism and nihilism, that is what awaits him without anything but a vacuum to ground our actions on. This is Derrida's legacy, decent man that he seems to have been.

Have I been too hard on the two men? I think and certainly hope not—only on their insistence that their deconstruction is the only way to deconstruct. They and the devotees to such a deconstruction remind me of those people who used to try to interpret everything according to Freudian psychology. We had to spend a long time digging out of the damage of such an approach. Now the same seems so with regards to repairing the damage of Derridan deconstruction. People who think this is the only way to unravel the mystery of what and who we are do a disservice to us. No, we are not only our language and our lineage, but the whole of life in us, with a presence that is definitely more than their deconstruction can offer. It is but one of the ways of knowing we have as humans, and we have so many ways of knowing, from logic to love, from wayward memes to wordless music. We are creatures with a mind that always wants to get past the story into the mind of the author, or into the theory of everything, or into its own very self and soul, even into what seems impossible, into the Mind of God. Such is the very life-blood of being human, this liberty proper to the human mind!

It is that very liberty that has ventured to our minimal certainty in life. Therein is the beginning of our answer to the purely human spirituality we are building towards, and who knows, maybe on a day when the wind blows southerly even a way to get to We-Know-Not-What? Have you stumbled upon me praying? If so, it might be out of an inability to pray, or maybe in a prayer out of the bowels of being itself.

My Old English moans when I talk like that. He'd rather we go into the garden, sit in the shade, and eat cake. *La dolce vita* is his philosophy after all, as he reminds me yet again today. The cockatiels scold him, of course, saying that one should sit in the sun in order to eat cake properly. He calls them birdbrains and tells them how silly that would be, since the sun will always be there, but shade is a passing thing, and so must be caught while it can. I am privy to such philosophical arguments between my Sheep Dog and cockatiels on a daily bases. It's far more interesting than those in the philosophy department, but, finally, I interrupt the discourse by reminding the hairy one what his Vet said about him eating cake. I won't tell you what he said in response, but after a stern stare, he seemed to want to avoid any further contact with humans and went off to the garden.

I was tempted to follow after him and play the day away like any philosopher worthy of the name. After all, didn't Nietzsche say he ranked philosophers according to their laughter! I know what you are saying. My publisher and the pedestrian minds from Harvard he has reading my manuscript say the same. They drive one to drink—and that is their only contribution to this book, believe me. One I openly thank them for, of course, and will again, and again, and again. But reluctantly I must put both gayety and *Grey Goose* aside, for I am gadfly-bound to take up our venture again.

The immediacy of such a demand is that we have come to a very important segment in our sojourn, one that will carry us deeper yet into our evolutionary horizon, where the rich meaning of presence will become all the more clear to us as we continue to pull together the swarming multiplicity of evolution into the entity called ourselves. Fasten your seat belts, it going to be a bumpy ride.

What we already know thus far with regards that evolutionary horizon is that what is essential to us and in us is *a consciousness in the cosmos*. Matter has given forth to life, and life to this equally astonishing phenomenon, awareness, and not only that, but an awareness that can want, wish for, will better worlds than exist, that can laugh and cry and love and die. It is an awareness of selfhood, each mortal one of us his and her own conscious being, the *myself* we speak of, the thisness or *haecceittas* that Scotus tried to get to way back when, the *hereness* as I would say, the beauty of individuality that you and I and all of us are. *Awareness know thyself* has been our mission from the start—and still is! As I said the purpose of this chapter is to establish presence and then to penetrate into it, with profundity. Since we have found that consciousness is the sine qua non for the completion of one's presence, we have to continue to pursue this self-awareness, this conscious matter that can say I am, now centering in on its origin, the question of how it might have come about in the evolutionary horizon? And in that penetrate all the more into what we are really, we conscious creatures that can want, wish for, will, want better worlds than exist, laugh and cry, love and die.

Mud stood up and thought and then talked about it, talked about the sun and the moon and stars, talked about the mystery of itself too—how did such a thing come to be and what is it? The inscape of incarnation happened how? When? Why? Where? And what is it really? This thunder throne of thought and flesh and bleeding psychic scars and screams and schemes and seeing through the sky to a singularity, this phenomenon called conscious matter came about how? I put down my cup of cerebral stimulant, but still the question is there, much deeper than any caffeine soaked dendrites. In this year of Darwin's bicentennial, conscious matter, show thyself for what thou art! Tell us how queer and obscure that first awareness, how sharp and immediate rising into such a baffling incarnation! Show us the amazing architectryonics it took to reach this reptilian, mammalian, fermenting on to frontal vision thing, a fusion of thought and form, a concoction of mud and mind that could love. We have no full and unquestionable authority to tell us how but you yourself conscious mud and muddle.

Yes, in essence it is a plea to ourselves. So what's new? "We venture ourselves," as Nietzsche so aptly said, appropriately continues to be our modus operandi, because really there is no other.

We as conscious matter, we as conscious matter conscious of itself, we as conscious matter that can be compassionate, we as conscious matter in conflict with the raw elemental energies of evolution out which we came, in conflict because of that conscious compassion, that giving of ourselves, that love, know that each of us as human beings can emerge from our lowest level to our highest by means of his or her own doing, his or her own inner decision, and that struggle is the sojourn of breathing. But how did our self-awareness come about in the evolutionary horizon, that evolutionary horizon that I am so enamored with, what is its origin? And will pursuing that, one way or another, one way after another, with yet greater chaodiveness, give us any more a profound penetration into this phenomenon than we already have?

Within the evolutionary horizon one can go either of two ways with regards conscious matter. One is that it grows out of the brain per se, as already mentioned, becoming *more* than the brain per se within the evolutionary sojourn, as the brain itself did physically with regards itself, going from reptilian to mammalian to neo-mammalian. The other is that *a parallel* symbiotic evolution of consciousness took place showing up in different forms and taking on different levels of awareness all the way to the symbiosis in our human heads. Here we can still use the neutrino as a model, where something can be one thing and another, again as already put forth; with the caveat of course that the parallel symbiotic evolution of consciousness only takes place inside heads, since we don't see consciousness floating around outside of them. However, here, in the parallel evolutionary hypothesis, still consistent with it not floating around outside, we can also take a position a la Da Vinci and suggest that it doesn't just take place in heads, but in different ways embellishes the whole form. Remember me saying, it is my own sense, that in time consciousness will show itself to be throughout our form, as Da Vinci suggested, the brain offering one kind, the heart another, and so forth?

Jumping way ahead of myself here, but staying true to the chapter and our present pursuit, I would like to say something out of the ordinary on the subject of consciousness and dare again to openly agree with Da Vinci. The primeval conversation between darkness and the mysterious nothingness before everything cannot be grasped by the human mind and the threshold where they engaged is not visible to us; but, nonetheless, the big bang happened and spacetime with it. So, too, with regards to consciousness; at least as I sit here in my den writing away as my dog re-enters with half a bush attached to his mounds of hair. No one knows, not the anthropologists or anyone else, when consciousness began, how, or what it really is. I have a tendency to think, once we exhaust the study of brains, we will move closer to Da Vinci on this, but it will be a process, possibly a very long one, then as now with a lot of ex cathedra statements from neurologists who think that sitting on said chair gives them a right to forget what else they are sitting on. Meanwhile I remain a lone voice speaking to future generations with regards to my Da Vinci leaning; but maybe not completely so. Doctor Gary Schwartz, a professor of psychology, medicine, neurology, psychiatry, and surgery at the University of Arizona, and director of its Human Energy Systems Laboratory, has come to accept a version of what Da Vinci says, even as he never mentions Leonardo and personally holds that consciousness came first.

Schwartz rightly says that the "brain first, mind second" hypothesis is the prevailing model in contemporary science and in many quarters treated as dogma. He holds the opposite point of view.[60] Since no one knows either way, take your pick. I personally see nothing wrong with it arising out of the brain as I explained, or in a parallel symbiosis, maybe even before and outside even a parallel symbiosis, as the good doctor holds. Although I am not going to go to war with Schwartz when he says he holds that consciousness came first, in the way he says it does, I do have to point out that because he does, he is forced into a real duality. This ghost in the machine approach bothers me, in that it is a statement outside of the realm of existence, and existence is really all we have to go by. To hold that a soul exists in some limbo awaiting transport into a body is the stuff of Scientology, maybe fun to discuss on a spooky night in the playground or around a pool in Hollywood, but, unless you can go to limbo, well you get my point. I might add, that since many besides the good doctor, folks like Ron Hubbard, robbed this duality of body and soul (σωμα και ψυχη) from antiquity, I think I can make mention of it in that context, that is, the context of the thinking coming out of antiquity, without, of course, taking Mr. H's stopover in Venus as a thetan, or ingesting mushrooms like some New Age prophet proclaiming yet another brand of phantasmagoria. For antique thinking, especially of Socrates, does not go about it in that way, and so Greek thought, especially when it comes to his, is a serious discussion we can take part in.

Before we do, however, let's freeze frame our sojourn here, because I want to plunge into a discussion of this ψυχη, not the soul Socrates spoke of necessarily, or what has come to mean soul since, that much abused term, but the one I can speak of, even as I always use it with caution myself because of the baggage it bears and therefore the misconception that would be fostered, and probably is right now with the reader as I mention it.

That said, allow me to give you straight out my particular contemporary insight into ψυχη: *presence at its deepest moment or level of being*. It is that *something deeper still* I referred to without definition. If all were known, what would it tell us about itself? That there *is* something deeper still—or that each of us is indeed a psychic crystallization around an abyss? Then with Hopkins we would indeed have to say, "I wake and feel the fell of dark not day." Yet, even there and then, there is this I witnessing such a situation, this awareness. This *awareness* then is a word that could as well replace the word *soul, presence at its deepest moment or level of being, awareness at its deepest moment or level of being*. Without repeating our whole process of presence let me hit upon some highlights that bring out *awareness* in this light and show how it is what I certainly can use to at least give soul, or if you prefer ψυχη, an understandable and contemporary meaning, although still incompletely developed. In light of what I say about presence, it can be seen as a profound awareness that permeates the whole of the body, but as the deepest level of our being. Put another way, it is the root-reality, pervading the whole of our form, with the body as the extremity of this essential of our being, the body the level of our existence where our awareness meets the material of space and the process of time. I could say that when we reach this profound awareness, we reach ourselves in the deepest *level* of our being and begin to touch upon that mystery each is, that *something deeper still* each is. Again, this is not a duality, I am not suggesting this as a duality, never; rather as the deepest level of what is happening in and throughout our being, the essence and existence one, and at its depth, what cannot be grasped directly. No one grasps oneself directly, for awareness as such cannot be objectified, it is always the awareness looking at—something we must and will penetrate further. Meanwhile, we can say that an appreciation of this awareness grounds everything about us and illuminates our life. You would simply be an empty receptacle without this awareness; you would have no real identity, no place where your life gathers, no chaord. *Your whole presence is this awareness*—even as it penetrates to a profundity that can never be objectified, whose absence would make you anonymous and without a within. For the time being let that suffice, as I said, knowing that it will be further developed when we come to a later segment in the chapter, wherein I shall use other words, words, words to try to express this something deeper still, without I must make mention ever making it an object, since it is always subject. Until then allow me to conclude here by saying that as levels of being replaces duality, so, too, with our understanding of presence, *awareness* can be used for soul, as long as understood the way I am using it. I should make mention while we are at it, that another Greek line of thinking might bring this out more clearly than does ψυχη; namely, Plato's cave, and I think that goes hand in hand with my reading of Plato as talking about levels of being and an awareness level within all that we must awaken. If I am inflicting my notion of levels of being on Plato, and Socrates with him, I apologize, but I do think they are talking in those terms. Again, if not, I am.

That said, let's unfreeze our frame about my refinement of the word soul and backtrack to Socrates and his use of the word, and do so because of Schwartz, as well our present search, not to mention for our own edification and enjoyment. To help us do that, because it has a bearing on the word soul in Plato's use of the word, and thus Socrates', let's start with those very beginnings of Greek thought and once again as promised look at Parmenides' famous phrase, Χρη το λεγειν τε νοειν τε εον εμμεναι. Heidegger, as I stated, and thank him for it, is correct when he says 'the making-to-appear' and 'letting-lie-before-us' is, in Greek thought, the essence of λεγειν and λογος, and 'take-to-heart' the essence of νοειν, and thus the beginning of Western thought and thinking rooted in Parmenides famous phrase, Χρη το λεγειν τε νοειν τε should be understood thusly; namely, 'Needful is the letting to lie-before-us also taking to heart too . . .'[61] Where we part company is in the last two words in the phrase, which I mention again, namely, 'εον εμμεναι.' He would translate it as 'beings in being,' and says it is in keeping with Plato's duality. I still think the translation should be 'being, to be.' It makes better sense when we come to Plato, which I say does not promote a real duality, something we shall go into more descriptively when we come to the cave, but which I shall at least discuss here.

The theme that ancient philosophy and our present one struggle with—that which calls me and you to this think thing—is existence. The place of this existence, Plato's and the Delphi Oracle with him, is the self. Plato calls it η χωρα, *the locus;* this is why *know thyself* becomes the centerpiece of all thinking, it is where thinking thinks and existence exists. You don't think outside of yourself or exist outside of you. It is the center of existence for each of us, *presence* in our parlance. This presence thinks about itself and then in turn about that which made it be, which is what Aristotle did in coining the word metaphysics and Plato before him without such word. Heidegger makes a duality, a distinction between what he calls something blossoming and the act of blossoming, something called being and the act of being, what I can only interpret as one between essence and existence. It is as I said, where I differ with him, for essence and existence are the same for us in this real breathing world. I think they were for Plato, too. He was always really talking about more in us, levels of being, and when he uses the word μετεχη, and μετεχειν, which Heidegger takes up in his defense of this duality, Plato was trying to work his way through existence, as he himself says in *Parmenides*, with the words, "but you are always this presence throughout existence. Therefore at all times you exist you are both present and becoming."[62] What Plato is saying is that you are still you, even as things around you change, including levels of your own being. This is talking in the flavor I am. Ever since I was a kid and water was free I have been me, even as I now have to pay for it as my father said we would have to someday and we all laughed. When Plato uses the word μετεχη I think it is in the contextual understanding I am giving it, maybe even with an aside as well. *Participium* in Latin, μετεχειν in Greek, and *participate* in English, do not gives us or mean duality when it comes to our presence, but exactly what it says, participation, or as I am putting forth levels of being in the one presence. That is just the opposite of duality. Aristotle takes this up when he ask: τι το ον, what is this existence, this presence, who I am, or put in the way of that famous invitation, *know thy self*, so fundamental to Greek thought, because it is so fundament to existence. The struggle to answer that is the journey of life and living. It is what calls mortals to thinking and does so out of necessity. It makes a difference in everything that follows, for how we understand existence decides how we act in existence.

Again that is so important, to Plato and Socrates with him, not to mention the author of this work; and when it comes to presence itself as precisely the presence of what is present, it makes existential sense to approach it as will and the action following as coming out of our presence, not separate from it, otherwise what is so important, namely, how we act in existence, is without a grounding, and where does that leave us, not only with regards how we should act in the face of existence, but who the hell are we as well. Willing is part of what presence does in being present. But then, who am I to argue with Heidegger, you are right, so if you want to make Plato talking in terms of a duality instead, fine, but humbly I maintain Plato and maybe Parmenides too was not doing that—*certainly I am not*. In any event, I think I can at least make the statement that Western thinking begins with existence, saying it is necessary to lay-before-us and take-to-heart being, to be; that is existence. Again, if I am even wrong on that, which I don't think I am as that is the very foundation of the contribution the Greeks gave to us, but even as I began to say, if I am wrong on that, I am not wrong on what I say about presence and its levels of being, or philosophy having to examine existence up and own its levels of being, even unto any ground of being.

With that backdrop, let's return specifically to Socrates and the soul, which follows upon Parmenides and his famous phrase that it is necessary to lay-before-us and take-to-heart being, to be; that is existence. Socrates tried to stay true to that I think; stay true to what he came to in his existence and only that. He spoke of soul as the word ψυχη itself as already mentioned, and as his δαιμων, something he sensed and guided him. For now let's stick only with the word ψυχη. I won't take up the whole spectrum of what the Greeks meant by 'η ψυχη, for the Greek concept of 'η ψυχη is all over the place, from Homer on into *De Anima*, though Aristotle one can say seems to try to clarify it. I can sense some of you pulling away from me. Why all this Greek stuff? I hear you. Put on some real rock'n roll! Good Golly, Miss Molly . . . I found my thrill on blueberry hill . . .

I have to admit to you I am of two minds on this. Which brings Cicero to mind. Cicero talks of us in terms of a duality within us, *credo deos immortales sparsisse animos in corpora humana*, which one cannot say he got merely from his reading of the Greeks, since he was a great thinker on his own and most likely came to it in his own right one starry night out looking for his thrill on palatine hill. I get the feel is time for a break.

After a late Sunday martini with two olives and an hour of comic relief with Louis Black and my Old English, I read some Joyce for a while . . . "For you had—may I, in our, your and their names, dare to say it?—the nucleus of a glow of a zeal of soul . . ." and found myself our bridge back to my I-Mac.

It may be that 'η ψυχη, *the soul* Socrates and Plato spoke of as immortal does precede life and returns to its origin after death, and that certainly is a clean or clear-cut way of approaching it and may even be the way it is, Marcus Tullius, and Dr. Schwartz with you. When we speak of the soul, our identity at its deepest level of being, that something deeper still, *presence at its deepest moment of being*, we have come upon the most numinous and mysterious of questions about us as humans. The self is not like anything else in the world, even as it is in spacetime, yet simultaneously somehow beyond it as well, with an antique awareness about it. That traditional thinking can be so, even in my contemporary framework, and I am not saying this is not so, but that is not demonstrable in any way, so it is not going to help us lay a universal grounding for a purely human spirituality based on the only thing we have to go by, existence itself. Granted a radical division between the soul and the body in a real duality has been around, well since death struck our species, and it is understandable why. First, because humans fear dying, and with a separate soul, that offers an opportunity for one to say the soul continues on. That offers another opportunity as well, for some imaginative folk to then describe what it continues on to. But even as we know what dying is, and it is not pretty, we don't know what happens or doesn't after we die and they shouldn't be so ready and willing to tell us. It is outside our privy, and to say it isn't is untruthful. So since they can't point to someway in existence to back up their claims, such people rely on one faith-based system or another. True, outside of such faith-based systems one can at least speculate about it and we do as a species and individually, but we won't here, for our endeavor here is not to speculate on an after life, but to venture into this one, for we are attempting *to build on a grounding that can be shown and is universal to our existence, and from that a way to act in the face of it.* Speculations about an after life, nor faith of any kind about anything, are not going to do it, there has to be evidence of and for what we say. God help us, but we don't need yet another faith-based movement, whether based on an honest mysticism, mushrooms, or Mohammed. We don't need yet more rationalistic nonsense either, awash as it is with its own stifling myopia. Both approaches take us down an already slippery slope. Yes, it's hard climbing the mountain of reality; ask Sisyphus.

Dark humor aside, Schwartz, contrary to my understanding and translation of Plato, holds onto what the Arab philosophers reinforced in their interpretation of Plato's writings, which was afterwards carried over into Medieval Europe; namely, that Plato (and Socrates via him) talked in dualistic terms, whereas with a careful reading, one sees the great philosopher is talking in terms of levels of being. In the Cave story, found in his *Republic, Book VII*, Plato is not talking about the end of you, or one of you here and one there, but the same you enlightened to a higher consciousness, enlarging your embrace of existence and entering into the highest level of being, where the Greek reads *an ascent to!* What follows is also very important, for then he goes on to talk about taking that enlightenment and helping those still held in the shadows. Remember, above all, Plato, like Socrates, was concerned with rendering humans morally better. He would have liked to ground this in the divine, but from his own 'prayer' we see he still stays true to existence first and foremost. "We must take the best and most irrefragable of human doctrines," the great thinker tells us, "and embark on that as if it were a raft on which to risk the voyage of life. Unless it were possible to find a stronger vessel, something holy, some Sacred Meaning on which we might take our journey more surely and with confidence."[63]

In the *Symposium,* as well, we see his sense of levels and his desire to awaken us to a higher life, but still staying true to you and me. "This wisdom of which I speak found sleeping at our depths must be awakened through the images of it that are found in sensible things, and from sensible things it must arise to the invisible and supreme beauty, which is nether born nor dies, but forever."[64] But it is you doing this as you. We are dreadfully ever present, even in becoming philosophically enlightened. It is you going deeper into being. Again, as I said when discussing Parmenides' famous phrase, even if I might be wrong about my rendering of Plato's levels of being, which I do not think I am, no matter, Socrates, Plato, and any philosopher worthy of the word is always trying to make us better animals. When all the dust settles, and all the footnotes written, this was really what Plato was trying to do, make us better by making us see the truth as he saw it. He even creates a whole *Republic* to that end. Buddha was trying to do the same in his way, and Lao Tsu, too, even as he was discussed with humans and fled into the desert, and likewise Mohammed even as he was coming out of one. Dare I say Camus and Christ were attempting this as well, as was the man from Rocken with his *ubermensch*, not to mention a certain hopeless author residing on Clown Alley and this pantaloony attempt of his to make himself and all of us better sentient creatures. Do humor him and read on as he sets his sights on answering the third question of philosophy, while asking who's on first, all the while with his eye on second. He actually insists that you have to go to first and second before third and home.

I have already stated that whether the brain creates consciousness or consciousness has its own parallel evolution it doesn't matter to the outcome. So, too, in truth, with regards to Socrates' notion of soul it must be said, or our own. Therefore, no matter how it came to be, consciousness caught up in matter or not, it is still incarnated awareness or conscious matter. And with matter, whether an incarnation of it or not, comes entropy, by the very fact that it is matter, and consciousness is subject to that, however it came to be, and so suffering and chance and the perilous perhaps enter the picture. Death happens! Yet, in all this, with consciousness also comes love. So, in this evolutionary horizon, we still come up with and are back to a consciousness in the cosmos, a consciousness in the cosmos that can love, existence and the deepest experience in existence. Our evolutionary horizon still gives us a consciousness caught in the thrill and throes of matter, a ride where . . . well where no matter what, we are still present, where one can say I am, I am and I can give of myself. Yes, love is there no matter how awareness came to be and is here; and what is more, we know how to act in the face of the world because of it, conscious matter knows how to act in the face of existence, the self, no matter how it came to be out of whatever stark abyss, knows how to face the cosmos, awareness up against a swarming multiplicity realizes how to encounter the earth. *Our "redemption" is built-into the beast*, it is awareness's choosing to give of itself, even over the raw elemental energies and entanglements of evolution and despite the possibility that it may even be alone and an aberration in the universe.

I think I should say here, at last, that where I do agree with Schwartz is where he agrees with me, first, in that "the brain first, mind second" doctrine has not been proven, and second, a la Da Vinci, that consciousness may have other residence in us besides our brain. Schwartz speaks of it in relation to the heart, and he does so in a non-metaphoric way. I would rather go along with Leonardo and speak of it in regards the whole form, as you saw I did in discussing awareness already. I think consciousness, one way or another, permeates the whole of the body, even as consciousness resides most obviously where it does, the way it does; and no matter what self-being is before or after spacetime, in spacetime it is one in-with-and-of the body, in a single presence, and *explainable in levels of being*. We know outside of the brain, the gut is where we have our largest nerve center. This gives room for conjecture as to whether there, too, there is not some form of consciousness present. When we get to Christof Koch we shall see that even he discusses the gut and consciousness. Certainly when we worry, we can feel it in our stomach. The Japanese actually thought that the soul resides in the stomach. Perhaps they are a people that worry more than most. While we are in that part of the world, I should mention that the Chinese might have touched upon what I am talking about as well, when they talked about *the vital breath, ch'i*. "When the *ch'i* is expressed in visibility," the Chinese sage Chang Tsai says, "its visibility becomes apparent so that there are then shapes. When it disperses, its visibility is no longer apparent and there are no shapes. At the time of its visibility, can one say otherwise than that is but temporary? But at the time of its dispersing, can one hastily say that it is then non-existent?"[65] The phenomenal manifestation of being is there, yet it is more than the subatomic particles, it is the vital breath as the earliest Taoist tried to express in talking of being itself, the vital breath each of us is. So that Tao scholars don't panic, I should mention that I realize he carries this to that which is behind the yin and yang, both of which spring from it. Also, I should mention that I brought up both the Japanese and Chinese notions not to say that they are saying what I am, but only to show that there is at least some thinking there that might at least be seen to touch upon what I am putting forth. In any event, traces for thinking in terms of consciousness permeating the whole body in different ways or levels is certainly not out of the question, and thus we can dare say this awareness we speak pervades the whole of our being. Leonardo may have been onto something. I tend to think so.

Even if I hold for consciousness only in the brain, or even relegate myself to accepting "brain first, mind second," consciousness can still supersede its neural structure as already shown, establishing a difference between the two in observable fact, as well as *levels of being* in a presence. Notice, too, no matter which way we go with this we still have a presence as our grounding in existence, and awareness as its essential.

Schwartz rightfully carries on exhaustive experiments trying to prove what he holds, while maintaining, unfortunately before the fact, what sounds to my somewhat postmodern ears like the dualism of old in New Age verbiage. Both the philosopher and postmodern in me cringes at what is called New Age, it is sloppy and without grounding. We, in our venture, always demand that we come back to *a grounding*. So as we continue our trek into the self and its evolutionary horizon, we come back to that grounding and again what comes out of that. Any philosophy or spirituality, ethic, or morality—all three really variations of the same theme—must have a grounding based in existence, and existence does give us such a grounding; namely, our only real and universal certainty, existence itself, and the deepest experience in it. From that existentially established foundation each of us must work our way, like a detective, always measuring everything in the light of that grounded reality, even as one ventures into the second part of our subtitle for this book.

Without going over it all over again, which would be cruel and unusual punishment, let me say that all things stand at the threshold of my presence, of your presence, and that neither of us can evict ourselves from ourselves and ever know either who we really are or really what existence is for us as humans—and if we don't know that we will not know how to truly act in the face of it. The deep reality of presence stands as our fundamental grounding. It is the deepest here-ness of being for each of us, so one must be aware, here as it were, and capable of acting out of that and the deepest experience in it, choosing thusly, all the way to love's highest realization, if one is to act in the fullness of our being as humans.

Again, to act out of that consciousness, in spite of our toiletry, in the face of the will to power within each of us, requires *an inner decision,* an inner decision based on this profound realization the gravedigger J C speaks of in his humanness, and that inner decision is *the will to love.* The pull of naked nature and the forces out of which we emerged and uncoiled will always be there—but so will the possibility of being sensitive to the deepest part of life and living.

Let me repeat and repeat as many times as I must, what we are talking about is *the* basic tension within us. We can no more give up our body than we can our consciousness; and within that tension we choose who we will be, at what level of ourselves we will act out of, both in action and re-action. My starving body might scream to keep the whole of the bowl of soup for itself; but my consciousness, which can decide to go along with that natural instinct, decides instead to share it with some stranger sitting beside me who is starving as well, whether in Dachau as we know it took place, or in downtown Des Moines as we might surmise. We know from science that the brain is fed first when a starving body takes in food, it is built into our biology, yet, here, conscious love supersedes even a starving brain crying out to survive. Again, how beautiful and clear a demonstration of consciousness offering each of us the choice between instinct and itself, the deepest part of itself I must point out. In this startling act of sharing we see concretely, and in such a truly human way, straight on, not only that we can love, but do so even at the peril of our own survival. As Nietzsche rightly said nature's *will to power* is present in our experience, so, too, is what we have found, *a will to love.* So it is I have to ask myself, although love is not an easy experience to express and not an easy road to walk, can it be that this mysticism without ecstasy, because of what it is in experience, can it be that it leads me to what I am looking for? In a very real way, I think we all know the answer to that. *And at that moment—that eureka—we reach a purely human spirituality.* It comes out of *being sensitive to the deepest part of being*, wherein a person realizes something so very profound, so real and so profound as to require action on his part, on her part.

It is straightforward. Existence and the deepest experience in existence give us our grounding for a purely human spirituality: *I am and I can love.*

Of course the tragedy is that what we can refuse to attend to cannot reach us, and even if it does we can choose not to recognize it in our life, we can choose the will to power and be unable to realize any form of relationship with the other except absorption or possession, use and even abuse. But contrary to that will to power rooted as it is in the blind and sometimes blinding elemental energies of evolution, is an aware creature, you and me and each of us, that can choose out of the deepest experience in its existence, sensitive to it and realizing life in and through it. And so it is that we can honestly say we have reached a spirituality, a holiness, an ethic, a morality, *drawn out of the depths of our very humanness.* I said concerning that which is most fundamental to us—that if we couldn't trust it, we really couldn't trust anything else, but since we could, the deepest experience in that existence becomes all-important. The truth is once the door of love is opened, you can never look upon the other as merely the raw elemental energies of evolution, and our treatment of all life changes. Even of a horse in a piazza. Yes, the raw elemental energies of evolution are there within us, instinct and survival, and survival of the fittest to be sure, all of it, from gene drive to our whole material make up—but so are consciousness and this profound experience that is as irreducible as the individual who does the loving, whether beneficent Buddha or caring Christ, an atheist or an agnostic, you or me.

Again, consciousness in the cosmos adds a level that is not there without it—and so most definitely does love. As conscious existence gave us a higher form of evolution and our one minimal certainty in the cosmos, love gives us our deepest experience in that conscious existence and a purely human spirituality. Yes, it is straightforward. Existence and the deepest experience in existence give us our grounding for a purely human spirituality: *I am and I can love.*

Note that I have kept it all in the realm of existence alone and the deepest experience in existence. I have kept it all on what all have and any can achieve, based on life and living alone. That is the daring of this spirituality. It is rooted in existence and existence alone. Different paradigms, philosophies, politics, pious-nesses, and the like, come and go, the root-reality is what matters and if not that, then nothing. Vocations, non-vocations, holy books and unholy ones, all that is *indifferentia* when we speak of spirituality, what is real is the invitation to give of yourself; that is the calling to a purely human spirituality, the grounding of it. It would be a tragic mistake if we named love wrongly and tried to make it into something it is not, into a pious legalism or scrupulosity or asceticism or—well I think you get what I mean. And if not, remember where it comes from, that it is rooted and grounded in our existence, as existence itself and the deepest experience in it. That keeps it outside the preview of faith or phantasmagoria, outside the preview of a tragic *on-going* mistake. It even keeps it outside the preview of any God. God or no God, it is still what it is. Of course, if it can further be grounded in an Ultimate Grounding, that would add significantly to our stand on love, relieving it of its lonely stand in the cosmos. But that is a discussion of another chapter. Meanwhile, I have kept it out of the realm of religion, and always will, for being spiritual is ultimately one's own 'religion', one's own 'metaphysics,' as much a part of a person as his or her being itself. It is freedom personified. You ultimately choose to be holy or not, to become actuality-conscious or not, to be sensitive to the deepest part of life and living or not. If you only look at the raw elemental energies of evolution you will come to the conclusion pre-equine Nietzsche did and define yourself thusly and thus act accordingly. But, unless you are purposefully myopic, you will see that you really are as J C so graphically realizes in his toilet. Yes in his toilet where evolution reminds us who we are everyday—but not stripping us of, as he tells us, an awareness as well of something in us called love, giving us that fuller human reality to act out of, choosing what consciousness has to offer at its depth, for therein is everyone's deepest definition and decision.

It is an *individual* decision, an *individual* growth; a person attempting with his or her *individual* act to surpass the indifference without with a caring within, one that supersedes levels inside of each that are tied lock, stock and Serengeti to what is loveless, and instead digs past that to the depth of one's being and *chooses* to give of one's individual self and soup and space and time to what is loving.

It is the most important decision in life, for it will ultimately define you. *How you choose to act* in the face of the jungle both within and without will fashion who you are, even as you are.

This ability to choose or *willing* has to give us pause. Just as one's presence can't be ignored, neither can this fundamental function of choice in us. We are not just conscious witnesses to life; we are conscious doers as well. My dog just came into the den making funny sounds demanding something. It sounds more like "let me out," rather than "I want another cookie," so I will open the French doors and let him out into the garden. His interruption demonstrated concretely or if you want existentially that a presence can't be ignored—it is a presence! A precious presence, as each is! But there is also a choice on our part with regards that precious presence, how we treat it, that other presence. That at bottom is what we are talking about when I mention willing. How we *choose* to encounter existence. At what level of being a presence chooses to live in the face of the world! Once consciousness comes into the picture, it is no longer instinctual behavior but what is consciously realized, a person choosing, and at bottom choosing between acting out of the deepest experience in existence or not, between what I called the will to love and what Nietzsche rightly called the will to power. Each of us is the deep truth of that being. That being or presence I speak of does not proceed nor come after your essence—essence is existence, existence is essence—they are one in the same, with you and me and each of us completing it, completing our own self-being, *by our choices*, alive in the levels of our being. Each of us is our own evolution in this. How Looking-Glass-like that the self is the very source of its own final creation! What you will be in the end is up to you, despite all the heavy baggage you carry with you in both DNA and the day's experience, the psychic scars and physical ones, humanity as a perennial disappointment and divinity gone missing, your soul soaring when the butterfly flutters in a southern sun, but shivering when the wind blows out of a northerly nothing! Fairly or not, despite and in spite of all of it, who you will be as you finish your journey in the Wonderland of breathing is the person you created, the presence you completed—with the measuring rod how you gave of yourself, everyone's deepest definition and decision.

Remember me saying, in a humorous way to be sure, but true nonetheless, that you can't proceed in anything really, Buddhism, biology, or being Beelzebub without this sine qua non we call consciousness? It is the tool that gives us the ability to choose; and that is our defining moment in being. We already know what we *fundamentally* choose between, so now let's continue with *the ability to choose itself.*

Penetrating further into this presence and its ability to choose, we begin to see what I meant when I said that we are dealing with our very presence's core definition when we talk of choosing or willing, and that has to involve *a fundamental freedom* to choose at all. If I didn't have this freedom, there really wouldn't be any choice or choosing. You might say OK to that, so we don't have any real choice or choosing. But we have seen that we do have choice and we already know something very important about it; namely, that whatever it is, this *willing* can even choose what is *contra natura;* which, in turn, argues not only to the fact that it is, but to something that is at a higher *level* of being than the raw elemental energies of evolution in that it can supersede them. *Or to put it another way, is more than the primal forces within organisms that are instinctual.* Again this difference is rooted in our very presence as we saw in discussing the interiorization that takes place in the relentless evolutionary process.

Freud's mistaken assertion, which I merely mentioned when I mentioned Frankl, I will now elaborate on here, not only because he is mistaken, but also because his view is so close to what many have mistakenly taken up as the truth about us, saying that we cannot overrule instinct and there really is no free will or choice involved. Sigmund once asserted: "Let one attempt to expose a number of the most diverse people uniformly to hunger. With the increase of the imperative urge of hunger all individual differences will blur, and in their stead will appear the uniform expression of the one unstilled urge." But a man who experienced what Sigmund only talked about and thanks heaven that Sigmund did not have to experience it, overrules him with actuality, speaking out of his laboratory of fact called Auschwitz and then Dachau, where he tells us just the opposite took place and people showed their individuality, choosing to be swine or saints.[66] Freud's pronouncement was wrong, it was not based on the fact of who we really are. Frankl on the other hand was not proclaiming from a couch what we were or would do when starving, but actually starving and relating what really took place. The conclusions by Freud were colored by his own conscious and perhaps unconscious bias and assumptions, and then presented as fact, even scientific fact; when in truth it was a spin, spin-science as I like to dub it. Science is always what is demonstrable, and here Frankl was more scientific than Freud. I underline that because we are going to see others like Freud in this regard.

Before we do, however, I want to say that I don't want to mislead here, and so we are going to have another one of my famous freeze frames. Although I mentioned choice and an awareness in that, I am not talking in terms of something without other factors entering into it; as the people in the camp had that horror enter into their choosing. Sometimes, sickness might make our body react in such a way as to make it nearly impossible for a person to overcome its effect, thus more than complicating the choosing, but actually nearly closing it down. We are creatures in spacetime subject to the physics of the place—I will be crushed by a truck if I step in front of it, no matter how I might will otherwise. I am going to die, no matter how I might say I will be the only person who never will! So, too, deceases might so affect our chemistry as to make it so much harder for us to act in a way we might want to. I make mention of this so you have a fuller sense of what I am talking about. Also, I don't want to mislead you in another way. I am not talking in terms of or from rationality as the source or force here. Perhaps love is reason completely developed, perhaps not, but from existence, which is our only real guide, being intellectual, or if you will, being rational, is not the necessary or primary; love is beyond reason per se, in a place all its own, a consciousness beyond even good and evil touching an actuality with its own reasoning. Even Aristotle, the practical ethician knew that. However, I don't want to get into a discussion of the ancients, for I do not think the Greeks and the Romans have the same primary in this as I do; nor the ancient Hebrews either. Love of course being what it is has to be seen coming through in both Greco-Roman and Hebrew writings, nevertheless, for the most part, the Greco-Romans in their approach, as well as the Hebrews in their righteousness, seem never to have put love as *the* primary in their ethics/morality/spirituality, let alone their institutionalized legalistic and ritualistic religions, and that has to be taken into account. When Cicero speaks of the cardinal virtues in his *On Supreme Good and Evil (De finibus bonorum et malorum)* he mentions wisdom, justice, fortitude, and temperance. Yet, at the same time he and Socrates with him want philosophy to be not only thoughtful, but also deeply felt—in other words move us to action and be our very way of life. So some form of push or pull is required. I think, therefore, we can see a certain sense of will in the Greco-Roman philosophical ponderings, and most certainly a sense of love in their private lives. We have only to recall how Cicero suffered at the death of his beloved daughter Tullia. There is most certainly a sense of love in their private lives, even primarily so. So why the hesitancy in their philosophers to say so? Why the hesitancy in ours? *It is a remarkably bold step to make love as the primary in ethics.*

But that is what we are doing—and it calls for explanation. A whole book of explanation! "Oh, is that what that written scream of yours is supposed to be," my Old English mumbles from his throw rug of comfort. I pay him no heed, realizing he is upset with me for not getting up to get him yet another gingerbread cookie. Where was I? Yes, addressing the source of our purely human spirituality and saying that it is more than a call to right reason.

In this regard, unless one can show that love is reason completely developed, (which I would accept if shown) what we are saying is that the sourceforce is different than something *purely* intellectual, though it most definitely is within consciousness. A person can know something is right, but still choose not to do it. Enlightenment requires more than reasoning about it; or to put it another way, *love is more than logic.* Will is involved in this, something more than rationality. I think the Greeks knew that, but never centered in on it, although Socrates, via Plato, did talk about the mystery that moved him. He brings this out when he talks of his δαιμων. I mentioned this before in discussing the notion of soul, and now do again, and again I am going to use only the Greek, because if I gave the usual English translation for the word, it would mislead what Socrates was saying. It expresses a familiar force, which he fails to fully grasp intellectually he tells us, but which is a part of him, at his deepest level of being, as if a primary intuition, one that pulls him to the profundity of his being and action. Philosophy was more than an intellectual exercise for Socrates, but rather, for him, *who he was, in a very real sense, and his guide in life, with his δαιμων that mysterious within that guided him to action; it was to lay-before-himself and take-to-heart being, to be, that is existence, and carry what he found there into action.*

Such a notion and the writing around it brings out *the holistic quality* in Plato and Socrates when it came to philosophy, and one that almost talks in terms of a will to love and it as primary. Plato brings this out in the *Symposium*, which I bring up again, the first Plato I ever read coincidentally, as a fourth year student in prep school, enthralled with what I was reading. Of course, I did not fully appreciate it at the time, especially when Plato tells us of Socrates as he talks in terms of love as the communion which "mixes and murmurs" with the Mystery that made us. It contains Plato's innermost conviction, often not addressed, even by him. But Plato does not stop short here in what he says about love, he identifies it within the depths of Socrates, as it is in the depths of all humans, and even uses the word δαιμων when describing it. "Love is δαιμων, and the intermediate, communication, communion between the divine and the mortal." "It is the mediator that spans the chasm which divides them." "For God mingles not with man; but through love all intercourse and converse of God with man, whether awake or asleep, is carried on. The wisdom which understands this is spiritual."[67] Throughout he gives a sense of what we ourselves are about here in this our venture. Granted we have had over two thousand years plus to refine our notion of love, and see Socrates and everyone else struggling in the *Symposium*, at times some of the dinner party seemingly almost ridiculous in their utterances, but that is the genius of all those dialogues, they are thought-provoking, even enigmatic, wanting to be seen with different approaches and appeals, leaving an openness and multiplicity of layers to get to—and that is in keeping with Plato's way of thinking. An important insight often overlooked when looking at Plato.

We see Plato has his *Symposium* via Socrates talk in terms of levels of being, starting out with beauty as seen and ending with the beauty that is unseen, within at the depth of each of us. From there Socrates says we draw ever closer to the Mystery that made us. To a communion that love leads and is the highest expression of. But Plato ever the teller of truth has love challenged with the interruption by our baser drives in the form of Alcibiades crashing into the gathering—how appropriate, how true to life. Yet, in the end, Plato has even Alcibiades realize what Socrates is saying; even as we are left wondering if it is a full realization and that he will now act upon it.

Of course, I am not saying that the *Symposium* or Plato himself is saying what I am saying, but there certainly is a sense there that he is heading in that contemporary direction, and I think a read with that in mind will show I am right in my rendering, despite all the splashing about in the *Symposium*, which as I explained is true to all those great dialogues, and what makes them so thought-provoking, arriving at the human truth in all this, which again was their great contribution in thinking, something even expressed in Greek art, where the beauty and true form of the body became their break-through and what they passed down the ages to us. What Plato added was the penetration into something within us which we call love.

Something is still lacking in today's philosophy, and that something is the main thing, the taking to heart, love; yet without it there is no wisdom, so how could one say they are doing philosophy, the love of wisdom, when both the love and the wisdom are not there?

Plato was there, and Marcus Aurelius, too, as was Buddha and Lao Tzu, and Jesus with them—and our only difference with each being that I went about it in the way we have. Please don't misunderstand me, I would be ripe for the lulu bin if I thought I am on a par with these giants or make such claims. No, I am not saying that, I am saying that because of the age we are alive to, even as we come to the same conclusion, we had to find our grounding differently. Whereas, for example, Buddha, because of the age he was alive to, could put forth a way to behave based on his own mystical experience gained under a papal tree on the banks of the Neranjara, our way had to be through a non-mystical way, one applicable to all of us, and thus through existence alone. Our method of getting to what we did differs, not our respect for Buddha. However, it has to be said about all of them, Buddha and Jesus included, we can come upon this even if none of the above ever existed, for all we need is existence itself. Again, although Jesus never tells us how he came to the conclusions he did, in other words what he based them on in his life, we can conclude that his conclusions were arrived at via his own experience in everyday existence, or like Buddha, via a mysticism of his own, we just don't know. If by his own experience, however, when he said, "I am the way," he could have easily meant that to apply to each of us, in our own incarnation, as well as to himself. Whatever which way, whether he did or didn't, we could argue ad nauseam; whereas we can't deny that the foundation we have come to is applicable to him, as he is a human being, a *bar'enas* like each of us. It is applicable to his statement about himself, as it is applicable to all of us—and that is the point, precisely what we have been trying for in this postmodern global era of ours, *a grounding for a purely human spirituality*. In any and all events, whether I am a Buddhist or a Christian, an atheist or an agnostic, left handed or right, I am as long as I am, and can as long as I am, can experience the deepest experience in that existence *and act out of it*.

So, after our detour into reason, right or wrong, Greek or straight, not to mention our mention of an Emperor, a Buddha, and a Christ, let's unfreeze and take up *acting out of this self* again, that is, our discussion of *willing* in our contemporary setting—*the giving of one's self to*—which prompts us to revisit the choice I spoke of. I could merely say with William James that my first act of free will is to exercise my free will in saying there is free will and leave my say on the matter as that, but I feel obliged to say more, since more has been our signature word of this venture so far. Let's start by saying quite frankly that when those in evolutionary psychology, or behavioral genetics, or neurobiology, or biology itself deny a real presence for each of us, or choice out of that presence as real as well, the burden of proof—real proof—falls on them, because they are denying what is fundamentally present to each of us and fundamental to everyday life itself. Yet we shall see they do this, make such a life-denying statement, without proof, whether scientific or from existence itself. What they do instead is use a half-truth, namely, that we are made up of the raw elemental energies of evolution, and forget the other pull in the tension within our humanness. That is and will remain throughout their basic blindness or myopic view. They make the same mistake Herr Freud did and Frankl corrected him on. We have already seen earlier in this chapter that they make numerous conclusions about the biological base of I-consciousness, but none of the groups mentioned above or any other can connect the chasm between the neurological processes and consciousness. The fact remains that brain-biology researchers, along with those in the quasi-scientist of evolutionary psychology, have no demonstrable (*ergo truly scientific*) proof to offer for their pronouncements. All of them merely make paralyzing proclamations masked over with scientific jargon—and offer them with the assertion of infallibility, all decked out in white lab coats as they speak ex cathedra. So what I would like to do, *choose to do*, is address these proclamations and take issue with them, because free will or choice is necessary for any ethic, morality, or spirituality, not to mention life itself as a human being.

Before we start, let me say so no one misunderstands where I am going with this, as awe-inspiring as the brain is, as elegant as DNA and messenger RNA is, as exciting as the current happenings in paleontology, molecular studies and the human genome, all of which I hold to dearly, again let me underline, there is still more to us, there is consciousness, too. A holistic approach must be embraced and that embrace includes the deepest experience in the fullness of our presence. The παντα ρει continues in the flow of life within molecular biology. The whole new field of biotechnology will be wonderful in the treatment of diseases. Or monstrous if misused. Again there is more to us you see. Darwin's framework of evolution is without doubt correct, but it is only part of what it means to be human, only part of our humanness. The fusion that occurred as we evolved from apes has left its DNA imprint and there is that FOXP2, but there is more still to this phenomenon of humanness. "Our complexity must arise not from the number of separate instruction packets, but from the way they are utilized."[68] That is precisely my third question of philosophy again. It always comes back to that and that back to the first, who am I—that is why we must take up the time to deal with these follyforgers.

How did life arise? How did self-replicating organisms arise in the very beginning of the great process of evolution on earth. It is honest to say we simply don't yet know. As we really don't know what consciousness is and how it came to be. At present the scientists are even arguing over what caused the Cambrian explosion. The wonder-filled world of DNA sleuthing is a noble endeavor, saying there is no self is not; and not science as well. And trying to patten genesis the will to power run amuck. It is all part of that third question of philosophy, and that part of the first. I am glad that James Watson resigned in indignation at the push for pattens for the genes of the human genome; but there is a grounding why he did and must. In light of that, we take up our sojourn through the drivel of the follyforgers.

Of course, as I already said, I find it fascinating to be shown the DNA molecule. Traveling through the outer backbone of ribboned phosphates and into the inner sanctum of the blueprint of life with its rungs of laddered chemical components in A, C, G, and T each a particular shape, has to make one giddy, and giddier still as the messenger RNA moves in an inner $\pi\alpha\nu\tau\alpha\ \rho\epsilon\iota$ into a place called ribosome and converts into an amino acid. I would be dead not to appreciate that! That spelled out, you know from whence we approach the follyforgers who betray that very science, and in doing so commit crimes against humanity, or at least allow for crimes against humanity to be committed.

And so, as promised, I will address the parade of follyforgers in this masterpiece; but if their "head-hunting" is too much for you, by all means skip over their skullduggery and move on to the segment that follows, proving either way—by not doing so or by doing so—your ability to choose as you enjoy, knowing no matter what they say, that you can, that you can, and are real, as are they, unfortunately. I resent having to waste time on their follyforging. Theirs is "a haven of the booboisie, of boobs and bounders and all brummagem mountebanks," as the great Auturo Bandini might have put it had he wandered into their midst from his one-night cheap hotel. I would prefer to further pursue what we have before, not to mention the wonders that yet await us in our venture of tying the air together in a divine dialectic, but alas I must show them for what they are and that they are as well, even though they would deny that to themselves and me and you and every last one of us. It'll be like going through hell to get to heaven, or something like that. And so come suffer with me. *Nel mezzo del cammin* . . .

The parade of follyforgers!

It has become the vogue in so many circles to deny a real you and real choice by you, invoking natural selection or neurology, or both together, as if two half truths somehow will do the trick of making you disappear. The fad is pushed on by a swarm of books from sympathetic publishers apparently eager to do so one can only imagine because of a needed excuse for their own behavior in the jungle of the publishing world—this way they had no choice in the matter of being sons of bitches and bastards. *O tempora, O mores!* I have lumped those who deny self and free will all together because in truth they are all in the same parade, following the same bongo beat, though they might *choose* to protest to the contrary. No matter, each and all deny what we are centered in on here, free will or real choice rooted in the root-reality of self; and instead each and all offer biological or mechanistic definitions of us, both of our selves and our free will, denying both. Because of the media and other misinformation, it has become a knee-jerk reaction among too many in our postmodern world to embrace these follyforgers as gospel, as if their hype—because it is put in the lingo of clinical neurophysiologic conditions or the raw elemental energies of evolution—has to be the truth, the whole truth, and nothing but the truth, enough to explain everything about us, from presence to choice, and everything in between.

I am reminded here of the revelations about the FBI lead bullet 'proof' as a forensic tool. For forty years the FBI believed that lead in bullets had a unique chemical signature, and so it was possible to match bullets. It was accepted in courtrooms and send people to a lifetime behind bars if not to their death. This went unchallenged until it was revealed that the basic premise had never actually been scientifically proved. In a very real way, the biological and mechanistic proclamations are like that. First of all in that they have not been proved, and secondly, like the misstatement about the bullets, these misstatements are detrimental, for social as well as individual harm can come from these forgers of folly who put forth that we are merely a mass of neurons, or merely mechanisms to propagate genes, or merely molded by modules from our evolutionary past, and can do nothing about how we behave in the face of all this, especially since there is no real self there to begin with.

Primal behavior is not the only way we can chose to act; and to say it is, divests us of life at its human level. I will borrow the phrase "nocebo effect" here, to bring out that negative expectations can become self-fulfilling. These folks, whether evolutionary psychologists, genetic behaviorists, sociocultural determinists, neurological reductionists, radiologists, or whatever other name they want to give themselves, all build everything upon a primal and/or neurological conditioning as the *only* real factors in our being. Although the evolutionary biologists might protest my lumping them with the biological determinists, or neurological reductionists with sociocultural determinists, the fact is together or separately, in point of fact, whether evolutionary psychologists, biological determinists, or any of the others in their parade, they ultimately all deny a real you and you having real choice. In this they are on a march to nowhere, all following a primitive bongo drum banging away inside of them, and only that! As you know in your sleep by now, I have never denied the raw elemental energies within our make up, and never would. I have supported that as a truth, but I have also said that making this the *only* criteria would not be existentially factual, and lead to a primal ethic based on nature wherein the will to power would ultimately be the guide to behavior, and would have to be, for primal nature alone would be the foundation for behavior. The raw elemental energies of evolution are of course "a factor in determining the distribution of traits and properties within these constraints. *A* factor but not *the* factor," as Noam Chomsky so aptly puts it.[69] We have already seen that this pull from biology within us is there, but so is another, one that cannot be overlooked or dismissed, namely, consciousness, which is the most intangible of all the levels of being in us, and one that has eluded both science and philosophy because of that, even as we see it supersede the very brains in our heads. Both, the raw elemental energies of evolution and the phenomenon of consciousness, together set up a tension within each human being that has to be recognized and acted out of—there is a choice to be had between those instincts and the deepest experience in our existence as humans. Therein is the grounding of ethics, morality, and spirituality at its root-reality.

This is so even in the most horrid of circumstances, as we saw. That is not bias talking as in the case of our neo-Darwinians, but life itself. No not bias, but Buchenwald! Of course, each of us carries his or her narration with us, and that can either help or hinder in one's ability to choose, lessen the window of opportunity as it were, as even our DNA might, and certainly a damaged dendrite would, so please don't think I am totting a bible-belt brain here, one without a backdrop of all that we have talked about. But, that said and again underlined, the window for willing is still there, whether in Dachau or Detroit. Our actions are not rhetorical grooming as these folks would have us believe; and it does come down to a belief on their part, despite the fact that these true believers say that they are being scientific. They would put forth a half-truth about us as I said, and then swear that is it the whole truth and nothing but the truth—so help them biological determinism one says, another evolutionary modules, another this synaptic gap or other, *all forgetting the explanation gap*. Theirs is a morbid self-scrutiny, one that leaves out a very vital part of life and living. For a thrilling instant I wish they would honestly look at themselves and realize what they are looking out of.

Their myopic understanding and appreciation of humans is a forced fit, more applicable to ants or maybe flies. Although some try to build a sense of mutuality, justice, generosity, etc on the primal ethic that comes out of their primitive interpretation of us, it doesn't fly—so in face of their science fiction I think it applicable to use something from science fiction itself, apply called *The Fly*. An eccentric scientist begins to transform into a giant man/fly hybrid after one of his experiments goes horribly wrong; the tagline reading "be afraid, be very afraid." Although I joke, the truth of the matter is that their primal ethic based on their primitive interpretation of us would lead to nihilism and would have to if the raw elemental energies of evolution were the only grounding for our behavior. That wasn't funny the last time that happened in our history when the will to power became all the rage. If a global ethic is to be had, it has to be built upon the fullness of what we are as humans; and that has to take in not only the raw elemental energies of evolution, but a consciousness that can and has superseded those instinctual urges, superseded them with among other things acts of compassion and love; acts of compassion and love not as "reciprocal altruism" rooted in tribal/gene propagation as these people would have us believe, but coming out of something deeper still that *consciously chooses* to act thusly and must be addressed for what it is, another part of the human puzzle.

Of course evolution prepared the way to both consciousness and the love and free will contained in us, as well as our brain, DNA, and instinctual make up. That it all led up to us as we are is no problem, except when one gets stuck in what went before and denies what we are now, creatures who can supersede what went before. The neo-Darwinists fail to carry through with evolution in denying the results of love and free will and instead try to make these stuck in the swamps out of which they, with consciousness, surpassed in the evolutionary process that came up with the human being. In essence they are denying us our very humanness.

They live in a basic contradiction, which I think you already see—but let's go and meet them head on in their individual posturing, even as we have lumped them altogether in their myopia.

Our first stop down this one lane highway through the rainforest is with Cyclopes of a particularly peculiar persuasion, those who look at our species and come up with this conclusion: that our purpose is simply to generate more genes. "We believe the things—about morality, personal worth, even objective truth—that lead to behaviors that get our genes into the next generation. What is in our genes' interests is what seems 'right'—morally right, objectively right, whatever sort of rightness is in order." So writes Wright, Robert Wright, in his book *The Moral Animal, Why We Are the Way We Are: The New Science Of Evolutionary Psychology.*[70] I start with this lot because they may be the most myopic. I should make mention here that Aristotle, for a time fell under the spell of the perpetuation and propagation notion, being the biologists he sort of was. Of course we have instincts and are part of the raw elemental energies of evolution, which has a drive to carry on the species, but these folks have carried it into folly—further by far than that prolific Greek intended or fact demonstrates. "What is in our genes' interests is what seems 'right'—morally right, objectively right, whatever sort of rightness is in order," is nothing else but ultimate nihilism, anything goes, so long as our genes propagate. In what they propose, interiority, choice, and the very mystery and warmth of our individual personhood itself have no place in the ultimate definition of humans—we are here primarily to procreate. Although it uses evolutionary wording, it is like Schopenhauer's "blind incessant impulse," and again we all know where that led, because it had to, and always has to. So rightly we might pause at their invitation to such a final solution of ourselves and ask of these folks what a scientist who gave us the singularity theorem asked of them: "if consciousness serves no selective purpose, why did Nature go to the trouble to evolve conscious brains when non-sentient 'automation' brains like cerebella would seem to have done just as well?"[71] We really don't need all this to procreate. Even if I use their basis of thinking, it appears that the musings, mumblings, and mutterings of yours truly, for example, are necessary in the natural order and selection of things, since consciousness is so fundamental to us, but why would that be so if we were here *merely* to pass on genes? It has been said that not by lasagna alone does a person live; the same thing could be said of DNA. The biological exaggeration of such men must be addressed for what it is.

This particular brand of so-called neo-Darwinians would deny the very sine qua non of our being and relegate us to the blind incessant impulse of ants. Ants with *reciprocal altruism*! That seems to be one of their catch phrases, which, sadly, so many postmodern scholars have fallen victim to, looking for a way out of human behavior as only "discourses of power." Reciprocal altruism under the pressure of natural selection is obvious nonsense as even George Williams among others have so properly shown to Edward O. Wilson and his fellow Formicidae.[72] For those not familiar with Wilson and his work, he likes ants. He likes them so much that he makes them the model of life, doing what they have to in a blind perpetuation and propagation of their genome—as he says we do also. There is no free will here, let alone love. However, though he forgets the flowers and champagne in the human condition, as he grows older he does seem to be using them to entice us, we human ants, to his position on the biosphere, in one chapter of a recent book even using the word love. Of course, when you see what he means by love you cringe.

As for Wright, the journalist in the grips of evolutionary psychology, for the moment I will be kind and say he meant well in his attempt to create a moral animal, and I am sympathetic with his attempt, since underneath it all it is the wish of every philosopher to do the same, make us better creatures. Evolutionary psychology, however, is not the way to do this. In point of fact, it is a strangely inconsequential exercise and I must add, not even a science as it purports. It can't prove its evangelical fervor, to use a catch phrase about it from somewhere or other that I can't recall. In the end, Wright ends up having to say that we must end the moral bias built into us by natural selection. How? By choice? It appears so—for he calls for us to follow Darwin, not in his natural selection findings in this case, but in Darwin's own selection to go beyond the call of nature, to help those who aren't likely to help you in return, and do so when no one is watching. So what is the actuality that makes up our deepest internal drives then? The question has to remain for him, if he is honest about it.

It really is ironic that he ends up at the end of his book, without realizing it so it seems, where we are in ours, namely, realizing there is and has to be more to have more, more than the blind incessant drive of the raw elemental energies of evolution winding their hit and miss way in a path of natural selection, or to put it another way, *more* than the primal forces within organisms that are instinctual. In countering such a meltdown of mentality in me and you, I believe it was John Horgan who said that *Hamlet* is not just a survival guide. I would just drop the word just. It is *not* a survival guide! On the contrary, it is a marvelous depiction of what I am saying, in that the Bard portrays the human condition as it is, depicting Hamlet having to choose throughout, and mixing that with the primal forces within his make up, being the genius Shakespeare was. At one point Wright seems to agree with William: "We are potentially moral animals—which is more than any other animal can say—but we aren't naturally moral animals. To be moral animals, we must realize how thoroughly we aren't."[73] Wild Will and this peasant rouge of an author along with him would remind Wright that what he would have us realize involves a choice over those raw elemental energies. But Wright already had the teeth marks on his neck, the lamia of genetic/evolutionary determinism had him in their grip, and so these lapses into the really real were put aside, and, instead, he returned to being a propagandist for neo-Darwinism. Sadly, he admits this right at the beginning of his book: "This book is, first, a sales pitch for a new science; only secondarily is it a sales pitch for a new basis of political and moral philosophy."[74] As for his first endeavor, unfortunately, there is no new science here; there isn't even a science. And as for his secondary effort, he needn't worry; there is no basis for a moral philosophy here either, although scarily maybe a basis for a political one.

Evolutionary psychologists say we can uncover basic laws of psychological development and are convinced that they can do so *only* with Darwinian tools. If you want to know how anything is adjusted by early experience, you must ask why natural selection made the adjustment. *Everything is explained by that* according to them. So much so that there is a way to act forged by natural selection that eliminates free will. That is their one throughline of thought; and although they might call it evolutionary psychology, it is nothing more than neo-sociobiology, of the ilk of Wilson, the ant man, or a mix of cognitive science and biological adaptation a la the loquacious psycholinguist, Steven Pinker. Although he might protest that the mind like another private part was engineered merely to perpetuate our foreparents' genes, one has to at least ask if perchance, unlike the penis, it wasn't engineered to think? And choose! We can at least venture that possibility, I think. And, as such, a different choice than the fixation evolutionary psychology puts us in. We are neither genetic survival machines nor molecular process computers made of meat. It is hard to overstate the nonsense of such limited views of reality. *If you look at life only as biology, you are going to come to merely a biological conclusion.*

Perhaps the most detrimental question of this neo-sociobiology is the one Wright asks, ironically in praise of it: "Does knowing how evolution has shaped our basic moral impulses help us decide which impulses we should consider legitimate?"[75]

We have already seen what nature is—to follow it as our *moral* guide will end up with a different level of being within one's presence than the one that allows you to share your soup, no matter how you cut it, or spoon it out to keep the metaphor apt. It is the phenomenon of consciousness, the opposite level from instinct within our presence, which gives us the tool not to follow the raw elemental energies of evolution as our moral guide, but rather share our soup with a stranger. Sociobiology, old or new, will always lead to the will to power, because . . . well you know from all that went before in this book: it is based on the raw elemental energies of evolution, even as you soft peddle nature as an aphrodisiac.

As for giving someone soup, Wright, following orders, doesn't call it love, but altruism, and "altruism," he says, "can now confidently be said to have a firm genetic basis."[76] Natural selection! So says Robert Wright—and goes on to say such moral sentiments are switched on and off in keeping with self-interest. In other words, altruism and love are really self-interest. If you define love as an act of possession instead of the giving of one's self, as in league with the will to power, than of course it is in line with natural selection, but that is not love, rather the very opposite of what love is. They do this a lot, these evolutionary psychologists, not only give their pseudo-science a new name, but morality and love itself new definitions that fit into their neo-sociobiology. Wright goes on to say that this refined theory of natural selection, which is called evolutionary psychology or neo-sociobiology or neo-Darwinism, "is so powerful as to explain the nature of all living things."[77] Quite a mouthful; but I think he chokes on it; he has bitten off more than he can chew with such a statement. Natural selection may have a food chain in its make up, but I can chose not to follow it, and he can to. I can even choose to give my soup to a starving stranger, and not for any self-interest; in fact quite the opposite to my survival-drive, which, of course, is part of me as well.

In the last paragraph of his introduction, Wright writes: "Darwin's 'excessive' humility and morality, his extreme lack of brutishness, are what make him so valuable a test case. I will try to show that natural selection, however seemingly alien to his character, can account for it. It is true that Darwin was a gentle, humane, and decent a man as you can reasonably hope to find on this planet. But it is also true that he was fundamentally no different from the rest of us. Even Charles Darwin was an animal."[78] How refreshing that you should say so, Robert. For that is precisely the point we have made, that the raw elemental energies of evolution were within him as they are within us—but so was the consciousness that gave him the choice to be the decent man he was, as it gives us the choice to be such. If his or any morality were based on nature, it would, by that very fact, be the opposite of what he chose to be. Wright forgets the basic tension in us as animals. He is myopic in his view, failing to see the whole of the person called Charles Darwin. A holistic approach to our being and the actions coming out of it would be far closer to a true picture of the animal Charles Darwin was, and the animals we are.

Finally, let me say with regards to Wright in his discourse on love, which is anything but that, he quotes biologist Robert Trivers as saying, "The personality and conscience of the child is formed in an area of conflict."[79] Partially, yes, for the will to power is in every human society, rooted in those raw elemental energies that are in all of us. But, again, the child can also be exposed to the opposite when, for example, a mother points out that the robin's blue eggs are her babies and he mustn't hurt them but care for them. As nature is innate in us, so is love. Not as natural selection for the propagation of our genes, but as something *more. We have evolved to more than our biology, our very biology has.* Wright's oversimplification of us is really the problem with the whole of this evolutionary psychological approach that wants to explain *everything* according to natural selection, when everything can't be explained according to natural selection. In fact, just the opposite, consciousness and the deepest experience in it, love, elude their Cyclops-like explanations. Like behaviorism and sociobiology before it, this too will pass. But, unfortunately, before it does, it will, via a false premise, continue to affect society with a wrong definition of what it means to be human, one that gives legitimacy to acting out of the underbelly in our make up, even saying we *should* act thusly. It leaves a noirish tone all about, a hollowed out humanity if one is honest about it, devoid of what makes life most human; namely, a real presence and a real choice in our existence, one that can really love and be loved. If what they say were true, we would have no choice but to accept our ant-like fate. Thankfully, that isn't the case. It isn't true, only half true.

Of course, again it must be stated, not all biologists and neuroscientists fall into the heart of darkness I have been rallying against. As far back as the nineteen twenties, in his *Essays of a Biologist*, and thereafter, Julian Huxley had been attempting to define and evaluate the evolutionary process differently. Although some biologists indeed claim that the mind is generated solely by the complexification of certain types of organization, namely, brains, such logic appeared narrow to him. "The brain alone is not responsible for mind, even though it is a necessary organ for its manifestation."[80] More recently, Francoise Wemelshfelder appears, in her own way, to be trying to crawl out of the black hole and existential despair biological exaggerators would put us in. She acknowledges the reality of 'first-person' perspectives, and does so not only for humans, but for animals as well, even quoting of all people, a philosopher, Thomas Nagel. Thomas Nagel is known as an advocate of the idea that consciousness as a subjective experience cannot at least with the contemporary understanding of the physical be reduced to the brain or brain activity. One of his more famous pieces is: What is it Like to Be a Bat? Brian Goodwin, following upon this, takes a longer stride away from the biological exaggerators than does Francoise, when he writes in his book, *How The Leopard Changed Its Spots*, "Of course, the further implication of this position is not only the reality, but the primacy, of the first-person, subjective experiences." After pointing out how it is a curious paradox that a large number of scientists who work in the area of artificial intelligence and in the cognitive sciences in general deny that consciousness has any fundamental reality, and say it is only an epiphenomenon of brain activity (the electrical processes that go on in brain cells), he goes to say: "This is just like the denial on the part of many biologists that organisms have any fundamental reality that cannot be explained by genes and molecular activities. However, the recognition that organisms have intentional agency that comes from the self-completing action of immanent causal process not only gives organisms a reality that is not reducible to their parts, but also creates a space for subjective experience—what it is like to be a bat or any other species of organism. For us it the experience of being human, and the awareness of the condition of consciousness."[81] He ends his book saying that this necessarily would lead to bonds of sympathy, mutual recognition, and respect for other organisms. But I must add to that, that these don't have to be acted upon. A person can choose to treat another animal in a very unsympathic way, whether a human or a horse. It is interesting how this biologist, like the journalist Robert Wright, reaches for the moral, which means choice. In the end, as mentioned, Wright ends up having to say that we must end the moral bias built into us by natural selection. But again how? By choice? It appears so—for he calls for us to follow Darwin, not in his natural selection findings in this case, but in Darwin's own selection to go beyond the call of nature, to help those who aren't likely to help you in return, and do so when no one is watching. So what is the actuality that makes up our deepest internal drives then? The question has to remain for him and his ilk, if they are honest about it. Though coming to opposite conclusions both the biologist and the man who would be a spokesman for evolutionary psychology recognize something here that I propose comes from deep within our very being; something not provided by the raw elemental energies of evolution in their natural selection, but by something deeper still that surpasses it. And it takes a real choice to do so, will, free will, sometimes calling for the giving of one's self and expecting nothing in return.

Noam Chomsky goes beyond the other critics of these neo-Darwinians when he suggests that consciousness and free will, among other aspects of the human mind, are indeed mysteries; mysteries that seem insoluble even in principle, perhaps forever. What is Chomsky touching upon here? The fact that physical evolution does not answer uniquely human attributions? Without speaking for him, he seems to say so when he talks of other immaterial properties and our own dear subjects of consciousness and free will in this manner. Yes, consciousness is mysterious, I agree—a mystery within our being that cannot be ignored.

It is a mystery within our being that our friendly anthilleans, unfortunately, and unscientifically, would do away with—denying this parallel part of the evolutionary puzzle altogether, the part we call consciousness. For them, we are gene-driven creatures, with natural selection itself based on that, and upon this proposition they posit everything about us, even as they give lips service to the plasticity of the human brain. The position they take denies both our daily experience and a true picture of evolution; namely, that it *must* contain a place for the parallel progression of consciousness other than merely natural selection, as I already discussed. This, as well as genomes and the bone and bodies they bring forth, is the holistic picture I would put forward.

Without being too argumentative or testosterone driven, I'd like to bring in a prizewinner of Sweden's high honor now, the co-discoverer of the biological double helix. For all his British humor, Francis Crick's myopic faith in DNA does not provide us with all that is necessary for knowing about ourselves. The double helix double-crosses him when it comes to consciousness and choice. He says he wants to eliminate the possibility that there is a you, and a you who can really choose, and begins his book, *The Astonishing Hypothesis*, as such: "The Astonishing Hypothesis is that 'you,' your joys and your sorrows, your memories and your ambitions, your sense of personal identity and free will, are in fact no more than behavior of a vast assembly of nerve cells and their associated molecules. As Lewis Carroll's Alice might have phrased it, 'You're nothing but a pack of neurons.'"[82] He subtitles the book: *The Scientific Search for the Soul*. A bit of double talk here he would have to admit, if he were still with us, since that very first paragraph is anything but science—nor does he ever *scientifically* prove it. In point of fact, there really is no search at all for Francis. In the end we can say not only was the title deceptive but the book that followed.

No matter how Crick would wish it so in his exclusivity, neural mechanisms are not the full scope of our being, though of course part of it. We must always remember, what Crick has forgotten, the whole of our being—the consciousness, brain, and body we *are* in spacetime. This full presence! Those, like Crick, who say love and free will are *merely* chemical *reactions* must prove it so; which they have not been able to do. Even neuroscientist Christof Koch, Crick's collaborator when Crick was still with us, in a lecture at a Tucson conference had to say: "This is the binding problem." Yet, even so, they seemed not to realize what it means to what they are advocating. Walter Freeman, one of the scientists listening, had to point out to Koch and indirectly to Crick, that what they assert as the key to consciousness is no more so than oxygen intake or blood flow or other ubiquitous phenomena.[83] Since those the likes of Crick can't prove scientifically what they say as scientists, they revert to that old standby, the future. I heard Koch, too, just recently talk in terms of us having to take a promissory note on what he says. I would just remind him and others of his clique, that that is not science; it is a leap of faith on their part to posit a proposition based on their bias, one that says that what they say will someday be proven. The fact is, to equate consciousness with DNA and choice with merely neuronal mechanism as Crick and his left-behind clique would have us do, is to be stuck in too narrow an approach, and despite all his gloating, he was and they are just old-fashioned material reductionists and warmed-over behaviorists, and what they propose amounting again to really nothing more than biological exaggerations. And funny to boot! Just listen to his comic routine. He says he earned the right *to do what he likes*—even as he denies free will. Of course, I would never have argued with what he might have *choosen* to do with his own life. Even that he had the right to love whomever he pleased, though playfully I would have had to say I feel sorry for said person—solely and merely the reaction of his neuronal mechanism and nothing more. Love is not an erection, or a mere neuronal mechanism either. Perhaps he should have added in his funny book something about his first night of marriage with what's-her-mechanism and what it really meant to him. I'm afraid that in the particular matter of consciousness, he was over his head (or forgetting what was inside of it). However, I would say to him if I could, "Don't worry, Ducky, there will be plenty for you to find out."[84]

Crick was a bright man, and I am sure he wouldn't have minded me having fun with him, or with what his mother told him in the above quote when he was in a struggle with himself of all things. Of course, besides Crick, the parade of such reductionists continues on, ever fighting among themselves over what to reduce us to.

Christof Koch is more diplomatic in his approach, maybe because his father was a diplomat. In any event, in my personal Koch-encounter, I found that when he tries to explain his position there seems to be a contradiction inside of him; on the one hand an ardent follower of Crick, on the other saying "we have no accepted theory of consciousness," with the happy addenda, at least for me, that he loves his dogs. A moment later, he even makes the quick point that because mammals have consciousness he never eats their flesh, which tells me he has a personal bushido, and therefore is choosing—even as he makes fun of free choice after saying as much and falls back into his Crick allegiance. At another juncture, in that charming German accent of his, he even said, "we don't know if consciousness requires a body." What does that mean? That it is non-material? I don't think he meant that, but when I heard him say it, I thought of the possibility that maybe there is a duality after all . . . and the fact that consciousness is so out of place in so many ways is because it is not of this material cosmos? Is Socrates, and Schwartz after him, right after all? I have been saying there is no duality, that the brain and mind are in a simultaneity a la a quark or photon as a role model—but maybe perennial philosophy is more on track with its sense of a duality; a strange sort of one to be sure, but a duality. In truth, it could be either way. In any event, it still seems to require a form of some form *in spacetime*, so until someone can show me otherwise, namely, consciousness floating around sans a form of some sort, I'll hold onto my position. Consciousness in spacetime needs a form to form, perhaps the whole of the form as Da Vinci says.

When Koch spoke of the gut as another brain, the Da Vinci in me listened carefully. He went on to explain that and asked, "but is it conscious?" Isn't that in line with what Da Vinci said, what we got into when we discussed the Schwartz's experiments? He went on to talk of the character of consciousness changing in dreams, attention as not the same as consciousness, and consciousness as perhaps pre-dating self-consciousness—but, again, isn't that all really what I described as levels of being? Perhaps even with a nod Leonardo's way in the process I might rightly wonder.

Don't get me wrong, I think Koch is intellectually in Crick's camp, of course, they are joined at the frontal lobes. You see this throughout his work, and certainly with statements I heard him personally say, such as "consciousness is more about measuring things." But, as he says that, he makes sure to mention it is *the mechanism* of consciousness he is talking about. There is wiggle room here, as there is with his statement that science has been working on correlation and needs to go from that to causation. At that point, he stopped, and then made a mean attack on philosophers who say that science will never be able to tell us what consciousness really is. Who knows is what I say, but so far science's promissory note is not going to do it, especially since it's based on denial of self-being and free will, on the denial of a real you and your really choosing.

Promissory notes aside, one thing I do firmly agree with Koch about, besides his love of dogs and not eating conscious creatures, is when he says, "subjectivity is the most important thing we have." I know I have already mentioned that quote, but this is the sine qua non of being human. The sine qua non of being us is the self-being I refuse to turn over to slaughter *by men who know very little of what they are dealing with*. Finally, I found it rather rewarding to my sense of more, not to mention irony, that Koch got further enmeshed in our chapter without realizing it when he ended where all philosophy does, namely, the third question of said philosophy, *now what?* How do I act in the face of the world? And in doing so, the man from CIT actually posed some of the very questions to be faced once science defines consciousness, questions like who will live, who die, whether it will be OK to use the parts of babies without consciousness for those with consciousness? Of course he didn't go further than that. If you do away with the self and free will or real choice as his friend Crick does, where do you base your ethics, on what cold calculation froth with human error and the ever-present will to power? Obviously, Koch is a moral person, but I would love to ask him what he basis his morality on? What he is dealing with is far more than his friend Crick realized, but perhaps Christof Koch does.

But not Ms. Peggy La Cerra and Mr. Roger Bingham! Another pronouncement masquerading as science whose high-priest and priestess know not of what they do or are doing, bears the title *The Origin of Minds*. Ms. Peggy and Mr. Roger maintain the minds they are speaking of are merely the gray and white matter of the brain, a la others of this ilk, but go on to argue against their former comrades that our ancestral inheritance is not a set of fixed cognitive tools or DNA, but at bottom what they call "an adaptive representational network" that exploits pliable brain tissue, changing the brain with new life experiences. Of course the brain is shaped by our experience to the unique brain each of us has, but that does not argue to what they say is the cause of this, and it certainly doesn't explain the self or do away with real choice. Again, the very title is spin since they never show scientifically the origin of the mind as they maintain it is, then expect all of us to swallow our redefinition according to Peggy and Rog. A redefinition that in essence is our literal disappearance, and all choice with it I am obliged to point out.

Though Ms. P and Mr. R became evolutionary psychology revisionists, they remain victims of the same Cyclopean view of you and me, claiming that their "adaptive representational network" is not metaphoric but the true definition of us at our bottom. They say this, but never prove it. One could as easily say consciousness exists before matter was made and enters the material world to find its way. At least I use the neutrino or quark or electron only as a help model or simile in trying to get a sense of something the same yet different simultaneous, like the brain and the mind. I am afraid we are going to need more from P and R before we allow ourselves to disappear into merely 'adaptive representational networks.' Scientific jargon aside, what it adds up to is nothing more than reductionist dogma refried.

Ms. P and Mr. R tell us (sans the soul of the scientific method, demonstrable proof) that it all boils down to an "adaptive representational network" that is the fundamental unit of intelligence, in a flexibility that leads "to a surprising range of human abilities; namely, the creation of selves and personhood, the generation of unprecedented thoughts and metaphors, and the ability to make inference about our world and the people with whom we share it." Now, of course, we do all that, but they don't show it is because of their made-up explanation, this so-called 'adaptive representational network,' again which they insist is not a metaphor but the real thing. I suppose we could, a la a Freeman to a Koch, put it directly to them and say, 'since you say consciousness is nothing more than what you say it is, show us!' They have chosen science as their field after all, so we are not being unreasonable in our request. They want the cover science offers without doing science. Like the other reductionists, they have reductionism without a base, and so they make up one. And this they maintain is the definitive definition of us and any choice in us. They really should work out of the Magic Castle, Hollywood's famous magician hang out, make themselves disappear before our eyes as we toast away, waiting for the next act or Irma the invisible piano player to play "It's Still The Same Old Story." Though P&R try to explain more than the traditional evolutionary psychology they were once such advocates of, one has to say 'so what?' They are still stuck in the same problem as the rest of that pseudo-science. This *is* the binding problem with these folks.

To merely stick within the raw elemental energies of evolution and try to define us solely in that context misses the fuller picture over and over again—and that is what all these cohorts in crime do, no matter what their act. Of course we have a neural architecture—but the truth of the matter is, they and everyone else with them don't even know what that is, let alone what *we are* at deep reality. You don't come into the chamber shouting that you have discovered the mystery of life and us because you have hit upon DNA! Biology is but part of the picture, my fellow witnesses to being. We have to use both our 'eyes' and all our ways of knowing to arrive at the actuality of ourselves and deep reality—and even then we still might not.

Which brings me back to Pinker and a fond stopover to be sure, for he has a sense of humor and I am a sucker for a good laugh. Steven Pinker, the author of *How the Mind Works*, says we can understand the mind only by determining what it was *originally* designed to do. He reminds me of those who deny the Constitution is a living document and instead say we must find out what was the intent or in the minds of the Founding Fathers and base everything on that. Our minds here and now are the living study! Yet, he says and continues to say that once we accept that our minds—like our eyes, hands, and other features of our biology—were engineered *to perpetuate our foreparents' genes*, we may gain similar insights into our thoughts, emotions, and compulsions—in other words how the mind works.[85] He further goes on to add that once we do accept that, we then see how the mind *has to work*. Mindlessly, I would have to say once again to the man. The root-reality of the mind and thought is not merely to perpetuate genes. Just as love is not an erection, thinking isn't either. I am not the only one who expels Pinker from Clown Alley because of a bad joke.

Claude Fischer, a sociologist at Berkeley, did as well when Pinker's punch line was that when modern mothers kill their newborns it is due to an innate psychological module. Claude Fischer responded that such nonsense, "illustrates how silly evolutionary explanations of human behavior have become. When mothers protect their newborns (which almost all do), it's because that behavior is evolutionarily adaptive. And now, when a few mothers kill their newborns, that's evolutionarily adaptive too. Any behavior and its opposite is 'explained' by evolutionary selection . . . Thus, nothing is explained."[86] Noam Chomsky is right when he says, "Darwinian theory is so loose it can incorporate anything they discover."[87]

In any reading of Pinker, however, despite trying to incorporate anything and everything into his neo-Darwinian theory, he is quite specific about his intent. The theme of his book, he tells us is, "that the mind is a naturally selected neural computer."[88] Every age has its metaphor for the mind. Sadly, however, this is not a metaphor for him. Perhaps he'll grow out of it, as Jerry Fodor did. He was a strong proponent of the computational description of the mind, but later changed his mind; and in reviewing Pinker's book, said that dividing the mind into many little dedicated computer parts, or modules, leaves unresolved the problem of how all these modular computations became integrated; how consciousness actually arises to use my own parlance, and what it *actually* is. Fodor put forth that in essence evolutionary psychology was running away from the basic problem, the crucial missing ingredient, and therefore wasn't grounded.[89]

Towards the end of his book, Pinker talks of the meaning of life and asks how we might understand not only psychology, but humor, art, religion, and philosophy itself within the theme of his book. I'll pass over in silence his depiction of humor because even Arthur Koestler's seems a barrel of laughs in comparison. It's better to tell a joke than try to explain it. Anyway, he goes into a misrepresentation of art and aesthetics after that, raging against phony people and missing the point of art, aesthetics, and the true artist. That could be forgiven, as he is not an artist. However, what follows cannot, for he goes on to say that he would have us be "alien biologists" when looking at our existence. Here he is again proposing that we have no grounding at all! Unless you are an alien biologizing your own alien existence that is! Of course, you are not, and that isn't what he is saying, he means for us to abstract ourselves out of our existence and view it literally as if alien to it. You cannot abstract yourself out of existence and know either existence or yourself. Your self is your existence! He would take the very presence we are that witnesses and acts in existence out of existence and replace it with a Dalek. Absurd as that sounds, he would have each of us become a Dalek who would witness it all as a Dalek and come up with a Dalek interpretation of us and our existence. He gets so removed from finding the truth about us here that

I have to wonder if I shouldn't take him out to Angelo's for a dish of pasta, and of course some vino to get his blood flowing again, or maybe just call in Doctor Who, then again maybe just Fatty Patty will do.

Ironically, Pinker proves my point, he can't view the work as a Dalek, admitting: "This book has been about the adaptive design of the major components of the mind, but that does not mean that I believe that everything the mind does is biologically adaptive."[90] Like Wright at the end of his book he has to come back to being human.

That reentry was hinted at I believe when he came to music. For as the poet Hopkins says, "music was before instruments and angels before tortoises and cats." Though I must sadly report, Pinker still treated it in the fashion he did everything else. He starts off with the words: "Music is an enigma." And had to admit that: "As far as biological cause and effect are concerned, music is useless." Yet he will force it into his worldview no matter, going through the same labyrinthine style he did for everything else, saying a lot of a lot, but ultimately saying what? He asks and then answers: "But if music confers no survival advantage, where does it come from and why does it work? I suspect that music is auditory cheesecake, an exquisite confection crafted to tickle the sensitive spots of at least six of our mental faculties." [91] He goes on to end the segment on music by saying it doesn't adapt to his discussion of the mental faculties in the rest of book. However, that doesn't stop him from still trying to make his case, suggesting perhaps it is "a resonance in the brain between neurons firing in synchrony with a sound wave and a natural oscillation in the emotional circuits? An unused counterpart in the right hemisphere of the speech areas in left? Some kind of spandrel or crawl or short-circuit or coupling that came along as an accident of the way that auditory, emotional, language, and motor circuits are packed together in the brain?"[92] When I finished the section, in my own mind, I could only refer him to Beethoven, the man, and the music coming out of the man. Ludwig lifts us into our transcendent depths. As music is not only the scale and structure, neither are we; as music is more, so are we. Yes, again, of course, there are neurological processes taking place, but simultaneously something more as well, giving us a holistic sense of our being, something our one-eyed Steven refuses to acknowledge except with a begrudging wink, followed by a yes; but it is still only an accident of the auditory this, or short-circuit of that, or perhaps an oscillation out of joint, or maybe a hemisphere . . . In truth, he doesn't know what he is talking about, so he tries to overpower us with scientific jargon. However, in the end, all's well that ends well, and as I said and repeat, Pinker concludes his book by coming back to being human, as we all have to in the end.

My first reaction to him, however, as I began his book was, 'what an arrogant little prick.' Hubris is never appealing. Pinker is a young man trying to make a name for himself, I noted, but he is a young man neglecting so much in his attempt to fit it all into natural selection. The MIT professor wasn't saying anything new in the jargon of evolutionary psychology, I concluded, and perhaps subliminally he just wanted to surpass that *mensch* at MIT, Noam Chomsky—"which would be in keeping with the will to power and those raw elemental energies of evolution via natural selection," I told my dog with a naughty wink of my left eye and then my right. I even had to smile when I saw Pinker enter the realm of scripture, pontificating to his readers on what Jesus meant about the little children coming to him. Most of all, I found that he criticized others for making assumptions about how the world is put together, without realizing his own assumptions, all of which were bases on a quasi-science he was defending like a true believer quoting from the bible of biology. In any event, he was forcing it, and as Fischer later said of him, he was disavowing his own view without realizing it. By the close of the book, he not only sensed his own humanness again, but entered the postmodern world as well. No, he had not given up his assumptions or his biology bible, but, there was hope for him, because now, at least, he realized there was more, even saying, "and perhaps we cannot solve conundrums like free will . . ."[93] He concludes that free will, consciousness, the self, and other riddles of being human are most likely unsolvable by us.

On this he takes what I call a postmodern view, and what others call a mysterian one. Either way we have to be uncertain about so much. Life remains profoundly mysterious, despite evolutionary biology and all the rest. At the finish, he pens words I myself could have written: "But there is something peculiarly holistic and everywhere-at-once and nowhere-at-all and all-at-the-same-time about the problems of philosophy. Sentience is not a combination of brain events or computational states . . . The 'I' is not a combination of body parts or brain states or bits of information, but a unity of selfness . . . Free will is not a causal chain of events and states . . ."[94] An he goes on to write on literally the last page: "Our thoroughgoing perplexity about the enigmas of consciousness, self, will, and knowledge may come from a mismatch between the very nature of these problems and the computational apparatus that natural selection has fitted us with."[95] Here he has landed smack into the postmodern uncertainty of things and finalizes it all with: "Our bafflement at the mysteries of the ages may have been the price we paid for a combinatorial mind that opened up a world of words and sentences, of theories and equations, of poems and melodies, of jokes and stories, the very things that make a mind worth having."[96] Now if he would only push a little more with that awareness worth having, deeper into the presence he is.

In the past, Crick and Koch, and their like, tried to transform consciousness and free will with it from a phenomenon with many levels to *merely* neuroscience, and then folks like Pinker tried to combine that with natural selection, only to end up in mysterianism, as Koch himself thought we all might when he conceded that a neural theory of consciousness might not solve such ancient problems as the mind-body conundrum and the question of free will, and that these riddles might simply be beyond the scope of science.[97] Consciousness in the last analysis may not be able to provide an explanation of itself; even as it explains the cosmos all around it. Neuroscience has yet to achieve its reductionist eureka.

One who said he had, however, was Gerhard Roth, starting with statements out of his Bremen lab that there is no real choice, in essence that everything is a neurophysiologic condition. He states that the "ultimate decisions of human beings" are in fact not decisions at all, but due to switches for muscle coordination, found in the limbic system with the basal ganglia.[98]

Since ganglia were mentioned, let me elaborate—they are located on both sides of the limbic system, in each hemisphere. Like the cerebellum, they are concerned with movement control, particularly with starting movements. In the human brain, these exquisite networks of cells are well developed and large. Although they are functionally rather different, the basal ganglia and the major structures of the limbic system are next to one another because they are both closely interconnected with the highest level of the brain—the cerebral cortex. In much of today's writings it would seem as though we know a lot about the cortex, but in fact we know very little about how it works.[99] One thing we certainly don't know is how choice is made in the brain. In the book, *The Amazing Brain*, there is a sentence that must be underlined. "Study of the higher brain functions of the cortex is, and probably always will be, the frontier of research in the neurosciences, and applying all our marvelous cortical abilities to unraveling the mysteries of their operations is a challenging, and maybe impossible task."[100]

What we are concerned with here is one activity and ability in particular, choice. Roth says there really is none. He says the conscious-I is "not the real master of our actions," and "freedom of will" is a delusion.[101] If ever there was a statement personifying spin-science it is that. So much so, that later he and eleven other leading German scientists had to admit ignorance about the decisive levels of the brain. All of it amounts to an ignorance precisely at the decisive level of choice we are centered in on. At one point in their *"Manifesto on the Present and Future of Brain Research"* the following must be underlined in red. "We still do not understand even the beginning of what rules the brain works by; how it depicts the world in such a way that direct perception and earlier experience fuse; how the inner action is experienced as 'its' activity and how it plans future actions. Furthermore, it is not at all clear how we can investigate it with present possibilities. In this respect to some degree we are still at the stage of hunters and gatherers."[102]

I want to make mention here of Giacomo Rizzolatti. When the neuroscientist Giacomo Rizzolatti, while working with monkeys, discovered what were called 'mirror neurons' in the pre-motor cortex known as area F5, he didn't rush out and say this is the way it is in humans as well, even as he might feel excited about his work and might suggest mirror neurons in the human brain as well, in the Broca's area of area F5. The reason he didn't run out and pontificate about mirror neuron in his own head and mine was because as a scientist he didn't know it to be so scientifically, so didn't say it was so scientifically. But, contrary to that, along came Susan.

The psychologist Susan Blackmore's simplistic rejection of the self and freedom is built on nothing but her saying so—which in itself is a free act. She takes Rizzolatti's cautious findings of the mirror neurons and without any scientific proof but her say so, builds her say so, ending her say so with the following I told you so, saying 'I' am only an illusion, 'a fluid and ever-changing group of memes,' 'a vast memeplex,' 'the most insidious and perverse memeplex of all.'[103] In short, she holds for a complete determinism and that she doesn't really exists except as memes and memeplexes. Ron Hubbard, at least, calls his science fiction a religion, and therefore doesn't require proof. She is telling us her say so is . . . well what is she telling us other than it is her say so. And she is free to do as she pleases. But please let's not call her psychobabble science—or even serious my Old English just added. It's more like she's talking out of her baccala. I am sure I heard Giacomo say as much! Oh, why not have fun with these people—my meme made me do it! Or was it the devil? Of course, I could have chosen not to, but there you have it, I chose to. *Forsan et haed olim meminisse jubabit . . . some day we will look on all this and laugh.* But why wait?

The sky outside my window is in concert with the Gregorian chant coming from the outer room, it is *valde mane* and I am tired, tired of these types telling us we don't really exist or defining us merely as dendrites, so I thought I might throw a Jon-Stewart-like rant in the following wordplay, a la with merry Andrew. In doing so I decided it would be in keeping with Stewart's show and my own naughtiness to ask my telephone-wire rat to compose something to send to the Big Blue Brain at Lausanne for it to decipher. Why so? Henry Markram, the Director of the Blue Brain at L'Ecole Polytechnique Federale de Lausanne has boasted that his Big Blue Brain computer has the ability of processing 22.8 trillion operations per second, that is just enough to model a 1-cubic-mm column of rat brain. What if my telephone-wire rat used 2-cubic-mm columns? No, I will not torture a machine! It is beneath me. And his machine beneath a real rat for that matter. So, instead, I decided to send the following to Henry Markram himself, *mano a mano*. "If you want your model to represent reality, then you've got to model it *on* reality." Yes, I know I am quoting Henry Markram to himself, but he seems to be forgetting what he said. So let's remind him! Remind him that we are more than his doctrine of dendrites, more than his neurological neo-cortical religion and Big Blue as the new idol to bow down to even as he doesn't give a rat's ass or real brain what we have to say.

OK, I am exaggerating about the dear man, but Henry Markram doesn't think he is exaggerating about us when he tells us we are merely a binary code, a loop of electricity, and nothing more, debunking consciousness as he does and mixing it up with a ghost in the machine nonsense, while all the while refusing to penetrate into the profundity of his own presence and acting as if his computer will tell him who he is. "His machine myopia has gone to his head," I hear Jon Stewart say in my own.

I am all for his pursuit to know the processes that dendrites and axons offer, but I think he's a little loopy and nothing more when making statements like, "There is nothing inherently mysterious about the mind or anything it makes. Consciousness is just a massive amount of information being exchanged by trillions of brain cells. If you can precisely model that information, then I don't know why you wouldn't be able to generate a conscious mind." Which is a tedious way of saying I don't exist, you don't exist, Jon Stewart doesn't exist. Even as we all do as I write. Scientists like Henry remind me of the Puritans of old, they sap life out of life and think they have the truth. A machine, Monsieur M, will never be the laughter, for the laughter is more than the joke, Beethoven more than the notes he writes. There was something deeper still in Beethoven that gave the music the more I speak of, coming from more than merely a binary code, a loop of electricity creating it. When we listen to the music as well. There is more to us when we laugh at a joke by Jon or any other sit-down comedian, yours truly included. You saying we are just a binary code, a loop of electricity is just that, you saying it and not science, and certainly not a model based on reality as you yourself advocated. Monsieur Markram is looking at computer and saying it is Markram, or you, dear reader, or Jon Stewart. Of course, Henry, brain cells are part of the human cerebral process, but we are not just dendrites and axons, nor exploding singularities either, even as all of that is a necessary part of us in our many levels of being.

To torturously continue on in our stay with these folks, I certainly don't deny the raw elemental energies in every one of us, and firmly hold that biology has a real and strong input on us, but of course. However, it must be said about neo-Darwinism and any thought pattern like it, including the siren of neuroscience as the eureka to everything, that instead of being in himself or herself a unique and irreplaceable value, the individual is reduced to the state of being simply the bearer of genes, or neurological programmed reactions, as if he or she had no other ontological function than to permit genes to exist or merely function like a programmed robot or yes, a Dalek. That is myopic, to say the least, certainly when it comes to the human presence. Again, we are not genetic survival machines nor molecular process computers made of meat. It is hard to overstate the nonsense of such limited views of reality. If you look at life only as biology, you are going to come to merely a biological conclusion. *And that holds true for neurobiology as well.* If you stay only with the raw elemental energies of evolution and leave out consciousness as it is, saying it is merely an epiphenomenon of DNA and we merely a pack of neurons, adding an adaptive representational network to that or not, you can never arrive at the actuality of you and me and the deep reality of our being; nor can you build a morality or ethic or spirituality, but must end up relegating yourself and everyone else to what is a modern behaviorism, which is nothing more than a myopic faith in bad biology. Bite the bullet and know it isn't the final proof. Consciousness down the ages and in each of our own lives shows a much wider picture of personhood. We don't know exactly what we are, but we should resist impoverished accounts of our being that deny or trivialize our basic human experience in existing. We have evolved to more than our biology, our biology has. That is contemporary evolution, not the passé one still clung to by so many. Blackmore's determinism is as dead as a Laplacean's is. My contemporary evolution accepts the fact that we have evolved to more than our biology, our biology has. I am and I can . . .

D. J. Chalmers, the author of *The Conscious Mind*, states that it is necessary to realize that "conscious experience is an irreducible feature of being."[104] And within that conscious experience, even as a network of nerves is integral to each presence, a network of nerves does not decide for the will to power or the will to love, the presence that I am does the choosing. You are one presence, from the invisible quanta to the strange qualia! Each of us is one presence that goes from one to the other, from neutrinos to the raw elemental energies of evolution on earth we call nature, to consciousness in the cosmos, and the choice that goes with it. That was what all this was for, this human venture, not to do battle with biological edicts, but to further penetrate into this presence each of us is in order to honestly explore that choosing. There is no activity without a neuronal substratum, and yet there is something deeper still, or as I always say *more* to it all. Of course all mental processes are closely connected with the electrochemical processes between nerve cells in the brain, but there is something in our presence deeper still that allows for the fundamental choice I am discussing here. *That might in fact be the totality of the presence, drawing upon the whole of its being, including a sourceforce at its deepest level.*

Is the string theory, or the balloon theory, or the brane theory or megabrane theory, or even the brain theory provable? Well, of course, the string, balloon, brane and megabrane ones are not—they are beyond the pale—as is death. We can only speculate and make choices or not about all them. The brain, however, is closer to home. And what is home? *Moi!* Yes, you are more than the particles that make you up; more than the neurons, too, even as the brain is in so important, as it is where consciousness comes to be and hangs out.

Charles S. Pierce, one of that New England gang of philosophers in the nineteenth century, might offer his fawning definition of absolute truth as whatever the scientists say it is and nothing more, but that is so passé under the telescope of truth in the twenty first century. No, on our deepest level it is not scientifically that we prove our existence, nor empirically, nor conceptually either, though we will use all of them now and hereafter. At its deepest level, it is done through another way of knowing. As we stand awestruck before the silence of the universe and the mystery of being, *it is self-evident to each of us that each of us is*—and that is what we are most certain of no matter how some might protest. We must stay with the chapter. Our existence is our only absolute, our only certainty, *fundamentally present to us and grasped as such.* Even death, though each of us knows it will happen to us, somehow doesn't seem as real as that I am. And it isn't, because life is what is most immediate to us, and death only what *will* happen. And no matter if you argue one way or another about us existing or not after death, you can't say that you don't now exist. Even if someone were to become Buddhist and deny a real you or me at bottom, still he or she would still be choosing to follow the four noble truths and the eightfold path and the five moral rules and the six *paramitas,* the seven factors of awakening, the twelve turnings of the wheel, not to mention sitting or not on his or her *zafu.* And when you do decide on being a Buddhist or not being a Buddhist, on taking philosophy or being too wise for such foolishness, that *something* deeper still in each of us making the inner decision is our *self-being*—me and you at our deepest—me and you at our deepest actuality, exercising our unique being in conjunction, composition, and concert with the many layers of life we have lived in the labyrinth of the time allotted us. We went from the very beginning of everything to this point, as you recall, *ab ovo ad omnia et animo et consilio paratus, from the egg to the seat of will and consciousness.* With Hamlet's gravedigger we have to say "cudgel thy brains no more bout it"—for even if you try to make it an object or argue against it—there you are! And it is self-evident that you are! You grasp your existence instantaneously and with the deepest certainty you can possess. It is not an eureka, for you and I don't come to it as a knowledge or flash of insight, *it is a deeper intuition still,* one which each of us has as the very core of his or her being, irreducibility my very self, your very self, each person's very self. It is absolutely our most basic grasp of reality, each person's *basic* intuition of one's being, *what is innermost to each of us and most fundamentally present to us.*

It is the presence of the presence looking out at the universe. It is the bottom line of being for each of us, truly, as I keep saying, what is innermost to each of us and most fundamentally present, sans thinking about it. There are different perspectives in this presence; we realize a tree is its particles on one level or from one perspective, but a real tree in another, wherein everything that is that tree gathers, comes together into its very presence, its treeness. You are your particles on one level or from one perspective, but a real person in another, wherein everything that is you gathers, comes together into your presence, your very *haecceittas*, your very human hereness. Science is one way to behold being; but there are others, and they give us real although different perspectives. To fall into Pierce's blunder is not the way to go, nor the way existence itself does. Science tells us what science can and should, but so does music, and poetry, and love. I am reminded here of what Chris Botti said. When he plays his trumpet he is present in the music—and he kept repeating that and how that presence is all-important. He was struggling to say what we are struggling to say. Our presence is in everything we do and it is all-important, all-important because it is what we are and in everything we do, from our toiletry to the will to love. Yes from our instinctual drives to our greatest expression of free will, an expression as nothing else, in that it is the very giving of one's self, which no one can do for us, or make us do either.

With that, we conclude our stay in Hades and this segment on the follyforgers and all their willful pronouncements on the lack of free will or real choice. No matter who they be and despite their nametag, each in their own way would have you and I be those machines starting with D, and because of that are worthy of the name follyforgers, for they truly do forge folly, even as they insist that they are not really there and this is not a folly of their own making since they have no choice in the matter because they are not there to have a choice in the matter and free choice is an illusion of our own making, although of course we are not there to make it and so 'twas brillig, and the slithy toves did gyre and gimble in the wabe . . . Yes, like the architecture that takes its name from postmodernism, I can be playful, even as my fleshed-out, in the flesh, plucky description of their nonsense must be taken seriously, for they affect people's lives with their science fiction and jabberwocky. So let the word go forth that when it comes to these folks who say *that you don't really exist as you and have no real choice or free will,* do please remember that it is all merely spin science, analytical mythmaking, a man's opinion, a good read, a good laugh, a con job, a snow job, a job, in most cases no doubt scatological humor without knowing it is or meaning to be on their part, and you should never let any of it rob you of your birthright. There is the toilet, of course, but there is also—well you know. *Laughter is real, love is real, you are real, and there is real choice.*

As I write at my computer, I can again hear little Mark yelling out "Papa" across the street. It is so beautiful. It is indescribable, all that is contained in the sound coming out of that little boy. A protest, a trust, an appeal, a love . . . I have no idea what he wants from him or why he is calling, but there is so much contained in the call. Of course little Mark exists, and his Papa, too. They exist as unique and precious individuals, not wheels or waves or aggregates, or merely a bag or bunch of neurons either. You are not a lie, nor is life, and to tell yourself you don't really exist really is the biggest lie you can utter—and the worst siren call you can fall victim to. No, not a wheel or mere wave in an ontological ocean, nor bunch of aggregates or neurons either—but rather a real being each of us knows and calls by name, centered in who each ontologically is, myself, yourself, Mark and his Papa. The beast of the abyss is to 'lose' your self . . . that is the devil we speak of metaphorically, the darkness we dread in the very unmetaphoric reality we call death. Just look to insanity as a painful reminder of it on the physical level; where one suffers that unimaginable loss except for all too brief glimpses out of a void of darkness. If hell is anything it has to be that. We all pray that we never lose our ability to be the conscious person each of us is. My Grandpa used to say as much when I was a little boy like Mark: *Signore, rammentate mi la mente (Lord, never let me forget my mind)*. To do so on the level of your very being, to deny your very self, is the ultimate in insanity and suicide both. It is the unforgivable sin. You would be denying life itself—yourself, along with the loved ones in your life. Mark would be denying Papa, and Papa Mark, and each the love they have for one another. Yes, to do so is to be insane and suicidal both, no matter how you sugarcoat it in a scholarly or saintly spin.

The gift of self-being is everything for us, it's where you and I hang out, it *is* you and I, at our depth and many levels of being both—for me, from that which is most fundamentally present, my very self at its mysterious depth of being, to me typing my philosophy out and listening to little Mark—for you, from that which is most fundamentally present, your very self at your mysterious depth of being, to you reading what I have typed and listening to what it says to you. What I have just described is unassailable truth. To deny it is to deny life and your sanity with it. Self-being is our very birthright to be. To be and to find out what that means. To be and to choose how to complete, finish, fulfill what we know as ourselves. To be and to experience the most profound experience we can in being, love, which in a strange turn around proves yet again, in yet another way, the very being of the conscious reality who is loving, for there is a radical realism to direct love—love demands I exist, you exist. Who among you would say your love is unreal, the person you love unreal? Who could? Yes, there is a certain loyalty to being itself that speaks out to us in that. If we make ourselves deaf to this, we chose to betray ourselves, our love, and being itself. The choice is ours. For our deepest experience in being speaks to both our reality *and our freedom*. We make so many choices as human beings, so many mistakes, but where each of us is profound—even Jimmie in his chapel—is where each of us does indeed love. There life itself becomes profound and teaches us—as the only real teacher we have—the profundity of our being.

Perhaps I should waste a page or two on some fellow philosophers here and talk about analytical philosophy because they, too, have a Dalek tilt in their undertaking of philosophy, their philosophy of lovelessness—even as such a posturing is on its way out and a new paradigm in the wings. Analytical philosophy as *solely* analytic has a violence built into it, one that reduces everything to object, including life and the person alive to it. It leaves out the deepest experience in existence and thinks that's perfectly OK, even as philosophy is the love of wisdom, where I dare say, wisdom turns out to be love.

Analytical philosophers of that type refuse to be guided by or discuss their personal experiences; that would be wrong according to them, when just the opposite is true. You cannot know existence if you abstract yourself out of it. Texts interpreted by other texts as the way to philosophize doesn't do it, nor contextualism even more so. When you read their works, which are so choked in Academese they sound like parodies on themselves, and so detached from reality that they truly do become vampiric, sapping the very life out of the subject and making it distant and as dry as death itself, you must realize they are not talking about you, or really themselves either.

Life is not the index of a book; nor is philosophy an analytical algorithm. A book of aesthetics bores the "holy shit" out of me, our very humanness if you have forgotten; but Beethoven doesn't, nor Da Vinci, nor . . . the actual art is what is real, the aesthetics removed, an abstraction, a concept posing as an intuition, an arrogance that thinks it somehow superior to the real thing, that somehow it is the truth stripped of "the mere experience" while getting to the analysis of the mechanics. We see this attitude in the whole of analytical philosophy, its followers acting as if they are the keepers of the gate to truth and dismissing any holistic approach and unfortunately wisdom with it—and thus true philosophy. True philosophy is mostly forgotten and made to seem naïve and romantic as put forth by these would-be coroners of the human surge. The tragedy is that what they refuse to attend to cannot reach them. *Art is chaord, as we are*. It deals with the chaos and order in us, the everyday of flesh and blood and bloodied flesh, too, and more, always more, in the outcry and the insight, the inscape and the landscape of our being. Art speaks in the unspoken language of intuition, even as it is spoken, or shown, or savored by sound. Philosophy has to include that, and science, too, dealing always with existence, the whole of it in a holistic way, using all our ways of knowing in its pursuit, yes, even love, that deepest experience in existence.

It is a remarkably bold step to give love its due in philosophy, as it is to make love the primary in ethics, and we must encourage those who do so in both—and challenge those that do not. For what they say sadly has an effect on the way they approach and answer the third question of philosophy, and that in turn affects people, how they perceive themselves and act in turn. I won't allow myself to go further in that regard here, except maybe a last plea—philosophy, be significant! And an essential part of that is having to ask and trying to answer the fundamental questions of life, who am I, and how do I act in the face of existence? If anyone's philosophy can't answer that, he should start all over again, from scratch with the only thing he really has, existence alone, and a presence in it.

In his *The Structure of Scientific Revolutions*, Kuhn told us what caused a new paradigm. Although the book's most profound proposition is the postmodern soul of the man, namely, that we can never truly understand the real world or even each other, there was a little matter of paradigms he mentioned which I would like to bring up by stating the following: there are anomalies, phenomena that the paradigm can't account for or that even contradict it, and so a paradigm shift takes place. Dare I say I am at least trying a paradigm tilt? We are on a venture, though unworthy in its execution, still in its pursuit the same as both Odysseus and Dante in each of their endeavors. So far, we have at least gotten home to ourselves, and we cannot abstract ourselves out of that human dwelling place, our very existence; otherwise we can never know what it is or who we are. Those that do abstract themselves out of existence end up ultimately denying they could ever know it, because, sadly, they refused to take themselves along in finding it. You cannot find deep reality without you deeply involved with what is deepest in you.

Consciousness fits into that as its very center; but bringing with it an uneasiness. An uneasiness we can rightly attribute to the fact that although a fact—in fact, the fundamental fact for each and every one of us—it is still difficult to describe, and still eludes us as to what it really is. I have argued that reduction of it merely to matter may be impossible, and so have said that there is a strange simultaneity of mind and brain in spacetime, one that makes conscious matter behave differently than anything else in spacetime. This lends itself to us talking about our situation as matter and maybe-meta-matter existing at the same time in a unique sort of symbiosis in spacetime, and as such rooted in our presence, where all our levels of being come together crowned with the awareness we are discussing. This all came about in an evolutionary process, but one that is more than the pedestrian one that is the norm today, which is simply the current way of thinking. The truth is, this conscious presence is the mystery of our evolution and our very being as such. Yet, mysterious as it is, we know it more directly than anything else. Granted we 'define' ourselves in a host of ways, but it is not the way we know our very existence. Again, that is fundamentally present to us in our deepest way of knowing and our only real certitude. As my/your primary intuition, however, it is more than an eureka-like insight as in science or Zen, it is the core intuition of my/your being and self-evident so that each honestly can say: *I am!* To deny that is the height of insanity and the most unreal thing we can utter, it is the unforgivable sin, the ultimate betrayal of one's very being and the gift of being; it is to disavow what is most fundamentally present to each of us, to forsake our interiority, integrity of being, sourceforce, dynamic constant, to vacate our most necessary ingredient; it is to say no to the very depths of our hereness calling out to us, to naysay the primary experience in existence, to play Judas to one's very self-being, to play Brutus to your very presence, to estrange yourself to yourself. You cannot be explained away! *Io sol uno* is as real as it gets for us; and it does not yield easily to analysis. As such, it always is that *something deeper still* manifested in our actions, that subject that can never be object, even as we try to articulate it. It is the self-evident basis of everything for each of us in our journey of life, involving real choice as we saw. *Yes, I am and I can . . . can love, or choose not to love!*

All of that we have been privy to in our venture. But as you recall I said we would further penetrate into this awareness with yet more wordiness. I openly admit, however, that I have problems with words directly expressing this something deeper still. I have at times used words such as sourceforce and the like, but words like that have terrible limitations; they sound to me like talking about the chemistry of pasta rather than tasting the actual wonder. So allow me to complain of this compulsion of mine in warping and stretching, compressing and inverting, reversing and dissecting so that I might have a keen enough verbal skill to articulate what can't be while at the same time realizing it as our most fundamental reality. No, it is not like the White Knight complimenting Alice on having keen enough eyesight to see nobody at a great distance down the road. Bear with me, then, as I inflict words on you, as well as myself, in an attempt to fulfill the mission of trying to penetrate further and further into the profundity of our presence and get a grip on this something deeper still within each of us. The words that will be employed I am hoping will help bring out a reality for us about us, each in their own way, even as they are only words and I using them more like that quixotic knight than the white one.

Let's start with sourceforce, since it may be the most slippery to get hold of. Each of us *is* a sourceforce, and I can show how the word *sourceforce* shows that, and is gotten to so as to show that. I will start by using a model from science to try to bring this out, reminding the reader that it is merely a model and should be understood only as such. That said, in science, with regards energy and elemental matter, so much seems to be a convenient way of expressing *effects*. In essence, that is what we will do with sourceforce. Just as scientists talk of energy for example without knowing deep reality, we can do the same with regards the source of our willing. Briefly put, when it comes to deep reality, the scientist are at one another's throats and their opinions are legion. If you are interested in the different schools of thought on this, confer *note 105, a to m*, of this chapter.[105] Meanwhile, without getting into that fun house, which in and of itself boggles the brain to migraine, we can say that although deep reality still eludes the scientists, we have a model from science that can be used in the same way for our purposes here.

With that said, let's move on and state just as in science energy is arrived at because a force is there to be explained by effects, and from this a name given, so, too, one has a force to be explained in willing, even though we don't know what that force might be in and of itself when it comes to our presence. What it does is bring an objective fact to light and gives the source of it a name.

Granted this is only a word, using a scientific example which may change tomorrow, but the process gets across what I am attempting here, to give a name to something from its effects, without knowing what that something deeper still is in and of itself.

In what I call *me* is the ability of willing. It is an integral part of this unifying subject that each of us is, this wonderful *io sol uno*. Such a presence contains levels of being, the deepest of which we give a name even as we still really don't know what it is in and of itself, except something deeper still that is source or force or both, a dynamic-constant that each of us is in our self-being. You are still you as you read this book and will be years after, even as your narration has grown and you have added layers upon layers to that dynamic presence in the universe, some of them by choices or a willing with you as the source or force, the sourceforce.

I could leave it at that; merely giving a name to it from its effects, but I would like to add to that something I already mentioned way back when. I said that this was always subject and never object. What I was trying to get across and am now again is a sense of *pure activity*; this sourceforce as *semper in actu, always in action,* not a noun, but a verb, or better only a verb in the present tense, that is, pure activity, always in action. That is what I am trying to get across at this juncture of our venture: *existence further creating itself out of the source of its very being.*

To further confuse us, this can be looked at as a *dynamic-constant,* which I already mentioned and will now elaborate on. Again it is only two words brought together, like sourceforce, but again helpful to our endeavor. Of course, I agree that everything physical is in flux, Heraclites was right ($\pi\alpha\nu\tau\alpha\;\rho\epsilon\iota$), as was Buddha, as is modern science, yet that doesn't eliminate two opposites as one and real, a la a dynamic-constant. For as we saw and I mention again, in modern physics, at least as I write, two things can be the same yet different at the same time, and this helps us with regards to grasping an intrinsic quality about ourselves here. But we don't need science to show us this, because everyday life itself show us this. Tomorrow you are not going to get up as someone else, even as today is today and tomorrow tomorrow—and this fact about *you* will be so a hundred years from now when you are on your deathbed, even as years have gone by and your looks lost to entropy. Our identity not only empirically acts like a dynamic-constant, but is such, and thus can be called that, trying to capture the fact of something deeper still which acts at the core of our interiority throughout the journey of life as just that, a dynamic-constant in a flowing physicality in which it chooses, remaining the same and changing simultaneously as it does, constantly chaordinating, not as substance or separate, but always in action, *semper in actu,* a la a verb, a verb in the present tense. Perhaps if merely understood as such, acting, willing, as never being made object, at bottom always a verb in the present tense, one can see what it is I am trying to explain, and mention yet again in that attempt.

As I type that, I can't help but noticing my ole shaggy lazily pawing at a balloon with a face on it as he lies there beside the cooling fan. How perfect an example for the dynamic-constant! No, not my lazy dog, the balloon! The balloon, with a face on it, gives me the sort of geometry I need to bring home my point. I lean over and take it up. I let out the air and then start blowing it up again. Do you see my point? The face stretches or contracts, and so it is never fixed, but there is still a constant in the process. It is dynamic and yet constant.

Consciousness is in a constant drive within to maintain order in existence, a chaord of sorts against the chaos given to pull to disorder—the self thus becoming the successful struggle in spacetime against oblivion and chaos, like the word chaord itself connotes, like the word dynamic-constant does. This core of consciousness in all the hurly burly of living—the blow ups—is that which we experience as the self, me not you, you not me, the sourceforce within each of us as we make the journey of real love and real loss, real laughter and real living, and real entropy in union with all our levels of being. In truth, being a dynamic-constant is our most immediate experience in existence, today as it will be tomorrow, and everyday of our lives. There is an idiom in popular culture—"pull yourself together"—which acknowledges what we all experience, a self, a dynamic-constant, that it is indeed our focal point in the face of the swarming multiplicity of being. Granted, "pull yourself together" is only an expression, yet it does bring home in its innocence a fundamental truth about ourselves that we all experience, the reality of a self, a dynamic-constant, a chaordinator in the cosmos.

Allow me one last limping attempt at it before I move on—one I use on my amazed philosophy majors, one I mentioned to you way back when—look at your forefinger! Now try to touch the tip of your forefinger with the same tip of your forefinger. You can't, of course. So, too, the source-I we having been talking about in different ways; it can never be made object. You can reflect on it nonetheless. Again take the same forefinger and place it to a mirror; you are now touching the tip with the same tip. It is a reflection. However, the tip itself can still not be made anything but what it is, the source. Of even the reflection of itself! So, too, I am saying with regards the source-I. I tried explaining this to my Old English, as handily as I do my students, and after careful consideration, he told me where else I could put my finger.

I get no respect. By the by, that is one of the great lines in comedy—and we all know why. But even if we don't, we still know each of us is irreplaceable and hopefully irrepressible. Even if you and I have no idea what I am babbling about with these limping attempts, we still know ourselves. And as we know ourselves we know that there is in each presence something as concrete as life itself, one that can and is lived and realized in a way that an abstract principle, a universal norm, an intellectual system or scientific and sociological one is not. It makes possible in a very real way acting above the madding crowd and exploding cosmos too, one coming out of the depths of our own being, this hereness each is, this *haeceittas* that makes this unique individual this unique individual only, not only in brain and body but very self-being and presence, with the greatest freedom each of us has as such; namely, the giving of our selves. Again, always staying true to the chapter and therefore life itself, only you can give of yourself, only me of myself, only each of us of ourselves, so much so that even the Whatever the hell that made us can't make us love. It is our primary freedom.

At the well of willing itself is the deepest willing we have, what no one, not even that Whatever that made us, can make us do, only each of us for ourselves, this giving of one's self. Staying true to the chapter and therefore life I have to add that this causes the fundamental tension within each of us between the depths of our being, this will to love, and the "selfish gene" that comes out of raw elemental energies of evolution, what shows itself in the phrase, the will to power. When we choose power over love, we inevitably condemn ourselves to an estrangement to ourselves, retrogressing into the lowest level of our presence; we fall into the swamp again, residing with the proverbial reptile within us.

Steadfast to staying true to the chapter and therefore life itself I have to say that at what level of being my presence chooses to live becomes the decision that determines who I am once I am, who you are once you are. Of course everything in this chapter and in me hopes that both you and I hold onto our purely human spirituality in this, one that tells us that acting out of the deepest experience in our humanness is thus acting most human. However, one can, as I mentioned, estrange one's self from one's depth of being and that is the only real 'sin,' a lost humanness. It is such a wasted opportunity. Like every great piece of literature coming out of our species all the way back to Gilgamesh, it is this journey of a person through existence that is the true story and subtext both, for it is our human story and subtext. The variation of each voyage is obvious, but what matters underneath the soldier, sailor, tinker, tailor, underneath the doctor, lawyer, Indian chief, rich-man, poor-man, every man in a line, is being fully human, and that is ironically accomplished by the giving of one's self, by loving.

I must add, forever staying true to the chapter and existence itself, that the age has arrived which appreciates that any interpretation of the cosmos remains unsatisfying and incomplete unless it contains interiority. Science already appreciates this in a rudimentary way with its anthropic principle, and only awaits a complete physics that will, one day, achieve the inclusion of *us* in a coherent picture of the universe. *And that will have to include love.* Why is that such a revolutionary statement? It shouldn't be! Love is our deepest human experience, even if it turns out to be an aberration in the universe, like consciousness itself.

But we are not at the end of the chapter, so I will cut off this semi-summation and staying true to my Old English tell a joke. Two Englishmen are sitting in their private club, high-back chair to high-back chair, when one says to the other, "Did you hear about ole Chumly?" "No, what about ole Chumly?" "Well he went off to Africa?" "Africa!" "Yes, and got married." "Married!" "Yes, to an orangutan." "Male or female?" "Female of course, there's nothing queer about ole Chumly." I needn't tell you who told me that joke, but his shaggy body is leaving the room in disgust at my attempted British accent.

After a plate of afternoon linguini for both my Old English and myself, I am forced to remind you that the proof of the pasta is always in the tasting. Wittgenstein said that any and all factual statements about the world have to be explained without fundamental facts or "primitives" as he referred to them, because there are no "primitives" that serve as the foundation for our knowing. But we have seen we do possess both a fundamental fact about our very existence and another about the deepest experience in that fundamental presence. We have not one but two "primitives" in our human existence—our root-reality and the deepest experience coming out of that root-reality—and from them we do indeed know something about our actuality and thus perhaps even a peek into deep reality itself. Therefore, let's not have any premature closing off of our encounter with existence, or knowing "primitives" either, primitives that serve as the foundation for our knowing how to act in face and fact of life. See what a little pasta can do! It really is 'soul-food' for philosophers and other various sorts. If only Ludwig would have liked pasta instead of sauerbraten, his whole philosophy would have changed.

Enough pastalytizing I hear you say. Fine, but let me say here, continuing on from what was said, that when I mentioned a peek into deep reality itself, I should mention that we already know our own deep reality as humans. In point of fact, we arrived at a *self-assured* answer about it. In truth, we couldn't get any more *self-assured* in our encounter with human actuality than the root-reality of our own human existence and the deepest experience in that existence. One being the very meaning of self-assured; the other what Viktor Frankl explained, you remember, as *Was Du erlebt, kann keine Macht der Welt Dir rauben—something when experienced no power on earth can take from you.*[106] Of course, to realize this, again *a choice is involved*; but it is not a choice out of nowhere, a real presence is here to make that choice; you are real and so is the love that comes out of that very real you. These are the *two necessary ingredients* for attaining a *purely human* spirituality, our choice to realize such, grounded in what are the two fundamental facts or "known primitives" of existence as humans.

So it is I can say, even if we are caught in a fractal universe, chaos chaording all around us in unfathomable and gloriously indifferent-to-us ways, and closer to home, even if caught between global dimming and global warming, a man-made Scylla and Charybdis haunting our every breath, a corporate monster making the bottom line the rubric of life itself, or a communist one creating its own monster, or one calling itself God's will or al-Lah's will, or Yahweh's will, with us alive to a breathing filled with an uncertainty so pervasive humankind today is like no other before it, whether with a god or godless no matter, each knowing a broken heart awaits with the death of someone we love, again with a god or godless no matter, even if caught in all that, we can, within this human context, in spite of it and because of it, attained a purely human spirituality *and know how to act in the face of existence.*

Imagine that, with all that surrounds us and permeates our postmodern age, and, one way or another, troubled our humanness since it first stepped foot and nail onto the evolutionary stage, gaining its Fox P2 gene on the way, we can actually say that we know how to act in existence in a wholly holy way, that we have a purely human spirituality!

We have achieved our quest for one minimal certainty, and within that presence how to act in the face of the world, no matter what that world is or will become, whether with a god or godless. We have come to a purely human spiritually based on existence alone; one applicable to everyone because our grounding is what each of us is, a presence that can choose to act out of the deepest experience within our presence. *I am and I can . . . love.* It is a choice, make no mistake about it, but one based on breathing, and sensitivity to the deepest part of it, the deepest part of you and me as we cross the street or the stars. Even if this venture is mistake ridden on many other points, this basis is as sure as it gets: you are a real presence in the world, and you can really love. Each of us can say *I am and I can . . . love.* And from this fact of life we build our answer to world and how I act in the face of it. We do not live in absolute night.

I am a presence; you are a presence, everyone on planet earth is a presence. And there are levels of being within each of us, within this presence each of us is, going from invisible neutrinos to nature and its toiletry, and on to consciousness and its ability to choose between the will to power that arises out of that nature of big fish eating little fish and the will to love that arises out of a sensitivity to the deepest part of our being in this odd-yessey of breathing, this odd-yes-sey if we but choose to give of ourselves. All of it is real and so are the consequences that arise out of it, from the darkness of a Dachau to doing whatever good you can on this globe daily. And what is remarkable is that in all of this we have a way to know *how!*

I sit with my cup of coffee, at a midnight diner wondering, pondering, pursuing. It's raining outside the large Deco window as I manage a creased-lipped smile across to the bag lady in from the night. I can only wish that the Mystery that made us cares for her, for me, for the stray dog outside in the drizzle. Or is that trying to domestic the wind? Is what we call God just different and we alone with our kindness? Just the bag lady and me against the whole of everywhere, is that the way it is, just me sending a bowl of soup over to this hungry stranger?

That says it all.

It synthesizes it all into a lived moment.

I could end all my fumbling and jumbling, my near Joycean humptyhillhead attempts to explain it with that lived moment—for if you understand that, you understand, and me with you.

That done—part of me asks if I can now quit all this philosophy and become a clown at last? After all, as I said, like Nietzsche I measure philosophers by their laughter. What's that, you think I already am a clown? At least a sit-down comic did I hear you say? Well it certainly is giddy stuff I'm sitting here typing out in my pajamas, striped blue and white flannels, which oddly enough look like I might have commandeered from a passing covey of clowns. At least that's what my Old English is saying under his bad breath.

"I forgive," I murmur, "both of us for being born of the flesh." No, I am not talking to my Old English, but to myself, and to you. Well maybe him too. I went off to take a stretch in the garden and read some in the shade with my big shaggy. By chance I just happened to turn to the above from the play *Venice*

Preserv'd by Christopher Fry. I hadn't read the play before and this particular piece of dialogue came as a surprise, since it was close to my own thinking, at least the way I interpret it.

> I forgive
> Both of us for being born of the flesh
> Which means I forgive all tossing and turning,
> All foundering, all not finding,
> All irreconcilability,
> All the friction of this great orphanage
> Where no one knows his origin and no one
> Comes to claim him. I forgive even
> The unrevealing revelation of love
> That lifts a lid purely
> To close it, and leaves us knowing that greater things
> Are close, but not to be disclosed
> Though we die for them.

I think it is close to all our thinking when all is said and done, because being born of the flesh means being vulnerable and uncertain, which in a very real way is the very definition of being human, as is our love, which leaves us knowing that greater things are close, but not to be disclosed, at least not as clearly as we would like or need at times in the face of it all. And yet . . . and yet, we do have a compass in the chaos.

That compass is at the core of each of us. Ironically, we can never really lose the vulnerability and uncertainty, but we can lose our core in the face of it all if we so choose. And if we do so choose, we become a stranger to ourselves whether we know it or not, whether there is a God or not. We say to the deepest part of our very being, "I am not interested." But our spirituality as humans is not to be estranged to ourselves, to the depth of our own being. Therein is the holy in each of us—rooted and found in our human condition, in our own incarnation and interface with the universe—and the giving of the very self that finds itself in the vulnerability and uncertainty of it all we call the human condition.

As I already said in this piece one way or another, if postmodernism is not to become life-negating, it has to accept the reality of love, that we can in this breathing of ours, half-abused, half-amused, and the other half appalled at it all, still speak with the authority of existence itself.

If I might be allowed a stream of consciousness, reminding you what consciousness is before I do, I readily admit, although I hold hands with a postmodernism decrying "fossilized formalism" to be sure, my dear Soren, I nonetheless approach it differently than most postmodern deconstructionists, among whom a different shift than mine has taken place. They would move away from the realization of self in relation to itself and other selves, reducing us really to a peeled onion, and with it ultimately nothing. Mine is not a deconstruction that destroys self-being, leaving a vacuum at the end of the process, but one that realizes we can deconstruct no further once we get to that root-reality. *Io sol uno* stands face to face with the deconstructor who denies that depth of presence, going on as he does to promote a pretzelled justice he must then root in a vacuum he calls faith, a faith awaiting a future in a Derridan desert. Believe me, I sympathize with anyone in the faceless desert of uncertainty we are all in, oh yes I do, but life has given us a way to face it here and now—and if I can continue the wordplay—one each of us finds in the face looking back at each of us in the mirror. Granted it is a glass darkly and each of us must admit the misery and mystery of that, but as we also admit the love in our lives as well, even if a person ends up the only one loving in his or her fading journey, old and alone and without a divinity to shape our ends. Or a deconstruction that does either. It is not about some *tout autre* in waiting; the messianic moment is you, your own flesh and blood here and now. My venture to go *beyond* postmodernism means that you do not deny yourself or the other, or that all-important thump in your heart. Quite the contrary, it is what everything ultimately is based on. This is not a secret, it consists of what we know deeper than anything, ourselves as a presence in the world, and the deepest experience for us as that presence.

That is what I must underline, because life does; so when I do, I don't want someone hiding behind a postmodernism filled with contortions more contorted than those they would flee, with an end-run around existence, one that results in a negation of the two planks and a passion we call life, and as such one that absents itself from the suffering and afflicted flesh that love can never absent itself from. This is not *an obligation* as one postmodern would say it is. Rather I would say it is *an invitation*. Not "without whom," as another adds, but most definitely with a who! One that acts out of what is deepest in each of us, to the core, to the giving-reality bursting in the deepest self.[107] To put it as simply as possible, there is a will to love with a real self actually willing it, even as that happens in the midst of the cosmic night. There is a human spirituality based on this! There is not an "end of ethics" and how to act in the face of the world, but the beginning of an ethic beyond good and evil, in the person of a human love, and this is so because we do know who we are—at least where it matters. This is the outcome of a much deeper thinking and so very beyond postmodernism.

Everything follows from how a person answers the first question of philosophy; and in answering it one cannot say that he doesn't know who he is—not on a person's most fundamental level, not on what is fundamentally present to you and the deepest experience in that. Let's speak of deconstruction, but also deconstruction to a root-reality; let's speak of the darkness, but also the love in that night.

In fact, because of that *love* in that *night*, we can actually say with Derrida that the messiah is always coming, but *with me* always here as well. On the one hand, as so beautifully put, we can honestly have *"a longing and sighing beyond the scope of what we can possible imagine."*[108] But we also do indeed have love here and now, which is not beyond the scope of what can possibly be imagined, because it is life's deepest revelation, leaving us knowing that greater things are close, so close as to be beyond at our very core. The desire in the desert and deepest experience in breathing, taken as the realities in life they are, do not leave us in a mutually exclusive situation. You can merge the two in a magnificent thrust to our everyday depths . . . and existence shows us how!

It is true that whatever we have forged out of the flux cannot only be un-forged, but is so over the span of our ongoing species' ongoing, giving rise to the uncertainty we as humans contend with, knowing as we do that we live in a swarming multiplicity of meanings, where mouths come and go talking of Michelangelo, or the Mahabharata, or the Mandelbrot set, or the Membrane hypothesis, or a Marx/Moses a la Monsieur Jacques, or a diner Darwin/Christ a la moi, not to mention the price of peppers in Rio a la Carmen Miranda. But simultaneous to all that *vive la difference*, there is a dynamic-constant in the mix and the mud, and any moananoaning and meaning given to it: one that gives us a way through it all based on what we ourselves are, our very human existence and something equally as universal to our species, the mystery called love.

Perhaps it is shade-stroke from my short stay in the garden with my shaggy, but I have to say that since language began and long before in grunts and groans, the human spirit has been struggling with its existence, struggling for a vocabulary that would give a true expression to our being, from the nethermost regions of suffering to the all too human and wonderful laughter in life, from the harrowing hallucinations of madness to the profundity of this mysticism without ecstasy which is "a madness" all its own, from the all too perilous perhaps of being flesh and blood to the overwhelming experience beyond expression that love suggests, the overwhelming something, somehow, somewho called up in us, whispering of some perhaps-possible-unknown-win-some, weather permitting, maybemysterium we could in our wildest, most wonderful moments, beyond the pale of night, right, or left brain activity clumsily try to give expression to. And when we do, we are left suffering and struggling both as to whether such an Incomprehensible is applicable to the world and we in it, applicable to our heartbreak loses. Yes, we are left wondering as we look up at the night sky out of our transcendent depths, out of our intimacy and what might be the most revealing of revelations, called forth in our very make up. I am again talking about love, our tainted human nature's solitary boast.

Yes, we must also always add, *tainted, tainted with* the cosmos we are alive to and in. Not in any Manichean sense, lest you miss my point. Nor Puritan, nor Pauline in his flesh-hating tirades either! No, never—for what I am speaking about is, despite everything, life affirming, *self-delighting*. For love is the self delighting in the giving of itself—even as this confuses us in that the giving of the self enhances the self. Even as the giver is the gift! A gift given without expecting anything in return one must add, therein reflecting something we have yet to get into. Although this does something 'strange' to the giver, giving a spiritual sense to such a person, it doesn't let him stop the world and get off. He is still naked to the cosmos, and the world he lives in, left trying to breathe as a loving human being in a milieu, a mind set, a quasi religion of sorts, that tries to mold him, from childhood on, into a true believer of brand names, advocating its doctrine that states it is indispensable, remarkably efficient, and responsible for the good life, while behind all the hype is a concern only for the almighty bottom line and making him an addicted consumer, plotting as it does to patent even the blueprint of life for its profit motive and beyond that, the ever present will to power in every movement and monument. Yes, if this quasi religion of the contemporary world isn't the culprit out to swallow him up, something reaching out of the past in the form of religion itself telling him to live by by-gone and barbarian laws that would enslave us all in the name of being a slave for God. And in all this and more he is still left hoping that it is true when he says God can't be a mathematical formula and a mere set of Mandelbrots, a pious legalism, *malin genie* or a volcano, that it is true that God can't be such; even as he wonders with babies born so broken and nature being so brutal and his babbling brain feeling so alone.

Some may sadly remain on the outskirts of themselves and live and die without ever wondering about the brain that gave birth to the awareness they call themselves or the grubby grabbing they have made their life, whether in the western hemisphere or the eastern one of the world, the right or left hemispheres of their individual brains as well, plugged into everything but who they really are and how to act in the face of it. That is a tragedy. As is postmodernism when it proposes to answer the most fundamental question in life with: "We do not know who we are—that is who we are."[109] With such a take on one's self, a person is not going to be able to build a way to act in the face of the world, except maybe in a relative way, which ultimately leads to anything goes, no matter how one might protest. Whether postmoderns admit it or not, and although many would hope for justice and democracy as they say, they have no grounding for saying so. In light of that, some revert to saying theirs is a position full of hope, faith, and affirmation—but based on what? Sadly, it becomes a word game, sometimes verbally adroit, but a real dodging nonetheless.

I have offered an alternative, rather existence itself has in the person of your very person, the presence you call yourself, the presence I call myself, the presence that each of us calls his or her self and the deepest realization in that presence. *The purpose of this chapter is to establish presence and to penetrate into it, with profundity. Without that we can never really know how to act in the face of the world or come to a purely human spirituality. I must remind us all of that, and then mention that we have done this.*

Often, however, even if there is love in our lives, we humans are too busy living our lives to extend our love beyond the walls of our immediacy; yet the deeper we get into the mystery of love that is exactly what we are invited to do. The embrace gets greater the more we know the mystery, until our love embraces the whole of our species, other species, all life and the earth itself, on into the embrace of . . .

Suddenly, my keyboard refuses to type out any more words, my stream of consciousness contracts, for I can hear a question rising out of the mist and rolling towards me like a tsunami.

You base everything on existence and love. OK, I know what existence is, I can't help but. But what is love? Yes, what exactly *is* love?

"Don't you think it's about time you tell us?" Zero mocks from my play within a play. "Since you have placed the sun the moon and the stars—everything—upon its shoulders, my loving philosopher, don't you think you should at least tell us what love is, exactly is?" Like a chorus of faces behind him, I can see each of you asking the same question of me, my five or six readers.

A long silence has to follow here, as you wait and I with you.

For . . . *love is its own revealer.*

It is very difficult for anyone to pass on such an inner sense of being—*love can only be understood directly.*

Love is beyond words and even reason, in a place all its own, a consciousness beyond even good and evil touching an actuality with its own reasoning, somehow bringing us to perceive differently, somehow almost as if a stranger to the goings on in our surroundings.

True, words can be used in an attempt to describe it and have been. I myself have talked of it in terms of *the giving of one's self.* Those may be the words closest to describing it, and so I dared to describe it as such. And Dante touches upon the same in his *Inferno* with a passage about fire, as might be expected in a poem about hell.

> *. . . come la madre ch'al remore e desta*
> *e vede presso a se le fiamme accese,*
> *che prende il figlio e fugge e non s'aressta,*
> *avendo pui di lui che di se cura . . .*[110]

Love shows itself ". . . like a mother who is awakened and catches sight of ferocious flames licking at her, and in panic grabs up her son and flees without let up, caring for him more than for herself." This is how the great poet writes of love, ending with those so insightful words; trying to capture in those words the heart and soul of love, the giving of one's self. That other Medieval giant, Thomas Aquinas, tried to capture it as "a reciprocal abiding," *mutua inhaesio*. Wild Will admitted he couldn't capture it, "O, learn to read what silent love hath writ! To hear with eyes belongs to love's fine wit."[111] Paul of Tarsus, in at least one of the letters we are sure he wrote, tried to relate nonetheless what silent love could only write, penning, "If I speak with the tongues of men and angels, but do not love, I am a sounding brass or a tinkling cymbal. And if I can prophesize, and know all mysteries and knowledge, and if I have all faith so as to move mountains, yet do not love, I am nothing. And if I distribute all my possessions to feed the poor, and if I deliver my body to be burned, yet do not have love, it profits me nothing. Love is patient, is kind; love does not envy, is not pretentious, is not puffed up, is not ambitious, is not self-seeking, is not hateful and wishes no evil, nor rejoices over lies and deceit, but rather rejoices with the truth; bearing with all things, believing and hoping and enduring. Love never falters and is forever, whereas prophesies will disappear and tongues will cease, and knowing things pass. For we know in part and prophesize in part. We see now through a mirror in an obscure manner, a glass darkly, but then face to face."[112] But beautiful as his words are, or Dante's, or Wild Will's, or as magnificently synthesized as Thomas's, they really don't tell us what love is. Love will always be its own revealer. *Solvitur ambulando, solvitur amando*. The solution to walking is walking; the solution to knowing what love is, is loving.

The tired mother who gets up in the middle of the night to care for her crying child; or the father who works two jobs to provide for that child; the son and daughter who care for their aging mother, the old man who spends the little he has so his dog can get a needed operation, the presence of one person so enjoying the presence of another—the solution to knowing what love is, is loving.

It is true enlightenment. It is the profound illumination of our presence in the world, this giving of ourselves, the light shining in the darkness.

We light the way when we love. But no one can give of yourself but you; it is a private, totally personal act, your deepest freedom. I cannot make you love me; even God can't make you love, me, him, or anyone else.

To experience love is to have a realized life. We must fight against deadening our own depths, for much of the world would have us do that. We must always be present where we are, and present with the depth of our being; present with the will to love braving a world that would distort us into a way to think and act and be different than loving. It takes a strong person to be loving, a person who refuses to deaden his or her depth of being, who refuses to do such harm to himself or herself.

I cannot overlook that *never harming intention* to all others as well, essential in love, or the *sensitivity to all life* I keep mentioning—but this is all for you to see for yourself, in love itself. Love is its own revealer. It is very difficult for anyone to pass on such an inner sense of being—love can only be understood directly. It is like existence in a way, certainly at the depth of our presence. All that said, the solution to walking is walking, the solution to realizing what love is, is loving.

Love is like that.

It's what's unwriteable—as clumsy word-wise as that clumsy word itself! And yet once experienced, no power on earth can take it from you. Even death cannot take away the love you have for the one you loved and is now gone forever. "Thou art the grave where buried love doth live," Shakespeare quietly whispers across the ages to us, for he, like us, knows that when you face that seemingly surreal situation of someone you love dying, you still keep loving.

The Nazis had this experiment that showed one's deepest presence most graphically. They would tie electric wiring to a mother and her daughter, with a red button each could press. If the mother pressed it, she would receive the shock, if the daughter she would. Keeping meticulous notes as they did, the Nazis found that nearly every time, the women would vie to take the pain onto themselves and not have the one they loved suffer. That, in turn, shocked the Nazis, my friend Meier Rubin told me, a man long since dead who had fled the Nazis and told me of this horror. Two things can be seen in this, one a human showing her essential presence, her source-I, and yes, that love can supersede survival itself—even as it is done without hope, hopelessly loving or loving hopelessly—*just the giving of one's self without any hope of change in the situation except the giving of self.* The Mengeles of the world tried similar experiments with fathers and sons, siblings with siblings, friends and friends, and got the same results, again with the same self-giving. All again we have to say done with a hopeless love in the face of darkness. There is a picture in my mind's eye still, of the two men the Nazi doctors put in ice-cold water to see how the body would response, each man looking at the other is such a sorrow in face such darkness. No, I never deny the darkness; but never the love either. A friend of mine, John McNeil, a scholar and psychoanalyst, who was a prisoner of war in Germany during the Second World War tells of a guard who, putting his own life in danger because he would have been shot if found out, would, when he could, toss a potato to John who was starving and cold. It was an act of love from a perfect stranger. It moved John so much that he decided then and there to give his life to giving. We know from other sources that strangers chose to stand in for others and get shot; and as already mentioned, that strangers in concentration camps shared the very little soup they were given with other starving strangers. We know a lot about ourselves from concentration camps, whether called an Auschwitz or a Gulag Archipelago or an Andersonville. Not only about a darkness we are capable of, as was the case with those who chose to act less than any beast on the Serengeti; but also about the exact opposite of that, those who choose to love even in hell, to love with a hopeless loving, merely giving of themselves. Besides my friend John McNeil, the famous doctor of psychiatry and neurology, Viktor Frankl, also talks out of a laboratory of fact called Auschwitz and his words have a profound ring of truth to them, resting on real experiences too deep for us to ignore. After talking "of the soul-destroying mental conflict and clashes of will power which a famished man experiences," and how "every day, every hour, offered the opportunity to make a decision, a decision which determined whether you would or would not submit to those powers which threatened to rob you of your very self," he makes clear to us in his rock bottom research of the human condition his conclusion in and through it all, and this time let me quote him directly. "Then I grasped the meaning of the greatest secret that human poetry and human thought and belief have to impart: the salvation of man is through love and in love." He goes on in Latin, "*Et lux in tenebris lucet,*" reaffirming what we said about light shinning in the darkness—and then in German, too, as I have already quoted.[113]

I use this again and the previous extreme examples to bring home the point of love as the deepest experience in existence, superseding all our other levels of being, even hope and survival itself. But we needn't go to Auschwitz, and thank heavens we don't have to, to find the fact of love. It exists in people's daily lives. However, Auschwitz does provide us with such a clear picture of it when we see a starving man sharing his soup with a starving stranger; for we know from science that the brain is fed first when a starving body takes in food, it is built into our biology, yet, here, conscious love supersedes even a starving brain crying out to survive. That is significant, and so I repeat it again. This choice that a conscious self, stripped to naked existence, makes in the face and fact of the raw elemental energies of evolution, contrary to its own brain's natural drive to survive, not only suggests to us that love is more than the neurons of the brain, but also shows us love as a choice.

The irony of it! The irony that in such darkness such a profound light calls out from our human depths and challenges the will to power with the will to love, revealing in hell itself a redemption found in our very being, a salvation in our very selves. It is the unforgivable sin to deny one's self-being, for without a real you there is no real love, and you lose the deepest experience in existence, you lose your "salvation" in the swarming multiplicity, ending in the vacuum of a loveless world and where that has always led and would again. If you deny what is fundamentally present to you and the deepest experience in breathing, you really have nowhere to go, unable to trust in anything, including your abstractions. When a person deconstructs as well, he must do so at a deeper level of inquiry, deconstruct as it were all the way to the rhapsodic ruminations of our humanness itself, beyond the pale of different cultures or the tyranny of the prevailing thought in our age which says we can't unravel the various strands that hold our traditions together and therefore cannot access some extra-contextual reality, or any firm reality at all for our beliefs, values, judgments, and truths. The fact is, we are *not* accessing some extra-contextual reality, but driving to the very heart of our reality, universal to our species, and has been since mud stood up and thought and then talked about it "contextually."

"If this be error and upon me proved. I never writ, nor no man ever loved."[114]

Love is a fact of life. Those with winter in their laughter will ridicule, of course, saying no doubt with a wry smile and sophisticated smirk that this is like finding Neverland—too childish foolish for this world. Although I readily admit I personally am too childish foolish for this place, and readily confess that I never want you to lose the little boy in you, or the little girl in you—when the first baby laughed humanity was born after all—still, this is past our melancholy for any loss of innocence or any hardening of one's heart as a supposed survival skill on planet stress either. Rather, this is you and I grown to our fullest, finding ourselves, our fullest human selves, *our purely human spirituality*.

Let me say it straight out, summing it up, this fundamental tension within each of us between the toilet and something that goes thump in a one's heart, between *the will to power* coming out of the raw elemental energies of evolution and *the will to love* coming out of the phenomenon of consciousness in the cosmos, this fundamental tension within each of us ultimately gives us our purely human spirituality, one that comes out of the deepest level of our being, where a person chooses the will to love over the will to power, sometimes hopelessly loving or loving hopelessly, true, but loving nonetheless.

There is real self-being and real suffering to go with it, and with it too real laughter and love. What it all means is at least that! That each of us is real in it all, that each of us is present, a presence in the face of the facts of the world, among them our suffering, and our laughter and our love!

If this be error and upon me proved, neither of us, my great Bard, ever wrote and no one ever loved! However, we are not in error, the grounding is most definitely there for our purely human spirituality, right smack in the heart of our human condition. But, again, to live according to that is a choice on our part; we are creatures that choose, even as we create ourselves by and through that choosing. *I am and I can love* doesn't mean I will choose to love, only that I can. One can act *in a moral or amoral or immoral way—this is the spectrum within each one of us.* I can eat the soup for myself and follow my natural urges and brain's hunger; I can share my soup and act more than nature and neurological instinct, or I can take your soup and let you go hungry and die. And we have seen there is a grounding in all this, rooted in what we are made up of, one that comes out of existence alone, one that presents our presence with a choice: either follow the raw elemental energies of evolution that made us or go the way of something so profound within us that we would give of our very selves because of it.

Yes, looking with the eyes of love and listening deeply to the cries of the world, one knows how to act, expecting nothing in return.

The deepest encounter with existence is thus. It is beyond good and evil, in that it is done as more than, above, even aside from and without reference to either. Here the man who hugged the horse in Turin was right: "What is done out of love always happens beyond (*jenseits*) good and evil."[115] It is the greatest act any creature can do.

It stands at the zenith of ethical or moral or spiritual action, and what is emphasized in that action. The lowest ethical action is one of law (which in truth can be moral or immoral), and sadly where most books on ethics get stuck, in a rationalistic and legalistic approach. Don't take my word for it, read them on your own and see for yourself. But as I said law is the lowest form of ethical action. Above it is justice, and above that righteousness or moral indignation at injustice, and above that compassion, which 'suffers along with' as the word connotes, and, finally, above all, love, the giving of self, expecting nothing in return.

One can show the graphic starting from law at the bottom and building up:

Love
Compassion
Righteousness
Justice
Law

Thus we see the levels of ethical or moral or spiritual behavior, and although the zenith can contain all that went before, it need not as well.

The point, of course, is, looking with the eyes of love and listening deeply to the cries of the world, and then not only knowing how to act, but choosing to do so—that is the realization I am speaking of. Oh how important that is—the choice of love—it affects everything, but most importantly how we look at another. And when I say that, I am including other life forms as well. Here I would like to quote something I. B. Singer wrote; something many have so misunderstood and attacked him for. "As long as human beings will go on shedding the blood of animals, there will never be any peace. There is only one little step from killing animals to creating gas chambers a la Hitler . . . There will be no justice as long as man will stand with a knife or with a gun and destroy those who are weaker than he is."[116] When all is said and done, the spirituality we are discussing is an indefinable simpatico. It is an indefinable simpatico that, yes, embraces a suffering horse—one that includes and affects how we look and act towards every sentient being. Love is all-inclusive in its embrace. But such a sensitivity to the other—be that other human or another feeling creature—doesn't happen by osmosis; a person has to make a profound decision to be sensitive, to be spiritual. For the most part the world will not respond to your love; it will be indifferent or perhaps even dismissive and even hostile. But the point is you still must keep from hardening your heart; *you must keep sensitive to the deepest part of being.* For even if a person knows what is right, it is still a choice on his or her part to act upon it; as Dostoyevsky so poignantly portrays in *The Brothers Karamazov.*[117] I am referring to the part in the novel where Christ returns to earth during the Inquisition and Dostoyevsky has him once again perform miracles, even raising the dead back to life—making the point that he is definitely recognized as Christ. The Grand Inquisitor has him seized and brought before him, and asks Christ, "Why have you come now to hinder us?" Freedom is too difficult and frightening for the people the Cardinal argues, and declares he will have Christ burned at the stake—to which Christ says nothing in reply, but only kisses him on the lips. Christ is telling the truth of things without words, the great writer tells us, but the Cardinal will have no part of it. "The kiss glows in his heart, but the old man holds to his idea." This little scene brings home the inner decision still necessary, even if you are face to face with the answer that the kiss so beautifully displays. I like the fact that Christ in the piece doesn't *say* anything; he *does* it. He acts out his love and his answer. That fits right into what I have stated about the will to love, as well as contemporary thinking, for contemporary humankind is action-oriented in its thinking. So must be our spirituality, combining both awareness *and* action, an action firmly rooted in our deepest personal experience as human beings. Thus it is I can say, yet again, that a truly human spirituality is an awareness in action, or more precisely, love in action. *Amor in actu!* There, I even said it in Latin! No matter what language we put it in, it must be a love that is active across the board: privately and publicly. In Washington? Yes, and in Nero's court as well. *Anywhere and everywhere; each doing so in his or her own way.* For it is a love each must stamp with his or her own personality. It can be done in the silent prayer and solitude of an abbey if that is the life one chooses, or in the midst of the crowd as the most gregarious of practitioners.

Yes, I know, for most philosophy departments the mere mention of love is anathema, and every example of it met with a crooked smile, if not a cerebral yawn or open claws; but I shall continue not only to incorporate love into philosophy as it must be since in it is the deepest experience in existence, but I shall even use the example of breathing men and women to bring this home, unlike some who roam the corridors of so many philosophy departments, abstracting themselves and everyone else out of existence and thinking they can better know existence that way. One of my colleagues asked me why I put so much emphasis on love and how I can say it is so important as I do? I said it would take a book to explain, but in a shorthand attempt then asked him if he had ever loved in his life? At which he grew very indignant and said that was personal. I told him that was the point—that all life is, and philosophy with it; that what we refuse to attend to cannot reach us. It's ironic that they are called philosophy departments, knowing that philosophy is *the love* of wisdom. Too many along those hollowed halls, at least in their philosophy, have closed themselves off to what we are speaking about due to a false notion they have of what it means to be intellectuals. "Coppola is no longer a scholar," one says. "Never was," another adds in a scholarly smirk. In answer I say, "To children I am still a scholar, and to thistles and red poppies, too." Yes, I am quoting Nietzsche. If you want to know what I think, read his take on scholars and bring yourself to tears of laughter, if not profound belly laughs. I'll wait, go head. And while you fetch *Thus Spoke Zarathustra*, allow me to continue in his spirit of fun-making and be un-loving for a moment more, stating that philosophy departments (at least in America) have become places set out to train people to become, oh let's say it, practitioners in "Ambition, Distraction, Uglification and Derision," dear Alice, the departments themselves of course calling it being analytical. They are producing sophists that argue all points, and at all costs—most tragically at the expense of what is the deepest experience in existence and the wisest. The will to power is alive and well in analytical philosophy, one-upmanship the flavor of the corridor. *Basta!* Enough fun with the funless! Though I am tempted to go on, for I do enjoy a good tease, my point is made, so henceforth I hope that anyone hearing the mere mention of analytical philosophy in their presence will burst into laughter as if someone were talking about limbo.

Meanwhile, putting aside my naughtiness, and moving from limbo back to the serious discussion at hand, it shouldn't seem strange to us that what is loveless, under whatever disguise, even intellectual pursuit, will always try to take love out of the picture and leave a person estranged to his or her deepest presence. In today's world we have forged a way of looking at life based on an economy of growth that in the present state of the globe cannot continue. It is unable to envisage any form of relationship other than absorption or possession and this is the will to power personified, ironically in the unreality of a corporation as a legal person, with the added directive that profit above all be its legal obligation. "Love show me your politic," a lyric in a song bursts out. Unfortunately we relegate it only to songs.[118]

Yes, the tragedy is that what we refuse to attend to cannot reach us. As a species we have a structure that has estranged us from own depths. Perhaps it is an impossibility to structure a state, economy, and ecology on love, and the raw elemental energies of evolution and what comes out of it always win in such an arena; like death in life. But at least individually we can listen to the call out of our depths, realizing love makes a person harken to the innermost and outermost boundaries of his existence, of her existence, and each live his or her life accordingly. I call attention to what I said in the overture to this symphony: Even if the whole world goose-steps down *Les Champs Elysee* to nature's drum, I don't have to. Even if the whole world says whatever it does about whatever it does, I must be honest to who I am and the love at the depth of my being, to existence and the deepest experience in it. On the other hand, I believe it was Mahatma Gandhi who said all revolution begins with and within the individual, so maybe there is hope for a better world. On some days we all feel so and we do a jig of joy, while on others hope grows gray hairs and our eyes become Cassandra's.

Politics as it is practiced for the most part is what is called *realpolitik*, which, when all is said and done, is based on a will to power. But love does tell us its own politic. This is not naïve nonsense; it recognizes all too well the world of *realpolitik*. It recognizes how easy it is to revert to authoritarian and self-serving policies in organized political movements—ever sabotaged by the will to power in each of us. We carry the cause of it in our very make up. Even with the best intentions, people often act out of a will to power. Though they might be on the correct side politically, they are on the wrong side *personally*. Politics is replete with such people, people who work out of the same Serengeti as the people they would replace. And when they do, one way or another, they end up like them. "I am the revolution," Marat screams out in the powerful political play, *Marat/Sade*, but he has no idea what that really means. No more than his political enemy, Sade. Both are still firmly rooted in the hiss in our heads and a place without love. Such a place can never achieve what I am talking about. Something fundamental in us has to change—or better found and willed forth. We don't behead people and call it a revolution, but rather enhance what are in these heads at the core of each consciousness, the will to love. Genghis Khan or Gandhi, conformity or Christ—the choice, the very hard choice is always there, in everything we do really, whether in the serious realm of hard politics or the silly pettiness of office politics. Acting out of the Serengeti in us is the easy way out. *To live love on the other hand is often lonely, and often requiring courage.* However, once a person does find the meaning in the mess we are alive to, it becomes his or her call from being itself, despite the herd instinct or the hiss in our heads.

And thus all politics *is* personal. If a person appreciates that, he knows what the politics of *amor in actu* is and entails. If a person appreciates that, she knows how truly personal politics has to be. It is our inner decision to love, now carried into the polis we are alive to and live in. That makes it, of course, something quite different than the platform of *realpolitik*, which, no matter the rhetoric used to soften the true agenda, has always been historically the will to power, whether practiced in ancient palaces, by-gone politburos, in theocratic Persia or in a city on the present day Potomac. That is the elephant in the room as I write—throughout history and into our present. Nero is in his court, but are we to play the part of Seneca? Of course, don't be so naïve as to think what's waiting in the wings to replace this monster is not a Caesar of its own, a Cyclops of its own, driven not only for more of the pie, but controlling the pie as well. Caesar always replaces Caesar and anyone who wants to realize a new politic must not be coned into thinking what is called the opposition will do it differently. A Caesar by any other name is still as Caesar after all. Racism with a different pigmentation is still racism. The will to power still the will to power. So where does that leave us? Always in some Caesar's court? Where it leaves us is where it always will. Each of us has a personal choice to make in all this, one between Cerberus' howl in our heads or what is the deepest experience in our being. We have that choice in politics, in business, in everything we do. We cannot separate or compartmentalize it. It has to be an awareness of love in all our action.

Lest anyone is still confused—such a politic is not left, center, or right. It is the politic that love shows us. How each of us answers its call is part of our personal confrontation with the cosmos. The will to power will always be out there, everywhere on planet earth; but so will the way for a person to meet it—with a will to love. It is the greatest revolution there is, the greatest rebellion, the most radical and only real politics for building a better person, polis and planet, a better place in the sun for all of us—with no one thrown off our spinning spaceship as it were. The politics of love is the most democratic and egalitarian of any politics concocted—and the only one based on those two all-important ingredients in life, existence itself and the deepest experience in that existing. However the understanding of that comes—whether from "just sitting, collecting the heart mind" or up from the gut—when you or I realizes it, it becomes absolutely evident to us that love for our fellow creatures, for all sentient life, becomes our absolute guideline.

At times it will indeed, and I must make mention again, take a desperate courage, especially when we appear ridiculous in the eyes of the world of *realpolitik* and feel we might actually be so. We might even feel abandoned by all that is good. That means you have to go beyond the norm, leaving behind what we can call the present political animal. Nietzsche declared that our humanness is essentially still undetermined—it has not be found or secured, and that is why we are still unfinished animals. That is so in many ways, but we still have a root-reality and finding that is what we have been going about here. That doesn't mean we know the future of our species, or ourselves in our many levels of being, and when it comes to our non-physical or metaphysical make up, we are certainly as yet under-conceived and so far undetermined creatures. But I think, even as the man from Rocken never finished telling us in writing what he thought *der ubermensch* was, only what it was not in *der undermensch*, he showed us in that rainy piazza what he himself knew it was and had to be, even if he and the rest of us and the horse with us have to eat bitterness.

The rational animal that we consider ourselves has to yet be brought to its full humanness, which is more than rationalism; but this can only be done by ourselves, and that means individually at least, by our willing to open one's self to the depth of our humanness, which is already there, and which we can validate in our daily lives in the reality of love, the deepest experience in that human nature, even if it be an aberration in the cosmos, as it seems consciousness itself might be. Metaphysically, Nietzsche's love had to be hopeless as there was no metaphysical grounding other than the abyss which is no metaphysical grounding at all; and that may be the way it is, even as love is our most real moment in being. However, if we can give this loving hopelessly a metaphysical grounding, that of course changes the metaphysical thinking and any adverb or adjective applied to love. That is the second part of the subtitle to this human venture, and must await our honest tasting of the pasta in this regard, no matter the outcome, even if we have to look into the abyss.

Meanwhile, never look for a politic of love in those characters who have pushed their way to power in the polis as it chief functionaries and so-called leaders. They are not *der ubermensch,* either Nietzsche's nor the one I am talking about. They are for the most part, no matter how talented or intelligent they may be, *der undermensch* in their mentality. For the most part politicians are poot-boys for the power elite and in reality more in the mode of a Judas-Brutus. At best, they are Seneca in Nero's court, while some even pose as scholars of holy books and as holy themselves, at the head of monstrosities called theocracies, perhaps the most hypercritical of all politics.

When it comes to politics all of us who are at least trying to be loving have to end up feeling like Lao Tsu when he went off into the desert disgusted with humankind. That is a noble realization and worthy of Voltaire's "we must cultivate the garden." Or if I might add, on a personal note, my grandpa's enigmatic toast to life, as he lifted his glass of red wine with a twinkle in his eye and would say, "I'ma bigga bum again." Of course he was one of the holiest men I ever knew, up to and including this moment of remembrance. I have said and say again, the purely human spirituality we have uncovered within our humanness requires that a person perceive his or her personhood, knows it is present and the profundity involved in that, evolved in that as well. A person exists as holy only to the extent to which he or she is open to his or her own self and only so far as each realizes that depth of being in their actions. I saw a person who did, and stand like Nietzsche coming out of the cave, asking myself and my heart: "Could it be possible? This old saint in the forest has not yet heard anything of this, that God is dead?"[119]

With that, I pour myself a glass of red wine and give a toast, and with it conclude this segment on love, cautioning again that refusing to attend to the phenomenon of love will leave you estranged to yourself, stripping you of the two necessities for any hope of achieving what each of us can be, a wholly and holy human being; one who looking with the eyes of love and listening deeply to the cries of the world knows how to act and choose to do so, regardless of the world's response to you or if there is a Mystery that surrounds us.

"Was mich nicht umbringt, macht mich libender."

A problem still remains however!

Indeed, a problem still remains, for even as we know ourselves and the deepest experience in existence, we are still left with the haunting question: where's the wisdom in the waste? Life's haunting question about suffering is still there staring out of our eyes. It comes with the territory. Any real answer to it has plagued conscious creatures one way or another since Gilgamesh and before, no doubt all the way back to those humanoids that buried axes with their dead. The problem of suffering, like the phenomenon of love and the very mystery of presence itself, has to be—has to be—part of any pursuit for a purely human spirituality or it isn't worthy of its name. And this is true of any philosophy, or any theology as well as we shall see when I address and have to address suffering with regards any Mysterious More—the proof of the pasta is in the tasting, and that goes for God, too. Suffering has to be addressed with regards to any talk of the Mysterious More, that compete Other in postmodern thought, at root completely Other maybe because of suffering.

The truth is that the problem of suffering will raise its ugly head throughout this work as it does in life itself. Like a seductive theme in a symphony it will keep coming back, for it is central to breathing on planet stress, and perhaps the biggest stumbling block in the way of any when it comes to any Mysterious More. Stendhal's bon mot, for which Nietzsche envied him, has to come to mind here: "The only excuse for God would be for him not to exist."

As I turned to the bag lady in the café to give flesh and blood to what I was talking about, let's pause and again give flesh and blood to what I am talking about here, this time through a young man dying of AIDS in New York on a cold February day and the soul-letting penned on that day.

> *I am looking across at myself in the mirror. What's become of me that is. I wonder what Jesus would have thought had they hung a mirror in front of him—what had become of him, too?*
>
> *Would he have said, I had such a beautiful body? Now look at me? Even my family looks at me as if I am a Martian. I felt that way when I went over there for Thanksgiving. Their visits have become almost non-existence. Phone calls are the way to keep your distance, huh, folks. A nice Catholic boy should have known better than fool around with other nice Catholic boys. Actually, most of them weren't. Not that it matters. Except to those crazy nuts on TV—so called men of God—who say God sent this to me to punish me for my sins against nature. It was nature that made me this way, you sons of bitches! How could I be sinning against nature? God made me this way! Or allowed it to happen.*
>
> *He made others the way they are, too, or allowed it to happen. Like that baby born a vegetable. I was a nurse. In one of those places they keep kids like that as they get older. Every day I heard a mother, a father, a couple, question a God who would allow what I was witnessing. I took care of them, those poor kids. I took extra care of them. Who else would? There was one in particular that comes to mind. "My daughter is extremely engaged when*

*she comes to see him," his father told a lady visiting with
him. "To 'Little Anthony's house,' as she calls it. You saw
how she says hello to all the kids, whether they respond
or not." His other son just hugged at his leg. I don't think
the boy knew what to make of it. I could certainly relate
to that.*

*I saw his daughter go to the cookies and bring one
back and set it on Little Anthony's wheelchair tray. He
raised his head, as if to acknowledge her gift, and then
sank back into the looping riffs in his head. Nobody knows
how much he comprehends. That's what the doctors put
down on the chart. No matter, Little Anthony turned his
head towards his family. This time he even reached out
his arm.*

*"One time," his father Tony told the visiting lady, "up in
Albany, he started to cry when we left. He started to moan."*

*I had to leave the room. I didn't want to cry in front
of them. That night, I had to write about Little Anthony
in my diary. It tore me apart working there. It made me
freeze spiritually . . . trying to see God in this . . . trying
to see the face of the God that made this, could allow this.
God why have you forsaken me? Now with Little Anthony
and Jesus I cry out the same thing.*

*The lady visiting with Little Anthony's family turned
out to be some woman journalist from the coast who came
to the place to write an article about these kids, or maybe
just about this particular family. Anyway, I recently ran
across it. The way she ended it made me feel that pain all
over again. It was something about this family saying they
love the son they wish they hadn't had. But does God?*

*I still remember that little guy. Hopefully his suffering
will end soon.*

*Today has been an especially bad day for me. My
former lover called from San Francisco and I could hear
it in his voice—when? It's coming on fast. I think he
wanted to help me prepare for it, but he didn't know how.
It was clumsy.*

*God, this is an awful disease. I look like I just came out
of Dachau. And feel I have. I feel betrayed by everything,
my body included. Not to mention You-Know-Who. How*

like you I feel, Little Anthony. How like you, sweet Jesus.
Will we all meet in Paradise? And will Little Anthony be
able to eat his cookie this time?
I hung up the phone and started to cry, and started to moan.

From the first piece of literature's outcry all the way to this journal's, suffering has been scratched out of one's soul onto stone, paper, or computer screen in an attempt to express our astonishment at the fact. "Tears, lament, anguish, and depression are within me. Suffering overwhelms me. Evil fate holds me and carries off my life. Malignant sickness bathes me," writes a man thousands of years before our male nurse and his outcry. "Why am I counted among the ignorant?" another asks eons ago as he sat letting out his soul along the banks of the Tigris. "Food is all about, yet my food is hunger. On the day shares were allotted, my allotted share was suffering." Although I have displayed a euphoria over existence, we had to ultimately face this problem that has been with us since consciousness first became aware of where it was and what was happening to it. So it is we must bring everything to a grinding halt here and look directly into the eyes of suffering. Into this world of vulnerability! For none of what I have stated answers the problem of suffering. None of it answers why life can be so brutal and creatures suffer so? Why nature itself is so brutal? Why babies are born monsters? Why each of us is so left to chance that it sends a shiver to one's very soul? Yes, I could theorize that the mysteries that created us created the universe to evolve as it would—to be free to do so—in order that we who evolved out of all that would be free as well; but still that doesn't answer the horror of suffering. Suffering silences all reason. And at that silent moment, the lack of any wisdom in the waste leaves us empty. Is the heart prepared for such an emptiness? Catharsis, dear Aristotle, is not the same as honest emptiness. My talking about it isn't either. Suffering is empting, and therefore wordless really. We will always be creatures looking up at the night sky about it, aghast at the amount of suffering that plagues our planet, up and down the levels of being on it. *What immortal hand or eye could frame thy fearful symmetry?*[120]

Because of suffering everything becomes questionable—and should! In suffering, the primal meaning and value of existence itself becomes questionable. What is the point of it? What did evolution have in mind, if anything? Of course, when you suffer, you don't theorize about it, speculative arguments fade and fall apart . . . they are as helpful as a lecture on the chemistry of foodstuff to a starving man.[121] It seems everything becomes futile at that starving moment, reality itself. In truth, how could we talk of reality when we don't know how to answer this everyday reality for each of us—consciousness looking out at all this suffering? Yes, we *must* stop here and look at suffering. We can't move on without doing so. It might very well be the very cause of why we even search for a spirituality, and a Mysterious More with it. Are we in some sort of vicious circle then? A real comedy of sorts? Perhaps a tragicomedy after all? Or better a comic agony as I am want to describe it? The wine dark sea is out there ready to drown us and we know it! Just when we thought we were enlightened, the Ichneumon wasp eats the caterpillar while it is still alive to the pain and Darwin and I both bemoan the fact and have to wonder and weep. Yes, the problem of suffering has raised its ugly head yet again. Abstractions and dimensions and simultaneities have been pulled back to flesh and blood and the dissecting of real creatures in life's labs, not mermaids in our minds. We have love, but we also have suffering! We have love, but we also have suffering and the added problem about any real meaning to all this that it poses!

Add humankind's brutality to evolution's remorseless, pitiless, indifference no matter what the cost in suffering and one definitely has to look out at the night and wonder what is this place? Are we not seduced and then abandoned by life when you think about it? Whoever we are, our attitude to suffering is connected at the deepest level with our attitude to reality as a whole, and visa versa. "If Nature were kind," writes the supreme Darwinist, Richard Dawkins, echoing Darwin, "she would at least make the minor concession of anaesthetizing caterpillars before they are eaten alive from within."[122]

Why, one has to ask as well, did evolution evolve the way it did? It could have evolved differently. So why did nature design creatures to prey upon one another and, at the same time, instill into such creatures a capacity for intense pain and suffering, thereby causing untold suffering among these creatures? I saw a documentary in which a crocodile pulls a deer feet first into the water and as it cries out begins to eat it alive. It made me remember reading about a young Peace Corps worker with all the best intensions meeting a similar fate in Africa. When the crocodile was killed later, they found parts of the young man in its stomach. A conscious giving creature ending in such a horrid way. Imagine it, creatures *eating* other creatures—imagine you being eaten! And if not by another creature, by a micro-biotic entity, leaving you, like the caterpillar, eaten alive from within! How can we make sense of the universe, given the fact of suffering? What's the purpose of all this suffering? Where is the wisdom in the waste? It does seem to be a tug of war between nature and our consciousness here—and not just human consciousness. The American Indians tell of a story of the buffalo standing all day and night at the site of one of those all too many slaughters and raising a moan never heard before, as if from the earth itself. I have seen in heartbreaking documentaries the trumpeted cries of the elephants as they knowingly look up at helicopters and the rifles pointed at them and so can painfully relate to the bison doing what these plains people related. All conscious creatures cry out. The periodic starving of chickens to stimulate egg production, the rigid confinement of calves in forever cages for veal, pigs in crates too small for them to turn around for the entirety of their lives, slaughterhouses that cut the hooves off live cattle—all part of humankind's contribution to nature's brutality; to the brutality of a brutal food chain to begin with and then humankind's diabolical contribution to it. And then, so someone can be fashionable on Fifth Avenue, there are those Chinese fur farms that skin the dogs and cats alive as they cry out, marking their furs as mink, as if that should make a difference to us. Conscious creatures cry out across the planet because of what we do to them in the name of profit or the so-called pursuit of science. I say so-called because in truth what these labs are performing on these innocent creatures is nothing but scientism, and all the more so as we now know Petri dishes and cell and computer research offer a true science with far more efficient results. I pass over in silence what we have done *to one another,* and still do—we all know that all too well. If nature doesn't get you, humankind will. Like Seneca in Nero's court, can a moral man survive in this system? Seneca, of course, did not, either as a moral man or a live one.

Nietzsche, the father of meaninglessness in the modern world, struggled over all this as we already know—his embrace of the beaten horse breaks my heart, the last straw for him it appears. It shows so much of the man. How could you not love Nietzsche? Isn't he all of us in that embrace?

Suffering and chaos had opened up the deadly cold night of nihilism for him. But again Nietzsche could not live without love—his embrace of the horse shows that. All his suffering and struggle comes out in that embrace. In a very real sense I have to say again his greatest statement is this silent one. When someone is in the depths of depression, or gripped by a madness that somehow one is aware of even as one is mad, or even coming off of certain drugs as addicts tell us, the brain is exhausted and the person feels emptied, as if in a black hole, adrift in fear and tortured by great psychological pain, as if nothing has meaning and ending is the only way out.

This possibility of nihilism—which does manifest itself in life—puts reality itself profoundly in question. It constitutes a basic challenge to our consciousness. Meaninglessness is possible; and suffering makes it all the more so, as it brings all the more suffering in the meaninglessness.

Certainly William James found it so as I mentioned. His visit to that insane asylum still has to stick in our cerebral claw as it did in his. Here was a human who couldn't be anything but honest when he told of the "black-haired youth with greenish skin, entirely idiotic . . . moving nothing but his black eyes and looking absolutely non-human. That shape am I, I felt, potentially." James was left with a "horrible dread at the pit of my stomach, and with a sense of insecurity of life that I never knew before, and that I have never felt since."[123] Like Nietzsche,

James is left struggling with the dread of an abyss, especially after looking into it. Like our nurse, James is left struggling with the visibility before him, the reality of this abandoned creature locking horns with any notion of a caring God, any caring but his lonely self.

Such a snake pit is part of all suffering—no doubt its result—and there a person stands, sits, or lies supine facing a meaningless universe. We all stand, sit, or lie there one way or another—at one time or another—each of us left crucified on the crooked cross of existence, abandoned and betrayed by existence on our own Golgotha as it were, on that horrible hill. Yet, somehow, even then, maybe especially then in such utter abandonment, love, stripped of everything, is finally realized as the only thing that makes sense in the universe. In the face of even an absolute actuality that seems meaningless, love is still meaningful to us! Like the nurse's love for that baby, and our love with his! Even after the loss of someone we love to death, and that empty incomprehensible almost surreal fact of them not being with us—even after that our love for them continues in the pain and the hole in our life, and we find the only real meaning *was* our love for one another when all is said and now done. All now done but our love, for we can and do still embrace them in our loss, with a love that both causes the suffering and soothes it. Truly our love for one another was not meaningless. Mortal but not meaningless. Love is the confronter to any meaninglessness in life. Even in the face of the absurd.

Camus comes to mind here, where he says, "children will still die unjustly even in a perfect society. Even by his greatest effort man can only propose to diminish arithmetically the suffering of the world. But the injustice and the suffering of the world will remain and, no matter how limited they are, they will not cease to be an outrage."[124] That there is suffering, any suffering as well as so much of it, is not only the root of our sense of absurdity, but of our outrage, and our outcry as well.

Why is suffering built into being, at least being on planet Earth, at least in conscious matter? Where's the wisdom in the waste? And yet . . . and yet, although our love might be as vulnerable as we are, it is there nonetheless, as long as we are, defying suffering and the meaningless abyss with it. Even without a caring God there is love; even without any cosmic meaning whatsoever! Even if suffering is built into matter and the Second Law of Thermodynamics decaying it and us with it, even so, I am and I can . . . love. And I know my love is real. I can at least believe in my own love, even if the world and universe with it is meaningless. Yes, love protests, it demands, it insists that the outrage be brought to an end. Love is our outcry!

It has become clear by now, no matter what one might say, that one's basic attitude about actuality is ultimately a choice, a choice to let love be, or not, to let love be or not in your encounter with the bag lady and the monster child, in your encounter with the stray dog and starving stranger, in your encounter with life. In your encounter with love striving to know, as well! Let love be! No matter matter itself! The stress within each of us is this tension between the will not to love and the will to love. This instress is in our very inscape of being and there is no escape from it for any of us, a choice has to be made one way or another, whether any Mysterious More or not. Indeed, one's basic attitude about life is ultimately this choice, this choice not to love or to live a life of loving and say this is my answer to the world.

The poet tells us that it is better to have loved and lost than never to have loved at all—and so does our own experience of love and loss. Heartbreaking as it is. That wisdom from experienced existence goes for living life in its entirety; it is better to have loved . . . No, love does not end suffering. That ends only with our own death. Until then, life includes suffering in all its very real concrete occurrences. Love does not solve this problem of existence. It does not protect us against suffering, but somehow love is still the most precious thing in life, even in the face of suffering. *It is the wisdom in the waste!*

My madman Zero says as much out to a darkened audience after the loss of his dearest friend in the lonely madhouse. "Dressing for a burial is slow. The empty feeling in your stomach follows you in its vague reference to everything, and yet you know you should and must celebrate that life." There is a near invisible nod as he stands there. "The hard thing, ultimately, the one that gets you, is not just to live in the world, but to live missing what's missing." A long stare follows. "But what's done out of love is in spite of the missing. In the face of it. With a desperate courage if that's all that is left to us. No, love does not protect us against suffering. What it does is—well you know. And death and everything inanimate must be so jealous of that."

Not so long ago they discovered a black hole in the center of our own Milky Way and saw it eating away at matter . . . the gravity so thick no light could escape past the event horizon. What is a black hole and why? And why in every galaxy, as they tell us? What is this universe really? And why? Especially since we know there is love? Why is it that we can love and the vast universe around us cannot? No one knows. No one even knows why things are, rather than they are not. If I knew I would tell you, believe me. As I would about suffering! "Nothing is certain in life except its uncertainty," Pirandello states, a man whose characters are shot through with laughter, albeit sometimes grotesque. Why do you think that is so? Because life is sometimes grotesque as well—grotesque because of this suffering that is so prevalent on planet earth. Pirandello asked this before Camus, and before Pirandello someone else, all the way back to the first conscious creature that looked up at the lonely sky. Why does this dimension we live in have to have so much suffering?

In answer, people say things like "it is a testing ground." But that only compounds the problem. What kind of a testing ground when a person can be so short-changed by nature and humanity? The truth is, so many people are born with such disadvantages, that one has to wonder how they could even or ever begin the expenditure of energy necessary to be what we might foolishly call enlightened? Where is the testing ground for Little Anthony or the baby starving to death in Africa? And no they aren't props for our spirituality! There is so much suffering and loss . . . even monsters born . . . what is this place? What am I doing here? Or you? How can we put together love with this universe? And yet . . . and yet there is love and there is this universe. Perhaps we can't put them together. We certainly can't answer the problem of suffering. But in the midst of it all, we *can* love. It is our deepest experience as conscious creatures as we look out at the wine dark sea or up at the night sky and wonder.

Allow me a breath of madness here . . . again returning to the two planks and a passion we call a play and Zero standing looking at a wall, alone in his cell and soul both, pondering aloud . . . or perhaps really talking to his wall. "So we continue where we left off—ever wondering about me. You're a good listener, I have to give you that. But why are you so quiet all the time." He stares at the wall. "Yes, it may be the only answer. To stare quietly at it all. But I have to tell you—break this sound barrier between us—I know that there is a radiantly joyous afterlife! I have had visitations telling me—no showing me so!" Silence. "More tub therapy is called for you say?" A pause. "The man down the hall says just you wait and see! He must have had visitations as well." A nod. "And so I have chosen to live in the world, but not exclusively of it. Though nothing could be more exclusively of it than this place." He laughs then goes all serious. "It makes you wonder why . . . why that side of the great divide is the way it is and this side is the way it is? Who knows what's what?" At that he turns to the audience, a long look. "Life is like talking to a wall." A sort of shrug. "Or talking to God." He laughs some. "They say I am mad. Damn mad if you ask me—over being mad. I gotta be honest with you, it doesn't make any sense to me. Me being mad." A pause. "Someone being sad. A tad too poor. Even being a lad . . . with a purse." He laughs then goes all serious. "I have to let you and"—he motions with his head towards the wall—"the wall, in on something. It has to do with me." He continues on in a near whisper. "You too. Oh now you're interested." He holds, letting the audience wait. "But why tell you what you already know. And if you don't, we should really change places." He laughs and comes back full voice. "To talk to the wall, to laugh out when no one else is . . . to love when the whole universe doesn't . . ." He quiets. "The final conclusion of my reasoning, or is it the final solution of my reasoning, anyway . . ." His voice drops off, returning with a somewhat smile. "And that, even as I continue on in this comic agony, firmly floored on two planks and a passion. A passion to tell you the only thing I know for sure . . . I am standing here talking to you. Of course, some people say that I'm not all there . . . but that is different than not being all here." He grows suddenly sad at that. "Believe me." He blinks. "Oh, there is one other thing I am sure of. An aberration in all this. Maybe an apparition as well. It is a word I dare not utter in polite society. You know what it is. You and my dog, Sperabamus, wherever he is." He stares at the audience, but doesn't say what it is. "Am I mad?" He turns away from them; then turns back even more quickly, goes to say something, then doesn't . . . as the spot dims on him.

The hard thing, ultimately, the one that gets you, is not just to live in the world, but to live missing what's missing. Oh, yes! But that truth has another with it. There is the gift of life, of course, but the gift of the gift of life is love, even as suffering comes with it, and a missing what's missing.

Perhaps like Augustine I am really writing my confessions here; so let me mention what I have only once before. I remember my mother being overdosed in the hospital even after we told her doctor she was super sensitive to medication. She became like Anna Magnani, her hair wild, her eyes bright, telling us she saw Mercury on the wall, and she was very paranoid about someone in the hospital trying to kill her (perhaps that was so who knows, since she died because of their negligence)—but her love reached through all that and she trusted us her children telling her that she was only seeing these things because of a reaction to the medication, the things weren't real. Her love was so strong that it could do that, reach through what she saw with her own eyes and thought with her own mind. Love can defy even the universe we find ourselves in; it is rooted so deeply in us, almost as if spanning more than spacetime itself. Perhaps that is why it is so hard to get to what it is. But love is its own revealer; it doesn't need me to tell you what it is. Yes, we are all left looking up at the night sky wondering, the desperate encounter between our human inquiry and the silence of the universe so real; yet so is our love.[125] The question is, how do we bring it all together? No one has answered that—not the scientists, not the philosophers, not Buddha, not Jesus, not the Wizard of Oz, *even after we opened the curtain and found him to be all too human.* Especially then! For not a one of us humans really has the answer to the question of suffering.

How, dear Galileo, do you bring together the rotating earth and the love you had for your daughter? That is the real problem here. Both are real. To deny either is only half the picture . . . half of the existence we are trying to explain. We have to answer the problem of putting it all together somehow, but it can't be any half-measure approach, or even a full-measured one, as it contains the un-measurable, at least partially so. So again, how, dear Galileo, do you bring together the rotating earth and the love you had for your daughter?

John Nash wrote the following in his autobiography for the Nobel: ". . . rationality of thought imposes a limit on a person's concept of his relation to the cosmos."[126] What can we say about our relation to the cosmos? Honestly say about it all? A Mona Lisa smile crossed a fat face when asked that . . . "To love, to live, to lose with grace, to just play the melody," the great comedian answered. Out of the mouths of babes, madmen, and comedians.[127]

Are we then all comedians locked in a madhouse from birth? Telling jokes without any real punch lines? Like Sack's people, each and all in our own asylum? Like Frankl, each and all in our own concentration camp? Is creation a madhouse? Is it a concentration camp for consciousness? There is so much suffering. And we definitely seem abandoned to it by the mysteries that made us. No, there is no philosophy or religion that can explain away suffering. In point of fact, there is just too much suffering! The litany of loss is so long and loud we can't ignore it. No, we can't ignore suffering. We can't and shouldn't. *In fact, it is part of our spirituality not to!* So what do we do, fight windmills? Or am I saying there is a way out of this? Some hope for humanity? At least for individual humans? It is always an *individual* inner decision after all.

Again, let's return to the journal of a dying man and this passage penned in it about walking in the park one rainy night, perhaps after reading Dawkins' or me—who knows?

> *Musuku, Africa's strange cemetery, called out in my drenched head. I had seen the place as a teen on a safari with my rich uncle after my brother's death, no doubt taken so as to get my mind off of it. How ironic! It was a place where the universe's fixation on death, in the form of an invisible gas—carbon monoxide—breathed out of a volcano called the Mountain of the Moon and blanketed everywhere around, in wait of any living creature to ventured into its domain of dreamless sleep. I remember seeing such a creature actually do so—and then find itself gasping for breath, its mouth open in shock and its eyes oxygen-hungry tongue covered with mucus in a matter of a moment. What thought up such a place?*
>
> *The absolute solitude that followed almost seemed to tell me, then as now. With an odd congruity my pondering pale eyes thought of the rat I once trapped with stickeem. The only thing in all my life I had ever killed. And in such a*

horrible way. I saw it shivering and squealing in pain as it died. The little creature merely ventured out of her hole . . . in the house me and my brother had recently moved into with our mom and sisters after our father passed away. My brother—the image of him brings back such a remembered pain. First my father, then my brother . . . "Tiger, tiger, burning bright, in the forest of the night, what immortal hand or eye, could frame thy fearful symmetry?"

My thirtysomething year old body stopped and felt a sudden chill shoot through me in that park thinking those things. "Whatever reality is, our suffering is real," I told those dripping trees, and now the icy windows I am looking out of. "The trick is to . . ." I remember stopping with that phrase for the second time that rainy night. "The trick is to . . ." My voice fell off and I said nothing after that for the longest time as the fog thickened around me. Finally, I got up and headed back home, the dogs splashing through the puddles beside me, obliviously enjoying the thrill of being alive. My lips cracked into a Mona Lisa smile despite myself and the demon night we three soaked creatures were making our way through. "Our suffering is real, but so is our love," I whispered to my two Old English, Tristan and Isolde.

No, Roger never wrote that page in the journal, I did, and put those words down as his these many years since he died, remembering my last phone call to him as I typed. Death had marked him and he was quite alone. Love doesn't end the suffering; it gives us a way to face it. Issa writes, upon the death of his child, this sad *haiku* showing his humanness and the world as so much more than what the Zen masters had told him.

This dewdrop world—
It may be a dewdrop,
And yet—and yet—

Love is the deepest experience in existence. You cannot have a philosophy without that fact as an essential part of it, nor a human spirituality either. The truth is, even if I never know the so-called Other, or solve the problem of suffering—I have existed! And I have loved! And Issa and Viktor Frankl, too, and Roger and Russell and . . .

Such is a human's most honest ontogenetic and ontological assertion both, no matter the time or place, no matter if these clever animals who inhabit this planet go far beyond it. Till death do us part and apart! And it may even be that the finality of death is what makes love so noble. Of course, neither you nor I nor anyone knows what death is, since we haven't experienced it for ourselves. It might lead to a radiant joy for all we know, as my madman says, and something mystic in me might hope. For, it may be that once the self comes into being, no matter how, it cannot end, and at our depths each of us knows something more essential about death than we think we do.

The poet John O'Donohue, who died not too long ago, wrote about the after-death in his beautiful book titled *Beauty*. It is similar to what I philosophically argue to, and I want to mention it for that reason, and also to pay tribute to a wonderful writer. "In much contemporary thinking," he writes, "there is the tendency to view death as simply dissolution whereby the body returns to mother earth and the spirit slips into the air to become one with the universe. While this claims a certain elemental continuity, it cannot be described as the eternal life of the individual. This view would accept death as a reversal and unraveling of the mysterious and intricate weaving of an individual life and it seems to offer very little. Indeed, all it delivers is a bland description of death as an elemental physical process. The intimacy and mystery of the individual life is merely loosed into anonymous, vague energy. In contrast, the resurrection promise is the continuity of the individual life in transfigured form. We will be ourselves."[128]

Death is the courage of absolute divestment, at least meeting it is, and in truth I don't know what death does to consciousness afterwards, but the actuality of death itself, dying, has always been ugly to me where I witnessed it, and any resurrection of the actual body per se sounds a primitive note to my ears. Yet, not the mystery of another dimension nor transfigured form, for it may be that once the self does come into being, no matter how, it cannot end, and at our depths each of us knows something more essential about death than we think we do, just as I said. Again, who knows? My point here being the marvel of what we do know: our existence here and now, and our love in it, despite everything, even how desperately hard it is to love at times, even at times left hopelessly loving, loving hopelessly, only with the giving of one's self and the loss of the one we love.

Love is still the wisdom in the waste. No, it doesn't end the waste or the emptiness left behind because of the waste, but it gives us a way at to face the emptiness, a meaning in and to the mess, even if a passing one, even if a hopeless one, even if one lone protest of one lone person, a voice crying in the wilderness, in the waste. No matter, it is real, more real than anything in us and for us. It is the most honest human holiness there is.

Russell wrote in his *Autobiography,* "that in human relations one should penetrate to the core of loneliness in each person and speak to that." Love does that.[129]

To see all the mistakes committed in the past, I would say one has to become some sort of a postmodern, uncertain to say the least. For from our contemporary vantage point we can see the marching orders of humankind in the past have been all over the place. Lives can be wasted on worthless causes or misguided ones and that is a cause for deep concern. But the guiding light in this is love itself allowed to be itself, something that always seeks to help not harm, to render kindness and not cruelty, something warm, unconditional, actually beautiful and good, a truth like no other in life, our tainted nature's solitary boast. In all the material as well as the mental swarming multiplicities and their misguided allegiances, in all the causes and isms, even as some are better than others for sure, just the point that I exist and have this light in the darkness is a major grounding in the uncertainty and *gives us a way to evaluate* each cause and ism, paradigm and politic, religion and ritual. The problem may be in the vessel itself, but so is love, so is the beauty and goodness and truth of love. Even as we have the raw elemental energies of evolution and that very selfish gene in us, there is this last best hope in us and for us as well, individually at least, even as a world might goose step down one avenue of worthless cause after another, ultimately even destroying the very planet we all are alive to. No I am not Cassandra, nor was meant to be. But this globe is in great trouble. Perhaps, as I already said the only 'salvation' is a personal one, even as we would save the planet and every living creature on it. But that is love—that very desire to do so, even as we might fail in doing so! That call to give of ourselves is love calling up from the very depths of our being. We are not deconstructed to a void or vacuum for there is a universal grounding in our existence and in the deepest experience in that existence, and in these we know a certainty, and a phenomenon called love in that certainty of presence. This is the basis and call coming out of this chapter.

Poetically I might call it the Eastering of existence, a *contemplatio ad amorem*, the final dharma, the supreme koan, ultimate karma, the gardening of the Serengeti, true tikkun, or a litany of other expressions, but it simply comes down to love, the beauty and goodness and truth of love. Awareness at its greatest profundity is *amor in actu*, this love in action. It is each of us at our greatest profundity.

As daunting and nebulous as this odyssey of being that is ours seems, it provides the way, to living and to dying, too, when that event comes calling and consciousness faces what it has created of itself. Who I am and the deepest experience in me, in communion with what I witness without in the form of beauty and goodness and love speaking to my own depths, gives me my grounding in the universe of things. Once this reality coming from the depth of our own humanness is grasped, one can only want to live and die accordingly. Yes, looking with the eyes of love and listening deeply to the cries of the world, one knows how to act, expecting nothing in return.

The deepest encounter with existence is this. *It is our purely human spirituality.*

Have you ever wondered where the unedited, uninhibited, unharnassed mind would lead? Of course there is no such mind, in *any* human head, but dare I say, our choice to love is the closest thing to such a thing. To such a freedom! Each of us in the face of existence can indeed be the incarnation of love, since that is within the make up of our humanity and the purely human spirituality that comes out of it.

No, Dorothy, there is no Santa, but there is a purely human spirituality. And when looked at honestly, it is, my dear, far better than if a Santa existed, for the gift here is better by far. We humans have found a way to live, and a way to die—one within our very breath and being. We have the gift of life and the gift of the gift of life love, even as suffering comes with both, and a missing what's missing, too.

Everyone surely agrees that the context in which we live our lives matters; matters if for no other reason than that it affects us and others. We have not been superficial about this; we have talked about the deepest meaning within our make up. It remains for us to realize it. Despite the siren songs coming from the sea of uncertainty all around us, when we are sensitive to this deepest part of life and living, the deepest part of our humanness, not only do we attain the basic truth about ourselves, but when we do that, *and act upon it*, we are alive to and live human holiness as the wisdom it is. It is an enlightenment and enactment of and about existing, existing as who we are. As I groped to give it expression, to embellish and enhance on it, I used different words and phrases, variations on the theme as it were, all honest in their grasp of spirituality, and I hope fully appreciated as such. Yet, but, and however, all that is really needed to know about our purely human spirituality is what you already know. It always comes back to this for each and everyone of us: *I am and I can love.*

"This above all—to thine own self be true." That is Shakespeare's advice to you, and mine as well, but most important, existence itself tells you this. We listened to existence in our venture here in the first chapter of this book, and because we did we laid the foundation for the rest of our sojourn. The purpose of this chapter was exactly that, to establish presence and to penetrate into it, with profundity. Without that we could never have come to a purely human spirituality.

Staccato thoughts shot and shouted out of me, not as a system, but as the soul of life and living, of *moi et toi*, this marvel called presence. So very many moons after I "conceived" of presence, I came across a phrase in Heidegger that both delighted and stunned me: "presence of what is present." "So he used presence, too," I told my Old English. I could make light of it and say great minds think a like, but rather will say what it really means, that it reinforces the minimal certainty we all come to, whether you ever heard of me, or me of him, or he of the Greeks, or the Greeks of God. What it speaks of is what we nearly but never achieve in words, our very existence, what is fundamentally present to us and which we must take to heart. Of course, even when we do there is no assurance of anything, and yet there is, an assurance about ourselves as that very presence, and in it, the deepest reality in being present . . . and maybe, just maybe, even an insight into the Mystery that made us. Of course, our own presence gives us plenty to pursue, but to add the Mystery, well, yes, it is like trying to tie the air together with that impossible injection into our venture.

No matter, it is the double-helix I spoke of in the introduction to this masterpiece, not merely as a venture coming closer to understanding *moi et toi*, but the added one of finding the Source of *moi et toi* and everything with us. I have the foundation, now I want to know the Foundation. This is the totality of the venture. "Madness personified," my shaggy shadow says as he wonders aloud why I just don't enjoy the moment and play in the sun and splash in the glorious puddles after the downpour. He may be right, of course, and I, this presence *moi*, mad in such a double-dare pursuit, which may double-cross me in the end, but here I am trying to explain to him, and you, dear lone last reader, it's who I am. And I think all us with me in our truest moments. Who can deny the venture, the adventure, of finding God? Not me—it is consciousness, awareness, wondering about the depths of its own being, delving and diving into its own love. Where many stop with being and only being alone as their pursuit, for me a deeper drive must be pursued, the ability to give of that very being. This radiant self-manifestation of what is our deepest awareness maybe of some importance in this divine discourse, dialogue, dialectic at our depths that we must uncover, discover, disclose to ourselves about ourselves. Oh what an adventure it is to be *moi et toi!*

So, remembering both the inscape of our very humanness and the landscape of the world without, and realizing that the communion therein, namely, of who I am and my deepest experience in being, along with what I witness without in the form of beauty and goodness and love gives me the confirmation of my grounding in existence itself let me end this chapter of our venture by saying that I must challenge the prevailing punditry in postmodern and perhaps all philosophical thought. I must challenge it based on what we have dug up here from existence alone, within the sinews of our being, in the unedited, uninhibited, unharnassed depth of it, namely, something which has braved hunger, pain, and the survival drive itself and established for us, past the tyranny of the thinking of our own age, even until some human on this or whatever far off planet is the last of our kind, a truly human spirituality. From that, and that alone, rooted as it is in existence and the deepest experience in existence, though we are still confounded and confused in so many ways and still tinged with hesitation, *can I dare to say that there is now* a possibility of somehow someway venturing into the Mystery that made us? Does the root-reality of our being, *I am and I can love*, stop there for we conscious creatures in the cosmos, having led us to more in life and living, or can it lead us not only to more but to More, the Mysterious More?

Stopover At A Cave[1]

"Candide," Zero prompted, "what's wrong?"

The flames from the fire fought off the cold air and dancing shadows on the tall cave walls encircling them. Candide shook his head no. He obviously didn't want to talk about it. "It doesn't matter," the other man responded. "I can tell. You're a man who lives in his eyes."

Candide lifted his eyebrows some, then pulled the blanket he had wrapped around him a little tighter. After a short stare further into the cave he put another damp log on the fire.

Zero watched him. "Don't you think you ought to take your medicine?" he asked in that way of his, his continued chatter cutting into Candide's need for quiet.

"What medicine?" Candide asked.

Zero never answered; instead he confused the former gravedigger with yet another question out of the blue. "Would you have killed them?"

"Killed who?" Candide asked.

"Them," Zero said pointing to the animals. "When we got really down to the bone. Is that what's making you so moody? So goddam morose? That you're not—"

"No," Candide answered firmly, shaking his head.

"No, that you wouldn't have or no that's not what's bothering you?"

"Just no!"

"No, I don't believe you would have, Candide," Zero said, as if honestly thinking about it. "But I'm not sure what I would have done," he added so matter-of-fact it gave Candide pause. "Left here alone with them and hungry."

"What do you mean left here alone?"

Zero laughed as if it were a ridiculous question. "If it's the other way around, just promise you'll dance on my grave," he insisted. "As I will on yours," he promised. "Whoever goes first. Promise me, Candide, you'll swirl around on top of me in that old red terry cloth robe of yours. Dancing about like a silly ole—"

"Let's just stop it, huh!" Candide interrupted.

"Stop what, dying?" Zero teased.

At first Candide didn't answer; then he mumbled out what sounded like 'eating ourselves up with nonsense.'

"But if a man is starving?" Zero pressed.

"You eat your heart out," Candide answered with a trace of impatience and plopped his socks down.

"And if you have no heart?"

"I thought it was no head—you've got to keep your story straight. Otherwise . . ." Candide's voice dropped off, he was obviously tired of this.

"Otherwise?" Zero insisted; then cocked his head in wait.

Candide merely shook his head in answer; unable to contain a yawn that went on for three larger and larger mouth openings and a long sigh as its finale.

"Tedium. Tedium. Tedium." Zero glared at the man across the fire from him. *"I'll try to be more entertaining from here on in,"* he screamed at the top of his lungs, throwing whatever was closest to him—a glove—into the fire. "Keep my story straight," he mumbled, as if that had bothered him far more than the yawn. His face hung in a flushed contortion, his pale eyes holding as if in some encounter with the primordial forces that formed us.

An uncomfortable stillness fell over the cave. The foul smell from the burning glove prompted Candide to poke a stick into the flames and push it aside. "We're not that hungry yet are we?"

His effort drew only an exasperated sigh from the madman. He was obviously annoyed with Candide, but as well with himself for some reason or other; and when the other man's pale eyes pried, Zero lowered his.

"Remember what you asked me? About what's wrong?" Zero looked up at the questioner. "Everything." Candide sat on the phlegm rising in his throat. "There is no redemption," he managed to get out, getting hold of himself as he did.

"Why, what did you do, Candy Man? That there's no redemption for you?" The voice out of the other man was taunting and meant to be.

"I wasn't talking about myself so much as everything. But since you asked. There are things I can never do over again. Never repair. You can't repair the past. It's irreparable."

"Does this have to do with what I think it does?"

Candide didn't take the bait. Where he had just been sapped any fight on his part. "Let's just say helping out a young madman does not correct it," he answered, and then nearly succumbed again. "Nothing does . . . even being heartbroken for what I've done," he murmured, still leaving unsaid what it was.

A painful moment passed. Zero went to say something from across the smoking flames; then, instead, he shook his head and looked away.

Candide's face tightened. The former gravedigger felt he had missed something very private and very painful in Zero's reaching look. "Zero," he quietly invited across to him. "Zero?"

Zero turned back. He studied Candide with the same intensity the odd-shaped man was studying him. The handsome man lowered his head and began to sob. It was with such bewilderment that Candide got up and went over to him.

"It's nothing," Zero said in the thinnest of voices. He sniffled, wiped at his nose with his sleeve, and then looked directly into the flames instead of at the man standing over him. The fire's light glistened in his concentrating eyes. Its glow played off his fine disheveled hair creating a halo effect. He could have been an angel by Caravaggio. Candide liked his comparison.

"Do you want to tell me?" the older man asked. The smoke from the resisting moisture in the burning wood circled around the fire, drifting across to the two of them wrapped in their Quechua blankets. The question was said in a tone of such genuine concern it made the younger man turn and look up at Candide with a face full of confusions.

Zero shook his head no—as if denying what he heard in the other man's voice with an unmistakable and sudden hardening in his own. "Forget it. You love them. Would die before you hurt them. That's that. Sorry I brought it up."

"Well I wouldn't have eaten you either if it'll make you feel better," Candide informed him with the threat of a little grin teasing at his lips; wondering how they got back to that.

The younger man again studied the face looking down at his. "You're eating me alive, Candy Man."

"Actually you're more than I can swallow."

"Likewise," Zero shot back, suppressing his irritation.

Candide could only nod as he watched Zero drop the Quechua blanket from his shoulders and stand stretching his neck and wiggling his strong back. Out of nowhere Zero smiled a beautiful smile over at Candide, a young man's virility breathing out of every pore in his splendid body. The sudden, almost abrupt change in Zero left Candide looking like dumb Dora. The older face smiled back, clumsily; Candide telling himself it had to be the cave. Not enough oxygen was getting to the brain he concluded—his own included. Especially so with the notion that was running through it at the moment! What a ridiculous thought, he told himself, holding on the smiling young man. What was he trying to do here?

Hadn't he just told Zero that nothing could redeem that! Yet, wasn't he trying to do just that, replacing one with the other in his pathetic way, the pale-eyed man scolded at himself.

A gush of cold wind found the mouth of the cave and was swallowed by it, leveling the fire's flames momentarily. The old fluffy sheepdog licked at the man with no name's hand and immediately proceeded to sit beside him and lean his body against Candide's. He was joined by two wobbly pups dragging their fat bellies, and then a woolly stray—all, in turn, mimicking the leader of their furibund pack and finding their way to Candide and then a place on him to call their own. Like intent detectives they began sniffing for that certain smell that is known only to the tiny gray cells in each canine head and finding it, laid their chins and paws and whatever on the amused fat man.

"How does it feel?" Zero asked, as if in suggestion of what he himself might want, whatever it was. A strange sensation came into Candide as he watched the laughing man—as if they had indeed shared a cell together other than this cave. It's the lack of oxygen, the former gravedigger reminded himself yet again, and gave his full attention to watching a memory—no, not a memory at all—but what could have been, but wasn't, his mind murmured. Zero bent down to pull his *amerindio* blanket back over his shoulders, and as he did, caught Candide's studied stare out of the corner of his eye and turned directly towards the sad man.

"What's wrong, Candide?"

A long pause followed. It was obvious Candide wasn't going to answer again.

"You remind me of mad Joanna," Zero said in a graceful whisper. "The daughter of Ferdinand and Isabella," he explained, trying to lighten the mood of the man.

"Yes, I know the story," Candide said quietly. "Everywhere she went, she carried with her, the embalmed remains of her husband, Philip the Fair." The words had none of his usual comic opera in their tone. Not even philosophical catharsis. It was a tone of flat fact. Pure authenticity. The pale-eyed man looked at Zero as if the former gravedigger was himself one of his corpses, if not the remains of Philip the Fair himself. It sent a chill through the madman.

"What's wrong?"

"Nothing," the younger man answered.

"Are you cold?"

"No."

Candide put yet another soggy log on the fire just in case Zero was being needlessly brave; then he turned and went to make sure the blankets at the back of the bird cages had no drafts coming through. After that, like a watchman doing rounds, he checked that the front of the cages, which were opened towards the flames, were not too hot for the birds . . . that the rabbit, goose, and cat were comfortable . . . and that the pups were not too close to the fire.

Zero watched him all the while. "Candide."

Candide looked around at him.

"Even if you would end up an old man living without a pension and no children to look after you, no wife to care for you in your decline; unloved and alone until a mechanized gravedigger buried you"—his flickering face held but a moment—"so what? You've had thoughts no man has ever had."

Candide made no reply one way or the other at first, and then smiled a weathered smile at the younger man. "Is that to be my posthumous revenge on life?" he asked. "Engraved on my tombstone? *Here lies Candide, a man who had thoughts no man has ever had!* I think we've both been in this cave too long," he said ruefully.

The flames from the fire danced against Zero's shadowed features. Whether from the cave's stingy supply of oxygen or actual cabin fever itself, Candide swore those pale irises looking back at him were guardians of unspoken secrets, of places seen which no trespasser could ever touch upon without forfeiting his or her own salvation . . . be it called sanity or a soul. Again, like some odd déjà vu he felt they were together again in a strange whereabouts. Candide was ox-eyed.

"What's wrong now?"

"I'm getting senile," the former gravedigger responded, brushing off his escapade in the twilight zone as he called it. He came and poured more cognac for both himself and his fellow cave man.

"Let's all get barmy and join the army," the fat bartender started up, downing his amber liquid in song and going on in his own rendition of *Die Dreigroschenoper* . . . *"See the world in all its mirth!"*

"Let's all get barmy and join the army," Zero joined in, swinging his glass of cognac with the beat . . . *"see the world in all its mirth!"*

He waited for the next line from the Maestro. Instead, Candide hugged at the surprised Zero, holding on as if for dear life while lifting and dancing him around the fire!

"What's up?" his surprised partner asked happily, like a child being introduced to a new game.

"What's up? What's down? What's upside down?" Candide answered and whistled over towards the birds.

The parrot punctuated his sudden outburst with a loud squawk. It started up the cockatiel who whistled and tweeted away. *"I luv ya. I luv ya. I luv ya,"* the littlest bird instigated; his parakeet bravura making the two men burst out laughing.

"I luv ya, too! I luv ya, too! I luv ya, too!" Zero mimicked, looking around at Candide's menagerie of big and little eyes looking back at him in amazement. *"All of ya! All of ya! All of ya,"* he went on in an orchestrated whisper of buffoonery that cocked every dog's head and made the old cat extremely suspicious.

Candide interrupted his part of the laughing duet with a sudden choking that soon became a coughing fit. It broke off their dance and left Zero practically holding up Candide. "My breathing is bad tonight," the purple face said through his asthmatic spasm and apologetic nod. "It must be the smoke from the wet wood," he managed to get out as he sat down with the help of the firm hands holding him.

For a moment—the blink of an eye—those hands felt like they belonged to someone else. And Candide felt those steely eyes again—staring at him—and himself naked and cold. A moment more and all the dogs were around the coughing man suffocating him with their concern. Noses and kisses came at him from all sides; the old shaggy actually sticking his own face directly into that of Candide's to see for himself what was the matter with the apple of his one visible eye. The birds quieted and watched intently, turning their heads just so to see. Even the rabbit and the old cat interrupted their secret thoughts to find out what was the matter; one with a head half-lifted towards the raucous, the other with two funny ears listening intently to all the goings-on. The goose stopped her fidgeting and waddled closer with a few pesky honks, joining the others at ringside.

The 'crisis' subsided and Candide's breath came back to him. "Feels good, huh?" Zero teased, laughing and then telling the ringside audience the fight for life was over, they should go get ready for dinner. He smiled coyly with that remark and Candide stopped himself from laughing. He had no intention of starting up his damn coughing again.

Zero took up the large hunting knife from the cutting board by the fire. It froze Candide for a mistrustful moment, but he didn't let on. "Not by laughter alone does man live," Zero said, and cut some cornbread. He winked Candide's way and hung the pot filled with the last of their black beans over the fire, stirring at it with the same large knife as the rich hot sauce of mountain peppers begin to bubble. With the precision of an impeccable European restaurateur he handed a tin plate to his senior partner, along with a bent spoon, then gracefully put his own banged up plate and dented spoon down in front of himself, reaching half a torn towel over to Candide as his napkin and taking the other half as his own. That done, he stirred once again at the bean stew Candide had concocted.

After he fed the dogs some of the cornbread and beans, he fed cornbread to the birds and then the rabbit and hungry goose—and woke the old cat who didn't want to eat just yet. Finally, what was left he served to the former gravedigger and himself.

Candide had watched the whole affair with surprised delight. Besides, it was nice to be served for once. The two men ate away at their bean stew, dabbing their crumbling cornbread with a touch of hot mango jam every so often and downing it all with some black coffee spiked with cognac to warm their shivering insides.

When the devil-may-care feast saw the end of their provisions swallowed up and every plate empty, Zero asked if he could read to Candide. "It's what I thought about," he explained, "when I was alone with myself and told only the laptop." Candide teased that it would be a nice way to fall asleep and nodded for him to go ahead and read.

But Zero never opened the laptop. Instead, he just sat there sipping at his cognac, listening to the windstorm howling outside.

"Do you really think it's hiding some secret? This funny ole world?"

Candide went surprisingly silent.

At first Zero seemed to think Candide was wondering how to honestly answer him. Answer himself for that matter. But Candide's continued silence changed Zero's mind and he decided it was a form of mockery. He nodded a vigorous nod and laughed defensively. "You're right, I'm starting to sound like you. All head and halloween."

"That's what a gravedigger's about," Candide replied with a cover of his own. "Even a former one," he added, his whimsy abruptly dropping off, as though his pales were suddenly somewhere else, lost in some grief buried deep in the recesses of his past and remembered yet again this cold night.

"Are you thinking about that baby again?"

The engrossed eyes looked over at the questioner.

"Yes and no," Candide answered honestly; for he was indeed thinking about a baby, just not the one Zero meant. But since he asked about it, he had a question of his own concerning that hapless encounter. "Why didn't it bother you?"

Zero didn't respond.

"It doesn't leave a hole in your heart? In life itself?" Candide asked so poignantly it brought a surprised smile to Zero's face.

"Surely, gravedigger, you've seen somebody dead before," he answered across the fire.

"Worse than that—dying," Candide responded, refusing to make light of it.

"Why is that any worse?"

"If you ever saw it, you'd know."

Zero's face took on a stiff defiance. "Have you ever seen someone go mad before your very eyes?" he asked of his gravedigger bitterly. "Before your very mirror?" he added, his face contorting. "There's no trust to place anywhere after that! And despite what some Zen shitmaster might say with his fucking little koan, you're real and know you're fading away before your very fucking and frightened eyes. Does that make me in the know about something worse than death?" he barked at the other man.

Candide's silence hung in the heavy air.

"Apparently, you know the mirror I'm talking about," Zero said.

"Life is the madness I was thinking about," Candide answered him. "Is there a point to all this struggle . . . all this suffering . . . the death of that baby," he pause a beat, "or any other?"

The fire cracked and the flames' ghosts played against the damp walls of the still cave, while outside the winds howled and the night's mirthless storm swept across the mountain, drowning the cries of any creatures lost in it.

Perhaps we're all lost in it, Candide told himself. Lost with a long horrible laugh coming out of it, he added, thinking back on those abandoned to their wired windows of madness. He could hear their lost laughter in his head. It was abysmal. The savage shrill glued the gravedigger's requiem eyes past what he was looking at to what he was hearing. In the temper of their surroundings, it sounded to Candide like the laugh of laughs behind it all . . . laughing at the laugh itself. He mouthed that to himself, in a dry silence, his jaw slightly ajar because he knew it did unhappily touch at something incoherent deep inside of him—something primordial that surpassed understanding, monstrous and meaningless—something so alien and chilling Candide cringed—how could any consciousness not—left as it was, standing as what, crying out to what?

"How do we cope," he asked aloud.

"If you want to know how I cope," Zero answered, thinking Candide was being facetious, "I stay alive with the courage of your hallucinations."

Candide didn't look up from the flickering fire. The inscape behind those holding pales was deep into itself, thinking back to what had to be the earliest of thoughts, before words, and that same forever question, passed down through a cave like this and fire just like theirs, from a time before fire and cavemen and hallucinations, at the dawn of consciousness itself, when consciousness awoke to find itself in an unconscious cosmos.

The thoughtful man poked at the burning logs, wondering if awareness could ever figure out itself . . . know itself without any fall or fire fables, or ones coming out of our latest pantheon, from follyforgers posing as profound in fields sounding so imposing to the modern mind?

"Candide."

He heard his name and looked around at the nameless man sharing the cave and fire with him. "Do you," Zero ask, his bright pale irises seemingly smitten with some strange reprieve, "do you—" he stopped as suddenly as he had started.

"Do I what?"

"Do you really believe that there could be more, more than—"

Zero's words broke off, and Candide didn't help him finish what he wanted to ask. Instead, the former gravedigger's own pale eyes betrayed any declared resolution. Something of a solemn utterance called out of the layers upon layers of complexity that made up the creature calling himself Candide—but like some pondering pendulum his mind swung back the other way, a question-mark burned into the walls of his skull, asking yet again if this was only born of fear to get him through the night, or a door that opened upon a beyond, in quiet moments acting upon the mind and removing it from the mundane to something more, as if on invisible wings, our intuitions tasting at things unknown and hidden, but there nonetheless, and so much more than this our world and the raw elemental energies of evolution that formed it and us in it? A frown came to his face; his lips readied as if about to say something. His hesitancy in doing so, however, brought a hesitancy of its own to the younger man.

The failed philosopher shrugged.

"What is that supposed to mean?" Zero asked, a hint of impatience in his tone.

"I always felt there would always be, magic in my life," Candide disclosed. "That I was, sort of anointed. From my earliest remembrance I always expected special treatment from some mysterious more and had this strange feeling, beyond and yet the very core of me." A muddled something or other followed, mingled with deep lines of pain that gained prominence on his shimmering features.

"And?" Zero prompted.

Candide and his more than half a century of living let out a sigh. "Sitting quietly, doing nothing, time goes by, and the grass grows."

The crackling fire reflected against the pair of faces. Candide pensively held at his cognac and Zero held on his; then the younger man smiled in such a quiet despair, murmuring something Candide couldn't quite catch. The former gravedigger was about to ask him to repeat it when Zero reached for the laptop, but taking it up, still didn't open it. Instead, he drank down a whole mouthful of burning cognac; giving himself a shiver.

"I read what was in your laptop while you were gone to Saint Hilary's," the anonymous madman confessed. "That's how I knew why . . . why you continue the search for a soul. Despite your—well despite what you just now displayed. It's because you know everything is riding on it—for you—and someone else as well."

A long time passed before either of the two took up talking again after that. "If you must know," Zero said, filling the void, "I added some stuff of my own to your laptop—to what you had written. But I already told you that didn't I." The odd-shaped fat man nodded, but didn't remember Zero saying he added to what *he* had written. "I should read it to you," the handsome intruder went on. "What I put in." A little grin creased at his nervous lips. He waited for Candide to say something; but he didn't. "Aren't you going to ask?"

"No."

"I'll tell you anyway."

"I sort of thought you would."

"We must take the best and most irrefragable of human doctrines and embark on that as if it were a raft on which to risk the voyage of life. Unless it were possible to find a stronger vessel, something holy, some Sacred Meaning on which we might take our journey more surely and with confidence." Zero stopped reading from the laptop for a moment and then continued on. "Plato's prayer shows us that the groping genius realized the struggle—searching as he did for something *more* in us that will show us a more certain way to knowing our inner selves and the truth of being." Zero laughed a little laugh. "What shit! That's what I added to what you wrote," he said with scholarly testosterone.

"Yet you say you stay alive with the courage of *my* hallucinations, nonetheless."

Zero toasted a touché Candide's way. "No greater *love* is there than that a man share his hallucinations," he added, making it obvious to Candide what blissful hallucination in particular he was mocking.

"To borrowed quotes and borrowed hallucinations," Candide said, holding out his cup.

"It's essential for a man who couldn't possibly have any of his own," Zero added as he swallowed at his bent cup of distilled wine, then pointed to his head to remind his traveling companion.

"To borrowed heads," Candide said in a near whisper. He touched his bent cup to Zero's, drinking to that and pouring another. And another after that!

On the round after the round after that, or the one after that, or was it the one still being downed, the building response inside of the fat imbiber burst out of the perspiring man. "Still, even if you're right and I'm drunk wrong and foolborn—merely sounding off in a bottled bliss—still," he made an effort to point out (the subject matter of his pronouncement apparently left hanging in air as well) "still, even if Candide *is* only a failed philosopher reaching in the dark and stumbling along, from comic womb to incoherent tomb, *still* we still have to still figure out how to still live over it all, through it all, in the midst of it all. Before the elements that make us up pull apart and we are no more."

"And we have!" Zero protested with a drunkard's laugh; his penetrating eyes alive with a boldness beyond the cognac and mere cavalier; seemingly tempting the fates at the very edge of giddy sanity itself. "I already showed you! Remember?" he underlined Candide's way, laughing away with eyes as icy as they were on that mountaintop, when they found the dead baby.

Candide held on his handsome drinking partner, almost sober. "Yours is an empty offer," he murmured. "An empty offer."

"No, Candide, yours is the empty offer." Zero picked up the empty bottle they had already finished and turned it upside down, pouring out nothing and looking at the former gravedigger. "As empty as this bracer you down every day to get through the night."

Candide grabbed the bottle out of Zero's hand. *"I have witnessed,"* he said through his teeth as he shook the bottle at him. *"I have witnessed . . ."* Candide's words fell off and the shaking bottle came to a standstill. He set it down.

"Yes?"

Zero waited.

"Something . . ." Candide was like a man pondering aloud, his voice low, as if not knowing how he might put it.

Zero looked at him with emaciated eyes and only half a smile, mockingly taking his drink away from him as if he'd had much too much.

Candide pulled it back and drank it down; then grabbed at a full bottle and poured himself another, and one for his madman, too. "I have witnessed . . ."

"What, gravedigger, what have you witnessed? I hope you're not going to tell me about the opaque vision of yours again!"

Candide shook his head no. "Whether it be madness, sanity, a dream, or a divine comedy, I have witnessed . . ."

"Yes?"

"The only thing that makes sense in life," the odd-shaped fat man asserted in a committed pose, holding his bent cup out as if a drunkard about to have armed combat with ocean waves and the cosmos itself. He waited a breathless beat, and the cave with him it seemed, and then nodded vigorously with what looked like too much wine in his will.

Zero's smile widened to a near shit-eating grin. "Yes, and as I already told you, that's got to be the best *hallucination* you ever had, Candy Man. Certainly in the same league with those I heard coming out of the padded cells in Ward Z. Actually WXYZ," Zero added in a distilled drollery.

Candide blanched, his bracer at his lips. "If that's an hallucination," he said in a near whisper, "then so am I. And you as well."

At first, Zero didn't oblige his thoughtful drinking mate; then he shrugged. "Who can say?"

"I can!" Candide insisted, standing—somewhat—"I can!" he said, trying to free them both from the awkward moment of committing the unforgivable sin. He blinked or his brandy did. "Can something that isn't real run this river? Struggle? Strive? Shiver? *Feel!?*" he underlined. "Feel loneliness, the call of freedom, the stretch towards forever, the chill of its own ending no matter, the horrendous heartrending loss of those loved and so often failed, the longing to see them all again, the world-weary wonder, ghastly grief, and giddiness of being?! I am hardly an hallucination! I am and I can love!"

And with that and a clap of thunder as his lead-in, Candide opened his mouth and began to belt out the aria of another famous clown, as if seized with life's absolute truth or absolute folly.

Zero could only double over and laugh, laugh his ass off as he often said. Yet, the old trooper didn't break character; he delivered his lines as his grandfather—who used to direct him in kitchen versions of Pirandello, Plautus, and Pagliacci—would have demanded, singing away as if he no longer knew what he was saying or doing, and hurling the liquor in his cup high in the air as if to prove his point. No, he no longer did know and he didn't give a damn or a flying shit. It was New Year's farchrissake! And would always be! For him! Wasn't that what they were arguing about! Him!? Whether he was real and could love?! "*Tu se' Candido!*" he challenged, coming back on his challenger with a comic grimace covering his flushed face, the language of his ancestors ringing out that he must laugh even as he suffers over love. "*Ridi, Candido, sul tuo amore infranto!*"

By then, all the animals were up and in a fuss; the old shaggy barking away—even Zero himself swept up in Candide's sobbing merry-go-round, the somewhat comically shaped fat man repeating over and over again his awkward rendition urging everything and everyone and everywhere to laugh!

The wind outside their snug surroundings howled across the battered mountain as though in some long laugh of its own. A horrible laugh. First the animals and then Zero, and finally Candide as well quieted, listening. No, it was not answering them—it didn't even know they were there. They could be there or not, still the indifferent storm would rage on. And did. The wind roared and a tree fell making its sooty sound. It didn't matter whether they could hear it, could see it, where alive, or not. And certainly not whether they laughed or cried. Or even loved. It suddenly became bitter cold. The two men, and all the animals with them, huddled around the fire and held on it for the longest time. Outside, the storm raged on and another indifferent tree fell somewhere. Candide couldn't help wondering if earlier cave men felt the same way. Absently he petted at his shaggy 'wolf' and Zero sipped at his 'fire water'.

The cup seemed to stick to Zero's lips and he held on the eyes looking into his own. It was more than uncanny. Candide again had that feeling of elsewhere and he seeing past the profound mask of flesh and bone into something so strange it defied interpretation—other than to say it felt *foreboding*. Was it the storm causing this reflection in the pale eyes looking back at his own—in some odd challenge that told them of the madness we all are at bottom?

Out of the blue, as if Zero had become the very storm itself, the quite young man sitting beside him went super-nova on Candide. It was with a murderous fury. A rage roared out of him full of snarls and guttural growls, his stiff hands clawing, scratching, smashing his cup to the ground and hurling what was left of the bottle of cognac against the cave wall. In the blink of a startled eye Candide found the only other human in the cave with him glaring into his eyes like a rabid cannibal preparing for the kill.

"Get behind me, Candide! Get behind me!" he yelled out in an enormous voice. *"You and your temptation!"*

Just as sudden, with that, the nameless man sank back, exhausted. His bright pale eyes cooled. The contortions vanished. He was back again, in a strange fixation, his sweating face held riveted on the cave entrance. "Because you're wrong, Candide. All wrong." He nodded somewhat, gesturing out towards the cave opening with an indefinable sense of wrongness about it all. "All wrong, Candide."

The older man found such a forlorn face looking back at his own. It told Candide through a cup too many perhaps, that he was indeed wrong—the cognac turning tannic in his thinking processes—silent and very serious staccato thoughts telling him that this thing called living *is* wrong. *All wrong!* A poem he had written as a teenager traveling with his father came to mind—he wrote it after their last visit to the Dark Continent. He had lost parts of it with the years.

Vaguely Candide heard himself turn towards Zero and even felt himself nodding. "I always wanted to sing like that," he said, in what sounded like some tangent answer to both himself and the younger man. "My mother was an opera singer after all. Used to sing a lot in the kitchen. One time in particular sticks out as she was cutting onions for the pasta sauce. I had just witnessed a little bird caught by chance in my father's lens. As well as the mouth of a Raven," he added with remembering eyes. "I ran from our hiding place. And my sister with me—to protect me as she always did! This time from my own outrage! I screamed up the tall tree at what I was witnessing. The squirming bird was gulped down in disappearing swallows no matter. My soul suffocating with its! When I told my mother about the horror on our return home, a long silence ensued. Until, that is, a single note from her lifted out of the quiet . . . and then another . . . and another after that . . . until what sounded like a bittersweet aria filled the kitchen, confusing the younger mind, and this older one still."

The tears rolled down Candide's face.

"Why are you crying?"

"It's the onions." The older man let his eyes wander across the dreary cave, then come back and settle on the shaggy dog beside him. He reached over and petted at Ubermensch with a remembering hand. "We had hoped . . . were hoping . . . that's what his name meant. My *first* dog, Sperabamus."

The younger man's glare cut across the fire as if he wanted to say something; something profoundly private; something universe-shaking he had to say to this gravedigger. Candide meanwhile, unaware, bend over and kissed the ole shaggy on the top of his hairy white head.

Candide's innocent gesture only perplexed the handsome listener all the more. His bright pale eyes were dancing in his head; as if indeed they didn't belong in that borrowed skull and wanted out. It was obvious he wanted so badly to say whatever it was he had to say; but before he could, Candide, without looking up, stopped him with a peppery interruption. "This one I called Superman," the odd fat man exclaimed with a touch of the aria still left in his strained throat. "Cause Superman can't die!"

"Yes, he will, Candide."

It wasn't said maliciously to hurt the former gravedigger—or sadly either on his part. Just as fact. Plain fact, devoid of anything else. Candide looked over at the other man in the cave with him. "You do have a way about you."

"I never met anyone like you either. You're insane, Candide. More so than any and all the nuts in every and all the madhouses there are or ever will be." Zero shook his head as if amazed, annoyed, and confused all in one by this stranger! "Insane!" he underlined, seemingly more for himself for whatever reason.

"I suppose I am," Candide vocalized softly to his younger companion. He lifted his eyebrows as if for no particular reason, his face holding on some thought or other behind it. "I suppose I am," he repeated ever so sadly, looking across at the other man in the cave with him. I lost my little boy, he wanted to tell him. That would drive any man crazy. I couldn't protect him. Couldn't save him. I saw his mouth gasping for air. He died like that . . . so brave. *A bitter blessing . . . because . . .* Candide could barely get his thoughts out to himself, let alone to the other man. We cremated him . . . the gravedigger cremated his only begotten. Of course, I wasn't a gravedigger then. There was a mental pause and then he went on. He was gone and it was forever. For the blink of an eye, full sentences fell off into a sorrow without words. His death destroyed my world . . . my trust . . . my God . . . my everything. A long moment followed. It left a hole in me forever. I lost my little boy, he wanted to tell him. "I'm tired, Zero," he said instead. "Very tired."

The agony in his words puzzled Zero. "Candide?" he pressed, his concern obvious. He poured more cognac for him while finding another cup for himself.

Candide took up the cup and barely drank at it. He nodded a thank you to Zero who nodded back. "Too bad we don't have some Cointreau and lemons. Then we could make that drink you like so much." What Zero was referring to was a drink Candide concocted in honor of his dead sister. The older man smiled a soft smile, a somewhat sad smile. "Let's make the best of it," he said, taking up the bottle of cognac and pouring for Zero and then himself, and making sure their cups ran over.

They both drank to whatever that meant—and everything else it seemed after that—first one and then another cognac, and another after that, toasting even the price of peppers in Rio as they went, until everything was irreconcilable, a cave and world aglow with irreconcilables!

"The hard thing," Candide said ever so quietly, "ultimately, the one that gets you, is not just to live in the world, but to live missing what's missing." A long pause followed. "Behind the sitting quietly, the time going by, the grass growing," Candide said with the bent cup to his whispering lips, "behind all the geese a flying, all the sages down the ages, the rages, the pages upon pages . . . missing what's missing."

With that, the toasts began to linger on their tongues, and the libations to they're being foolborn began to slow to a pie-eyed pour, the fatter of the two imbibers finally putting down the bottle.

"Yes," the odd-shaped man asserted. He waited a breathless beat, and the cave with him it seemed. "Yes."

"Yes?" Zero asked.

"One can make a leap," Candide answered. "Despite and in spite of everything."

"A leap?"

"A leap of love!" the intoxicated man said most definitely.

"To where?"

"I'm trying to find that one out. I don't know and am trying to find out," he repeated as if talking to himself, then nodded, and then nodded again.

"Are you sure?" Zero asked mockingly.

"It's my unfinished symphony. I'll finish it when I'm sober," Candide slurred, "good and sober." He paused but a breath and then laughed.

"And when will that ever be?" Zero asked with a wide grin. "You're like what's his name, Candide. *Khurshid kamandi sobh bar bam afgand*," he said in

Farsi as if to give a hint, *"Kai Khursro i roz badah dar jam afgand, Mai khur ki manad sahr ga Khizan, Awaza ishrabu dar ayam afgand."* The handsome face flickered in the light of the fire, waiting for his drinking partner to guess.

"When eagle-like I flew from my world of mystery, upward and ever upward, no sage stood there to greet me with the truth . . . I was brought to birth and learned nothing from life but wonder of it; and so must leave—still uniformed of why in the world I came, or went, or was! Omar Khayyam," Candide declared in an erudite intoxication of his own, still wondering where Zero had learned Farsi.

"I couldn't help memorizing it. He would scream it out every night," Zero rallied. "Wake up the whole of Ward Z. His real name was *devounee* of course," he added without translating the Farsi word for *crazy*. "At least that's what he called himself when he talked to al-Lah. After he made his leap, of course. Out of a window one moonless night." He held on his cave companion with that, and as he did, he took a deep drink of amber liquid from the bottle itself; then offered it across to Candide.

They drank like that for a long while, in the shadows of the cave, when Candide's face softened into that famous smile of his, where his lips turned downward and he appeared awash with a wordless wisdom. "To why in the world we came, or went, or were," he said punctuating his remark with a minimalist's shrug.

"You know," Candide started up again as if to speak to the futility felt by the two of them, "Plato, in his cave, thought about these things, too. Like us in ours," he quietly added, gesturing around towards their surroundings with his head. "And if he were here with us now, I would tell him he was wrong."

"Wrong?"

"We have to go inside our breathing selves, not to some ideal place."

"To do what, Candide?"

"To find the wisdom in the waste."

The two men merely sat silently in the somber cave after that, the animals asleep all around them. All except for the tiny parakeet, Rainbow, who spread his wings as if trying to convey some comic catharsis to the silence surrounding the two humans in the cave with him.

"I luv ya. I luv ya. I luv ya," his parakeet voice burst out.

The man with no name winced. He got up and went to the cave entrance, looking out at the storm. The rain swept in and his blanket bellowed in the wind, and Zero did nothing. He merely stood there with the night beating against him.

The former gravedigger pulled himself up with difficulty and went and stood behind the taller man. The icy rain whipped around the pair and made echoes inside the hollow of the cave itself.

"Com'on," Candide beckoned, "let's go sit down by the fire."

"Yes," the taller man said almost too quietly to be heard, refusing to budge. His body was trembling. "Yes," Candide heard Zero repeat, touching that desperate part of a person where one goes to take a stand against it all. At least that's how Candide felt it to be for his madman. He pushed aside the lama wool and pressed it around his charge. The engrossed madman stood there looking out at the night, shivering uncontrollably and dripping with rain, his hair windblown, his eyes wild. "Yes," he vowed.

"Yes?" Candide quietly asked.

"You have dug up more than you know, Candide." He paused as if thinking about that, his body trembling so violently that Candide put his arm around him to lead him back to the fire. But again he couldn't budge the stronger man.

Zero held out his shaking hand and looked at it as if it were some strange new find; his bright pale eyes studying the scars on it (those odd bites Candide had wondered about). A blink later and he gestured to the air with the same hand, immediately looking back at the odd-shaped fat man after he did. But Candide had no idea what he meant to tell him, either by his look or by the gesture. That's all the former gravedigger knew was that the eeriness of both, along with the cold, made him tug all the more at the stronger body; and this time the taller man seemed persuaded. Zero allowed himself to be led back to the fire.

The heat from the smoking flames had to feel good to his shivering body; they did to Candide. He even said as much, but whether or not Zero heard him was another matter. After he sat him down, Candide let go with a hesitant hand and the younger man nodded what had to be a thank you. It was almost imperceptible, but there. He pulled his blanket more tightly around himself, and then let out a bitter little laugh. "It'll be fun, my aging Huckleberry Finn, my old honeybunch of frolic," he insisted. He nodded and nodded again. "Standing in the cold or sitting by the fire aren't my only options, Candide. I sat down this time. But remember one thing, gravemaker." Abruptly, his face contorted with his thought. "One thing about the man with no name. I will make that leap." A brooding obsession fell over him, riveting his fixed eyes on the smoking flames.

After a while he looked up at Candide, as if somehow in answer to what he was frantically grappling with high above the pedestrian thoughts of the sane. He bit at his lip and held for the length of a long minute on the shadowed face holding on him. He turned away and put his hands out to warm them over the fire, lowering his pale fixation to the ground. Neither man broke the odd silence; the crackling fire and the howling wind the only sounds in the cave.

Ubermensch's one showing eye followed the movement with a dutiful concern. The big dog got up on all fours and went directly over to Zero to investigate the problem. The eyes behind that mass of hair stayed on the object of his sniffing black nose until Zero yielded and hugged at him with an assurance that he was OK. The genuine warmth of the hug surprised Candide. For a moment he wondered if he wasn't just mimicking him, the way he always hugged at Ubbie.

"You're right, Candide," Zero said, rubbing his nose against the dog's. "It's no shaggy dog story," he offered coyly. With that, he got up and said nature called.

Candide found him at the bottom of the ravine, bruised but breathing.

"Couldn't you see in the dark?"

"I saw alright," he said bitterly.

"So how did you fall?" Candide asked, taken back a bit.

Zero didn't answer at first. "I didn't fall, I leapt," he said softly. "Leapt into your love, to see if it would change the world, Candide."

It was Candide who didn't answer this time; then sighed. "It doesn't work that way."

"Oh," Zero said, something numinous dancing behind his eyes and beckoning as if out of nowhere, the voice that followed sounding half-amused, half-aghast, "and here I thought listening to you it could make the blind walk and the lame see, tie the air together and know the Mystery we call God."

Tying the Air Together

Here at the edge of America, and possibly my sanity, too, I do indeed find myself blinking at what was said at the end of chapter one and then two; namely, the author asking if we can venture into the Mystery we call God—tie the air together as it were! Does the root-reality of our being, *I am and I can love*, stop there for us, we conscious creatures in the cosmos, having led us to more in life and living, or can it lead us not only to more but to More, the Mysterious More?

The proof of the pasta is in the tasting has been our guide all along, and must be as well when it comes to this chapter. Can existence as we know it be elevated to the unconditional validity of a Mystery we call God and what that Mystery might be?

In a statement resounding out of truth itself, you and I and everyone with us honestly know the Mysterious Source of being is unfathomable and we humans in an inescapable space-time pit, where anything said of that Incomprehensible other than that it is Incomprehensible is a forgery, a fake, a fiction stretched over nothing; so much so that many postmoderns, with ultimate resignation, foreclosing on any grasp of what many call God, rightly regard the Mystery as the complete Other or as the Absolute Anonymous. This leaves us with something essentially un-thought and un-thinkable, and thus for this author to even attempt to say anything about it would indeed be like trying to tie the air together. It is an impossible feat—hubris if not madness personified a chorus of voices shouts out at me! My own voice included. What was I thinking with such a ridiculous challenge?

And yet, and yet *de profundis clamavi ad*—yes, *from the depths I have called out to*—to what? The nagging question is still there—still haunting me out of the deep, rooted as it is in something numinous that dances behind the eyes and beckons as if out of nowhere. Are we half mad when we talk this way?

Half-amused, half-aghast? Is the call a siren, is the sacred a siren? Is God a dream of prayer and suffering being itself? Is it humankind's last stand against our loneliness in the cosmos? Why don't I bury the venture in my breakfast butter and take my dog for a ride, avoiding this Mountain of the Moon in my mind? It's much ado about nothing anyway! Un-thinkable and un-inkable! Good God say amen to it! And yet, and yet, dear fellow adventurer, siren though it might be, and dream, too, mere poetry, something numinous still dances behind my eyes and calls out as if out of nowhere, and I must find out what it is. I must unriddle it! "I must go nowhere and see," I tell myself with a nervous laugh, cerebrally chewing on the challenge and fortifying myself with humor. I might end up uttering "quaquaquaqua," as Pozzo's partner in my own version of *Waiting For Godot;* in my own version in that, unlike Beckett, I shall go in search of Godot, go in search of the impossible, and without any leap of faith, Soren. No, there must be evidence of and for in existence, in my own innermost and everyday being as well as in the landscape outside my own personal inscape, leaps of faith need not apply! I can't trust my truth to just nothing! Yet, paradoxically, the journey that follows seems to be venturing into a call out of nowhere.

A call out of nowhere? So where then do we begin with this impossible venture?

Let's begin where everything banged in to being, where everything and everywhere began, an event called the primal singularity, the big bang, one that against all odds, as Hawking once pointed out, produced the likes of us, an alarmed awareness looking out at it all. After a long process, before present day inflationary theories and string theories, too, a presence burst onto the scene that could wonder about itself and everything else—consciousness was in the cosmos! We have no idea when it arose in the evolutionary process, but it did, and then found itself pushing that wonder about itself and everything else all the way back to where it all came from, the Mystery called God.

Aristotle is said to have said that wonder is the beginning of philosophy; theology, too I would add. Were the Neanderthals who wondered about death and laid flowers on their graves the original philosophers then? Were those conscious creatures long before the Neanderthals, living in a world before fire was tamed, the precursors to any talk of God when they wondered about what would come after this world, laying a pristine rose-colored quartz ax as they did among their fallen? And what about our own cave ancestors who painted larger than life animals on the walls of their caves, making them into prehistoric cathedrals—were they transcending their world in a search into something More as well? Faced with the human condition, we could certainly argue that they all did indeed wonder and try in their own way to address the mystery that surrounded them, perhaps pushing it back to the genesis of it all in the only way they could explain it at the dawn of consciousness. Though we now have a string theory where Plank lengths vibrate the plethora of elementary particles into existence, like some grand Beethoven symphony, and though we have the M-theory to go along with that, M standing for Mystery or Meta-unification or Matrix or *Mater* (take your pick)—*our* way of explaining it—the beginning itself, the actual beginning sans math or myth, at its microflash, still remains a wall behind which fuzziness holds court and all the king's scientists and all the queen's philosophers can't put the one and only, original and real Humpty Dumpty together again. Not at the spaceless timeless start that started spacetime called the initial singularity! "It is not just matter that was created during the Big Bang. It was space and time that were created."[1] So far then, we have at least gotten back to the beginning of the universe.

Plato got into this search as well, how could he not? He called it a *Khora* out of which the material world came. In classical Greek *Khora*—χωρα—has the following meanings and roots: the space in which a thing is, to make room for, begin, to spread. Plato tries to describe what he means by using the word in the sense of midwife, womb, matrix, giving space to. I like the *giving space to* interpretation best. It is rather clever of Plato. Actually, the *Khora* could very easily become the big bang for us, that which pulls spacetime into being, the beginning, giving space to, time too. But, despite all our fascination with *Khora*, it is *the nowhere* out of which *Khora* pulls the universe into being, *the nothing* out of which the symphony of strings of modern science begins, *the silence* before the stars and the speed of sound that interests us here. For it is that *nowhere nothing silence* out of which a somewhere comes that we must penetrate, and when it comes to that *incomprehensibility* (Capitalized or not) we are still in the dark, not unlike philosophy's proverbial blind man in a pitch-black room looking for a black cat that may not be there. In this case is not there, since there is no there there. So we are nowhere looking for the source of it all.

Whether in *philosophia perennis* or modern physics *that source of it all* has been unknown and unknowable, and still is, no matter contemporary scientists maken melodye with megabranes and chasing their own tales. It is unknown and unknowable not just as to why—why are things rather than they are not—but from *what* as well? Even when we get past Plank's wall where all physics breaks down, we still know of a singularity, it is *what* is before that big bang that stumps us! If we knew that, *what* that is, we might even know the *why*. But we are in the dark, wandering in a soundless sightless nowhere trying to see—trying to see we know not what!

Without anything to go on, not a where or there, not even a moment to steal away with, we have to close the case, Inspector Clouseau. There is nothing, *nihil, niente, nada, neant*!

Sadly, I must admit that we do end with *nothing* for our effort. And yet . . . dare I say, we know it is *a nothing that gave forth to everything*. So let's do a very human thing in our human venture and give that nothing that gave forth to everything a name, a word that connotes that. Let's just call it what it is a GIVING, a GIVING out of which the big bang and everything came, all being everywhere, even other universes if such exist. Actually, that GIVING should be without any article, either definite or indefinite, for it is nowhere and nothing, just GIVING, not anywhere or anything, nothing and nowhere. Of course we can't think in such terms, we are concrete creatures in a sea of spacetime and such a notion as just GIVING is incomprehensible to us. Even as I say that, we are trying to give it space in our minds, hanging it nowhere even as we attempt to imagine a nowhere and a nothing. We just can't get our human minds around it. In this sense the postmoderns are right when they refer to God or what I have been calling the Mysterious More as totally Other. But dare I say maybe not *totally!* True, in the perspective we have taken, it is so out of our scope that we can't grasp or even imagine it, for as I said and you certainly know, unless you have residence in a padded cell, humans can't think in no-space and no-time concepts.

Kant says as much when he posits the impossibility of doing away with space and time in our thinking. Scientists, too, have talked this way. "So, if we live in a three-brane, there is an alternative explanation for why we're not aware of the extra dimensions. It is not necessarily that the extra dimensions are extremely small. They could be gigantic. We don't see them because of the *way* we see."[2] "Right now, right next to you, right next to me, and right next to everyone else, there could be another spatial dimension—a dimension beyond left/right, back/ forth, and up/down . . ."[3] So writes Brian Greene in *The Fabric of the Cosmos.*

Notwithstanding our present state of blindness, and despite those in science locked like us all within the confines of space and time, still many leading scientists say that space and time, "although pervasive, may not be truly fundamental."[4] Space and time may have emerged from some other more fundamental whatever, which we have yet to identify. Notice how they are entering into philosophy here, if not tempted by some strange theology—where we ourselves are venturing I must add.

Yes, for we are on our way, daring to go where no human has gone before, past the beginning of everything and everywhere, carrying no baggage with us, no holy books telling us what is there, no scientific compass to help us in such a non-place, just a word, GIVING. Even if we choose to throw it into the Mac trashcan later, let's see, like good detectives, where we end up with it.

So far at least, without maken melodye, we can only say that the big bang at its inception (at which all our physics breaks down) comes out of GIVING—which is Incomprehensible. The primal conversation between darkness and GIVING cannot be grasped by our humanness; but, nonetheless, the big bang happened and spacetime with it. So, at least we can say we know the cosmos came into being out of a beginning, event, or happening we call the big bang. What does that give us—well we might add from that, that Plato was on to something, that the Mystery only allows the cosmos to be made possible, but is not the direct cause, since the big bang is the direct cause, as we know from science. However, that is not the ultimate ground and foundation after which we seek, nor the one that haunts the heads of scientists who would be philosophers, not to mention strange theologians. We must venture further than the singularity that gave us the sun and moon and stars, *and we have*, into the ambiguous, abyssal, beyond thinking nowhere nothing silence; and concocted a name for this space-less, time-less, article-less incomprehensible as I mentioned at the top of this paragraph. So it seems we are back where we started—nowhere, with nothing for our effort but a name for it.

The big bang hung from nowhere and nothing and burst into us! And that's it. We've gone about as far as we can go using a journey past space and time; all our instruments broke down at the singularity, and then we did after that, finding ourselves nowhere with nothing for our efforts, no matter math or our maken melodye with it. I sit here with my stymied sight and insight both, again pondering the profound *clamavi* within me, left with nowhere and nothing, not even the echo of what could be, the shadow of what should be. It is beyond our ability and our access.

We have to try another way.

But is there one?

The big bang hung from nowhere and nothing and burst into us! The sentence at the top of the above paragraph and now this one may offer us just that. Not at its beginning, but at its end. Yes, in the word *us*. That way we will be using what is far more accessible and by far more immediate. Our venture will be out of and rooted in our own existence!

Turn the spaceship around; we have to get back to terra firma. It is not past the primal black hole we will dare to find our answer—no, not by going there, but staying here, staying here and looking into our hereness, something intimate to us and what we know best. By now, it is clear that I am a person who likes to ground my approach to anything *in existence*, since it is all we have; so, when I bring up God, I am not asking you to fly off with me past the first moment anywhere and everywhere while scribbling away in some padded cell at Saint Haha's. Nor, in the more sober world of academia, am I assigning myself, and you with me, to a resignation that closes down any possibility of seeing beyond the blindness some postmoderns say, with unbending certitude, our humanness imposes on us with regards to the Mystery that made us, this despite the principle of uncertainty they say is their touchstone, or should that be tombstone. Rather, amazingly, I am now looking for a way to this Mystery in that very human existence itself. And I must make clear that I am trying to penetrate to the real God. I am not talking about God as *a* God, nor a supreme *being* either, not an entity in any way, otherwise that which created it would be God—the Mystery I am talking about *is* God, the God beyond all Gods, beyond being and non-being, GIVING. And let me repeat, rather amazingly, I am looking for a way to this Mystery in our very human existence itself.

"Wipe your glosses with what you know," Joyce said, and he was right. What we know and know best is our own existence; it is our one minimal certainty. So I am making the claim that herein is our avenue to the Anonymous and Nowhere! In the never-to-be repeated distinctiveness of *moi et toi*. Is that one cocktail too many or can it be that there is some clue, here, in our only certainty, some opening to the Mystery that made us—in us? Can I dare say that although we don't exactly know what the Mystery is—it does seem, nonetheless, that we do?

What we call God is without argument Incomprehensible, all the more so when we view the long dark dash of evolution . . . awareness waiting in the wings, only, finally, after a sustained draught to arise on planet stress. The blood-blameless tide of evolution gave forth with a litany of hit-and-miss heads along the way called hominoids, only at long last becoming us. Why the hit and miss, why the dinosaurs before? Where was God for the Neanderthals? Did they hear any whisper of what God might be as they struggled to survive and lost out to the tide of time? We stated they might have, but who knows? And we suffer because we don't really know, suffer that horrible empty anonymous fear in the wee hours when we sense a loveless force behind the morning still, something alarmingly alien to us and that poor abandoned species before us. Such is the onslaught on consciousness—it is a mysterious voyage each of us is on, admitted or not, committed or not. The postmodern mind is no different than the most ancient in this it seems, no different than the Neanderthals lost forever to us, or the supposed oldest of our hominoid line called appropriately Dawn, hanging on his tree, either having fled there from a predatory beast or hung there as the food of that predatory beast. Each of us is a variation on the same theme, the same through-line of thought since the beginning of this strange phenomenon we call consciousness, each left wondering on the crooked cross of existence about ourselves and the mystery that surrounds us.

Uncomfortable with the answers of the past, and with those of our own age as well, our kind continues the pursuit; continues to venture into the unknown seeking to know. But instead of looking without, let's, as I said, look within, within our own presence in the universe and the deepest experience in that presence. Perhaps at our depths, each of us knows something more essential about life than we think we do, something that escapes us unless we do indeed pause and give it utterance. Using what is most immediate to us, then, we may have a way to appreciate what GIVING might be, maybe even has to be, according to our own depth of being. It is a Mysterious More that cannot be less than us the philosopher and poet in me both argue, no not less so but more so. This is still through a "gloss" darkly I must make mention; and mention again lest you think I am having visions of God here. Or saying you will. God in the absolute sense cannot possibly be known by the human mind. But that, dare I say, doesn't close the Incomprehensible off to us. Rather, without a leap of faith or a surrender to the postmodern notion of any knowability lying totally beyond the limits of human understanding, I am daring to say that by our very existence, there has to be a way to know the Mystery that gave us existence.

That is not a pompous pronouncement, but, rather, a most humble statement of possible fact. Looked at in its starkest terms, the truth is we are creatures and experience is all we have. If perchance there are any a priori things in our heads, they must still come out in and through existence. It is the labyrinthine river we must all travel looking for the truth about ourselves, and for any Source to all this as well. It can only be revealed to us in the mortal waters of life and living. So it is here each of us finds the truth about his or her self, and it is here we must find any truth about the Mystery that made us. Only in this way can we find out what it is we call out to from our depths. Only by going to our depths to see if the Mysterious Source is present in our presence! *In the midst of our humanness!* That is the refrain one must never forget. *In the midst of our humanness!*

That is fair enough for anyone to tolerate, even the most unbridled postmodern.

So let us go to the deepest part of our humanity, again, as we did in the very first chapter of this book, the section that gives us the grounding for what I am about to say and must ask; namely, if it allows us to be privy to a profound possibility, the profound possibility of sensing something more in being, more than the emptiness that postmodern philosophy has become, more than money as the measure of all things that is the god of our society, more than the passé mechanistic-materialism still all too prevalent in intellectual circles, more than bibles and holy books of any kind, East or West or In-between—if it allows us to be privy to the profound possibility of knowing what is unknowable? In other words, to ask straight out, can our human love be elevated to an unconditional truth about God?

Think about it—really think—not with a reflex-response out of the tyranny of thought out of our own age. Love allows us to sense something more in being, why not even the profound possibility of knowing being itself in its profundity, of realizing the numinous dancing behind our eyes and beckoning as if out of nowhere? From the depths of our own being, I have to say and ask, can we reach the depths of the Source of all being?

The answer to that question threatens the entire enterprise called existence when you think about it. Either our existence is a means of telling us the truth or it is not. It is all we have, so if it is not, we are indeed left to the wind as it were, left to the wind and long-winded discussions signifying nothing, not only about the nowhere nothingness of the Source of all being, but about everything really. In such a reality, the truth would be that anything then goes, since everything went, or at least couldn't be gotten to. But I am saying that we have from the first chapter on shown that existence shows us a truth of a different kind, and that it shows us the foundation for this truth; I am and I can love becoming the conclusion of a long existential inquiry. Now in that and through that and because of that am I maintaining that we have a way to the Mysterious Source mentioned at the start of this chapter? The long and short of it is *that* is what I am maintaining, or existence is in me, in *moi*, in *toi*. It is in our own breathing that the incomprehensible, indefinable, imperishable, unseen and so very hidden, even as such, becomes intimate to us, intimately present somehow, in our loving, as if telling us what it is, in our realization of love, love at its purest, *a love that seeks nothing in return, not even love.* Just giving! Just—dare I say it—GIVING?

Why do I hesitate? So priketh hem nature in hir corages. Whether due to the temperament nature gave me or the way postmodern society has come to affect all of us, I find myself having to ask, does love really give me and you an opening to that *what* in my *clamavi?* From the depths of our own giving, can we really reach GIVING itself? Can our human giving be elevated to unconditional validity in the Mystery we call GIVING and GIVING to unconditional validity in our human giving?

I have to stop and catch my cerebral breath, go for a walk in the garden, or better yet, drive to the university and my aquatic exercise, submerge myself in the bubbling waters, and as we did in the far past emerge with a pristine consciousness, like some aquatic ape gazing into his surroundings without any gods or God to fix on, only survival on the Serengeti.

Is that it? So what do I do with love? It's there, too. We all know that. I see it every time I go to those bubbling waters and watch someone helping the crippled body of a friend or family member into the water. Past all my mental arias, my run-on theatrics, my ebullient comic confabulations, which for all their brilliance fail to work and love maybe does, is that what I am being shown? Am I so bold as to say that past bibles and sutras, qur'ans and upanishads, past philosophy of the abstract persuasion and politics as our salvation, simple human love is the way to the depth of being and the wisdom in it to the Wisdom in it? Let me be sure I know what I am saying here. Am I daring to put forth here—that love is telling us what the Mystery we call God is? That the Mystery that is un-thinkable and thus un-expressible is like our own giving in its most beautiful expression, a love that expects nothing in return? That the Mystery that is the unedited, uninhibited, unharnassed depth of love, GIVING, is grounded for us in what is deepest in us?

At the moment and for the moment, although it remains to be thought about further in this damn dialectic of and on the divine, I will allow myself to say that we resonate with this GIVING at our deepest being; our primary "memory" of it is here in our own giving. The Source of all being is not absent in the cosmos. For the Source of being to be absent in being would be untenable. Therefore, yes, yes to my quest and question! Wisdom before the big bang is the same as wisdom after the big bang, GIVING! And that means in me and in you and in each of us! The gift GIVING gives is itself, *GIVING gives giving* . . . we are giving, too, at our depth of being. GIVING entrusts love to us as our essential destiny, and our hearts are truly restless until they throw in with that incarnate realization of the divine within them. Are we beyond the pale here? Yes! God in truth is the Mysterious More. Yet still knowable to us! Our deepest level of being and essentially our very truth of being is revealed when we give of ourselves, when we love, and so too is GIVING revealed when we do. God has remained as problematic as ever, because God is before being, and we can only think in terms of being. God is pure GIVING! That is impossible for us to grasp, with one exception, our own giving. Though God comes through being to us, it is not through being per se we know the Mystery, but through what the Mystery is, giving, love. That in which we have our being is this GIVING and in this we are at our deepest level of presence, we are in the image and likeness of GIVING in our own very giving. It is turning being back on itself to its very root-reality, and so our own. It is only logical that we should reflect the Mystery that made us.

Am I going too far from the street, the everyday, too *meta* with this way of putting it? Let's bring it closer to everyday then. Angel food is not our dish, pasta is!

The reality of who I am and the deepest experience in that, along with what I witness in those waters, what I witness without in the form of beauty and goodness and the beauty and goodness of love, gives me human confirmation of what I have said. God is as personal as our own presence and love is to each of us. Metaphysics leaves something essential un-thought and un-thinkable, and thus un-inkable as well: God! But at the same time known to us! The appearance of love, the awareness of love in spacetime brings God as well as humankind's essential existence together, in our own giving, our own love, that which bridges across the whole of being to the Source, beyond at our very core. The Mystery we call God is manifested in us! Yes, God is found in love and the beauty and goodness of it we witness without and at the depth of our own being within. To be in touch with the divine presence means to be in touch with the beauty and goodness of love within and without. The mystics say the knowledge they have of God is the knowledge God has of himself. Well maybe, but still only in the way that we can as humans; first of all not by starting with or using mysticism, but rather the knowledge we have of ourselves, the deepest knowledge within us, and *that* is the knowledge we have of a presence that can love, that can carry his friend or family member into the healing waters, that can give of himself or herself. This is as real as it gets for us; out of what is the deepest reality for us we reach the Deepest Reality. It is the reality check love is. Our very existence at its deepest moment leads us to the Mystery that gave us existence! The proof of the pasta is always in the tasting, even when it comes to God. As it was with our purely human spirituality, so to with God, *in the midst of our humanness!*

Was all that much more than the human condition could sustain?

I sit here in the middle of the night, knowing for sure there *is* love, and shake my head and the caffeine in it, wondering and having to wonder if that giving, that final phase in human love, that deepest experience in our being, *is* finally where we do indeed find the Mystery that made us? It does seem that if we cannot find the Mystery that made us in our deepest experience in existence, then truly we can't find the Mystery anywhere. That's all that one can really and honestly say. The rest *is* silence.

But before that drop into such an abysmal silence, before I am pricked by hesitation once again and my courage wanes back into our postmodern milieu, I have to state once more the profound possibility love offers with regards to knowing something so unknowable as the Source of all being. Maybe that more we sense in love is only more than the unconscious cosmos has to offer—consciousness looking out into the vast unconscious cosmos. But maybe also it is a way to know more than that, maybe a way to know that GIVING we spoke of that gave being to us—that *our* giving does indeed give us a sense of GIVING, past the blind groping in the nothingness of nowhere and past the surrounding Serengeti, too. I shouldn't give up on our own giving so easily with regards to GIVING itself. The giving at the depth of my being and yours at least suggests some profound sense of something profound, some intense reality. Maybe at the truest moment of it, it is communion with the Mystery that made it, one that gives us an intimacy with what-can-not-be-put-into-words, yet known to us through what is so familiar, simply our own love.

The existence of love and its effects are extremely real, and thus the conclusions about a Mysterious GIVING based on it are grounded in our deepest reality and certainly allowable, not as a proof of God, but more like touching upon that something numinous dancing behind the eyes and beckoning, inviting, calling as if out of nowhere, a sense of the Mysterious More, a theology out of existence itself, an intimacy, a living prayer. Nietzsche had to shrink back in terror when it came to his eternal recurrence; and that is because it is the most horrible metaphysics ever concocted, in league with the notion of reincarnation until you get it right, which would be never, and which would make the Source of all this, a true *malin genie*, a monster god, void of the depths of our own being, and thus unloving and truly Other. But there is a deliverance from this nightmare metaphysics and the theology coming out of it, and it is the one coming from the depths of our own presence and the metaphysics and talk of God coming out of that; namely, love. That sustained thought is a grounded metaphysics, one that even if love stands alone in the cosmos, it is more, *meta* than the physics of it all, and if out of the Source to all this, even More. Love dares us here! Double-dares us! It says if you go to the deepest part of your humanness, to the greatest intimacy in your being, love, *there, in that*, you can dare to touch the Mystery that made you. Incomprehensible still, but intimate! Beyond yet at your very core! Only in this way can the indefinable, imperishable, incomprehensible GIVING be realized. In *our* giving! In *our* love! When all is said and done and words have fallen into silence, it is the invitation of love, the dare of it, no matter what, that speaks a wordless wisdom at the very depth of our humanness, and in the everyday life of it. Love itself tells us that when we become estranged to our own depths we can never know ourselves—and now never find the Mystery that made us as well. So it is I can dare to say, in the logic of love, in the reality of it, the existence of it in our lives, that if we go to the deepest part of our humanness, love, we do have an intimacy with the Mystery that made us, even as on this journey of breathing we still utter our forever outcry *sperabamus—we were hoping*—about life and living, about this and that, about . . .

I am mentally back in those bubbling waters, in my mind's eye watching, the twisted bodies of those crippled people, a young man in a wheel chair being lowered into the water, unable to control his shaking legs, a middle-aged man, his son or younger brother hugging him into the bubbles. We were hoping . . . My thoughts have to center on that outcry. Because of it, the Mystery that made us will always remain a mystery to us, vacillating in us between what we see without and what we know within, and within, too, between my love and my love. No, not between what I might poetically call the battle between the Serengeti and the self, a conflict that makes up every human, rather here within between my giving and GIVING! That outcry I spoke of, our *sperabamus*, makes existence complex and contradictory, and the Source of all this utterly confusing. For in all this, whether we live "lives of quiet desperation" or "rage against the night," whether we say as my play character shouts out, "if nature doesn't get you, humankind will," or just utter our forever outcry silently, alone and to ourselves, we are forced to admit, despite our love, that what we call God is still Incomprehensible—Incomprehensible because of that outcry. Where does that leave us? Isn't God back to being Other?

The proof of the pasta is in the tasting has been our guide all along, and must be as well when it comes to God.

I realize that for the most part I have used the subjunctive in this matter, that is, always as possible, and that the argument *from being possible to being is not conclusive*. I even said it was not a proof. Yet love exists, love is, and is on solid ground. When all is said and done, it is our most sure-footed way along the edge of the abyss towards any meaning in existence. But does that extend to this Mystery that allows so much suffering in that very existence?

Although there is much to be said for Nobel Prize physicist Steven Weinberg's statement that "the more the universe seems comprehensive, the more it also seems pointless," as well as his conclusion that "the effort to understand the universe is one of the few things that lifts human life a little above the level of farce, and gives it some of the grace of tragedy"[5]—it can also be said that within that mix arises a meaning in our human existence that challenges the cosmic indifference and gives a greater grace to life than any other, even as we still live in the shadow of Clown Alley, living out a comic agony, and that meaning, that challenge is this phenomenon we call love. That giving of ourselves, which somehow enhances the self giving, even if the giving is only a hopeless loving on our part, still gives meaning to life and living. It is within this context that we travel our spiritual journey, either to end in loving hopelessly or somehow sensing in love the Mystery we call God.

My attempt to do truth to existence as a whole in all its levels of being, both within us and without in the cosmos, this holistic approach, does present us with this situation with regards love, with regards that deepest experience in existence and our desperate encounter with the cosmos, either *meaning or Meaning*! Either loving hopelessly alone alas along the riverrun, the Source of all this as remote and removed from our humanness as the unconscious universe, or somehow someway sensing in our love an intimacy with Ultimate Meaning, Ultimate Love! Either way love is still there. Either way it is the most profound act a human being can do in existence, the giving of himself, the giving of herself. So, if it is not registered as a hopeless act in the face and facts of the world, then the other possibility is possible. At least that, I would have to add honestly. So what I am daring to put forth is that since it is the most profound reality when all is said and done, our own giving is what brings us, invites us, leads us, if anything can or does to the first and last reality of everything and everywhere, what we call GIVING, and does so as nothing else does or can. Our own giving gives us the profound insight into GIVING.

Again, you see I am trying to penetrate to the real God. I am not talking about God as *a* God, nor a supreme *being* either, not an entity in any way, otherwise that which created it would be God—the Mystery I am talking about *is* God, the God beyond all Gods.

Even if I were to say, "there is no God but God, and Its name is GIVING," it would be incorrect, for GIVING is not an It, or He, or She. GIVING is without an indefinite or definite article, or pronouns of all sorts, even as we use and must use them. GIVING is simply GIVING. Even the word *is* and the word *simply* should be dropped.

The Mystery will still be a profound mystery because of that, no matter what I, or any of us, say or sense, philosophize or theologize. I suppose as the Source of all being how can it be otherwise? Yet, nonetheless, an embrace out of the depth of our own giving of GIVING itself is there for us, but not in some abstract way, rather, as the word *embrace* connotes. As *direct* as love itself. Such is *our decision in favor of love*, of love as the deepest most real way we can go because *it is* the deepest and most personal of our experiences, our most intimate. Either that or our most deeply held spiritual sense is and has to be disappointing.

Is my tendency to create better worlds than exist now being extended to God? Am I creating a better God than exists, than could possibly be?

I readily admit if God is love there is very little of God in the world, either in nature or human behavior . . . yet, no matter, there still is love. What is a possibility because of that love is an approach which calls out of that love notwithstanding and not to mention our twisting guts, glorious gossamer truths, humiliation without relief of genius, and all the rest that goes with it called life and living in the human condition. It is this possibility that makes the impossible possible—that is what I am daring to say!

This is so even as we know GIVING is beyond things and places, voids and notions of a theistic entity or supreme being. As Augustine said, God is "wholly other" and yet *interior intimo meo*, "more inward to me than my innermost." The man from Hippo also used similar phrases throughout his writings, "*acies mentis, acies, cordis, acies animi, oculus mentis, oculus cordis*—all bringing out the depth of a person, that interior and intimate—*the mind's gaze, the heart's gaze, the soul's gaze, the mind's eye, the heart's eye.*[6] All this to bring out the *interior intimo meo*. And it is an interiority universal to our human condition, as we saw in our purely human spirituality, not just to one's own civilization, though of course it is nourished or not by that civilization. Wherever one happens to happen there will be this interiority of being, from Gilgamesh searching and seeking *balatu, the self, the breath of being within*, to Augustine and his own *interior intimo meo*, through to me and you in this postmodern world and whatever expressions we might give it. There is where we must go in order to say that *God is the giving we experience in our own so very human love,* totally involved with me in the depths of my own very *personhood*—and can only be approached thusly—*intimately.* This assumes a degree of awareness in existence on our part—both of that minimal certainty we all have, and the deepest experience in that reality. All theology is autobiographical, personal, ultimately intimate. *In love, my very and so human love, I would and do understand God, even as God transcends all thinking.* Thus I can and must say the Mystery we call God can be addressed, talked to, loved in return! The impossible is possible!

That possibility makes the impossible possible is what I dared to say and still am daring to say!

God is not dead; GIVING is a living God, in beauty and goodness and in the beauty and goodness of love. To this we are invited to give our hearts to and *act out of it in our lives.* Which brings me to a very important point, one I shall return to further on in our venture, but feel I must still mention here because it is central to this venture; namely, *unless God affects the third question of philosophy for us—how do I act in the face of existence?—there is really no point of bringing God into the conversation or our lives.* Although I am still on the outskirts of fully developing that, I think it can already be seen how God, the God we have come to so far, as such, enters into the conversation about our lives and affects the third question. The very grounding of our purely human spirituality is deepened, human grounding given absolute grounding, human love given absolute expression, validity, and truth in the Ground of all being, and this despite our outcry, a fact of existence that will always be with us, and one that not only makes existence complex and contradictory, but also the Ground of all being, this God we are attempting to know and name.

> Within each
> The Ground of being pulls up
> Gravity down.

Are we back in J C's so human toilet? Even when it comes to God? "You bet your ass, the one sitting on that toilet seat, on a cold wooden toilet seat with stale wine on your breath and your own waste filling your nostrils. Funny things can happen to you in the human condition. Like being holy and still having to shit," J C yells out from the wings. Is he being too human with that? "Try to say it more philosophically," my Old English whispers my way. Ok, let me say it more philosophically, by first asking: Is God close to us in spite of everything? Is it just that God is hidden from our human condition because those old-companions of struggle and suffering, the tide pools and Serengeti have their own truth? Yes they do, as does love! Presence is the gathering of everything in us. As long as we are alive to spacetime, both God and Gravity will be our reality, both love and the outcry. This is the way it is, don't ask me why, I don't know, if I did, I would tell you, believe me! And, oh, by the way, nobody knows why.

Let me say, with that outcry always in our human throats, maybe because of it, humans have been seeking to know and name the Mystery that made them since the chaord called consciousness happened haphazardly in their heads and they stood erect in the savannas, or returned back out of the seas, or wherever we first happened and got that glint in our eyes and faced the swarming multiplicity. Suddenly we had a face and we wanted to know the face of the Mystery that made us and left us to the volcano. It is so species-specific! Listen to what we called it over the eons, so no doubt we could call upon it for help, yes, listen to the different names given to this Mystery by members of our species along the way . . . Yala, Kwoth, Hananim, Thixo, Gatt, Kyala, Bari, Ruata, Agaayun, Rabi, Bathala, Foy, Tanara, Bao, Junzi, Wain, Mawu, Bhaganwan, Ngai, Leza, Tentei, Shen, Yataa, Asila, Dio, Kalou, Ishwar, Hyel, Prajow, Madaru, Siyeh, Akua, Abai, Ala, Were, Nyasaye, Gaia, Dumnezue, Isor, Maxam, Dioz, Perendia, Chiuta, Yah, Isten, Ngewo, Arnam, Ualare, Asdulaz, Pai, Naibata, Waqa, Hera, Nyambe, Amut, Gedepo, Jee, Norin, Shangti, Droue, Ormazd, Shido, Banara, Gado, Owo, Dok, Devel, Godimli, Sikwembu, Zambe, Deews, Bozymy, Nun, Paz, Xwede, Sibu, Gaddel, Gospod, Igziabiheir, Gud, Kami, Shango, Bog, Shiva, Rongo, Zin, Tane, Chaacs, Olorun, Vishnu, Dieu, Indra, Mulungu, Amma, Jumala, Deus, Theos, Brahma, Chukwu, Soko, Zikhle, Gutip, Yamba, Boh, Imana, Unguluve, Efozu, Tumpa, Shashe, Nan, Amaterasu, Khong, Ibmel, Rua, Kot, Torym, Muneto, Oco, Nialic, Lubah, Nzua, Tswashe, Oghene, Tev, Manitou, Khuda, Nzapa, Ramwa, Nom, Tsuku, Owuso, Ywa, Nawen, Jincouac, Rum Oqmasi, Nkulukumba, T'ien-chu shiho-i, Shang-ti, T'ien, Tao, Nirvana, Adonai, Elohim, Yahweh, al-Lah, Devas, Dio, Dios, Dieu, Gott, Guth, God, and a legion of others I have left out—the last name of all, known to God alone. That is, if there even is a name!

In truth there is no name for the Mystery we call by many names, but if words are to be used at all, I would like to say that in human terms existence itself has given us the profound realization of one; namely, GIVING.

What we are really concerned about is *what* God is . . . not necessarily the name; though the name GIVING helps us in that. We are aware that GIVING is no-thing (nothing) and no-where (nowhere), but it is the name we give to the unfathomable mystery of the activity that is God, since no one can argue—no matter what they might say the Source is—that it is not Giving. And using our deepest experience in existence, our own giving gives us a sense of what this might mean and thus a sense of the Mysterious Source; not only that *what* we *clamavi* to out of the depth of the existence, the existence given to us by this Mysterious Source, but how that very GIVING then affects us.

The purely human spirituality grounded in existence and the deepest experience in existence is completed in the Mystery that made us. At the moment one becomes aware of this communion, past the swarming multiplicity and our aloneness in the cosmos, and acts upon it, a person is alive to and living a holy existence—and thus, again, the Mystery we call God does answer the third question of philosophy for us. It is the Ultimate Grounding for that behavior, that how to act in the face of the swarming multiplicity that has been in our face since we had one.

However much anything else accords itself with the cosmos and its laws and chance within those laws, we should orientate ourselves primarily on the grounds of the needs of our human consciousness rather than something else, for consciousness is our deepest reality in the universe, and love the deepest experience in that reality. If the laws of evolution are a tendency towards fitness, one that drives evolution inexorably to that at the expense of the less fit, in other words, the principle of natural selection or survival of the fittest, it doesn't mean that consciousness, aware of a difference, has to act out of survival of the fittest, as big fish eating little fish. Survival of the fittest shouldn't be the tyrant of thought and criterion of human action, but rather what consciousness adds to the puzzle of personhood, something that can supersede survival of the fittest by the sharing of a bowl of soup with one not so fit in coping with the world—and that something we call at its deepest level love. This is open to all, you can give of yourself, love, even as it sometimes makes you a stranger in a strange land. This as I mentioned before and yet again can be done without any reference to anything other than one's own human love, that giving of one's self. Yet, therein as well is our way to GIVING, and if followed to that conclusion shows how the Mystery does indeed affect how we act in the face of the world. We act from what is deepest in our conscious experience, and, in that, act out of a puzzled communion with GIVING itself, the primal ground and primal support of the love within us, as the Original or Ultimate Source of our very being and it most profound expression. The gift of giving is made a gift itself, and thus we recall in giving that to which we owe thanks for the gift of being and how to be in the face of being. In other words, we have a purely human spirituality, rooted in our reality as human beings, that is the grounding for our getting to God. It tells us how to act as a human in the face of existence whether we take it all the way to God or not, but, if we do, ironically, we see it is grounded in God, giving that same human spirituality an ultimate holiness.

And yet . . . and yet, we must say, as the morning darkness is filled with the smell of the fires burning in Southern California and animals and people are running for their lives in the surrounding hills, we must honestly say that our outcry is still there, no matter, and has to be because of what we are witnessing.

Witnessing and confounding us! That is why I said puzzled communion. We are stymied by suffering. And yet . . . and yet as well, even if there is no primal ground, primal support, and primal goal of the whole of the evolutionary process, a meaninglessness to it all, there is still love, and that does put meaning into it for us. Even if there is truly total solitude and the Mystery that made us could care less, there is still human love. But we need not have to accept the fact of a hopeless loving or loving hopelessly, though that would be enough in facing the meaninglessness; an alternative presents itself with and out of that very human love, namely, the absolute beginning of all love, showing itself in us whenever we in turn give of ourselves, give of ourselves in overcoming the outcry in the world.

And so it is a puzzled communion we have come to, not on our part, but on what we cry out to. We can only follow our own inscape, our own innermost, in this matter; it is our only way into the everywhere and everything, into the nowhere and nothing. "God is the greatest mystery or nothing at all," the main character says in a play I wrote. But I must correct that now: God is the greatest mystery *and* nothing at all. And Incomprehensible because of that! *That and the fact, the very real fact, of suffering!* Again, since the beginning of being aware, the problem of suffering is the shadow that haunts every human head and the very sinews of our being, each of us left to struggle for some explanation, some wisdom in the waste. In suffering, doubt about any caring Mystery has to and does arise within us. We can never escape the problem that suffering poses. It leaves us in a sort of astonishment at our situation and with regards to the Mystery that made us as well. Truly, and all the more so, the Mystery *is* Incomprehensible.

However, following our own inscape, our own innermost, I dare say there is an intimacy that dwells within us that makes us want to see the same in nature, and past it into what is beyond and behind everything—to see our likeness, a presence, aware and caring, beyond nature, space and time, in the very Source of it all that is Incomprehensible. A total Incomprehensibility, a total Other, is never at peace in our human psyche, for we know within that same psyche that intimacy with beauty and goodness give us peace, a strange peace that transcends us. Yes, the Mystery/Source is Incomprehensible, and yet . . . and yet at the same time in the everyday experience of beauty and goodness, is a call, especially in the beauty and goodness of love. Almost abruptly so! Personally so! At the deepest level of ourselves, in the truest moment of being! Since we are a naming species we want to name this intimacy, and we do with the same name as the experience itself, love. In this truest moment of our breathing and very being, somehow, we silly-smudged mammals sense more and perhaps More still, perhaps the very More that made us, touching at us in the beauty and goodness, in the love—so much so that we can indeed dare say, in contrast to all that confuses us, that *we actually know* God, even as we don't simultaneous to that. God does not degenerate to a complete otherness from us in our humanness as we stand looking openmouthed at the loveless universe; on the contrary we sense we know God via the deepest experience in our being, despite everything else.

But is it merely a construct? The question does still arise to the pursuing sleuth inside all of us. Everything might indeed be a construct to deal with life. Culture and the Christ concept, religion, Nirvana, enlightenment, government and God! But what then is the really real—what is actuality? *The truth in the visibility of a person's life is all we have.* "But in all that what truth will there be?"[7] Listening to Vladimir in *Waiting For Godot*, we might give out with our own sigh, and then a nod. Isn't that the truth! In all this what truth will there be? What really real? What truth in my silly search for a purely human spirituality, let alone a God of love? Are we not all really waiting for Godot, as I suggested in the very beginning of this sojourn, whatever Godot is, our particular Godot? As Vladimir alias Beckett says standing beside his tree: "It's indescribable. It's like nothing. There's nothing. There's a tree."[8] But what does that mean? That there is simply what is? Or some meaning in the tree? Even in, one might ponder, the meaning of that tree on Golgotha?

Maybe the Incomprehensible has only existence to offer—for better or worse? "I don't understand," Vladimir says and every man, woman, and child with him who is honest with themselves. "What does Godot do?" "He does nothing, Sir." "Christ have mercy on us!" *Silence.* "What am I to tell Mr. Godot, Sir?" "Tell him . . . tell him you saw me and that . . . that you saw me."[9] The visibility of one's life—in suffering, laughter, love, and very existence—is all any of us have! In that we have and find our actuality, and our spirituality in that actuality.

'But who or what is God in that actuality?' we almost hear ourselves asking as if Pozzo, and not just called such as in the play. "Who is Godot?" ". . . he's a kind of acquaintance. Nothing of the kind, we hardly know him. True . . . we don't know him very well . . . but all the same . . . Personally I wouldn't even know him if I saw him."[10] When any of us talk of the Mystery we call God, Godot, Godet, Godin, or whatever, we can only approach via the visibility of our lives. We can only see the Mystery . . . in the face of someone we love, and in our own as well.

Is that it then? No more than that? Is that it? Under a tree or on one, it does seem so. In our visibility, our existing, we know love is the deepest meaning in life . . . so it must tell us something about the Incomprehensible we call God as well. So we are back to where we started, *ourselves . . . with life and love.* Fine! For we have found a human spirituality in ourselves, in our own life and love, a human spirituality found in our humanness, in the midst of our humanness, one coming out of our depths and daily life both, and one that can possibly lead us to the Mysterious More, more honestly than any other because it is our own most honest moment in the visibility of life and living.

But what of those who have never been loved? Who don't know that experience? We can only know and act out of experience—so what of them? That's where we who have loved and been loved come in—by our acts of love we show them 'the face of God.' The gravedigger in my play was so right. *When you show a person love, you show him the depth of your being, and you show him the depth of his own as well.* Yet, keeping true to our motif, a caveat for any who would think they can "raise the dead" by merely showing them love. Even if you or I do show a person love, each person must still become alive to it himself, herself, *see* for his or her self, and then *choose in the visibility of their own lives,* as we saw in the Cardinal and Christ piece Dostoyevsky presented for our consideration in the first chapter. Of course, we can argue the Cardinal didn't see; that the Cardinal saw but he didn't see. But we can also say that it was given for him to see, no, not as the great Russian might have put it, not in a religious sense of the Galilean standing before him, but as Jesus standing before him in his own humanness and inviting the Cardinal to respond to the love he was showing him by the Cardinal calling up his own love. Whitehead has an echo of this in his *Process and Reality* where he writes that what stands before the Cardinal ". . . dwells upon the tender elements of the world, which slowly and in quietness operate by love. Love neither rules, nor is unmoved; also it is a little oblivious as to morals."[11] There is a word that comes to mind here as I sit with my birds enjoying themselves in the sun breaking through the clouds, my shaggy asleep in the shade, and opera faintly playing in the background, a word I will mention again, *Ephaphatha! Be open!* That word is the road sign to appreciating the tender elements of the world, including the most tender of all. *Be open!* And when we are, it would not at all be a bad conclusion about the essential mystery some call God to describe this Mystery GIVING as inviting us to do the same, inviting us to be open to the profundity of ourselves, inviting us to communion with our Source. In this, a human being dares to know who God is and has to be if God is anything at all for us as human beings, as conscious creatures that can love in an unconscious cosmos that cannot.

One cannot simply dismiss the deepest experience in existence for us, nor forget the impulse within humans to see behind everything and everywhere with the inscape of our own being. One might say with a certain cerebral satisfaction that what I just said was anthropomorphic. Everything for us is anthropomorphic! We always see through human eyes. That is why is it called a human venture! Everything is such for us, seen through human eyes. Just as my Old English can only see through his canine eyes. We can only go so far as our human awareness can take us. He only so far as his dog awareness will. This maybe more than we imagine, but still one can't get way from it, from one's being *as is*. And if you dismiss the very depth of your being in the visibility of your very breathing, how really can you honestly say anything about yourself. You ultimately are existentially paralyzed, and must admit, as I previous pointed out, that you have fallen into the abyss of nihilism and will at all times metaphorically be marching on Poland, or you are lying to yourself, and lying to one's self is the worst of lies. Instead, accept who you are—to your very depths. *In the midst of our humanness*—remember! So again, one cannot simply dismiss the deepest experience in existence for us, nor forget the impulse within humans to see behind everything and everywhere with the inscape of our own being. Which in turn brings us back again to trying to tie the air together—do what is impossible for us, know the Mystery we call God.

There are those who say God as compete Other is impossible for us to know, and they go to our humanness to argue their point. I do the same to argue mine. For I have dared to say, it isn't impossible for us, but built into our being, related to the depth of our own being, *in the midst of our humanness* that we must go if God is ever to be discovered—that is the profound possibility love presents in our presence! Yes, always in the subjunctive and even conditional as long as we are in the human condition, and yes the Mystery is and will always be Incomprehensible as along as we are in that human condition, and yet . . . and yet at the same time in the everyday experience of beauty and goodness and love, especially in the beauty and goodness of love, I venture to say God becomes visible for us. Personally so! Intimately so! At the deepest level of ourselves, in the truest moment of our being, *in the visibility of our human love!* This is why I say that knowing God is a *belove* rather than a belief, a profound possibility rather than completely impossible.[12] It is embedded in each of us. It is our love, our giving. And so it is that God is not the complete Other! Opaque, but not Other! Anyone who abides in love abides in the Mystery, and the Mystery in them. Only our own living love is the basis of this, that mysticism without ecstasy that is open to every one of us.

Rudolf Otto was in a sense a postmodern theologian in that he makes God totally Other and in that, totally other to the position I just put forth. In his book, *The Idea of the Holy*, Otto uses *mysterium tremendum* to describe God. Although I read his book after I finished my own, I added this segment afterwards because I didn't want anyone to mix up my use of mysterious with his. I certainly can accept *mysterium* in my own use of Mysterious More, but I don't accept *mysterium tremendum, a mysterium that is one of dread and terror, a mysterium we must fear and tremble before,* one we must approach in "awe" in our worship—as he puts forth. That is a primitive approach to God. We shouldn't fear God, but love in return.

The inner sanctum of reality is not esoteric but everyday; it is love. Putting aside his *tremendum* for the moment, we see Otto talks as well in terms of wholly other, the opposite of everything that is and can be thought, which has a truth about it; but not completely so, for it is not *wholly* other, or opposite of everything that is—we have a existential line to God, past the void and vacuum, the otherness and the incomprehensible, and that is in the mystery of love, an everyday mystery that surprises our sense of other with intimacy, a mystery that prompts discovery of the divine, one that may even surprise that forever requiem in every creature's eyes. But, even if all that I have said of God, discovery, and death is mere poetry, we still have love. It gives us the way to act in the cosmos, even as we continue our guessing game about the riddle of life and the irreducible Mystery at the heart of things and before things and why they are rather than not. That much we do know: I am and I can love.

I think I realize what the ancient Hindus were struggling to express in thinking of God as "the Self seated in the heart of all creatures"—it is love. This giving. When the self awakes to/experiences love, it awakes to/experiences the All-Giving Mystery that made it. I say All-Giving again out of our human love . . . out of the deepest level of it, namely, a love that seeks nothing in return. There—at this deepest level of human love—is where I think life for the Hindus, for this hard-headed American, and for every other human allows us our approach to GIVING/GOD—and, as well, know our purely human spirituality most deeply. When all is said and done, past sacred books and piousness, past prayer and popes, preachers, prophets, pulpits and muezzin calls everywhere, GIVING'S revelation in the world is love.

Everything about God changes for us with this realization. Love changes our relationship to God. There is all the difference in the world between worshiping or adoring God and loving God; the first stems from without and God as Other; the latter from within and God as Intimate. One is a blind bargain with something other. The other anything but other or blind really—rather rooted in what is deepest in us, what is familiar and warm, seen in the faces we love and who love us. "Keep your metaphysics warm," I might playfully tell my three or four readers, something that can be perfectly understood in the *realization* of love.

Such a realization can be said by some to be a gift, a grace, a glee, a gnosis, by others a desperate courage despite everything, and by others still a creature's last hold out in the face of the abyss. I could accept all of them, remembering what is central here. It is in that, what is familiar and warm, and so personal and very real in human existence, our love, that we must seek the hidden face of GIVING, and thus as it were keep our metaphysics warm and real, certainly our theology so. We cannot abstract ourselves out of existence and ever know either existence or ourselves; so, too, with the Mystery that gave us existence.

Our venture *is* grounded, and grounded *in us*—in us and our very human love, where we find ourselves, have our deepest access to one another, and dare I say any access to the impossible that proves possible.

Love challenges not only the cosmos, but the notion of God as complete Other; namely, totally unknowable, or, at best, only in the experience of unknowing. The truth of the matter is, that when it comes to God, yes, we are, of course, in an un-say-able realm, but also in a very existential one that lets us somehow sense what that wordlessness might be . . . Yes, in the experience of unknowing, but also in one of profoundly possible knowing as well. Although we still have the sense of beyond, of not being able to grasp the Mystery we call God conceptually, of not being able to embrace the whole of this Endless Mystery, even disbelieving in it, yet we simultaneously do sense this More, intimately, out of the very deepest experience in our being; and any disbelieving, legitimate as it might be, is challenged by the fact of this mysticism without ecstasy we call love. We 'discover' God in it—still un-say-able, beyond the limit of language and concept both—maybe belief as well—but also through and in and by what is most real to us in the human condition. If postmodernism is not to become life negating, it has to accept the reality of love. It has to accept that we can in this breathing of ours, half-abused, half-amused at it all, still speak with the authority of existence itself, and in that of God.

It transfigures you and the world with you. Not literally, but in the realm of action on your part. The will to love becomes the way you meet the challenge of the cosmos, the way you meet all sentient creatures, and if you so choose, the way you meet the Mystery that made you.

My fellow ad-venturers, we who go to, take up, carry out, give ourselves to the venture given to us called human, must stay human in all this. It is in that, the only thing we have, *our human existence*, and then *the deepest experience in it*, that we could ever discover, in an incomprehensible intimacy, the Mystery that made us, even as we struggle with the forever problem of our outcry. There is no name for the Mystery we call by many names, of course, but if words are to be used at all, I would like to say again that existence gives us the profound realization of one; namely, GIVING, or LOVING.

One can, of course, sink into a quagmire of qualifications when it comes to God. However, approaching God in that way misses so completely the profundity I am talking about. Staying true to that, we can at least say that what Whitehead calls the tender elements of the world *are* there for us to see, in ourselves and others. We have only to see them and we see what love is—and when we see what love is, we see what God is and has to be, if God is anything meaningful, even as we are left dumbfounded in this dialectic to, on, and of the divine. We are related in an essential way to what we witness in love. We take the gift it gives when we give as well, when we realize giving. We can't define love, as I have said, but we still know what it is when we see it, and when we do, we realize that it is always expressed in giving, the giving of one's self. It's ironic, love takes one out of one's self while simultaneously taking one to the depths of one's self and enhancing that very self. Love is the mother of all koans, and because it is, God is. As such, we come to one mystery, the Mystery that made us, with another mystery, the mystery of our love. I dare to say only when we understand that can we possibly grasp the greatest mystery of giving, and grasp it directly and intimately, and thus do the impossible and know the un-nameable we call God.

Is there still a problem? A problem and a choice both! How can it be otherwise and we still be human? Like a refrain in counterpoint nature returns vying for our commitment; truth against truth confounding us, in a dialectic like no other, as there never is a synthesis, never a solution, never a satisfaction. Every artist and philosopher, too, is haunted by something that disturbs him and to which like a theme in a symphony he keeps returning to over and over trying to dig deeper and deeper into it, always excavating something deeper still, until he can dig no more, and we call that last ditch, death. This book and the play in it, as well as the book before, all the way back to my first poem, contains my own haunting wound in this world of wounds and wonder, the quest of how to tie the reality of love with the cosmos that surrounds us, with *la Stravaganza, the extravagance* we call nature, or more pointedly with the Source of *la Stravaganza? Something is wrong, oh so wrong, the shadow of what could be, the echo of what should be,* I penned so long ago as my first poem. The monstrosity of dinosaurs and the brutality of nature, the indifference of the cosmos, the reams of suffering, evolution itself, all of it has to give us pause, coming as it all does, from the same Source of everything. And I haven't even mentioned the reams of religions, the failed struggles to get to the Mystery over the eons, the shear difficulty of it! It does seem, looking at this swarming multiplicity, that the Source is indifferent and loveless, beyond our comprehension and truly Other.

Science tells us that the fabric of space below the Plank length is a seething cauldron of frenzied fluctuation, and the scientists go on to try to explain the chaord of the cosmos coming from one source or another, as do the different philosophies, and the plethora of religions.

So given that there is a Source—what the hell is it? Is the Ground of Being really a dehumanized whirlwind, leaving us in a windswept desert of desolation? Does the cry at Auschwitz ring in our ears, "Do not forget humankind, your creature?" Is the human relationship to the Source always the dark night of the soul? In the end, can there only be a dread silence? A complete Other—not only in the sense of un-say-able, unknowable—*but loveless as well?* Does Aristotle trump Augustine? Even if we re-establish a metaphysics? Have we come to a

God that is not only beyond our comprehension, *but beyond our love?* Maybe our love is only and purely that, *our* love—and we alone with it in the universe as we so often sense. We are once again haunted by that reality.

Life is this through-line in counterpoint, and any talk of God is always haunted by it. Yet, again, love does exist. And in our existence love stands against that lovelessness, against the whole without of the world we might say. Of course, we would be wrong in saying that, for love is out there in the faces of those we love and who love us, in the faces of so many. However, it still stands in counterpoint to the litany of lovelessness in the world, and it does so as the strongest deepest most wonderful experience in breathing. So what do we do with this? It is all from the same Source, so what is this Source then? Even if one says as Teilhard de Chardin, that God is imminently working out some eschatology in matter, one that can see evolution as the "Golgotha of God" to paraphrase Hegel, still why have monsters and suffering in the process? What does it tell us about God? We are like a tide washing in and out on the beach of existence, coming out of the vastness of the ocean, in and out, confused about those very waters we came from. We know there is a Ground of Being because there is being, but what really is it?

"What tremendously easy riddles you ask!" The statement is from the broad mouth of none other than Alice's egghead friend and displays the hubris before . . . well, we needn't get into that, only remind ourselves to proceed cautiously here; and honestly. But it is bewildering. Just when we thought we had worked out a modus vivendi in the cosmos with a grounding the ground is pulled from under us.

How, Galileo, do I put the spinning world together with the love you have for your daughter? How the indifferent unconscious cosmos and the love within me with God? Does a reality check destroy our enthusiasm, "the God within," which is the Greek root of the word? It can! Not only because the Source of all being is beyond our comprehensions, but also because we are left with love in face of it all, as if this love and the consciousness that chooses it were an aberration in the cosmos, with the Source more like the cosmos than us.

"Are we here to teach God how to love?" the mad gravedigger in my play asks. Or does love have to be without a why as Eckhart says?[13] With that we reach yet another realization in our venture; a very important one; namely, whether or not we can fully answer that ceases to be important in love, only that I send that soup over to the bag lady. In that act, whether God even enters my mind, somehow, someway, our horizon of being changes. *Looking with the eyes of love and listening deeply to the cries of the world, one knows how to act, expecting nothing in return—this is the deepest encounter with existence.*

At such a depth, looking with the eyes of love and listening deeply to the cries of the world, love is its own revealer, leaving one with a profound knowledge of how to act, expecting nothing in return, and in that one can dare say realizing *love is our correspondence with Love Itself.* Still uncertain; except in that love. Let me repeat that, still uncertain, except in that love.

Though Sophocles might have his chorus utter, *"Μη φυναι τον απαντα νικα λογον"—Not to have been born is best, when all is reckoned with*—and though we might be as blind as poor Oedipus at Colonus when it comes to so much, still the love in our lives stands as a challenge in and to the human condition and the cosmos itself, and tells us it is better to have been born and to have loved. It is a realization so profound that I am daring to say that it is the Mystery that made us calling out from the depths of our very incarnation. From the depth of our very incarnation—*in the midst of our humanness!* Yes, I am daring to say that the Incomprehensible we call by many names speaks to us in our human love and becomes Intimate. In human love in and of itself! The original call to love is made by God, present in us as our very creation; *our choice in life is our answer,* still uncertain and hesitant, except in that love.

It is not a conclusion without *a leap* over the outcry, or through it, past the twisted bodies and struggle, but always with an eye on the love. Just as in our purely human spirituality we never denied suffering, so, too, here when it comes to the Mystery we do not. *De profundis clamavi ad*—yes, *from the depths each cries out of one's suffering and one's own giving*—to what? To Love, Love beyond at the core of you and me, something we know as we know nothing else, our own love, and God in that, despite the outcry, despite the black hole that would cannibalize us. The nagging question of suffering is still there, still haunting me out of the night, but so is love here, rooted as it is in something numinous that dances behind the eyes and beckons as if out of nowhere. The problem of suffering makes the Incomprehensible all the more incomprehensible, but this giving of one's self makes the Mystery intimate as nothing else can. *It is that Intimacy we leap into.*

It requires a leap past our outcry—*a leap into love.* I have to answer the abyss with the only thing left to us! If we are to use this deepest experience in existence and profound sense it gives, when we are faced with the problem of suffering, we must make a leap into love.

We cannot deal with this leap without the preparations needed to make it, that is all that went before in this venture, but more particularly all that must go before in your own selves. Such a thing always remains a questioning act, that's why it is called a leap, but subjunctive or not, love is still the real foundation upon which it is built. In other words, we take what is most real, our deepest experience in existence, and we trust in that in talking about the Mystery that made us. It is not a whim or a whistle through a graveyard either; it indicates what is present more deeply than anything else in the presence we call ourselves. That is what theology ends up being, for a person to let lie before him or her and take to heart presence, his presence, her presence, to be present. In that way one finds the way, actually the only real way one can take to the Mystery that made us. Our presence speaks more immediately and directly to the subject matter of God than anything can. The only danger is ourselves in the matter, that a person will not take the way of love, but the way of power and end up in phantasmagoria and phony baloney nonsense and call it this religion or other, this mystical experience or other, pill induced or power induced as it may be. He who abides in loving, abides in God and God in him; she who abides in loving, abides in God and God in her.

Faith is not required here. If a leap has to be made, it must be one of love. A belove not a belief as I already mentioned. Faith is by its very definition, to believe in something without evidence of or for it, but love is at the root of our reality and so a leap of love comes out of what is known to us, so very known and real, and thus a leap of love is different than a leap of faith. One is grounded in existence; the other is not. Of course, *credo* can also mean *I give my heart to*, and thus even belief, at root, is love. Faith as love as it were. I am not going to argue over the point, only to restate that there has to be evidence of and for what we are talking about or it is like believing in Santa Claus, sweet and nice, but not real. I said God is not a Supreme Being; God is not Santa Claus either. There has to be evidence of and for this Mystery and there *is* evidence of and for what we are talking about. It is not a passion for the impossible, but one out of what is so very real to us, our own love loving past our outcry to the Intimacy of that love and all love, into embracing it and being embraced by it. Our evidence of God is a personal one, and love is as personal as it gets—and I can't stress that enough! God is not a person, but relates to each of us personally. So, when someone says they don't believe in a personal God, they have it wrong on two counts; not only is it not a matter of belief, but belove, and secondly, although God is not and cannot be an entity, a person, *God is a personal God*, as God can only be gotten to personally, through the most personal intimacy in our being, love—and in turn gotten to us the same way, for that love is God. The proclamations of certain postmoderns about God as Other are all defensible, yet all inadequate. So too with regards to those that say we must accept God on faith alone. In both cases, they leave out the deepest experience in our very being. The sense of divine intimacy and warmth, as well as the numinous depths of God become empty if we do not approach God personally. Given that love is the deepest experience and one of the most beautiful experiences about being human, it follows that we must have that same experience with God, or it loses the depth of our own existence, and is anything but in the midst of our humanness. Our encounter with God cannot be less than our human love; God cannot be less than it either, but rather the deepest source of it. The notion of the infinite Presence that is pure love is the deepest way to and embrace of God, one a person must never abstract or distance himself or herself from; God is a personal God.

I wrote the following paragraph in my notebook this morning and I think it applicable here. What is called postmodern theology too often forgets the moment embedded in our being where we do know even as we don't. It is through our words and world of course, but something more is present in the mix and mystery of it all. There is such a thing as a pure moment, when past the clutter, chatter, and though through a glass darkly, we still sense the more of it all, and in that strange purity of being realize a naked communion, a presence that is beyond paradigms and bloodless philosophies, where life, the life in us here and now, senses a meaning to it all, perhaps a piece of eternity, but really a sense of life itself, at the depths of our being in the mystery that surrounds us, in a Mysterious More. And that comes to us in life, in our presence, in our flesh and blood, our excitable cells and electrochemical signaling of beauty and goodness, of the beauty and goodness of love, and, so it is not devoid of breathing for us, yet it is breathless. That delicate balance between the unknowing/sensing and the deepest experience in our knowing is what postmodern theology forgets and would build everything on a "faith in faith" and not the realization of life at its deepest in love. No, it is not a faith in faith, but a love that allows us to trust in more and More too, and if that is what your faith is built on, fine, because it is rooted in the deepest experience in existence; but not a faith in the future or a faith in that of which there is no evidence of or for, a faith in faith that makes mockery of us and our suffering and our love and ultimately of life itself. Our journey in and into life should not be a reduction into faith any more than it should be a reduction into biology. We are not merely a mass of deconstructions ending in a vacuum, and though we do not know what to expect next, we do know that love is real, and life is more than a secret that is withheld from us. We have something in life that gives us a way to live and breathe, and in that, life itself becomes our way. Some might say, "we haven't a prayer" as the saying goes, meaning that it is hopeless, but existence itself is our prayer. Existence is all we have and somehow in that, existence itself, we do sense a more, a more that carries us, confused-and-all, past the abyss that would swallow up our psyche, and, instead, brings us into something beautiful, deep, and enigmatic we can only call More. I might be walking along the beach with my dog at sunset and sense it, something beautiful, deep, and enigmatic I can only call More, and yet I know it. We all can, in and at its depth in ourselves, in our existing. God presents what God is *in our presence*, here and now, not in some upcoming messianic whatever. Seeing someone sending the soup over to a bag lady is stumbling upon God present here and now, even as the soup-sender is still a question to himself and God is still Incomprehensible to him—even as I am still a question to myself and God is still Incomprehensible for me watching as well. No, the scene is not like Kant reducing God to ethics! It is embracing God as love, GIVING itself. Does God remain a Mystery, of course, as does the problem of suffering and the self itself, and why all this was even necessary, but we are not without the certainty of existence and the phenomenon of loving in that unique presence each of us is in the face of the cosmos. Such a presence in the face of the chaosmos, as Joyce called it, or a chaord, as I might, still presents the problem of creation itself, no, not why things are rather than they are not, but why this swirling multiplicity of matter we call the universe is so alien to what is our very presence; namely, our existence and the deepest experience in that existence, as it, this cosmos, is without consciousness and therefore sans love. Why are we strangers in a strange land? Why does consciousness and love itself seem an aberration in this creation of ceaseless indifference and each like a voice crying in the wilderness, wondering "why in the world I came, or went, or was!" To send the soup over to the bag lady - we almost become paratactic explaining it, even as it is seamless - approaches the adventure of being with the best of the only thing we have, being itself and the deepest experience that comes out of it for us, this phenomenon we call love.

Without getting into an argument with saints and scholars, allow me to say that somehow love cuts through the language barrier in being, through the theological one, too. It cuts through the exploding super nova to the very human thump in our hearts, and does this despite the humps on our backs. It surpasses all spiritualities and even supersedes our toiletry. Our toiletry tells us everyday that we are made up of the raw elemental elements of evolution, and our love shows us that we are more than that toiletry, that we have something in us that can supersede even the primordial drive of evolution in us, that we can give of ourselves. This, in turn, somehow lets us *realize* God. Uncomfortable as we might be in making defining statements, we say and can say that, say it because of our own human existence and the deepest reality in it. No, it doesn't solve the problem of why evolution and nature with it are so indifferent and brutal, it doesn't solve the problem of suffering, it doesn't solve the dagger of death, all that is the reason a leap is necessary. But not one of faith, rather, one out of what is the truest moment of our being as breathing humans. Isn't it logical that in the gift of being itself, at the depth of it, we somehow someway sense the Source that gave us that gift, GIVING revealing Itself at the depth our very being? The Mystery we call GIVING remains an unspoken pervasive mystery, yet manifests itself the only way it can, as it is, as it is and as it made us, loving us into existence out of what it is. That emanation of love is still emanating in us. In each of us, but only if we allow it to. Only if we make a response!

Again, the original call to love is made by God, present in us as our very creation; *our choice in life is our answer.* It is a free act. In truth, our deepest freedom! I can make you fear me, but not love me. The same is even true of God; the Mystery that made you can't make you love back. That's how free love is. It is as I said *a choice*, as is the God you choose as well.

Is there still a problem? A problem and a choice both! A problem in that very choosing!

Just as there is a choice between the will to power and the will to love within each of us, one based on the raw elemental energies of evolution or nature, and the other on the deepest experience in our consciousness, so, too, with regards to the choice we make concerning God. The double-dare of love I spoke of earlier. If you go without, using nature as your guide, you end up with a volcano god, one that is rooted in power and awe, alien to your deepest experience; a *mysterium tremendum, one you must fear and tremble before.* If you go within, you end up with the God we are speaking about, an intimate God, one of love, rooted in our deepest experience in existence; even as it sometimes contradicts the world we live in and so much of our evolutionary baggage.

The world we live in, as well as that baggage of DNA, the selfish gene, and all the rest, do of course dictate certain behavior in us as I have said over and over again. But when all is said and done, we don't have to follow their dictates. It might be harder in given circumstances, of course, as Frankl pointed out. I won't go into those circumstances again, but I do want to say what those circumstances showed: that despite being alive to raw and bare nature, a human being can act out of what is deeper still in us and make an individual decision to give of himself, to give of herself. It is for each of us our deepest decision in the face of the world without and the will to power within.

"The experience of camp life shows that man does have a choice of action," Viktor tells Sigmund.[14] As in the camp, out of it as well. There as here, here as there, life tells us about ourselves and about love. One of the most important insights it tries to teach us is that love is the only way to grasp another human being in the innermost core of his personhood, of her personhood. It is the truest moment of our being as breathing humans not only between God and us, but also between one another in this odyssey called existence. *Love changes the way we see ourselves and others.* There is a certain 'insanity" in this sanest of acts in our species. It is like Francis of Assisi stripping himself naked in the city square. No, I am not suggesting such an act literally. The point is to *realize* the love each is, even as we might feel naked to the world. To realize it like an enlarging circle, rippling out from those we most immediately love, to others, on until it takes in the whole of our species, and out still further to all sentient creatures, then the earth itself, until we finally get to Love Itself, answering the original call from Love Itself without expecting anything in return. Just naked love! Such is the deepest appreciation of God and ourselves. Such is our purely human spirituality, found in life itself.

"Holy shit!" I hear Zero again yelling out from the recesses in my head.

I'll attribute this 'outburst' to the fact it is two thirty in this sleep-starved morning. No matter, I must remind you as my loveable loonies did—that is what it means to be human! We are at twos and threes in time, torn between our toiletry and the thump in our heart, and unable to put it all together. How postmodern of J C, Zero, the loonies, and me and you with them! The theory of everything eludes us! There are even times a person can't help but wonder if each of us isn't merely a psychic crystallization around an abyss. And when we look into the abyss, it might even look back at us, as Nietzsche warned. Accepting the fact of bad hair days and very real nights, let's still never commit the unforgivable sin of denying our own existence and the love that comes out of it—nor forget that an *individual* response is called for in this chaord we call the cosmos. In this is our true and human spirituality found, and dare I say someway somehow a true sense of the Mystery that surrounds us as well. No, love is not going to stop the world and let us get off. It doesn't end suffering. But it does give us a way to face it: to face it and to see the face of God, too.

In the *Mahabharata*, one of the longest poems ever written, the story ends with a pilgrimage to heaven. Only Yudhisthira, the holy man, journeyed all the way, accompanied by his faithful dog. When they reached heaven, he was told that the dog could not come in. Yudhisthira replied that, if this were so, he would stay outside heaven, too, for he could not bring himself to desert his dog. He even argued with God. It was a long argument, as the poem is long. Finally, both dog and holy man were admitted and the dog was revealed as Dharma itself. This had been the last test of Yudhisthira's spiritual greatness . . . love. With that he passed into the Being of God that is immortality.[15] Besides the Hindu tradition saying that the true and final dharma is love, the Buddhist traditions tells us that the last Buddha will be the Buddha of Love, and the Jewish tradition teaches that the greatest commandment, to be said by a devoted Jew every day, is to love God with your whole heart and with all your soul and with everything in you, and your neighbor as your self.[16] Jesus says yes to that, then turns that around, saying God reveals himself in that call to love, loving us the same way, with all God is, and asking us to be like him in that, no matter what.

One can go to the secular world as well and find the same, as Camus, Feyerabend, Frankl and Eiseley, among others, including Nietzsche that night in the Piazza, all point out, one way or another. For this is a purely human spirituality, one based on existence alone. It is in that, at the depth of our being, in our purely human spirituality, I maintain we find our way to the Mystery that made us. It doesn't mean that God is no longer Incomprehensible to us. Hanging as we are on the crooked cross of existence and suffering what it means to be human, and postmodern to boot, the Mystery that made us will always be Incomprehensible! But the venture doesn't end there. Rather, in that very humanness, and out of that very postmodern uncertainty, we can still venture into the Mysterious More! Again, isn't it reasonable that the Mystery that made us—that gave us the gift of existence—allows us to find the Giver in and through that very existence? In my giving! In yours! In the end, it is the very human giving we find in ourselves. I might say poetically God puts on a human face so to speak, sometimes a bag lady's, sometimes a baby's, sometimes what each of us sees in his or her mirror when we love. Yet again, the original call to love is made by God, present in us as our very creation; our own love in life is our answer.

I mentioned that Meister Eckhart said for him the highest way that he could name love was without a why. Not for milk, like one loves their cow, he said—but selflessly, past petition, rewards or punishments, in the giving of one's self.[17] Though he reaches this via a mystical ecstasy, we have through everyday existence and the very human experience of love, *a mysticism without ecstasy*, open to everyone. Love is totally egalitarian! Everyone is not a mystic, but every human can arrive at what I have put forth, through his or her very humanness. It is at the root-reality of the human condition, *I am and I can love.* And in that, one can love a cow, too, not for its milk, or you for anything but yourself, the real presence you are. I love you for you, and the cow for the real sentient presence she is—that is important enough to underline; lest someone miss what love really entails. There was an actor who played Christ in a movie, and in one of his many interviews to promote the movie said that he loved God more than his wife. What a misunderstanding of both God and any love he had for his wife. There is no separation. When I love you, I love you! I know it is hard to grasp, let alone to explain, but separating God from love misses it. God is not *something* that loves; God is LOVING, without I must make mention the two words that started the sentence! Just LOVING! LOVING! We can't help but think of the source and the act as separate, but not in God's case. When the actor said what he said, he missed the very Jesus he was playing. The genius of the presence called Jesus was that he tried to realize LOVING for people, not in the abstract, but with the warm word *Abba,* most particularly in his parable of the prodigal son, which is about the *Abba*, the father, more so than the son, a warm *Abba* of unconditional love, which is what God is he was telling his audience through his metaphor and parable both, and doing very deep theology I might add. Where he found this

God, I don't know; but we know how we do, and I imagine he did likewise, in the beauty and goodness of love as he experienced it. But whether Jesus would have ever existed or not, existence itself does, and what we have found in it. The historic Jesus, or Yeshu, was not unlike any other human in this then, and said as much when he told everyone over and over again that he was a *bar'enas, a human being,* and to be open to it, *Ephaphatha!*

Since Derrida and Caputo both use Abraham to bring out their cerebral circumcision, as I already mentioned him, I think I might use Jesus here, not because I am a person who lives in the structure and stricture of religion, but rather one who lives on the open shores of a purely human spirituality, as I image Jesus to have, and so do the same in this piece I concocted, my gospel, the gospel according to Vincent, wherein I try to show how Jesus *in his humanness, from existence alone*, found his notion of unconditional love and thus the Mysterious More. I have no idea what went on with the real historical man, as I believe no one else does either; the New Testament, gospels and epistles both, are written by men who never met him, each with an agenda of his own, in the idiom of their own times. The abiding inner figure I have of Jesus is somewhat different than the gospels, as well as the present day scholars who would make of him merely a pedestrian Palestinian Jew of his times. So when I write my own gospel about him, it might be poetic padding, but I think not, for the love in the storytelling is still the deepest experience in human existence, his, or ours as humans like him and him a *bar'enas* like us. Hopkins in one of his poems put it thus: "I am all at once what Christ is, since he was what I am . . ." And so now my gospel.

When Yeshu got to the deep desert, the struggle became far deeper; there he wrestled with darkness itself. The barrenness of the place seemed to challenge any notion he had in his heart about Yahweh. The brutality of nature always made him go silent. Suffering of any kind did. It had bothered him since his youth. He asked why, but the desert was without a why. He asked the sky, but it too was silent. When as a child he had asked why the mamma bird fell from the tree and her babies left to starve, no one really had an answer. And as a young man, when he heard the Pharisees explaining it among themselves, he scoffed at their nonsense. That's what he called it, to their faces. There was a certain anger, even rage in him about suffering. It left everything he held dear as if bleating away, like the lambs he saw hanging in the marketplace. And like the lambs it drained him. And his God with him! "Nothing is really there," he wept, alone in that barren place he had come to seek the truth. Without a name, without words, without a heart or soul—nothing, he told himself. "Only an endless desert." A haunting filled his gaze.

He spent many days and nights in its grip, a darkness felt deep inside of him, as if it were the very background of everything and everywhere. His soul echoed the emptiness and he murmured a muffled outcry. He twisted and turned for forty days and forty nights, doubting the deepest part of his heart because of this shadow that fell over it. He cried out to something unfathomable he hoped was deeper still, but heard nothing in return.

He grew lean and his eyes hungry.

He sweated in the day's sun and shivered in the night's chill. What was out there in the world and what he had always felt deep within his heart said different things, came to different conclusions—came to different Gods!

He found a cave and shared it with the darkness.

For three days and three nights he had such a hopeless sense that behind it all there was nothing. He looked, but his gaze did not pierce the question mark in his soul. He felt he had been brought to a place where no one could find him, not even himself. At such times a person opens his mouth to escape suffocation.

He blinked. A hill he had seen outside of Jerusalem called the place of skulls held in his mind's eye. A strange mist blanketed the land all around it in-wait for any living creature who ventured into its domain of dreamless sleep. He saw himself actually do so; and found himself actually gasping for life . . . his mouth open in shock and his tongue covered with mucus. A dreaded silence followed, when something sounding like his own voice told him to find the secret spilling from his own dead skull.

He held in his stare as one minimal certainty climbed into his eyes despite everything. He screamed it out at the night sky. But the darkness all around seemed to challenge it—challenge the deepest part of him. His mind raced within him . . . is Yahweh this loveless nameless silence, this faceless emptiness, this abysmal indifference, totally other than and from me?

A snake slithered by in search of survival. Did it hear any whisper of what Yahweh might be? Or the dried bones partially covered by the drifting desert sands? Sticking out as if grieving for a God! He swallowed hard.

In the wee hours the sense of a loveless force behind the morning still, something alarmingly alien to him and even the desert itself grew stronger. He had no idea what it was or if it was in answer to his question. But what he did know was the one minimal truth that was still in his stare . . . and clung to it!

"I don't understand," he whispered. A string of words followed. One strange one stood out . . . and he uttered it with hesitancy . . . the last part falling off into silence.

Again, that something deeper still inside of him he could not shake off filled him, telling him something totally different than all he was witnessing.

It made him scream out. He felt as if Yahweh was beyond him, yet at his very core. Which sense was right? What he got out of this desert, or what he got out of his deepest self?

A long stare followed. "Is love nothing more than a bastard in this world? Like me? Even as it is what is most real for me?"

Yeshu listened. He begged this unfathomable sense of something inside of him to be more clear. He was in a desperate situation, when all prayer fails and not a word can be spoken. He waited, but it remained an unspoken pervasive mystery.

His eyes followed the walls of the cave to the entrance and back again with a hairsplitting silence. He could actually hear the silence. A hesitancy filled him . . . Yahweh is truly unknowable when it comes to the life we are alive to. "I can never know."

Suddenly, a shadow appeared at the entrance of the cave. It startled him. The leper, a middle-aged woman in rags, stood there looking his way. It was obvious she was thirsty, no doubt abandoned out here by her relatives. Many lepers were. Left to wander until they dropped. Yeshu nodded and managed a creased-lipped smile across to the woman in from the heat. "Just you and me in the whole of the desert, is that the way it is—just me bring this bowl of water over to you?"

The poor woman took the water and swallowed it down. Yeshu touched at her and that made her stiffen some. No one touches a leper. "Who are you?" she asked him. The touch made her think him mad. Yes, who would share the little water they had in the desert—and with a leper, a leper whom the stranger even touched? The woman left him with that strange look and disappeared into the barrenness.

He needed someone to touch him, too, he told himself. Suddenly, a thankfulness still tinged with hesitation overcame him. "Is the hidden presence present in our love?" he said almost silently, as if his words were sacred, sacred with the profoundest attitude towards life. "When I hear and feel, taste and touch, think and dream in the tones of love, do I know Yahweh?" The whisper carried across out to the barrenness and he nodded telling himself something so strange: *that love seeks nothing in return, not even love.* Is that how to interpret Yahweh, he wondered.

Alone in the desert cave that was all Yeshu had. Himself and his love! A love that told him to seek nothing in return; not even love.

"I am the way," he barely got out of his parched lips. "My love is the way to Yahweh. Yahweh and the way are one. Yahweh is love."

Tears ran down his cheeks as he sank to the ground, leaning his tired back against the cave wall.

The stone-deaf desert can't wonder about a stone-deaf God. But he could . . . especially as he somehow someway sensed an extreme beyond at the heart of him. And Yeshu wept. Hard.

The last of the desert silence ended with an intimacy, with a thankful trust still tinged with hesitation, but with a wordless grasping of what was ungraspable.

He was blind in a barren desert, yet he could see. It was silent, yet he could hear. He was still crippled in so many ways, yet he could walk. The sitting man did just that; he got up and went to the cave entrance, looking out at the wind and the waste.

He whispered something silently to himself.

He knew the desperate encounter between himself and the silence of the desert would always be there . . . as long as breath was . . . yet so would his love.

Yeshu blinked at what it meant to be human. We are torn between the desert and the deepest part of us. He took in an intense breath. He had found the way, within himself, if he would be but sensitive to it.

All this I heard much later, from his own lips, and I told it to John who wrote it down as you read. Since I cannot read Greek, I can only hope he told it as I told him and Yeshu told me. Knowing John as I do, I suspect, of course, it is a little dressed up here and there, as is his way with words. But I know the heart of it is there, the heart and soul of what Yeshu found. I met him at the desert's edge as he came out. I told him I was about to head in to find him. He smiled—"I think I already found me," he said. He looked so vulnerable, his eyes tearing suddenly.

"I think I found my father, too."

"What are you talking about?"

"Yahweh."

I shivered. Had he lost his mind in the desert? At the time I didn't understand what he really meant. People still don't from what I hear from those who say they follow him. "I love you," he said in answer to my shivers, as if it were the answer to everything.

His life went on like that after the desert, he trying to tell people what he tried to tell me. He wanted to share it. He said that old sense he had had since a youth, that somehow he was protected was back again . . . that he felt, despite all his uncertainties, connected. I had no idea what he was talking about. Months later he said he sensed a presence in the presence of his own presence, that is what he told me one rainy night, and then broke off. But his eyes went on, trying to tell me what he meant. Maybe trying to tell himself as well.

Here Nietzsche comes to mind, and a mirror into his own inner conflict. Even as he gives a sympathetic picture of Jesus as one who lived love, he says it is "ungraspable," "inconceivable," "against the instincts of life" to do so.[18] Of course, he was right—and wrong at the same time. The instincts out of nature, where he rooted what he called the will to power, are there of course, but so is what I call the will to love within us that can override even those raw elemental energies that make us up in the textures of the presence each of us is. We are more than just one will or the other, and one can act out of either. Nietzsche was his own best rebuttal to what he said, by his embrace, lovingly hopeless for him, yes, but open to and acting upon love nonetheless—*love realized*. I suspect the historic Jesus had his own moment of a lovingly hopeless realization on Golgotha, far worse than his desert struggle, when he like Nietzsche looked into the abyss and it looked back, empty and loveless, and he gave his outcry that sounds down the ages, my God, my God why have you forsaken me?

In our so very human outcry, the Mystery we call God becomes nowhere and nothing for us, as much so and more than anything before the big bang offered—so again where does that leave us, *really?*

I look out the window of my den at the rain and wonder. *Che speraza sta, che speranza more*, an old Sicilian saying tells me . . . *those who live with hope die hoping*. Is that it then, dear Pirandello? Is that it then, dear Archimedes? Have we reached a point that is pointless? Are we back to where we started, adrift on that river of relativity with uncertainty as our compass? In and out like a tide? Forever lost in a divine dialectic? Does the bump on your head tell it all, dear Aeschylus? Dear Aeschylus, who died so haphazard on that same Sicilian isle, despite writing some of the most beautiful lines ever written? "God—who is he? Whatever name he chooses, by it will I cry out to him, mortal as I am and to whom wisdom is won in suffering! Yes, even in our sleep, pain, which cannot forget, falls drop by drop upon the heart, until in our own despair against our will comes wisdom through the awful grace of God."[19]

Has life become *de trop*, too much, like swallowing the ocean we came out of, just too much, our daring venture as ridiculous as that blind man in a bitch black room looking for a black cat that may not be there? We could forget the haphazard happening to the first playwright, and instead remember the depth of the creature who thought up such thoughts, but where would that leave us? It would leave us in denial of the funny sort of situation we call human, wherein as witnesses and actors both there is a part of us that says we don't know who we really are and what part we really are playing, even as we suffer, laugh, and die, pondering if everything perchance is haphazard, even our being here, not to mention the Mystery that supposed to have made us. It all appears a comic-agony to be sure. Are we humans, who are alive to the second millennium of the common era, aware of what no one before could even conceive; namely, that we are all merely watching ourselves in a music-hall rendition of astonishment at death and disfigurement as performed by the Fratellinis, with a curious chorus of lunatics in counterpoint, and a madman calling himself Zero winking out at it all from his tub and telling us in a stage whisper: "Ladies and gentlemen, show some style, pull down your pants and head up the aisle!"—is that it? Are my Mediterranean roots mixing with my particular and peculiar kind of postmodern American intellect and creating a whimsical fatalism?

My Old English just groaned for whatever reason, no doubt because my legs are blocking him from getting under the desk—and now leaving again even as I moved for him. He is restless about something, perhaps the cataracts he has developed and I must have removed, but hesitate to do so, not just because he just had his eleventh birthday, but because in preparation for that operation he was diagnosed with Cushing's and his immune system thus weakened. I do love him so, and the thought of losing him sends shivers down my spine.

Like him, and me with him, we are all in a struggle over this situation we find ourselves in. It is the reason for philosophy, poetry, and prayer. If we were Cyclopean witnesses all this might be easy, but we are not. Rather we posses a dichotomy to our being—a dilemma—and must, in the end and through it all, bear witness to existence with both these eyes, even if it leaves us cross-eyed with an *embarrass de choix*. "It's hard being me, farchrissake," my madman tells his mirror. Perhaps he was driven mad because of it, because of what he knew to be in those two eyes looking back at him. Who might not be when you think about it? For at the same time as there is a hiss in our heads, there is also a profound mystery dwelling there, a phenomenon we call love, at the depth of our presence, which senses something more, mysteriously more, perhaps even opening us up to eternity—and all that may be too much for a creature to contain. For there is a part of us that thinks it all a shame and a sham, too—one, as I said, that returns like the tide to wash up on our psyches and make the postmoderns sounds in our heads. In the end even great Plato was driven to just wanting a laugh or two to get through the night, tucking his copy of Aristophanes under his pillow, no doubt with a resigned smile parting his lips, even as a silent prayer still showed in his eyes, hoping Aeschylus-like for his Aristophanes to be joined somehow by a divine whisper in his slumbering ear.

Plato did, of course, hold for such a whisper. In his Cave he tried so hard to explain it and kept asking if Glaucon understood, almost as if he wanted to make sure he himself did. He even talks of people half here half there—spiritual people who live in two dimensions simultaneously and seem at times strange to the rest of us. Like Jesus did to the leaper lady in the desert. At one point Plato even states how hostile the rest can become towards such a person. "And, as for anyone who tried to free them and lead them upward, help them ascend, if they could somehow get their hands on him, wouldn't they kill him?"[20] And didn't they. Both Socrates and Jesus. This "ascent to what is" makes someone stand apart, Plato suggested, when it really shouldn't, if only humans were true to themselves, that is, their own deep-rooted and real selves and the spirituality that comes out of that I must add. Love realizes the silent beauty of the ordinary, even as it touches upon the profound.

It's so easy to forget, dear Plato. And even when we remember, still difficult. We are caught between being witness to the haphazard and the holy in our breathing—and within that perilous perhaps must somehow still choose—hopefully choose love—which I think with all my heart to be something lingering in us before our very presence! A final thought before the dreams beneath our frontal lobes take us into that strange place the brain goes in sleep for whatever reason. Look at a baby. As I say that, the two in that TV ad pop up in my mind's eye, probably because they are so cute, one trying to sing and the other shushing him. Yes, look at a baby, any baby, of course the world has meaning—and if it doesn't, we do, and should put that meaning we call love into our world. But I have maintained thus far in this chapter and dare to say again that the Mystery we call God is found *directly* in this love. That there is more and More, too.

There is a line of poetry that comes to mind here: "For I greet him the days I meet him, and bless when I understand."[21]

And with that I sign off for some shuteye, my Old English already snoring on most of the bed.

A thought in the middle of the night injects itself into the dark, the black wind howling outside, the Muses in my mind churning up a dance of chemistries and calls from out of a nowhere as if not in spacetime itself. No, we are not the center of the universe, and yet each of us is. And that tension between one reality and another causes us heartache and mindache both. It isn't easy being us, with inner and outer worlds, those that were, and those yet to come. It makes for the crooked cross of existence we all sail existence on; but also a passion for the possible, the Mystery "Eastering" in us through it all, that is, the victory of love in us. Though I use religious phrases in a poetic sense having gone to bed with Hopkins in my head, it is not philosophical mysticism, even though it be in the middle of the night and about a mysticism without ecstasy. It is the wisdom of the ages and before the ages, found at the depth of our everyday existence, even as it was before existence was. Herein is the final measuring rod of everyone, whether Wall Street Wizard or the poorest of the poor, whether you and me or those thought of by you and me as a bit less centers of the cosmos than you and me. This is deep reality, even as those on the surface of things proclaim it to be banks or bibles, borders or boardrooms, this ballyhoo or that, all part of the landscape to be sure, as are those raw elemental energies within us and the will to power with them. But there is also another phenomenon, a consciousness that can, can choose love, that will to love in all of us, *if only*. The basic tension in all of us is that. Some, however, are so removed from love as to be another species (for we do judge a species by their actions), and that presents a problem. Yes, when the eyes of the other are flat, like a tiger tiger in the night, or intelligent with the intelligence of rock solid, glacier cold abstracts, goodness and beauty and truth and love perishing in their parade, that presents a problem. It is all watched and witnessed by human love—and in the despair a tension and temptation both there to join the parade, or stand alone on the curb, in our draining despair, in doubt as to the "dawn of a doom or a dream" or a maybe divinity, in a lower case or Capitals, who knows? Is my philosophy a waste of time, christening people who were never born and curing people who were never sick—do I live in bat-like darkness and shout out of a self that is dreaming even itself up? Is it all wasteful *Kulturkampfs* between Augustine and Adoph? What comes to mind is the wasted life of Hopkins with his superiors destroying the poet with their nonsense and he still clinging to such nonsense. Am I too a destroyed poet clinging to such nonsense? And yet . . . and yet, I and you with me do know love, watched and witnessed in us, in others, in everyday human love. Yes, there is an Adoph and the will to power, but also—oh you already know, I needn't tell you. You knew before you read this book! And because of that same depth of experience, it is not forced reasoning to say that the Mystery we call God is—oh but you already know that, too. You don't have to stay up late for this. That most prolific of composers, that God of everywhere and everything, of the sounding strings and far off planets and places and people so different than us, in atmospheres undreamed of by us—except, except there too would have to be love, since it is from the same GIVING. I break off my thought there, the dream world already at the door of my psyche and seeping into the construction of my sentence with its incoherence.

I turn off the lamp and put aside the pen—and turn the lamp on and take up the ballpoint again.

"Night is for sleep, not poetic philosophy," my Old English scolds, the light having disturbed his dreams of gingerbread cookies and romps in the green glens in far off isles. I turn off the lamp and put down the pen, close my eyes, awaiting the sobering dawn and computer cold logic to pass as truth and theology too, so publishers uptown and downtown will take me seriously and an imprimatur be given by the pedestrian and pedantic, while the Muses disappear into the truth of things. Yet, one thing still sticks in my cerebral cereal as I make a quick breakfast for myself and my ever-hungry sheep dog, morning's minions doing nothing to alleviate it.

God will always be Incomprehensible, not only conceptually and verbally, but also because of *what I witness,* witness in the supernova exploding or the volcano erupting or everything in nature eating everything else—and of course that all eats at me. I admitted as much, and must again, and maybe again after this. And so the divine dialectic continues without synthesis or solution . . . It is like a refrain in our humanity, making me ask the question each of us must: *is the Source of all this loveless?*

"I thought you answered this!" I hear my last lonely reader yell out as she or he or someone from Mars throws the book against the wall. "Yes I thought I did, too, hesitantly, so," I must answer. "Ok, defiantly so, but still with a human hesitancy in my hoarse voice, hoarse from the outcry. So I must revisit it. God is still problematic. We all belong to this rendezvous when all is supposedly written and done. We are so overcome by it, we have to stop and ask all over again to make sure we got it right! Spend concentrated time on it!" So, my lonely reader, for this writer, unfortunately, sans sugar or surge, on a decaffeinated note, after a dream-filled night, there is still the problem of suffering, *God and Suffering.* We can't shake it! It is the strongest reason for disbelieving everything I have said about the Mysterious More, leaving us stripped naked in a different way, without any 'logic' of love about a God who cares, and grieving for the death of such a God in our journey. Yes, like a seductive theme in a symphony in counterpoint it keeps coming back, for the problem of suffering is central to breathing on planet stress, and is indeed the biggest stumbling block in the way of any when it comes to God. Forget Stendhal's bon mot, Weinberg's outcry is far more powerful.

Weinberg doesn't know how a rational person can believe in a God who cares for us. Having seen cancer, Alzheimer's, and the Holocaust of family members, it had to give him pause, as it should. "I have seen a mother die painfully of cancer, a father's personality destroyed by Alzheimer's disease, and scores of second and third cousins murdered by the Holocaust," he tells us in *"A Designer Universe?"*—asking us to face up to it with his devastating question.[21] This metaphysical rebellion or absolute negation as Camus calls it, is certainly understandable, given nature or what happens to humans because of other humans. Nature of course is the bigger problem, because humans choose to do the cruelty; it is a choice on their part, whereas a more haunting question would be why is nature so indifferent and brutal if God made it and cares? Of course, even with regards to human acts, why somehow doesn't God protect us from these people even as they chose to do evil, if he cares so? Weinberg's outcry is all of ours, one way or another. It is certainly a fundamental wrestling match for me, being left to this. So one has to ask such a question about the Mystery that made us, that is if we did not appear through sheer happenstance and will vanish through the same or our own stupidity! Yet, at the same time, in all this, is love, the love Weinberg had and still has for his mother who died of cancer and his father who vanished into Alzheimer's. What do we do with this very real love? We live and realize it! But what do we do with God? Stendhal would answer that he doesn't exist.

Yet a Source of being does—and so you and I with you have to ask, 'but what the hell is it?' 'Really?' We're caught in a vicious circle here and back where this venture began, not to mention consciousness itself! Perhaps the postmodern mind is right and we should just label it as Other and close the book on it. But even then, a question seeps through the closed cover—where does love come from in all this—and also why does this Other allow for such a place as this? What are we to think except what Lucretius did? What are we forced to think except that the Mystery that made all this and us with it is a monster; or at best what Aristotle did, just a First Cause, as cool to its creation as indifference itself? As loveless as a mathematical formula! We use the construct of math after all to explain the universe—why not God? Or perhaps we could deny suffering a la the Buddhists! No, it is still there, we can't escape suffering, or the problem it presents, even as we call the Mystery Other, or anything else, or say with the height of insensitivity that the lady chewing at her lip in the cancer ward isn't really suffering, or brought the cancer on herself as so much of New Age nonsense spins out. No—suffering is real. And what it might mean as well! A nightmare far worst than any silly defense as the word atheist might offer, a word that merely means not a theist. It is a nineteenth century mentality to talk in those terms. Dawkins like so many are still in the nineteenth century fighting the passé fight between science and religion. The mind of today has accepted science and spirituality both, even as it might put aside religion and theism, accepting the Ground of Being as complete Other; that is, not being able to say what it is. This book is a book of our era, so I will now leave behind Dawkins, as well as Hitchens in his beach house stupor, having used one and now abused the other, and move back into our century, even as I face the forever problem of suffering and the nightmare it could conjure up about the Source of all this.

What do I do with that forever problem of suffering and the Source, or whatever you want to call this Wordless Whatever from which being itself came? No, the philosopher in me, nor the peculiar sort of postmodern that I am, doesn't hide from the reality of suffering, or the seemingly insolvable problem it presents, not even the nightmare concerning that Ground of Being it might conjure up. So is that it? Are we left with saying it is insolvable and in a very real way because of that, calling the Mystery complete Other as our way out? Oh, how easy it would be! Or to be a Dawkins or a Buddhist and bury my head in Eastern and Western denial, and that's it. But I must ask where's the wisdom in the waste? For there is waste! Wasted lives and wasted labors! Suffering is in the very evolution out of which we came—suffering is systemic to life itself. It leaves us in the labyrinth we find ourselves in and cannot deny, facing a Source dilemma, as well as an honest definition of ourselves.

No, I am not going to be Pollyanna-like about this, or postmodern either, or take the cowardly choice of denying suffering for sure, for suffering is real—*but*, oh yes *but*, so is the love that is called up inside of us I have to add. And that *but* only compounds the problem!

As I can't bring Galileo's love for his daughter together with this spinning earth, so, too, I can't bring this spinning earth together with the God of Love in this divine dialectic. Suffering is and remains the most human incomprensible when it comes to GIVING, The Mystery of Love we call God. There is something more I must yet discover, yet uncover about this - I can almost taste it! Something more about the Mysterious More and suffering!

Here you and I stand, real with a real capacity to really care; but what does it tell us about the Source really? We can stay here as I said we rightly can, but the problem of *what* still hangs before us—*what* is the Mystery that allowed such suffering? Yes, using the most real of groundings in us, we dared our leap in saying what the Mysterious More would be because of it. But that again only compounds the problem and makes it more unanswerable still. How can the Mystery allow such suffering? Have you ever seen suffering—how can a caring Mystery allow for such a happening? Yes, there is more to discover and uncover in our venture!

Like an albatross around our necks, we must make this sojourn of breathing with the problem of suffering always with us. Even as we laugh, and you know by now I am all for that, still out of the corner of our eye we are watching, and you know for what. In the first Chapter I covered suffering, but without bringing God into it; and in the Cave Chapter I covered it too, and again in this very Chapter, for I will never be able to be finished with God unless I face the problem of the Source of being and suffering, once and for all. Unless I pursue what is at the tip of my psychic tongue, something more I can taste about the Presence we call God.

We are left with my lunatics as they all blink away, looking out at us from their invisible stage as they and we with them stare into the Invisible trying to figure that one out. "He does that a lot," one cries out. "Fills our head with ideas," another nods. "Only we don't know exactly what they are," yet a third complains. "Being crazy isn't all it's cracked up to be," a skinny one explains. "And we're lunatics in case you don't know," a fat one to his side confirms. "Words applied to something unknown, doing we don't know what, are not unusual for us," they all end in a chorus of confusion.

A chorus of confusion fills my head as well! We can't confine the confusion over this to insane asylums in plays, because it isn't, it goes on in real hospital wards as well, only not so funny, in fact not funny at all. I remember reading of a woman dying of cancer musing from her bed of pain: "What if there really is a God? Won't that be extraordinary? I grieve for a God—no, not just a God, I grieve for a God who cares." Doesn't she echo Weinberg? Don't we all echo her?

Can you taste her situation? See her Mona Lisa smile or perhaps wide-eyed stare as she chews on her lip in pain? Is the extraordinary maybe real? Is the impossible perhaps possible? No, we didn't dillydally about suffering, but it finally had to come to this—not whether there is a Ground of being, for there is being, but if such an Unborn, Unoriginated, Uncreated and Unformed, Incomprehensible, Imperishable, Indefinable Mystery cares for us? We can leap into our own love all we want, but is God love? Does God care? Is there a providence—individually and for the cosmos as a whole? And does 'talking to this God' really matter? With dinosaurs in evolution . . . and a Cambrian explosion . . . with the plethora of possibilities within this material world which can go any which way, so much so that evolution as well as so much in spacetime seems so alien to us, the question even goes further than that. Can the possibility of a caring intimate Mystery be possible above all the rest of what a God might be from what we witness in existence? A profound pause comes over our page. What really is this Mystery some call God? Even if we rip away all else and merely approach the Mystery as the Source, what the hell is that? Were back to page whatever it was. Have I gotten lost in my labyrinth of love and has it lead us astray? People live their whole lives without God and seem to do just fine; at least no different than those who embrace God and die of cancer anyway. So what are we talking about when we talk of God?

In suffering, doubt about any ultimate caring has to and does arise within us. Our only support is knocked from under our already uncertain stand against it all. In the pain, fear, anxiety, weakness, in all the emptiness and so real suffering, when all prayer dies out and not a word can be spoken in its defense, when the fundamental trust of the most radical kind, love itself, falters in its struggle to sustain us, any Intimacy seems far away indeed. So what do I and you with me do with what is still waiting to be uncovered in this - discovered about God and Suffering?

A purely human spirituality will always admit the reality of suffering. It is so very real. And that has to give us pause . . . every time we say it! Or think it out of the corner of our eye. Yes, like a refrain it comes back over and over again to haunt our venture, interrupting our very discussion of God, and make it seem indeed that we are trying to tie the air together in a madness not a metaphor. Is our only *real* answer the final act in Nietzsche's sane life, the embrace of a fellow suffering creature? A gesture beyond despair, in the realm of total hopelessness—hopeless love his only final response to all the pain? Ours, too? I think I understand Nietzsche in that embrace from a hopeless one I myself had. The event is for no one's consumption but my own; but it was something that made me pen the phrase *hopelessly loving, loving hopelessly, because that is what I experienced.* I remember it now, and always will. How horrible it was and how hopeless, leaving me only my loving and a realization I cannot truly express. Even after all my writing about a God of love, the truth may be *that* hopeless loving, *that* loving hopelessly.

Yes, we still love, it is still our deepest human act, but is it all without remedy? Or prayer, I might add? Remember Nietzsche's own prayer. "I want to know you, Unknown One, you that are reaching deep into my soul and ravaging my life, a savage gale, you Inconceivable and yet Related One! I want to know you—even serve."[22] Yet, again was his prayer heard? His embrace of the beaten horse breaks my heart—the last straw for him it appears. It shows so much of the man. How could you not love Nietzsche? Isn't he all of us in that embrace? In lovingly hopelessly, in hopelessly loving, loving without remedy?

You protest from your bathroom or your bed or your backyard, that he saved that horse; but not the next, or even that one after he was gone. Our love is like battling the ocean, and the cosmos beyond it, the cosmic ocean, the ocean of the cosmos. Whatever metaphor we use, there it is, loving hopelessly, in hopeless loving, loving without remedy.

So it is that in our trying to get to *what we cry out to,* existence itself becomes truly troublesome, for it is that which is crying out, and me only part of it. I know that at times it does *seem* there is a divinity that shapes our ends, roughhew it how we will. I could have died a number of times in my life but didn't. It only adds to the confusion. And even if I myself lived a life without suffering, how could I not ask about the starving baby in Africa, his skin sticking to his bloated stomach and skinny arms, his eyes wide in shocking question? How could I avoid it in the helpless eyes of the old, or those I see struggling in their aquatic therapy, with bodies that betrayed them? My heart goes out to them and my forever question does as well. How could I not ask about my beautiful little white bird with red circles on her cheeks dead in my hands because of a mistake, or the death of my sister because of a mistake, or that dear baby the dying male nurse wrote of, made a monster by a mistake? How could I not ask about nature itself? Where does human love lead us but a question mark, not about what we should do, but about what the Mystery should!

Is the face of God a blank slate once one has suffered? We have to live with that question. The problem of suffering will not go away. We must face it. In truth, as I said, we cannot really not. Not only reason and love, but life itself, forces us honestly to face suffering here and daily—for it is all around us and *constantly* challenging us and any honest response we try to settle on.

The only solution to suffering is death—our own individual one. But that is a solution without a solution. Unless, perhaps we'll know *why* then, find out the answer to the brutality of nature and the suffering of the innocent and the old, or the hurt of anyone anywhere? Meanwhile—though there might indeed be a radiant joy afterwards, which thus argues for at least a good God, although certainly for an incomprehensible one—suffering remains for us here and now, and remains something that can argue to an indifferent Grounding to all being, or maybe worse, a naïve notion of God on our part. We protest the impotence of love from on high. When all is said and done, the scream of atheism is built solidly on the fact of suffering, better to deny any Ground of being, even as we know there is one, than have to admit to what it might be. For wouldn't love turn the universe upside down if it could? I would for love. You would. So why not a God of love? Thy wisdom be done people might say, but where's the wisdom in the waste? Like a refrain it returns over and over again. Suffering will not get its talons out of our flesh and blood—it is there and I will not dismiss it with pious nonsense or saying it doesn't exist or even with an aria from *Turandot* sing away that I will overcome. Suffering silences any aria, any symphony of the soul, too. It leaves us in a sort of astonishment at our situation. "Not to understand, to be stupefied—this is the closest one can come to understanding the un-understandable," a wonderful playwright once said as I already mentioned.[23]

The predicament of suffering does indeed leave us astonished and stupefied. Just when we might think we have it all figured out . . . with love . . . we are left with this, all over again, even into our chapter on the Mystery itself and our tying it all together. Does life need to feed on life to survive? Do creatures up and down the lattice of life have to suffer the way they do? Couldn't evolution have thought up a better scheme of things—or God have? Is it all really a spiritual vacuum, one of no meaning and no God, or worse—is that it and we afraid to face it? Is the Mystery an opaqueness, a darkness so empty of anything remotely close to us and love that it would be better not to have been born—in Colonus, on any of the seven continents, or in the cosmos as a whole? Or is God and love somehow in this astonishment—in this un-understandable stupefaction? If not, we really are at the mercy of what? Where is God for the poor little stray cats looking in astonishment at another creature being petted and loved as they are abandoned to the cold? Where is God, or any meaning, in suffering? Where was God for the poor beautiful white bird the cats got and ate? Where was God for the little boy in Chechnya staving in the cold and actually living in a hole in the ground? Or the little girl in Indonesia eating raw rice spilt from a truck she was so hungry? Like her raw rice, this is not digestible. Have we gone beyond the pale with this God of love idea—beyond the probable—beyond even the possible? Truly, where is God when a person relies on God's love? Where is God in the greatest need in a person's life? In that most truthful of moments? When we trouble deaf heaven with our bootless cries? Where is God in this world? Where where where is the wisdom in the waste? There is too much suffering in the world. Just too much, and we have to be honest about that reality.

Everyone knows this and is forced to react to it . . . Buddha who ended up having to deny it as real, the Mediterranean three, Judaism, Christianity, and Islam, which, one way or another, relegate it to a fall . . . what could we have done to merit this? I know it is only a myth to try to explain it, but it is still ridiculous. The universe was what it was long before humans. But even evolution baffles us with its brutality—it could have so why didn't it evolve differently? The way it did is but only one way of the zillions of possibilities. And even if there is only nihilism, still why such a suffering one? The truth is it is the suffering that brings about the nihilism, as it does other reactions as well, Buddhism's, Judaism's, Christianity's, Islam's, and all those unmentioned and even unmentionable others.

"I proclaim that I believe in nothing," Camus wrote at the beginning of *The Rebel*, "and that everything is absurd, but I cannot doubt the validity of my own proclamation and I must at least believe in my own protest."[24]

The protest against suffering sticks in our collective throat. So, too, the impotence of love. Christ may be one of the more beautiful spiritual concepts we as a species created as an example and exemplar for ourselves, and a God of love perhaps the most beautiful concept of any God. It would be nice to live that 'loving lie' even if it isn't actually so—to rise above actuality itself with a choice of love. Such a magnificent courage! Such an insane generosity! And it would be insane, in the sense of not accepting reality. Maybe that is the whole of it, to rebel against reality with love?

But what is reality? All around us, the struggle for existence is nature's principle of life—and Galileo's famous retort, "*E pur si muove*" does draw us back to the round and very real rotating earth—a real earth that does indeed challenge any concept of a loving God; of any primal meaning to it all as well. Even to any primal meaning to evolution! There is no escape hatch there. Of course, I can argue that the mystery of being is bigger than nature or this dimension. I can even quote the man who said he must believe in his own protest and afterwards coined the phrase *insane generosity*: "Christ came to solve two major problems, suffering and death, which are precisely the problems that preoccupy the rebel.

His solution consisted, first, in experiencing them. The man-god suffers. With patience. Suffering and death can no longer be imputed to God since God suffers and dies. The night of Golgotha is so important in the history of man only because, in its shadow, the divinity abandoned its traditional privileges and drank to the last drop, despair included, the agony of death. This is the explanation of the *Lama sabactani* and the heart-rending doubt of Christ in agony. The agony would have been mild if it had been alleviated by hopes of eternity. For God to be man, God must suffer despair."[25] Yet, once again, this doesn't answer the problem at hand, certainly not the problem of suffering . . . the *why* of it?! Suffering still is in our face here and now, and that God suffers with us doesn't explain it away, though it might explain away metaphysical rebellion and certainly make us love such a vulnerable God in return. But even with such a giving God, we are at a loss, wondering why . . . why 'he' allows 'himself' to be so vulnerable and us with 'him' . . . even as this Incomprehensible enters matter and suffers out of love with us? I am afraid the refrain of suffering is still with us and we can't shake it or say why a God of love allows it—even as he cares! The refrain of suffering is still with us as the inexplicable counterpoint to love, and to the God of love, even as naked love is the most beautiful and most real thing we know, even as it is everything we are capable of in the face of suffering.

"The faith," Jurgen Moltmann tells all, "which springs from the God event on the cross does not give a theistic answer to the question of suffering, why it must be as it is, nor is it ossified into a mere gesture of protest, but leads sorely tried, despairing love back to its origins. 'Whoever abides in love abides in God and God in him.'"[26] All we know is God is love and that's it?! Or should say about it?! Or could? Each of us still left on the cross of existence and wondering why? Aren't Moltmann and Camus both there with us, despite what they say, both still in the same impasse as ourselves? One man holding out for an abiding, the other for an insane rebellion against all this—and our very souls still screaming at them why suffering in the first place! Naked as we are against evil evidenced hourly everywhere on earth, we might stammer out that evil is man's choice, not God's. But what about suffering, suffering which is systemic to spacetime itself? If humankind doesn't get you, nature will. Naked love does stand in direct opposite to this stopover in spacetime. So where do we go with that?

Nietzsche, the father of meaninglessness in the modern world, struggled over all this as well, as we already know—and because of it, over the incomprehensible 'unknown God' that he had lost and wanted to recall. Yes, I hear you say, we know that, you already told us. Let me tell you once more. In his own *de profundis,* he cried out: "I want to know you, Unknown One, you that are reaching deep into my soul and ravaging my life, a savage gale, you Inconceivable and yet Related One! I want to know you—even serve."[27] Yet, was his prayer heard, I remind you, being honest to suffering as I requested in this daring discourse, this divine dialectic. "No—come back, with all your torments! Oh come back, to the last of all solitaries! All the streams of my tears run their course to you! And the last flame of my heart—it burns up to *you*! Oh, come back, my unknown God! My pain! My last—happiness!"[28] Thus spoke Nietzsche, as himself.

We are lost in our labyrinth of love and life both, and everyone is lost with us, whether a postmodern person or a primal one. Perhaps because I can't seem to find a way out, or yet uncover what I sense as more to the More concerning this, what is still there at the tip of my psychic tongue, I should pause and remove myself from the abrupt reality of facing it as myself, and instead ponder our problem by means of an old philosophical device. Therefore, bear with me as I compile our confusion into a dialogue . . . after all what would a philosophical work be without a dialogue of some sort stuck in? So with a nod to Plato, I will concoct a confabulation among postmodern men on a rainy night as they try to tie the air together with us as their audience.

Dialogue On A Rainy Night

The warm drizzle fell all around the veranda looking out on the distant beach; the lonely trees holding still in the sounds of the night as a harvest moon hung without motion in the silent sky far above the drifting moisture, playing peek-a-boo through the darkening clouds. Seven men sat drinking an assortment of libations, martinis of gin or vodka, and one lone guest red wine, their conversation up until now about a Mysterious More many call God. Beside the host himself, there was the guest, cane in hand, seated closest to the host, then a poet friend, a defrocked priest, a retired professor of philosophy and his twenty-something-year-old friend, and finally a rather reticent man, that only one drinking red wine.

"Does God contain and constain everything?" the guest seated closest to the host asked, swirling the ice in his long stemmed glass.

"Tiger, tiger burning bright in the forest of the night, what immortal hand or eye could frame thy fearful symmetry?" the poet added, smiling a slight smile. "Poetry is all we have when all is sad and done."

"No—existence is all we have when all is said and done, sad or otherwise," objected the man who once taught philosophy before retiring to his garden. "Correction, sad *and* otherwise," he went on and then stopped, studying the faces holding on him.

"Sad because whatever existence is, it isn't what I am saying it is. Or can! It is *otherwise,*" he added, clarifying his explanation. "We are incapable of knowing what it really is—natural selection didn't give us a brain to do that. So we are at sea, and know it. That much we do know."

"All we have is the uncertainty of life and the certainty of death," the guest closest to the host advised and nodded afterwards. "A requiem is in all our eyes. Let in the clowns."

A polite laughter filled the veranda and drifted out to barking seals in the distance, the dogs barking back.

The host seemed to think a moment about something and his expression quieted the dogs. "Shakespeare said untune the strings and hark what discord follows," he offered. "And when you do—do untune the neural cords and synaptic gaps—is there still a presence present perceiving its own discord, lost at sea and knowing it?" He looked over at his philosopher friend.

"You and that presence you keep holding out for," the retired professor of philosopher countered with a deceptively bland expression. "All that's true about life is the chemist's broth."

"And that is your answer to the Delphi oracle's communiqué to Socrates?" the host queried with sham dismay.

"And you a philosopher!" the poet pounced.

"Me a postmodern man," the retired philosopher answered, and then pounded on his chest as if a savage or a superman, an ambiguous smile cutting across his face.

It didn't cause the response he intended, instead, a seriousness came over the host and he reached over for a notebook on the end table beside his whicker chair. "One man sees a red fox running through a shaft of sunlight and lifts his rifle," he began to read, "another lays a restraining hand upon his companion's arm and says, 'Please. Let it live. Let it run.' I read that and had to put it into my notes." He turned the book of scribblings over on the page. "There is in us both an urge to act out of the Serengeti as well as an aching at the very heart of our being because of the brutality of it. Some go the way of nature; others the way of that something deeper still. Whether it be creatures killing creatures with razor sharp teeth or with rifles, something in us, at the depth of our presence," he stopped on the word, and then went on, "wants to protest, protest this place we find ourselves in and its brutality.

That has to tell us something about who we are. Know thyself," he advised, turning back to the retired philosopher.

"It is the odd man out who would put down his crosshairs," the guest closets to the host said, perhaps too quietly.

"True, look around you. What do you see?" the retired philosopher stated more than asked, missing the mood of the man who just spoke. "As Feuerback said—

"I hope you're not going to say what I think you are," the host interrupted.

"'We are what we eat,'" the retired philosopher went on, waiting out the interruption as if not paying it any mind, "and he meant it literally."

"Humans are for shit. Present company included," the retired philosopher's friend said with a laugh. "We have no choice in the matter," he finished as if it were from a lecture by the retired professor he had heard ad nauseam.

"*Holy* shit," the defrocked priest made sure to add as a correction, a little uncomfortable with his own remark.

"I see you have been reading that maniac," the friend of the retired philosopher countered. "His new book?"

"One idea with a new title," the retired philosopher chimed in, describing the author with dismissing distain. "Like Dante he dared to write his autobiography into a universality."

"But unlike Dante he is no genius," his former student enhanced with a false heartiness. "Although he does prove at least part of the good padre's definition of humankind with his writing. *Merde, merde reel.*"

With that, the retired philosopher turned towards the defrocked priest. "There's nothing holy about us, padre," he challenged as his friend nodded with assurance.

The poet grew immediately grave, running his forefinger along the rim of his tall drink. "I think there *is* a holiness in humanity," he countered very pointedly.

"How poetic," the friend of the retired philosopher said as if the word was unfamiliar to him, his former professor laughing at his antic.

"It's a call of evolution within us to yet evolve," the poet offered in defense of his position.

"Bongos to become Beethoven!" the former professor offered with a smirk.

"An"—the poet seemed searching for a word, for himself rather than in answer to his taunter, and then gave up and went on instead. "It goes back to the oldest piece of literature known to us. 'Let me uncover a secret thing for you, Gilgamesh,'" he said quoting the ancient work. He waited as if for his memory to catch up with him. "'By which a man can get life within,'" he finished with a nod.

"But you have to admit the human journey comes close to crushing Gilgamesh," the host was quick to add.

"Right—life is just a bowl of fucked up cherries," the retired philosopher interjected.

"Not that you fucked any of them," his smirking friend and former student said leaning his way.

"But," the host went, despite the duo's interruption, "Gilgamesh has learned to love. And with it he has learned the secret of the mystery called the Opening."

Three mocking claps followed from the retired professor, but they didn't deter the man sitting in the wicker chair opposite him. "There you have it, the wisdom of the most ancient piece of literature and the ages," the host said leaning over towards his mocker in mock imitation of the professor's friend.

"From Gilgamesh to Jesus," the poet took up as if he and the host were a chorus in a Greek play, "to the most contemporary of humans."

"And all of it bullshit," the friend of the retired professor of philosophy added. "Just cultural constructs."

"Jesus"—the defrocked priest said and then paused for whatever reason—"used the same word, Opening. *Ephaphatha* in his own tongue. He would have humans carry that opening to beyond the crooked cross of existence, past your cultural constructs, past the hypocrisy and bullshit. Into God."

"Back to God," the friend of the retired philosopher said with a groan of dismissal.

"And back to nonsense," the retired professor added. "Since you can't see this God *anywhere* in the world," he went on, looking from the defrocked priest back to the poet, "you are forced to say we are e-volving to him, her, it, whatever the hell it is."

"Evolving to a more understanding of whatever the hell it is," the poet corrected.

"The brain has radically reorganized itself in evolution, so anything is possible—even your mysticism," the man closest to the host offered the poet's way, his quiet sarcasm changing the other man's expression.

"Anything is possible," the defrocked priest added too quietly, "even prayer." He looked around at the rest of the faces looking his way. "Something I have not been able to do," he went on with a seriousness that took the group by surprise.

The host looked to the others for help.

"You asked whether God contains or constains everything," the defrocked priest pressed. His stare held on the others sitting around in their veranda comfort. "There is matter, and with matter comes entropy and with entropy suffering. Is there a hand of God in that suffering or not is what you are really asking with your constain—your tiger—your poetry. In our succumbing on this day or that, by this means or that—is there a providence that shapes our ends, roughhew them how uncertain life will?" The pale-eyed man stopped with that. "I'll tell you all a secret about myself," he said and then spilled it out in a suddenly much slower delivery. "In a certain matter, very important to me, I thought God was working in mysterious ways." The rain began to fall a touch harder and its scent stole onto the veranda along with a fresh burst of balmy wind, the moon now buried behind a patch of thick blackness. "But he wasn't," the defrocked priest finished in a near whisper, his eyes moving from the faces around him out to the rain. "God is not the Good Samaritan."

"As I said, we can't know and have a naïve notion of all this." The retired philosopher paused, but then did not go on, his gray eyes watching the man who had spoken before him, his expression, like all the others, as if saying 'we all have shared silences. Things we can't talk about.'

The balmy wind seemed to hold still, as if in wait, drifts of fog along the beach hanging in silhouettes at different places. The host got up to refresh the drinks and the old fluffy Sheepdog immediately proceeded to circle the veranda floor for the perfect spot to rest his big old mop of a body and its arthritic bones, his hind legs shaking some while the other dogs just watched. Like an intent sleuth he sniffed for that certain smell that is known only to the tiny gray cells in each canine head, going around and around in a strange circular pattern.

"How like us," the retired philosopher commented with a head motion towards the old dog, "chasing our own tails. Or non-tails as the case may be." Finally, the Old Bobtail flopped without further delay, making those little grunts of comfort dogs do on such an important find, the ritual ended.

"Visiting the grave, the old dog leads the way," the host said pouring as he did. The haiku poem seemed to have given him a way to lighten up the party again as well as the drinks. "On my tombstone they will write," he offered, opening up a new bottle of expensive gin, "this man was an utter failure except he had great dogs."

"The truth is I can't image you without them," the retired philosopher added, slightly exaggerating his last two words.

The host laughed and poured away, merely passing the Vermouth bottle over the martini glasses. "I will try to enjoy each moment with them." And then looked a sad look over at his Old Bobtail. "He wouldn't be with me much longer and I don't know what I'll do when he's gone."

"I think dogs—all animals—but dogs in particular know stuff. Know we are naked to the elements and are on our own." The man closest to the host drank down his martini. "Sans any divinity to shape our ends," he added more quietly, as if suddenly alone on a troubling tangent. "Jesus found that out on the cross," he murmured. "When," he went on, answering the cocked heads, "he hung there alone and realized his life had been spent for an illusion, in the end his God was not there. For him or anyone else, including old dogs."

"That's funny you should say that, because I wrote a poem about that very thing," the poet followed.

"About old dogs? Were they visiting graves," the friend of the retired professor asked with a smirk.

"*Christ's Thoughts On The Cross* I call it," the poet went on, paying no attention to the other man's smirk. "I am all alone. I will die all alone," he begin without waiting to see if they wanted to hear it, "No more trying to make God into something he's not."

"No more trying to make God into something he's not?" the host responded in a tone that sounded like a mock scold, then laughed a little laugh, carrying a tray of drinks back towards his guests. "I think Jesus died still clinging to love." He stopped. "And I think love is the memory of something lingering in us."

"God," the only man drinking red wine said to the host as he was handed another glass of Borolo. He had been silent up until then. He looked into his wine dark glass, and then up at the rest. "The way I see it, or hope it, is that God is love.

"On what planet do you live?" the friend of the retired philosopher asked and rolled his eyes.

The only man drinking wine nodded. "Everything argues against a God of love but love itself," he said. "But," went on in a voice of protest, "love is the deepest experience in our existence. The most profound. The most meaningful. Either that accounts for something, otherwise—"

"Otherwise what?" the guest closest to the host asked. "We'll realize life is saturated with emptiness?"

"Even as your martini runneth over?" the host offered, taking up the man's hand and bringing it to the stem of the martini glass.

"Perhaps we can't save God," the defrocked priest said to the blind guest and then the rest with a look around.

There was a long grating silence. "I don't know," the host answered. "All I do know is I want God to be God!"

"Which is what?" the defrocked priest asked in a tone that was more a challenge than a question.

"Which is the God of my youth," the host answered. "One that cares and . . . and I don't know . . . is there for me."

"Like grandpa," the retired professor mocked.

"Why not?" the only man drinking wine offered. "Or Abba, or Mamma mia! Someone who cares."

"Why?" the retired philosopher shot out.

"Because I do! I care! I am more than my bones and their marrow, more than my liver and lungs," the only man drinking wine shot back.

"Isn't the ancient Roman notion of *Dis aliter visum* closer to the truth than our God—yours and mine?" the defrocked priest asked. "The gods think otherwise," he added for those not familiar with Latin. "Virgil may have been right."

"Or our wine drinking friend and God is love lingering in us," the host answered for his put-upon guest, then smiled as if what he was about to say needed a comic cover with this crowd. "It comes down to more with a small m argues to More with a capital one," he added gesturing with his head towards the sky.

"Talk about a leap," the former professor said, shaking his head. "It's childish and foolish."

"Perhaps I am too childish-foolish for this world," the host responded with a light-hearted laugh.

The lone wine-drinker swirled the wine in his glass. "You are right, it is a leap, professor." He looked over at the confused man.

"Please explain," the poet asked, carefully taking his drink from the host's tray.

"Please don't. It's as vacuous and silly as all the rest of the proofs of God," the friend of the professor interrupted. "Give me nihilistic gaiety," he offered with a flair.

"But it's not meant to be a proof," the wine drinker said, looking at the friend of the retired professor. "Only a call out of my own love for such a God," he explained.

There was a long moment.

"We know you lost your whole family, my friend, and need the comfort of such a God," the guest seated closed to the host's empty wicker chair gently intervened. "But wouldn't what happened to you make you suspect the opposite?" he added quietly and with a cautious care in his tone.

"Everything argues against a God of love but love itself, and maybe that most—" The lone man drinking wine stopped before he would or could finish. "You're right," he offered instead. "I need the comfort of such a God, and I suspect there is no such God at the same time, even as I hope with everything in me that my loved ones died into God and God is caring for them."

"Even as he didn't on earth?" the friend of the professor interjected.

"I don't know that," the guest with the wine glass in his hand answered.

"The proof the pudding is in the tasting," the friend of the retired professor informed him.

"And what is that—that God is loving me through this, or that he caused it? What flavor of pudding do you choose?"

"I choose what really happened! That he didn't stop it! Allowed it!" the professor told the wine drinker outright. "So how does he care?" the retired professor followed as if a prosecuting attorney. He turned to his jury. "I am sure that is what my friend meant."

Some of the other guests were taken aback at the pair's insensitivity.

The only man drinking wine smiled. "What *really* happened? I thought you said we couldn't know that."

"Hoisted on his own petard!" the host said with a laugh. "There are more things in heaven and earth than are dreamt of in your philosophy, Ho-ratio."

"All I know is I lost my faith over the problem of suffering," the defrocked priest said in a near whisper.

"And me over reading the gospels." With that, the blind face sitting near the vacant host's wicker chair laughed a little laugh, and his empty eyes looked over at the man drinking wine. "These eyes are my answer to you."

The defrocked priest looked from those empty eyes to the man looking into them. "There is some very private part of us that always remains loyal to what we have loved," he offered, it sounding like he meant the man to his loved ones until he went on. "Like the sweet God of my youth and that trust," he said the host's way. "Even as it has proven chillingly untrue," the man still wearing his collar finished looking directly at the only man drinking wine. "Look at me, have sympathy on me, for I am alone and alone," he finished quoting a Psalm.

"And so we are all left on the road to Emmaus," the man closest to the host's wicker offered with a slight nod, "saying everyman's prayer, 'we were hoping.'" His empty eyes never moved off of the other man.

"Yet he still clung on," the poet interjected, almost as if a reminder to himself and a protest to the others.

"Who are we talking about now?" the friend of the philosopher asked too cheerfully.

"Jesus," the poet answered, almost ignoring the man he was addressing.

"Jesus!" the friend of the retired professor of philosophy shouted out.

"Clung on to what?" the defrocked priest challenged the poet's way.

"His *empty* loyalty," the blind man interjected knowing what was coming.

"Why do you call love empty?" the host asked cocking his head just so. "It was real on his part—true?"

"Jesus died too early. He should have grown too old for truth," the retired professor offered with a sip at his martini. "Like me," he assured with a feigned noble nod. He looked over at the poet. "Do you have a poem for that?"

"I do," the blind man answered, and as if reading from a torn sheet out of his memory, his empty eyes danced in their sockets, and words began falling out of his mouth as if written on the surrounding night, hanging there, his voice sounding in everyone's ears . . . "We all compose our own requiem, Dear Amadeus/Each done doomed day/Having been to hell and part-way back/When those we love die/And what word wisest/Left living a paean to diespair/Left to call out to, to cry out to/A terrifying empty/That hole left in our world/In/Us/Lear-like/Almost gone with them when/The radical unmappying/Begins the dizzying depths of self/ To somehow live on/Composing/Composing our own left life/And what's left of love/A world changed forever/And a God with it/Eli, Eli, lama sabachthani/For wasn't God all the while that love."

The applause seemed to stop the blind man in his muse, but then he smiled. "And so dies Jesus and us all."

"Yes, prayer is so one sided. You always end up talking to yourself," the retired philosopher added.

"One day solitude will make you weary," the poet took up after the man as if chastising and describing him both.

"And on that day I will hug a horse and go mad. I didn't know you read Nietzsche," the man closest to the host's vacant wicker said to the poet without looking at him. "Plagiarism is of course the best of flatteries." Nothing moved but time. "You blush," he responded to the poet's silence. "You are too young to realize everyone is a plagiarist, at least of his own memory."

"Thank God we stopped talking about God for godsake," the friend of the retired professor said bringing his martini to his lips and saving the poet further embarrassment without meaning to. "Like what's-his-face, ole Fatty, it's the only thing to do. It's all naïve chatter."

"I don't think he meant to say that when he stopped talking about God," the host said with a laugh.

"Who?" the poet asked, looking the host's way.

"Why—do you want to 'quote' him, too?" the friend of the retired professor responded with a touch of naughty *l'amour bleu* in his laughter as he looked the philosopher's way.

"I remember," the defrocked priest interjected, "if I might plagiarize my own memory some. I remember," he said prompting himself, "while a missionary in the Amazon, preparing a sermon on providence, and while I was, a jaguar struck and a wild boar squealed in the bush." He looked back from the darkening ocean. "Does that tell us anything about God? Something not naïve chatter?" His steel eyes held on the friend of the retired philosopher and the host handed him his martini with a twist.

"Humans do the same don't we—eat other creatures! It's nature," the retired philosopher rebutted to one an all with a look of 'so what?'

"But nature is not worthy of us," his younger friend said in a feigned scold towards his older companion. "I remember taking your class and hearing you say it yourself."

"No, nor is nature worthy of any God worth his name either," the retired philosopher added as if a bon mot and not to be taken seriously.

"I agree." The defrocked priest set down his drink and stared at the rest, very intently. "Why would anyone want to adore a God that allowed the jaguar to eat the poor pig who wanted to live and run free? Why a God that allows the ichneumon wasp to eat the caterpillar while it is still alive—alive without anesthesia? Nature is not just indifferent, it is diabolical." His voice trailed off into a silence as he held on them all.

"Who knows what's what?" the guest seated closest to the host's empty chair said, tapping his blind man's cane in a nervous gesture. "We're back where we started. Does God contain and constain everything—including cruel nature? It is one notion of God, Reverend Father. That such a Mysterious Source contains yin *and* yang. Good *and* evil. The shadow as Jung called it." He went to take a sip of his martini, but then stopped. "As for me, I myself hold that such a Mysterious Source is beyond good and evil. Where *nothing* swims in the primal energy that is the basis of everything, where there is no meaning, only a motiveless primordial urge to be. The whence, whiter, and why of you and me is oblivious to that—it is beyond good and evil, men and minds, shadows and suns. And love, too, my dear wine drinking friend."

"Yet, you and I exist and we can't be oblivious of that," the defrocked priest began. "And no matter how any of us might deny it," he was too fast to add as if in a debate within himself, "no matter how any of us might disregard or denounce any dichotomy or duality in that existence, we are still forced to deal with what every human being must, the difference within us, between this presence you speak of"—there was a pause as he looked over towards the host—"and this thing called nature around us, even as we are part of it. Let me repeat that another way, since it is elementary."

"Elementary, Doctor Watson," the friend of the philosopher interjected with a little laugh.

The defrocked priest gave him a look that could kill, and then merely went on with what he was going to say. "While we are alive, no matter who we are, a chain-smoking Zen master or a defrocked priest downing his gin"—he shook his glass—"we are forced to deal with that difference. Indifferent nature and a conscious even caring creature caught in the midst of it all."

"What the hell is that supposed to mean?" the friend of the retired philosopher shot his way.

"That we are like my man in the woods," the host answered with a nod.

"Shoot the damn thing I say," the retired philosopher added with a carefree drink of his martini.

"And be done with it and God, too," the retired philosopher's friend followed up with exaggerated eyes as he nonchalantly picked up the notebook the host had laid face down and began to read from it, as if at random. "I felt somewhere deep inside myself when I looked out at the lonely vistas empty of human coloring. No, it was not sweet, but rather naked, stripped down to a contented barrenness touching at something strangely true." With that, his sky blue eyes looked up again at the men around him. "We are all," he went on in apparent agreement, still holding the notebook and its anonymous quote, "merely a mosaic of faces at the end of Fellini's *Satyricon,* and nothing more."

"I didn't see that," the blind man said with a touch of wickedness.

"Mais ou sont les neiges d'antan?" the poet asked, looking around at the group. "Isn't that what Fellini was asking?"

"I thought it was Villon's question," the retired philosopher added, purposely missing his point while adding salt to the poet's still festering wound concerning his first quote.

"Analytical philosophy has left you a pain in the ass," the host teased with a laughing follow up.

"Now there is a subject for consideration—"

"My ass?" the retired philosopher interrupted.

"Philosophy," the blind guest offered. "Philosophy as taught today by asses. It is more harmful than helpful."

"Really, that is *de trop* even for you," the retired philosopher responded with a shortness in his own tone as well.

"It cuts our wings," the blind man went on as if he hadn't heard a word of the interloper. "It has become an institutionalized tyranny of thought." He tapped the tip of his cane as if in a rhythmed but quiet rage. "Present-day philosophy is really a conspiracy of the cerebrally pedestrian—their word games adding up to nothing more than a tower of babble. Like yourself, Herr Professor, they are committed to an unfit, unfounded, unforgivably quibbling counterfeit life."

"I hope you're not taking about what I think you are talking about," the friend of the retired professor said rather pointedly.

"I'm talking about analytical philosophy—which is as anal. Certainly its advocates have it ass-backwards," the blind man responded. "You can't abstract yourself out of existence and hope to know what it is. You stop a person at the borders of inward expansion with your damfoolery—with your anal-ytical philosophy. It just doesn't work," the man closest to the host's chair ended with annoyed tap of his red and white stick.

"You're talking about what I gave my life to," the retired philosopher answered with a little smile, trying to mollify the moment.

"Then you have wasted it," the blind man said without smiling back. "Exterminate, exterminate, exterminate—you and your ilk are like those soulless mutations housed in armor—"

"Daleks?" the poet asked, a touch surprised at the improbability of the blind man knowing about Daleks and Doctor Who.

"All you want to do is exterminate the human spirit," the angry man went on, paying the interruption no heed, "the human surge. Your ilk is the distillation of all that is evil in the universe," he finished, narrowing his eyes and cementing it in his mind. In his frustration, as if nowhere to go with that, he lifted his red and white cane towards the defrocked priest. "Does religion have anything to say about this?"

"All religions are merely the will to power," the retired philosopher said dismissingly.

"But I," the defrocked priest added holding on the retired philosopher, his eyes moving to the blind man, "wasn't discussing religion, I was discussing God."

"Yes—and so what convinced a hairless ape that he was the object of divine affection?" the retired philosopher shot back.

"Troglobites," his former student answered as if on cue.

"What is this some sort of a gig you two worked out," the poet shot out with distain in his voice.

"Like you and all those men you quoted," the retired professor offered with a continued smile the poet's way.

It was then the wine-drinking guest came back from what appeared to have been a roaming in his own thoughts. "Jesus *was* anointed," he shot out. "Anointed as to tell us, show us something—to cling to love no matter what."

"Emotional turmoil has taken hold of the poor man," the friend of the philosopher said with a sip at his drink.

"Next he'll tell us there will be a resurrection of the body," the retired philosopher added.

"No," the only guest drinking wine answered, "But we do die into God. It is a changed state of being," he explained, going on it a rapid pace, the word spinning out of him. "We are transfigured and spiritualized, freed of the limitations of space and time, freed from the restrictions of matter, without doing violence to our identity, the same yet different, and in this and as such enter into an eternal embrace of Love. As does all that dies, including our beloved dogs and birds and all the wonderful animals. Of course, we cannot imagine such a state of being, such a *joyous rapture!"*

With that he fell silent and so did the room.

"About those bygone snows," the host interjected, trying to lighten the moment, "Camus playfully writes in his *Notes,* that he believed in God but not in immortality."

"What does it matter what Camus thought?" the intimate of the retired professor asked, too cavalierly.

"'Fuck you,'" the host shot out, "would rightly be our response to"—he turned back to the others—"a divinity that betrayed us so. God would be the Absolute Judas-Brutus!"

"Well isn't he?" the friend of the retired philosopher burst out, and then put an olive in his mouth as he looked the host's way. "That is, if he existed. Unlike you," he was sure to get in looking the host's way, "I don't fumble about over a God. I could never be a metaphysician of sunsets and snowflakes."

"Nor I," the defrocked priest interjected, but not in the younger man's cavalier attitude, "for I have seen nature for what it is—and maybe God, too."

The retired philosopher laughed a harsh laugh. "These intelligent design folks don't know what they are asking for—a *malin genie*," he said with a nod.

"I hate what nature has to say about God," the poet offered in agreement. "Nature with no mind to plead, no heart to feel," he went on as if beginning one of his poems, but then his voice dropped off realizing that no one was listening.

"Sipping at our thoughts here on a rainy night, doesn't—" the host paused making sure to gain everyone's attention—"love *demand* that God not be unaware of love—not be less than us? As our friend over here suggested?"

"The tide pool is less than the brain that eventually came out of it, so why not?" The blind man waited for an answer from his host.

But it wasn't the host that answered.

"Like the brain is more than what it came out of, the brain too has something deeper still in it that is more than the brain it came out of," the only man drinking red wine said across to the blind man. "Of course, in truth, whether the brain evolved to it or was there before buried in the brain, or in eternity, I have no idea, but somehow, someway, somewho, this something deeper still senses a divine intimacy," he added, but with a hesitancy in his voice. He laughed, as if at himself. "Oh God," he offered, "see what happens when I drink too much wine."

"Yes, you become silly," the blind man nearly snorted his way.

"That seems to be what any notion of God has to be," the retired philosopher interjected.

"My notion of God may be silly, or naïve as was said before," the wine drinker quietly said back to both men, "but not my experience of goodness and beauty and love. That is truth itself. God—who really knows? I grant you that. But goodness and beauty and love I know. And so do each of you."

No one said anything until the retired professor finally did. "One of my students asked me this very common and honest question. How do we know love is not just a biological side effect? Isn't it instinctive for a mammal mother to love and nurture her offspring? How can we prove love is not just a biological need for the continuation of our own species? I gave him an A for the course just for that question."

"And what did you give yourself for the answer?" the poet asked.

"I give myself a failing grade," the defrocked priest interjected, gazing up from his drink out to the rest. "I say that not because I am without a family or a companion, or even a career anymore, but because without God anymore. No—not gone, but now so very different." The tall-stemmed glass shook slightly in his hand. "The things that happen to us have to show something about God." His intense eyes looked out and held on the darkening ocean. "Now God seems so different, so other, without warmth or intimacy," he went on, as if to both the blind man and the man drinking red wine, without turning their way. "One that doesn't have any sway over the aftermath of its creation." A near silent sigh followed. "But what was the purpose of the whole of it then? Was all this necessary?" With that, he looked back at the rest of them with a nod. "We have since day one till the present had and have very naïve notions of God. And no God, too."

"You have to reset your watch, padre," the friend of the retired philosopher offered the defrocked priest's way. "You just told me a while back that you didn't have a naïve notion of God." He gave dramatic sigh. "Besides, no one cares these days about any ole God. Or no God either. It's all as passé as a Dolce & Gabbana scarf from last year. And less significant."

"One thing is for certain, this divine myopia we are discussing will lead to madness," the retired philosopher protested, more than ever enjoying the antics of his former student who blew a stage kiss his way.

"As I said, who knows what's what," the blind man said towards whatever he was looking at with his empty eyes.

"There is a line from Brecht—'I don't trust him. We're friends.' For the most part, that is our most honest relationship to God," the host said with a sip at his dry martini.

"I don't trust him. We're friends?" the poet questioned. "How can you be friends with someone you can't trust?"

"Would each of us on this veranda trust the other with his life?" the defrocked priest asked the poet directly.

"Yet we are friends," the retired professor said, nodding with a little laugh. "Relatively speaking."

"Does that mean like with relatives—cause I hate mine," his friend said over to him.

"It's hard to trust God with our lives," the man still wearing a collar said, but in so thin a voice that only those closest to him heard him. He looked back at the poet.

"Fine—but then you are not friends. The same here. If I can't trust you, you are not my friends. Not really." The poet rested his case.

"The poet Blake asserted that he saw into a further world than this," the blind man said as if a description of all poets, his eyes following the direction of the voice that had just spoken. "I see only what is and hope for the rest."

His eyes hung in a stare.

"My hope, my genuine desire, it's that the lion lie down with the lamb," the host took up as if a challenge to the silence. "That the wasp doesn't eat the caterpillar alive or dead, that the school of squid don't swarm in a cannibalistic food frenzy on a lone squid swimming in its killer waters, that there are no Komodo dragons eating out the heart of a downed deer as it looks up in terror—"

"That we don't eat out our hearts for a God of love because of all that," the man closest to the host interjected.

"Do I see too much in love?" the host asked over towards his old blind friend.

"God seen through the lens of love is—"

"The Greeks thought the gods were capricious," a voice interrupted before the blind man could finish. "And Lucretius downright hated them. I love the way his poem ends with the sanctuaries of the gods swollen with the accusing corpses of plague victims. And you can't say that the God in Job is anything but psychotic," the poet went on with a surrendering shrug. "Me thinks the East had it right with yin and yang after all," he finished with a look the blind man's way.

The host put down his tray of drinks, took up his notebook and turning some pages began to read. "There is that which cannot be told, the nameless before heaven and earth, above existence and non-existence. How calm! How indistinct! How dim! How confusing! It stands unchanging though ever acting everywhere, untiring. To its accomplishments it lays no credit. It loves and nourishes all things, but does not lord it over them. It is the gate to all mystery. I do not know its name." He stopped and put down the book again, taking up his tray and handing out the last of the refreshed cocktails. "The Tao is beyond and before any yin and yang," he said as he did, looking directly at the poet.

"Oh, goodie, for the Chinaman," the friend of the professor offered with a false enthusiasm as the host sat back into his wicker chair with turquoise pillowing. "Except, if it can't be told, why did he tell us about it?"

"Exactly! How does he or any of you know what God is?" the retired philosopher said. "Even if I grant you a wordless Source before all this, it is totally Other than we could even imagine."

"And doesn't seem to have any say or sway in spacetime," his friend added with a period in his voice.

"But if it is the Source of existence, there has to be a way in existence back to the Source of it," the blind man said half asking in tone.

"And what way are we speaking of?" the retired philosopher asked after a pause, and then squeezed the cut of lemon into his tall drink. "Catholic? Buddhist? Jewish? Moslem? Your God beyond good and evil?" He smiled the blind man's way. "We're all children crying ourselves to sleep—that long sleep where dreams are said to vacate. Where did I read that?" He laughed, turning to the host. "As for your hope, hope is the enemy of truth."

"Those who live with hope, die hoping," the blind guest added. "I heard that on a visit to Sicily. In the city my maternal grandmother was born."

"God how fatalistic!" With that, the poet took a sip at his cocktail.

"But true nonetheless," the retired philosopher said. "The Source of all this is completely Other than we could ever know or even imagine, why don't we accept that?

"And what do we do with our love?" the host shot back.

"Live and die with it. Like Jesus. Cause God doesn't care one way or another," the defrocked priest said, suddenly dejected.

"How do you know that?" the host asked quietly of him.

"Because babies are born monsters and old people die as vegetables," the blind man answered for him. "Let's have no more naïve and silly notions of God. Let's have no notions of God."

A long silence filled the veranda and seemed to roll out to sea, a stillness filling the air.

"The question is—what does one give one's heart to?" the blind man add.

"And if I still say a loving God?" the only man drinking wine asked. "What if I still have this love?"

"What can I say?" the blind man answered.

It seemed to be what everyone was saying silently to himself. The friend of the retired professor sighed and then asked, "Can we have something to nibble on with the drinks?"

"We might as well be worshiping a volcano," the defrocked priest burst out, interrupting the moment. "A fucking volcano!"

"I think that trip to the rainforest clouded your catechism, dear father," the poet offered his way.

"Of course it did," the defrocked priest shot back. "I already told you that! Once you see nature in the raw, any notion you have of God has to become suspect. Didn't I already tell you that!"

"As well as not to have any notion as I recall," the friend of the retired professor said, rolling his eyes.

The defrocked priest turned out towards the ocean for whatever reason. "The argument of the earth is strong," he whispered.

"Wrong?" the poet asked, not hearing him clearly.

"For sure! Something's wrong, oh so something," the host suggested, but before he could go on, a quiet voice interrupted his.

"The echo of what could be, the shadow of what should be." Everyone held on the lost look on the blind man's face.

"So it is. And it's for us to set it right," the host quickly added, patting at his blind guest's hand as if to quietly call him back, and the defrocked priest as well.

"Yes, our host would have vegetarian lions. And bears that sing arias no doubt," the retired professor of philosophy added with a mean toast of his tall gin, missing the hand placed on the old man. "No," he went on, settling back comfortably onto his chair's turquoise pillows, "I am afraid one's personal drama is just that, and there is no good or evil out there." He waited for the man looking out at the ocean to respond, and when he didn't he went on. "Like with God, it's only in one's head."

"Some things are very real and very really evil outside one's head," the host said across to the retired professor, a suppressed anger coming into his eyes.

"Like what?" the man asked back, almost rising out of his wicker chair, as if this was an old battle between them.

"Like the Gulag, or Andersonville, or Dachau," the blind man responded for the host.

"How do you know they are evil?" the friend of the retired philosopher shot out, showing his own allegiance.

"What kind of nonsense is that?" the host replied, holding the stem of his martini glass in his left hand, his knuckles almost white. "Is Dachau only in our heads?" he challenged towards both the retired philosopher and the man's postured friend.

"When I was a young student," the retired philosopher replied, "I had a professor who quoted a Zen proverb to me about a student asking his professor why shit smelled so badly?"

"Yes, and he said if you were a fly, it would smell sweet. And the smell of the chimneys of Dachau sweet to a Nazi! But that's comparing shit to slaughter, answer my question, was Dachau in and of itself, per se, good or evil, irrespective of the Nazi?"

"Describing such things in human values has a humor to it that always puts a smile on my face," the retired professor answered with a smile.

"Yes, I am sure gas chambers are funny," the host said with a glare. "How Zen! Being thoroughly vacuous while attempting to sound clever. I see now why you are a *retired* philosopher."

"To witness the slaughter of innocent people and say it is not bad, is not Zen," the poet challenged.

"Yes it is," the only scholar on the subject corrected him, tapping his cane all the while. "Suffering is the forever problem," he said, his cane going as quiet as he. "We are all as blind as me when it comes to that. Zen masters most especially."

A quiet filled the veranda, and lasted into embarrassment.

"Should I put on some music," the host suggested, covering with an offering nod.

"Put on Mozart's piano twenty seven," the guest seated closest to the host offered, gaining his composure and smiling some. "It's the one where he looked back on his life."

"And?" asked the poet playing along.

"And realized it was not what he wanted to accomplish. So he writes this work as his answer to it. As I do mine," he added, again reciting from some scribblings in his mind. "It is me me mourns for/The dying death of/Self-taste/That youth and then/Young fire laugh/Potential lost/In the potting shed of/Life spent/Without genius/And God-wondering/Providence if any at all/Seeming so imperfect—"

"A million-fold contrivance and chance/Everything arguing against/A God of love/But love itself," the host added as if an old thing between them for one to start a poem and the other to finish it. He nodded a small laugh. As he got up to leave, the wind blew in a gust of rain that lifted the white tablecloth on the makeshift bar causing the display of bottles arranged so orderly on it to be shrouded in wet linen.

"Ghosts," the poet offered, pointing at the shrouds.

"Speaking of which, I maintain that dead people help us," the host offered, almost at the French doors into his home. "Hopkins in you writing poetry," he went on as if he had been thinking about it all the while, "Beethoven in my writing music. Shakespeare in someone writing plays, and so on."

"We're not very good channels though," the blind man offered with a laugh.

"Let's talk seriously of death," the retired philosopher said towards the blind man, stopping the host dead in his tracks.

"I thought we already did," the only man drinking wine interjected.

"Would you agree it is our final defeat?" the retired philosopher asked as if he had not been interrupted.

The blind man shot up out of his wicker chair and got down on the floor, curling himself up in a fetal position at the foot of the shrouds. "Tell us what you see, having died and now here again." The invocation hung there. A moment passed. The lone man drinking wine looked as if the he was thinking about those he loved long ago and lost and not here again, the blind man, too.

Lying there, the tired man found himself staring straight ahead. He gave out a groan and turned, curling up now on his right side. But fetal or not, it was futile. He couldn't seem to get past whatever it was. "Death our final defeat? No, life is," he concluded aloud. Yet, even as he spoke the words, his eyes still wondered in that odd way of his as if someone else had spoken the words and he listening. "Yes," he went on, getting angry with himself. He actually nodded, a vigorous nod. "I need no test—final or otherwise—to see that."

There was a pause.

"The wind," he said in a spinning speeding voice, "or is it the silence . . . maybe the touch of the alcohol on some synaptic spark traveling down a dendrite spin to an enigmatic engram in his cerebral cortex . . . or maybe just drifts, desert drifts and snow drifts in some distant delirium . . . something prompts these hopeless pale eyes to hesitate . . . as if to hope they are wrong."

Again he stopped, then went on at a more normal pace.

"One particular in my life paradoxically gives my sour eyes hope again," he said. "It is something I could never forget. An individual mercy—*that I will someday die.*"

He lay there on his side looking up at the shadows playing against the ceiling; listening to the silence. For whatever reason or non-reason the former actor sang the rest out. "How could you believe me when I said I love you, when you know I've been a liar all your life?" He stopped and his head shot around towards the others. "That's God's song!" he screamed, shaking all over. It took a minute or so, but then he calmed again, with only the slightest of tremors. "How oddly the mind works in the face of nothing," he diagnosed, almost nodding at his thought. "A song, a scream, silence," the slightly shaking man went on, listing the options. "Take your pick. Just so long as you know. Even as we really don't." He nodded at whatever it was they were supposed to know and whatever he meant; and again looked back at the faces all around. "Do you hear it too? Still! Despite everything!

Whispering to you . . . of . . . some-perhaps-possible-unknown-win-some . . . weather permitting maybemysterium we could in our wildest, weirdest, most wonderful moments, beyond the pale of night, right, or left brain activity, grasp nonetheless . . . something underneath the underneath and the undertaker, too?"

With that, he got up and sat again in his wicker chair and laughed a big laugh as if he had put them all on. "Death our final defeat? No, life is," he said in a bon mot voice with a toast their way.

They all laughed and toasted him back, applauding his performance, apparently agreeing among themselves that though he had not acted since his blindness, the old talent was still there. "The gloomy glamour of death," he offered their way.

"I still think death more gruesome," the poet had to add, looking around. "The body in such a throes, urinating and defecating, the breaking asunder! Dying is blanking, becoming blank. That's what is seems from this end."

"Yes, so it does seem," the host agreed, "and yet I have had an experience that told me after-death is so different. That told me of a radiant joy in a difference I couldn't understand, just as our wine-drinking friend said. Was my experience from somewhere beyond the skull? Timelessness in time? Or merely a chemical shot the wrong way in my head?"

"I'll tell you," the retired philosopher offered without hesitation. "When all the illusions are unmasked, stripped and torn away, there is only the naked reality of that skull."

"But if you look at a skull, you have to wonder what had been its dreams. No, I am afraid there is more than merely the skull." The statement from the only man who was drinking wine almost sounded as if he was thinking aloud.

"Do you think the same after you dig up the bones of a dinosaur, my friend? What had been its dreams?" the retired philosopher queried.

"My point exactly!" his friend burst out.

"Of course," the man drinking wine answered the pair of them. "And what a pig thought knowing it is heading for slaughter. Or a chimp in a lab readied for experimentation. Consciousness everywhere meeting this loveless world."

"How ridiculous," the retired philosopher responded. He pointed to a tree just outside the veranda. "Next you'll go and hug that fucking tree out there."

"I just might," the only man drinking wine answered. "And a horse, too. And afterwards maybe even go mad because of this fucking loveless world."

"You have to admit, my professor friend, we are a long way off from knowing what consciousness really is," the poet interjected. "There are scientists studying plants to see—"

"Yes, I know—to see whether they react," the former professor interrupted with a look of disgust on his face.

"Life is always an incomplete investigation," the blind man began. "Isn't there this investigation in contemporary science to prove a bone-headed dream in the skulls of physicists that says the other dimension exists side by side with ours, in ours, but we can't see it?" His face turned into a questioning expression, his blind eyes the only part of it remaining unreadable. "Just as we can't see the whole spectrum of electromagnetic radiation, or quanta, maybe when it comes to the dead or consciousness or—well you see what I mean." He smiled.

"Yes, what is naked reality," the host added with a nod.

"I seek the world of the first baby who laughed," the only man drinking wine offered with a healthy taste of his Borolo.

"What is that supposed to mean?" the friend of the retired philosopher asked.

The only man drinking wine put down his glass. "If you don't know, I can't tell you, young man."

"Our wine drinking friend exists in Neverneverland. No, make that in his wine glass," the retired philosopher mocked. "It's our host that exists in Neverneverland—and together they make one wit." The former professor looked around at the others, but no one seemed to want to play his game, so he finished his drink and held out his glass for more. His host merely turned and entered the house.

The retired philosophy professor shrugged and got up to pour himself another drink from a bottle with an ugly Queen on it. As he did, a murder of crows flying in the rain cawed overhead and the defrocked priest downed the rest of his martini in a swallow, holding up his glass towards the disappearing birds. With that, he got up and walked with a nearly imperceptible sway towards the makeshift bar and the ugly Queen. "Does God," he said in too loud a voice, "work his way through whatever I fuck up? And does he do the same through whatever nature or evolution does? That seems to be the final defense for those of us who would hold out for God," the defrocked priest finished as he stopped and stood there watching the empty sky the crows had passed through as if mesmerized by it.

"How? How does he work his way through evolution?" the poet asked him with a genuine sincerity in his voice that surprised the gathering. It seemed he was wondering if the defrocked man agreed with his earlier statement.

"How, indeed?" Suddenly, the sightless guest's voice mimicked the host's near perfectly. "I tell you, it is all traceable—God in evolution—traceable in the phenomenon we call love."

Everyone laughed and applauded simultaneously at the blind man's skillful mimicry. "Encore!" most of them shouted out. He obliged only with a bow.

"Even though you let in the clowns with your performance, I'm glad that you didn't continue with the charade," the retired philosopher said towards the man looking the other way. "Because," he explained, "I for one am tired of listening to what our dearly departed host has to say. It is all awash with unutterable, tip-of-the tongue twattle and tommyrot, mumbo-jumbo and applesauce, bull and balderdash, horsefeathers and hogwash, trick and trumpery, bilgewater and baloney," he added with more than a touch of meanness in his toast to the absent man. "Dearest host, you hang your hope on air/Your resolute on nothing/Your love on only love./ And is that really enough?/ Lost as it has become and is?/ Or does it linger still in eternity?/ In the timeless tomb beyond at the core of us?" he finished with a flurry of makeshift mockery in the form of a poem, as if an added argument of what he thought of his host's position, mere poetry.

"It's all like a sex scene in an Ayn Rann novel—it does nothing for me," his former student added and made a face towards the rest of the party. With that, he took a swig of his drink; then followed with raised eyebrows at the choice of music the host had put on, Corigliano's *Of Rage and Remembrance* heard coming out of the house.

"To rage and remembrance!" The retired professor lifted his glass.

Half the party joined his toast; the rest did not.

"Wherever two or three are gathered in my name," the defrocked priest started in, then stopped and laughed a silent suppressed laugh to himself, the host returning and sitting again as a lull fell over the group.

"I remember. I remember. Remember." The Chorus's words sounded from inside the house as if on cue.

"All I remember is that no one wants to kiss an old man," the guest closest to the host added, encouraging laughter with his bon mot about the music's lyric and himself.

"That's not true," the retired philosopher inserted with a follow-up smirk as he sat. "At least not for me. You see how relative it all is," he added looking over towards their host as his companion encouraged him on with a barrage of nods.

"What was it Jesus said about not casting pearls to campy Vaudevillians calling up a routine," the host responded towards the couple, a touch confused by their blitzkrieg.

"It's really not inviting calling your guests swine," the friend of the retired professor said, "even if you think it."

"Darkness and deserts today, daylight and desserts tomorrow, daylight and desserts today, darkness and deserts tomorrow, and tomorrow and tomorrow . . . it's all relative," the retired philosopher ended. "Isn't that the truth?"

"Aren't we all having a peachy good time," the blind man said in a mock-menacing tone, as if to tell the couple to cool it in the coolest way.

"Not as long as our host chooses to be silent like Jesus—silent before Pilate when asked about truth," the friend of his retired professor offered, drinking down the remainder of his drink and getting up to pour himself another.

"Or confronted with it," the retired philosopher said, adding to the indictment.

"Why really was Jesus quiet?" the defrocked priest asked, interrupting their game of get the host, his mind racing ahead as he looked around at the faces accentuated in the Chinese lamps' shadowed lighting. "Because he didn't know what to say in the face of reality—the reality of power," he said in answer to his own question. "He who had contradicted all possible metaphysical and historical ideas of God with his God of love was now facing reality. Love was. It had to be silent in the face of it. *In the face of fact!* He could suffer no greater contradiction, for love meant everything to him. Everything he did was based on his understanding of love, yet here it was failing in the face of the facts of this world."

"You're supposed to receive confessions not give them," the poet said leaning his way. "But didn't our wine drinker say as much when he talked about Jesus and love?" he added turning to the others.

"No—he made it sound like a good thing, and missed the problem it presents for everyone who talks of love in the face of the facts of this world," the blind man corrected.

"God *is* a leap of faith no matter how you look at it," the poet answered in his own defense, suddenly considering for a moment. "A leap over the exploding stars and the strained satire. Over the—"

"Oh please, a leap of faith is nonsense. I don't believe in faith," the retired philosopher interrupted, enjoying his own play on words, then turned back to the poet shaking his head. "You and Kierkegaard are—"

"Yes," the man drinking red wine interrupted, "you are right. No leap of faith, please."

"I thought you said you were for a leap?" the poet challenged his way.

"A leap of love," he answered. "Different thing," he added and smiled a soft smile, and then downed the rest of his wine in a thoughtful swallow.

"Do you see what he's saying?" the host asked the poet's way as if to help him to do just that.

"The way we see has an impact on what becomes visible," the blind man interjected in the thinnest of voices, tears threatening in his pale eyes. "It must be the music," he covered.

For a long while no one spoke and merely sipped at their drinks.

"Is it that voice of thin silence inside us?" the host finally said, as if to save the moment, looking around at his silent guests.

"One Kings?" the only man drinking wine asked aloud.

A bird lost in the dark sounded its cry as it flew on into a distance Doppler shift, its call fading into a faint echo beyond human hearing.

"It's all beyond human hearing and seeing," the defrocked priest said quietly. "Beyond scriptural references, too."

"It can't be beyond existence. It's all we have," the host said pouring more Borolo for the sole wine imbiber. "Even you said as much, *mon professeur*."

"*His* idea of existence," the friend of the professor objected.

"His idea, your idea, existence is existence," the blind man said towards the friend of the retired professor. "It's all there, but as I said, the way we see has an impact on what becomes visible."

"So you agree with me then—it is all relative," the retired professor said.

"No! Just the opposite! It's there for us to find, but there!" the blind man protested. "So don't give me your postmodern relativism shit!"

"Which leads to nihilism and anything goes," the host added, subtly bringing up their Dachau argument again.

"So tell me then," the retired professor shot back, "on what do you base this so-called morality you are spouting out?"

"Existence and the deepest experience in existence," the man drinking wine answered. "Our purely human spirituality," he finished with an existential confidence that surprised the lot of them.

"Yes, perhaps there is a *human* spirituality and it is different than—more than nature—but you still haven't told us how that relates to the divine? It is only human," the defrocked priest obsessed. "And also, why is nature so different than our human spirituality?"

"Because you can choose to do no harm, and the volcano can't," the host told his defrocked guest.

"What he is saying is, despite the amount of alcohol consumed by us, we are still conscious creatures," the blind man said with a toast their way.

"Relatively speaking." The retired professor held on those who had spoke before him.

"Only so far as we caused the relativity," the blind man answered back.

"Even choosing what form of alcohol to intoxicate ourselves with," the lone man drinking wine added.

"But how does any of this answer if God is constained and contained in—"

"Back to that?" the friend of the retired professor burst out. "Why don't you just tell us and be done with it!"

"I don't know," the defrocked priest answered with such an honesty in his tone it drained the ridicule in the friend of retired philosopher's statement.

"The truth is we postmoderns are right," the retired professor said, "this Mystery that started—that is the Source—is totally Other and we should just accept the fact and get on with what we are about."

"But what are we about?" the poet asked of them all.

Again a silence followed, until the man drinking red wine turned towards the poet. "Existence!" With that, he turned towards the retired philosopher. "Existence and the deepest experience in it. The same *more* that makes you more than nature. The same more that makes us aware of a capital More, the Mysterious More."

"But how can you be sure of that—the part about a capital More?" the blind man asked.

"I'll tell what I really think," the retired philosopher shot out, as if past endurance with all this, "he can't! Whatever you call God, or Mysterious More, or Source of everything and everywhere is completely other than us and a *feeling* isn't going to change that. A feeling of *more*, a feeling of *love*, or anything else!"

"Feeling? Love is more than a feeling."

"No, that's all it is, this love of yours," the retired man challenged the only man drinking wine, actually pointing at him with his forefinger. "Yours is just another still-born God," the retired philosopher challenged.

"Was it merely a feeling when you nursed your former lover during his final months?" the host asked the retired professor directly.

"What are you the lawyer for the defense?" the retired philosopher responded with a bitterness in his tone.

"The divine defense," his friend added.

After a mean laugh, the retired professor went on. "You all keep saying it comes from our innermosts—the deepest experience in existence—isn't that what you all have been saying?" he went on with a touch of frustration in his tone. "But what do we really know about our innermosts—know thyself and all that shit? And as for love, it is at best an aberration in the cosmos."

"And even if so, it is real—real and more than a feeling. Did you nurse him, clean his waste, spoon-feed him—"

"Stop it!"

"I'm just trying to show you what you already know," the host said to the shouting man. "Love is the deepest experience in existence."

"And if you saw how he looked in the end, you would have to say not in any way connected to this God you all speak of!" The former professor held on his host.

"No, I am afraid we must teach God how to love," the defrocked priest said with a firmness in his voice, as if trying to overrule himself and any moment of weakness.

"As I see it, and I do see it," the blind man offered, "we are all troglobites. You're right without knowing why, my silly young man," he said turning towards the friend of the professor. "And hopefully you never do and stay as silly as you are. Troglobites all," he assured, and then stopped in his attempted sarcastic whimsy, becoming suddenly very serious. "Like them, in perpetual darkness no matter where we stand on anything, ourselves, more than ourselves, love, and especially God."

"Quod ergo amo, cum deum meum amo?" the host asked looking over at his blind friend, knowing his history as he did. *"What therefore do I love when I love my God?"*

"Or when I say God loves me?" the blind man challenged. "That was a long time ago, my dear friend, before that fork in the road." He nodded. "You *see*, like Sophocles' Oedipus, if I might be allowed another simile, after my eyes were ripped out, I saw the truth."

"What are we supposed to do, believe every word that comes out of your mouth because you're blind?"

"I think the liquor is talking in all of us," the host said to the friend of the former philosopher, the young man no doubt still smarting over his dismissal as silly. "Let's calm down."

"Yes, and forget any talk of God. It doesn't change the price of peppers in Rio or bring back the snows of yesteryear," the blind guest interjected, taking up his drink.

There were swallows all around and then a lull.

"All I know is I am and I can love. The rest is the rest." The only wine-drinking guest smiled and held up his glass towards the group. *"In vita veritas!"*

"This is another fine mess you've got us into," the defrocked priest said up at the night sky, and he actually laughed, and everyone with him.

"What does it all mean? We haven't got a fucking clue," the host admitted as if the voice for all of them.

"Father, will you take our confession?" the poet asked and the man he had addressed made a mock sign of the cross over the lot of them, each left with his own confession, rage, and remembrance, and his own life and love as well—and with the Mystery that surrounds us, *still*.

With that, everyone toasted out towards the rain as the seals barked and the dogs barked back. The winds came up and drove everyone inside just as *Rage and Remembrance* ended.

We are left, of course, with our own confession, rage, and remembrance, and our own life and love as well—and with the Mystery that surrounds us, *still*.

"What may I hope?"—Kant's third great question haunts us here as we exit our dialogue. Perhaps our only hope is an embrace, Immanuel. Perhaps you and all of us with you are left like Nietzsche, looking into the Abyss, and the only response left to us an embrace. Life took him to the edge, and perhaps even caused him to fall over the edge—but not without first embracing this other suffering creature. Nietzsche could not live without love—his embrace of the horse shows that, nor it seems could he live without a why. "He who has a why to live can bear almost any how," he tells us.[29] All his suffering and struggle comes out in that embrace—loving and still asking that why as he did, that why of so much suffering, the why of life and living. It shows so much of the man. In a very real sense his greatest statement is this silent one—this silent one of caring. He who rejected both the credo and the cogito and concluded that there is no fundamental certainty could not reject caring in the end. He embraced this other suffering creature. Such an embrace does indeed become our only answer to suffering, with or without a caring from on high, with or without a why. It is our answer on *how to act in the face of suffering!* This is so whether secular or sacred in one's outlook, Nietzsche or Christ. To live love is the only answer—for the man who said *Gott ist tot* and the one called the Revealer of God as love both.

Each held on to their love, even as each asked why. "My God, my God, why . . ." Neither in the end weathered the madness called the human condition, one crucified and one confined to a madhouse calling himself the Crucified. We are caught in the cold snows of reality, with that dog at the gravestone, left to die alone and wondering why. It leaves each of us a yearning presence, poised between love and a why before we die. Perhaps all this makes for impossible thinking and a lifelong dialectic. Perhaps, too, whether or not we can fully bring those two together is not what is really important, only that I send that soup over to the bag lady. In that act, whether God or an answer to the why enters a person's mind, somehow, someway, the horizon of being changes. *Looking with the eyes of love and listening deeply to the cries of the world, one knows how to act, expecting nothing in return—this is the deepest encounter with existence and, in that, the deepest encounter with the mystery that surrounds us, even as we still ask and have to ask a why.*

We can talk of God, do theology, even without a God, or more accurately perhaps without believing in one, at least clearly so, but we cannot have a true human spirituality without love. A person must tap into that deepest of human experiences to be all a human can be, as he or she faces the mystery that surrounds us. Again, I employ a cyclic progression back to the tonic truth of this whole work: stay true to the two necessaries in life and you will have grasped a real spirituality, a purely human one. Even if one believes the world absurd, the moment can be meaningful, life can. The random selections of my sheep dog may be absolutely random—bringing me his toy to play with him, making me laugh, hollering at me for a cookie may all be random nonsense. However, despite the despair in such a reality as randomness, I can transcend the absolute meaningless of the universe and give meaning to it—give love to it—give a cookie to it. Yes, let's love and laugh at our predicament—it's the only way to defeat it—by putting meaning into it, by putting love into it. Knowing as we do that love is real. Live and love, that much we can do—and maybe only as much.

"Wie veil ist aufzuleiden!" How much suffering there is to get through, the poet Rainer Maria Rilke wrote. And love asks why, but never stops loving; this as it looks at everything with a stunned stare.

Quo vadis, Vincentus? Where are you going with all this?

Like those in that dialogue on a rainy night—still onward into our venture! Deeper and deeper into doing our dum'dee doggerel on the divine! Past postmodern persiflage and hoping you've got your hair well fastened on . . . to something so serious it is silent. To that something at the tip of my psychic tongue still not spoken! So bear with me, for a venture into God is a voyage into a great Mystery. One yes always in the subjunctive, a subjunctive silence, that is, always as a possibility of more, a wish for more, always a hope of and for more. "Please, Sir, I want more." Isn't that everyone's outcry? More to all this! Like Oliver Twist just to sustain we do need more! Sustain spiritually! Sustain spiritually so our love doesn't become loving hopelessly, a hopeless loving devoid of a final grounding other than death! But, therein lies the pain as well as the promise, for as love gives us more, it may very well give us More! Beneath the frenzy that goes on behind our frontal lobes, marooned in each moment as awareness is, the true sense of love lives and belongs to our inner mystery of identity, of presence, where perhaps we touch Presence itself, in and out as it goes, gaining deeper meaning, losing meaning, and regaining it, never as absolute, rather always human—our so very human love always asking for more—more with regards to More! Even the impossible! That the Presence be that love, that unconditional love! That is as honest as it gets, and earth as good a place as any to learn humility. Have I proven anything? Only that we can love . . . and only when we can . . . and yet . . . and yet this so human love gives us a sense of, a hint of a greater life . . . true, interrupted by driftings into a challenging weariness of why . . . but with a slow transformation through duration and daring *back to the will to love no matter what—the what* of our original quest and question? *De profundis clamavi ad* . . . And when we come back to *that what* of our *de profundis* we are still caught in our own embrace . . . of a horse or a God . . . caught with the horrible question still staring back at us in the mirror. The refrain of suffering is still with us as inexplicable *with regards to God*, even as naked love is the deepest thing we know, even as it is the most human thing we are capable of in the face of suffering. We who are capable that is—unlike the starving baby suffering such an ending to his brief and brutal life. Yes, like a *da capo* repeat out of a great musical composition, we come back to and must face the fact, the fact that although love is our deepest encounter with existence, the *more* in it, it does lead us into a labyrinth all its own making *with regards to God, the winding hallways all still hollering a silent staring stunned and senseless why!* Hollering why at *a what* it doesn't know! As in Beethoven's so very philosophical final quartets, we see our theme of love, the resonance of it, lead to an inversion that is contrapuntal, so too here. Is that where love must always lead? To a bewildering maze of keys? To a God that doesn't make sense?

Again, *Vincentus*, where are you headed with all this?

To the fact that we are all born with the gift of laughter and a sense that the world is mad, or at least should be! But what does that make our Maker? What God is, is truly incomprehensible when it comes to the life we are alive to. Theodicy (a vindication of the Divinity in allowing evil to exist) is a "delusion of reprieve." There is simply no explanation to the problem of suffering! No answer to the why! So how is it possible to say yes to a God of love—that God is love—in spite of this?

I am still in conflict with myself here, for I rightly could protest that I know love, for sure, but do I know God for sure? Perhaps I do, with a special kind of awareness, one that doesn't obey the usual criteria of coherence. One at the tip of my psychic tongue but that I can not say. No matter, why doesn't this Incomprehensible-Intimate I call God intervene? Intervene in sickness and injustice, in deafness and deceit, in suffering? Perhaps God does in an Incomprehensible way . . . or perhaps not. That is the most honest of answers anyone can give. But what it means is up for grabs. Can it really be answered? No! Neither the question of providence or the *why* of suffering can really be answered; though people are always telling us they have the answer. We are in a maze the mind has no way out of; the moods of the mind going one way and then another. *Miserere nobis.* Love is real and suffering is real and how do we put them together with God? We are left in the choppy waters of life, still and always asking. Do I fly towards an ever-receding sky, mixing metaphors in my mix up? Sometimes Buddha seems right and it is all somehow an illusion—or the Existentialists seem right and it is all absurd—or just is—and nobody is right. Beethoven's inversion is sounding in our ears! The stone-deaf creator is wondering about his stone-deaf God. Especially as he hears Him in his head and expresses it so mystically in perhaps his most personal work, his great Opus 131. Here the suffering man is confronted in his love before it reaches for the impossible. The last of the great fugues in order of composition (Opus 132, Opus 130, and Opus 131) ends with an embrace of incredulous relief, with a thankfulness still tinged with hesitation, but with a coherence of the profoundest attitude towards life and the Mystery that made him, with or without a deliverance from the why screaming in his deaf ears. Existence is that at its most profound breath, confronted love leading, leaping, beloving to . . .

Quo vadis, Vincentus? To that!

Somehow, no matter anything else, to realize love is to realize God—and it has to be as wordless and whyless as love itself. Do I intuit an entire theology out of my loving, my beloving, beloving to, leaping to that? Yes! However, when I murmur or shout out *leap*, I must remind myself the leap is not into something strange, alien, other, but is into everyday beauty and goodness and love, and maybe not a leap at all, but a walk in the midst of our humanness. It is as familiar as the faces we love and who love us, as warm as *familia*, the memory of grandpa holding you in his arms as a toddler and loving you so; the generosity of your older sister, loyal to you no matter what, who, when, or why; the smile of your mother; a father who would give you the shirt off his back. Is that domesticating God? Yes—of course—if you mean by that getting through our love to Love, using what we are, humans in love to get to Love itself, what-we-are showing us the way to *the what* we cry out to from the depths of our being where the Call calls!

God is not complete other, dead, or impossible, but living love within us, and in the beauty and goodness of love we witness without. To this we are invited to give our hearts and act out of in our lives, and thus and in this our purely human spirituality is carried to communion with the Call. Yet there is more - more to the More; that something still at the tip of my psychic tongue about God and Suffering! What I mentioned and must yet get to!

I just finished a book about a boy called Rex. Without going into a whole narration of his life, he was born with a gigantic, fluid-filled cyst in his brain that had to be operated on, then later he was diagnosed as blind, and later still as autistic. That is enough to send any parent into the abyss. Yet, his mother's love was unrelenting in battling for her "broken son." Ultimately, his road out of the dark world nature had thrown him into was through music. How like Beethoven. Perhaps there is something in music that goes back to the vibrating strings at the base of our becoming. "How could he have such a flawless sense of space when seated there in front of the keys and yet get lost in his own living room?" his mother asked. In the last chapter, called "Reflections," after telling us about her despair, about being left blank and confused both so often, his mother writes: "Then I would hear Rex's piano music, and it would take my breath away . . ." She goes on to say how she felt God's presence in the music, and in the next to last page of her account of her journey with Rex, says, "I began to see God's truth revealed. Initially vaporous and blurred, that truth gained clarity in the emergence of Rex's spirit, pure and beautiful, from out of the darkness of his own imprisoned body and mind." She more than suggests that God send her Rex, and the suffering, to make her hear "each note resonating with His truth."[30] Her reaction was contrary to Weinstein's. But in truth, I have to honestly say I don't agree with either Weinstein or this wonderful woman, in that, one way or another, each seem to be saying God sends us the suffering, whether one rejects a caring God and the other holds for one. I don't think God sends us suffering, but loves us through it. That's why Beethoven speaks more to me. *I don't think God sends us suffering, but loves us through it.* There I think I've got it! I think I've said what my psyche has been trying to get out, what my presence has been trying to express, the more about the More that now adds yet another level to our venture.

The why of suffering remains a mystery to be sure; and Falls of all sorts as toted by religions of all sorts, and everything with them, do not explain it. Whatever might or might not be, the truth has to be, if God is love, God is not the cause of suffering. Of course it gives us a different God than most are use to, that All-Powerful, Et Cetera—but still one closer to our own deepest expression of being; and since existence is the only thing we have to go on, dare I say this choice is the strongest one I or anyone can make during this sojourn called breathing. It is a walk in/leap into our own depths. And when you or I leap into that love, walk and wait and wonder in love, you and I can say with the assurance of beloving—*and only that*—that God doesn't sends us suffering, but loves us through it. Just as love would! So with the confidence of love and within the confines of the subjunctive and my very self-being, I can say within that human horizon that God is love and as love loves us on and through and into a realization of Love itself. I am and I can love, and in that love realize God - and realize that God leads us through suffering, loves us through it!

It's a blaring hot day outside, nothing suggestive of shadows and shaded groves, only bright cutting clearly distinct and indifferent reality, devoid of me and my sentient self. I leave my den and wander into the living room where my Old Bobtail is snoring in dreams of green grass and wild winds on rocky cliffs off an island shore. "It has dawned on me late in life that no one loves me," I say to him. "Well maybe my dog." He refuses to wake to my humor. This is a hard room to work. Vegas would be easier. I straighten out the painting of myself, the gift from a now dead friend, and then cross the room and put on Opus 131.

Each one of us has to connect the connections for his or her self, but it is so like Beethoven in his reach of confronted love and cuts right through you. Just listen to Opus 131. The suffering man is confronted in his love before it reaches for the impossible and achieves it. The last of the great fugues in order of composition ends with an embrace of incredulous relief, with a thankfulness still tinged with hesitation, but with a coherence of the profoundest attitude towards life and the Mystery that made him. The suffering genius tells us, as only such an insight into life can, that relief from suffering comes only in this embrace of the mysticism without ecstasy, even as he lifts us into ecstasy. How like the blind man in one of Fellini's films, where the movie ends with him playing away on his accordion as he sits on a wooden chair alone on the sand save for his straggly dog, his head back and he lost in his wordless wisdom. Here is the true *ubermensch*—where one overcomes the *untermensch*—and knows love, and in that knows something wordless even as he doesn't know the why to this world and the wounds in it. Here, in this wordless wisdom is where I dare to head to find the Wisdom before the big bang still in the world, that Wordless Wisdom of *that what* that began this divine dialectic. Of course, my fellow ad-venturer, it does require, call it what you will, a leap into love. *But since love makes sense in a way only love can, so does a sense of God as love only in the way it can.*

Yet, with regards to that, it becomes necessary here to point out a reality to which we all too often fall victim again and again, namely, that the world keeps whittling away at our sense of loving, first by showing the loveless universe we are alive to, and then by the ways of humankind itself. The brutalities big and small that are done by human beings does drain one's hope, and yet . . . and yet we still can and do hopefully love on, live on without hope in humankind. Our hope in place in Love itself. However, without that we live on in a universe, a world, an existence without any hope—afloat in the face of just what happens, at the mercy of chance, chaos, or universal contingency, alone alas along the riverrun, even with our human love. Perhaps, we conscious creatures cannot face that, because it is too awful.

Of course, the opposite might be true, that we cannot accept such an awful actuality because it is not actually so, and a wordless wisdom tells us so, despite the world and its willowing. Love understands what God does not say, and we cannot—is that it then?

After a chapter, a cave, and now in the midst of our humanness and yet another chapter, and we are only on a subjunctive stage shouting out to a silent heaven, still only human? Yes! No, not in the subjunctive about our minimal certainty and the love that comes out of it—but when we approach the subject of God, yes of course, subjunctive and only human! *But since love makes sense in a way only love can, so does a sense of God as love the only way it can. Everything argues against a God of love but love itself. But love is the deepest experience in our existence. Either that accounts for something, or nothing does really, both in our human endeavor and divine one, not if what is deepest in our being is meaningless. And so in the light of that we make our leap into love, from the most in our being to the Mystery that gave us being, from or own giving to GIVING itself, from love to Love.* Look what we can accomplish in the midst our humanness!

Nietzsche warned to be careful because if you look into the abyss, if might look back at you; but, I am saying the opposite, be hopeful, because if you look into love, it might look back at you—no, that is wrong, it will look back at you. But we must look in the first place, in order for that to happen. The goodness and beauty and truth of love is in life, and when we see it we sense more, and in that more, something that fills the moment and the abyss both, showing us, even if only for a moment, that God is not dead, but a living God, in that goodness and beauty and truth of love; that we are here to love and dare I say, even be loved. Is that too much? Asking for too much and too much, too? Not when you really look at the beauty and goodness and truth of love in life. When the first baby laughed humanity was born I said earlier in this venture, and must add now, that when that baby first loved, the divine became visible in his eyes, in her eyes—and ours looking into his and hers. And this goes for all love. Each of us has to be opened to it, be sensitive to the tender elements in life. The way we witness has an impact on what becomes visible. This takes will! Try loving in the face of ugly behavior. No, loving is not for cowards. Socrates was not a coward. Jesus was not a coward. Anyone who loves in the face of this world is not a coward. Loving, like growing old, is not for cowards.

Way back in the first Chapter we penetrated into the profundity of our own presence in the cosmos, and realized the deepest experience in it. With that we could speak to all who claim to be human, say to an Existentialist that we came up with a an Existentialism of love where we put love into the meaninglessness, or to a practitioner of Zen that we came to a Zen of love where we met the void—the empty moment—with one alive, alive with love, our limping all-too-humanly beautiful and real love to be sure, but there no matter. However one wants to call one's self, tinker, tailor, soldier, spy, Existentialist on the Left Bank or CEO in one, one's presence tells of a real existence and the deepest experience in that existence; it realizes one's root-reality. That is no mean accomplishment. With or with out a God, holy books, religion or anything of the sort, love exists and we proclaimed it as such! Who among us would say that it doesn't—that our loving those we love is without value? That it is meaningless? That it is unreal? We cannot bring ourselves to say that love is unreal, without value, meaningless—because it isn't. Not to any of us who have loved. We sense a loyalty to life itself in this—and so in the midst of that humanness we found ourselves with a fundamental choice arising out of this experience of love; a choice about one's basic attitude about actually itself. No matter whether you are a materialist through and through or someone who holds for more than the material, you still can choose to love or not to, still fight for your loved one's life, for your child's life, for your husband's life, for your mother or father to live, for your wonderful dog and cat and bird to somehow be saved, for the planet itself to be! It became all too clear, we exist and can love, but that deepest of experience is still a choice to embrace or not. By penetrating into the profundity of our own presence, we realized a purely human spirituality grounded in existence itself, one summarized and summoning us in the words: I am and I can love.

This inner decision is existentially called for, one way or another; our very make up is a tension between the raw elemental energies of evolution and a consciousness that can love. It is the through-line to everyone's opus, the opus of one's life, to love or not to love. How odd that what is at the core of our being defies the universe we find ourselves in—telling us in our very depths that there is more to all this, there is conscious love in counterpoint to the cosmos. Yes, there is love, love as the deepest experience in life. "No, it does not protect us against suffering. What it does is—well you know. And death and everything inanimate must be so jealous of that . . ." Yes, there is love no matter what—despite the deafness for a man who has to hear to create his music, and does in a way that confounds his physical deafness and the despair he faced because of it. There is love no matter what, and despite the silence of the universe, it is there as if spanning more than spacetime itself, as if telling us in our very depths that there *is* More to all this, giving that person a horizon that is beyond any other, and the second choice mentioned in our sojourn, the leap into love to Love. First the choice to love, then to leap into love to Love!

Despite being left to chance and change, circumstances and the cold laws of the cosmos, left deaf to it all, and daft, too, dying on a cross or in a madhouse or in an appallingly dirty and uncared for sickroom; love is its own revealer and it is into that love one leaps, into its intimacy and tearing warmth, into its legitimacy, sensing in it that the Mystery that made us doesn't send us suffering, but loves us through it, as love itself. Yes, we are all left like Ludwig aroused in his deathbed, or Friedrich so alone in his, or Jesus hanging abandoned on a tree, or the blind accordion player alone on the sand, all left looking up at the night sky wondering . . . the desperate encounter between our human inquiry and the silence of the universe so real . . . yet so is our love, and love as its own revealer, revealing a wordless wisdom, and with a leap into that revealer, the Call is revealed, the Wordless Wisdom, the Mystery of the what we call out to. In your own love then you will find the answer, either more only, or still More, and if the latter it will be in an embrace of the impossible become possible, with a thankfulness still tinged with hesitation, but with a coherence of the profoundest attitude towards life.

That is what came of our venture.

One more time, Sisyphus! Let's see if our divine dialectic comes to the same divine diagnosis, one that came to a God of love. So can one continue to hold for a God of love despite grief, disappointment, and death? Can one continue to give one's heart after it has been broken? Friedrich, Jesus, you, me, each of us must face suffering at one time or another in our lives, as I pointed out, lie there on that contrapuntal cross, each of us crucified on the cross of existence, the cross of crooked existence, abandoned by God himself on our personal Golgotha as it were, on that horrible hill, wondering where's the wisdom in the waste—but can any of us continue to give our hearts at such a time? Silent Nietzsche and silent Christ both tell us in their actions, tell us the refrain of suffering always returns *with a refrain of love as the answer!* Let's stop right there! Are we embracing a dead horse here, clinging to love because we fear it is our only option, and if we let go we will collapse into a mad cosmos and a dead God? We have love, OK. But our question here is not about *our* love, we have firmly grounded that in existence, and even in hopelessness, if need be, our question here arose and arises again even as I write this recapitulation, arises about God's love? Not love from our end, but from the other! We know we can love, but can God? "Or are we here to teach God how to love?" a serious scherzo again calls out from the two planks and a passion called my play.

In the comic agony off stage, in life itself, the question still hangs there for me, for you, for all of us. Yet, somehow, even then, maybe especially then, in such utter abandonment, love, stripped of everything, is finally realized as the only thing that makes sense in the universe. Yes, the refrain of suffering is always accompanied by the refrain of love. I remember writing that—because it is true. But is God that?

In the face of even an absolute actuality that seems meaningless, love is still meaningful to us. Even death cannot take that away. As anyone knows who stood over a coffin, looking with that empty incomprehensible almost surreal fact in one's gaze, the fact of loss, the loss of someone you loved not being with you and it breaking your heart—yet your heart still loving, with a certainty about it more than ever before; a certainty telling you that love is the only real meaning to life when all is said and done. We know to live love is the only answer, even as we suffer. I remember writing that—because it is true. But is God that?

A blink comes to my eyes here, in the midst of my supposed recapitulation. Am I to be thrice tempted like Christ in the desert? My musing eyes may look past the more in them to More, but is it only a half-beckoning wisdom, maybe even half-baked? We must give dreams their looking glass I might counter, but is life merely telling its old joke to new generations here? I'm too tired to recapitulate my recapitulation. At least let it keep until tomorrow. I gaze towards my French doors out at the dark garden. It is actually raining, with thunder and lighting, in Southern California of all things. I get up and open both doors, looking out into the fresh smells and cracking clouds. Does love understand what God does not say, even as it doesn't understand? None of it seems to interest my Old English, he turns and hurries down the shadowy hall with Grandpa's and Grandma's antique pictures looking down, his shaggy body already on the bed before I head for whatever space he leaves for me.

Whether it was the thunder and lightning outside my window or whatever was bounding around inside my head, I woke up at two thirty in the morning and found I couldn't get back to sleep, so I chose from a pile of books at my bedside, coming up with *Darkness Visible* by William Styron. I felt such a vulnerability reading it—that people are abandoned to such a fate. It seemed he was not Dante going through hell, but was himself hell. I have never heard the scream of madness in my head, but after reading Styron's memoir of madness I found my lips whispering my grandfather's prayer: *Signore, rammentate mi la mente.* 'Lord, never let me forget my mind.' Grandpa never did, living to eighty nine in full awareness and as holy as always. But what of those that do? What fate allows the brain to deteriorate into mush and madness, and forget the 'me' inside of it? And if not fate, what? Evolution, nature, chance, God? What is so impervious to the warmth and personal as to allow for such a loss as one's mind, unless it is without warmth and impersonal, and mindless itself? Alien to awareness! Such a happening has to cause religious terror in us. Existential terror! Suffering is more than a vague representation of all the evil in our world—no, it is not a simulacrum but a scream, our outcry, our outcry in what we are above all else, conscious creatures, conscious creatures in what seems an alien cosmos.

In such an outcry is God really relevant? In such a world as ours, is God relevant at all? What I thought I could put off until tomorrow was staring into and out of my wide-eyes. Such involvement is the soul of a dialectic about the divine.

I said when we experience beauty or goodness or love, we sense something more, and maybe mysteriously More as well. Of course enhancing beauty and goodness and love for others and ourselves becomes relevant for them and us—sending the soup over to the bag lady—but does it enhance the relevance of God in the world? Do we sense God's relevance and *what* God is in that?

I quietly watch the rain from my open bedroom window. God cannot be an abstraction, an idea or concept to which nothing really corresponds; it must be incarnated into our lives, and thus have a relevance . . . my thoughts drop off . . . waxing and waning within my wide-eyed stand in the wee hours of the night.

"Is love the messiah?" I hear myself whisper to the wind now knocking at the windowpanes of my French doors as I carry myself into the living room. *"Oui, le messie est l'amour, Jacques.* Yes, the messiah is love, Jacko." But is *what* I cry out to that, and thus relevant? Only so far as love is—is that it? So if we are but open to it, so open as to leap into it . . . do we *realize* God?

Like Nietzsche in his embrace, and Christ on his cross, I or you, Jacques or any one of us, cannot give up love—it is what saved Styron from suicide in his darkness visible when the temptation to end himself cried out of the pain and hopelessness of it all. He writes, late one bitterly cold night, when he knew he could not possibly get himself through the following day and sat in the living room of the house bundled against the chill watching an old film . . . "the characters moved down the hallway of a music conservatory, beyond the walls of which, from unseen musicians, came a contralto voice, a sudden soaring passage from the Brahmas *Alto Rhapsody*. This sound, which like all music—indeed, like all pleasure—I had been numbly unresponsive to for months, pierced my heart like a dagger, and in a flood of swift recollection I thought of all the joys the house had known: the children who had rushed through its rooms, the festivals, the love of work, the honesty of slumber, the voices and the nimble commotions, the perennial tribe of cats and dogs and birds, 'laughter and ability and Sighing, and Frocks and Curls.' All this I realized was more than I could ever abandon, even as what I had set out so deliberately to do was more than I could inflict on those memories, and upon those, so close to me, with whom the memories were bound. And just as powerfully I realized I could not commit this desecration on myself."[31] He did not give up on love, and it seems love did not give up on him. At the end of the book he mentions the *Alto Rhapsody* again and tells us how his own avoidance of death may have been a belated homage to his mother. "I do know that in those last hours before I rescued myself, when I listened to the passage from the Alto Rhapsody—which I'd heard her sing—she had been very much on my mind."[32]

Like Nietzsche in his embrace, and Christ on his cross, Styron in his darkness visible, or us in this venture, we cannot give up love—and in that very love we transcend and are immanent, and in that, dare to say we realize More, even as we still don't know the why or wherefore, only the wherewith to this Mysterious Meaning. And how do we know that—from the ultimate meaning in our very human lives.

God did not send the darkness visible, but loved him through it, in his own love for and of his mother and those close to him—to realize this is to realize God: that we join in God when we love. No, it doesn't answer the why of his suffering; and it confuses us all the more, and makes for this very divine dialectic, when we read that his daughter wrote after his death that in his last years he succumbed again to a lesser form of chemical/clinical depression, finally dying of pneumonia at eighty one. A moment of joy, a moment of happy rest, rest-a-bit, respite was not to last for him; his own chemistry a Judas-Brutus in his head, as if mocking my more and More with it. I suppose in the hell of a darkness visible a person would have to laugh at me saying there is a Mysterious Meaning and think me naïve, but at those moments when we get a glimpse into such a realization of what I speak we touch an inner time . . . although outer time does have its say in the matter of us. God is inner time. During countless ages monstrous creatures mangled other creature in and out of ancient seas, and after yet more strange outer time the tide pools came forth with us and outer time does have its say in the matter of us, in the matter of our make up, even as we are strangers on the Serengeti. We are strangers because of love! Not because of the raw elemental energies that make us up. We are strangers because of love. Even as the world of whittling and whittlers would have it otherwise, it is our most authentic moment in living as a human being, one in which we finally realize that love only shows us love, not whys and wherefores. Once we love somehow we know, even as we don't know, the human truth another man uttered out of that other darkness visible, his words still echoing in our ears: "The truth—that love is the ultimate and the highest goal to which man can aspire . . . the salvation of man is through love and in love." Both Frankl and Styron saw love was possible even in hell; that it happened despite the darkness. *Von allem Geschrienbenen liebe ich nur Das, was Einer mit seinem Blute schreibt,* Nietzscshe wrote. *Of all that is written, I love only what a man has written with his own blood.*[33] Certainly Frankl and Styron wrote with their own blood and so what they had to say has to be taken very seriously, listened to, listened to with our own blood. On the final page of his book Styron quotes Dante at the end of his own *Inferno*, *"E quindi uscimmo a riveder le stelle;"* and who knows maybe emerging to once more see the stars, he realized the same poet's words at the end of the *Paradiso,* which to me has always been a prayer . . . *"l'amore che move il sole l'altre stelle."* Yes, maybe like Dante, in the end we are moved by the Love that moves the sun and the other stars.

I cannot explain the dinosaurs or the their demise, nor our own discarding and dissolution of any sort, not in terms of sanity or the scared. Love does not give us freedom from the instinctual powers that make up nature, from the tireless tyranny of situations we find ourselves in, from the lovelessness all around us, and we cannot explain those in terms of love, or explain them away in terms of love. But love does give us something both sane and sacred, something of great resonance, as though we have gone beyond life on earth into another realm to a truth without words; this even as we have not but are still here as we face the doubt and drain and finally each of us the double-cross of our own bodies. I say these things, remind us of suffering and our whittling world, not to make any of us depressed, but do so as a caution to you and me and all of us; a caution never to let these things rob us of our love, which they are quite capable of doing. Fathomless permutations do exist in our breathing as a human being, and in the sweep and sully of things, despite how a person has been wounded, scarred psychologically and damaged in so many ways, so vulnerable we have to wonder, there is still within each of us a holy place of deep love, here on planet earth. If God is to be found, it is there—*and there relevant.*

I know what you're thinking, at least I know what I am thinking—this *still* doesn't answer why Styron or Hyman's patients had to go through what they had to go through. Of course I am not talking about the immediate cause of clinical depression in the one case study, or dementia in the others, I am talking about the root cause of suffering, be it in evolution or elsewhere, maybe even powers and principalities we are unaware of. No, it doesn't answer that, because, again, no one can answer that, with or without a God. Sentient creatures suffer by the mere fact that they are sentient, that seems to be the bottom line, and we can only help lessen that—that is what is relevant, or to put it another way, the giving of ourselves is relevant, so very relevant. If God is to be found, it is there—*and there relevant.*

Unless God affects the third question of philosophy for us, there is really no point of bringing God into the conversation or our lives. I stated that during one of my sweeping statements. Dare I say it again? Yes, because it is so. The only way God can be relevant in our lives is in the way we choose to act; namely, *God as realized in loving, our own love acting in the world in communion with, abiding in, the image and likeness of Loving.* Maybe that is what our times will finally grasp. Finally grasp—devoid of the divisions and distractions of dogmas and doctrines, rites and rituals, religious rules and regulations—finally grasp as the most honest and relevant way for humans to the Unborn, Unoriginated, Uncreated and Unformed, Incomprehensible, Imperishable, Indefinable Mystery that is God.

I am convinced of love, it is the most authentic moment in breathing; and in it we find our most authentic moment with God. Love gives us our purely human spirituality and the way to God both—for *ultimately* they are one and the same, both the human spirituality and the way to God. *God and the way are one.* Can I finally say that my parade of wobbly acrobats and contemplating clowns has come to a synthesis in this divine dialectic? I stare at my computer.

Since I made mention of the Principle of Uncertainty at the very beginning of this masterpiece, it might be appropriate to mention Werner Heisenberg by name here. Beside Plato and myself holding for levels of being, Hans Kung writes in his latest book, *The Beginning of All Things,* that Herr Heisenberg had a "theory of layers" in reality and spoke of a bottommost layer which was casual connections of phenomena and processes in space and time and could be objectified, and an "uppermost layer of reality in which the view opens up to those parts of the world which can be spoken of only in parable: the last ground of reality."[34] I think we can speak about it in parables, and in philosophy and theology, poetry and plays, as well. But best of all, I think each of us can *realize* it in our lives, in the full sense of realize, and therein "the last ground of reality" becomes everyday reality, and there and then so very relevant. Aren't the parables and philosophy and poetry and plays ultimately to bring that about; namely, to realize our humanness to its depths, to move us to breathe out of that? And even in the most bitter of landscapes a poem or play or our lived human condition can present, our human love can be there and real.

To relax from so much relevance, my dog and I watched *Looking For Richard* late into the night as the storm continued to rage outside. Al Pacino's documentary is about a group of very talented actors discussing and then performing Shakespeare's great play about a man who cannot find love, and in the last act knows he is alienated from his own self. "A horse, a horse, my kingdom for a horse," is more than the immediate cry for a horse to escape the battlefield; it is a cry for a way out of this—all of this! But he has closed off the way out. "I am not in a giving mood today," was his daily mantra. It is a masterpiece of deep personal choice throughout, with regards each of the characters; one surrounded as it is by a swell of politics that unmasks the true soul of that will to power, especially the way Shakespeare so beautifully puts forth the sophisticated hypocrisy of slippery words with motives totally opposite. Nothing has changed, not politics or the personal choice involved for we who live in our own postmodern play.

No, I did not escape the call to relevance; it followed me to the DVD and spoke out again through the words of the Bard who told me I cannot escape my own inscape. Great art will always do that.

"Oh, Jesus, to love in Lyons is so difficult," we might cry out in frustration, echoing Anne of Lyons moanananoaning through what was happening to her and her city during one of the endless wars humankind seems addicted.[35] Be it with Anne in Lyons, or with some career-hungry actor in Los Angeles moanananoaning in another kind of war and addiction, wherever any human happens to be, each of us faces the same problem; namely, that the affirmation of our deepest human experience flies in the face of our world. So how does one continue to love in a world so loveless? Half fool, half corpse, and half mad as well perhaps, I answer—as anyone can—by choosing to do just that: continuing to live that deepest affirmation. Yes, even and despite the lack of any providence we can recognize, left as we are to the facts, the hard facts of a world that really doesn't give a flying expletive if we live or die, starve or breakdown on the road to Emmaus or anywhere else. And so we make our way in the world, all of us longing with a transcendent hunger, praying our poetry and looking for a crack in the sky. Yet, half fool, half corpse, and half mad as well perhaps, I still love, you still love, each of us that does still does. But is such a choice as continuing to live that deepest affirmation unreal, especially with reference to any Deepest Relevance, as silly as hoping that Peter Pan will fly again, the summer wind blow again, as silly as saying the lame will see, the blind walk? Though part of me wants to answer so what, let's be silly, I have to honestly say no—for love is not silly, despite the will to power everywhere, in nature and in the very brain stems of our species, despite a darkness visible in our world that whittles away all trust in a providence that shapes our ends! Sitting by the bedside of someone you love who is ill is not silly. Struggling to feed someone hungry is not silly. Having an unsettled and insatiable love to help all sentient creatures is not silly. Love is not silly! It is the other necessary ingredient in existence besides existence itself. It is the deepest affirmation of life and the Mystery that gave life.

That very night, in their stop over in the Roman-styled city, Yeshu left the others and went out on his own, traveling through the Roman section with his dog at his side and ending up at a tavern next to the baths. The tavern owner must have thought him a Roman because of the dog, even though he had a beard, for he asked him in Latin what was his pleasure. Yeshu ordered a cup of wine and a hunk of Roman bread, some olives and cheese. As he partook he noticed a man watching him. Yeshu nodded at him and the man got up and came over to his place. He sat besides Yeshu and placed his large jug of wine between them. "I know you," he said straightaway. "You are the sage who talks of love. That the true God is such and loves us no matter what."

"Yes," Yeshu answered, "no matter what."

The man took him in for a long moment. "God loves us no matter what, but can I love God no matter what?"

Yeshu held for the longest time without a word.

"I come from Rome, the Court itself," the Roman went on, "and have seen too much, too much to make me hold as true what you say. Though I would like to." With that, he reached over and poured more wine into Yeshu's cup from his own jar. "Can you love no matter what—even if the mystery that made us turns out not to be love and the world is without meaning—as Augustus said *a joke*? When he died you know, he asked if he had played his part in the comedy well. He had seen too much too apparently. Do you know who the great Greek Plato was—well he is said to have died with a copy of Aristophanes under his pillow. Aristophanes was a writer of farce. In the end, did great Plato, too, think it all a joke?"

"But what do *you* think?" Yeshu asked of the man after letting him finish.

"I don't know what to think. Travelers from the East tell me that their God is dreaming and when he wakes we will all disappear. And others from that far away place say that there is nothing but a great void out of which everything came and suffering is an illusion."

"But what speaks to *you*? You will have to decide from all this for yourself. Ultimately, by yourself."

"And you have decided for yourself? Not from anyone else?"

"I have decided from myself and for myself. And I have chosen love. Even, as you say, if everything turns out to be a joke, a very bad one . . . or a great void. But I have it on good authority that it is neither. That it is indeed love." Yeshu laughed, but the Roman didn't.

"What authority?" the man asked almost with a plea in the wine he was sipping at.

Yeshu waited and then poured for him this time. "Have you ever lost someone you loved to death?"

"My eldest son," the man answered quietly.

"And when you did," Yeshu said touching at the man's hand, "did you still love him? Yes," Yeshu said as he watched the man nod slowly with a distant suffering in his eyes. "Even death cannot take that love away. As anyone knows who stood over a pyre. The fact of loss, the loss of someone you loved not being with you and it breaking your heart, yet knowing your love was still there, there with a certainty about it more than ever before—what did that tell you?"

"That it was the only real meaning to life when all is said and done."

"You have answered your own question."

"But not why your God of love allowed it," the man said directly to Yeshu. The Roman let out a deep sigh. "As I said to you, I have traveled the world. Where was God for the little boy in Thrace staving in the cold and actually living in a hole in the ground? Or the little girl in Egypt eating raw rice spilt from a wagon she was so hungry? Like her raw rice, this is not digestible. Where is God in this world? Truly, where is God when a person relies on God's love? Where is God in the greatest need in a person's life? In that most truthful of moments? When his child is suffering and dying?" The Roman was quiet for a moment. "There is too much suffering in the world. Just too much, and we have to be honest about that, my sage."

Yeshu nodded and kept silent for a long while. "No, love does not end suffering. It does not protect us against suffering. But somehow love defies it," he said in a quiet voice. "And—" he stopped for the length of a long look at the man—"and only a God of love suffers with us."

"I grieve for such a God," the Roman said.

Neither man said anything for a while after that; then the Roman ordered another jug of wine. "It's from my region in Italy—supposedly the best in the world," he said with a little almost silent laugh, still harboring his grief. "I have heard you say, 'I have come that you may have life and have it to the full.'"

"We all have," Jesus shot out. "We all have come that we might have life and have it to the full."

"And you are saying if one loves one will have life to the full?"

"To its deepest breath."

"And thus know God?"

"In the love, yes," Yeshu said to him.

"Of the many callings I have heard in this world, your invitation is like a cry inside of me—a cry telling me it is the truth." He looked at Yeshu with a sad look. "But how can I be such in Tiberius' court? The world is very unloving, Yeshu of Nazareth."

"But you needn't be. Live the soul's journey. And the soul's journey in the world is to love. In Caesar's court or in the back streets of Tiberias."

"You would turn the world upside down, Yeshu of Nazareth. Make a selfish species share its soup. An empire, and a temple with it, act *contra natura*," he said, reverting to his native tongue. "Only special people it would seem can do this."

"It is within all of us to do this." Yeshu poured some wine out of his cup onto the table; then with his forefinger made a circle in it. "Think of it as a widening embrace. As you loved your beautiful son, now give of yourself to others "—again he made a circle in the wine—"and after that embrace the animals"—and again—"and then the earth itself, until, finally, you are in God's embrace." With that his forefinger pulled some wine to the very edge of the table as if into infinity itself.

"And where is the emperor in all this?"

"He needs love, too," Yeshu said with a little laugh.

"Surely, you are the Son of God," the Roman said in amassment.

"As you are," Yeshu made sure to tell him. "Never forget that. Never ever." With that, Yeshu put down some coins to pay for the wine, and when the Roman insisted that he pay instead, Yeshu said we must never charge for God's gifts. "If anyone says he has something sacred to tell you and takes your money for it," Yeshu joked with him, "you know it is a good sign that he isn't mouthing the truth." Yeshu smiled and bid the Roman goodnight in the man's own tongue, exactly as he had heard it in the baths of his youth, and he and his dog, Balatro, left the tavern, and the next day the town.

Yeshu wrote down his encounter with the Roman and made a secret decision soon after. He told his friends to go to their families and homes while he did the same. They were all to meet in Jerusalem afterwards, sometime before the Jewish Passover, which he himself had never celebrated and that confused us. Only later would I see that he intended to use it to challenge the temple itself by saying God does not dwell in the holy of holies, but within each of us. Meanwhile, he would return to Nazareth and rest. And he did. Only after the third day home did he tell me as well that he was going down to Jerusalem, "for the last time perhaps." It was then he gave me his writings. As he did, he paused and unrolled one scroll in particular and began to read aloud to me from it. I held onto to what he gave me until John urged me, years later, to turn the writings over to those who follow the Way in Jerusalem. What a mistake that was!

The segment he read to me that silent still night when we were alone in the house he was raised in, is what follows. I must mention that his heart was heavy that night. He seemed to be wrestling with the desert again. Though he never said, I could see that. He was wondering, going back and forth, intermingling love and doubt, undecided on what he should really do. He had been calling for each of us to follow our heart, for each of us to be sensitive to the deepest part of ourselves, but the world was heartless, nature itself was, and the argument from earth was strong. "Am I a fool?" he asked aloud, looking out the window at the world. "The court jester in the comedy?" he whispered. He turned those sad eyes and smiled a strange smile my way . . . it was then he read what I spoke of.

"I was as it were in a watery wasteland. Deep inside a great sea's twilight, watching the strangest creatures I could ever imagine. Cruelty was everywhere. It appeared the stuff of creation all around me had taken on any haphazard form in the chaos. Firewater shot out of great chimney-like mounds, creatures blindly groping for prey in the murky depths. Great ells gulped down giant-eyed fish, and forms I can't even describe tore at the dead carcass of a leviathan. Monstrous-mouthed reptiles lying in wait never moved as strange near skinless fish swam into their swallow. Fish as if carrying torches inside themselves glowed all around me as I sank deeper into the darkness. It was like falling into a great chasm, and the further down I went, the darker and more brutal it became. Finally, no light was to be seen anywhere. Nor any love. What thought up such a place? It was heartless. Nothing made a sound. Or seemed to have a soul. It was abyssal emptiness. 'Where is God in all this?' That is what I stammered out and had to. And out of that another even more frightening question arose inside of me . . . so what then do I love when I love my God? 'There has to be a source for all this,' I cried out, my mouth dry despite the oceans of visible darkness all around me, my tongue sticking to the outcry running through my soul . . .

Suddenly, I was nowhere. I was nowhere and without sight.

Without sight, but seeing, too, face to faceless face with what was nothing. There is no speaking of it, no name, no knowledge. Darkness and light, good and evil—it is none of these. It is beyond everything! Yet there like a great embrace! Beyond at the core of me! An Incomprehensible that was Intimate!

I say that because despite that which was beyond my wildest understanding, there was something as familiar as myself, too, something warm and trusting, something I somehow knew even as I didn't. Don't ask me what it means—I don't know.

We clumsily try to give expression to the word *God*. And when we do, even the word I have used *Abba*, we are left suffering and struggling both as to whether such a confusion is applicable to the world and we in it, wondering as we look up at the night sky and then back to that intimacy deep inside of each of us.

It is then and there we find . . . *God* . . . both as beyond our comprehension and yet totally intimate in our love."

With that, Yeshu stopped and sat silently for a while until he reached over and touched at my hand. He held on me for a long moment after that. "Somehow in the intimacy of love I know the Mystery who gave birth to me, who gave me birth," he said in a near whisper. "As long as I love, I will never be abandoned by this, by God, or could ever abandon this, abandon God. No matter what is to come," he added, as if he knew.

But, of course, how could he? How could anyone have any idea how horrible it would be.

The very next day he set out for Jerusalem. "Whatever happens in Jerusalem, I want you to know I love you." Those were the last private words he spoke to me.

Thus Yeshu entered his Passion and was crucified, died, and was buried, never losing that love he spoke of, not even as he hung on that fateful tree suffering such physical, soulful, and spiritual pain, feeling abandoned by God and crying out so. But, of course, as long as he loved, he would never be abandoned by God, or could ever abandon God. At that moment he was the exemplar of how to be *bar'enas*, a human being, all things to all men, because he is like all of us, all things to all women, because he is like all of us.

Mary's son has been over the ages conceived and reconceived again and again and come to be an exemplar of what a human can be—in that each of us can honestly make him say as each of us can, "I am and I can love!" That is the miracle from Mary and every mother, the miracle that each of us is. It is our own very incarnation. It comes with being an aware animal called human—from the first one on. We have over the ages refined it, articulated it, enhanced it, as did this man making his way through life on the outskirts of significance, yet becoming an historical catalyst of what is everyone's story. The striking thing that gets through about this everyman was, despite the gospel agendas and nonsense after, his sense of being, and that message gets through because it is our own. It gets through despite gospel writers and their first century mind-set, it gets through despite the Hellenistic terminology on trinities so contrary to any I could concoct, and theologies, too, it gets through despite our own present-day preachers, priests, and pop religions meeting in giant settings and the money-changers running them. In my humble opinion, all that destroys the case to be made for Jesus and by him. *The simplest and most honest approach to this person is the best, a human being who opted for love, who said we must live in the mystery of love to its depths, and who only came to this after his own search, as did Frankl and Feyerabend with him, and each of us with them—all of us in the midst of our humanness.*

I think we have, despite the drastic detours, as a people, over the ages, found in the person of Jesus what is in ourselves and told our story through his and him. Jesus is the incarnation of ourselves, the Passion a great rendering of life's journey, even more powerful than Odysseus' for it is historically rooted. Jesus then and Christ now is a false divide understood in this way; his passion, death, and resurrection become consciousness-itself's drama in being, Easter the victory of love in our human hearts. The story of Jesus as told and retold over the millennia is so powerful because of this tie-in to our human condition—that is why I say again the simplest and most honest approach to this man, as well as for ourselves, is the best; he, and we as human beings with him, opting for love, in a spirituality that tells us we must live in the mystery of love to its depths. Each of us, like him, only coming to this after our own search, and like him crying out on the crooked cross of existence. Of course I love Jesus, I see what is most beautiful in us in him. How can you not love him!

I think ultimately whether in one tradition or another, past deconstruction and deserts both, each comes to that purely human spirituality when one is honestly human, honestly one's self. In the plethora of possibilities surrounding us *is a grounding*, simple and everyday—one that gives us a way to act in the face of it all. Existence and the deepest experience in existence is that. Jesus, or Frankl, or anyone else mentioned in this venture never need have existed to come to that in our consciousness, because it is there in our consciousness no matter. Of course, we cannot pretend to be like Augustus and nearly everyone else in the Roman Empire and know nothing of the birth of Jesus. Jesus, no matter what your take on him, changed history. Historically speaking, we can say Jesus became a catalyst to consciousness's realization of its own deepest reality, and thus the way to live and meet the world that is within each of us. *Love is the messiah*, and he brought this home to us in his life; if we only could get through all the trappings and titles inflicted on him, all of which have buried him and *his life's realization*, that love is the way—the medium, the message, and the messiah.

Nietzsche said, what does not kill me makes me stronger. Of course, it can also make you daffy, end your days, like him, in a madhouse, signing your name the Crucified. It's a dark hymn of de-creation one can be alive to . . . from the fact of the ichneumon wasp eating the caterpillar while it is still alive, all the way to a stunned human witness to it all quietly saying, "there are thing which must cause you to lose your reason or you have none to lose."[36] We all hang out here, in life; at times it becoming a lonely cross of dark doubt and despair. Easter aborted! And yet . . . and yet, a yes surges up in us! A yes to love! For life itself would be aborted, unless, like another human mentioned in this piece, and another after that, and yet another after that, we hold onto the deepest affirmation in living, that mysticism without ecstasy called love, and do so as our fundamental choice in life, whether on a cross or on holiday, whether as hopelessly loving or somehow realizing in the goodness and beauty of love that the air can indeed be tied together.

"I have always had this head-on judgment about life, that it should be happy!" my gravedigger says as the very first line of my play. Yes, coming from a gravedigger's mouth it's meant to be comic. We are all in on the humor because of our human condition, as we are all in on this purely human spirituality that comes out of that human condition as well. Striving indeed to be happy, yes, but, above all, striving always to live love. A love that is never silly, though playful at times, a love that will find itself in whatever and wherever we find ourselves, a love that must somehow tell us how to act—and does!

When Augustine asks *what is it I love when I love my God*—I answer love itself! As does existence! As does your own depths, pondering reader, and Jesus with you, and Jacques, and every other *bar' enas* who ever lived or ever will. Our fulfillment as humans resides and depends on venturing to the *love within,* and to the goodness and beauty of the *love without* as seen in all those around us, human and non, until past loving hopelessly we somehow sense in that very love what our venture humanly and therefore hesitantly has arrived at, *l'amor che move il sole e l'atre stelle.* No, not as impossible, but possible! No, not as Other, but as Intimate! And I dare to say familiar and warm in that intimacy—never to be feared or adored, not even to be approached as awesome. The way to appreciate this, the way to this *most* personal of all approaches to the Mystery that made us, is love itself, and only love. The way to God, the primal Mystery of reality, is not a judgment of pure reason, nor a speculative fantasy, is not a faith, nor a pharmaceutical, but rather an honest choice that is supremely personal, one that can only be made in the logic of love, with the evidence of love, with the basic credibility and courage of love, in the living reality of love. It is our tainted human nature's last refuge of hope and its best.

It is what gives us a sense of a greater life, interrupted by driftings into a challenging weariness to be sure, even at those lonely moments of suffering questioning aloud any meaning to all this, let alone any God . . . and in that lovingly hopeless, hopelessly loving pain, thinking that that is all there is left to our love and us with it, even wondering if that isn't how it should be after all, our humanness found only in that lonely stand against it all, we sweat our flesh and blood . . . until with a slow transformation through duration and daring we are faced with a decision and we leap into love, and with a thankfulness still tinged with hesitation we grasp God as this enduring and daring loving, and in that see past the abyss, past any transcendent and immanent, into a wordless embrace beyond at the core of us. *No, this is not a proof of God, but a way to realize God.* And so have we tied the air together? For the moment at least with Beethoven I might answer in that thankfulness still tinged with hesitation, yes. There is in that affirmation a coherence, a communion, a closeness of the profoundest attitude towards life and the Mystery that made it.

This doesn't come to us out of a vacuum or a Void, it is a revelation life itself opens to us, and our journey in life is to *realize* it. We breathe-in our understanding of it, the only way we can, through ourselves. This realization I am speaking of, as such, is *inspired* revelation in the root meaning of the word, *infused by breathing.* The philosopher in me likes that, that existence alone is used—even when it comes to God.

Nietzsche described what happens in inspiration *as taking but not asking who gives*. Yet, at the same time he tells us, letting Zarathustra sing out to all, "Write with our heart's blood, and you will see that the blood is spirit." Kazantzakis has his own hero do the same. "Odysseus felt his brains would burst with a longing," the noble Cretan tells us about Odysseus, as he makes him set sail on the sea of seeing in search of a soul for sentient life.[37] Aren't we all Odysseus, for we, too, with a passion for the impossible have set sail on the sea of seeing in search of a soul for sentient life, wide-eyed with what we found but never turning our eyes from it; *our Venturer,* like Odysseus, realizing that the success or failure of the spirit depends on himself, not on nature and its amoral urges, or the cold cosmos, but on what is vital and sentient in his own embattled being, and though in many ways he is a squandered man, scarred to his very soul, vulnerable and so very human because of that, he realizes the final truth for himself in his struggle with all the levels of his breathing is in the mystery of love which surprises life itself.

The passion for the impossible becomes possible in love. By our own life and love! In that we sense there has to be more to it all—*because we are more.* That is as much a part of the human inscape as nature is of the landscape we find ourselves in.

My birds are in ecstasy listening to Carlo Maria Giulini's conducting of Verdi's *Requiem*, something I saw him do in person as my mother and I were able to get the last two seats, in the very last row, in that horrible huge building used before Disney Hall. The rendering was magnificent as is the recording now while I think about Carlo and Carmen both gone. Maybe that memory and the music are the cause of what I am about to write as I listen, thinking . . . as life itself can retain its beauty and goodness in spite of its tragic aspects because of love, so can the impossible become possible for us, our own giving giving a way to the GIVING that gave and continues to give . . . *exaudi orationem meam; ad te omnis caro venit* . . . what we call God transcending all our notions, concepts, ideas, imagery . . . *mors stupebit et natura* . . . but if we go to that which is most real in existence for us, the deepest human experience, this mysticism without ecstasy . . . *Sanctus, Sanctus, Sanctus* . . . have we perhaps then, just perhaps then, indeed heard the true theme of the Mystery? In such an absolutely desperate situation, when all prayer fails and not a word can be spoken, in the silence of love, does God come to us, and, in the forthright admission of our incapacity to solve the riddle of breathing, inspires us, that is *infuses by breathing itself a way to realize the impossible?*

Gerard Manley Hopkins, in his final year, when he felt squandered, having been wasted on nonsense by pedestrian men acting as superiors, wrote: ". . . birds build—but not I build; no, but strain, /Time's eunuch, and not breed one work that wakes. /Mine, o thou lord of life, send my roots rain."[38]

From his depths he cried out, from that radical selfhood each of us is, questioning whether he had been squandered! His friend Bridges thought so and wrote upon his death: "That dear Gerard was overworked, unhappy and would never have done anything great seems to give no solace. But how much worse it would have been had his promise and performance been more splendid. He seems to have been entirely lost and destroyed," Bridges adds bitterly, "by those Jesuits."[39] And yet, Hopkins held on to such an abuse, because of his notion of what? Without knowing or passing judgment upon this wonderful poet, we can say in general that there is always the danger that we have a mistaken notion of whatever, including *the what* to which we *clamavi*. One can waste one's self on nonsense. Yes. People do everyday. But there is a safeguard for us in our spiritual journeys. The closer any spirituality is to our human love the more real it is as a spirituality, the more real it is to life's deepest encounter. This is so from Gilgamesh's ancient passage on what it is to be human all the way, hopefully, to this present venture and its say on the matter.

In life spirituality is beyond religion, with the Incomprehensible remaining an unspoken pervasive mystery manifesting itself the only way it can, as it is. *What-that-is* has been our venture here. In this recapitulation and before. It is that into which we leap regardless of whether the attitude of the silly superiors change or the world itself does, regardless of whether we can write poems or not. Our final trust is love, and in that leap, God does not "degenerate to the contradiction of life,"[40] but is seen in the light of our own deepest experience in life, even as we face the Serengeti of spacetime, even as we are Time's eunuch, even as we know we will become the snows of yesteryear.

"You build everything on love," I hear you say, no doubt afterwards thinking with a condescending smile of a line from Kazantzakis, where he writes of Death lying besides Life and for a brief embrace dreaming it is Life. Like death do we dream of the Impossible? Only to wake and say *sperabamus*? *"We were hoping?"* And with God gone but love still real, are we left to build our answer to life, our construct of life over the abyss, in an ecstasy of hopeless love, loving hopelessly?

I put aside my keyboard and take my bundle of hair, even as he is losing it with his Cushing's, out for a ride, his big white head sticking out the window and wind blowing into his joy. How he enjoys the moment, regardless of everything else. Do you think dogs walk upon the earth to teach us that, or ride in Ricotta White BMW's as the case may be?

From reading this venture, even thus far, one realizes that I do not deny the temptation of the abyss, even as the beauty of Cecilia Bartoli's voice singing *"Lascia la spina"* drifts out of the car radio. No, Cecilia, I make no apology for this personal approach; it is all we have, each and everyone of us, magnificent artist with her music or man in his car with his thoughts. Nor do I deny the undertones in all consciousness whose cause is recognized as only something that threatens, something missing, without being able to say what it is, only at times as a fear of futility and at others a melancholy in matter itself, stiff old age in wait, our body and bones aware of something strange and queer to it all, if the truth be known. And doesn't that after all put things in their proper light?

Or is love itself the struggle, maybe squandered struggle, to liberate God within us, each of us a fathomless composite and construct both, of roots that plunge down to the primordial origin of things and Theos both?

The unceasing creativity of life, casting up and discarding individuals and species, whole solar systems and galaxies, to mere experiments on its way towards more and more liberation, is what Bergson and Kazantzakis meant by God, this onrushing force throughout all of nature; but it is not what I mean by my More, because my human more, my human love, challenges such a coarseness and has-to-must rebel against such a God if that would be "the final ground of everything" a la Kant, the "Ultimate Concern" a la Tillich, Plato's this, Aristotle's that, or whatever other names and notions for the numinous. Love, the deepest experience in my being tells me no, that is not God, do not look for God in the loveless landscape of the cosmos, but in the lovescape at the depth of your very being, beyond, yes, but at your very core. *Everything argues against a God of love but love itself.* That is the conclusion yet again in this go over, as it was before. Yes, I am taking the road of what the world might call insane generosity, venturing a spirituality based on love, a happening in my human horizon that has always told me, and anyone who has loved, that it is the deepest wisdom. To challenge the undertones in our very make-up, we have ventured, hesitantly, to dare carry on right to the end of our intuition, and the deepest happening in it, to a purely human spirituality and the Possible that comes out of it.

Back in my den, my Venturer does not dissolve himself herself into passive contemplation, a bliss of renunciation, utterly abandoned to the impersonal powers, nor does he she cast a veil over the chaos and the coarse, but in the midst of his her humanness finds the bearing in bared being. The only thing I have ever seen out of my own eyes and the only thing out of the eyes looking back at me that made God possible is that of love. Here truth ripens, so much so, that I can say, even if we are wrong about God, we are not wrong about love. If God isn't love, God should be!

And what is more, if God isn't love, then God is Other. And I am not just wrong, but totally and completely wrong. And so is life with me.

Metaphors and similes, allegories, fables and legends, mysticisms and philosophies, none of them can take the place of simple profound human everyday love. At the heart of spirituality is the awakening of and to real presence. In that is found our purely human spirituality and in that somehow we must find the Mystery that made us. This is the true epiphany, the real eureka, the most honest easter, *I am and I can love*. Upon that I dare to disturb the universe.

Black-eyed necessity got conscious and burst into giving of itself . . . loved . . . such is the evolution that continues with us, with us now choosing the course it will take or not take, within the fact, the very real fact, that love is hard to come by on planet stress and its people. As a species we might not evolve, but as individuals we can . . . even as we accept the given conditions and work within a whittling world, even as, like Odysseys, our Venturer, too, sees with horror a troop of blind ants devour a baby camel, and then a human infant, and forever after keeps this in his mind's eye as the loveless truth behind omnivorous nature and the raw elemental energies of evolution within each of us, which only a conscious willing of love can combat, even if a lovingly hopeless hopelessly loving battle . . . and even if only that, still more . . . but maybe More, too. No, this is not a proof of God I have put forth; I am not such a rank amateur in life or love. No, it is not a proof of God, but a possibility in the face of the impossible, a way, a human way, to the Mystery. So one must at least ask, is that more I speak of a call of More itself, Love itself, God, calling out to us in our senses and soul, in our own individual incarnation? That is for each of us to answer for his or her self, but the very real possibility is there, while still facing the fact of brutal nature and even more brutal human behavior, and only because of the very real love in our lives! This is what my Venturer and I are saying, not with the certitude of a mystic, but with the hesitancy of a human being who knows love.

Either that or God is Other, and Aristotle does indeed trump Augustine, and a cold truth trumps the thump in our hearts. *But since love makes sense in a way only love can, so does a sense of God as love.* I rightly can say that I know love, for sure, and so do know *more*—more than that which cannot love hanging in the cold stare of otherness. Our odd-yssey is as odd as love in the cosmos, but in that love we have arrived at a way to live in the face of that cosmos. This is true even if God is Other, but all the more so if God is More, if God is Love.

Love is God breaking in on the world—in between the determined and indifference, in between nature and the cold cosmos—all the scurrying verbs of life and living giving way to the verb of love as each of us takes on God's face. Suddenly, that something deeper still in us, finally, unmistakably, is grasped and our recap ends as before with our giving at one with GIVING, our loving at one with LOVING.

Everything changes for us with that, even evolution. A theory of evolution based on our venture's arrival at *l'amor che move il sole e l'altre stelle* makes us look at evolution with different eyes. Without attempting a whole discourse on evolution, or saying this is definitively it, I would nonetheless like to brainstorm about what could be because of what we have said thus far. Think of it as my own "contribution" during this bicentennial of Darwin. I had an idea festering in my forehead for some time now about the Source somehow still in spacetime after the singularity it allowed, and I somehow think I might somewhat have now plotted it out, that is, somewhat can articulate it. In doing so, I put aside any divine sundering into bits and pieces, as well as any Omega points or process theologies or Ultimate Earths in the works. I suppose I should also state that it can be called an existential evolutionary approach in that my humble brain is brainstorming backwards from here and our hereness. That is the method of my madness, arriving at what might be dubbed *an evolution of hereness*. My Old English likes that, and since English is his native tongue I'll go along with it, after all I only speak American, and that with a hard a.

The evolution of hereness

Viewed in its biological mix, the phenomenon of awareness is not peculiar to us. It is a basic property of all conscious life and as such it embraces in its varieties and levels all forms of conscious matter, whether an elephant or an Englishman. In such mammals, it is easily recognized, whereas the lower we go in conscious matter the less so, and maybe not even in the mix, maybe only instinct or a blind process-to-be as both Schopenhauer and Nietzsche professed, or maybe still the contrary as Chardin would put forth, a sort of élan of consciousness from its most rudimentary form, in the nascent forms of matter, all the way to the human mind and hominisation, with all energy psychic in nature, and *radical* energy always drawing forward, culminating ultimately in the highest degree the perfection of consciousness, the illuminating involution of the being upon itself, hyper-personalisation, so not a requiem for the future, but fulfillment. Or maybe it is Kazantzakis' credo of an unceasing and renewing reconciliation and cooperation with antithetical powers in the universe, and harmony with that as our highest endeavor and redemption.

Without pursuing a discussion about any of these other hypotheses here, I think I should stage the basis of mine; namely, consciousness as the zenith of evolution, and the love within this awareness the highest expression of it. So it comes out of our very existence. Jumping from that foundation in chapter one to the chapter we are in at present, it is in this love, present in the presence each of is, that the ultimate Source before the singularity itself shows itself. This is God in evolution. No, not as a planner to anything, Omega, or anything else, not as fate, just there, rather, here in love.

It is not an energy to return to, though as a young man writing his thesis I called it a "love energy," influenced no doubt by a desire to combine the energy from physics with the love from life; not to mention the times I lived in and the influence Chardin had on the Jesuits and they in turn on me. But no, it is just love, beyond at the core of us, transcendent and immanent, before spacetime, yet expressed in spacetime, the *more* in us, the *Mysterious More in spacetime*. Don't look for a process or a God of process in the material, just *the more* that is there *here and now*, and *the More* in that. I have no idea what is going to become of the world, let alone the universe, other than that both will end—the rest is speculation about that, arguing from strong or less strong arguments; but that *I am and I can love is immediate and so is GIVING immediate in that.* In our pull between the will to power and the will to love, we might as a species chose power and in the process end the planet, or we might as a species choose love and build a better society—that is for us to do or not to do; *there is no divine plan other than that each of us love.*

There is no divine plan other than that each of us love.

"As simple as that?" I hear you complain. What about Whitehead or Chardin or Hegel or . . . This is as simple and profound as it gets. There was in the very beginning, GIVING allowing the singularity to take its chancy course, and then its historical constrictions. It could have all evolved differently, as it can all end in different ways, but GIVING still is in the cosmos, in the conscious creature's core and choice, emanating that GIVING. Within the form of humankind is a level of our presence that can indeed act contrary to the determinate without, and if carried to a discussion of the divine, this freedom to give of ourselves is where GIVING acts within the world. It is truer to evolution as no other theory is.

Why? Because it combines the within and the without; there is no discarding of the determinate without and consciousness as the pinnacle of the process, nor is there no discarding of the determinate without and consciousness within us—only levels of being expressing each; we are both the raw elemental energies of evolution and consciousness, a consciousness that can choose to act at the depths of its being, that is giving of itself. That level within us in the process of evolution brings us closer to the original Source, the Mystery that made the happening of everything and everywhere happen, in that in our giving we manifest the Mystery in the world as the Mystery does itself.

But what of the without, mustn't the Source be in that as well? I don't know how to answer that except to say the end result is an actuality of aware love, as we saw. Somehow the process came to that and must to express the Source, just as consciousness is needed to examine the universe. I might put forth that *Giving, God, in the pre-conscious is the potential in evolution working its way to actuality in aware love.* That of course is looking back from the end result and having to say at least it had to potentially be there to be here, as it is here and we know for sure it is. The cosmos was driving towards consciousness and achieved this actuality. But in that we still have to give of ourselves freely, to complete the evolutionary process, no one can give my self but me, even God cannot make me do that. Evolution had to work its way to an awareness and a freedom within that to give of itself, love, *because it did*. And when it does the Source is manifest in it and us. Therein lies a four-fold synthesis; namely, the material, the mind, the spiritual, and the Source.

My accumulation, me, is the evidence of and for me of the possibility of what I said, there being this holistic theory of evolution, or this hereness hypothesis of it. To put it another way, therein are both the metaphysics and physics of the universe; a synthesis that stays true to what we find both within and without. It is only as strong as consciousness in the cosmos is—and that is so even if consciousness is an aberration in the universe.

The notion that God directly created the cosmos, of course, has to be put aside, for we know that the big bang did. God didn't create the cosmos, not directly, anymore that God created you or me directly. We happened in the process of evolution. But the Source, God, is still present in the evolution; namely, as God is, and we needn't go into that yet again. Of course, I don't want anyone to die over this hypothesis. It is put out there for what is called thinking. But like this whole venture, it has its roots in the very root-reality of our presence, our presence here and now, hence a hereness hypothesis.

As you can see, I accept Darwin, and evolution, and the different additions that some like Gould and others might put forth—it is all there for us to see, suffering and love, the whole plate of pasta. Even our purely human spirituality, for *how we act* in the face of existence now can resonate with God in spacetime. Willing love, the will to love, giving is at the core of this evolution, not as Schopenhauer's primal unconscious will in nature, nor pre-equine Friedrich's will to power coming out of nature, but another will, which when manifest manifests the Will that brought being into being, and with it the big bang and the process that evolved out of that including consciousness and the highest expression of consciousness—so it doesn't leave out any of the so-called wills, nor the natural selection of Darwin either. In fact it builds on Darwin's evolutionary process, realizing the fact that we have evolved continuously, to more than our biology, our biology has. You can build whatever Utopia or Ending you want on that, using process theology or eschatological judgment days, or whatever other future, but the fact of what I say here and now still holds, my more simple, yet profound evolutionary hypothesis built on hereness. *This is God in evolution.*

Let me explain, so you don't confuse this with any of the present explanations. The cosmos is what it is, and we are what we are in it, and God what God is. Whether we evolved as anti-matter, or silicon based, or nourished ourselves by osmosis, or evolved to any other unimaginable forms and minds, still, at our core of being, GIVING would be present in the phenomenon of our own giving. All else is evolution in whatever form it takes or took or will take. Granted, now that we have taken over, at least on planet stress, evolution will take whatever form we push it towards here on earth, though obviously not throughout the vastness of spacetime.

As I write here, the elusive Higgs boson—whose existence would help to explain why matter has mass—seems about to be proven either at Cern's LHC (Large Hadron Collider) or Fermilab's Tevatron, and that will be what it will be. It is part of the evolutionary make up. Notwithstanding, as beautiful as why matter has mass is, there is still more, more in the process of evolution. I am not speaking of ourselves as if we were a fully settled matter . . . nor God either, at least for us. Certainly there is more to discover in the mysteries we call ourselves, but the Source will always be the Source, GIVING, and GIVING manifested as that, as what God is, within the swarming multiplicity of time and space.

No, God is not the volcano, nor is God the universe either. God is not the chaos or the order, nor a chaord conclusion. *God as God* is only in the universe in one way or finding or manifestation, wherever GIVING is present in the swarming multiplicity that is spacetime.

Let me be as clear as I can about this. The existential meaning of what I am saying is that God comes to us through our incarnation, our humanness; that we encounter the Mystery we call God in our very human love. It is an intimacy of which we can't form a representation, except to point to beauty, and goodness, and the beauty and goodness of love. God is both mysterious and manifest, revealed in the actual relationship with what is most real in our lives, love, without which our formulated notion of God would be impossible and God Other, not to mention not directly involved in spacetime. In love we encounter the reality of the Mystery we call God, and it is as true as our very human love is, the deepest experience in existence, in our humanness, in our incarnation. Our presence makes-to-appear, letting-lie-before-us and take-to-heart the Mystery that made us, and thus God is known to us and acts in the universe, in fact, is the underlying foundation of our purely human spirituality, our very way to act in the face of spacetime, like God, LOVING.

We are far from playing etymological games when we say that or put forth this evolutionary theory. Everything before us in our lives, not to mention evolution to come, is ambiguous, but we still have our one minimal certainty and the deepest experience in that. We are more than our biology, but we never deny our biology, it happened the way it happened, and we did. We could have happened differently, but not GIVING in any spacetime. From this we come to God and the God as manifest in the universe.

This is not Hegel's God, or any process one, which ultimately has to make God Other and Indifferent, a pure process of power, lost of any love, a notion of

God which forces a person's inner life down to a primitive level, and in essence merely makes a more sophisticated volcano god, no matter what the advocate might say. Even the famous Catholic process thinker Chardin talks of his God and his Christ in terms of power in *Hymne de l'Univers.* "In the beginning was *Power*," (his italics); and then goes on to write: "Radiant Word, blazing Power, you who would mold the manifold . . ."[41] And further: "As long as I could see . . . in you, Lord Jesus, only the man . . . the sublime moral teacher, the Friend, the Brother, my love remained timid and constrained . . . . But now, Master, today, when through the manifestation of those superhuman powers with which your resurrection endowed you you shine forth from within all the forces of the earth and become visible to me, now I recognize you as my Sovereign, and with delight I surrender myself to you."[42] Though filled with pious devotion and surrender to this Power, again it is not the spirituality I am talking about, not the God I am talking about, nor in fact, not the Christ I would be either. My point being that even Chadin within a process philosophy falls victim to what a process philosophy has to ultimately concede and can't get out of it, a volcano god, a god of power and submission, not the God of love I am talking about, not at all. *Our subjunctive is stronger than their suppositions.* I think that has to be clear by now, my tribute to Darwin and Divinity both is quite different, evolution took place and there is no divine plan other than that each of us love.

I might mention here as well that this is not a Theistic Evolution, nor a Deistic one either, for both ultimately end up with a God of Law, either of the physical kind or moral, and GIVING is above law and Law too. Suffice it to say, law doesn't replace love, and to do so brings back the volcano god and all that that entails. Again, I think that has to be clear by now, my tribute to Darwin and Divinity both is quite different, evolution took place as it did, and outside of that we can only say there is no divine plan other than that each of us love, both with a foundation in reality, and one taking place within the other. We have evolved to more than our biology, our biology has, but no matter how evolution would have happened, GIVING would be manifest in it as GIVING. In a sense, everything else is commentary when it comes to God in evolution.

So it is the God out of darkness shines through paradoxically, and we in turn love, love with a love that is a mutual love. There is no fear and adoration, nor a slaving surrender, nor law either. Love is our salvation, whether in a concentration camp or a concentrating mind, whether in a world ending or one's self coming to an end. It depends on you loving, even as the whole cosmos came in with a bang and will go out with whimper, and the world with it, or you alone in a one night cheap hotel with bad wallpaper. Evolution is in process, as is one's own spirituality, but not God. God is forever GIVING—and when we do, we manifest

God in our lives and God is manifest in the world. *Evolution took place and there is no divine plan other than that each of us love.*

That is my simple and profound hereness evolution. I suspect by now even I know what I am talking about.

Later, a day or a trip to Arcturus and back, one early morning hour when sleep again evaded me, I got up and headed for my den to jot down some new thoughts on this bicentennial contribution of mine. My Old English, of course, was under foot all the way, more interested in gingerbread cookies and some healthy frolic than in Darwinian metaphysics.

Loren Eiseley writes in *The Invisible Pyramid*: "Many millions of years of evolutionary effort were required before life was successful in defending its internal world from the intrusion of the heat or cold of the outside world of nature."[43] Whether his "internal world" or my own "interiorization," such a notion, one way or another, runs through human thought since we started jotting things down, and that is so because this interiority is so. Eiseley followed up with this, which I shall quote at length because it helps establish an important point: "Close to a hundred years ago the great French medical scientists Claude Bernard observed that the stability of the inside environment of complex organisms must be maintained before outer freedom can be achieved from their immediate surroundings. He meant that for life to obtain relative security from its fickle and dangerous outside surroundings the animal must be able to sustain stable, unchanging conditions within the body. Warm-blooded mammals and birds can continue to move about in winter; insects cannot. Warm-blooded animals such as man, with his stable body temperature, can continue to think and reason in outside temperatures that would put a frog to sleep, in a muddy pond or roll a snake into a ball in a crevice. In winter latitudes many of the lower creatures are forced to sleep part of their lives away . . . One of the great feats of evolution, perhaps the greatest, has been this triumph of the interior environment over exterior nature. Inside, we might say, has fought invading outside, and inside, since the beginning of life, by show in degrees has won the battle of life. If it had not, man, frail man with his even more fragile brain, would not exist."[44]

Here I would like to quote what the mystic Thomas Traherne wrote, "'Infinite love cannot be expressed in finite room. Yet it must be infinitely expressed in the smallest moment . . . Only so is it both ways infinite.'"[45] At first I had no idea what this meant, but since it talked about love, infinite love, it drew my attention.

To make sure I knew what I was babbling about in my version of evolutionary hereness, after a good breakfast of veggie bacon and eggs, and of course coffee to set the heart beating, I decided to spend some quality time with my I-Mac revisiting the subject, even as I would still be writing in the subjunctive. With both Eiseley and Traherne already on the electric page, I have to honestly ask once again, if all of it, what they said and what I did, can really be seen in modern evolutionary terms? I have to say, whether because of the landscape and its lightening or the inscape and its enlightening, that I think it can and so will again try to explain why. To cut right to the chase, I think conscious love expresses the final triumph of Claude Bernard's interior microcosm, as well as both Eiseley's and my interiorization or microcosm, in its battle with the macrocosm. Consciousness can roam at will within the cosmos, traveling faster than light itself. And that same consciousness can give of itself! As for "project infinite love in a finite room," we ourselves do that in that love, project the GIVING. In this year of Darwin's bicentennial perhaps a greater insight into evolution *can be* fostered by looking within to that consciousness and love as the deepest expression of it. It will create a new paradigm of course, but we can use one, especially one taking in the whole of it; a holistic one, that is one not leaving out our own hereness and what that brings to the universe and its evolution.

I have to ask: Is the Mystery behind all this somehow, after the big bang banged into its chancy expansion and then the "historical contingency" after that, still working its own way through evolution? My answer was and still is, yes, in the highest expression of being; namely, the one that manifests the very Source of being! Although evolution could have evolved a billion different ways at its beginning, even to antimatter, its started the way it did, and came to this interior that could love and thus express the Source directly.

Had we rolled back the film and started all over again as Gould said and I said he said, we would have a different pathway. Good heavens even on our own planet it has taken different paths on two different continents. But still, though it is true it would have as Gould says taken whatever path, it is still true I think that somehow—whether creatures that were sustained by osmosis and of a totally different form, matter, and even intelligent interaction with the without—that somehow, still, the within would have emerged as an awareness that could love, and in that an evolutionary and existential communion with the Source.

Kant, in his last work before his death, the fragmentary *Opus Postumum*, seems to be trying to connect God with human moral consciousness, a connection that would make God totally immanent within our human moral consciousness. Although I admit he wasn't saying what I am here—nonetheless he had the same intent as I did with our purely human spirituality and God. Whereas he went his way, I went mine, and made love that connection. For that is what I am saying is taking place. The Mystery remains Incomprehensible, except in this connection or communion, this love, this giving and GIVING, and thus our purely human spirituality accomplishes what I set out to do—once I realized it that is—give it an absolute grounding if I could.

We are not deceived by existence in the end; we are not merely a phagocyte in a cosmic body totally unaware of "the pouring tumult of creation it inhabits," without any awareness of it.[46] Loren Eiseley has a sentence I shall use here, though he didn't mean it quite in the way I am using it: "Strangely," he writes, "these men [he is talking of the wise men of our past] have never spoken of space; they have spoken, instead, as though the farthest spaces lay within the mind itself—as thought we still carried a memory of some light of long ago and the way we had come."[47] I think we do and I think the evolutionary process led up to our awareness of it. Does the anthropic principle have a home, a basis in evolution? Yes, the way I use the anthropic principal it evolved to an awareness that could love and reflects in that the Source of being itself, with the ability to find its way back to the Source via that, and a way to act in the face of evolution. GIVING is within evolution, but not as Hegel might have thought God immanent, or even Chardin, but only as GIVING itself, still allowing evolution to be chancy and have its historic constrictions and consequences; yet still a Presence in our presence. So it is I can say that the profound awareness or consciousness within projects infinite love in a finite room. I think even though it be in existential and evolutionary terms for me, I see what the mystic meant, and I suspect should even present my finding to Kant for his consideration.

In 1990, I had the notion that the Source gave of itself and 'broke asunder' into spacetime. I think I can enhance that and carry it to a closer understanding with the notion of the Source as GIVING and still manifesting itself in giving, not as something breaking asunder but as a manifestation in communion with the within in evolution, in communion with creatures of the cosmos called human. It could be with others as well, but we can only know as humans and for humans. Though we might all agree or not that epistemologically a human cannot know 'things' in themselves when we look out at the cosmos, however, we do know ourselves and how we do does give us some inkling past the swarming multiplicity into the mystery that surrounds us, maybe all the way to the Mystery that is beyond at our very core, if love has its way with us.

There is in this a line of thinking on the evolutionary process, one that takes in the whole of evolution, without and within, the whole of the experience of being; one that is different than those of the past; one that allows for the chancy determinate and freedom, the raw elementary energies of evolution and conscious love.

Evolution, too, has to be true to the without and the within.

Yes, evolution too, has to be true to the without and the within. There is within the cosmos conscious matter, conscious matter that can overcome the very matter that makes it up, that can give of itself, conscious matter that is aware love.

Although I can at times speak of love as a winsome even whimsical phenomenon, I can also say that it is so strong a reality in us that it can even supersede survival of the self in its decision of giving; in a giving that must never be harmful to the other, otherwise it is not love and not at the deepest level of being within us. So it is that we have the ultimate inspiration of actual existence, remembering what inspiration means at its root meaning. Spirituality, our purely human spirituality, is acting out of our deepest level of being—it is rooted in the depths of existence itself, and through that, in the Depths of the Deep Itself, beyond yet at our very core.

Of course on rainy days I have a different sense, and bleak thoughts prevail. Maybe a cyborg is what evolution is to be, as cold and removed as a formula or as indifferent as nature itself . . . and we like cavemen with our love, with our God.

Like Gilgamesh must we settle for less? Is love a lonely stand against it all? Is love to be, finally, merely a casualty of the on-going process of everything . . . to become as dead in some future paleontology as are the bones of the dinosaurs today? A passing phase in the meaningless drive of it all? Even now I see very little love in the world . . . so are we merely cavemen to the cyborg, a link on the way, and our stand a lonely one, with the cosmos as indifferent to us as it was to all that went before? Is the mind melancholy because at the back of it, it knows this? Or is there something still beautiful in us, to yet be called forth? Is the construct we have created in Christ-consciousness with its unconditional love, or in Buddha-consciousness with its all-embracing compassion, somehow rooted in us and thus the calling forth of these from some root-reality hidden by secretive evolution even from ourselves, except in these strange callings forth? Is this divinity calling at the depth of our being? But it all seems so devoid of divinity . . . a divinity that shapes our ends. I see no wisdom whatsoever in the waste . . . except waste itself as wisdom. Everything, volcano, universe, and evolution itself argues against a God of love but love itself—and me and my foolish would-be God. And yet I know kindness is better than unkindness, and compassion better than no compassion, and love . . .

I sit with my cup of coffee, at a midnight diner wondering, pondering, pursuing. It's raining outside the large Deco window as I manage a creased-lipped smile across to the bag lady in from the night. I can only wish that the Mystery that made us cares for her, for me, for the stray dog outside in the drizzle. Or is that trying to domestic the wind? Is what we call God just different and we alone with our kindness? Just the bag lady and me against the whole of everywhere, is that the way it is, just me sending a bowl of soup over to this hungry stranger?

I think you see now why I said this little scene sets it all up for us, and how it really comes down to sending the soup over to the bag lady. *God is as simply profound as that. And in that profundity we find God.* It and it alone, despite the rain and the night, despite a natural as well as a social Darwinism, and a cosmos as cold as a witch's tit to boot, it and it alone, the act of love, loving, brings out the depth of being and us in it.

Somewhere behind the *mysterium* of evolution, or within it, with it still, is GIVING, showing up in giving, in love, in beauty and goodness, in the beauty and goodness of love, in our truest moments of being.

Without confusing the issue, I would like to add that a caution immediately comes into play here, something I have already touched upon with the process philosophers and theologians, and obviously a carry over from that crinkle in creation I offered, but which I would now like to pursue more specifically; namely, *naming* God wrongly. Neither Sweeny Todd's God nor beautiful Beckett's is the God we have realized. Sweeny for reasons known speaks of "a dark and vengeful god;" Beckett "for reasons unknown" of a punishing Godot.

"A strong and heavy wind was rending the mountains and crushing the rocks—but it was not God. After the wind there was an earthquake—but God was not in the earthquake. After the earthquake there was a fire—but God was not in the fire. After the fire there was a tiny whispering sound, ever so gentle, a voice of thin silence." Here *1 Kings* touches upon something very significant. You will not find God in nature, but rather in a thin place, a whisper within, ever so gentle, a voice of thin silence. Thus comes the Mystery to us. No, not in the demonstration of power, but in a quiet giving, in a cup of coffee, in a bowl of soup.

Beckett and the barber with him sought God in the wrong place, and therefore named the Mystery incorrectly.

Dare I say, Abraham did as well?

In the Hebrew and Christian Bible and the Qur'an as well, not to mention in the tears and prayers of Derrida and Caputo, is the story of Abraham, all using him as the precursor of their religions or religions without religion as well. I will use him, too, but with a profound difference. In doing so I will center in on the most famous account of this man out of Ur, the part of the story when he was "told" by God to sacrifice his son. This story has affected people down the ages with this strange God, even Paul of Tarsus falling victim to a God who sacrifices his son, rooted as it is in what God asks of Abraham.

As one on a venture myself, I can and do honestly sympathize with Abraham, after all he was both historically and symbolically traveling into *Terranova* with his spiritual sojourn; and aren't we doing the same somewhat, so in that sense he is much like ourselves. However, I can still admit my differences with this ancient and *his* notion of God. Why? Because in a very real sense he had made God Other.

Let me explain. It was not God, it was Abraham, who in a sort of religious scrupulosity, thought he had to sacrifice what he loved most—that if we are to be holy we can't enjoy love and life—that we have to give up everything to be spiritual, to approach God we must shed our deepest human qualities, and that is what God wants! "Here am I" or "I am here," is his refrain throughout, which, of course, is the beginning of every spiritual journey. However, Abraham stops there.

I-am is necessary, but there is *more* involved, and first and foremost it is not making God into some sort of a volcano god who needs a blood sacrifice. Abraham doesn't see the face of God—the face of God in Isaac. Instead, like the actor who perhaps was mimicking him, as so many have down the ages, Abraham makes the abysmal mistake of thinking he must sacrifice even his human love to get to God. That one must follow a pious legalism or spiritual scrupulosity or harsh asceticism is a deception that snarls so many who think they are approaching God, and in doing so, name God thusly. We see this in practically every religion.

No, Benedict, and all the rest, too, pious legalism and purity codes, righteous rituals and reading sacred writings, calling out from minarets or ringing bells from towers, singing Halleluiah or swaying back and forth in front of a wall, donning robes or lighting incense as you sit on your zafu, all of that and religions, too, don't do it. That really doesn't give us God. It is all *indifferentia* as Heloise so aptly put it—all that religiosity. Heloise was correct in pointing out that these exterior acts common to truly pious souls as well as hypocrites (I gather she meant Bernard) get in the way of wisdom, at least are not what matter—only the interior act really counts.[48] Love instead of asceticism is of course right-on. Love instead of adoration as well. Love over the law, over the rule, over religion. In point of fact, religion when followed as a law stifles true spirituality and thus the way to the Mystery that made us.

Abraham was struggling, and that is the scary part, that one can struggle in a search for God and still make a mistake—Abraham was struggling but nonetheless was stifling true spirituality, and in doing so stifling his very search for God. Again, as one on a venture myself, I can and do honestly sympathize with Abraham. However, always humanly hesitant as I am in my own divine dare, I can still admit my differences with this ancient and *his* notion of both spirituality and God. He was not grounding his spirituality in the love he had; and in doing so he was 'naming' God as Other.

As Rabbi Norman Cohen says in his interpretation of the story of Abraham and Isaac, Abraham just won't let up in his wrong-headedness, one can almost see him put his hands around Isaac's neck even after the angel's visit. I agree with the Rabbi, and would add, it seems Abraham has shackled himself with this

God, *a God outside of his deepest experience in existence,* and would impose his wrongheaded God even on God, let alone everyone else, including poor Isaac, not to mention so many others down the ages, perhaps even our poor actor. Paul of Tarsus, as I mentioned, is definitely caught up in this when he says God sacrificed his son for our sins. How negative an interpretation of Golgotha—if anything, this Yeshu hanging on his cross of physical pain, psychological aloneness, and spiritual abandonment has a positive interpretation, strange as that sounds; namely, that a human being, no matter what befalls him or her on the crooked cross of existence can still choose to love, as Jesus did. Circumstances crucified Christ, not some negative interpretation of God wanting a sacrifice of blood for our sins, which, rooted in Abraham's mistaken notion of *Elohim,* Paul, in turn, carries on into Christianity and down the ages. Circumstances crucified Christ, circumstances he couldn't change, but he met them still clinging to love, and in that showed the way and the significance of the cross, what it should symbolize. Only the God out of antiquity wants sacrifice, law, ritual, and all the rest people posit as holy. The God of love wants us to love, simply to love, though that isn't simple, especially as we are still left with the circumstances. But, whether the circumstances change or not (even as we pray they do), love is the way to live and the way to the Mystery that gave life. The Mystery that made us tells each of us this in our very make-up! To grasp that is to grasps our own creation and what I am saying here. *The original call to love is made by God, present in us as our very creation; our choice in life is our answer.*

Of course, there is the historical explanation of the Abraham story as well—the Hebrews at the time did sacrifice children, and this may merely have been a story to tell them not to. So much of the Bible and all holy books with it are just that, stories that we have turned into the word of God and made sacred. They are tools that can be helpful or not. But we are not here to give a scripture course, rather to get past all that, and through our universal grounding to find a way, a way past the past and postmodernism as well, to the Mystery we call God. So allow me to continue by saying that there is the possibility with regard to this particular story that it merely was conjured up by an ancient writer who concocted such a God out of what was prevalent at that time. However, no matter the source of the story, or if any historical intent, Abraham's notion of God is different than the God we have arrived at. In that Abraham named God differently than what was to be found in the depth of his humanness, differently than love.

When I say naming, we are of course talking about *what* God is, the 'naming' telling us *what* we call out to. Historically, Abraham called the Mystery *Elohim.* But that tells us what he meant to say about God. One can argue as some scholars do that the most likely derivation comes from the word *alah* ("to terrify") or *alih* ("to be perplexed, afraid; to seek refuge because of fear"). *Elohim*, a plural word by the way, therefore, would be "They who are the object of fear or reverence." Today, of course, it would be translated, as, "He who is the object of fear or reverence." But I would like to change it to one closer to our own meaning of God and say, "He with whom one who is afraid takes refuge." Why not? However, again, our efforts here are not to get stuck in scripture studies or scholarly disputes, but rather to find our way to the Ground of Being via the deepest experience in our being. Abraham would have been embracing Isaac had he done so, seeing God in the face looking back at him.

There is no doubt that Abraham's God and Jacob's God who leaves him behind wounded, or the God of pestilence and the three thousand massacred, or Jephthah sacrificing his daughter for Yahweh, and so on, and on (at least in such passages) connote a God of demonic features, and in this respect I think not unlike the pagan gods and the pagans whom the Hebrews made holy war against and slaughtered in the name of this God, a God who took up arms with them and slaughtered their enemies. It is the God of past centuries, not dissimilar to those of the Central and South American Indians or the Pacific islands or any of the others including the Greek Gods and their capriciousness, and Shakespeare in his *Lear* as well when he pens, "As flies to wanton boys are we to the gods. They kill us for their sport." He must have read Lucretius, or his Plato, who on a bad day at the Acropolis called humanity παιγνιονθεου, *a plaything to the gods, God's toy*. We see such a notion of a cruel or indifferent, at best all-powerful and judging God, up and down the centuries and into ours as well. There is a reason for it, of course, one we shall return to, but for now allow me to say that, in a sanitized way, the God promoted by religions of the Book today, with their insistence on a God of power and pious legalism, the Law, even trying to interpret love as the fulfillment of the law like so much of Christianity today, is certainly a carry-on of the God of old, no matter what their denial. Such people quote their particular holy Book with a blindness bordering on . . . well we won't get into that. Ultimately, I think their God is a God that comes out of the underbelly in us, the will to power, lifted to divine heights. And I think it is naming God wrongly.

Knowledge in and of itself is beautiful and good; and when used for beauty and good is loving. Knowledge can also be robbed of its beauty and goodness and used for power and any absence of goodness and beauty as we showed in the so-called science of Dachau and the doctors doing it. In a very real sense it was not science, but as Bronowski dubbed it, scientism. God, too, can be misused and abused as history shows, naming God incorrectly and turning Beauty and Goodness and Love Itself into a tyranny of thought and a suppression of our true human spirituality. I could use the Inquisition here, or the Crusades, or the suppressions in the religion of Islam today. In that vein, I am reminded of Al-Hallaj, a Sufi who in 922 was crucified by the Islamic leadership of the time.

He said before his crucifixion that one must not ask a person to adopt Islam or any other faith over what is fundamental. "My heart has opened to every form . . . I practice the religion of love," Ibn`Arabi said centuries later, following another crucified man's exact insight, though no doubt having arrived at it through his own journey, which we have said each of us could. No, there is no divine right for any religion, but we might say there is for each individual, a divine right of birth to find the truth of being. Religions are institutions, structured strictures with some sort of sacred scripture; but no organization or its Bible, its Sutras, its Vedas, its Torah, Talmud, Gita, Qur'an or Mathnawi can speak for us, or actuality, or the Mysterious More. Our personal journey in existence does that and what is fundamental to it, but we must be open, open to the deepest part of it.

The prophet is an *ish haruach*, a man driven and emboldened by the spirit of God—or by madness. A so-called prophet can be either and that is important. "In madness you think you are exceptionally enlightened," John Nash said, a man who had a lot of experience with madness.[49] The truth is anyone who starts spouting out about God can be nuts. Yours truly, included. So spirituality requires our attention, our full attention, because it will lend itself to our God-talk or theology. We started with venturing to establish a spirituality that was rooted in our very being, in our very human being-ness. It is only thus that we can honestly ever arrive at what is most real for us in naming God. But what's in a name you say—a rose by any other name is still a rose. As true as that is, the name we do call this Mysterious More affects our attitude towards It, ourselves, and others, and so does become important—it verbally tells us how we answer the *what* that started this chapter. As Martin Buber has demonstrated, the syntax of this question does not connote an inquiry as to the name of God but an inquiry into the character revealed by the name. He says, "Where the word 'what' is associated with the word 'name' the question asked is what finds expression in or lies concealed behind that name."[50] He used "Absolute Person," and I suppose I should say, again, the Source of Being cannot be a person per se, though I see what he was trying to get at, as he is advocating the God of the Hebrew bible and thus a God that is a Thou. I prefer my own use of Intimacy or Loving Presence with regards this Mystery, which accomplishes a personal *mutua inhaesio* without reducing God to an entity even sideways. Buber's God is different in other ways as well, most particularly, when he says we should fear and stand trembling before him, he who can suspend goodness and ask us to murder our child.[51] This is too close to the volcano god for me; and his reliance on faith, too, is not the way our venture has taken or could have. I should also make mention here what we have been doing; namely, theology; and go on to mention that theology means 'God talk,' 'to talk of God,' from the Greek $\theta\varepsilon o\varsigma$ and $\lambda o\gamma o\varsigma$. I know I should definitely make mention of what one of the greatest theologians said of theology. It is perhaps the most profound and precise thing ever said about it: *to talk of God is love striving to understand.* For me, personally, that *is* it. It is so beautifully put—the deepest experience in our existence striving with a desperate courage to understand, to see past the problem of suffering, brutal evolution, past the nonsense of pious wrong-headedness and wrongly naming God, past the whole of this postmodern planet of stress, and somehow someway understand the Mystery that made us and allows all this. That is and must be my definition of theology. Theology is not texts and technicalities, but ultimately *love striving to understand.* Actually, I can say, life is that as well.

I think you can grasp the whole of this endeavor we have undertaken in that, *love striving to understand. Love striving to know.*

I dare to say that each of us indeed is given in the course of our lives, glimpses into the heart of the really real, and, surprisingly, what one sees in that special encounter is something found in our everyday lives and open to us all; namely, the utmost simplicity yet very depth and profundity of actuality itself, love, the love that moves the sun and the stars as Dante so poetically put it at the end of his own spiritual journey. In the everyday mysticism without ecstasy we call love, at certain moments in time and space, we sense the connection of this to *the Mystery that surrounds us.* Somehow, love, the love we experience on a golden afternoon or a rainy winter one, too—our everyday and every kind of weather human love—does indeed give us a sense of something more, something even More. Something that is not a thing at all, but wordless and only sensed, yet seen in that everyday and every-kind-of-whether love, seen in the faces of those we love and who love us, and yes seen in the face in the mirror looking back at you. In the end, like that fat theologian we quoted who put away all his tomes and merely loved, perhaps we will do the same some day. He had come to an understanding. Let's say that we are still striving; perhaps that should have been the subtitle of this book: *love striving, love striving to understand, love striving to know, love striving to realize.*

Of course, a period can never be put at the end of anything said about God; it must always have an ellipsis . . .

Paradoxically, though the Mysterious More is always More and More still . . . we have been given a way to such an Incomprehensible that takes us to the very core Truth of God, of GIVING.

Let me say here that there are other experiences, perhaps even mystical ones, that can give one an insight that one might not otherwise have and they have to be allowed a voice, even trusted, but always done so within the horizon of one's whole being and the deepest experience in our existence. Love is our safeguard in anything and everything spiritual, including and maybe especially when it comes to mysticism.

So that we are on the same glorious page then, I must say that pure spirituality is not what is referred to as traditional mysticism. Since most people are not mystics, discussing it might be a waste of time, but people so often identify it as both spiritual and in touch with the divine that it has to be addressed, or undressed as is the case. Traditional mysticism is a rapture where the body/brain/mind meet in a swoon of ecstasy in spacetime, but that does not necessarily have anything to do with being spiritual or with God either. Again, love is our safeguard in anything and everything spiritual, including and maybe especially when it comes to mysticism. If mysticism lacks love it lacks both spirituality and God as well. And even if any ecstasy happens now and again to come along with love, it can be of great help, if and only if, understood properly, always remembering it is the love, the very human and everyday love that is what is of importance.

The word mystical comes from the Greek μυστηριον *(secret things, secret worship)* μυστης *(one initiated)* μυειν *(to close the lips)*. What it meant was that it was a secret, not open to the uninitiated, not open to everyone. That is totally contrary to what I am saying about love as the revelation in life and reality open to one and all—as love is. Traditional mysticism tends to perpetuate a privileged kind of spirituality, when, in fact, true spiritually is just the opposite. It is as egalitarian as existence itself. Spirituality is not the property of any particular group, though people are always tying to make us think so, people like all these gurus and so-called masters, and even these traditional mystics in their own way, for they, too, would give off the impression of something special needed. All of that robs us of our birthright of achieving a pure, true, and human spirituality. There is no privileged pedestal. Consider that and you see what I am saying. And I think what Heloise might have been saying as well. Traditional mysticism, enrapturing, ethereal, and ecstatic as it might be, is still *indifferentia* when it comes to spirituality. Spirituality is something found in the deepest expression of our being in the everyday doings of living, from the smallest of acts of love we are called upon to do, to the biggest and most stupendous. That embrace of existence at its deepest expression of being and that alone—not myth, mysticism, or monasticism—leads to answering the meaning of breathing and the three basic questions we must ask about it. And if we let it, it tells us what the Mysterious More is as honestly as a human can possibly hope to achieve. If God exists, God is open to all. There are no chosen people or super race or higher caste or any such nonsense.

We might argue for a mystical approach, or even as some are doing, the use of drug-enhancing mysticism (which I will address specifically further on), or we might argue for a path of righteousness, or a blind leap of faith, but we know love is rooted in our deepest reality and it is where our deepest spirituality must also be rooted, and so our most profound, honest, and human approach to the

Mysterious More. It is true that each new discovery is potentially one that will change our horizon or the perception of our place in the realm of reality—for example dimensionality—but still within all that is the constant of love, down to earth and very real. *I am and I can love* is still our root-reality, the deepest experience in our human journey, and our way to act in the face of it all.

In love we find hope against the outcry! Against spacetime itself! My first poem so many moons ago, as you already know, was that *something is wrong, oh so something, the shadow of what could be, the echo of what should be.* There is a Hebrew word for correcting creation—*tikkun.* Traditionally it is understood to be a path of cosmic restoration or correction, and the fundamental task of humans to do this. I am rather fond of this word because I believe it implies my notion of *love in action* against the outcry. My *amor in actu!* Might I suggest, without being a prophet or mystic either, just a human like us all, vulnerable and stumbling along, might I suggest that the deepest *tikkun,* the truest *tikkun,* is just that, living love. It may be too childish-foolish for this world, possibly even an aberration in the cosmos it is trying to correct, but love is still our deepest experience in existence in this cosmos and our very real protest against the suffering outcry of time and space itself, certainly against the suffering of all the creatures within this odd creation. I don't know what the readers and practitioners of the Kabbalah have in mind when they use the word, but that is what I do, for in love we find hope against the outcry! And here I dare to add that in this living love we find *our living God.*

As the abyss looks back when we look into it, so does love, and when we look deeply into that love we see God looking back. What kind of God is this? One that cares, that loves us through this odyssey, that has some kind of relationship with us, some kind of Presence. This profound glimpse of God is in each of us . . . and so, here I dare to say again, that in this living love we find *our living God.*

I want to stop and dwell on something once again, because it is so important *where* we *choose* to find our God. I quoted the poetic words of *I King* at the top of this segment. Let me expand on what I already said about them. Going *without* will give us a different God than going *within!* Nature will give us a different God than the deepest experience in our existence! "Is there any cause in nature that makes these hard hearts?" the Bard asked in my favorite of his plays. "Yes," we must answer. And since we have, let's amplify on the fact mentioned already, that the search for the sacred itself can be a siren. A person attempting to get to the ultimate truth of being has to be cautious; identifying the source for doing so becomes all-important, otherwise one can end up identifying God with a volcano. You laugh, but don't. People do that every day, metaphorically today, and literally in the past, because they have gone and continue to go to nature to find God. Nature will give you what it is and thus a God based on power, the volcano God who must be obeyed and given worship and sacrifice as I pointed out. One can refine that, and people have, so that God becomes the All-Powerful, the All-Mighty, the Majestic and Omnipotent who must be obeyed and given worship and sacrifice. All of it can be and has been refined even further, into a plethora of theologies we witness in the plethora of religions and carryings on we see across the globe where their God is described thus, one way or another, for all of them are rooted in the same source. One that does indeed, old Lear, make these hearts hard, at least hardened to love, and instead give themselves to a credo of power, one they find without and not at the depths of their own being and the deepest experience in it. They have estranged themselves from their own essence and the very Ground of their being, and that is what 'sin' really must be; to estrange one's self from love, from your own essential self, saying, no to the invitation, the call within, I mentioned. Such a person rejects the greatest gift life offers, and his or her only way to God.

I can hear them now, those with ice in their laughter. "As he has gotten more unconvincing, he has become ever more ear-piercing and uncontrollable in his philo-soso-phy. It has festered into a messianic complex wrapped in a disillusionment about everything he calls the world. Anyone can see this in how his writings are now absorbed in theologically driven throes and twists." In answer, what can I do but let my sheep dog eat the cookie I gave him, and hope that those with ice in their laughter all get sheep dogs. In that spirit, appreciating how crazy as it might sound, I would like to continue in pursuit of unmasking those who would name God wrongly and why I must do so, because *by naming we give rise to acting.*

Without getting into naming a specific denominational service, I recently watched one of those events on television which all of you must have seen at one time or another where the congregation is ecstatic in their worship. Even as I told myself that it was their way of getting to the Mysterious More I was in an argument with myself. No, it is not getting to the Mysterious More, rather it is merely an expression of this culture's superficiality, I concluded, perhaps overly upset about the 'dumbing down' of America at the time. Upon further reflection, I admitted that the roots for such behavior go deeper than our education system or our mass media of breadcrumbs and circuses. It is rooted in the tide pools and dark rainforests of our past, and shows us that getting to God is not a relative thing, one way as good as another. I know white wine is being spilled all across California after that statement. But let's use some extreme examples to bring out the truth of that statement. Santeria shamans slicing up live creatures is not good, no matter political correctness or the Supreme Court—nor is a congregation of Vodoun worshipers making people into a deathlike stupor as zombies for the Loa, the deities of the voodoo faith.

What is being displayed here is the underbelly of evolution, what is faceless, loveless—as empty as that faceless, loveless zombie. Neither of these is the way to the Mysterious More; nor is any other religion that is based on nature and the fascination with and allegiance to power that arises out of it, even though less extreme than these two primitive examples. If you go to nature, you always end up with the will to power as primary and an All-Powerful All-Mighty God, whether accompanied by bongos or Brahms.

My point in all this is that there is a choice involved. One that displays the forever tension involved between consciousness and the cosmos. By the choice of either you shall know the source of a religion and its God; that is, whether closer to consciousness as evolved to its deepest experience, or its opposite, the primeval waters we came out of. That might fly in the face of the sacred cow of all things being relative, including cultures and ethics, but it is what a closer study of the situation we call breathing truly shows us. A zombie is a body without character, without will. To do that to another person in the name of whatever, Gods or religion included, is hardly the same as not doing it. In point of fact, it is functioning out of the rawest and darkest of what we call evolution. That becomes especially obvious to any of us when we think of it being done to us: the very thought of being a zombie has to send a cerebral chill through us, an echo of the unconscious abyss hissing out at our terror from a place without love. We feel the dark primordial underbelly of evolution swallowing us as some indifferent predator might—which the one doing such a deed to another would be, no matter the tolerant understanding on our part of the social conditions of how he or she might have arrived there.

I am reminded of Clairvius Narcisse in this matter, a person who had been drugged into a zombie state by his brother to gain control of the family land in Haiti. Narcisse told of his ordeal, as Wade Davis, a Harvard scientist who traveled to Haiti and reported on his findings, relates in his book *The Serpent And The Rainbow*.[52] Clairvius was, according to his own account, in a sort of stupor and was sold into slavery where he worked from sunrise to sunset on one skimpy meal a day. His life had the quality of a strange dream, with events, objects, and perceptions interacting in slow motion, and with everything completely out of his control. In fact, there was no control at all. Decision had no meaning, and conscious action was an impossibility, even as he remembered being aware of his predicament, of missing his family, and of wanting to return. Like all such happenings, the shaman who spun his fate used an ingenious poison that served as a template upon which the victim's worst fears might be amplified. Still, in the end, it was not the powder that sealed Narcisse's fate, it was his own mind, Davis goes on to tell us. Narcisse believed that the other man, called the *bokor* in voodoo, had sent for his soul. The victim strove desperately to communicate, but with the paralytic poison, he found it impossible. It was in medical terms an autoscopic near-death experience, Davis explains. Totally paralyzed, he may have been a passive observer of his own funeral, the Harvard scientist speculates. Since he worked as a slave after that, I gather he meant psychically or volitionally paralyzed—at least after the initial dose and ceremony; at least one can draw that conclusion from the way Narcisse described himself.

In my further readings on such practices, one is witness in a Vodoun ceremony to a litany of creatures being tortured before someone who had been made a zombie is brought in. As the one brought in demonstrates, the individual, left with little intelligence or will, is slowly perishing. It is a scene of such singular horror to the human psyche that people relating such ceremonies can only think of escape from such a place. It is matter without mind . . . giving evidence of the terror I spoke of in all of us. Lest you think I am limiting this behavior merely to third world societies, highly technically evolved societies can be as un-evolved as these un-technically evolved ones. Haiti or Hitler so to speak. Santeria shaman or Stalin! In both and all such cases, throughout the spectrum of societies within our species, it is evolution stuck in the raw elemental energies where consciousness has not evolved to give evidence of something more within their own being *or* rejects it and embraces those naked forces out of which we emerged and uncoiled, and does so with fancy philosophical and political phrases like 'will to power,' or 'dictatorship of the proletariat,' colorful religious ones like *mange moun* (to eat people) or *coup n'ame* (capturing the soul of an individual). No matter, we are involved in what is truly primitive, primordial, and primeval in the root meaning of such words; namely, the raw elemental energies of evolution. A 'holiness' of this sort has too often been history's henchman, as we certainly are witnessing in today's world, where in the name of God such horrors are being committed. Impelled by urges that are primal, humans have deified that and given a religious base to their drives to dominate and destroy.

I have a short fuse for those who 'play church,' or go off on trips of tarot cards and the like, not to mention into the sophomoric if not scatological notions of New Age nonsense. What they are really involved in, when all their machinations are shoved aside, is the will to power—if not over others, over the elements, and that is the root-reality of their religiosity no matter what they might call it. We have all met such people. They name and maim spirituality and God so wrongly as to merit a Dantean Circle all their own. But alas, dear Dante, we have no idea if there is any justice to come, there certainly isn't any here on planet stress. Let's at least hope for a purgatory! Meanwhile, they cause hells and purgatories for other people, luring them to islands as de-spiriting and ultimately as dehumanizing as the one Pinocchio went to by way of a lie as well.

In such a hit and miss situation as life, humans are left in a quandary trying to solve the sacred, because of a fundamental dilemma in our make up; namely, the unceasing and pitiless, blind, prehuman, dark and lustrous powers out of which we emerged and uncoiled, in light of the phenomenon of consciousness and its sense of the mysterious more of being. Here the footprints of existence within us show themselves, ascending from inorganic matter into life and from life into consciousness and love . . . leaving us with an inner choice each conscious creature must make in its reach for the profound depths of its being. In our attempt to reconcile what seem to be antithetical powers, as different as lust and love within us, one stemming from the natural drive to procreate, and more primal still, to survive, the other from something more in our being, reaching for something More in being itself, humans have come up with all sorts of 'salvations,' ranging from those stuck in the elemental forces that made us, to those that push on further (or deeper). It might all just be the creature trying to cope, with religion and philosophy itself still secretly guided by survival, and humans driven by physiological and psychological requirements in order to maintain sanity and society both in such an abyss as spacetime offers. Certainly we have to admit as witnesses to existence that does indeed seem the innermost nature of nature itself, merely a blind incessant impulse without cause, without rest, without goal, merely a drive to survive, to live, with no meaning in this groundless existence other than this unceasing, primitive, dark, blind, shapeless, discordant drive which takes on a swarming multiplicity of forms, and nothing more. It drove the witness Schopenhauer to end his great work *Die Welt als Wille und Vorstellung* with the words "this our world, which is so real, with all its suns and milky ways—is nothing."[53] This is the shout out of the abyss in all our ears—and yet, and yet. As with Issa and his *and yet* in the face of his Zen void when it came to human love, we have ours in the face of the nihilistic abyss.

Perhaps what Jesus saw on the cross was the abyss—that there is only the void and no God of love—but he still held onto love as a human being no matter. There is that side of the puzzle. Even as there is the other, with warmth and beauty, and goodness and love, as a guidance from a God.

In contrast and choice both to Schopenhauer's last word, *nothing*, there is *love; love as the last word, in the face of the puzzles within puzzles and the perilous perhaps, in the face of the desert of postmodernism, in the face of pain.* In this we realize our humanness to its depths.

I said that those seeking enlightenment itself must be attentive to what they are about, always guided by the light of love; otherwise it really will not be as enlightening as they might hold. I am especially thinking of those who seek to achieve mysticisms of different sorts through drug-enhancing means. We have already mentioned traditional mysticism, here we are talking about a modern take on that which involves drugs, often referred to as entheogens by their devotees and their dizzying array of doctrines. Of course drug use has been administered by primitive religions all the way back, but here it takes on a different twist, even as it is the same; namely, based in the way and will to power, call it what you will. Though these entheogenic mystics often use modern technology and modern terminology, there is still the forever self-aggrandizement involved in these endeavors; totally opposite of the giving of one's self. In point of study, these entheogen-takers can so easily end with delusions of grandeur, purporting to be mediums to what no one else can know about heaven, hell, voids, and visions of God almighty. Yes, today as in the past, it involves an elitism, which the very word mystic connotes from its Greek root as I already put forth. My point again being they are indeed rooted in the will to power, *to give the person using them powers.* This is the furthest thing from true spirituality or enlightenment. Also, often users fall into an abyss-worship mode, making their so-called "meaningful" hallucinations into a drug-based Zen, with all that goes with that, from denying self to denying anything as good or bad, but rather "depending" or "relative," until they really are in the abyss, the abyss of nihilism where anything goes. It is for so many of them, "just the evolutionary process of genes and memes playing itself endlessly out—and nothing more."[54] Does that sound familiar? Yes, old Susan again. "The big butana!" Giacomo, please! These people's derealizations and deperonalizations are more sophisticated forms of the vodoun—but they are based ultimately on the same thing—and should be known for what they are.

True, there are those among the so-called modern mystics who take a different approach, but again still rooted in the same place and ending up the same way. "I don't put God with a capital G right up at the top of everything, I'm pretty much oriented towards Mother Nature in all her guise," a rather famous such person puts out, and ends up saying his spirituality is "the cool, clinical, detachment of a mirror."[55] I am sure that moves him mightily to share his soup; and with that I end wasting my time with these types, hoping my soup reference brings home to you, my lonely reader, what is wrong with these gurus and their pathological narcissism, narcissistic even as they deny they really exist ironically. One last thing I must mention before we leave these people who can cause such irreversible harm; namely, their smugness when it comes to suffering. They are indeed cool, clinical, and detached as the mirror they are looking into out of what they have chosen to be.

In their attempt to be mystical and have power they miss the real mystery of life and living, the mystery that surprises life itself.

What I have been attempting is to unstuckify you and me and everyone from the God of the will to power, not to mention the silly and sometimes sadly dangerous spiritualities saddled on us because of it—and, instead, have each of us look at ourselves as the only source of-and-for a true spirituality, one rooted in choosing to be sensitive to the deepest in us, and because it is the depth of our being arguably a call from the Mystery that made us, which becomes our guidepost to that Mysterious More Itself. For each of us, spirituality rests on such a personal inspection and decision, and so does our way to God if there is to be any. That doesn't make this Mysterious More an abstraction from life, but rather only attained through each of us *realizing* a spirituality that does not lie beyond or outside our humanness, but constitutes the very depths of that humanness, and in that a human being's way to the Source of that humanness, call it the Mysterious More, God, or what one will, even that which has no name—no matter—it is still and only our realization of love that brings us to it, hesitant and human as it is, carrying all the luggage that it does, even the forever question *was all this necessary!*

If there is to be a mysticism that is real it must entail that busy buzzing brain of ours beloving in this so human way, beloving the Giving, grasping at God, the God behind all others, even as God is not Other. Here the mystery of the mind forgets words, has done with doom, and simply knows in an different kind of knowing. That comes from the mysticism without ecstasy we can all experience. It is from it that we ground our purely human spirituality and so answer how we can all act in the face of the world, and in the face of the ever present problem of suffering that goes along with that.

The non-conscious, selfless abyss, a place without love is always there. We have not left that out, as we have not left out the brain-stabbing reality of suffering. Nor have we left out the biology of our body. If I might add a postmortem to that even as we have laid it to rest, allow me, since this is a far more serious position than the entheogenic devotees pose, allow me to say that in unraveling our biology, we humans delve deeper and deeper into our material make up, as such specialization is expected to do—but those who imagine that they can prove *our full make up* simply by uncovering ever more material findings, are blind to the depth of our being. When looked at in an historical perspective, biochemistry has become for the present day our particular panacea, in a sense the faith of our day, and those who propagate it the new priesthood of authority who speak out of the findings in a new kind of entrails hunt. So we should not be so smug as we look at our voodoo practitioners. Biology cannot encompass reality, especially as it tries to compress it - those words stick in my mind's eye. Greater empirical adequacy will lead to greater empirical adequacy; but we reach the limits of empirical verification at a certain point. Even my fellow funny man Crick had to admit that he didn't think "we'll be able to explain everything that we're conscious of."[56] And the point of all this, specifically with regards to spirituality and God? That if you pursue spirituality and God in the raw elemental energy of evolution, not only will you come up with this raw elemental energy as representative of you, but with a representation of that as 'God' as well, as we saw in the misplaced spirituality that started this particular segment—whatever you might call your God. Such an approach, be it of a primitive or present day rendition, can only render its notion of deep reality through the mud out of which we emerged and uncoiled, leaving out the greatest mystery in the cosmos, consciousness, and what is more, a consciousness that can love. *We should never allow anything to lead us into a place without love.* Even if we choose not to pursue it to God. But if we do, it must be done through the fact of this greatest of mysteries we are alive to in ourselves, the mystery that surprises life. To paraphrase Planck with a little plunk: neither biochemistry nor blood tests, holy books nor *bokor* bloodletting can solve the ultimate mystery. And you know why. In the last analysis, we ourselves, we at the depth of our being, are the ultimate mystery; which, in turn, contrariwise to the cosmos but not consciousness, gives us access to . . . to what?

Dare I say tying the air together?

"These are the things I think when I am, when I am not I don't know what I think." I echo my madman, who said those same words to the gravedigger at the asylum. I think you can figure out the significance of it without me; meanwhile, the immediate question before you might be: does this somewhat sort of fat author—no, not a roly-poly, just a somewhat oddly shaped man whose weight seems to gather around his stomach and rosy face, while his nearly hairless arms and legs remain thin—does such a man have it right? Does he have it right when he says that presence is our beginning and our end, our alpha and omega? That everything for each of us is, and has to be, within that presence? Not only the inner choice between the raw elemental energies and being sensitive to the deepest part of our being, but even finding any *real* God as well?

How do we not stay in the realm of raw elemental energy, but move on to a place where we don't turn another into a zombie, an object, call it what you will, but, instead, share our bowl of soup? That is the inner decision each of us must make, first and foremost; and, again, it is not one made in a vacuum, but rather out of depths of our own conscious life itself. It gives us a way to act in the face of the primal forces that we can so easily give ourselves over to, even giving them fancy names and constructing religions rooted in them, religions, which, when all is said and done, find their God in what I call the underbelly of evolution.

If a person stays there without looking at more in his or her own being—that is, consciousness and the depths of what it shows us—he or she will indeed wrongly say that this tide pool tilt is the way to go, even as he or she does not recognize that is what he or she really is saying, even as there is, in fact, another way, sensitive to the deepest part of life and living. When I say consciousness is in an evolutionary tug of war with the raw elemental energies, pulling evolution towards its own depth of being, that is not saying evolution or nature is evil. What I am saying, again, is that the amoral world we find ourselves in is not worthy of us. We know of another kind of existence. We know of love. We know of an awareness of love. Herein is the depth of our being. It is here we find the mysterious more of ourselves *and* in leaping into that the Mysterious More we call God. Nietzsche says only a few can attain what he called *der ubermensch* and that *der untermesch* or unfinished man will knock such a greater human off the tightrope and never allow him to get across to that fullness. Maybe that is so about both his statements, and maybe not, but, despite the legion of petty people Nietzsche speaks of, and they are there of course, what I speak of is open to all no matter how they finally choose how to act—because existence is open to all and it is in their very existence they can find this. Our purely human spirituality is alive and has its roots in this, and so does the God it can come to. Such a God cannot be taught by harshness, by any amount of harshness, not even by morality, by any amount of morality. Love is the source here; it is where we choose to find the unfathomable mystery of being, and only when that is undertaken can the Mystery that made us be realized by us and GIVING understood in the fullest way a human being can grasp the God beyond all Gods. In realizing that we do indeed tie the air together and the impossible becomes possible.

It need not be, as I said, like Francis naked in the square; and if you looked like the entropic entity authoring this masterpiece you certainly would not want to impose such a sight on man nor beast. Rather it could be a quiet loving, not yet sure even, but there, with a God of love as our last best hope, and if not so, at least our human love, our human love still hanging in there—to lead us in our face off with the world. I don't mean to be obsessed with the third question of philosophy—how do I act in the face of existence—but really that is what matters. I suppose I must further add that that too can be done in the hurly burly of the square, or done in the quietude of a retreat from the world, a retreat within one's self, or actually as the case may be into a place apart. *The point is to act out of the depths of your presence in existence.* We are in the eight day of creation when we must do the creating . . . and so how we act in the face of existence *is* important.

Since no one can really deny his or her presence in the world, our presence is really not the issue here, the mystery of the presence of God is. It is said that among Yahweh's words to Moses were these: "I shall hide my face from them. I shall see what their end will be."[57] That may be so; namely, that God has hid his face; or it might not be so, because of love. Our venture has said that the testament of love is God's revelation to us—of the divine presence, in us and in the face looking at us, bag lady or leper—and when we realize that we realize

God, we breathe in God. That is ultimately each individual's choice, but seeing love, knowing it, the beauty and goodness of it, I think does tell us something about realizing God.

There is grounding *and* God in that! That is what I said. Our very own grounding gives a grounding to God for us. God is grounded in our grounding! Damn but that is exciting! It is a drama of Aeschylean proportion, a theology of Augustinian dimension! Is it the coffee again causing this surge in the circuitry of my brain, or is it perhaps the thrill of the truth?

For the moment at least let's answer in a thankfulness still tinged with hesitation, and say a yes to it, even as midnight might bring the exact opposite in this divine dialectic we are involved in. For the moment at least let's dare to grasp the moment and say yes there is a coherence here of the profoundest attitude towards life and the Mystery that made it. *Carpe diem et etiam eocum Deum.*

A thought in the subjunctive at five in the morning: God is loving, pure and simple, nothing more need or could be said. That is hard to get my head around . . . just loving. Not power, not providence, not other, not anything but loving. Not expected to do anything but! That is very hard to get one's head around. God is that which directs us into love. Not someone we call love out there, rather Loving, just LOVING. In a sense that is scary, because we want God to be all-powerful, to protect us, and we lean that way as is only natural, and maybe that is so as well. *But God loves us even as we die!* Even as God allows us to die—and that tears my heart out and my head inside out, for I don't understand, and that twilight thought bangs out in my brain. Why did God allow for such a place called spacetime and dying? Was all this necessary? Our questions become more questioning, and we can't help but think in questions, live in questions. The chill around the words empty and abyss are real and haunt all human heads. A call out of the empty, leaving us face to face with the abyss is there for us to experience—and with it a monstrous conclusion. That chilling encounter will cause misery to any person who is honest with himself, with herself. God always remains a questioning in us, one that leans the baggage we carry first one way and then another in an ongoing problematic, a divine dialectic.

It is an unfinished symphony we are composing, but one we are doing so with and a la Beethoven! So for the moment at least let's answer in a thankfulness still tinged with hesitation—yes to loving—and to a beloving of God as well—even in the silence all around us, and at times as if crying out to what seems not to be there, at least as we imagine.

Love is both our most profound presence in the world, and at the same time, our most profound transcendence to include more. When we have this synthesis within ourselves, we are both ethereal and very much down to earth. Simpatico for ourselves, our fellow humans, and for all other living creatures is as flesh and blood as it gets—but also there is this touch at transcendence within it, suggesting to us something beyond at our very core, as contradictory as that sounds. Love brings with it all of this. It is our very incarnation triumphing! All the elements of our experience are included, with nothing ever omitted. But the way in which we see them transforms us and them, even as the world goes on as it is. In spite of my stammering sincerity a truly indescribable synthesis has been achieved. *Here, in love, each presence is the most pure and profound of prayers in and of itself when it loves.*

Of course I am not talking about what is conventionally called prayer. No, it certainly is not a prayer of adoration or awe, or even a prayer of petition. In fact, I wonder if I should even mention any prayer at all. Perhaps the only authentic prayer is *sperabamus—we were hoping.* For how many have asked and it was not given to them, knocked and it was not opened, sought and did not find. As I write that, Peter O'Toole in *The Ruling Class* comes to mind, perhaps to soften that reality. When asked—I think by his psychiatrist—why he thinks he's God, he answers: "Simple. When I pray I find I'm talking to myself." You might ask, isn't that what we are doing as well when we pray—when we ask and it is not given, knock and it is not opened, seek and it is not found? In fact, can postmodernkind even pray? Should we? It may merely be the outcry in us. In fact, I think it is. The outcry of existence! I don't see why we should get bent out of shape because of it, as long as we realize what it is. For God is the Mystery of appeal.

Prayers of petition ask that those praying be spared another draught or flood—another suffering. Of course God does not send the draught or the flood in the first place, or any suffering, and to think otherwise is to revert back to the volcano god. Notwithstanding that, to petition for our daily bread and to be delivered from evil is going to be a part of us for as long as we are human, knowing how vulnerable we are—and that is OK in and of itself, to talk to God about one's needs is fine. As just to talk to God is. There is a line in another movie that comes to mind here, when C. S. Lewis, in *Shadowlands,* says he prays because he must. That asking and crying out to, pondering and petitioning, looking and wondering, questioning and quieting into stillness, leads us into a more profound look at prayer.

Do we pray merely because we are prey, or is there a deeper purpose to prayer—from something deeper still? Something in this sojourn, I suspect, should be said about that. Each of us has to look up at the night sky and wonder about the mystery that surrounds us at one time or other in our life, every consciousness has to eventually, even if it is to cry out for a horse or over one. Out of the misty millenniums of the past we see civilization after civilization trying to deal with this wonder and worry both, trying to deal with this *mystery of more* within the context of their conscious existence, knowing both their vulnerability as well as a sense of more. Each civilization had its own notion of what that awesome mystery of more to which they prayed might be, from the most primeval society to the most sophisticated. It ranged from cruel and mean gods to the Roman notion of *numen* which had neither shape nor name and very near a mere presence; from the awe of the vastness of the universe and what might be behind it, even a Void, all the way to a sacred sense of love that moved the sun and other stars. Oswald Spengler remarked that human choice is only possible within the limitations and idea-forms of a given age—yet I have to say there are still 'moments' when we are given in the course of our lives glimpses into the heart of the really real. It reveals to us the true fabric of actuality, beyond the tyranny of thought of our own age or normal limitations. Geniuses show us this in the flesh, of course, each opening his or her age to a new paradigm or possibility. But my point here is that the λογος σπερματικοι—*the seminal meaning of being*—of this sense of more, *the mysterious more,* has been there from the beginning of human consciousness, with humans, as individuals and as whole peoples, trying to attain it—and today is no different, people are still attempting a crack in the night sky, still attempting to 'pray.'

Following up on what we came to in this chapter, we can say a type of prayer that comes out of that, a type all its own, *a prayer of presence.* So let us in this pursuit of prayer accept what the chapter has to say, even if you yourself can't pray or chose not to. Remember me saying that God is decidedly not a person, an entity like us—yet, still is capable of being addressed at any time in a personal way, in an intimacy, in a love. *God is an embracing relationship between our presence and Presence.* That is going to be the basis of our prayer here even as it will be developed more clearly, a prayer of presence. It is as personal as anything is personal. This is open to all, and it is rooted in our deepest reality. So real prayer is rooted in our deepest reality. Mystics come and go, talking mumbo jumbo for the most part, but here is an honest and human way to the Mystery that made us, using the deepest experience in each of us to do so.

Prayer is to give your heart to, to love God. In other words, the very thing in us that corresponds to God. It is communion with God through love, reaching past the emptiness and darkness of the unknown, even with tears in your eyes, to Love. *It is being present, the holy here.* Prayer is being alone with God, in the mystery of divine love. It is warm and personal, unique to each one in a special way. There are many levels of being, we are talking about the deepest, love, in which we transcend to what barely penetrates the threshold of cognition, but is there in our presence, that which reaches beyond spacetime and illuminates and purifies our understanding, where one can sense a silent presence beyond the chaord of the cosmos. Again, it is an embracing relationship between your presence and Presence.

That said, namely, that loving in and of itself is prayer, let me elaborate on that.

Because ours is an age, especially perhaps in America, where, in the hurly burly hubbub of our daily lives, people more and more are seeking out different kinds of access to this mysterious more, call it what we will, even a restful moment, or peace, or oneness, or emptiness, let's look at one of the more popular endeavors to achieve such attainment, one of the more prevailing methods of attempting to get to what is behind our brain and being, too, one of the more personal ways to attaining access to this mystery of more so deeply rooted in us; namely, one of the deepest kinds of prayer, *meditation or contemplation*.

Bear with me, for as I said I was talking about something different than the conventional notion of prayer, what I am going to talk about now is different than what is usually promoted as meditation or contemplation. Please stay with me on this until I have explained this prayer of presence in full. Often it is said, that at the root of all meditation is *silence & swallow* so to speak; that is, being silent and having the self swallowed up, to put it succinctly. But I am offering an alternative meditation or contemplation: one where you are not swallowed up, where you don't empty your mind and presence with it. Instead, you are alive to that presence, and in it to witnessing everyday love, and beauty, and goodness, and the sense of more they give . . . and the sense More as well. Here is the *beginning* of the contemplation I am speaking of. One that carries the sense of being alive to love all the way to being alive to Love Itself, the Love beyond and at your very core—consciously so. Let me try to give expression to that: it is to share the moment—share the moment with Mystery—to share that moment with all the love in you . . . without the reservation of even the problem of suffering and all the blood under that bridge, despite the hesitancy of your trust and all that goes with it, despite the world and the silence of the Mystery in it, despite the fact that you might be foolish, a failure, and fat, and without trying to have to remember any 'proof' to argue to anything . . . *to simply sense and swim in love*.

Prayer, profound prayer, is a presence embracing Presence. It is giving your heart without the luggage life has given you, or maybe with all of it, but without the head having to prove anything, being open to what you sense in love and going all the way with it. This type of contemplation is a venture of love into love—consciously so.

In such a contemplation you are in a profound 'co-mingling' with Mystery—a *mutua inhaesio* or reciprocal abiding in the most intimate of ways, *direct love. This is you at your deepest self, alive to Incomprehensible Intimacy.* It is you in a profound 'moment,' alive to actuality, to the depth of being, to the interiority of the really real, living in the spirit, living in the dimensionality of actuality with the deepest insight into being one can have, in fact, beyond being and nonbeing—one with GIVING, where you are still and always conscious of the your own profound presence, but in communion with direct love itself, God's Presence—and because of that, to an awakening or awareness *to act out of that love. Prayer is a leap into love and the living of love out of that.*

Complete or fulfilled meditation is ultimately action oriented because of that profound realization—the within becoming the without because it has to, has to be swept back into the vast current of life with a matchless insight into it, daring to realize that insight, softly or with a shout. Yes, I am saying that meditation will take to action, *an awareness in action* that is expressed best in the words you already know, I am and I can love. Prayer, which started out as a leap into love, returns giving us what we might call the grace to fight on—no, not the awful grace Aeschylus speaks of, or the god-awful scrupulosity Hopkins calls grace, but a loving grace, that is, what grace itself is—LOVING itself, GOD.

Always and everywhere by *God* something is understood which is the mystery that fundamentally determines all being. *What* this is has been a species-specific search since humans began, as it was our very own human venture. A venture one could say that somehow tried to penetrate past the planets and awe-inspiring space that is too large and too impersonal and too indifferent and too much—to venture past it all into the Unseen, Unoriginated, Uncreated, Unborn, Unformed, Uneverything! What we have done intellectually; we now do in a prayer. Words wash away or become dim, and, somehow, in a direct line that is, as I said, without the reservation of even the problem of suffering and despite a postmodern hesitancy still hanging around in our heads, without trying to have to establish anything anymore, we simply give ourselves to the sense we have touched upon in love, leap into it, share the moment with Mystery, and 'touch' the Presence of God. Such a moment of direct love is one where words fall off the page. That is the first step in giving your heart to contemplation, wherein you get to the article-less Mystery beyond any Void or *Hsuan,* or any metaphysics or religion as well. But getting there is not always easy. Sometimes, as when certain people spoke of "the dark night of the soul," or what might just be called "a bad hair day," a person will register nothing at all, only the will to do so. For whatever reason such things happen in meditation or contemplation, just flow with it—*the will* to love is all that matters, the will *for* communion, just flow with it, without any straining. If you are frantically trying to bring yourself into that, it will not happen, and you will wear yourself out, almost falling into the will to power disguised as prayer. Rather let it be—just look at beauty and goodness and love and let that lead you into the sense of more and More with it, *and give your heart to that.*

That makes it different than other meditations on two counts. The mysticism of ecstasy a la the Christian mystics or Sufi mystics, or the emptying of everything a la the Buddhists, including present-day American ones who advocate a mysticism that ends in a void, all of which make the self disappear, is not what I am talking about when I speak of meditation or contemplation. *Just as real love requires your presence, so too profound prayer.* And here is the second great difference. Our meditation or contemplation is complete only when you realize it, *realize* in the root meaning of that word, to grasp and bring to bear in your living, your everyday living, embracing all of life and its creatures in a love that is not separated from that meditation. It is upon this point that we must compare all other meditations. *Complete meditation is love in action, this awareness in action.* As love is a verb, so too ultimately is contemplation. Though it might be, that to achieve what I called the beginning of meditation one gives attention to a quite sit without distractions, allowing your whole being to bathe in the communion, *complete* meditation is not over with that, but carrying that on in and with action, and in that action carrying on in that contemplation. It is not losing the self in the sit so to speak, which ironically can be a selfish act, but rather fulfilling the self in giving and doing—love in action, *contemplatio in actu.* This is deep-rooted spirituality—*complete* meditation a means to it. The particular action depends on yourself of course; you merely act out of love in whatever you do, be it monumental or modest, in a monastery or as a movie mogul. It is a love that each of us stamps with his or her own personality—in an awareness in action, an awareness that comes out of this *carried on 'moment,'* this *carried over 'moment'* you act from, out towards that all too real world. It is a continuous contemplation so to speak; an awareness in action as was said—living love, to reiterate what's all-important, *amor in actu.*

The heart of meditation is as if always present with you afterwards . . . with maybe an occasional, instantaneous attention to it as you do what you are doing. And it doesn't have to be without words . . . or offering up of a hardship . . . words or offering might in fact activate God's Presence for you as you act. But closer to it, it is like breathing after a while—always with you—a certain awareness in action or continuous contemplation. So, in a very real sense, it is to be alive to yourself, *alive to the deep down love that comes from the center of your being, where you and the Mysterious Presence have* intimacy, have *communion. To be alive to that always! Continuously!* No doctrine of renunciation or systematic practice of ecstasy is called for. It is not a spiritual Spartanism of self-effacement and unceasing effort in the training of the mind, practices that people so often equate with achieving enlightenment. It might be that you are in a postmodern mindset with regards to the very act of contemplation you take up, but still act upon it, and that is the important thing . . . for prayer is love. *Prayer, profound prayer, is living love.*

We pray, not for God, but for ourselves, that we might bring love out in us . . . otherwise it would be absurd to ask God to do what God already knows about and should have done. So prayer is helpful for us, has efficacy in that it brings love out in us. And the greater it does, the greater the prayer. And the greatest prayer is to be alive to the Mystery that is direct love. It is the deepest insight each of us can have and out of which we must act. Continuously. So if you are to pray, pray as deeply as you can, make it this contemplation of direct love that continues on in an awareness in action as you live in the very real world around you. Like the necessity of physical breath to life, it opens you up to the necessity of the breath of love in you, so you can live in the depth of such a realization as you go about your daily hurly burly life in the rush and rashness of modernity. He or she who abides in love abides in God and God in him and her, even as he or she be hesitant about it all and all of it, even as one be human and have bad hair days or bad heart days. No matter, as you never lose your presence, never lose the Presence of God.

Our venture from the start was and remains rooted in and from existence alone, where lonely love breathes within a loveless cosmos. No matter, because of that love I can truly pray, pray a different form of prayer. Yes, within that love is the ability for postmodernkind to pray. Not from its uncertainty, but from its reality. Not as prey, but as a very real presence. I do think that though we might be at sixes and sevens about suffering, and no matter our confusion about trying to tie the air together because of that suffering in this spinning world of space and time—when each of us witnesses beauty and goodness and love, in others and ourselves, somehow we do have a sense of more, and a sense of More, too, and in that, a leap into that, the giving ourselves to that, is prayer and this other kind of profound contemplation. God will never be unriddled, but in love we somehow sense what God is, and in that, this inner willing towards transcendence that is prayer. It touches upon a numinous and sacred sounding in us, a pervasive Presence in our own presence; an All-Embracing embrace, the swimming in love I spoke of. "I have immortal longings in me," Shakespeare rightly cried out from his own soul, and then penned the line, as I do, but here in a real context. For in prayer you touch the deep sanctuary within you. There is a dimension in our depths that knows despite the darkness or any glass darkly, and it is where our courage secretly gathers and where we pray. In prayer there is a suspension of this world, but a world taken up again now in carrying that prayer back into the world. In prayer our human presence is alive to its eternal depths, to the Mysterious More, to what we call God, to

GIVING, and we *realize* in our loving that we are alive to the call of GIVING in the form of flesh. If this be false and upon me proved, no man ever loved and so no man ever really prayed. To pray is to love, and to love is to pray; or perhaps better put, praying is loving, loving praying.

How ironic! We started off without a prayer in this world of ever venturing into the Mysterious More and yet here we are. I began this chapter saying I was at the edge of America, and possibly my sanity, too, and that I found myself blinking—and still do—now at what is being said at the end of this chapter. *De profundis clamavi ad*—yes, *from the depths I have called out to*—to *what* we asked, and though still stuttering quaquaquaqua in so many ways, we can now say *what* we have ventured into from the validity of existence alone.

This chapter has been a great challenge, harder by far than what went before; yet it was what was already written before that allowed for it. In that purely human spirituality we had our answer on how to act in the face of the world, grounded in our very existence and the deepest experience in that existence—but we still did not know the Mystery that made us, we had more but not More, the *to what* we cried out from our depths still eluded us.

Part of the problem was we were looking at it from '*to* what' instead of '*from* what.' It isn't outside of ourselves we have to go to get to God, but from the love we know as we know nothing else. And thus a choice arose. Just as there is a choice to live love, there is a choice in love itself—one that enhances the first: I am and I can . . . love . . . and can . . . leap into that love to Love.

The first choice may be a lonely battle; the second gives us communion with Intimacy itself. Both are a choice—both from the deepest experience in our existence. Therefore no other has such legitimacy as a grounding for a purely human spirituality, or I must add a way to the Mysterious More we call God. Yes a leap into this love is still required, but this is a leap of fact—that is, based on the fact of love, and into the fact of love. I should make known, however, as each of us fumble on in life, that of course each of us will be like a radio wave coming in and out of such a giving on our part, that our enthusiasm will be tinged with human hesitation even after we leapt, our decision tarnished forever with ellipticity. It will be a leap past or over or despite the lack of evidence daily for the planet in general having a providence. Yet, at the same time, there are undertones of something numinous, of something strange and queer to it all, if the truth be known, something like a sensed providence no matter. At times this sensed providence will feel like folly itself, foolishness, a fable, the fairytale it may all very well be, for although we love and have evidence of love, we only have evidence of it, and not of any God to go with it, especially when bad things happen. Would I be the savior of the world where no salvation exists? Consciousness got formed on the shores of insanity, which is life—isn't that what life itself tells us? When one baby starves to death on earth, don't all of us die of hunger—a hunger for a God that wouldn't allow for such a thing—*wouldn't allow Little Anthony to sink back into the looping riffs in his head, and start to cry when his family left and he started to moan. Can God hear Little Anthony moan?* Can God hear when we trouble deaf heaven with our bootless outcry? What is this place? What is my leap of love? No one has the answer—not Buddha with his nightmare of forever returning to this suffering until what—you become what—meanwhile trying to convince himself and me it is all an illusion and the Whatever that wants this what? A monster! No, not Buddha, nor Jesus either, hanging on his cross and sinking into the looping riffs in his head, tearing alone when his God left him and he could only moan. They later put out made-up stories to qualify that moan and make it seem reasonable, when it isn't. No, not for Jesus, or Little Anthony, or all of us hanging on to love trying to do what—to stretch the truth of love so as to contradict the facts of this world? Isn't that really our human venture, Humpty Dumpty humanity's patron saint and a moan our only true prayer? To miss that is to miss the problem present for everyone who talks of love in the face of the facts of this world. Can one experience counter all this? This is no dark night of the soul, this is truth telling us what is really so, life staring straight into our requiem eyes and asking us to see.

How can I sing the Lord's song in such a strange place? And yet there is love, love alone alas along the ellipticity, and in that each can still say I have journeyed to my very self. And to *realize love is to realize* . . .

To realize what? We are back to that!

I am too tired for leaps. And too tired for love? No. But tired out because of it. Where does the flame go when the candle is blown out? Nowhere. There is nowhere to go, nowhere but here, in our hereness, and I have to be honest with and in my hereness. Yes, I have to be honest, there is no Santa, Virginia, and existence can't give us a God of love, only love, Jimmy. Love is an aberration even theologically it seems. That may be so, Little Anthony, and all my 'offerings up' for you were to a Void. So dies Jesus, and Nietzsche, Little Anthony, Jimmy in his empty chapel . . . not without love, but without a God of love. The world will end not with a bang or a whimper, but with a moan, Little Anthony's and that of the rest of us.

God is unraveled in suffering, unravels, and we end up with nothing there, nothing here. Here, there, everywhere! But isn't that what I said God was at the very beginning? Yes, but GIVING also! What happened to that? It was the most remarkable thing I ever thought up. When I was a child, there was this woman who was a cashier at the Italian Supermarket, whom I was told lost her entire family, husband and three children. I used to look at her with such disbelief. It was unbelievable that she could even go on. That anyone could go through that.

How could that happen to anyone? How could God let it happen? My mother and father never explained. No one really did or does really. Not when I was a child and not now as I may be too old and too far-gone for words. Jesus, when Pilot asked you what is truth, you should have said. Well maybe you did with your silence, or maybe you were too far-gone for words. How can we sing the Lord's song in such a strange place? Where children are left orphans and mothers without children? Where babies moan and old women forget who they are? How can we sing the Lord's song in such a strange place? To talk of God seems like a feeble tale in comparison to all their suffering. I couldn't get my young mind around it when I saw that poor woman, and still can't.

You see someone dead, your eyes want to believe they are asleep, just like my love wants to believe it sees God. There is no echo of love in God. That is my own echo. And it dies with me, but hopefully not while I am still alive. I hope to love until I die, to love still, and no matter what. Funny, no matter what - who writes this stuff?. "I need a miracle to show me you love me," the little boy told God. And the old man said, "I need two, I lived longer than you." Is that our real clamavi - only love holding on to us and we to it—just love, only love? And God only the place, the thin place, where vanquished days secretly gather? There is this 'elsewhere' in all of us. Is that God? Like good detectives our divine dialectic gives us pause. God is too invisible, and human love defeated at every turn, even as it holds on to us and we to it.

How can I sing the Lord's song in such a strange place? I was born at dawn and with the suffering witnessed in life honesty can say rosey-fingered dawn has given way to the wine-dark sea. And yet there is love, love alone alas along the ellipticity, and in that each can still say I have journeyed to my very self. And to *realize love is to realize* . . .

Since antiquity, the human spirit has been struggling, struggling with a vocabulary that would give a true expression to the depths of our being as creatures, from the nethermost regions of suffering to the all too human and wonderful laughter in life, from the harrowing hallucinations of madness to the profundity of this mysticism without ecstasy, from the fathomless ordeal and black anguish of the abyss to the mysterious more that moves in every mind, from the all too perilous perhaps of being flesh and blood to the overwhelming experience beyond expression, the overwhelming something, somehow, somewho called up in us, whispering of some perhaps-possible-unknown-win-some, weather permitting, maybemysterium we could in our wildest, most wonderful moments, beyond the pale of night, right, or left brain activity clumsily try to give expression to with the word God, and when we have, still left suffering and struggling both as to whether such an Incomprehensible is applicable to the world and we in it, wondering as we look up at the night sky and that Intimacy. I have been so human in all this; I have struggled in our venture not only like those before me, but as a postmodern as well, which left me in the most uncertain of all ages and places. Yet, from the one minimal certainty in existence and the deepest experience in that existence, I have dared to say that the Mystery we call God does not "degenerate to the contradiction of life" if I am sensitive to the deepest part of life and living, seen in the light of my own and others own deepest experience as human beings. Boldly I have dared to say that the Mysterious More is in our own more, as everyday and present as the love in the faces of those we love and who love us, in the actual happening of love in our lives, when God is only love holding on to us and we to it.

Even on bad heart days, when each of us has to wonder what is this place and we trouble deaf heaven with our bootless outcry, our venture, our all too human venture, has maintained that the way to the Mystery that made us is embedded in each of us, through our very existence and the deepest experience in that very existence. Even as my drained presence might be dry to my bone morrow because of being's onslaught, I can *realize* in love a living Intimacy within me and thus within the world, acting in and through me. The measure of a man, of a woman, his and her holiness, is acting in and through this, in sending soup over to another across all the counters life has to offer. In this God is revealed to us and in us and through us.

Exsultate Jubilate is drifting in from the outer room, Cecilia singing over and over again Mozart's *Alleluja*—Mozart's, hers, and ours, with the love in each of us striving to set out and see and say the *exsultate,* the *jubilate*, the *alleluja* is so.

It has been a venture from the start that we have grounded in existence alone, and as such a philosophical sojourn. I have to pause here and smile my best Mona Lisa smile. Philosophy in its original Greek, φιλοσοφια, means the *love of wisdom*—how ironic that wisdom turns out to be love. Our long night's journey of uncertainty has led us into, at least, an uncertainty accompanied with love, even if only a hopeless loving or loving hopelessly, that much at least. But when the wind blows southerly and I know a hawk from a handsaw, or when the wind is my north, my south, my east, my west, and in that have a sense of More still, I know love is no longer hopeless. It is something open to all of us, as egalitarian and democratic as anything can be, for it is rooted in conscious life itself, in the presence each of us is and is conscious of as we are of nothing else - and in that more still, and with a human hesitancy no matter, More still.

You remember Plato's prayer. "We must take the best and most irrefragable of human doctrines and embark on that as if it were a raft on which to risk the voyage of life itself. Unless," the great ponderer adds, "it were possible to find a stronger vessel, something holy, some sacred meaning on which we might take our journey more surely and with confidence."[58] We have found *that*, and *that*, paradoxically, in the very humanness that is our raft on the river of life, our presence, which contains the ability to love, the sacred meaning on which we take our journey more surely and with confidence, as it is More as well, when God is love holding on to us and we to it. No, the giant of the Acropolis would not feel comfortable with my vulgar America definition of humankind as *holy shit*, but the groping genius seems almost to be talking of those same reptilian hisses and yet a hoped for 'place' within us where consciousness touches directly, at the depth of our being, something where the holy originates, where we decide to share our soup, where we touch the sacred and in turn are guided by it. He recognized the conflict—and felt the uncertainty within our human journey—searching for something that would show us a more certain way to knowing our inner selves and the truth of being, *as we have, and found it in our very presence.*

It is a presence that has thoughts that tell it that the lack of love "dulls to distance all we are." It is a presence that has thoughts that tell it, in the end, the beauty and goodness, truth and love you see and touch, smell, taste, and hear manifest God, is God manifest. "I am who am" tells us about God, dear Moses, and about ourselves. Where God is and where each of us is! It is a presence that has thoughts the day after Christmas and the day before, dear Jesus, because this is what it is to be human, thoughts that tell us that the beauty and goodness, truth and love you saw and touched, smelled, tasted, and heard, like our own here and now, is the Mystery manifest in our incarnation. So, circle the *Kaaba* of the heart, for *Hu* is as near to you as your jugular vein, dear Mohammed. And that is real, dear Buddha, because each of us can really say *I am and can love.* Love a dog, dear Yudhisthira, and all sentient life; in harmony with the Tao, dear Lau Tzu, when each of us does love.[59]

Within that all-important presence that can, can love, we have established a grounding for a purely human spirituality and ventured beyond-the-postmodern via that, into a coherence of the profoundest attitude towards life and the Mystery that made it. From our venture into the hiss and holiness that each of us is, we know we can answer yes to love, and in that yes tie the air together, coming to . . . words fall off the page here, but it is to that each can say I give my heart to. Our deepest outcry telling us if God isn't love, God should be! Yes, a million-fold contrivances, the swarming multiplicity, everything argues against a God of love, but love itself! And somehow, though the maddening crowd and the cosmos too might try to drown out that call at our core, when we see beauty and goodness, when we see the beauty and goodness of love, when we see another suffering and moan, we do indeed hear that call and know beyond the bullying and whittling world, beyond the disappointing *sperabamus* in all of us, we do hear that call to give of ourselves, plunging into it, leaping into it, praying into it, and in those sanest of moments, though it seems madness itself in its impossibility, with an embrace of incredulous relief, with a thankfulness still tinged with honest human hesitation, but with a coherence of the profoundest attitude towards life, in a crescendo of consciousness, we realize unconditional giving, *realize GOD*. This even as the opposite is true as well and the Mystery remains Incomprehensible, Unapproachable, and Other, and we seemingly alone with our love, making us lonely for what cannot be, for we cannot turn a blind eye to suffering, it empties God out of the world, but not our love out of it, and we are left with love striving to understand . . .

A Play

"I see it feelingly," I confess to my sheep dog sitting beside me in his plaid doggie coat. They shaved him at the Vet's. "O, let me not be mad, not mad, sweet heaven! Keep me in temper; I would not be mad," he says back to me, quoting Lear. He knows it is my favorite play, except for my own of course, the play that will never be done. I suppose I should make a confession here and tell you that no one understands my play, in fact, agents have stopped moving their lips while reading it as their mouths hung open in dismay. As for many an Artistic Director of many a successful theater, they have closed their transoms in terror that I might just have another copy to throw through an open one. The truth is only those on Ward A understood it, and gave up a roar of laughter listening to me reading it. I should remind you that nobody on Ward A can understand a word of anything—but they understood my play. It broke them up. Watching crazy people can be so much fun. All that jabber and jumping around. Contortions of all sorts. All over the place. Kinetic on one side—frenetic on the other! Makes you wonder why they were born doesn't it . . . why they came into this world? Yes, it is a comic agony, like the play. A play of Aeschylean proportions I must add half-appalled, half-amused. "It takes place in a madhouse—tell them," I hear my Old English say leaving the den in a grumble, not at all happy about his hair-do. Yes, it does take place in a madhouse, so I must caution you ahead of time. For it may be too insane for consumption . . . or too sane.

Tying The Air Together

A comic-agony in two acts

(The play that will never be done)

The actors play multiple parts in the play. It all works out, and actually adds to the madhouse motif. The Muses know what they are doing.

Jesus Christ—(Jim Chaord)
Zero—"God"—(Peter)
Lunatic One—Mother Mud/Bag Lady—Chief Justice (Alice)
Lunatic Two—Death—Blind Man (Wilbur)
Lunatic Three—Aeschylus—Orderly Two (Victor)
Lunatic Four—Disillusionment—Justice O'Daffy (Patrick)
Lunatic Five—Carmen Miranda—Lilith—(Loretta)
Director—Voice—Dark-haired Young Man—Orderly One
Beeshaleak—Justice Alles Zermelmer

Act one: a madhouse

(allegro con brio, e con una toletta molta expressiva)

(Alone on stage is a more than middle-aged man, in fact, Lear-like in age, dressed in an old red terry cloth bathrobe and happy as a lark, with very red cheeks and a glass of red wine in hand. This is "Jesus Christ". There is nothing taking up the stage with him but an old worn armchair, a fluffy bed, and an enormously large lopsided white window frame center stage. The empty frame looks out to darkness behind it. A flash of lightning streaks across it; revealing, but for a moment, five bodies—as if hanging in mid-air—standing within it at staggered heights; these are the Lunatic, in white pajamas.)

JC
(after drinking)
I have always had this head-on judgment about life—that it should be happy!

(In an instant, a man clad only in white pajama bottoms runs out from the wings, with another man trying to pull him back . . . this is Zero; the man trying to pull him back is Beeshaleak, wearing a suit and tie, the suit just a touch too small on him and looking rather foreign.)

ZERO
How can he say that? How—especially after what happened to him?
After what's happened to us!

DIRECTOR (UNSEEN OVER A MIKE)
What is he doing on stage, Beeshaleak?

BEESHALEAK
(still holding onto Zero; in an Indian accent and cadence)
I have no idea.

ZERO
I am protesting!

DIRECTOR (UNSEEN OVER A MIKE)
Protesting what?

ZERO
That line! My life!

(As the storm continues, lights immediately come up on the Lunatics, who nod in agreement.)

LUNATIC ONE
Right! Happy my ass!
Not here on planet stress!
LUNATIC TWO
The man's a lunatic.
LUNATIC THREE
Of course he's a lunatic.
LUNATIC FOUR
We're all lunatics.
LUNATIC FIVE
This is a madhouse.

ZERO
(out to the audience)
Ladies and gentlemen, show some style, pull down your pants and head up the aisle.

DIRECTOR (UNSEEN OVER A MIKE)
Can we stop improvising, please! Now, Zero, will you go back and wait your cue! And turn the damn lights off on those Lunatics.

LUNATICS
The lights went out for us a long time ago.

(They all wave little goodbyes. The lights go out on the Lunatics; meanwhile Beeshaleak has managed to pull Zero into the wing.)

DIRECTOR (UNSEEN OVER A MIKE)
Can we start from the top, please! Jesus, say your intro again.

JC
I have always had this head-on judgment about life—that it should be happy!

(A groan goes up from the darkened Lunatics; and then Zero screams from the wings.)

J C
(with sarcasm)
Despite the peculiar play I happen to be in. *(out to the audience, confidentially)*
It was written by one of our . . . inmates.
That's why my next line is rather, well, what it is.
(the line to the audience) There is this feeling I get in my head from time to time.
(All still in the dark)
LUNATIC ONE
That he is outside the universe looking in.
LUNATIC TWO
When we say things like that the doctors here tell us—
LUNATIC THREE
We're out of it all right!
LUNATIC FOUR
Not all there.
LUNATIC FIVE
Nutty as fruitcakes.
LUNATIC ONE
Off the wall.
LUNATIC TWO
Out in left field.
LUNATIC THREE
Daffy, bonkers, loony tunes.
LUNATICS
Have our heads up our asses!

J C
(on it; perhaps too quickly)
It's a funny feeling—like I'm face to faceless face with all that was or ever could be. Anyway, it's incomprehensible.
Perhaps it's God I sense.

(The lights shoot up on the Lunatics.)
LUNATICS
God?!

LUNATIC ONE
He does that a lot—
LUNATIC TWO
fills our heads with ideas—
LUNATIC THREE
only we don't know exactly what they are.
LUNATIC FOUR
Being crazy isn't all it's cracked up to be.
LUNATIC FIVE
And we're lunatics in case you don't know—
LUNATIC ONE
Words applied to something unknown, doing we don't know what, are not unusual for us.
LUNATIC TWO
(in a whisper out to the audience)
Like God.

(Suddenly, JC's mood changes and he becomes thoughtful; as if touching an authentic moment in himself.)

JC
It's an incredible thing to look into the eyes of the mad.
(looking out at the audience)
Makes you wonder. About God.
(with a cavalier acceptance)
In any case, whatever it is, I got this strange feeling I told you about—beyond and yet at the very core of me.
(He cocks his head some.)
I think it's because I died when I was a baby. That is, the silly doctor told my mother I was dead. But I wasn't.
At least I don't think I was. *(suddenly serious, looking into his wine)* I died some years later. But that's a story best left untold.

ONE OF THE LUNATICS
His secret!
LUNATICS
What happened to him!
LUNATIC TWO
You see his real name isn't what he says it is.

LUNATIC THREE
Then again, who knows?

(They all stretch their necks to watch him.)

J C
They always watch me from the tower. Until lights out.
It gives them something to do. *(with a raised voice their way)*
Mi casa es su casa. (looking back at the audience; translating)
My house is your house. They love to say that over there.
Often scream it out the window at passers-by. That and watching me is pretty much
their daily routine. As I said, it gives them something to do. *(A mischievous grin comes
to his face.)* Of course, I try to make it worth their while.

*(At that he turns, and with his back to the audience, facing the Lunatics, spreads
open his robe.)*

LUNATIC ONE
That's hardly worth our while.
LUNATIC THREE
Certainly not the price of admission.
LUNATIC FIVE
But you'll find out soon enough what is, dearest audience.
LUNATIC TWO AND FOUR
Right now, all is well with the world for this fly-by-night Jesus Christ,
LUNATIC FIVE AND ONE
our gravekeeper at Saint Hilarious's Asylum
LUNATICS
For The Hopelessly Insane.

*(J C, robe still open, turns back to the audience. He is wearing red polka dot
boxer shorts.)*

JC
They try to make everything sound foreboding.
(over his shoulder back at the Lunatics)
It's a comedy forchristsake.

LUNATIC ONE
The man doesn't even know what play he's in.

LUNATIC TWO
I don't know why they gave him the lead.
LUNATIC THREE
And not me! Or Julius Caesar over here.
(*one of the Lunatics nods in appreciation*)
LUNATIC FOUR
Ladies and gentlemen, we'll take a bow,
LUNATIC FIVE
Unseat your fat asses and leave the place now.
(*they all bow; looking up while still in the bow*)
LUNATIC ONE
What, still here?
LUNATIC TWO
You'll be sorry!
LUNATIC THREE
End up like us.
LUNATIC FOUR
Having to watch him!
LUNATIC FIVE
A man who—well we'll let you find out for yourselves.
After all you paid to get in here.
(*They point at the audience with a single laugh; then go all dead serious.*)
LUNATICS
Paid with your *minds* if this play has anything to do about it!

LUNATIC THREE
This play is the worst thing that ever happened to us.
We were all like you once.
LUNATIC FOUR
Until we started watching him.
Listening to him.
LUNATIC FIVE
Now look at us. How do you feel?
LUNATICS
(*sardonic smiles all*)
Dangerously well we hope!

DIRECTOR (UNSEEN OVER A MIKE)
Can we stop improvising, please! And where is Zero—he's supposed to be on by now! Beeshaleak?!

BEESHALEAK
(sticking his head from out of the wing; in an Indian accent and cadence)
I have no idea where he is.

DIRECTOR (UNSEEN OVER A MIKE)
(annoyed but taking it in stride)
Well try to find him. The rest of you *(a sigh)* just be still.
Gravedigger, carry on.

JC
Carry on?

BEESHALEAK
(in an Indian accent and cadence)
It says right here *(looking at his copy of the play)*—you're supposed to—*(he looks up towards where the Director is)*
He's supposed to pray?

DIRECTOR (UNSEEN OVER A MIKE)
(in a dry droll)
Oh why the hell not?

LUNATIC ONE
I wouldn't if I were you. Remember the last time you tried that.

(J C suddenly looks terrified, first at the Lunatic who said that, then out towards the audience.)

J C
Perhaps this time it'll be different. There's a certain technique in praying you see. Some intuitive way to get past the strings and the membranes. I'm Jesus Christ after all. I should know how to do it.

(J C stands up straight, readying himself as the Lunatics cross themselves backwards. He makes an attempt at a ridiculous flying pirouette and landing, twists his ankle—the Lunatics all pointing at him and doubling over in a silent guffaw as he limps over to the edge of the stage and they wave bye-bye to him as the lights go out on the Lunatics, leaving J C looking out at the audience.)

J C

You're right—what the hell kind of play is this? Confused as to whether it is a comedy or a tragedy! I know, I know, the playbill says a comic agony, but that doesn't make any sense.

A VOICE AS IF FROM ABOVE—GODLIKE
You want things to make sense?

J C

Did you hear that? I'm never sure when I hear voices.

LUNATIC ONE
(sticking her head out from the wing)
Me neither.
LUNATIC TWO
(sticking his head out as well)
It's a strange ghoulishly funny bit of business to be sure.

J C

(His eyes hold—a moment please.)
But who could be sure. About anything really. *(The two Lunatics nod in agreement and retreat back into the wings as he goes on.)*
I remember, when I first came to this mountebank Shangri-La, how I insisted I had risen from the dead. *(He takes a long look out at nothing, as if whatever it was he tried to forget is back again.)*
I did rise from the dead. Left standing at the grave. *(then)*
The doctors said that I had to put it out of my mind.

A VOICE AS IF FROM ABOVE—GODLIKE
I think he went a little too far with that.

(An unseen parrot whistles; then talks.)
Let's all go barmy! And join the army! Let's all go ravy!
And join the navy! *(Then it squawks.)*

J C

That's my parrot. I taught him to say that. For the lunatics—it cracks them up.
(He looks over at the empty window with a little laugh and a little goodbye wave as the Lunatics had done.)

Too bad they aren't watching. The lights went out too early if you ask me. And it's lonely talking to myself.

(looking back with a solemn wink) You know what they say about people who talk to themselves. That's what they would tease if they were here—the looneytunes. All crazy as bedbugs.

(considering; with a touch of sorrow) It's a strange ghoulishly funny bit of business to be sure. A real howl. *(coming out of it and back to the moment, looking towards the wing)* A real howl!

DIRECTOR (UNSEEN OVER A MIKE)
Cue! Will someone get the damn dog out here?

LUNATIC ONE
(sticking her head out from one of the wings; addressing the Director)
He refuses to come out.

LUNATIC TWO
(sticking his head out from the other wing; addressing the Director)
Somebody shaved him.

LUNATIC FOUR
(sticking his head out from out the lopsided window frame—one side)
Besides he doesn't like his line. He wants to say beautiful things!
Wear grand robes! Eat on fine dishes—and not dog food!
Instead you've given him—a howl!

LUNATIC FIVE
(sticking her head out from out the lopsided window frame—the other side)
He doesn't know what it means.

LUNATIC THREE
(a bald man comes grandly out to the stage itself; addressing the audience)
Before I went crazy *I* wrote plays. And I can tell you—a howl is ridiculous as a line! Of course the dog refuses to say it! What actor in his right mind would? Besides, somebody shaved him. He looks silly. A shaggy dog without hair—you would laugh at him.

DIRECTOR (UNSEEN OVER A MIKE)
Beeshaleak!

(Beeshaleak sticks his head out from one of the wings between the lunatics.)

BEESHALEAK
(in an Indian accent and cadence)
He just refuses to come out—and he's a big dog. I cannot budge him. This is the daddy of all drags for me. *(turning over his shoulder towards the wing)* Do not kindle my wrath, dog.
(meekly looking back) I am afraid I am going to have to do the part myself.

DIRECTOR (UNSEEN OVER A MIKE)
Oh why the hell not?

(Beeshaleak makes a high-pitched howl of comic despair—and it is taken up over a loudspeaker by another person, becoming more despair than comic. All the Lunatics and Beeshaleak, frightened, dart out of sight as the loudspeaker howl continues. Like a madman's trumpet at reveille, it shoots through the stage and the lights go out. A lone spot comes up on J C sitting on a stool.)

ZERO (VOICE ON A MIKE)
He really is one of our strangest cases you know, our
Jesus-whoever. Everyday they say he roams the place,
Looking for some sign of God. He can't quite put it altogether you see—what happened to him—with his God.

(The backdrop becomes a motion picture of the desert, a silent wind blowing over the dunes.)

JC
(as if reminded)
God—yes—I went into the desert looking for him.

J C
(using a third voice altogether)
A snake slithered by in search of survival. Did it, like the Neanderthals after it, hear any whisper of what God might be?

J C
(using the second voice)

And what about Homo heidelbergenis some three hundred and fifty thousand years ago? Did they have a miraculous rattle in their heads, too?

(The lights dim to a silvery tone, blanketing the stage; the sound of a light wind coming up with the visuals; J C reacting.)

JC
(using his third voice)
A strange hill pops into his mind's eye at this fragmented moment, a place where the universe's indifference blankets a hill of skulls all around, in wait for any living creature who ventures into its domain of invisibility.

JC
(using the second voice again)
He sees himself actually do so; and finds himself gasping for breath
. . . his mouth open in shock and his tongue covered with mucus.

J C
What thought up such a place?

(The backdrop disappears and he is left sitting alone in the murky lighting; the backdrop suddenly filled with a huge picture of J C's face. It starts to tear, as a haunting fills its gaze. J C looks from it out to the audience.)

J C
Each face is its own inscape.

J C
(using the second voice)
And I twisted and turned there.
(using the third voice)
For forty days and forty nights.
(using his own voice)
I asked why, but the desert outside was without a why.
I asked the sky above, but it too was silent.
I had been brought to a place where no one could find me, not even myself.
(using the second voice)
Who am I?
(using the third voice)

What's really real?
(the backdrop face)
And how do I act in the face of it?
(using his own voice)
Especially since I don't know what it is . . . or who I am . . . really . . . some psychic crystallization around an abyss?
(there is a moment of dead silence, and then the backdrop face)
I found a cave and shared it with darkness.
(All his voices at once, in sync)
At such times a person opens his mouth to escape suffocation.

(Both J C and the backdrop face open their mouths as if trying to do just that. Suddenly, the backdrop face's skull splits open and holds there in a freeze fame.)

JC
(screams)
I DON'T UNDERSTAND!

(The backdrop face disappears. A long stare follows. A bag lady, Mother Mud, pushing a grocery cart comes from the wing, heading his way. When she reaches him, she stops and looks out at the audience.)

BAG LADY
A soliloquy in four voices—how odd. *(then turning to J C)*
Hello, I'm Mother Mud. What's your name?

J C
Jesus Christ.

BAG LADY
(with an accepting shrug)
Anything to get you through the night.
(She takes out a bottle of wine, takes as slug of it, and then holds it out to him.)
Thirsty?

J C
(nodding)
The desert.

BAG LADY
(handing him the bottle)
You can change it into water if you like. But I'd stick with the wine if I were you.
Life is too brutal not to drink wine. And too short to drink the cheap shit.

(He takes a slug from it.)

BAG LADY
What do you think?
*(He says nothing; she laughs and takes a loaf of spongy bread out and gives him
a slice.)* I'm sorry I don't have any cold cuts to go with it.

J C
That's OK I'm a vegetarian.

BAG LADY
Me, I eat anything that moves.

*(J C reaches out and touches her. She stiffens some, and immediately backs
away.)*

BAG LADY
Why are you touching at me?

J C
Because you're a leper. Abandoned out here.

BAG LADY
You're strange.

J C
Yes, and I'm startled by my own strangeness.
(looking around) You see I'm torn between the desert and the deepest part of
me.

BAG LADY
(nods)
It's the reason for philosophy, poetry, and prayer.

J C

Oh, God, love me—that's my prayer!

BAG LADY

And?

J C

(using his second voice)

It's like talking to myself.

(using his third voice)

There is a strangeness in me all my own.

(The face of J C again appears on the large screen and then talks . . .)

I was brought to birth and learned nothing from life but wonder of it.

(J C using his own voice)

And so must leave *(as she does, waving a little ciao over her shoulder)* still uniformed of why in the world I came, or went, or was.

(As she disappears into the wing; the face on the screen does, too, leaving J C looking out at the audience. The lights go up on three Lunatics, all in tubs, smoking cigars and drinking whiskey in a room with drifts of steam in it.)

LUNATIC FOUR

You can't live your life and expect to know what it's about.

LUNATIC TWO

Yet, he refuses to accept that! And then there's this Jesus Christ thing of his.

LUNATIC THREE

(confidential-like)

I've been listening at doors and behind trees—and down chimneys—and I think he might really be him.

ZERO

(the lights come up on him, also in a tub with a cigar and a tumbler of whiskey)

Though not Jewish in his case. His case study. *(to Jesus)*

Off on one of your little sojourns again?

J C

Yes—I thought this time it might be different. I was hoping.

LUNATIC FOUR
(repeating it in bitter mockery)
I was hoping!
LUNATIC TWO
(sadly)
Everyone's middle name.
LUNATIC THREE
It's an incredible thing to look into the eyes of the hoping.
LUNATIC TWO
An echo of what should be, what could be . . . if only!

ZERO
If only.
(Just then the Bag Lady comes out pushing her cart.)

BAG LADY
If only.

LUNATICS
Rub a dub dub we're all in that tub.

THE LUNATICS, ZERO, and THE BAG LADY
(serious and terrified)
WHAT THE HELL IS IT ALL ABOUT, AND WHO THE HELL ARE WE?

JC
(J C looks around, confused.)
I'm frightened. *(out to the audience)* Really!

(The three Lunatics, the Bag Lady, and Zero shoot an angry look his way.)

LUNATIC FOUR
But do stop galumphing about it, J. C!
LUNATIC TWO
Watch television or something.
LUNATIC THREE
This is America forgodsake!

BAG LADY

Pursue your fucking happiness. We don't bother about what you're bothering yourself about here!

LUNATIC TWO

It's all Jabberwocky anyway!

LUNATIC THREE

So forget any venture to understand the Unseen,

LUNATIC FOUR

Unoriginated,

LUNATIC TWO

Uncreated,

LUNATIC THREE

Unborn,

LUNATIC FOUR

Unformed,

ALL THREE

Uneverything!

ZERO

Who better than we know that? We who have suffered an unbirthday!

BAG LADY

So forget it, whoever the hell you really are.

J C

I'm Jesus Christ!

LUNATIC TWO

And I'm the Queen of Romania!

ZERO

(about Lunatic Two; out to the audience)

He's really Hieronymus Bosch. Lives down the hall from me, in Ward Z. With Vincent Van Gogh. A real nice couple. Banded from all military parades though. By order of the Queen . . . of Romania.

BAG LADY
Who wants to be the only queen in the parade!
(She stares intently at J C.)
Like you wanting to be the only you-know-who.
But tell us, who are you really?

(It seemed everyone in the room is waiting for him to answer.)

ZERO
Too many unbirthdays—he can't remember.

J C
(looking a dead serious look at Zero)
Peter Pan will fly again.
The summer wind will blow again.

BAG LADY
(out to the audience)
If only!

LUNATIC FOUR
But something's wrong.
LUNATIC TWO
Oh so something.
LUNATIC THREE
An echo of what should be, what could be, if only.

JC
If only I could tie the air together.

ZERO
(deceptively bland)
When you find out how, let me know.

LUNATIC FOUR
And us.

BAG LADY
Not to mention the Mystery that made us!

ZERO
Then made us crazy.

LUNATIC FOUR
Eli Eli lama sabactani?

J C
God—yes—I cried out to him on the cross.

ZERO
And?

J C
A snake slithered by in search of survival.

LUNATIC THREE
And some homo three hundred and fifty thousand years old!

ZERO
Did he have a miraculous rattle in his head, too,
Jesus-whoever? *(He looks out to the audience.)*
So it was he found his way to our madhouse and became the gravedigger.

BAG LADY
Thinking he could dig up God.

ZERO
And tie the air together.
You see the desperate situation he's in. The doctors are trying to work it out of him—cold turkey if necessary. Though content rich plays like this work better.
(smirks out at the audience)

DIRECTOR (UNSEEN OVER A MIKE)
Will you stop it! All I ask of you is to say your lines as written.
And an occasional pause in the confusion!

J C
Yes—one minimal certainty in the chaos. Just one.

LUNATIC THREE
If there is none, that saves a world of trouble.
LUNATIC TWO
As he needn't try to find it.

(JC starts to shake his head vigorously, up and down.)

J C
I trust and mistrust at the same time a sort of sense of I know not what!

LUNATIC FOUR
What the hell is that supposed to mean?

LUNATIC THREE
(indignant)
Who wrote this play?

DIRECTOR (UNSEEN OVER A MIKE)
Since none of you are saying the written lines anyway, does it matter?

A VOICE AS IF FROM ABOVE—GODLIKE
Not really!

J C
Did you hear that?

DIRECTOR (UNSEEN OVER A MIKE)
J C! *(But J C is all caught up in staring upwards.)*
Case Study 1938, do try to pull yourself together.

J C
I have to go to the toilet.

BAG LADY
Christ goes to the toilet?

LUNATIC THREE
Of course! We all have to go to the toilet.

ZERO
(out to the audience)
But you have no idea what happens when *he* does.
You'll find out.

BEESHALEAK
(sticking his head out from the wing)
You're not supposed to tell them that! Are you trying to ruin the play for them?

(Zero with a deap pan look out to the audience.)

DIRECTOR (UNSEEN OVER A MIKE)
Will you stop that!

LUNATIC THREE
(scolding Zero's way)
Yes! A play is like a soufflé!

DIRECTOR (UNSEEN OVER A MIKE)
Right, you have to allow it to rise to the occasion.
Didn't Aristotle say as much!

ZERO
(out to the audience)
He lives down the hall from me. In a ménage a trios. With Carmen Miranda and Evita Peron. And what a pair they are!
One dancing up a storm on her red satin platforms and the other blaring away all night long. Don't cry for me, Argenthhhinna!
As if anyone would cry for either of them. Two pathetic loonies on tour together inside their overly coiffured heads. And don't for one minute think that's their own color. I know true tangerine when I see it. Anyway, he lives . . . down the hall with Carmen and Evita.

BAG LADY
And where does this one live?

(A black-haired youth of about 21 with greenish skin, entirely idiotic, moving nothing but his sunken eyes and looking absolutely non-human comes out from

the wings wearing white pajamas. He crosses over to the tub looking directly down at J C. The 'creature' lingers over him. There is a moment.)

JC
PROMPTER!

(J C seems terrified, and then so does Lunatic One, and after him the two other Lunatics. It leaves the 'creature' looking hopelessly around at them. Just then J C surrounded by the thin steam stands naked in his tub for a stern moment; then gambols and grins, shakes his sides, points his finger, turns up his nose, and finally shoots out his tongue.)

EVERYONE BUT JC AND THE CREATURE
PROMPTER!

(The lights go out across the stage. The sound of a strong wind fills the stage. This is followed by the sound of rain. The lights come up on J C and Zero together in the gravedigger's cottage, drinking wine, both in red terry cloth robes. There is nothing taking up the stage with them but an old worn armchair and a fluffy bed, with a bizarre quilt on the floor; again with the enormously large angled or lopsided white window frame center stage. The empty frame looks out at darkness behind it. A flash of lightning streaks across it; revealing only emptiness. Suddenly, two men in white, orderlies of some sort, come rushing in.)

TOGETHER
Is he here?

J C
Who?

ORDERLY ONE
The escapee! From Ward Z. We were told he was here.

ORDERLY TWO
Pretending to be an actor. Have you seen him?

JC
How does he look?

ORDERLY ONE
You'd know if you saw him—black-haired youth with greenish skin, entirely idiotic, moving nothing but those damn sunken eyes of his.

J C
(far away)
Yes.

ORDERLY ONE
Then you have seen him?

J C
But he's gone.

ZERO
Too far gone apparently.

ORDERLY ONE
(Orderly One glances over towards the toilet . . .)
Do you think he might be in there?

J C
(sadly)
No, he's not in there—he wouldn't know how to use the toilet.

ZERO
Though *(pointing at JC)* he's still hoping he might.

J C
(J C looks from him out to the audience.)
That's true. I was hoping . . . and still am. You'll understand as we go on with the play. If he can use the toilet . . . well, it will make all the difference . . . prove that . . . but you don't even know about him yet—what happened to him.

ZERO
Or what happened to you.

J C
(towards the wing where the Director is)

It's not right, Doctor Mortadella. My private life should not be used in this way.

ZERO
(explaining to J C)
He thinks the plays are therapeutic. Wants you to re-enact—you know—what you did—to him—to Jimmy—because he couldn't use the toilet and you wanted him to . . . for that strange reason of yours?

(Just then a spot comes up on the dark-haired youth sitting in the armchair. His face has that bewildered stare. It appears to drive the gravedigger to have to act, to do something, anything to get his intruder-guest to respond for his own secret reason.)

J C
Com'on, whatever your name is—George is it? *(tickles him)* Bucky?
(tweaks his nose) Frank? *(slaps him hard—but nothing—then forcing himself on, in pain)* How about a comic howl from the dog? *(looks towards the wing)* A song then?

(At that he starts to sing and soft-shoe it with a certain desperation in his burlesque routine; Zero just staring at his behavior toward the dark-haired young man.)

J C
'How could you believe me when I said I love you, when you know I was a liar like my wife? We had this situation since you were a youth. You must have been insane . . .
(his voice drops off in a trail) to think we'd tell you the truth.'

(Suddenly, he screams out.)

J C
COM'ON! COME OUT OF IT! SAY SOMETHING!
DO SOMETHING! *(nothing happens of course; hoarse as if in a sad memory)* Jimmy is it? *(tears fill his eyes)* Why? Why? Why?
Why? Why? *(His decrescendo ends as he wipes at the tears rolling down his cheeks.)* I hope you don't suppose these are real tears.

(There is a pause; then a sigh.) We'll decide what to do with you in the morning. There's this wonderful place called OZ. Just over the cliff from here. We'll go get you a brain. And me some courage.

ZERO
(out to the audience)
Some courage to tell the truth.

(A tired J C picks up the quilt beside him covering the catatonic man up to his neck with what has to be a creation from one of St. Hilary's inmates, from the looks of it. Almost paternally, he tucks the younger man in; snugly folding back the crazy quilt and with sad serious eyes searches into the empty stare.)

J C
You get some shuteye. *(He starts for the bed.)*
I'll be over here in bed trying to figure out the punch line.
In case you do have to go to the toilet during the night
(sitting on the bed and pointing) it's over there.
I hope—pray—you know how to use it. Oh, how I do.
It'll make all the difference. For both of us.

(The nameless creature just sits there staring straight ahead and J C lies down on the bed facing the audience. Lying there, he finds himself doing the same thing as his odd guest—staring straight ahead. He curls up into his favorite bedtime position—fetal. And with that he wipes the tears welling in his eyes.)

J C
No, I hope you don't suppose these are real tears.
(Some madhouse screams are heard; J C still holding on the audience.)
Or those real screams. Or that our little comic agony in two acts is for real!

(With that the tired gravedigger closes his eyes—the last thing he hears more night noises coming from the asylum . . . they fade into silence and everything goes pitch black. It lasts until it becomes uncomfortably obvious.)

ZERO'S VOICE IN THE DARKNESS
Welcome to Saint Hilarious's!

(The storm outside punctuated his remark. A flash of lightening in the night sky seen through the large window frame displays J C's rude awakening as he holds on the razor in Zero's hand, the dark-haired young man gone. A roll of thunderous drums follows.)

ZERO
(going on after nature's tantrum; the lights rising; but shadowy)
Holy Hilarious. Happy Hilarious. Hollow Hilarious . . . yes, hell is hollow—hollow laughter. And Hieronymus Bosch is definitely a three hundred and fifty thousand year old homo. He lives down the hall from me *(nodding)* with Vincent Van Gogh. A real nice couple. Banded from all military parades though. By order of the Queen . . . of Romania.

(The pale eyes looking at J C are dancing on the razor's edge, swaying between reason and some obscure presence, an eerie enthusiasm in their look, a ferocious immediacy at work behind their glare, as if he had to tell the other man something of the greatest importance.)

ZERO
Did you know that the laws of physics don't apply to the big bang?

J C
Yes.

ZERO
Well, did you know that they don't apply to me either?

J C
No, I didn't.

ZERO
You'd like that wouldn't you? The laws of physics not applying to us! To you, to me, to the dark-haired weirdo! To your Jimmy either!

(J C cringes at the name and Zero nods and his voice takes on a distant chill.)

ZERO
A strange ghoulishly funny bit of business that. You should have used a razor with that son of yours. Spare the razor and spoil the child is what I say.

(The alarmed audience of one staring back at him through the room's shadows holds still. Two men with the same still eyes are fixed on one another. Fixed as cat and mouse. There is a distant scream across the storm from the asylum. The man in the institutional red robe holds in their moment together, as if to listen to some conspicuous meaning in the inaccessible echo.)

ZERO

The Queen of Romania! Calling for a command performance!
Of course, she's not really a queen. Actually not really a she either.
Not even Romanian. *(After a brief giggle, which he immediately wipes off his haunted face, he goes on.)* Anyway—which is another way of saying enough of that shit—how about a song? You like songs.

(He nods, sets down the razor and with moving hands on an invisible piano burst into song. The tune is practically non-existent, but he stretches it to his words—or the words to his make-shift tune.)

ZERO

'I tell ya it's a world livin' on Clown Alley!
People lining up at the Italian deli.
The Fat Lady soaking in a tub, rub a dub dub.
This may be a bold assertion, but it has to be said.
Pasta is our salvation. Our souls have to be fed.
So start the water boiling, get out the olive oil.
Stir that sauce and cut that bread—it's not over, folks, till we're dead!
(His hands glide over the airy keys, his voice dipping into autumnal tones.)
Some people say life's a serious matter.
Play it safe and live to grow fatter.
But don't listen to all that chatter.
Take it from me the Mad Hatter!

(With that, flashes of light, like lighting, reveal the Lunatics standing in their window places, all with pasted on grin, singing in his fashion.)

LUNATICS

Isn't it all a ball?! Whadda ya say y'all? Isn't it all a fabulous farce?
Isn't it all a com-o-dy . . . a river run red . . . there's nothing more to be said the fat lady is dead! Tons of fun just drowned in her tub. Isn't it all a party on Mars!?

(Zero nods as if it's so, and with that speaks the rest as if an afterthought, his hands still playing the piano keys.)

ZERO
So what's the punch line? That's what we're all doing here, looking for the punch line. That alfresco revelation that makes us piss our pants, crack up, get the shits, double over and uproariously all *die* laughing?

(The Lunatics cover their eyes with their hands as if in anticipation and not wanting to look, and he winks with a solemn wink: holding his eyelid down as his other eye flares with some mad thought or other; riveted so intently on his host, as the lights on the Lunatics go out.)

J C
(nervous)
Why is your hand bleeding?

ZERO
The dog bit me.

J C
Why?

ZERO
I shaved him. Would you like a shave, too? *(With that he takes up his razor again.)* We could sing together as I shave—a duet—you on the piano and me—on the razor's edge as they say. *(giggles)*
I threw that in cause I know you like cutting humor.
(wide-eyed all of a sudden) I know a lot about you.

JC
Why did you say that?

ZERO
That I'm on the razor's edge?

J C
No—why did you say you know a lot about me? And in that way?

ZERO
That way—this way—up, down, and around—what does it matter, Jesus-whoever?
You're always asking questions!
Why this, why that, why the other thing—*(agitated)* why don't you just relax?
Look at me with what I know—and yet I'm relaxed. Totally! They don't call me
Zero for nothing.

J C
Is that what they really call you?

ZERO
Who?

J C
The doctors.

ZERO
What doctors?

J C
That take care of you in the asylum. You are an inmate or did you forget?

ZERO
(as if J C has to be pulling his leg)
Go on! *(Again his intruder-guest gives his host a solemn wink; with his other
eye this time.)* Next you'll be telling me you're the President.
And I know that's not true—he lives down the hall from me.
Wacky as they come!

J C
So you do remember!

ZERO
Of course I remember—what do you take me for a complete nut?
I'm only cuckoo on my right side—and only half the time. When the wind blows
motherly, I'm fine. *(with a laugh)* It's a funny ole world I live in. *(At that he
glares out the window in a jarring hilarity.)*
A person will do just about anything—no, anything—mutilate his firstborn—set
his mother on fire—bury himself alive.

(He turns back; screaming.) ANYTHING FOR IT TO STOP!

LUNATICS
(out of the dark)
ANYTHING!

ZERO
(He quiets almost to a whisper.)
But there is only one way for it to stop. You gotta disappear altogether! I did you know.
(He taps at his head with the razor.)
But, unfortunately, I resurrected. See how much we are alike.
Both raised from the dead to live out our unbirthdays.
(a quizzical look coming over Zero's exaggerated face)
But what kind of a resurrection is that I ask you?
(suddenly staring predator-like at his host, razor in hand.)
So I'll be kind and cut you out of the play.

J C
(yelling out to where the Director is)
That's not his line! What's going on here?

ZERO
(all teeth and wacko)
A play—we're in a play. A postmodern one to be sure—even as postmodern means not to be sure.
(He covers his mouth as if trying not to laugh, nodding away.)
I'll *play* along. If you do. I'd like to take a *stab* at it.
(singing) 'We gotta get going. Where're we going? Whadda we gonna do? We're on our way to nowhere the two of us
(with a wink at his razor) and you. *(then back to J C)* Are you ready? *(He stops abruptly; then becomes very sad.)* Are you going to help me here?

J C
Help you how?

ZERO
(gives J C a look of feigned incredulity; repeating it mockingly)

Help you how!? *(The tower of Saint Hilary's chimes, one, two, three, marking the hour. A pasted-on smile cuts across his face.)* Quasimodo is at it again I hear. Bats in his belfry. Certainly in mine.

(At that, the young man's pasted-on smile fades away, and he begins to talk aloud to himself as if to some inner query that possesses him; though all the while with a clever eye on his host.)

ZERO
Mine? But who am I that I could have a mine? A me that goes around muttering . . . 'Oh dear, what is the meaning of life? What's it all about? What is the Mystery that made me—and then made me mad?' Is that what drove you here, too—God? Did he offer you up on the crocked cross of existence? *(with an indication towards the audience)* Leave you talking to yourself and calling it prayer?

(The lights come up on the Lunatics.)

LUNATIC ONE
Another nut!
LUNATIC TWO
Nuts all over the place.
LUNATIC THREE
We better get out of here—where is the time-traveling machine?

ZERO
Yes, we'll ride the tide—the high tide, the low tide, the near tide, the rip in the tide of time itself—and you can tide me over till we turn the tide together! Where should we go? You, me, and Doctor Who? Traveling on our highwire? Our hotwire? Our haywire? Getting there under the wire? *(He glares at J C with that.)*
Help you how!?

(They hold motionless.)

J C
(sadly)
Yes, you lost your mind. I didn't forget.

ZERO
(with bitter accusation)
You forget a lot of other things though, don't you? I'd say so!
(He turns suddenly cheery.) But who am I to say—with my forgetfulness! Just
last night as I was taking leave of my senses, the blind, deaf, and dumb broad
down the hall said to me that life is an adventure or it is nothing at all. For me it
is the adventure of becoming nothing at all. Of course when I told her that, she
didn't hear me—and couldn't read my lips. But she laughed. I left her laughing!
(glares at J C) Don't even ask.

J C
I hadn't planned to.

ZERO
(with a sardonic smile, tapping him with the razor)
She looked like you. Rosy cheeks *(running it along one)* . . . sort of somewhat
fat . . . a *dead* ringer. *(J C clears his throat somewhat.)*
Even the way she cleared her throat. *(touching at J C)* She could have been your
twin. *(Zero blinks at that and looks away.)*
Twin. A redundancy on nature's part if ever there was one.
One of its little jokes . . . making two of you . . . then four of you when you look
in the mirror. *(He waits a look at J C.)* Leaving you doing a soliloquy in four
voices.

(They hold on one another.)

J C
A soliloquy, a symphony, a semblance in glass, what does it matter!
It's still me! Me suffering!

ZERO
(upset)
Do you think that fellow looking back at you in the mirror is you?! Hardly! He's
ass backwards from you forchristsake!
Sorry. *(after the mockery he just going on)* Looking at the world the other
way around! Trying to deceive you that you're shaving the left side *(his razor
accompanying his words)* of your face when it's your right! Trying to deceive
you that you are . . . are suffering. Don't let him, J C! In fact, stay away from
mirrors altogether. They're nothing but trouble! Believe me!

(With that he runs over to the window and roars out in a madman's pitch and pace, as a gust of the wind blows in.)

ZERO

FRESH AIR! IT FILLS OUR LUNGS WITH LIFE AND OUR
HEADS WITH . . . *(turning back to J C)* airy ideas. *(agreeing)*
I'm too much for me, too. That's why I have no mirrors.
Couldn't take two of me. Of course, they tell me it's all in my head.
Not in the mirror. To get real. Lay off the sugar. Take my pills.
Look at some television. Get in a play. *(He grins.)*

J C

I'm sure if you went back—

ZERO

No—my doctors are not philosophers! They never get to the root cause of the disease. *(nodding)* It's all due to the Higgs particle, of course. And Eve. Or was it Lilith?

J C

(on it)

How do you know about her?

ZERO

I know! I know—it was the fucking symbiotic spirochete. But that does nothing for me! *(His eyes dance after that; moving back and forth in wait.)* See! It did nothing for you, too. Fucking symbiotic spirochete is for shit. It's out of our routine. Holding your breath will draw bigger crowds. *(He lifts one eyebrow, and waits.)* Well?

J C

What?

ZERO

Aren't you going to practice?

J C

Practice what?

ZERO
Practice what—holding your breath forchrissake! Sorry.

J C
(obviously trying to end it)
Look it—

ZERO
You're right. *(Suddenly all the wistful assurance drains from his face as he comes over to J C.)* Perhaps we should stick to the script.
A strange ghoulishly funny bit of business to be sure. *(happy again)*
But who could be sure? About anything really. The only person I ever met who ever was was God.

J C
You couldn't have met God.

ZERO
I did! In Ward W, X, Y, Z. She was that far gone. But she still could fuck, the ole *tu sabes* from Rio. She screwed you I hear. But good!
(He holds on J C.) Or was it Lilith?

J C
(again taken aback at that name)
What do you want from me? *(a beat)* Mentioning her?
What do you want from me?

ZERO
From me . . . of me . . . mine . . . back to that . . . *(whispering the rest as if it were the deepest of all secrets)* . . . a mere psychic crystallization around an abyss.
Me! (stares at J C) How nice to be able to say it though. Me! *Io solo uno!* Do you read Dante? I know you do.
Your grandpa started you on it. Got you addicted to the ole Dago.
How would you say it? *I, myself, alone? Me, myself and I?* And why does he call it a comedy? A divine comedy no less? You oughta fit right in, don't you think? *(His eyes move towards the window.)* How nice to have a graveyard just outside your window.
We all really do you know. A hop, skip, and a breath away. A way a lone a last a loved a long the—well maybe not a loved.

(Lightning strikes somewhere in the nearby graveyard and the lights dim for a moment. It startles the younger man and that angers him for some reason. He lets go of the top sheet covering J C that they both are clutching at and laughs a weak laugh—holding the silly grin—his mind apparently somewhere else.)

ZERO
(screaming out of the blue)
CORRECTING THE HUMAN BRAIN IS A GRAND IDEA. UNTIL YOU SEE IT'S HUMANS DOING THE CORRECTING!
(A steely resolve comes into Zero's loony look.)
Rather a vicious circle wouldn't you agree? Huh, Jeeeeeeesssssssus.

(He lets the word drag out until he is out of breath; then let's his head fall to the side as if dead. A wacky wink towards the gravedigger follows; as if in mockery of being breathless.)

J C
Don't you think you ought to take your medicine?

ZERO
What medicine?

J C
I'm sure you must have some sort of medicine. To-

ZERO
To what? Make me into someone I am not?! Like you do with him!
With your 'Jimmy'!

J C
Stop it right there!

(The handsome madman bites at his lip as if about to tell J C something in the deepest confidence, and in warp speed.)

ZERO
Did you know, and I have it on the best authority, did you know that guts. I am
And I'm referring here to actual not metaphoric stuff to those simple conduits that
take food in one end and expel you-know-what those simple conduits that take

food in one end and expel advanced life forms. Would you believe it?! A mere
gastrointestinal tract was the highway up! To us! *Moi et toi!* And her toitness,
too! However it seems to have lost its way with regards to what's his face, his
green face, Jimmy was it?
(*He pats down J C's belly ever so neatly, then staring at him, gently touches at
the other man's wild hair.*)

ZERO

So don't blame yourself for whatever it was you did. It was all the fault of the raw
elemental energies of evolution. Made so by the generosity of God! An insane
generosity if ever, don't you think?
Or was it mere chance that brought us here—a universal contingency?
Maybe just the Queen of fucking Romania!

(*J C says nothing.*)

ZERO

Ah, silence—you are a chip off the ole block. *(then)*
Let's pray together, Jesus-whoever, and see if the Mystery that made us has some
revelation on the subject.

(*The unseen sheep dog gives out a howl of despair.*)

ZERO

Good, doggie! You're worth every cookie in your contract.
Dogs know ya know—but they'll only howl about it. Even when you try to get
them to enunciate more clearly, they won't. Not even if you shave them. Yes,
they know—somebody's got to know.

J C
(his voice fading)
Yes . . .

(*Zero giggles and then his face tightens into a white rage.*)

ZERO

Yes, somebody's got to know why your visual *(through clinched teeth)*
your verbal *(screams)* YOUR VISCERAL IDENTITY *(bringing both*

his hands to his head) is ripped out of you—your *very* inners right out of you—right before your eyes—in your looking glass! The one I fell through. Somebody's got to know the answer to that, Jocko—Jesus—or whoever the hell you are.

(J C goes to say something, but Zero holds up his hand; holding it there with whatever it is pulsating in his bright pale eyes.)

ZERO
The man down the hall from me says if he knew the why he could bear any how. He has a definite fixation. And fixation is the very definition of madness. So let's just say he's mad. *(Abruptly, he looks back at the window and the dark sky.)* Damn mad about it!

(He covers his face with both of his trembling hands, his wild eyes showing through.)

ZERO
Help me, J C! *(He seems fighting for breath as he looks at his host with muffled gasps, his eyes piercing out of some horrible place he is trying to hide from with his absurd mask.)* But not like you did him.

J C
What are you talking about!?

ZERO
A strange ghoulishly funny bit of business, to be sure. *(letting down his hands)* But who could be sure? Sure about anything really? That's what you said.

J C
Right now I'm more interested in what you said!

ZERO
What I said? *(dead serious)* I said they miscast you.

J C
What are you babbling about now?

ZERO
You tell me!

J C
If it's about what I think it is . . .

ZERO
Yes? *(He waits.)* I didn't think so—too close to the bone, hey, gravedigger? *(raising his eyebrows naughtily)* So let's continue to pretend! *(suddenly provoked into combative eyes)* Like pretending you don't know what I'm talking about!

J C
(obviously nervous about it)
I don't!

(A cell phone rings inside J C's pocket and he takes it out, listening . . .)

J C
Yes—I know!
(Then hesitating; he looks up at Zero who has gotten up off the bed and is looking back at him.)

J C
He's complaining that you're changing the lines again.

ZERO
Tell him I'm trying to improve your performance—make it more real. Believe me, that Doctor Mortadella knows nothing about Stanislavsky. *(to the audience)* I know you paid good money to find out what happens, but I'd leave while I was ahead!

(The lights come up on the Lunatics again standing in their places within the giant lopsided window frame.)

LUNATIC ONE
Ladies and gentlemen,
LUNATIC TWO
don't be such bores,
LUNATIC THREE
pull up your skirts

LUNATIC FOUR
and head for the doors!

BEESHALEAK
(sticks his head out, pointing like a schoolmarm at the Lunatics, accent an all)
Now stop that! You're not even supposed to be out there—and what have you
done with the dark haired boy with green skin?

ZERO
Don't ask them—ask him!

*(As if in a distant tower, a woman begins singing the wordless part of Lucia di
Lammermoor's mad aria.)*

ZERO
She knows!

(J C is very upset at hearing the woman, for whatever hidden reason.)

BEESHALEAK
(in an Indian accent and cadence; fumbling through his script)
No, I believe that is incorrect. I'm looking—hold on. There is no woman singing
a wordless aria—where are we?

ZERO
Haven't you been following along?

BEESHALEAK
(in an Indian accent and cadence)
Who could follow this hickey-dickey mess? It's making me popeyed!
I go home at night and ask my wife to tell me honestly if I still know my ass
from my elbow!

LUNATIC ONE
You'd better! Evolution is riding on it according to him.
LUNATIC TWO
But evolution has to be overcome according to the other one.
LUNATIC FIVE
Nature is amoral and not worthy of us he says.

LUNATIC THREE
It all comes out in the toilet scene.

ZERO
That's not till later!

BEESHALEAK
(in an Indian accent and cadence)
Well, what's now?

ZERO
I don't know—you've got the damn script!

(Suddenly, a voice distant and foreboding comes out over the mike; no one seems to hear it but J C.)

VOICE
Signore, rammentate mi la mente!

(J C looks up shocked; suddenly as if lost in memory; murmuring something.)

ZERO
Where were you, Jim *(correcting himself)* I mean Jesus?
And what was that you were babbling in Dago? More Dante?

J C
(only half there)
Far scarier stuff than his hell.

ZERO
(looking confused at J C who seems lost)
Mr. Chaord? Jim?

J C
Grandpa.

ZERO
You're not making sense!

J C

Oh but *he* was—I see that now.

ZERO

Who?

J C

(pointing towards nothing)

Don't you see him? Hear him?

ZERO

(taking his arm; concerned)

We gotta get you outta here. *(out to the wing)* Doctor!

LUNATICS ONE

Good—let's just cut to act two. I like act two better.

LUNATIC TWO

But we have to do act one first.

LUNATIC THREE

Why?

LUNATIC TWO

The truth is I was never good at answering that one. *(turning to Four)*

LUNATIC FOUR

I hope you don't expect me to tell you!

LUNATIC FIVE

Out here in public!

LUNATIC ONE

Not on your life!

LUNATIC TWO

Or your liberty!

LUNATIC FOUR

Or your pursuit of happiness either!

DIRECTOR (UNSEEN OVER A MIKE)

Let's at least try to approach what was written. Have you found the black haired kid yet, so we can get on with it?

ZERO
(in mingled admonition and pain)
On with what? Showing how the Mystery that made us is a carnivore? *(distressed; in a strained stage-whisper)* A God who particularly fancy brains! The black-haired youth's. Yours, mine *(pointing at the Lunatics who are wide-eyed with terror)* theirs. We're his menu! Of course, when I confront him with it, he says nothing. I find that rather funny.
(a stare) Maybe I have a warped sense of humor.

J C
(taking his arm; concerned)
Come and sit down.

ZERO
(as he's led towards the armchair)
He's nothing like you say, Sweetie-pie, you who won't eat anything with a face! Who passes over frontal lobes framboise! Sautéed pituitary glands with truffles! Chilled cerebellum with crispy arugula!

J C
Here.

ZERO
Be forewarned, God's a headhunter! Forget your thighs, it's your thalamus he's after!

J C
Try to stop shaking.

ZERO
With what I know?

J C
Try not to think about it. Like when you wake up from a bad dream. *(out to the wing)* Doctor!

ZERO
This is not about things that go thump in the night! Or little green bastards from outer space swooping down on a lawn party!
This is for real!

(The Lunatics nod yes vigorously.)
LUNATICS
We know what that is.
LUNATIC ONE
If nature doesn't get you.
LUNATIC FIVE
humankind will!
LUNATIC THREE
They're in cahoots with God!

ZERO
It's called the Incarnation. *(He nods a vigorous nod up and down; the Lunatics all starting to cry.)* I can only blink at what it means to be human. *(eyeing J C, runs his hand nervously through his tousled hair)* I must get on the Internet to warn people about it!

J C
(trying to soothe him; while looking over at the wing for help)
Can I get some help out here!

DIRECTOR (UNSEEN OVER A MIKE)
You're Jesus Christ, work a damn miracle!

J C
(sadly)
I don't work miracles any more.

(Zero's dancing bright eyes go wild! Warp-wild with a pale fury popping out of both of them with what he has to say—at a breathless speed.)

ZERO
It is possible—it is plausible that beneath the holy fable and fiasco of the life and secrets of sweet Jesus—is it plausible that there is hidden one of the most painful instances of a bothered and bewildered, betrayed and broken screwball ever to breathe on planet earth? *(looking directly at J C)* Not to mention down the hall from me.

LUNATIC ONE
The story of a poor unsettled and insatiable creature—a nut—who finally, finally, after he could get no satisfaction—driven past vitamins and the movies, health spas and at wit's

end—past everybody else's answer to the riddle of why we live and die, faced with the bare-assed truth—

LUNATIC TWO

Had to write his own comedy routine!

LUNATIC THREE

His own farce. With his own punch line.

LUNATIC FOUR

Yes, invent a God who was entirely different than the universe!

LUNATIC FIVE

One that loved. Loved him. And everything! A universe with a heart. Imagine that?

ZERO

A fairytoothfather. And all because the poor bastard was threatened with not knowing why! It was eating him up. Especially when the ichneumon wasp eats the caterpillar while it is still alive—alive without anesthesia.

(His pale voice holds on that as if accusing J C of something; immediately spreading out his arms in the form of a cross.)

He tried so desperately, and still does—to put together his toiletry and what goes thump in his heart. And all that together with the Mystery that made us. It drove him here, of course. To Saint Haha's.

(All hold as if in a freeze frame; J C nods a slow sad nod . . . turning and going to a spot with only a toilet bowl and seat, a sink, and mirror in it. As he modestly takes up his bathrobe and sits on the toilet seat, Zero and the Lunatics fade.)

J C

(out to the audience)

You really shouldn't be here. It's really not part of the play. Funny things can happen to you in here. Here where evolution proves its point every single day of one's life. Reminding us who we are. What we are. Then confuses us with . . . with what I feel. I feel, I feel sitting in this confusing toilet . . . on a cold wooden toilet seat with stale wine on my breath and my own waste filling my nostrils . . . I feel *(he stops as if he could barely say it)* love.

(A spot comes up on Zero listening, then the Lunatics doing the same; J C looking over at him, then the Lunatics, and back again to Zero.)

J C
A love that's the final phase of love in the mind of a person.
Maybe all humankind! Maybe everything! A love that asks nothing in return . . .
not even love. Merely love. Meaningless.
Empty of return. Different. Flimsy or even flimflam . . . almost beside
myself and this funny body. As if the whole world were alive with it.

ZERO
Holy shit!

(The Lunatics stare at JC.)

LUNATIC ONE
Look it, Candy Ass, all of us are having a difficult time enough just trying to
live in Ward W
LUNATIC TWO
X
LUNATIC THREE
Y
LUNATIC FOUR
Z!
LUNATICS
When we take a dump we don't want to have to figure out how it's holy!

*(J C shakes his head as if he concludes as well that he is just a silly ole man; a
Mona Lisa smile comes to his face and he gets up, goes to the sink, turning on
the invisible water to wash his hands and looking into the mirror as he does.)*

J C
You're right, that's a mystery perhaps best left unsolved.
(He traces his own face in the mirror.)
And yet . . . and yet, everything ultimately depends on that outcry and there is
no asylum from it.

LUNATICS
It's the reason for philosophy, poetry, prayer and plays.

J C
Each of them leaving us staring at ourselves trying to find out—

ZERO
something essential to us that we may not be able to find out.
LUNATICS
Yet imperative that we do!
LUNATIC ONE
What a predicament being born is!
LUNATIC THREE
(starting to cry)
Just ask the caterpillar being eaten alive by the ichneumon wasp, bit by bite by
bite by bit
LUNATIC TWO
(crying as well)
As it hangs there asking why?
LUNATIC FOUR
(crying)
Just ask the baby wildebeest being eaten alive by the laughing hyena, bit by bite
by bite by bit
LUNATIC FIVE
(crying)
As it looks over to its helpless mother asking why?
LUNATIC ONE
Just ask anyone in Ward W X Y Z being eaten alive
LUNATIC THREE
As we are left looking up at the night sky asking why?
LUNATICS
(yelling to the wings)
PROMPTER!

*(The lights go out on the Lunatics, only Zero left watching J C. J C looks away
from the darkened window, back again into his mirror.)*

J C
Yes—why? Like the rat I once trapped with stickem all my life ago. I saw it shivering
and squealing in pain—gasping for breath—its mouth open in shock—oxygen-hungry
and covered with mucus in a matter of moments, as if asking why? The little creature
merely ventured out of her hole. In the house Lilith and I had rented when she first
got pregnant.

*(A spot comes up with a beautiful woman in it; Zero going dark. She is pregnant.
The gravedigger has to turn away when he sees her. He looks again into the*

shadowy mirror, resting his forehead against the sweated glass of his own image.

He looks away, and then back again at the face looking out at him. With that he tries to say something—force himself to say it—but the words are lost between his clenched fist and never rise up out of his sore throat. He leans his head back, takes in a deep breath, and then makes himself look back into the mirror. His face has such a savage irony about it.)

J C
You frighten me . . . with what I know . . . know about you and that fateful night you decided to take matters into your own hands.

(As a spot comes up on the dark-haired young man with greenish skin in J C's bed as if dead.)

J C
It's a grief that lasts forever.

(J C's arms embrace both sides of the sink holding himself up; his head falling forward almost against the mirror—the dark-haired young man sits up from his dead sleep and looks out at the audience with his blank stare.)

J C
God was kinder to Abraham than he was to me.
(An onrush of sobs follows.) It was out of love. Out of love.
Love! I couldn't . . . my broken-winged baby boy . . . I meant well.
I hope he knew.

(His eyes glare into the mirror, his breath hot against it.)

J C
How could he . . . my mindless monster without significance or a soul? My poor baby . . . my poor baby boy.
(in a harsh loudness) My God, my God, why did you forsake me?
(in a whisper) My God, my God, why did you forsake yourself?

(The spot goes out on the young man and a spot come up on Zero, holding on the audience.)

ZERO

I warned him about those damn mirrors. It'll cure anyone of Narcissism believe me—a person staring back at himself—especially him, fixed on that one thing in particular in his case. In his case study. And we suspect what it is, don't we?

(J C lifts himself slowly . . . until finally his body isn't shivering any more. Zero meanwhile has come to the mirror.)

ZERO

Are you alright? I heard you scream. I thought I might join in.

(They both look into the mirror and SCREAM, then stop.)

ZERO

Now's as good a time as ever to talk about it. Maybe especially now, considering.

J C

Considering what?

ZERO

Considering that he came back from the dead to help you.

J C
(with quiet acceptance)
You're mad.

ZERO

At you yes—bringing him back to this! Does it seem a joke to you that the dead should continue to endure life? Lazarus was miffed about it, too—he told me so just last night. You really should stop bringing people back from the dead.

J C

Is that what you call it?

ZERO

Your prayer was answered. *(J C cringes.)*
I pray, too. *(looking up)* You-who! How cheerfully you seem to grin. How neatly spread your claws. And welcome little children in with gently smiling jaws. *(to J C)* I'm sure those are not the right words though—they never work.

J C
No—it seems none of them do.

ZERO
(Zero cocks his head somewhat at J C.)
I thought you were Christ?

J C
I am. A postmodern one.

(First Zero nods, and then J C; as if they are both understand.)

ZERO
(in a sudden grotesque whimsy)
Call me a cab. I gotta get back.

J C
Back where?

ZERO
Back stage!

J C
(pointing at the wing)
It's only—

ZERO
It's only what?

(He looks out at the audience.)

ZERO
You have no idea what really goes on backstage. It's a laborratory. *(giggles)* Laborratory. I like to say it that way—the way Boris Karloff did in those old movies—it sounds so spooky. And it is. Because it's unreal what they do to you backstage. Make pies out of your thighs, and lies out of your eyes.

LUNATICS (UNSEEN)
Self-sacrifice should at least be a matter of choice.

ZERO
(turning to J C)
Did he have a chance to choose? Even a self to sacrifice?
Did you even have a son? *(There is a long moment with J C staring at Zero.)* Do you know the story of Pinocchio and his lying father Geppetto?

J C
(hesitant)
That's not quite the version I heard.

ZERO
They all have funny names. Un-American if you ask me. Anyway, to straighten out the fairy tale—an oxymoron if ever I heard one—it was when the little bastard *lied* that he became a real boy. A chip off the ole block. And it wasn't his nose that grew either. Ask Gertrude!
And Brad! *(He laughs that off; and goes coldcock still.)*
The moral of the story being: never lie—unless you have to.
Especially to yourself—right, gravedigger?

J C
What is that supposed to mean?

ZERO
Nothing. Does everything have to have a meaning with you? Where I come from people laugh for no reason at all. *(laughs)* See? I'm laughing for no reason at all! Just call me flimflam's son and folly's brother . . . mother, sister. Twin. I really don't know who I am. Like your wooden son whom you tried to—well that doesn't matter—since there was no son there—but quite a New Year's Eve wasn't it?

BEESHALEAK (FROM THE WING)
(in an Indian accent and cadence)
I have no idea what page you are on. None of this is in my copy!
There is no New Year's Eve mentioned in my copy!

ZERO
No December thirty first to remember!

J C
And one to forget, too. If you can ever forget such a thing.
(out over towards the window; in which the Lunatics appear again)

Do you think that's why they scream—they can't forget?

ZERO
Our little get-together is hardly going as expected. Put the television on, dude! Let's learn how to plug into the rest of America's attention span. It might be fun. Did I ever tell you about the whole of Ward A going up in a roar of laughter watching television. Nobody on Ward A could understand a word of anything—but they understood what the Chief Justice was saying. It broke them up. Watching crazy people can be so much fun. The autistic, the catatonic, those with Tourette's. All that jabber and jumping around. Contortions of all sorts. All over the place. Kinetic on one side—frenetic on the other! Makes you wonder why they were born doesn't it . . . why they came into this world?

LUNATICS
Me phunai ton athanta nika logos.
LUNATIC ONE
Yes—perhaps not to have been born is best, when all is reckoned with.
LUNATIC TWO
Certainly for Jimmy.
LUNATIC THREE
Certainly to such a father.
LUNATIC FOUR
To a father who . . .
(each of them puts their forefingers to their mouths)
LUNATICS
Shhhhhhh.

(Tears roll down J C cheeks.)

ZERO
Yes, it is best left unsaid.

J C
(suddenly angry)
Look, I'm very tired. Do you think we can bring our party on Mars to a close?

ZERO
I'll ask Mission Control. (with a solemn wink between them) I know the Head very well. She—

J C
(exhausted)
Lives down the hall from me.

ZERO
So you do remember!

J C
All the time. "What's done is done and can not be undone."
I hear her every night, yelling at me from across the hall.

ZERO
She's not as crazy as she would appear.
Though dicing up her guests was hardly hospitable.

(The bitter irony in his voice fades to a mute sigh. Zero studies J C's face.)

J C
Why are you looking at me that way?

ZERO
What way is that?

J C
Like I'm your accomplice in some galactic conspiracy.

ZERO
No—your conspiracy is a lot bigger than that, J C. The salvation of God himself!
Why don't you just live your little life and die your little death? *(a moment)* There
is as much a chance of there being a soul for him as there was for the dinosaurs.
For any of us. Or a caring God to go with it.

(J C says nothing; merely looks at him.)

ZERO
Look it, we are all bubbles, so you mustn't dig too deep, gravedigger. Otherwise,
we'll pop. That goes for God, too.
(He laughs some.) Isn't that what you called him . . . Pop?

(Zero goes to the armchair, sits with closes eyes. The lights go out on the Lunatics and J C sighs as if he believes the night is over, going over and laying backwards onto the bed. The wind outside becomes the only sound on the shadowed stage, everything else still as could be.)

ZERO
(his eyes shoot open)
Was his name really Jimmy?

J C
I thought you were tired?

ZERO
Exhausted.
(He waves that aside with a dismissing hand; his look becoming menacing as he shoots up out of the armchair.) Just who do you think you are? *(racing across)* Calling me up from the dead like this? With me so exhausted! And for what? AND FOR WHAT?

(The expected detonation stiffens and the anxious man falls off into a private silence instead. It leaves one set of tired eyes holding on the other.)

ZERO
And for what, you silly nilly of a man? Well aren't you?
(His eyes widen and he nods as if he knows that for sure; a mad smirk cutting across his handsome face.)
Who else believes that to be superficial you have to be profound?
Or is it the other way around? You never know with him. He even puts shoes on the corpses he buries. And suits and ties.
New dresses and corsages. But enough of your sleight of hand, old man, we got to set it right! However, I have to warn you ahead of time—don't try to get me to dye my pubic hairs tangerine.
Paint my balls blue. Put a peppermint sock on my powerful penis and a comatose cork up my beautiful ass. Be profound on your own! I'm just going along for the ride.

(With that, he glares down the length of the crazy quilt, his bright pale eyes digging into the gravedigger's. Searching! He even leans forward some.)

ZERO

His brain was built around a funnel. He was slipping away synaptic gap by synaptic gap. What else could you do?

J C

I could ask you to leave!

ZERO

And leave you alone on New Year's Eve? Of all nights?
Lucky I could squeeze you in. I'm booked ya know. Dinner dates all over the place. What the hell I said—do it for Hecuba, ole cold tits herself. Where is she anyway? Ole plunderpussy?
My mother. Your wife.

J C
(jumping out of bed)
That's it—you're out of here!

(He starts to push Zero towards the door.)

ZERO

Same as before, huh, J C? Trying to push me out of your life? Or are you going to take care of me this time?

J C
(stops)
I did try to take care of him!

ZERO

You tried to *take care of* him alright!

J C

Don't be silly. You don't know what you're saying.

ZERO

What if I said no one believes you? Not me! Not the prompter!
Not the director! Not the audience! Not anyone!

J C

I don't care! How does that grab you and your blue balls?

ZERO
My balls aren't blue. That was precisely our argument, that you don't expect me—

J C
Jesus Christ!

ZERO
(a cappella)
'Superstar! Who the hell do you think you are?' Or something like that. I wasn't in that play. We put on a lot of plays here.
People play all sorts of parts. *(With that he starts up in a theatrical flair.)* 'Out out brief candle! Life is but a walking shadow, a poor player that struts and frets his hour upon the stage and then is heard no more. It is a tale told by an idiot—*(stops)* full of sound and fury, signifying nothing.' You were right to try to *take care of* him.

(Both men look at one another. J C looks out at the audience.)

J C
Is he a figment of my imagination or I his? My youth come back to haunt me? Is he the rest of me? The best of me?
My own unrealized madness?

ZERO
Unrealized?

(Zero sort of laughs slightly; then, after a realized beat, J C sort of nods.)

J C
But shouldn't you be getting back now?

ZERO
(arches his eyebrows)
Back stage? Or back on a ledge somewhere? The feel of fall in the air? A delicate balance to be sure—being at the edge of the why, the cry, the sigh—while looking up at the cruel silence in the sky. And since we're discussing it—my mental balance. Or yours! You can at least be sure about this—everything I told you is all wrong. A lie to be exact.

Yes, everything I told you was a lie. Well . . . not everything. Only when I said I didn't know who I am. *(He stops for a moment before his matter-of-fact statement.)* I am God.

(There is silence.)

ZERO
You're wondering about this little phenomenon aren't you, old J C Chaord, the only real clown left on planet earth? *(He laughs a carefree laugh.)* Put on your make-up, your top hat, your goofy shoes, those silly patched pantaloons—you've got a showboat to catch!
Me, too! We'll book ourselves in every port of call! They'll name babies after us! Elephants, too! Maybe even a mountain or two!
Certainly cities! We'll leave 'em laughing. J C and God!
(A puzzlement comes over his handsome face.)
That doesn't sound right somehow. I should get top billing.
But no need for a contract dispute, son.

(Just then there was a horrible scream from the window; coming from out of the darkness.)

ZERO
There they go again, remembering. *(out to the audience)* Let me let you in on a big secret. All of you—formerly hairy dog, gooney parrot on tape, invisible director and remembered rat, pathetic prompter and even more pathetic playwright, Lunatics and you our intriguing audience—*(He stops; then giggles.)* No, I'll let Jimmy break the news to you.

J C
That might be a little difficult. *(Zero looks puzzled.)* Jimmy can't talk. *(out to the audience)* He really did die you know.
The doctors didn't just write it into the play, it was for real.

(Zero holds on J C, a look of appalled amusement holding on his face.)

ZERO
Without any help from you? *(J C says nothing)* Always the joker that kid of yours. Do anything for a laugh. Was it a pratfall? I hope he went out with his make-up on! *(He touches at J C's red cheek and nods.)*

He always wore too much rouge . . . too much lipstick . . . eyes that were pure mascara. And he was far too green. *(An expression of pathetic bewilderment overtakes him and he looks directly into J C's flushed face.)*
Dead? Really? Is everyone agreed? *(J C nods.)* Despite all those hours he spent in front of that fading mirror reassuring himself he was there? *(He giggles.)* He was really unhinged that boy of yours.
(He goes all serious again, looking as if recalling him at his mirror; his one hand slowly rubbing at his face as if putting on make up.)
His basic disease is pretty much at a stand still now though . . . wouldn't you say, gravedigger?

J C
It does that to people.

ZERO
Well, it's against the Constitution! Let me tell you! Cruel and unusual punishment is against the Constitution! *(Abruptly, he is ox-eyed and straight-backed.)* Your constitutional, too, it would seem. We shouldn't have to die! To cry! To sigh! To have to—*(He starts shaking all over.)*

J C
What is it? What? Are you having a seizure?

ZERO
Only a grand mal. But let's make the best of it.

J C
Well what do I do—call the Rescue Squad?

ZERO
I've got a scoop for you. *(with a glare back at J C)* I forgot my line.
Where are we? *(sadly, in an Indian accent)* In our hilarious horror in two acts?
(somewhat dazed) Oh, yes, call me a Rescue Squad.

BEESHALEAK (FROM THE WING)
(in an Indian accent and cadence)
No—you're getting the lines all mixed up! The line is 'There is no Rescue Squad. I got a scoop for you. There is no Rescue Squad!'

(After a slow nod, and then another, Zero's face drains into such bewilderment, he looks pathetically over at J C, moisture in his haunted eyes.)

ZERO
What's going to happen to me? *(There is a moment, an odd moment they both occupy together.)* Help me. *(His face is burning with pain.)* Please! *(He lets out a deep, heavy, continuous, rolling sigh.)* I'm all tangled up like a snake tied into knots by a cruel boy scout.

(His hand grips at his head with such intensity, and he begins whispering the rest of what he says.)

ZERO
A boy scout who looks exactly like me in my mirror . . . but who doesn't care whether I live or die . . . isn't even indifferent about it . . . it doesn't cross his mind. My little horse must think it queer to stop without a farmhouse near.

J C
(taking him by the arm.)
Here, why don't you lie down. I'll get you some warm milk.

(J C nods, but Zero begins to hyperventilate at that—as if indeed alone on some shadowy road, all tangled up in some abandoned amazement.)

ZERO
Are you trying to help me? Like you did him? *(He says it again as if that would make J C understand.)* LIKE YOU DID HIM?

(The older of the two men puts his hand on the other man's shoulder to calm him. But the touch of another human being only seems to intensify his outburst and not calm him at all; the lights on the Lunatics coming up.)

LUNATIC ONE
It's hilarious! *(She laughs through her excessive gasps for breath.)*
Get out your cerebral pens, doctors.
LUNATIC TWO
Put this in our play—*(over to Zero)* the Constitution, too—we have a scoop!
LUNATIC THREE
I'll have two scoops, please.
LUNATIC FOUR
Maybe a cookie to go with it? Steal it from the dog.

LUNATIC FIVE
But no blood toping on the ice cream, please.
LUNATIC ONE
We wouldn't want to catch that mad cow disease.
LUNATICS
NO BLOOD TOPPING PLEASE!

BEESHALEAK
(*sticking his head out, in an Indian accent and cadence; exasperated*)
What are you babbling about? Lunatics—if ever there was type casting!

(*Zero holds still, his plotting eyes shift first one way and then another.*)

ZERO
There are no lunatics here! (*looking frantically out at the wings and pointing*)
Don't listen to them (*then back to J C*) all those white-coated pricks and polished
pusses (*his spittle covers his host's face*) primping themselves for this or that press
conference (*wiping at the one side of J C's face, as J C wipes at the other himself*)
while boiling our asses in hot tubs in preparation for their feeding frenzy!

(*He puts his forefinger and thumb to his teeth in a nervous gesture, biting at them
with tiny imperceptible bites.*)

ZERO
This play is the worst thing that ever happened to me.

LUNATIC FIVE
Us, too. Can we do another?
LUNATIC FOUR
Zero doesn't like his part.
LUNATIC THREE
The dog either.
LUNATIC TWO
And we must especially state our bias about being eaten alive.
LUNATIC ONE
There—it's all out on the table now.
LUNATICS
OUR FRONTAL LOBES FRAMBOISE! SAUTÉED PITUITARY GLANDS
WITH TRUFFLES! CHILLED CEREBELLUM WITH CRISPY ARUGULA!

(With that Zero dashes off the stage; the stage lights dim on everyone, except a lone dim silver spot light Zero dashes into—stopping dead in his tracks, he looks up at the sudden wind and thunder and lightening, and let's his red robe drop from his body, standing naked and shivering with a razor to his throat. A moment later J C dashes into the same spot light. Zero looks at J C almost sideways; his eyes tearing.)

ZERO
Things don't turn out the way we imagine, do they, Holy Shit? The way we hope.

J C
Not for Papa Bear, Mamma Bear. And certainly not for Baby Bear.
(His voice falls off; coming back in a hoarseness, as if forced out with the greatest of effort.) No, not for any of the fairy tales. *(His pale eyes enlarge to a hueless burn, tears running down his cheeks, the sound of rain starting up.)* Why is it I can think up better worlds than exist?

ZERO
You're only human after all. But mums the word. *(as J C takes up Zero's red robe and puts it around the shivering man; gently taking the razor from him)* What's wrong?

J C
Wrong—what could possibly be wrong? The lame can see and the blind can walk, right? What could possibly be wrong?
(as if forced out with the greatest of effort) Where's the wisdom in the waste, Peter?

ZERO
I'm afraid the love that moves the sun and the stars is only in your poetry, Jim. And in mine.

(The spot goes out. The end of act one.)

Act two: a madhouse

(allargando in C-sharp umano al fine)

(J C, in a Derby hat, dressed as if a ridiculous gravedigger from a comic opera, with both suspenders and a belt, stands in a solo spot, cheeks redder than ever. With swelling cheeks he blows a twisted horn to announce himself. Then he winks and the lights come up on the Lunatics in comic garb as well, on the stage side of the window in a bizarre rec room. Death and Disillusionment are on a seesaw, one in a weird mask of tragedy, the other a weird mask of comedy; Aeschylus on a rocking horse with his bald head displaying a fake crack in it, along with a toy tortoise; Mother Mud in a wheelchair, going in circles and wearing three hats; and finally, Carmen Miranda standing on the old armchair, with her grand head-gear of fruit—each playing their costumed part.)

MOTHER MUD
(stops going in circles, out to the audience; rolling her eyes)
What now?

(Zero, wearing a large fig leaf over his privates, comes out from one of the wings and stands looking out at the audience.)

ZERO
Allow me to try to explain. *(pointing back at the Lunatics)* Somehow, somewho, these people—let's call them that—these people are going to do act two. Yes, they're crazy. You would be, too. But you're absolutely right—this play is about us, not you. You're all there.
Here *(pointing)* and there *(again)* and everywhere. You're all over the place. Get yourself together! *(giggles)* Crazy people always think everybody else is crazy. *(bites at his lip impishly)* And just what are *you* thinking about me at this given moment? *(nods)* Yes—we can be insidious like that. So I must caution you now that you are all about to enter the asylum itself—as observers, of course—you'll never laugh the same way again. *(smiles) Mi casa es su casa.*

(He starts to turn, but doesn't, instead, he backs up towards the wing so as not to expose his bare behind, pointing at the audience and laughing as he does, then disappearing backwards into the wing; leaving J C and the Lunatics.)

J C
(out the audience; exuberant)

It's Carnival at the asylum. Fat Tuesday! A time to celebrate the flesh! A time to belch and break wind—when Jesus moons the congregation and Buddha does a dance in the tulip bed!

(He looks back at the Lunatics.)

J C
Right, Mother Mud? *(She blows her little Mardi Gras horn.)* Death? Disillusionment? *(Laughing, Disillusionment goes up and Death comes down on the seesaw.)* And you, Aeschylus? *(The bald man bites at his lip with joy and rocks harder.)* Miss Miranda? *(The lunatic dressed in a white suit with sequins and an elaborate tangerine hairdo with a tall hat of fruit, smiling away with delight, gives him the arm.)* Yes, it's Carnival at the asylum—

MOTHER MUD
And having the best costume is all that matters!

(They all blow their little Mardi Gras horns and spin their little sound makers. At that, Beeshaleak sticks his head out, trying to be calm, trying to be reasonable.)

BEESHALEAK
(in an Indian accent and cadence)
Stop it—all of you! You're supposed to be doing act two!
He just announced it to the audience forchristsake! Sorry.
Now, please do the play as written! *(to J C)* And it says right here in front of me—act two starts with an aria by Jesus Christ!

DEATH
That doesn't make any sense!

DISILLUSION
The playwright takes care of the sounds and allows the sense to take care of itself.

AESCHYLUS
(starting to cry)
Mother Mud! I thought we were going to do *my* play! You promised!

MOTHER MUD
I did, Beeshaleak. *(motherly rubbing Aeschylus' bald head)* And he spent all night in the tub writing it.

BEESHALEAK
(in an Indian accent and cadence; now exasperated)
You can't just drop this play and do another! Especially his!

AESCHYLUS
I'll have you know that before I went crazy *I* wrote plays.
Mind-boggling plays. In fact, I was the first playwright ever!

J C
(with a small non-committal smile out to the audience)
Have you ever wondered where the unedited, uninhibited, unharnassed mind would lead?

AESCHYLUS
(to everyone)
No—where?

J C
(turning to the Lunatics)
Troops, let's take it from page one of Aeschylus's
(to the bald man) what are you calling it?

AESCHYLUS
(proudly)
The Human Condition as Revealed by the Bald Wizard in His Tub on Ward Z One Rainy Night Of Genius.

(Exasperated Beeshaleak sticks his head back with a groan. Everyone waves him 'good-bye' out and Aeschylus goes to the other wing and carries out a broken manikin—its arms hung on in a haphazard way, its legs dangling, and its head on backwards.)

VOICE
(very deep; "out of nowhere"—miked; but obviously Zero)

How chic! So a la mode, gravedigger! Your boy certainly has a flair for the human condition. *(a diabolic laugh follows)*

AESCHYLUS
Who the hell is that?

VOICE
(very deep; "out of nowhere"—miked)
I know—you didn't write me into your fixation, but here I am.
Ready and willing to address your predicament.

AESCHYLUS
What predicament?

VOICE
(very deep; "out of nowhere"—miked)
See what I mean? Keep cool about this now. Sang-froid.
Steady as you go, all of you. Do have the presence of mind to remember something unknown, doing you don't know what!

(A diabolic laugh follows.) Your species is my specialty, dear audience. I've dug into the subject more than I care to mention. Why what do you think I'm doing at this very moment?

AESCHYLUS
(referring to the audience)
They have no idea.

MOTHER MUD
How could they?

CARMEN MIRANDA
They can't see you.

VOICE
(very deep; "out of nowhere"—miked)
Well of course they can't see me, you loony tunes. I'm the Almighty, the Ground of Being, the Incomprehensible hidden behind everything, Lord of the Lordies, Invisibleness Itself!

Of course, they can't see me. However—I'm going to make an exception in this case.

(The lights come up on Zero standing on high—a platform to the side. He has an operating mask to the side of his mouth and a mike hanging over his head—along with a brain in the jar in front of him on an operating table. He's a wild man; his hair like a mad scientist, little rimmed glasses parked on his nose, a white doctor's coat on—stained like a butcher's—with a flash of Frankenstein lightning every now and again popping off all around him.)

ZERO
(a big hello)
Hello.

DEATH
He's got someone's brain in a jar!

DISILLUSIONMENT
Good God!

ZERO
(with a haughty glare her way)
I hate that expression. It makes me feel obligated. Nobody likes to have to live up to expectations. It puts undue burden on a guy. *(turning suddenly towards J C)* Right, son? *(to the audience)*
Part of my therapy. Attacking the problem head on.
(laughs) I can't help myself. They just keep coming.

AESCHYLUS
I can't stand it anymore! He's changing my entire play!

ZERO
(turning out to the real audience; by way of irritable explanation; piqued)
He's obsessed with his damn play. He thinks he's going to find it in his play!

AESCHYLUS
Find what?

ZERO
You wrote the damn thing, you tell me!

MOTHER MUD
(slapping Aeschylus across the back of his head)
The answer, you bald ninny.

AESCHYLUS
The answer—I don't even know the question!

ZERO
Well lookie here then and I'll show you—all of you! Rub a dub dub, through this three pounder in a tub! *(He points at the brain.)*

AESCHYLUS
(worried)
Who's is that anyways?

ZERO
Nobody's. *(giggles)* Get it?

CARMEN MIRANDA
(dripping with sarcasm)
No, tell us!

ZERO
(sings)
'Don't Cry For Me Argentina'—and they won't anymore.

(Carmen bursts out in tears.)

ZERO
(looking down at his prize)
Now let's get back to our search.

DEATH
Our search for what?

ZERO
(Zero just rolls his eyes up at the ceiling, shakes his head)
Oh, Wilbur, please.

DEATH
Who's Wilbur?

ZERO
(too patient; his words cutting)
Yes, who's Wilbur? *(looking to each as he says a name—Mother Mud)*
And who's Alice? *(Aeschylus)* And who's Victor? *(Carmen)*
And who's Loretta? *(Disillusionment)* And who's Patrick?
(to the gravedigger) And who are you? We're getting to that—believe me. *(out to the audience)* Believe you me.
(he laughs a mad laugh, then stops, catching Mother Mud studying him)
Why are you looking at me that way?

MOTHER MUD
(still studying him)
You can't be God!

ZERO
How would you know? Have you ever seen him? *(aside to audience)*
Wrong place to ask that one. *(with a sigh turns his attention back to the brain, at which he starts poking around with his fingers)*
Like detectives, let's ponder the evidence, my biped featherless creatures who laugh at nothing. Will you look at this mess. Who's responsible for this? *(giggles; then a la an aria) Siamo contenti?*
Son dio ho fatto questa caricatura.

DEATH
(towards the wing)
Is that the aria?
DISILLUSIONMENT
I thought Jesus was supposed to sing it!

CARMEN MIRANDA
No—it wouldn't make any sense then—what he's singing.

AESCHYLUS
What is he singing?

(Zero just laughs and continues on.)

ZERO
The Dura Mater is unusually dropsied in this one. *(digging)*
And what's this funny fluid? *(he tastes at the fluid with his finger tip)* Tastes like
anchovy sauce. It's those amphibian roots—all this salt. *(a carefree ahh)* I love
doing this. I feel like an ancient oracle fishing for messages—from Myself.

MOTHER MUD
(aside to the audience)
This is not the sort of God one would be inclined to pray to.

ZERO
For purposes of descriptive ease, allow me to chop it into all its parts for you.
(and does! quickly like a Japanese chef) There . . . the hindbrain, midbrain, and
forebrain . . . *(looking up)* Strange, the frontal lobes are still throbbing . . . he
couldn't still be in there?
(down towards it) Hello!

(He winks out at the audience, and then turns back to it again; digging away.)

ZERO
It seemed a straightforward enough job when I started.
Willyalookie here . . . the Fissure of Roland . . . *(up)* More like the Rubicon!
Between mammalian and neo-mammalian if I recall correctly. It's been a while
since I put the damn thing together. *(sighs)* Ah well, mistakes will happen. *(He
laughs a little laugh and the Lunatics start to cry.)* Yes, cry, cause this is the only
way out, my fine bunch of banshees.

AESCHYLUS
No! I shall be the only man who will never die!

ZERO
(out to the audience)
Humor him. Humor them all. You never know with nuts like this.

(They all laugh and he quiets them with a glare; and then turns back to the brain with a little shivery giggle of anticipation.)

ZERO
We're almost there.

(He smiles, picking at the brain and tasting at it, and as he does, Aeschylus faints into Death's arms, distracting Zero but for a moment.)

ZERO
I hate vegetarians! *(with that he turns back to chopping and digging away)* Ah, the optic nerve—by which I myself in my living brain am observing this dead one, and you in your crazy ones me doing it.
Not to mention our audience out there—doing the same through *their* glorious brains. *(smiles their way, then immediately dives back into digging away)* Will you look at this . . . it's like a can of worms, all congregating on two planks and a passion.
(gives a wink out at the audience)
Everyone's real stage—all three pounds of it. *(a little giggle)*
At war on all fronts. Left frontal, right frontal. Thrashing about every which way. It makes you wonder what this man saw? I've heard of psychic scars before but this is too much.
(again a little giggle) De trop. It sounds so much better in Frog.

MOTHER MUD
(with terror)
So what *did* he see?

ZERO
We're getting to that, Mommy dearest. *(down to the brain)*
Carcasse, tu trembles? Tu tremblerais bien davantage, si tu savais ou je te mene.

MOTHER MUD
(repeating it in terrified English)
You tremble, carcass? You would tremble a lot more if you knew where I am taking you.

DEATH
(frightened)
Where?

(Zero merely laughs and proceeds with his digging; then looking down at them all with an exaggerated gawk.)

ZERO
Nothing! Deeper yet? Fine. *(doing just that with his wheeling knife)*
Towards your primal floor? Your basic flavor? *(cutting frantically)*
But where is it? This man's irreducible self? *(He give a snicker; and with that looks up out at the audience.)* Looks like everybody is a little bit of a fraud.

(With that, he turns directly towards J C.)

ZERO
And you say I never did anything for you. Here I am showing you that there's no one there to grieve over, to love and suffer for, to bury! Nothing underneath the underneath and the undertaker, too.
(holding dead serious on J C)
I'm afraid the love that moves the sun and the stars is as nothing as you, dear Jim. And your Jimmy, too.

(A cackle as the spot goes out on Zero. They're all left just standing there. J C looking around at it all, a little dazed.)

AESCHYLUS
Somewhat burlesque wouldn't you say? I myself would never have written so . . . so French. *(eyeing J C)* What's wrong? You don't look well.

DEATH
Peculiar to say the least.

MOTHER MUD
(giving J C advice; still somewhat terrified)
Forget it, whatever it is eating away at you.

DISILLUSIONMENT
It's all—much to do about nothing.

J C
(passionate, to Disillusionment) Was what you felt for your wife—nothing? *(to Death)* Or you for your dying twin sister? *(to Aeschylus)* Or you for that stray dog you took in? *(turning to Mother Mud)* Was it nothing when you were a bag lady and someone shared their soup with—

MOTHER MUD
(on it; agitated)
Stop it! *(almost too low to be heard.)* Having the best costume is all that matters.

DISILLUSIONMENT
(nervous; to JC)
Yes, having the best costume.

DEATH
(angry)
So don't bother us with your shit.

ZERO
(from the wing)
Your holy shit. (*a mad laugh; sticking his head out and addressing J C*) It's an aberration in the universe—the holy part! Evolution's mistake! It was a great mistake, my being born a man, I would have been mush more successful as a sea gull or a fish—sorry, *(out to the audience)* wrong play. We all make mistakes. *(stops; to J C)* Like you insisting on what's his face having a real face! When in fact he was faceless.

J C
You're a fucking liar! And this whole fucking play is a goddam shame!

DISILLUSIONMENT
I wish you wouldn't talk like that—being who you are and all. Especially in front of a nice Catholic girl like myself.

MOTHER MUD
You're a boy!

J C
(looking a very odd look at her—as if all the wind is suddenly take out of him)

But was he? *(looking around at them all)* It sucks the air out of me.

DEATH
It's a strange ghoulishly funny bit of business to be sure.

DISILLUSIONMENT
But who could be sure? About anything really?

AESCHYLUS
Einstein who lives down the hall from me firmly believes that the moon is there. *(sudden sad)* But who could be sure?

ZERO
Well, one thing is for certain.

CARMEN MIRANDA
What?

ZERO
(sticking his head out from the wing)
Right, J C? Ask the dark-haired youth with green skin—he'll be able to explain it to you.
(with a cackle he sticks his head back in the wing)

(J C just looks at the wing, and then back at them all; half there half elsewhere)

J C
No one can.

DEATH
He's gone.

CARMEN MIRANDA
So what do we do?

MOTHER MUD
Or does it matter?

AESCHYLUS
Since we're unreal!

CARMEN MIRANDA
Then why does it hurt so much?

AESCHYLUS
What a predicament—being unreal and yet having to suffer.

MOTHER MUD
Who wrote this fucking play—the Marquis de Sade?!

(As J C stands there as if a statue in a trance the toilet door opens and out darts Beeshaleak, script in hand, fumbling through it.)

BEESHALEAK
(sheepishly)
Did I miss anything? I had to go.

MOTHER MUD
We all have to go, eventually.

(They all laugh; including Aeschylus who stops suddenly.)

AESCHYLUS
That's hardly funny. Especially for me. I'll be left all alone.

MOTHER MUD
Oh please—you gotta know you're going to die! Everyone knows that.

AESCHYLUS
(shocked)
Everyone knows that I'm going to die!? *(then defiant)* It's impossible I tell you!

MOTHER MUD
You're impossible! You're as bad as that nut who said he's God!

AESCHYLUS
You mean that wasn't God? *(to Carman Miranda)* Well then who is?

CARMEN MIRANDA
Do I look like I would know?

(They all turn towards J C standing there like a statue.)

ZERO
(from the wing)
He's still digging him up.

MOTHER MUD
(screams at him as if at herself)
Doing the same thing over and over again, while expecting a different result is
madness!

CARMEN MIRANDA
(blasé)
Well we are in a madhouse.

AESCHYLUS
(shocked)
We're in a madhouse? I thought we were in a play!

DEATH
Of course we're in a play, you lunatic! *(out to the audience; apologetic)* Actors
sometimes get lost in their parts.

DISILLUSIONMENT
(also out to the audience)
After all, we're not rocket scientists—if you get my drift.

AESCHYLUS
You think rocket scientists know more than us! So they put together a machine
to carry us to the edge of the universe!
Then what I ask you!

DIRECTOR (UNSEEN OVER A MIKE)
Beeshaleak!

BEESHALEAK
(in an Indian accent and cadence)
Will you people please *please* stop this—you can't just say any ole thing! The playwright had something important in mind when he wrote the play—something vital he wants to get out to the audience through you his actors!

(Zero comes out mopping his brow and shirtless.)

ZERO
My dressing room is too fucking hot! And there are mirrors in it!

BEESHALEAK
(in an Indian accent and cadence; exasperated, tapping at his script)
Can I get someone to sing this damn aria!

ZERO
That's in the toilet now.

DEATH
The toilet—we're going to sing the aria in the toilet?

MOTHER MUD
And I suppose you want us all bare-assed to boot!

AESCHYLUS
There are Equity rules about nudity you know!

BEESHALEAK
(in an Indian accent and cadence; exasperated)
Oh, skip the damn aria . . . let's see *(pages turning and fumbled with)* go to the part on how Alice got here.

MOTHER MUD
(suddenly terrified)
Alice who?

ZERO
(naughty)
Those were her very words!

DEATH
When she first came here.
DISILLUSIONMENT
It all started with Humpty Dumpty falling off the wall.
DEATH
And being buried in Wonderland. A certain convocation of worms was called
to conviviality soon after.
CARMEN MIRANDA
And soon, the poor, dear, and hungry worms were mad.
MOTHER MUD
We are what we eat as the saying goes.
DEATH
And so the birds that ate the worms in turn went mad.
LUNATICS
And the hunter who made his stew from the felled feathery bipeds also went
mad.

BEESHALEAK
And the little girl named Alice who listened to her daddy and finished up all
her stew because he says it's good for her—she was carted off to the madhouse!
(giggles)
Asking *Alice who?*

DEATH
Can we please say our own lines!

CARMEN MIRANDA
That's what we're paid for ya know!

AESCHYLUS
We get paid?

CARMEN MIRANDA
Of course we get paid!

DISILLUSIONMENT
A jelly doughnut here.

CARMEN MIRANDA
More rec room privileges there.

DEATH
Extra tub time.

DISILLUSIONMENT
Extra time all around.

LUNATICS
(terrified)
Too much time!

MOTHER MUD
ORDERLY!

(The Lunatics become disquieted, looking this way and that, up and down, one banging his head against the window frame, another looking into one wing as if a blind alley and laughing a silent mad laugh. The lights go out on them; leaving Zero alone in a spot; then a spot comes up on J C, both silent and a bit uncomfortable with each other.)

ZERO
Why the suspenders *and* a belt?

J C
I'm trying to figure out how to be a complete clown.

ZERO
Try coffee enemas.

J C
With or without cream?

ZERO
It doesn't matter. As long as its at room temperature. Not hot, not cold, just right. Like Baby Bear's. *(very serious)* Why did you give up on him?

J C
It was the loving thing to do . . . the hopeless and loving thing to do. *(a pause)* . . . the hopeless and loving thing to do.

(Zero looks out towards where the Director is supposed to be.)

ZERO
I never understood that line. What's does it mean?

(The Director doesn't answer; and they both hold absolutely still. Then J C walks out of the light into the darkness. A spot comes up on Lilith with him walking into her spot; Zero left watching as his own light dims to opaque.)

ZERO
Mr. Chaord? Jim?

(The man he called Jim nods some and everyone holds as if in a freeze frame.)

J C
Lil?

LUNATICS
(in the dark, as if far off throughout)
It's a cold night in December. A December to remember.
LUNATIC ONE
Or forget.
LUNATIC FOUR
Forget what slouched towards Bethlehem to be born!
Well, actually, LA.
LUNATIC TWO
Go head tell'im, Lil. Tell us all.
LUNATIC FOUR
Tell us about your only begotten.
LUNATICS
Tell us, weeping *Lie*-lith! Mummy dearest!
We all want to hear what you have to say.

LILITH
(She hesitates; J C waiting.)
The baby was premature in more ways than one.

J C
(in his mind mixing both the past and the present)
Yes, I know . . . and he died shortly after.

LILITH
No.

J C
No.

(There is a breathless moment; she holds on J C.)

LILITH
He was born more deformed than could be imagined.
Very little brain tissue. A sac at the base of the skull.
It was seeping spinal fluid. He didn't even have a reflex to eat.

(J C, after all these years, still cringes with those words.)

J C
It was too much.
ZERO
De trop.
LILITH
I broke.

LUNATICS
Who wouldn't faced with that?
LUNATIC ONE
Witness to that?
LUNATIC TWO
Carrying such a heartbreak inside of them, J C?
LUNATICS THREE AND FOUR
Why was all this necessary, Jesus?
LUNATICS ONE AND TWO
We're half-wits and can't get it!

J C
(exasperated)
Tell them Lilith—tell them why he was born the way he was.

LILITH
(bursts out)

What does it matter now? They put him on maximum support and I decided to
leave any decision about what to do up to you.

LUNATICS
Lie-lith!

LILITH
I did! I did!

J C
Up to me?

(He shakes her; stopping as she stares at him.)

LILITH
I couldn't deal with it!

J C
It?!

LILITH
Yes it! There was nothing there.

ZERO
Why can't you accept that, J C?

LILITH
No, he never would—that's why I told them *(she stops)*

LUNATICS
Told them what, Mrs. Chaord?

LILITH
I told them . . .

J C
What, Lilith?

LILITH
They could do what they asked!

J C
Which was what, Lilith?

LUNATICS
Say it!
(She breaks down in tears.)
I took the sonogam—all was going OK. Then the premature birth—the way he
was—they were as shocked as me at what happened.

LUNATIC ONE
But what did happen? To it!
LUNATIC TWO
After the sorry mother it was born to and her medicine cabinet—
LUNATIC FOUR
her irresistible medicine cabinet!
LUNATICS
Yes, what happened then?

(Everyone waits.)

LILITH
Ask my husband.

J C
She put him in that place. *(his voice at first lost, then hoarse.)*
When I saw him lying there . . . *(he can't say it)*

(She nods.)

LILITH
And you were right to try.

LUNATICS
Try what?

LILITH
Listen to me . . . what I am going to say to you.
(J C controls himself; waiting.) It wasn't our son. It could never have been a son.
It wasn't a baby. It was—I don't know what it was. *(screams and cries both)* Its
eyes were flat—inhuman! There was nothing there, forchrissake!

ZERO
Why can't you accept that, gravedigger?

LUNATICS
Yes, why not, J C?

LILITH
(her hand goes towards J C's face to touch at him gently)
It would have been easier to do what you wanted that way.

(J C freezes.)

ZERO
Take care of him. Like you wanted to.

LILITH
I saw it in your eyes. The outcry in your eyes. At what happened to your baby.
Watching him lying there like that.

LUNATICS
Of course an outcry! How can we make sense of the universe—given a fact like
that?

ZERO
If God were kind, he would at least make the minor concession of anaesthetizing
caterpillars before they are eaten alive by ichneumon wasps—the minor
concession of having babies without brains never get born.

J C
(in a whisper; with a dry mouth)
Yes, he should have intervened and protected my baby.
Turned the universe upside down if he had to. *(erupts in bitterness)*
WHY DIDN'T YOU!? *(J C looks as if he's going to scream, but doesn't—only
stares.)* I trusted you.

ZERO
Peter Pan pales in comparison to you, Jesus-whoever.
You and your Neverneverland.

(J C turns and walks out of the spot; and in the dark we hear his voice.)

J C'S VOICE
I can never accept my son as soulless! I heard him moan.
I heard him moan.

(The lights go out on her, leaving Zero alone on stage.)

ZERO
No—he will never accept his only begotten's unbirthday.
And we all know why.

LUNITICS
(from the darkness)
Why?

(The spot goes out on Zero. Beeshaleak sticks his head out.)

BEESHALEAK
I have no idea why—or where we're at in this play. I do wish Brahman would
wake and end this for me! Until then, do stay seated and see how it all turns out.
It's as much a mystery to me as to you. *(pulls his head back in)*

*(The lights come up on J C, still in his clownish gravedigger costume.
He is sitting on the floor in the midst of the former carnival. Zero comes
and sits besides him with his bandolin, which he starts playing softly.)*

*(The lights come up on J C, still in his clownish gravedigger costume.
He is sitting on the floor in the midst of the former carnival. Zero comes
and sits besides him with his bandolin, which he starts playing softly.)*

ZERO
Gravedigger? Where are you?

J C
Saying grandpa's prayer.

ZERO
Signore, rammentate mi la mente. 'Lord, never let me forget my mind.'
(the trace of a smile) And if He did, you wouldn't remember anyway.

J C
(looking at Zero, dead serious)
No—there are things you never forget. *(confiding to him)* You know, I always
felt special before Jimmy—as if God was family.

ZERO
The God of my youth is gone, too. One morning you wake up and realize you
can't fly—and never could. *(sadly accepting what happened and happens)* Did
you know that the real Superman fell off a horse named Pegasus? Of course, he
really wasn't superman and the horse not really *(shrugs)*

J C
I wonder if it was the same one Nietzsche hugged? You know—on that fateful
rainy night.

ZERO
(a soft nod)
He saw a man beating a horse and stopped him, then hugged the horse and
collapsed.

J C
And when he woke, he was mad.

ZERO
The superman and his winged horse shot down over—

J C
Over the moon. Flying over the moon. The moon that Einstein says is there.

ZERO
Do you really think it's hiding some secret?

J C
Only the man in it. Just like this funny ole world.

ZERO
You're still holding out aren't you—for that something deeper still that stirs
deep inside?

(Zero nods a vigorous nod and laughs defensively.)

ZERO
You wouldn't answer Pilot, and now you won't answer me.

J C
(a Mona Lisa smile towards Zero)
I'll tell you the truth. I'm no more him than I am the man in the moon. *(sighs at the absurdity of it; then turns a serious eye towards the other man)* Why is it I can I think up better worlds than exist?
(begins reciting something he knows by heart)
Gravedigger, where are you going?
The life you pursue you shall not find.
When the mysteries that made us created humankind, madness for us they made mandatory.

ZERO
You're forgetting the best part of it.
(he begins to recite it)
Gravedigger, let your belly be full,
Make merry by day and by night.
Of each day make a feast of rejoicing,
Day and night, dance and play!

J C
(tears welling in his eyes)
Pay heed to the little one that holds on to your hand,
Let your life delight in love!
For all this is the way of humans.

(They finish and look at one another.)

ZERO
Life is sweet—

J C
When it works.

ZERO
And if God isn't love—

J C
He should be.

(There is a silence between them.)

J C
Did you know that the very first of our line—the oldest humanoid we know of, they call him Dawn—was found hanging in a tree. I have a deep affinity for him.

ZERO
Yes, you would.

(Zero holds on him.)

(The lights go out; there is a howl from a dog; then silence. The lights come up on a bizarre courtroom. There are dressed manikins as the court spectators, Zero in prosecutorial robes, and a panel of judges with Mother Mud as Chief Justice Peedapadee, wearing a large white wig, Disillusionment as Justice O'Daffy, wearing Carmen Miranda's hear-gear, and Beeshaleak as Justice Alles Zermelmer, wearing a Cardinal's miter. In the dock is J C.)

AESCHYLUS
(ringing a hand bell)
Hear ye, hear ye, my play will come to order.

CHIEF JUSTICE
(correcting him)
The *court* will come to order!

AESCHYLUS

The *court* will come to order! Chief Justice Peedapadee
(she waves regally), along with Justices O' Daffy and Alles Zermelmer will
preside.
(With that he looks out to the audience.)
I know you're all wondering about their names, so I'll explain.

CHIEF JUSTICE

Stifle it! Call the play to order!

AESCHYLUS

Hear ye, hear ye, the *court (giving her a look of correction) w*ill come to order.
Only three Justices presiding. The other six are in therapy session with Doctors
Mortadella, Mengele, and Torquemada. I know you're all wondering about their
names, so—

CHIEF JUSTICE

A playwright is not supposed to explain his play.
That is what he leaves for the audience to do!
(abruptly with the proper airs)
Now who is in the dock?

AESCHYLUS

Jesus Christ.

CHIEF JUSTICE

(aside to the audience)
You certainly know where this is headed with that moniker.
Proceed.

AESCHYLUS

Alias We-Were-Hoping, alias—

CHIEF JUSTICE

Whoever—get on with it!

AESCHYLUS

He stands accused of the unforgivable sin!

(Everyone is aghast. The Chief Justice rising from her chair.)

CHIEF JUSTICE
The implications of this are too staggering to mention, namely, that he can really miss meals, pass wind in the corridor, and do other stuff *(eyeing him)* in the toilet!

JUSTICE O'DAFFY
Outrageous! Who do ya think y'are!

JUSTICE ALLES ZERMELMER
Well whoever you are you won't get away with it!
Off with his head!

AESCHYLUS
No—first we have the trial.

JUSTICE ALLES ZERMELMER
What kind of a court is this?

CHIEF JUSTICE
(standing with pomp and ceremony)
The Supreme Court of the United States of America!

(She sighs and sits and then looks towards the wing.)

CHIEF JUSTICE
Now, will someone tell the defense lawyer to get out here so we can condemn this man!

(Aeschylus runs over and puts his head into the wing as if getting a message; then runs back to the others.)

AESCHYLUS
He refuses to come out! His hair still hasn't grown in.

CHIEF JUSTICE
(putting on her spectacles and looking anxiously around)
OK—then just proceed with the execution.

ZERO
The prosecution.

CHIEF JUSTICE
Whatever!

ZERO
Jesus whoever, you stand accused—

CHIEF JUSTICE
Of the unforgivable sin!

ZERO
He says he has a birthday!

CHIEF JUSTICE
(turning to the audience)
But since he doesn't, I don't want you to believe a word he says.

JUSTICE ALLES ZERMELMER
Just because he said it!

JUSTICE O'DAFFY
Exactly—it doesn't mean a thing. Jost act as ef he's not there.

AESCHYLUS
Certainly not all there.

CHIEF JUSTICE
You certainly can't deny that. Case closed!

J C
But you haven't told me why that is the unforgivable sin!
It's only a birthday.

CHIEF JUSTICE
Only a birthday he says.

JUSTICE O'DAFFY
The man is blind.

(A blind man comes out the wing; feeling his way across with a cane.)

BLIND MAN
Is that the gravedigger I heard? Finally?

AESCHYLUS
No—not yet. Wait for your cue!

CHIEF JUSTICE
He's here to testify against you.

J C
Who is he? I've never seen him before.

JUSTICE O'DAFFY
Of curse not, he's blind.

J C
I can see that.

JUSTICE O'DAFFY
Well thenk you're lucky star ya can.

JUSTICE ALLES ZERMELMER
Cause he can't! When the poor fellow looks in the mirror he's not there.

ZERO
Which proves the prosecution's case!
(to the Justices)
I think it's time for an opinion of the court.

CHIEF JUSTICE
(She stands and shakes her hips.)
I'll tell you everything I can, there's little to relate. I saw an aged aged man, ass-sitting on a gate. 'Who are you, aged aged man?' I said. 'And how is it you live?'

JUSTICE O'DAFFY
'I look for bubbles,' he answered. 'That lie inside my head.
And bake them into apple pies and sell them to keep fed.'

JUSTICE ALLES ZERMELMER
Remember—we are what we eat!

CHIEF JUSTICE
(nodding)
That's why we promote eating humans—to make you more human.

JUSTICE O'DAFFY
We haven't deeseeded what teastes best though.

AESCHYLUS
Yellow meat or white? Black, brown, beige or pink?

CHIEF JUSTICE
It would be politically incorrect to say.

JUSTICE ALLES ZERMELMER
As long as we do not wait till they are dead. You don't get the full nutritional value of what you eat then.

JUSTICE O'DAFFY
Yes—they must be eaten while they are alive.

CHIEF JUSTICE
Like with the caterpillar. Ask the ichneumon wasp.
(suddenly serious) And us!

AESCHYLUS
(terrified)
No—not *us*! We're not in my play!
None of *us* can be! Otherwise—

J C
(interrupting)
But how can you be trying me if you aren't here?

CHIEF JUSTICE
Not all here, there are six of us missing. Now do you know your rights? Unattainable according to the Constitution!

ZERO
Unalienable.

CHIEF JUSTICE
Whatever.

J C
What do you mean whatever!

CHIEF JUSTICE
Just what I said—whatever—whatever we say goes.
(sternly to J C)
And since you don't realize that, we'll teach you.

JUSTICE O'DAFFY
Reach you!

JUSTICE ALLES ZERMELMER
Breech you!

JUSTICE O'DAFFY
(angry at him)
Eat you!

J C
What?

CHIEF JUSTICE
Yes, we know—it's a slight deviation! But what the hell!

JUSTICE O'DAFFY
It's one wey to get rid of the evidence.

CHIEF JUSTICE
Just like you did.

J C
What are you babbling about now? If you're talking about *(stops)*

JUSTICE ALLES ZERMELMER
(prompting him)

Yes?

J C
(somewhat lost)
I couldn't—

ZERO
Yes, gravedigger? Couldn't what—can't say? No matter, we'll let *him* tell us
himself. Where's our main witness?

*(The Chief Justice nods and everyone turns towards the wing, waiting. A moment,
please. Then lead out from the wing by Orderly One comes the black-haired
youth with greenish skin, entirely idiotic, moving nothing but his sunken eyes
and looking absolutely non-human. As Orderly One leaves, on his own the young
man walks up to J C in the dock and stares.)*

ZERO
Do you recognize this creature, J C?
(J C doesn't answer.) No need to incriminate yourself. *(to the Court)*
He pleads the Fiftieth amendment.

BLIND MAN
Shouldn't that be the Fifth?

CHIEF JUSTICE
That are a lot of things that should be, that aren't.

BLIND MAN
I see what you mean.

CHIEF JUSTICE
Miracle—the blind man sees! Now if only the defendant would!
But we'll make him. *(to creature)* You there, didn't the gravedigger say in act
one, that you were born! Have the court read his very words.

AESCHYLUS
I have it right here '—it's what you've been *born* to—' his very words!
(insisting to the creature) Answer the question!

J C
He can't answer you.

CHIEF JUSTICE
Exactly! And why is that, gravedigger? Because he never was born!

ZERO
(a short wait; then turning to the creature) Better to have an unbirthday wouldn't
you say? *(to J C)* Wouldn't you say?

JUSTICE O'DAFFY
Ef the trooth bee knoown.

CHIEF JUSTICE
Yet you would condemn him to a birthday.

JUSTICE ALLES ZERMELMER
And us with him!
And thus have committed the unforgivable sin!

(J C looks a pathetic look over towards the creature.)

ZERO
And what are you thinking now, gravedigger. *(He looks at the creature, and
mockingly addresses him.)* Nevertoolatetolove, Jimmy?

J C
*(His voice has that slight tremble of uncertainty that finds expression in human
vocal cords when a person with no where to turn thinks about what comes next.)*
Maybe.
(It even has the thought of surrender in it.) That always haunted me . . .
and still does. *(to Zero)* You're right there. But wrong about the other thing.

ZERO
What is that, gravedigger?

J C
What I thought this was really about. *(There is a moment.)* I didn't have to do
that. *(As he stands there, a silvery spot comes up on Lilith silently looking on.)*
Bitter as the loss was, it was a blessing I had asked for.

ZERO
So why are you so tortured about it then? Because you wanted him to die?

J C

Profoundly so! But still that's not it. Any father would have wanted that. He was a creature who should never have been born . . . but was . . . did have a birthday . . . my poor baby . . . my beautiful baby boy whom I only named long after, trying to give him significance . . .
(his voice drops off, then returns)
Trying to remember him as bouncy when he wasn't.
No, this guilt . . . this profound guilt I feel . . . has to do with something else I know about myself and my son. *(He stops.)*

ZERO
What?

J C

I didn't love him. *(a stare)* Not as much as I thought. All my talk about ending his sorry state was out of love, yes! And my wanting him to die! And thankful when he did! Relieved really!
All out of love! But not for him—*for myself!*

(There is a moment.)

J C

Do you see—understand?
(Zero nods.) Even if I would have killed him, I wouldn't have been doing it for him—saving him by my thoughtful act. Just the opposite! I would have been saving me—my life! From carrying him through his! And so I never really loved him! Not really! Not enough to give up my life for his! Me for him!

(J C goes silent with those words. The sad face looks up again at the eyes studying him.)

J C

And yet . . . and yet . . .

(His voice falls off and Zero waits.)

J C

And yet *(finding his voice again)* I believe I would have. I vowed it.
Beside his bed the horrible empty day before I never saw him again—in the purest act of love in all my life. And I meant it, even though I felt I had descended into

hell and would stay there for the rest of my life if he did live on. It would have been the loving thing to do—the hopeless and loving thing to do.

ZERO
(shaken some)
No doubt you would have grown tired at times—weary with the daily care—as people who take care of a sick loved one do—grow tired—weary.

J C
Even lost patience. I was willing though—at that moment—willing to go all the way. But would you have, I ask myself in still moments—was my love for real?

ZERO
(Zero studies J C.)
You'll never really know that will you, gravedigger? You *didn't* have to go all the way as you say. So you will never *really* know will you, gravedigger? No greater love hath a man than he lay down his life for—

J C
What about his mind?

ZERO
Are you saying what I think you're saying?

J C
There are worse things than death. More generous, too, perhaps.

ZERO
An insane generosity if ever! (*smiles a mad smile*) Like your God, J C? To love expecting nothing in return, not even love? You preach a strange catechism, Jesus-whoever.

BLIND MAN
You're the looniest of the loonies, gravedigger!

J C
Perhaps, but as a gravedigger I can tell you—

BLIND MAN
Tell us what? About death?

J C

About something I suspect even surprises death.

ZERO

Even as we shit ourselves and piss our pants?

J C

And do our toiletry during life as well.

ZERO

(in a mocking tone)

And what about those that can't? Like Baby Boo Boo here? Creatures who can't even wipe their own asses? Let alone have a thump in their hearts!

BLIND MAN

Don't you see why he must say what he does?

ZERO

I see alright! What you want is preposterous, Mr. Chaord.

A preposterous hope of inter-connecting, myriad-level entangle—ments of neurological meat, which somehow can say *I. I am!*

Am on the lamb! Have some strawberry jam. It's all a scam.

Admit it!

CHIEF JUSTICE

Admit an unbirthday for him and for you! For all of us!

J C

No.

CHIEF JUSTICE

It's much easier that way!

J C

No—I am real, suffering is real, love is real!

CHIEF JUSTICE

Do you think you have victory over the chaos with this nonsense of yours?!

Victory over this? *(pointing at the black-haired youth)*

(J C does not answer, but goes up and kisses the black-haired youth on the mouth.)

BLIND MAN
He's hopeless. Hanging there in his mind. Abandoned by even the Mystery that made him. Yet still clinging to this aberration of his!

CHIEF JUSTICE
Yes—aberration!

BLIND MAN
Despite the hard facts of life proving him wrong! He who has contradicted life itself with his God of pure love is left hanging alone on his cross. Love is! It is dying with him. *In the face of fact!*
To miss that is not only to miss this man and what he has to say, but to miss the problem it presents for everyone who talks of love in the face of the facts of this world. I can even see that, Jesus-whoever!

ZERO
Out of the mouth of babes and blind men!

JUSTICE O'DAFFY
Llwyd Josus, Jim, what's this whiskey in you, telling you it's ne'ver too late to luv?

CHIEF JUSTICE
You ole fool, you ole fat fool, you ole fat *fatherless* fool. Can't you see what even a blind man can? *(turning towards the creature and pointing)* Accept that he's not there!

ZERO
(shakes the creature by the chin.)
Made so by Ole Mother Hubbard—with her peculiar cupboard?
(at which Lilith covers her face with both her hands) Or was it by God himself—with his peculiar caring? *(a heartbeat)*
Anyway, no one is inside of those eyes! Despite what J C over here would have us believe. *Niente. Nada. Nicht und null.*

CHIEF JUSTICE
Niente. Nada.

JUSTICE ALLES ZERMELMER
Nicht und null. No self and love! Much too late for that.

THE BLIND MAN
(as Wilbur it appears)
And yet . . . at such time we play music or he hears music in his unfortunate head . . . oratorios and passions, requiems and symphonies . . . heavenly choirs . . .

JUSTICE O'DAFFY
(without his Irish accent; as Patrick)
He forgets, as it were, his biology, his booboos, his bashed in brain, and a sense of great spacious satisfaction takes hold of him.

JUSTICE ALLES ZERMELMER
(as Beeshaleak)
And more amazing, not only can he repeat the scores heard, but create new ones . . . eerie otherworldly music.

ZERO
(laughs bitterly and goes on in an Indian accent and cadence)
What is going on here? *(totally exasperated; now mimicking an Irish accenty)* Is there any hupe for any of'em?
(accusation at all of them) Is there? Do you think giving Jimmy boy a soul will change it any—any of it?! Make what happened to him—to you—to Alice over here, to all you hopeless creatures any more bearable?! *(standing with accusation; he starts to rip off his cloths.)* Accept the situation for what it is—the naked truth!

MOTHER MUD
Orderly!

(Just then Beeshaleak's cell phone rings and he frantically answers it, coming to attention and listening.)

BEESHALEAK
(to the others)
It's the Head of the Hospital. I don't know what to tell him.

ZERO
(now half naked as he looks over at him)

Tell him that life is not symmetrical and people don't die alphabetically, Chutney.

(Zero laughs a mad laugh looks out at the audience, and then seems to lose his breath.)

ZERO
But that they do live and die . . . *(He is suffocating some, in dread.)*
I guess the physical laws do apply to me. And that's the punch line, Jim . . .
(trailing) The world, unfortunately, *is* real; I, unfortunately am, too.
I was born! We all were.

(His head falls forward—as those around him rush to him—Mother Mud yelling back towards Beeshaleak.)

MOTHER MUD
Fill in forchrissake!

(Beeshaleak, runs to the front of the stage looking out at the audience; and proceeds to adlib like a nervous stand up comic.)

BEESHALEAK
In India they do. Die alphabetically—we like things to be done—
Orderly! *(regaining himself)* For example, when men who say they can attain
remarkable degrees of control over their bodies, do so *(looking back somewhat to watch them pick Zero up and start to carry him towards the wing)* like bringing
their heartbeats down to zero—oh I do hope his isn't—a sensible procedure is
followed. We throw them in the Ganges. *(looks at the opposite wing for help)*
And wait.

(With that, he looks nervously over as the others proceed towards the opposite wing, like a procession, carrying Zero, the blind man tapping his cane as they go, leading the creature by the hand as he does. They exit and Lilith, like the painted howl, screams a silent scream as if in slow motion, the spot going out on her.)

BEESHALEAK
We keep waiting—until the elephants weep—looking up as they are
being chased by firing hunters in helicopters—dentists from America
out for holiday. Then we know. Oh, I do hope the elephants don't weep.

(The lights go out on the court; then come up again on Zero and J C. Both sit looking out the large crooked framed window, towards the rain, fun-house mirrors to either side of them. Both are in hospital gowns, each holding a bottle of red wine.)

J C
Zero?

ZERO
What? Is it dinnertime? No knives allowed I know. What are we having tonight? Chutney? *(looking a sad look back to J C)*

J C
Are you feeling better?

ZERO
Better than you—you look terrible.

J C
An old man has to look like this. It comes with the territory.

ZERO
Is that what I have to look forward to then?

J C
The older you get, more and more the past makes up most of you—until you're in the past tense yourself. Parsed out of existence just when you think you know what it's all about.

ZERO
What a sentence!

(J C looks around and catches himself in the fun-house mirror, getting up and walking over to one, standing there looking at himself in it.)

ZERO
You remind me of mad Joanna. The daughter of Ferdinand and Isabella.

J C
I thought it was someone else I reminded you of?

(Zero comes over and stands beside J C, both looking at their images.)

ZERO
Everywhere she went; she carried the embalmed remains of her husband, Philip the Fair. They put her away of course. Not in a madhouse. They didn't have madhouses in those days. Only ships. Ships of fools they called them.

J C
We all carry around our corpses. Trying to makes sense out of their coming into this world . . . and their going out.

ZERO
(makes a Tourette gesture)
Makes you wonder doesn't it?

J C
And end up a failed philosopher.

ZERO
(He touches at him.)
Even if you do end up an old man living without a pension and no children to look after you, no wife to care for you in your decline; unloved and alone until a mechanized gravedigger buries you in the past tense forever—so what? You've had thoughts no man has ever had.

J C
No—I am sure others have had these thoughts. Certainly everyone in here!

(An unseen parrot)
'Let's all go barmy! And join the army! Let's all go ravy!
And join the navy!'

J C
(bursting into song; pulling Zero to dance)
See the world in all its mirth!

ZERO
(joining in)
Let's all get lazy then all go crazy! See the world for what it's worth!

(Zero waits for the next line from J C. Instead, J C hugs at the surprised man; holding on as if for dear life while lifting and dancing him around.)

ZERO
(happily, like a child being introduced to a new game)
What's up?

J C
What's up? What's down? What's upside down?

ZERO
What's in?

J C
What's in? What's out? What's inside out?

(J C interrupts his part of the duet with a sudden choking which soon becomes a coughing fit. It breaks off their dance and leaves Zero practically holding J C up. Zero takes him by the arm and leads him back to a window chair—sitting him and fussing at him as only a spot holds on them.)

ZERO
Suppose I get you some hot soup and bread—with maybe a splash of cognac? Cognac always helps. *(touching at how cold he is; worried)*
I often use it myself when I'm cold. How does that sound to you?

J C
I'm so nervous. My mother was too. Just before—

ZERO
(getting panicky)
Then the soup will help.

J C
No, don't go.

ZERO
Don't you either!

(Zero sits beside J C.)

J C
(looking out the window)
It's a funny ole world. A funny ole world.

ZERO
Do you honestly think it *might* be hiding some secret on us after all?

J C
(looking at Zero; leaning towards him, almost nose to nose)
It's not hidden.

(J C touches at Zero's face, then suddenly J C falls forward, startling Zero.)

ZERO
What is it—are you having a seizure?!

J C
No—just dying.

BEESHALEAK (FROM THE WING)
(in an Indian accent and cadence)
Dying?! I don't have anyone dying. That's not part of the play!

J C
It's part of every play, Chutney.

ZERO
(panicking)
Let's change it. All of it!

J C
Think up better plays than exist?

ZERO
Call it a re-write, my right, setting it right!

J C
(studying Zero and his remark)
Your face resembles every face I have ever seen in this funhouse since.

ZERO
Since?

(J C's eyes take in the faces of the audience and he nods.)

J C
Did I ever tell you about my first day here, at Saint Haha's?
I hadn't noticed her.

(A spot comes up on a woman in a red terry cloth robe, looking sideways, so her face can't be seen, and clutching at a chalice.)

J C
When I first came in. She was standing to the far side of the foyer.
But the noise brought my full focus over to the weeping. She stood there in the stark shadows under the large cross on the wall, with a chalice in her hand. She no doubt had taken it from the chapel.
The poor creature violently shook at it—again and again.

(He pauses as if he can actually see her.)

J C
Finally, she just stood there staring as if waiting for something to happen. I went over to her and she looked up at me. There was someone inside those eyes telling me they wanted a better world than all this. Something deeper still than the neurological devastation she had become.
(There is a moment.)
A residue of someone with a name, however scarred and shattered, held on me. I was facing a ruined life, and yet saw at that moment, and perhaps only for a moment, the depth of the woman.

(He starts for her . . . and comes into the spot with the woman.)

J C
I tried to lift the holy grail from her desperate clutch . . . but the tortured creature clung to it. *(As she does.)* She fixed on it with a stare that sent shivers to my very soul.

(The woman turns out in full face—she is Lilith, but older. There is a held moment.)

J C
I had no answer for the wrenching question in that suffering stare. But she had one for me.

(He stops for a moment and the spot goes out on Lilith, J C walking out of the darkness.)

J C
She died that very night—without a rewrite. She was the first person I buried here. Lot eight, near the statue of Our Lady of the Unborn. *(Pause)* I was left to take care of the black-haired youth in Ward Z.

LUNATICS
(from out of the darkness)
The black-haired youth with greenish skin, entirely idiotic . . . moving nothing but his blank eyes and looking absolutely non-human.

ZERO
He reminded you of him? Like you remind me of Christ?

J C
I am Christ.

LUNATICS
(from out of the darkness)
A gravedigger always touches at the truth underneath the underneath and the undertaker, too.

(J C turns and looks at Zero.)

J C
I lost my little boy. I couldn't protect him. Couldn't save him.
I saw his mouth gasping for air. He died like that . . . so brave.
A bitter blessing. He was gone. I lost my little boy. I'm tired, Zero.
Very tired.

(Zero looks at J C and neither says anything for a long moment.)

J C
The world unfortunately is real; I, unfortunately am, too.

ZERO
Are you sure about that?

J C.
I am sure only of my own faltering human love and really nothing more. *(nods a soft nod)* You see I did dig up God.

(His voice falls off; a wind comes up and the sound of a distant train.)

LUNATICS
(from out of the darkness; exaggerated, a la a Greek chorus)
Ton thronein brotous odosana, ton patheimathos thenta kurios exein.

LUNATIC THREE
God—who is he? Whatever name he chooses, by it will I cry out to him, mortal as I am and to whom wisdom is won in madness!
Madness, which cannot forget, falls drop by drop upon the heart, until, despite us, comes wisdom through the awful grace of God.

ZERO
They think you've dug up more than you know, gravedigger.

J C
I've dug up God. Everyone I loved. Everyone who loved me.
(touches at Zero's face) Even if none of us can understand, not me, not them, we can love. *(There is a moment.)*
When I see beauty and goodness and love, especially the goodness and beauty of love—even if I am alone in a madhouse—I grasp God.

(Zero wipes at his nose with his bare arm, holding, as if thinking about what J C said.)

ZERO
It'll be fun, my aging Huckleberry Finn, my old honeybunch of frolic. Doing more plays together. *(He shakes his head up and down.)* It'll be great. I can see it now.

J C
I wasn't built for greatness, but to be the wind. Just the wind.

(looks at Zero, with such profound failure in his look) I never harnessed the wind, only fought windmills. Never wrote a symphony. Do you hear it—Beethoven playing down the hall?

ZERO
I don't hear anything.

(J C stars directly at Zero, a hesitation in his eyes.)

J C
But still, still in the still night, I have to ask, why, Jimmy?
Why did it still have to be the way it was?

ZERO
People suffer, what can I say, Jim.

(Just then the dog howls.)

ZERO
His hair is growing in. You think if I shave him again, he'll tell?

J C
He already has. Listening to the cries of the world, one knows—*(his voice drops off into silence)*

(Beeshaleak comes out from the wing, gingerly.)

BEESHALEAK
(in an Indian accent and cadence)
Mister Chaord—you're supposed to finish the line. *(prompting)*
'Knows how . . .'

(J C shakes his head no.)

BEESHALEAK
(in an Indian accent and cadence)
But it says right here, Mister Chaord, you do.

(The lights come up on the Lunatics standing in the great window; as Zero runs away as if he can't face what is going to happen.)

LUNATIC ONE
Knows how to what?
LUNATIC THREE
What are we supposed to know how to do?
LUNATIC TWO
Please finish the line.

J C
(He looks out to the audience with the trace of the slightest of smiles)
Our audience is much too intelligent for me to do that.

LUNATICS
Really?

J C
(as if listening)
He's up and at it again! Listen! The suffering genius is confounded in his love
before it reaches for the impossible and achieves it, his great fugue ending with
an embrace of incredulous relief—

LUNATIC ONE
What?

J C
With a thankfulness still tinged with hesitation, but with a coherence of the
profoundest attitude towards life and the Mystery that made him.

LUNATIC TWO
I don't hear anything.

LUNATIC THREE
Me neither.

J C
Listen! Listen, the suffering genius is telling us that relief from suffering comes
only in the embrace of this mysticism without ecstasy, even as he lifts us into
ecstasy.

LUNATICS
What ecstasy?

J C
Without ecstasy! *(he laughs to himself softly)*
I once knew a girl name Joanna. Who was as they say a *butana!* She road off one day. In a most unusual way.
Mounted on the Dali Lama!

(He laughs again, his little laugh; talking a hard breath, just as Zero returns.)

J C
There was a young man called Bright, whose speed was much faster than light; he went out one day in a relative way, and came back the previous night!

ZERO
(quietly)
He's up and at it again. He had enough of that mud, give him back his ole blood, being dead isn't all it's cracked up to be.

J C
(looks directly at Zero who appears to be waiting, tearing.)
Come to my arms, my beamish boy! O frabjous day! Callooh! Callay!

ZERO
(crying himself)
Now don't go all juicy-eyed on me!

J C
It's time. How hopelessly human of me.

ZERO
You can't go. You're the gravedigger.

J C
The man who dug up God. In ward WXYZ. He sits all day looking out at the night sky. Drooling. Murmuring he is the greatest mystery or nothing at all. Then gambols and grins, *(he starts to shake)* shakes his sides, points his finger, turns up his nose—and finally pees his pants and shits himself. Holding there until lights out. Making a leap of love.

(The wind comes up and the lights go out on the two, leaving only the Lunatics.)

LUNATICS
The play by the inmates at Saint Hilary's Asylum for the Hopelessly
Insane is over.

(*From their great window sadly they wave good-bye out at the audience with slow*
gambols and strange grins, shaking their sides, pointing their fingers, turning
up their noses—then shooting out their tongues with an odd pathos as the lights
go out on them, as simultaneously a lone spot comes up on Zero, at the apron of
the stage looking out at the audience.)

ZERO
I didn't want any rituals. I just wanted it to be honest for Mr. JimChaord, case
study 1938, alias Jesus Christ—like all of us.
Alias We Were Hoping—like all of us. Alias whoever—like all of us.
I won't go into what the death of someone you love does to you with its torturing
thousand if onlys and why nots—how it leaves you—except to say the world
empties and will never be the same. *(looking over towards the dark)*
I told him—if such things are possible, let's meet again. *(looking back at the*
audience) I already know what I will put on his gravestone: 'I'll love you till I
die . . . *(shrugs)* Jimmy.' He called me that you know—you all know why.

(*He wipes a tear from his eye and walks into a spot that comes up behind the one*
he was in, deeper into the stage, turning again to the audience.)

ZERO
He said he wasn't ready to go. Afraid some, to stay with him. And in such great
pain. He was so brave. I prayed for him to live, but . . .
Dressing for a burial is slow. The empty feeling in your stomach follows you in its
vague reference to everything, and yet you know you should and must celebrate
that life. No, love does not protect us against suffering. What it does is—well
you know—it ties the air together.

(*There is a slight pause.*)

ZERO
It was his challenge to the whole of everywhere. Holding it all at bay.
With the secret that surprises life. Death and everything inanimate must be so
jealous he would tell me. He was a madman you say? His last *mad* words perhaps
say it all. "I want you to know I love you."

(he chokes up) "I want you to know that love is the mystery that surprise life. I want you to know that I am and I can love." Did that make him too childish-foolish for this world, a drooling dying creature defecating and peeing his pants in the end—too insane for life on planet earth? Or too sane? You decide.

(With that, he walks into a spot behind the last one, further back, turning again to the audience.)

ZERO

You should know before I leave—know that he came to me. With a magnificent smile on his face. In a radiant joy. I don't know what the hell it means. Is love the mystery that surprised death, too? *(a soft smile comes across his face as he mouths 'too insane, or too sane?' and then shrugs as if to say you decide.)*

(A distant viola starts up and then the sound of wind. As he turns to leave, the spot goes out. It is over.)

Supermetaphysics

The play ended with these questions and stage directions: "Is love the mystery that surprised death, too?" *(a soft smile comes across his face as he mouths 'too insane, or too sane?' and then shrugs as if to say you decide.)* A soft smile has to come to my face as well. Is love about to surprise us yet again, take us somewhere over the rainbow, where Peter Pan flies again and the summer winds blow again? Or is it more like where a tiny whispering sound, ever so gentle, a voice of thin silence tells of a somewhere beyond rainbows and remembrances, poetry and plays, music and mere metaphysics? And is that too insane? Or . . .

From what we have ventured to so far I would like to allow the mind, in an unedited, uninhibited, unharnassed freedom, perhaps form of madness too, to go all the way with love and for a fractal, a moment, a chapter at least, past all the moananoaning and mud, mentalrot and mendacity, wonder about and wander into a Supermetaphysics. As the name connotes, it is not only meta the physical, but meta the meta itself. It is bound to make postmoderns sweat and swear, and seek a subpoena to search my mind for any sign of sanity, to be sure. Yes, I readily admitted it is already unharnassed and uninhibited, and now add unspeakable, too; that it is beyond the beyond . . . and yet, and yet, because of the same surprise that surprises our very breathing, I can dare to write what I will write in this chapter and call a Supermetaphysics. It is the way I would have it, if I had my way, true, and in that it may merely be a passion for the impossible, a compulsion for the quixotic, an immersion into towering babble and muttering mania—but then again it might actually be love surprising us with Love itself.

I can dare to say the latter, because and only because of the fact that what I am about to put forth here is firmly rooted in the foundation we have already established; even as it is already making my head wonder if it is still attached to the rest of my body. *Ma perche 'l tempo fugge che t'assona, qui farem punto . . .*

*e drizzeremo li occhi al primo amore, si che, guadando verso lui, penetri quant' e
possibil per suo fulgore . . . e tu mi seguirai con l'affezione, si che dal dicer mio lo
cor non parti. But though time flies as in a dream-like trip, we shall stop and take
our bearing here . . . and turn in our mind's eye to Primal Love, so that, holding
tight onto our version of God, we may penetrate as deeply as we can into God's
radiant Presence . . . therefore follow me with love so that what I say and your
heart share one way.*[1]

And so, with Dante ringing in our ears we enter beyond the portal of
metaphysics into love's surprise, and Love's, too!

I said when discussing prayer that it opens you up to the depths beyond
being and nonbeing both—what did I mean by such a confusing if not confused
statement? I meant that when you give your heart to a *contemplatio ad amorem,*
at a profound moment, sans any ecstasy and despite the winter in our eyes, a
warmth arrives and it opens one to a reciprocal abiding in the Mystery from
which all emanates, even as I am sure only of my own faltering human love
and really nothing more. And yet in the language of God I am. It's wordless.
It is entering beyond the portal of words and metaphysics both, into love's
ultimate surprise, a Mystery that loves you back. Therein is the true God,
beyond the awe and vastness of the universe, beyond good and evil, being and
nonbeing—where all words fail and fall off the page. No matter, on a wing
and a prayer, I will try to conjure up words despite the linguistic annihilation
that awaits me, I will attempt to articulate this impossible feat, I will fight my
own sure thing of limited fragile and faltering human love, and foolishly try
to tell of God's. "GIVING! GIVING! GIVING!" That all I can stutter out as
we begin! And maybe as we finish, too!

We struggled with it in the chapter on tying the air together, but that was
in the context of a divine dialectic on love. Now as we go beyond rainbows and
remembrances, poetry and plays, music and mere metaphysics, beyond any divine
dialectic and into GIVING itself, without anything further about more and More,
except to say this is the way I would have it, I suspect that sober minds will indeed
say we have entered Saint HaHa's asylum for the theologically insane. And in a
way we have, sitting with JC in his toilet and carrying that love he spoke of to
its unchained, unseen, unoriginated, uncreated, unborn, unformed, uneverything
ultimate, where not only reason but mysticism itself breaks down. Yet it is not
without reason and mysticism, at least the mysticism without ecstasy we call
love, and thus at least somewhat reasonable, in that we have experienced that at
least, even as we come out of the toilet repeatedly stuttering one word over and
over and over again, as if it told all, my overcharged brain suddenly bursting out
that "we have entered beyond the portal of metaphysics, beyond being itself,
beyond the great void, too, into the Incomprehensible Intimacy!"

Saints and scholars alike might rightly be upset with me, for such a notion as God has always been limited to Being Itself both in philosophy and religion, or limited to the absence of Being, the Void and nothingness & nowhere; either or, depending on where you are coming from, the East or the West, positive theology or negative theology, and so on. But now we are looking at it all in a different light; namely, GIVING as before being and non-being, yet without eliminating either.

As such, a different God comes into focus for us. We have already gone through the notion of GIVING, in the tying together chapter, so I won't go through that again; except to remind you that it was through our own love, our deepest experience in being, that we came to at least touch upon this Incomprehensible notion. Now, continuing on with this—from the other end this time—we can say that this article-less Mystery GIVING *loved* us into existence, loved everything into existence, even the nowhere and nothing out of which a somewhere and something came. Of course, by saying "GIVING loved" I have committed a terrible error, since it can't be in the past tense, since GIVING is without time. However, since we do exist in the river of time, I can at least use the past tense from our perspective, or use the concept of God entering time. It really isn't important to what we are about here. Also, while we are at it, I should mention that by saying "GIVING loved" I have committed a terrible redundancy, which by now I am sure I do not have to explain. Finally, it should be said, in all that, we still don't grasp GIVING as such, because we can't think in terms of no entity-agent acting, it is contrary to our head gear, but that is exactly what we have in GIVING, *just* (if I can use that word) GIVING, GIVING acting out of what it is, before being and non-being both, the unchained, unseen, unoriginated, uncreated, unborn, unformed, uneverything, the incomprehensible source GIVING, that is, LOVING. And what that means, and has to mean, is a different kind of metaphysics, one where love is primary, unconditional love.

I am not using being as the basis. For God is beyond being, though old metaphysics, as I said, always made God *Being Itself*, at least in the West, all the way to Heidegger who makes it whatever he does, the first principle it seems from one's read of the great philosopher. No matter, there have been different ways to express *Being Itself*, but that is the basic and universal idea, subsistence in *Ipsum Esse* to use old terminology. It is the *Seinsfrage,* that is, the Being-Question. All metaphysicians, medieval and modern, really ground our being in Being, whatever they end up calling it. Even a God coming out of the future as some do—a waited for God coming into Being. And in the East there are other ways of expressing it, there the absence of Being, or Void as final, as I already pointed out; Being still used as the definer, however now as its opposite. But I am saying that love can alter both these ways of thinking, and in doing so create a different metaphysics—actually a meta metaphysics.

How again?

To start, ironic as it sounds, let's use some old metaphysical terminology that might help in grasping the supermetaphysical; and that would be by carrying love to its absolute in the Absolute. This is done by Absolute Love acting, carrying out itself, the only way it can, with total love, totally giving of what it is, in true *mutua inhaesio* with regards ourselves, so that it is beyond at the center of each of us, which is what is meant by making us in its image and likeness. We will come back to that, but for now let's continue with God per se. There is no Abyss of Godhead underlying or behind this or anything else we have yet to get to, GIVING is it. This is so in all its mystery, beyond understanding except through the understanding of love. To grasp that is not only to grasp our own creation, but what I am saying here.

Let me elaborate, if for no other reason than to help me understand what I am saying here. In our present discussion of divine love, the veil is not lifted but becomes gossamer—so when we talk of GIVING, we do not really have a metaphysics, that is where being is the basic, or non-being either, but GIVING preceding being itself . . . and the nothing and nowhere that came before being as well. It is before the Void.[2] Concerning the Void, I would like to make mention that it was something some mean-spirited monk in Sri Lanka inflicted on Buddha, when Siddhartha more likely was talking in terms of the Unborn, Unoriginated, Uncreated, Unformed as he himself says of his mystical experience about Nirvana, or as it was written down and called five hundred years after his death, the Third Dharma Seal, which would better be approached the way I think Buddha intended. And if he didn't intend it thusly, we are past the Void anyway, into what gave forth to it. This sense of GIVING behind being itself, as well as non-being, the nowhere and nothing we spoke of, is what confuses metaphysicians and mystics alike—and stops me in my cerebral tracks as well. This is so even with Eckhart, whom I have mentioned before. I can only wonder how he existed so alone in the world he did with his insights, and admire him for it. Yet, the God he ends up with is very different than the God of this chapter. We go together only so far and then part profoundly. Let me explain . . .

To my amazement I was moved by some of the startling things he wrote, things that do border on my own tongue-tied talk of God. He talks of the divine ground *(grund)* that is the God beyond God. Though he says *Esse Deus est, Existence is God* or *Gott ist Istigkeit*[3], he also asserts that God is in some way beyond *esse*.[4] Had I met a soul mate? If one takes the conventional way of interpreting him, I had not. For example, he appears to have changed his thinking about beyond esse—or maybe clarified it—in his response before the Inquisition during the Cologne proceedings. Here, he invoked the distinction between the *esse absolutum, absolute existence*, of God, and the *esse formaliter inhaerens, formally inherent existence*, of creatures.[5] Being was still the grounding! And *Esse* was radically different between God and his creation.[6] God was Other! The God/self relationship was separated by a chasm that could not be crossed, no matter the cross or anything else, the discontinuity between human and God was glaring. Again, God was Other. Period!

If that is what he truly held—as conventional wisdom holds—then indeed we do part company, on two counts. For, at other times, he speaks as a traditional mystic, saying in his *Sermon 83*, "You ought to sink down out of all your your-ness, and flow into his his-ness, and your yours and his his ought to become one . . ."[7] Again, traditional mysticism, as I already stated, gets lost in this sort of thing and talk, as he himself admits when he finishes the above quote with that very notion of oneness with nothingness. When compared to the conventional take on him, these make him seem to be of two minds or two pens; and yet, in both he ends up with God as Other. First Being as complete Other; then Nothingness as complete Other. But in using traditional mysticism I am saying we still haven't ventured deep enough. Despite all this, I think that I could interpret Meister Eckhart in a different way, a way far closer to me and GIVING, or at least as a guide along the way to that God.

In his *Sermon 48*, he invites the presence each is to penetrate beyond to the purity of God, writing, "but it wants to know the source of this essence, it wants to go into the simple ground, into the quiet desert, into which distinction never gazed, not the Father, nor the Son, nor the Holy Spirit."[8] Though there are overtones of his traditional mysticism in this, especially with the use of the word *desert*, still it seems closer to what I am saying as well, that each of us has to go to the source beyond and behind the nothingness and nowhere, and being, too.

We have to be sympathetic with Eckhart; we don't have the Inquisition hounding us—only the Church of Analytical Philosophy, and of course, a plethora of religions, in fact, probably all of them, both in the West and the East, and maybe on Mars as well. Before his run-in with the Cologne crowd, he did describe this God as a formless abyss, and I certainly sense what he might have been getting at, since I have described God as nothing and nowhere at the beginning of our venture. However, he was never allowed to develop this. Without diverting into an opus on the Meister, I would like to say, dare to say, that I think those—both who are boxed into the traditional mysticism of the self disappearing or those among the postmoderns who are putting forth God as Other—will happily use and maybe even abuse Eckhart, but I suspect he is more complex than that, and think I could still argue for an Eckhart and the enigma he was as far closer to my position, or at least in a position so that I could persuade him of it.

But Being and being are stuck so thick in our thinking that I really wonder if I could persuade anyone to move past it to what I am saying, for in all honesty, our thinking has to begin with being. Even to the Pre-Socratics, though it appears as an abyss beyond coherence, it is being that is still the source of thought and wonder. I had to begin with existence; after all, it's all we have—that and the deepest experience in it, love. But once I do exist, and in that presence experience love, I find the way back to the Source, the Mystery that gave existence, GIVING itself at a much deeper level than only Being—so much so that I can say the truth of being is sourced in loving, the presencing of what is the Source.

That being the case, talk of God (θεο-λογος) has to be one based on love striving to understand. So theology for me is not *fides quaerens intellectum, faith seeking to understand*, but love doing so.

"Whatever we understand," Aristotle tells us, "or say about the First Cause, that is far more ourselves than it is the First Cause, for the First Cause is beyond all saying and comprehension."[9] This is true! And not true at the same time! As we have already shown in our venture, God is beyond our comprehension and yet known to us directly in love, that is from what we know deepest about ourselves, and thus both Incomprehensible as Aristotle says, and Intimate as love does; the Incomprehensible-Intimacy we spoke of. Notice I didn't relegate God to mere First Cold Cause. If you take love out of existence, of course, then Aristotle is right. But once love enters into existence and thus our discussion, the situation changes; even the word said to be coined by Aristotle changes; metaphysics becomes supermetaphysical.

What does that mean?

First comes GIVING, God. God is before being itself, before time, before space, before the nowhere and nothing out which spacetime came, before the Void. How can we ever get to such a Mystery? Though God is Incomprehensible, our way to God is still possible; again, it is grounded in the deepest experience in existence, and as love can really only be understood directly, so, too, Love itself, in that very Intimacy, and thus we get back to GIVING. The way to God and God are one—direct love—for that is what God is. Our being is called out of Love, and Love is only gotten back to through the love in our being. It is the only way each of us finds God really—*in this inrush of the real at the depths of who each of us is. We are loved into the image and likeness of the Mystery that made us—and it is only in this direct love we get to direct Love.* We are at our own core here. I cannot wholly objectify myself since I am made in the image and likeness, direct love, at my very depths. As for sure I cannot objectify GIVING. Nor can I articulate, or even article-ize GIVING. Yet, in love, we know God, even as we cannot comprehend God conceptually. Can then God be thought of? Only sideways so to speak—unless we do so directly in love! In the language and logic of love as it were. Thus the Mystery behind it all is not totally hidden or Other; there is a way to GIVING—in our own giving.

Let me *try* to bring all that back into the warm personal reality it is, for this is the symphony of the soul and our sojourn, you and me and each of us in our personal encounter with the Mystery that made us. We are called to fathom the gift of love here, to cherish it in its wordlessness. Each of us carries within our bodies crudities of former forms out of the carboniferous swamps, to be sure. The colossal debris of the ages is our baggage, while within the prowlings of our brains we call our minds invisible dimensions are denied us, not just those as yet unanalyzed by science, but those unanalyzable. We have arrived at just such a paradox here—something so fantastic it is beyond the pale of our comprehension, and yet is not, for it is found at the deepest experience in our journey on planet stress, telling us through that very consciousness something about the Mystery that made us and the very point of being. And here is something else as well . . . because of our *haeceittas*—that is to say that which makes *this person this person only*—thank you Dun Scotus for the word—each of us must find this for his or her personal self, as it is his or her personal self, for love is a radiant-self-showing, the self showing itself at its depths, presenting itself naked to the world, and God presencing as well. We are at our core in the image and likeness that gave in the first place, and we can find this out *if we are but sensitive to our own loving*. It is open to everyone—egalitarian as it gets! Yet, always personal! Always as this person and this person only, and this person in his or her naked truth, the unique experience of which should astonish us considering what it does. Yes, God can only be gotten to through the depths of our personhood, and so, paradoxically, although God cannot be a person, an entity, God is always personal in any relationship to us, always intimate. God can only really be approached intimately; God is Intimacy itself.

Though there is a radical difference between God and creation, there is not. Or to put it another way, God is still present in the creation this Mystery allowed; namely, in the deepest level of our own very being, where we in turn must turn to find this Mystery and experience it directly. God is 'hiding out' in the faces of those we love and who love us I can rightly say, and when we love them and they us, each of us sees God, knows God directly.

The parable of the Prodigal Son again comes to mind here.[10] The genius of the man called Jesus was that he tried to realize LOVING for people, not in the abstract, but with the warm word *Abba,* most particularly, as I said, in his parable of the prodigal son, which is about the *Abba,* the father, more so than the son, a warm *Abba* of unconditional love, which is what God is he was telling his audience through his metaphor and parable both, and doing very deep theology I might add; the deep theology of Supermetaphysics. He doesn't talk about God as Being or abstractly, but as Love and personally. Where he found this God I suspect was where we do and as we do, and my point in bring up the parable is exactly that, and thus showing Supermetaphysics in personal terms. God is unconditional love and when we realize that we come home to God.

For two thousand years whether directly or indirectly we have been an audience to what Jesus said, but nowhere, in words, does he spell out his theology more clearly than in this parable. I am not a bible-based religious type, my bible is existence, there's where God's revelation takes place, if there is to be any. But that is my point, existence itself does give us God's revelation, found in each of us. The very place, this very Jesus got his. I am and I can love, the unique and so very personal experience that should astonish us in and of itself, now astonishes us all the More, in taking us to a Supermetaphysics, which is this LOVING that continues to love us out of eternity and into the moment, the moment we hopefully choose to love back, each of us precious to God, for there is no hierarchy of love in LOVING; God loves all and everyone with the totality of divine love. Each and everyone one of us! That is so very important. God cannot love any other way. God is—excuse the word just—GIVING—the Mystery/Love before time and being and voids and nowheres, perpetual, eternal, forever unconditional LOVING. That is Supermetaphysics.

Thomas Aquinas said something I would like to mention here. I suppose since I mentioned Eckhart and Scotus in this chapter, to make the Jesuits happy, I should bring in Thomas Aquinas. By the by, I have already used Buddha, Lao Tsu, and the great Hindu story of Yudhisthira, not to mention Gilgamesh, so everyone is in the mix, because it all leads back to I am and I can love. But back to Thomas; although using the language of Scholasticism, with words like *substantia,* a word I would not use because of my levels of being approach, nonetheless, the following quote needs only the changing of one word to prepare it for saying what I am saying.

"By its act of existence, each being poses itself as an absolute, as a concrete totality, and imitates on the level of creature that sufficiency, perfection and exclusiveness that are the property of Subsistent Existence."[11] The word *imitate* implies the following of something as an example or model and does not necessarily connote exact correspondence, but if one but changes imitate to *is,* we have the following: "By its act of existence, each being poses itself as an absolute, as a concrete totality, and *is* on the level of creature that sufficiency, perfection and exclusiveness that are the property of Subsistent Existence." This is important because we have a real self that can really act and thus really love. Which brings us into the second part of my using Thomas for my own ends. Granted the rather substantial Thomas is talking in terms of Being, and I of Being's oblivion into Before—into LOVING—nonetheless, I not only think I can bring this earlier writing of his into the realm I am advocating about the self and its love, but the same with regards the self and Love, and perhaps convince Thomas of it as well because of what he said about all his tomes and God after his wordless experience. So over pasta and wine, and in his case a lot of both, I would say to the great mind and mystic of a man, "By its act of *loving*, each being poses itself as an absolute, as a concrete totality, and *is* on the level of creature that sufficiency, perfection and exclusiveness that are the property of *Loving*." I hope this helps at least some in our understanding of the replacing of being and Being with loving and Loving. Love is not an attribute of God, God is love, or more accurately, Loving; and when we will the giving of ourselves as God did loving us into being, each of us is in the image and likeness of God. That image and likeness notion is what I humbly suggest Thomas was really getting at; and I merely replaced the being he uses with the loving, making us even more so in the image and likeness, for though we can't give being *ex nihilo* as God, we can give love, give ourselves. Therein is our image and likeness; and our direct communion with Loving itself.

I suppose what I am trying to show here is that whether Aquinas or Heidegger, Scotus, Augustine, Aristotle, or whomever, we can get past Being and still have Being and being too, *but not as the beginning*. Although I have stated that this is more than metaphysics and Being, past nothingness and nowhere, nevertheless, in the enthusiasm of my venture, I don't want to dismiss anyone's thought, whether being or non-being, *Ipsum Esse* or the Void, *das Sein* or the Tao, but rather show how we might still proceed without doing so, and continue that here, though still within my own 'pasta' approach; that is, no matter how far we might travel, to do so always from what we can know and ground, build from and to, taste and can show from existence alone, and in that, the most profound phenomenon of the human self, love—which ironically points to something in us even closer to the Mystery that made us than the existence it is in. So if I abuse Thomas' thought or anyone else's, it is done out of love, love as that which gets us past Being's oblivion into Before, while at the same time incorporating what Thomas and others have to say on the way. If doing this is a push too much, a mental mile too many, and it may be, I do apologize, but it is still in the realm Thomas was advocating, only now using love and Love behind and beyond the calling into being. However, no matter what any of the metaphysicians hold or those denying metaphysics either, let me end this long, if not labyrinthine, sojourn into Scholasticism with the alpha and omega of Supermetaphysics: our very presence is at root-reality the source that can give of itself; and thus when we love we are acting most really as ourselves and most really as GIVING, the Source, that is

God, and it is only in this, this direct love that we embrace the Incomprehensible and know the Source, that is GIVING.

We can go no further. We have achieved an in-rush of the real! Yes, what we have as fundamentally present to us is not a lie, nor is the deepest experience in that existence, you are real and irreducible, a true identity, good and beautiful at your core of being, and love ultimately, as am I and everyone with us. And upon this we build our Supermetaphysics. GIVING gave and gives (a living God) such a gift, and in the process makes us in the image and likeness of GIVING, which we can choose, will, uncover and remember to do and be, or not. *Love is the freedom to act like God.*

For no other reason than to help out the glitches in my own brain, let me highlight that I said 'gave and gives,' and use *living God* to get across both the temporal and timelessness of God's love—*direct love*—to each and every one of us, now and forever. Direct love is timelessness in time. From eternity there is no other God than the One who manifests in love, manifests in giving. Our own direct love is our only way to this Intimacy. For the Intimacy is *direct love.* So when I say God is love, I mean it to the fullest. LOVE is God! Unconditional Love, article-less GIVING, before being and the nowhere and nothing out of which a somewhere and something came, beyond understanding, except in loving. No, we can go no further. This is the ultimate actuality of love, understood only through love. *Unfathomable GIVING creates us out of Unfathomable GIVING, sharing that mystery with us at our very core, really, unconditionally, so much so as to make each of us actually like itself and thus able to truly find our way back to GIVING itself.* God *realizes* us in his love, his giving; and it is there we *realize* the Mystery that made us.

Thus it is in turning in our mind's eye to Primal Love and holding tight onto our version of God, we penetrated as deeply as was possible and impossible both into God's radiant Presence, and by doing so we know ourselves better in this our human venture!

The cosmos, the world, or any other concealment or cave can not really change that, and in the enlightenment of early morning before the rest of the slumbering surroundings are up, as the linen curtains lift in the light night breeze and I sit alone at my computer, I have to register something that should astonish us, the fact that our very existence ultimately goes back to an act of love, this giving, that existence is an act of love. Yes, I have made the preposterous proposal that the Mystery that made us loves us! Struggling with this as an astonished awareness in spacetime, where if nature doesn't get you, humankindlessness will, my restless fingers go on to stutter out my stuttering soul . . . and in spite of my species and spacetime itself, past fruitless fables or fixations on false formulae, type out . . . that besides inscape and landscape we are in a lovescape, and at this moment, past the telling of any tongue, beyond the struggle of spacetime, in another rhythm and rhyme, in a Supermetaphysics beyond mere metaphysics, each of us as *io sol uno* is in communion with . . . with God!

Setting aside my hesitancy as a human, or the tortured theologian in me because of the problem of suffering, I have dared to carry love to its ultimate intimacy and the Supermetaphysics that comes calling out of that. The deeper we go into love, into the giving of ourselves, the closer we realize the Source of that is in us, and the more we bring to realization our lovescape. Therefore, though it sounds like a contradiction to grasp the Incomprehensible—that is exactly what we do in love. Directly! And in doing so we come to this Supermetaphysics I speak of, the only thing that truly brings God and us together, in our initial existence as well as in our own final creation, that is, the one we do ourselves by our love—or, sadly, lack of it on our part, and thus die lessening God within us.

The original call to love is made by Giving, present in us as our very creation; our choice in life is our answer. Thus we share in our own creation, the fulfillment of it. We are made in God's image and likeness even in that. Such an incredible God! So giving as to allow us to really love! To be truly in the divine image and likeness! Even in our own creation!

No—we *are not* bearers of a universal amorphous Being, as if called forth for no other ontological function than to permit Being to be, or Non-Being either. That is old metaphysics. Seen in the light of love we have broadened Being itself . . . *GIVING has* . . . out of a love that is total. So total it boggles the mind. But, in truth, could total love be any other way? Could God who is total love love any other way? It is total and forever. God will never stop loving us, each as the unique being each of us is and finishes as in our own love, which is the freedom to act like God. To forget that is to stilt if not still-born our own creation, it is to become estranged to ourselves and our own very essence, which is all that sin really is—and holiness the exact opposite, to grow nearer to that Loving with our own. Each of us can choose to act out of this or not, can give of one's self or not, and if we do love we are acting most really as ourselves, and like God—and if not, drawing away from God, and really ourselves, too.

Here we allow love to have its say, its total say, all the way; and, ironically, in that the way and God turn out to be the same. No, we can never deny our doubts, our confusion, or the perennial problem of suffering; but with Supermetaphysics we have a God who suffers with us. Love is God's salvation in that as well, for when we say God is love and suffers with us, because of that, we have the only thing that saves God for us. Otherwise Stendhal is right, or worse, that we have a God that is monstrous, wallowing in the will to power and as brutal, or at best, indifferent as the raw elemental energies of evolution and the cold mathematics used to compute it. Only love saves us and God from such a fate; for a loving

God opens up for us a God who suffers with us out of love, even as we do when we love. It is a love that loves us through the suffering, even as we are still left without an answer as to why suffering is allowed in spacetime, allowed by either God or evolution itself, for the whole of it could have evolved differently. In that God still remains Incomprehensible, even as God, Love, becomes our salvation—for us and God as well for us. The problem of suffering will not go away; but neither will love, and with that, Love.

No, even Supermetaphysics still doesn't answer the problem per se of suffering, but it realizes love to its fullest, in us and in the Mystery that made us. The battle over the problem of suffering will continue until we no longer continue, either individually or as a species, still as inexplicable as ever as consciousness confronts the cosmos, as awareness looks out at unawareness, as love looks at lovelessness. Yet, a God that suffers with us is impossible in any metaphysics. It is impossible to any metaphysics other than what I have put forth with and in a crowning Supermetaphysics.

Let's catch our collective breath here and state again what we have done, that here we carried love, in an unedited, uninhibited, unharnassed freedom, to its unchained, unseen, unoriginated, uncreated, unborn, unformed, uneverything ultimate, Unconditional Love, and in that dared to establish a Supermetaphysics.

This is grasped with a different understanding of existence than before. Here the reader must forget all about perennial or unperennial philosophy, East or West terms and terminology, past and future, rites and religions. He or she must aim at the utmost simplicity yet the very profundity of being alive. That is the great spiritual verity; let us not approach it pedantically or partially, but in all its profundity and warmth. It has something urgent to say, to each and every one of us. The ultimate in being is arrived at via a sensitivity to life itself, the life in each of us at the deepest breath of our being, at our truest moments, perhaps, too, at times the loneliness in terms of the terrain we are looking out at. No matter, the narration of each person in spacetime is really a story of love, though it often seems folly when it confronts the norms of our worldly judgment-calls and even nature itself. Against and in the face of this, love answers a deeper call and creates its own conditions, since it cannot accept the condition of lovelessness. For lovelessness in a very real sense is the profound absence of God, and we somehow know that. In the loveless logic of so much of the world we live in, let's be honest, love is not really valued. Yet, in our most personal and intimate moments, sometimes in our most suffering and sorrowful, we do know the truth of love, and because of that value it above all else as the most important thing in life. Here is where we meet God! In the value of love, we know the value of God! Simply carrying that to its fullest, we have Supermetaphysics.

Finally, summing up Supermetaphysics, ours is a venture that in the end says we exist in and because of love. This is not only a different tone of voice and a different understanding of metaphysics or denial of it; it is a different God! Love is the Grounding or Source. There is no Abyss of Godhead underlying this love, this *is* God. Love is the Ground of Being, the Source of Being Before Being. Therein is the true God, beyond the awe and vastness of the universe, beyond good and evil, beyond being and nonbeing, where words fail and only love shows the way. God is the unspoken pervasive mystery we somehow know in love. *The Incomprehensible that is before being and non-being is known in loving because* . . . but you already know. This is so, in all its Mystery, beyond belief; yet as normal to us as our daily breath and the soup we share in that breathing.

The world I have come to realize is a very odd place without love. This is made clear to those capable of discerning in the flow of everyday life the point at which the mundane world gives way to quite another dimension. Yet, even as love carries us beyond, it is at our very core, as everyday as the face who loves you and whom you love. Love is as real as it gets, despite the world and the cosmos with it, despite the long periods of evolutionary groping and the modern economy with it. Despite Dawn hanging on his atrophied tree and the Old Croghanman of antique times staked to the bottom of a bog, or us buried in our cerebral fog and hanging on the erratic cross of existence, this paradox of giving, somehow triumphs over life's limitations. And though it seems as silent as the airless moon when we look into the distant skies and exploding stars, and though we know that we are different than that because we are aware beings, what we have experienced, no power on earth can take from us. Only we can take it from ourselves. Only we can let the world rob us of ourselves and the will to love, hardening our hearts, and our heads I might add. Love is not a gratuitous grace that is not really necessary but potentially helpful if made available—it is the very soul of spirituality and way to God, where the way and God are one.

God gives ultimate meaning to our meaning, a forever foundation to our spirituality, and makes our love not hopeless. This is achieved not by mysticism but by everyday love, human love, a mysticism without ecstasy. When this is realized, action follows in our daily lives—a love in action. And that love is true existentially both on earth and in eternity, because we are truly the self-sustaining source of our own love, *in communion with LOVING itself*, not as something abstract or amorphous, but personal and intimate, warm. In a crescendo of penetrating coherence, we have in this, the profoundest attitude towards life and being, in that, it is life and being at its profoundest. Everything in this whole piece is premature until we come to that; and predicated on that, we can and do create *something more than metaphysics, something about the God that is beyond all metaphysics, our Supermetaphysics of love.*

Yet, yet, yet, yet, it is for you to investigate, to pursue, to be sure about for yourself, which is the only way to go, since it is your very self I am talking about. Your birthright to freedom is where this 'freedom fugue' must proceed from—not from me or anyone else. Again, each of us must make this odyssey of being for his or her individual *personal* self. Aim at the utmost simplicity yet very depths and profundity of actuality when you do, and you will achieve a presence that will take you all the way to a Supermetaphysics. For I dare to belove that each of us indeed is given in the course of our lives, glimpses into the heart of the really real, and, as such, that the fabric of actuality is open to all to pursue, and thus arrive at God, the real God, GIVING.

I think that respects both your freedom and what I want so ardently for you to see and hear and taste, smell, touch and be alive to. I once tortured a lecture hall with this sentence: "I insist we ground it—ground it by expanding our scope and centering in to what we know best at the same time, and in the process possibly arrive at that dream of a supertheory about being itself, grounded in what is most crucial to our own being." Good heavens, I think I understand what it means now!

William James in his *Varieties of Religious Experience* stood for the priority of religious experience, as for example in comparison with what he regarded as conceptual interpretations in doctrine and dogma. For him, the religious experience was "the feelings, acts and experiences of individual men in their solitude, so far as they apprehend themselves to stand in relation to whatever they may consider the divine."[12] Though I would certainly agree with James, as well as with Bergson who makes the distinction between static and dynamic religion in his *The Source of Morality and Religion*, I root and want to root what they call the religious experience, and I the spiritual one, a purely human one, *in the most concrete happening in everyone's everyday life, establishing our approach to the very fabric of actuality through that,* as I suppose not only the philosopher in me would, but the human being that I am. Again, lest you forgot within the scope of the last page, even the Supermetaphysics of love grows out of that root-reality, and is approachable only through it. True, because love is honestly beyond the power of words to express, and I had to use words to communicate with you, I used expressions like mysticism without ecstasy to try to capture both the intuitional quality and yet democratic reality of it. But the point of all these "words words words," dear long suffering ad-venturer, is to establish as clearly as humanly possible that the foundation is always you and the love you experience. That is the two-in-one reality necessary for all this, and now we see how love and being for us are one, are really one, that our being emanates from love—that each person is at one's source of self, one's sourceforce, love. *Lovelessness is the absence of the deepest level of you as you, and the Mystery that made you as well.* This is 'explained' when we reach the Supermetaphysical love that surpasses all words and really can only be fully grasped in a non-conceptual way, or perhaps better put, in a more than conceptual way. *For in truth, love is its own revealer.*

This is truly what it means to walk with God in this world. *De profundis clamavi ad te, Domine* is not a spiritual suicide that swallows me up. Rather, when I call out from the depths of my being to GIVING, I am enhanced, enhanced as I realize what no words could ever convey, above names, ineffable yet inevitable, LOVING itself. At that moment, even with all the luggage of the labyrinth of life we are caught up in, somehow we know the Mystery behind it all, and would give our hearts to it.

God is not a thing, a place, an Other, nor a being or Being either, nor a nowhere and nothing, non-being or Void, either, but out of forever, GIVING, unconditional LOVING! These are the only words that can come close to explaining the Incomprehensible-Intimacy we sense when we are not made crazy by this world and know a hawk from a handsaw in the warm winds of love itself, deep in the inscape of our very being, our lovescape.

Such is our *contemplatio ad amorem,* and our *amor in actu* combined, combined with the way I would have it, if I had may way—true within the boundaries and bullies of being on planet stress, but always there. I can *live love* and be in true communion with the Mystery. We have allowed our love to do that for us, in the unedited, uninhibited, unharnassed freedom that love is. In the unedited, uninhibited, unharnassed freedom that is Love. Our freedom, love, being, and birthright are combined, alive in the presence I am. We are alive not only to the more in us, but to More!

Journey's End

Halfway into life's allotted time for us, I found myself in a dark mass, a place far from the light that I sought in vein. It's hard to speak of, what it was like, that obscure oblique place, so brutal that even to think about it now grips me with unfocused dread. So bitter, it was like chilled extinction itself. Yet, still, I want to tell you the truth I discovered there; and to do so I am forced to tell you everything I experienced in that visible darkness.

Past thought on thought, so I ventured into that Strangeness: I wanted with all that was in me to see the way in which our humanness fit into the Mystery that made us, and find a place in it—yet my own mental wings were far too weak for that. But then the core of my very being throbbed with a profundity that surged through me and I realized what I had sought with all my heart and every utterance of a past prayer. At that height-depth-whisper of radiant joy within me, as if out of a forever force that was not mine, yet was, I was moved by the love that moves the sun and other stars.

From the beginning of the *Divine Comedy* to its end.
Inferno and *Paradiso*, my translation.

I started our venture with Dante, and now as we begin our ending I again use the great poet, as well as another Italian poet, Giovanni Pascoli, and appropriately so his *l'ultimo viaggio*. In a very real way, he and all of us with him take up where the Greeks did. They, those ancestors of us all, no matter our blood type, looked into space and experienced nostalgia. The word is made up of two Greek roots, νόστος, *going home*, and ἄλγος, *suffering*. Pascoli in his long poem makes his Odysseus nostalgic for a home he cannot return to, as gone as the waves he traveled and never to travel those same waves again. Pascoli's nameless man, or one carrying a name we all have, no longer can hear the Sirens sing, no longer outwit the Cyclops, Circe, Calypso, but his hero with no name except our own understands, finally, and nobody comes home to nothingness. In this so postmodern view of humankind Pascoli, nonetheless, still let's the magic linger even in the face and fact of *nihil*, and allows something so human in his hero, something as nameless as the hero himself to bring him into a timeless dimension, one having its own wondered-about reality. How close the man who wrote *l'ultimo viaggio* and we are here. We and our Venturer who dares to say there is more and More, too! Even if we put poetry, Pascoli, and paradise aside and turn our laughter into ice, we are still forced in our lifetime, no matter how we might deny or disregard any dichotomy, to deal with the difference between our consciousness and the cosmos around us, even as we are part of it—but not completely so, for we can love and it cannot. And in that we are forced to deal with a *mysterious more* inside our experience and very being, and ultimately forced to deal with a pervasive Mysterious More, too, even if only to deny it despite our own *mysterious more*. Yet there it is across the ages and into our own, perhaps only poetry, but perhaps also a nostalgia for what is there at the core of our creation and we suffer to return to.

Remote abysses do not give shelter to the soul, nor satisfaction either—so the soul seeks more, and More still here and now, immediately and intimately. One can say it is the projection of love beyond the boundaries of biology, by a creature yet born out of biology and evolution's struggle, who now knows something deeper still under its skull about which it can say little or nothing and calls by the name Sacred. It is as if personally and as a whole species the supernatural had touched somewhere in us without record, and out of the depths of a singularity, like a vaporous emanation, a consciousness had escaped the darkness to look around itself and wonder, and then love. And in that love, in a leap into it over everything to the contrary, the creature finds its way back to the Mystery that made it.

We seem to have immortal longings in us as a poet put it. And life is not a detour from that, but rather that longing rooted in our very being. When we come home from wherever, we are like Odysseus greeted by his dog, or Darwin by his, or Wild Will by his, or me by mine, and reminded in so concrete a way that more, a mysticism without ecstasy exists across the illusion of form and is the deepest level in our being, in being itself; for in that and all love is a sense, a whisper of the love that exists without form and before form took form, somehow lodged there in our make up, even as we breathe in uncertainty. Our only compass in such a storm of raging risk is within the depths of our breathing, the assurance in it all that our love is real, our love and those we love and ourselves with them. From that and only that we make our venture into the Sacred and can, with Dante, finish off our venture with a love before nothing and nowhere, a love that loves into the present, into each of us.

But I hear human doubt in my all too human head even as I write. Cyclops, Circe, Calypso, Coppola—am I my own entrapment?

Is my book a secret nostalgic farewell? Merely a diary of delicious words? My own delicate twilight? My own *delirious* twilight? Yes, the venture possesses some inventiveness, a few outrageous ideas, but does it really say the truth? Especially when it tries to explore the vast and vague geography of God? Is it merely a handful of metaphors? Is it merely my coloring book, with colorings of intonations already intoned in tomes much tidier and more thorough than my more and More? *Can I really insinuate the supernatural in love?* From my own human intimacy? In the giving of soup and overriding my hungry brain, in the sharing of soup and superseding the natural? Am I a scribe of God, or merely writing a book too childish-foolish for this world? Vanquished by reality in the end am I that lone knight tired of fighting windmills, too exhausted for enchantments, inside or outside this fragment of reality, this fractured fractal? In the end is it all the rhapsody of an imaginary identity? Both my own and God's?

The proof of the pasta is in the tasting even when it comes to God. Is God tasteless? Or is the little goodness and beauty and love we witness in the world God? Or are we just alone with our little goodness and beauty and love, all of it and us with it an aberration in the cosmos?

In a very real sense I may be clinging to nothing here, with what I call me no one until a chemical consciousness is born and borne both in my brain, my venture into the invisible only a swirling vapor in my head and I a clown-alley philosopher who fancies myself as possessing powers contained in my make up that give evidence of sacred roots, when in fact we are all truly nameless and heading nowhere into nothingness. Such a nihilism is always possible; the possibility of disappearing altogether always there looking back from the abyss.

The chilled consideration of nihilistic giddiness tempts us all, realizing as we do that we will come and go as a species, forgetting to talk of Michelangelo, and of Shakespeare, and of Beethoven, too, not to name yet to be named geniuses as well, all lost to memory in the tide of time, this planet, too, and then our sun, and finally the cosmos itself. That has to give us a melancholy or we are inorganic and non-sentient, not to mention without a mind and bloodless.

"To-morrow and to-morrow and to-morrow creeps in this petty pace from day to day to the last syllable of recorded time. It is a tale told by an idiot, full of sound and fury, signifying nothing." So wrote one poet and another after him, ". . . all is an enormous dark," and after him another that said the center will not hold. Shakespeare, Hopkins, Yeats, we write in snow and die to nothing—and for nothing, dear poets? Or is it enough to just having been? Should I relinquish the untenable, the unattainable? Is consciousness looking out at the cosmos and end unto itself? More than that too much to ask for? Life itself merely a happening that happened and nothing more? Or should this scrambling scuffling work give way to something more in each of us, and in that, still More, a Mysterious More breaking through and in and in between the bottom lines of economies, earth, and existence itself, breaking though in something as intimate to us as our love, so much so that we can say, though we are but passing we still have found the mystery that surprises life and maybe death, too, and in that become not a throwaway or makeshift, living on Clown Alley in a comic agony called life, but take on the face of God?

Such is the onslaught on consciousness—it is a questioning voyage each of us is on, admitted or not, committed or not, one way or another wandering through it all and wondering who we are, what the really real is, and how do we act in the face of planet stress. And in all that, admitted or not, committed or not, a search for the sacred, something more in us and to us, something that answers what the Mystery that made us is.

That is the human venture. We have taken it, and though we claim no infallibility on the matter or about matter itself, we have come to a place for us to stand, an eureka against the darkness and drain of time, perhaps an aberration in it all, a mystery we call love, a reality that turns the universe on its head and gives us an answer, a human answer in the midnight dark and daylight, too. "I am and I can love" rings out challenging the cosmos and its indifferent silence. It challenges all notions of God, too. If God isn't love, God should be! IF GOD ISN'T LOVE, GOD SHOULD BE!

Should I take this to the limit for my audience of—how many of you are left—three? Or is it merely me talking to myself?

In the swirling cerebral seas, and those endragoned whirlpools at the base of our brain as well, across the wonder of breathing, caught between love and lovelessness as we are, we can only take what is best in us and embark on that as our make-shift raft, risking everything on what we know most certain in life despite the laughless cosmos around us and the hiss tempting inside our heads. "Unless," as Plato hopes, "it were possible to find a stronger vessel, some sacred meaning on which we might take our journey more surely and with confidence."

There is no such vessel! We must seek salvation in the lonely personal, in the breathing creature that each of us is, in the only place we must find everything, in our existence. And there, ironically, is where we do find Plato's hoped-for sacred meaning, in the very human everyday mysticism without ecstasy we call love.

We will barely have time to survey the world and then be gone, but we can nonetheless say before we do depart, that, impelled by the contending forces of lovelenssness and love, we chose love, and for a moment in that love possibly knew God.

That is the dilemma of life, that choice. Are we merely the discarded rubbish of the past, the eye of an octopus evolved to another eye with human thought behind it, and behind that the need to seek out something more than the insentient place we find ourselves in, something more like ourselves, to which we give the name God? But we are befuddled. Is such a Mystery Completely Other than us? More like the insentient cosmos that surrounds us? Consciousness looks out at the unconscious cosmos and has to wonder, love or loveless? Is the Mystery that made me completely alien to me, or somehow connected? And if loveless, I can still love, and so am more than the universe and the Mystery out of which it came. But isn't loving hopelessly, hopelessly loving, then a principle of despair, a spirituality, perhaps stoic, but still ultimately one of lonesome despair, even as it is heroic? Yes—but if it is all there is, it is an existential fact and we must deal with it. That or that very love is our salvation and I am at my depth not hopelessly alone, but made in the image and likeness of GIVING itself and my own love tells me so. Love gives us that choice, for love is a fact of existence, the deepest experience in our existence, and we must deal with it, either as a hopeless love, alone in the cosmos, or one grounded in Love itself.

How odd that is! How odd that what is at the core of our being defies the universe we find ourselves in, as if spanning more than spacetime itself, as if telling us in our very depths there is more to all this, and if not there is still love in counterpoint to the cosmos and the Mystery that made us. There is love no matter what! This is the *ultimo viaggio* through spacetime on the only ship we have, with the only compass we have. We either come out of the darkness visible to find ourselves alone with our hopeless loving or with a love that moves the sun and other stars, and if not them, one that moves us at our very core, giving Ultimate Meaning in our own ultimate meaning, giving us More in our own more, giving us GIVING itself in our own giving itself.

Let's catch our collective breath here and allow me to state what I honestly feel, returning all the way back to our venture's very beginning. I have an expectation without knowing what I expect. The revelation of something! A message that will arrive, or one that doesn't, but is still meaningful. I have seen beauty, witnessed goodness, and known love. And in it all, I have sensed something mysteriously more about my life, the undertones in me of something numinous, of something strange and queer to it all, if the truth be known, something like a sensed providence; and with all that still, a somewhat sort of Presence. And yet, the opposite is true as well, for I cannot deny the undertones of something cosmological that threatens, something missing, without being able to say what it is, sometimes only a fear of futility and at others a melancholy in matter itself. One that tells me I am such stuff as dreams are made on, and my little life is to be rounded with a little death, unnoticed in the cosmos. One that tells me that I am nothing more than a psychic crystallization around an abyss, alive to a universe, a world, an existence without ultimate grounding—afloat in the face of just what happens, at the mercy of chance, chaos, or the universal contingency, alone alas along the riverrun. It leaves us all with psychic scars and psychic scares, knowing our vulnerability on the Serengeti of spacetime. Perhaps, we conscious creatures cannot face that, because it is too awful.

Of course, the opposite might be true, that we cannot accept such an awful actuality because it is not actually so, and a wordless wisdom tells us so. Half my mind says one thing, the other half another, and a third half says live an as if! Life leaves us in such a strange place. In this and so much more, we all are alive to the human condition, one where people do not die alphabetically.

Yet, in this condition, this all too human condition, our venture has brought us to one minimal certainty, and from that alone to the deepest experience in it, and from both to grounding a purely human spirituality, one that chooses the will to love over the will to power. A human can stop there and have a noble way to face the world; or one can choose to try to tie the air together with that love. We have chosen to do just that, to make the impossible possible! Yes, we have chosen to make the Incomprehensible intimate and immediate, not with any trick up our sleeve, but rather with the simple and straightforward everyday experience at the depth of our breathing. From that and that alone, in that and that alone, we have dared to say that we have intimacy with the Mystery that made us, what is beyond yet at our very core. It is thus we are made in the image and likeness to that which is GIVING itself, LOVING itself, the Incomprehensible-Intimacy that called us into existence and is present in our very presence. It is in this we have direct communion with the Mysterious More we call God, the Unseen, Unoriginated, Uncreated, Unborn, Unformed, Source of all being. Only after coming to that in our venture, could we dare to establish a Supermetaphysics and such a wonderful God.

To love is to grasp the purpose of being human, of being itself.

In truth I don't know much - except we are in a divine dialectic when it comes to God. I do know there is beauty, and goodness, and love, but I don't really know if God is manifest in that, or really is Other. And only Other because there just is too much suffering in this world. God doesn't seem to have any say or sway in spacetime.

So where does this leave me, us? *Sul ponticello,* with the bow close to the bridge, or the bone as the case seems to be.

Is the original call to love made by God, present in us as our very creation, *our choice in life our answer,* still uncertain and hesitant, except in that love? And does such a statement carry us beyond the postmodern and the postmortem, too, even as it brings along with it the baggage of our contemporary milieu, and I must honestly put forth, the baggage of existence itself?

God is more than we know, mysteriously more, and we naïve in what we say about the Source of all being; and yet, in beauty and goodness and in the depths of our love is there something more, Mysteriously More? Somehow does that make God not Other and us not naïve and alone in our love? Everything argues against this, of course, but love itself.

Lovelessness is all around us, to be sure, but love is here as well, here as its own revealer—and maybe even the revealer of God, even as we feel left to chance and change, circumstances and the cold laws of the cosmos. Even as we are left deaf to it all, and daft and deftless, too, dying on a cross or in a madhouse or in an appallingly dirty and uncared-for sickroom, or abandoned to the long goodbye of Alzheimer's, or to the lonely moan of a baby called Anthony. Yes, such suffering is in the very bone marrow of our being, with us left looking up at the night sky wondering . . . the desperate encounter between our human outcry and the silence of the universe so real . . . and yet so is our love, that which makes us have simpatico for those in the litany of sorrows mentioned and those unmentioned as well, that makes us put our final trust in love, our tainted human nature's solitary boast.

In the beautiful dedication of a book of his, *The Unexpected Universe,* the great American archaeologists and poetic paleontologist Loren Eiseley writes of his dog in haunting beauty: "To Wolf, who sleeps forever with an ice age bone across his heart, the last gift of one who loved him." I don't know about you, but to me that is exquisitely beautiful. It brings home so much of our humanity, one that echoes the *Mahabharata,* but in a very postmodern way. Eiseley doesn't know what death will bring, all he knows is he loved and lost, but it was better to have loved and lost than never to have loved at all. The poet who wrote that knew it as well—as we all do. And know as well that love crosses beyond the structure of form and species. In the oldest piece of literature known to us, an unknown writer spoke of the same realization I am writing about, telling us at the dawn of civilization it was an old story then, the story of our love, and ends with this so human insight into life.

Gilgamesh, where are you going?
The life you pursue you shall not find.
When the mysteries that made us created humankind,
Death for us they made mandatory,
Gilgamesh, let your belly be full,
Make merry by day and by night.
Of each day make a feast of rejoicing,
Day and night, dance and play!
Let your garments be sparkling fresh.
Wash your head by bathing happily in the river of life.
Pay heed to the little one that holds on to your hand,
Let your beloved and you delight in love!
For all this is the task of humans.[1]

Since this oldest piece of literature known to us was written, our human horizon has expanded to the point that modern science and technology can take us to the edge of spacetime itself, yet it is still within the depth of our humanity we must go to find the truth about ourselves. It is there—displayed in our daily life—the realization of who we are and what we are really about. It is there—to be found first and foremost. The ancient writer was right to include all that he did, but most especially love. It has always been seen to be the deepest part of being human. It is an enduring eureka, enduring in the sense of both lasting and long-suffering, for though it has always been at the depth of our very being, there is always the possibility in the event we call life, to lose sight of it, for life is not an easy road and requires attention on our part so as not to lose our way by losing our human root-reality. That is why the ancient writer in the earliest work we have about our human condition has to remind his hero; and that is why this present day writer these many centuries later has to remind himself and everyone else with him as well. Yet, no matter how difficult it may be at times, or in whole eras, it is from this root-reality we must make our inner decision about life and how we act in it. The universe may be silent, but not the consciousness inside us. Love is an assertion of the value of self-giving in a domain whose criterion of value is anything but love-asserting. Both nature and human society are anything but love-asserting. But because of the meaning and value we know to be so very real in the love we realize in both our depths and daily lives, we know and can act beyond the cruelty and indifference of nature and the world we live in. Only through love—this mysticism without ecstasy that is our very real everyday human love—can we see the meaning in life manifested, and each able to manifest it ourselves.

But does any of this tell us about the Mystery that that made us?

I quoted Eiseley as an introduction to one of the above paragraphs and I would like to again, now from the end of one of his books, not the beginning. He ends *The Man Who Saw Through Time* with this passage: "Across that midnight landscape he rides with his toppling burden of despair and hope, bearing with him the beast's face and the dream, but unable to cast off either or to believe in either. For he is a man, the changeling, in whom the sense of goodness has not perished, or an eye for some supernatural guidepost in the night."[2] We have kept an eye out for some supernatural guidepost in this night of uncertainty, and strangely enough we found it within our very humanness. One merely has to be sensitive to the deepest part of that humanness. If that is finding God, then we have and can say we have and God is a verb! The verb is within us. Love! That is the light that shines in the darkness, the stilled silence as ambulance sirens screech at us in the night, the ambivalent trust that we ride with when we are in those ambulances and speak to the Mystery that made us.

I am, once again, reminded of Beethoven here, a precursor to our era, if not perhaps the greatest postmodern philosopher in the last of the music he created, a prophet telling us what we would be going through, for as he himself said he wrote those last works for future generations. In those final quartets and one in particular, Beethoven's inversion sounds in our ears. The stone-deaf creator is wondering about his stone-deaf God. Especially as he hears Him in his head, and expresses it so mystically in perhaps his most complete work, the last Opus he wrote despite its number, his great Opus 131. Here the suffering man is confounded in his love before it reaches for and achieves the impossible. The last of the great fugues in order of composition (Opus 132, Opus 130, and Opus 131) ends with incredulous relief, *with a thankfulness still tinged with hesitation, but with a coherence of the profoundest attitude towards life.* The suffering genius tells us this, shows us this, and though suffering still, he still tells us of something more than the suffering, something that comes only in this mysticism without ecstasy, even as he leads us into ecstasy.

We are all Beethoven creating such an opus in each of our lives. One that tells us the Incomprehensible remains an unspoken pervasive mystery yet manifests itself the only way it can, *as it is, this inversion and conversion called love.* When a person hears and feels, tastes and touches, thinks and dreams in the tones of love, he senses the Profound.

Through the adagio, allegro, andante, I sit at this early morning hour in an awareness, an animal awareness to be sure, as a creature that knows the earth for

I am its mud . . . and yet a creature rid of nature's cold laws and brutal bend and instead morphed for a moment into more and maybe More, with me left to tell about it, my flesh-hindered fingers trying to pound out what is rushing through my skull onto an electric page.

The metaphysical rebellion in us, is, of course, justified! With membrane universes spinning in our heads and maybe in reality, too, who can blame us for our confusion about the Source of all this or even our rage against it? Lucretius lives in all of us. Rage and remembrance seemingly our only prayer! My mind's eye suddenly is back again in that Revolutionary graveyard with the stray dog couched behind an old gravestone, a bitter temperature falling towards death for the old furry canine. I wanted to save him with everything in me, but when I got to the suffering creature, he just looked up at me and my heart broke for I knew it was too late. In that moment I saw the snow turn yellow with urine and the shaking creature gasp a long shocked instant and then defecate. There had been no caring God for him. He had survived alone and now died alone, and I was expected to go back to Saint Andrew's and pray. Where is the wisdom in that? Aren't we all that animal in truth? Isn't all my writing, my philosophizing, my theologizing, my praying merely a piece of music in the winter wind? Is all that is left for us merely to live as if it made a difference . . . when in truth it doesn't? A sense of loss lingers with that thought. "Would I be a savior of a world where no salvation exists?" Isn't that Christ's real prayer and mine! Isn't it all merely music in the winter wind, Beethoven?

And yet, confounded as we might be, we can't be confused about the deepest experience in our existence, and when we are honest about it, we are not confused about it, but just the opposite, we know it as we know nothing else. It is in this same known and very human love we find our way past the whirlwind of whys and woes in our heads, and dare to try to realize the inexpressible! In love and love alone, in the intimacy of myself, of yourself! Why we love that lonely dog, or deaf Beethoven, or dying Christ! Or the madman from Rocken! Either the Impossible comes to us there or not at all. True it will require a leap, a leap over everything engulfing us, but one from the truest moment of our being as breathing humans! Such is our plunge into the depths of our own person; such is our dive into the divine. And if only into the depths of our own person, then at least we have the truth of our own being!

Love is life's hardest labor and its greatest gift, without any reference to God. And when we do refer it to God, sometimes it will bring us so easily to Intimacy, at times an Invitation that even comes without us doing anything, a Profound Presence quietly kissing us past our ideas, and even our wills, past everything, with an intimacy that is without words. But life might prepare a lonely dinner for us as well, one where we dine only with Lucretius and his cursing corpses, for sometimes that very love blocks God out of our lives because of the cruelty of life, a cruelty we blame on God, God's allowing it. How could little Anthony's parents trust the Mystery we call God? God has betrayed their love! Or a brother's for his dying sister! Or . . . Yes, God is hard to get to all too often because of love. Yet, the very love for little Anthony is beautiful and good and challenges with everything in us the cruelty we witness, the moan we hear. It is in this all-too human love, heartbroken because of it as we are, within a confusing contradiction, so very real yet so surreal, beyond brain serotonin yet drowning in it, with quiet tears and tunneled calm as if watching with an unknown knowing, in a thin place that seems almost beside us and this world, we again find . . . what? Dare I say God? If God is to be found and real for us, we find God in the depth of our own most profound statement of being, our own most profound expression and experience of existence, our human love, our human love for little Anthony.

When you are honest with this and to it, you touch the numinous, the nowhere and everywhere, you touch, though of course you don't touch, you somehow, someway, somewho understand and yet, of course, don't, and though you do will, it is without will. So it is we realize the Mysterious More or don't.

A rush of responsibility comes into my stare and moving fingers here, forcing me to admit to you that my computer is glitching on me with all this God talk. Perhaps it's because it's a postmodern computer and feels a touch uncomfortable with it, as I do sometimes. So maybe I should crack open a book and be "lonely in me loneness," or walk in the garden with a summer giggle, listening to the staring Calla lilies singing in the noonday sun, remembering my Old English biting at my heals and though missing him with everything in me, still smiling at his wondering about my hatless head and conducting arm, intoxicated as I am with Beethoven drifting out from the open window. O Freuden-Tag! O Halloo-Schlag! And then Bellini after that! Or maybe Bandini! O jour frabbejeais! Calleau! Callai! Or should that be O giorno fantastico! Callo! Calle! Anyway, O fabjous day! Callooh! Callay! Yes, my Old English is gone. Perhaps I can't save God. God and me both couldn't save my beautiful Old English. Not all the king's horses and all the king's men could put Humpty Dumpty together again. But I am able to write this no matter: Buddha passed—it was as I prayed it would be, quickly, at home, and without any long suffering. I just brought him back from the Vet and as he lay there I realized he was breathing heavily. I gave him some water, which he drank, but slowly. I laid my fifty-year crucifix on him and asked Jesus that he not suffer. After which I immediately called the Vet and as I was speaking to him, I saw the breathing stopped and he had defecated. I knew he had passed. I loved my old clown so very much, the house without his presence is so very empty, and there shall be a hole in my own breathing hereafter, like others I loved who have gone, the world changed forever.

It's good to play in the sun; it gets the winter out of our eyes, or at least mixes winter with warmth.

Didn't that anonymous ancient author tell Gilgamesh as much? Perhaps tearing as he did, as I am. "Day and night dance and play . . . bathe happily in the river of life!" It was good advice then and it still is, as is the end of that famous passage, wherein he gives Gilgamesh his deepest advice about being human.

That anonymous human writing at the dawn of civilization was right to include all that he did, as I said, but most especially what he ends with; namely, human love. When all the confusion settles, when the hypocrisy in human history admitted, when the heartaches past belief faced, despite the swarming multiplicity and the cosmos itself contradicting our love, when the proof of the pasta is tasted and told, our human love is still there. So to go from the oldest piece of literature known to us to my postmodern computer, I would like now to state what is absolutely central to this work—but I needn't, you already know it all too well, and yes, that's it lock, stock, and hammerclavier! The whole of it!

Ludwig von Beethoven said of his great fugues that they were *Zusammengestohen aus Verschiedenem diesem und jenem—pilferings from one thing or another*. Of course though his humor was shining through in this, in the fugues themselves we know it was the very outcry of a human being trying to reach through, through it all. Like Ludwig I should make known, with the laughter of one having no fear of exposing himself—naked to ridicule, especially to those with ice in their laughter—that I too have used pilferings, distilling this finale from one previous chapter or another that went before, from afterthoughts and perhaps non-thoughts, trying to reach through, through it all, through my own outcry and the outcry of being human that each of us bears if not bares. No, I am not Beethoven, nor was meant to be; but instead full of high sentences and a bit obtuse, at times almost ridiculous—if I might pilfer from T. S. and my own ridiculous venture. A venture when all is said and done that should have been called no doubt *my all too human confessions*. Or maybe just *love striving to know*! Then again perhaps, *wisdom after the big bang!* But no matter what I titled it, the truth and masterstroke of the work would remain and remains the same; namely, our minimal certainty, what is fundamentally present to each person, and the deepest experience in that presence.

From that, like Ludwig, I, and dare I say you with me in your own presence, hoped to stretch to a Presence beyond mine or yours, one that I and you yet sense at the core of my own and your own, and with that write our own fugue, our own daodejing, our own simple summa, realizing what cannot be told, the gate to all mystery, incomprehensible and beyond, oh yes so incomprehensible and so beyond, yet mysteriously known to us, intimately and directly. At least if I had my way. One we give a name, a name which we already know before we do, because we know the depths of our own selves, for the Mystery that made us tells us in the gift of our own existence what It is in those depths, in that deepest level of our being, in our love. At least if my love had its way. Yes, if I had it my way and love had it its way. God is not Strange or a Stranger as long as this is so; and we are not estranged to either God or ourselves.

We have come to the end of our venture, and in ending this sojourn, I will and can say that life is not an illusion, though a confusion. It is a fugue, a poem, a play, an aria into the wind and about it, too. But it is not coming from nowhere. *I am and I can love* rings out of each of us! It is life-affirming and life's very own affirmation! Though we might feel like twilit visitations to ourselves at times, wandering in the fog and drifts, just trying to breathe, let alone sing in the fractal gusts, uncertain where we are even headed, the moment is never empty—as long we never commit the unforgivable sin of denying we are there. There and able to love, despite it all.

In that, we have our deepest and most authentic moment, one that gives us a way to be fully human, found in our very incarnation. *Found in our very incarnation!* One that allows us to dare, notwithstanding our postmodern jitters, to venture into—into what? Into love at its most profound depths, knowing like we know nothing else that if God is anything, God should be love, and we say that because we know love like we know nothing else. But is God love? Or am I a foolish person in the face of everything? A failed philosopher, a theologian chasing my own tail, and finally a complete clown? No matter, isn't love the sweetest and most beautiful madness that ever was, because it is always fighting for what *should* be? Yes! And yes again! And yes again after that! So, if God is anything, God should be love. On this I am right, even if I am wrong.

But am I wrong? Of course, that is for each of us to answer for ourselves as we make our journey across time, hopefully along the way experiencing love, for it is in that giving of ourselves we do realize there is more to all this. And what is more still, that somehow in that thin whisper within there is a thunder that confronts the cosmos with its revelation. It is a simple invitation, yet an insight that shakes the very inscape of our being. It turns everything upside down, in the truest of revolutions, in the real revelation, and in that realizes . . . hopefully some Mystery at the depth of that giving. No, every tear will not be wiped away from our eyes, nor shall death or the mourning because of death, nor the morning after death, nor the outcry out of life itself, an outcry in each of us and everywhere. And that has to give us pause. But despite it all and all the rest, love's revelation is still there, still there to be found in life itself, my own and ever other, the insight and invite still there, to be answered by me and you and each of us.

"But God—what of God?" I hear you cry.

God?
Daylight or night dark,
Built of a chance-query
Self-quarried
Echo-of-earth and pasta pursuit?
A riverrun of sister, mother, father,
Dogs, birds, a grandpa and what?
God manic, God depressant,
Or is it just life alone that speaks?
Foreword fumbling
Trust taken and ending in a lie?
And I too old and too alone for words,
Thinking up a better world than exists?
And I too old and too alone ending with a sigh,
Thinking up covenants that never were?
No matter, the lesson of love is still there.

Does God matter in the world—perhaps only to remind us to love. And in that alone God is not complete Other. But again intimate, even as beyond and so different than the nature of things. All this is as weak as an argument from authority, the weakest of all arguments, unless you yourself love. That is the strongest argument and proof and realization of this book. I cannot think you there; this is merely an antipasto to the pasta.

Again, humbly, with the hesitancy of being human, and always with the chance that I along with you are both as mad as the Hatter by just being human, I have offered this deepest encounter with our existence for your pondering, and perhaps on some rainy night, a bag lady will come in out of the same night we all inhabit and you, too, wearing a Mona Lisa smile, will send a bowl of soup over to her, whispering what each of us can within, whether with words or wordlessly, *I am and I can love*. If there is anything to this book, it is that. *I am and I can love*. This is my synthesis and my soul, the synthesis and soul of a purely human spirituality. With that, I myself alone end my venture with a thankfulness still tinged with hesitation, hesitation because of a possibility that tells me I am such stuff as dreams are made on, and my little life is to be rounded with a little death, unnoticed in the cosmos, that tells me that I am nothing more than a psychic crystallization around an abyss, alive to a universe, a world, an existence without ultimate grounding—afloat in the face of just what happens, at the mercy of chance, chaos, or the universal contingency, alone alas along the riverrun with my lonely love. Perhaps, we conscious creatures cannot face that, because it is too awful. And yet, the opposite is true as well, with me-myself-and-I saying yes to a part of the human venture within me that bares and bears a thankfulness still tinged with hesitation, yes, but one alive to a transcendence past the dissecting of thought, and tears, too, past a hopeless loving into one of radiant joy. Of course, it could all be just a piece of music. Which is not to say that there is not a very real choice involved, simply said a choice to be on the side of love, to live love, aided by a whisper within me, as words fall off the page, telling me there is more to it, and maybe More, too, as if out of a forever that is not mine, yet is, and I moved by a love that moves the sun and other stars. It is into that moment, into that more, always guided by the truest and deepest experience in my being, my human love, I say yes there can be a coherence here of the profoundest attitude towards life and I leap, dive, plunge, plunge, dive, leap into love, give my heart to the ellipsis that is giving, and enjoying my own soup send soup over to the bag lady, *realizing God . . .*

> Either that, or I am too old and too alone for words.
> And yet we are creatures of words.
> I fear, my hopeless heart,
> What might be
> Or not be
> For blind children shake me to my soul
> And the brutal birth of monsters makes me cringe
> At what might be
> Or not be
> The horror and the havoc
> Of what we call creation
> The giant groan following
> A God gone from the horizon
> Of head and worse the heart.
>
> And yet . . . and yet
> I love
> Love the God gone still
> Consciousness what an incredible gift
> Organic matter aware!
> Aware of the giving of itself

Until it can give no more
No More?
And is left
Left to what?
I fear, my hopeless heart,
Too old, and too alone for words.

Remote abysses do not give shelter to the soul.
Look at me, Mystery, if you are love.
For I am alone and alone.
But there is no Impossible
Not even a providence to rough-hew.
Fault-filled ready for asunder
This make-shift make-do me
This potsherd presence without his shaggy shadow
Sans sister, brother, family and friend,
With only requiem in his eyes and no magic,
With nothing overwhelming, earthshaking,
Unmistakable, but only simply human love,
Simple human love that turns out to be
Hopeless loving and nothing more or More.

And yet, and yet . . .
The proof of the pasta finally tasted,
Tasted only in that love, and so left
To crave and carve an outlet
In the hesitant heart and head both,
And choose, determine, decide to live,
Knowing everything argues against a God of love
But love itself, and maybe that most of all,
Waking me to a winter and warmth
I do not understand still,
Still and though, in spite of and despite,
With "we were hoping" still stuck in my throat
And heart and head, in the very marrow of my bones
Yet so choose, determine, decide to live
Knowing who knows what
No matter, in matter, on the side of love
And asked and it was given
Knocked and it was opened

Sought and it was found
Jesus did not lie
How do I begin and what do I say?
Love was asked for and giving today.
The Mystery work invisible shown bright
Te Deum
And trenchant radiance became
A warm embrace
I was not buried alive
But for a time in space and a space in time
Knew through the drift of time and solid space
A wordless touch of happy tears
And I was not too old and too alone for words . . .
For I am and can love . . . Love

Notes

Introduction

[1]   The Mysterious More is what I often use instead of God, though I will also use the word God, along with the Mystery that made us, Incomprehensible Intimacy, et cetera.

[2]   I want to pay tribute to Loren Eiseley with regards my sense of evolution and, as well, Steven Gould with regards to a sense of chancy and historical contingency, at least as I understand him to mean; namely, as two levels of the same process, and not a contradiction at all as some would have.

One Minimal Certainty Please!

[1]   If interested CF Lilly Tomlin's play, *The Search for Signs of Intelligent Life in the Universe;* and for Karl Popper *Objective Knowledge. An Evolutionary Approach*

[2]   *Inferno*, Dante, my translation, Canto II, line 3

[3]   "Out of the Blue" page 9, Seed Magazine, March 22, 2009

[4]   *Hamlet*, William Shakespeare, Act I, scene V, lines 165-167

[5]   From a talk at CSUN 2009

[6]   *Man's Search For Meaning*, Viktor Frankl, New York, Washington Square Press, 1965 p 212

[7]   *The Man Who Mistook His Wife for a Hat*, Oliver Sacks, New York, Summit Books, 1985, p 36

[8]   *The Man Who Mistook His Wife for a Hat*, Oliver Sacks, New York, Summit Books, 1985, pp 37-38

[9] *The Man Who Mistook His Wife for a Hat*, Oliver Sacks, New York, Summit Books, 1985, p 199

[10] *The Man Who Mistook His Wife for a Hat*, Oliver Sacks, New York, Summit Books, 1985, p 140

[11] *The Undiscovered Mind*, John Horgan, New York, Free Press, 1999, p 69

[12] *The Mind's New Science*, Howard Gardner, New York, Basic Books, 1985; CF also, *The Undiscovered Mind*, John Horgan, New York, Free Press, 1999, p 72-73

[13] *Psychoanalysis and Neuroscience*, Wyman and Rittenberg, New York, Basic Books, 1992, p 332

[14] Mazziotta, interview in the *LA Times*, July 2, 2001, A 12

[15] In his book *A Leg To Stand On*, New York, 1987, Perennial Library

[16] *Scientific Autobiography and Other Papers*, Max Planck, Santa Barbara, CA, 1968, pp 33-34

[17] *Man's Search For Meaning*, Viktor Frankl, New York, 1961, Washington Square Press, pp 58-59

[18] *Man's Search For Meaning*, Viktor Frankl, New York, 1961, Washington Square Press, p 131

[19] *The Star Thrower*, Loren Eiseley, New York, 1978, p 309

[20] *Shadows of the Mind*, Roger Penrose, Oxford University Press, Oxford, 1994 pp 48-53; 64-65

[21] Without writing a book about it as Penrose so aptly did, let me merely state what interests me is exactly that; namely, as Penrose points out, the human intuition cannot be reduced to a formula, but rather has a freedom about it that simply cannot be put into a cage, category, or algorithm. And this from a mathematician! *Shadows of the Mind*, Roger Penrose, Oxford University Press, 1994, pp 50; 64-65

[22] *What Is Called Thinking?* Martin Heidegger, New York, 2004, Perennial, p 202

[23] "A New Refutation of Time," *Labyrinths,* Jorge Luis Borges, A New Directions Book, 1964, p 234.

[24] *Treatise*, David Hume, Oxford, L. A. Selby-Bigge edition, 1051, I, I, 4, pp 10-13

[25] *The Varieties Of Religious Experience*, William James, New York, 1961, Collier Books, p 138

[26] *Quest*, V. Virom Coppola, Xlibris, 2004. This is the book referred to; and the phrase "I am and I can love" is first mentioned and established in it.

[27] Again in the flesh and blood encounter already mentioned

[28] Rene Descartes, *Meditationes de prima philosophia in Quibus Dei existential, et animae humanae a corpore distinctio, demonstrantur*, Paris, 1641. The quotation is from the Synopsis prefaced to the Meditations, AT VII, 12.

[29] Ionesco, *The Exploding Stage*, Norris Houghton, New York, 1971, A Delta Book, p 150.

[30] Charlie Rose TV show with Stephan Gould as his guest

[31] Even Thomas Aquinas, stuck in the middle ages, sensed this peculiarity of our being, and struggled to express it, equating the fact of actually being and essence. He says that the *id quod est* (that which is), the *ens* (the being) can participate in something more than its isness, *scilicet praeter suam essentiam*. Here, Thomas equates a concrete being's isness and essence. He is talking about *id quod est* having something beyond *(praeterquam)* itself, its isness or *essentia*. He writes: *"consequens est verum esse quod hic diciture, quod 'id est est, potest aliquid habere, praeterquam quod ipsum est,' scilicet praeter suam essentiam . . ."* *(consequently it is true to say what this said above, that 'that which is, can have something, beyond, except that of its isness (that it is); namely, beyond (more than) its essence).* He is saying here that *essentia* (essence) is the way of saying the is (isness) of a being. This gives him a very interesting insight all the way back in the Middle Ages into a very modern notion of existence with regards the self—your existence is your essence at its innermost being; upon which you add a life's journey of choices which fashion the completion of that self into your own final creation of the being you are. Of course, Thomas did not put it that way, but he certainly seems to have that insight in the above quote from his *Expositio De Hebdomadibus*, page 174.

[32] *"siblings of the same dark night,"* is a quote from John Caputo, *A Passion for the Impossible*, edited by Mark Dooley, State University of New York Press, 2003, p. xvii. The quote that precedes it, as mentioned from Sir K. R. Popper, *Logik der Forschung*, p. xxv.

[33] *What Is Called Thinking?* Martin Heidegger, New York, 2004, Perennial, p 71.

[34] *Ordinatio* II, d.3.p1.q 2,n. 48; *Ordinatio* 2, d.c, pars 1, qq. 1-6, Duns Scotus.

[35] *Autobiography*, Bertrand Russell, George Allen & Unwen, UK, 1967, Prologue.

[36] *De Natura Decorum*, Cicero

[37] *The Man Who Saw Through Time*, Loren Eiseley, New York, 1973, Charles Scribner's Sons, p 60

[38] *The Man Who Saw Through Time*, Loren Eiseley, New York, 1973, Charles Scribner's Sons, p 87

[39] The quote is either Alan Mcglashan as Loren Eiseley says; or Albert Einstein's as other sources state.

[40] The Invisible Pyramid, Loren Eiseley, New York, 1970, Charles Scribner's Sons, p 145.

[41] The full quote is "Nietzsche could deny any form of transcendence, whether moral or divine, by saying that transcendence drove one to slander this world and this life. But perhaps there is a living transcendence, of which beauty

carries the promise, which can make this mortal and limited world preferable to and more appealing than any other." *The Rebel*, Albert Camus, New York, 1956, Vintage Books, p 258

[42] *Lady Windermere's Fan*, 1892, Act III

[43] *The Invisible Pyramid*, Loren Eiseley, New York, 1970, Charles Schibner's Sons, p 119

[44] Somewhere in my mind I want to attribute these words to Einstein and associate them with him, but I have never been able to find such a source for that.

[45] *Aus dem Nachlass der achtziger Jahre*, F. Nietzsche, in Werke III, p 661; "Revelations of all Values" in the Unpublished Material of the Eighties, Schlechta's edition.

[46] *Sex As God Intended*, John McNeill, Maple Shade, NJ, Lethe Press, 2008, p 44

[47] *Sex As God Intended*, John McNeill, Maple Shade, NJ, Lethe Press, 2008, p 58

[48] *Sex As God Intended*, John McNeill, Maple Shade, NJ, Lethe Press, 2008, p 60

[49] *Meditations* 2.15, Marcus Aurelius

[50] *Man's Search For Meaning*, Viktor Frankl, New York, 1963, Washington Square Press, 1963. All the quotes are taken from the following pages; p 48, p 104, pp 58-59, p 64, p 131.

[51] *Points . . . Interviews, 1974-1994*, Jacques Derrida, ed. Elisabeth Weber, trans. Peggy Kamuf, Stanford, 1995, Stanford University Press, p 83

[52] *"For the Love of the Things Themselves, Derrida's Hyper-Realism,"* John Caputo, July 2000, *Journal for Cultural and Religious Theory*, 1.3

[53] *Love Among The Deconstructibles*, John Caputo, JCRT 5.2 April 2004, p 44

[54] *Love Among The Deconstructibles*, John Caputo, JCRT 5.2 April 2004, p 47

[55] *Jacques Derrida "Circumfession,"* J. Derrida and Geoffrey Bennington, Chicago, 1993, Chicago University Press, p 34

[56] *Love Among The Deconstructibles*, John Caputo, JCRT 5.2 April 2004, p 55

[57] *Love Among The Deconstructibles*, John Caputo, JCRT 5.2 April 2004, p 52

[58] *Philosophy and Theology*, John Caputo, Nashville, 2006, Abingdon Press, p 39.

[59] *Philosophy and Theology*, John Caputo, Nashville, 2006, Abingdon Press, p 55.

[60] *The Afterlife Experiments* Gary E Schartz, New York, 2002, Pocket Book, p 267

[61] *What Is Called Thinking?* Martin Heidegger, New York, 2004, Perennial, p 202. I kept his translation of the Greek except for "needful"—I still hold the Greek is that and not "useful."

[62] Translation mine.

[63] *Quest*, V Virom Coppola, Philadelphia, 2004, Xlibris, p 84.

[64] Translation mine.

[65] *Quest*, V Virom Coppola, Philadelphia, 2004, Xlibris, pp 151-152.

[66] *"The Case For Tragic Optimism,"* a postscript to *Man's Search For Meaning*, V. Frankl, New York 1985, Pocket Books, p 178. ("The Case For Tragic Optimism", a postscript to Man's Search for Meaning, Viktor Frankl, New York, 1985, Pocket Books, p 178)

[67] Translation mine.

[68] *The Language Of God*, Francis S. Collins, New York, 2006, Free Press, p 125.

[69] *The Undiscovered Mind*, John Horgan, New York, 1999, The Free Press, p 178

[70] *The Moral Animal*, Robert Wright, New York, 1994, Vintage Books, pp 324-325

[71] *The Emperor's New Mind*, Roger Penrose, Oxford, 1989, Oxford University Press, p 408

[72] *Why We Get Sick: The New Science of Darwinian Medicine*, Randolph Nesse and George Williams, Times Books, 1994

[73] *The Moral Animal*, Robert Wright, New York, 1994, Vintage Books, p 344

[74] *The Moral Animal*, Robert Wright, New York, 1994, Vintage Books, p 11

[75] *The Moral Animal*, Robert Wright, New York, 1994, Vintage Books, p 10

[76] *The Moral Animal*, Robert Wright, New York, 1994, Vintage Books, p 12

[77] *The Moral Animal*, Robert Wright, New York, 1994, Vintage Books, p 14

[78] *The Moral Animal*, Robert Wright, New York, 1994, Vintage Books, p 15

[79] *The Moral Animal*, Robert Wright, New York, 1994, Vintage Books, p 169

[80] *Introduction to the Phenomenon of Man*, Julian Huxley, New York, 1975, Harper Colophon Books, p 16

[81] *How The Leopard Changed Its Spots, The Evolution of Complexity*, Brian Goodwin, Charles Scribner& Sons, 1994, pp 235-237

[82] *The Astonishing Hypothesis*, Francis Crick, Charles Scribner's Sons, New York, 1994, p 3.

[83] *The Undiscovered Mind*, John Horgan, The Free Press, New York, 1999, p 237

[84] In his autobiography, this is what he said his mother said to him when he revealed that he was worried that by the time he grew up everything would have already been discovered.

[85] *How The Mind Works*, Steven Pinker, New York, 1997, W. W. Norton & Company, p 175

[86] *The Undiscovered Mind*, John Horgan, The Free Press, New York, 1999, p 185

[87] *The End Of Science*, John Horgan, New York, 1997, Broadway Books, p 151

[88] *How The Mind Works*, Steven Pinker, New York, 1997, W. W. Norton & Company, p 521

[89] *The Undiscovered Mind*, John Horgan, The Free Press, New York, 1999, p 197

[90] *How The Mind Works*, Steven Pinker, New York, 1997, W. W. Norton & Company, p 524

[91] *How The Mind Works*, Steven Pinker, New York, 1997, W. W. Norton & Company, p 534

[92] *How The Mind Works*, Steven Pinker, New York, 1997, W. W. Norton & Company, p 538

[93] *How The Mind Works*, Steven Pinker, New York, 1997, W. W. Norton & Company, p 561

[94] *How The Mind Works*, Steven Pinker, New York, 1997, W. W. Norton & Company, p 564

[95] *How The Mind Works*, Steven Pinker, New York, 1997, W. W. Norton & Company, p 565

[96] *How The Mind Works*, Steven Pinker, New York, 1997, W. W. Norton & Company, p 565

[97] *The Undiscovered Mind*, John Horgan, The Free Press, New York, 1999, p 250

[98] *The Beginning of All Things*, Hans Kung, Cambridge, UK, 2008, William B. Eerdmans Publishing Company, p 176

[99] *The Amazing Brain,* Robert Orstein and Richard F. Thompson, Boston, 1986, Houghton Mifflin Company pp 29-30

[100] *The Amazing Brain,* Robert Orstein and Richard F. Thompson, Boston, 1986, Houghton Mifflin Company, pp 30-31

[101] *The Beginning of All Things*, Hans Kung, Cambridge, UK, 2008, William B. Eerdmans Publishing Company, p 176

[102] *"Das Manifest, Uber Gegenwart und Zukunft der Hirnforschung," Gehirn und Geist, Das Magazin fur Psyhologie und Hirnforschung*, June, 2004, pp 30-37.

[103] *The Meme Machine*, Susan Blackmore, Oxford, 2000, Oxford University Press, pp 241-242, 231, and quoted as well in *Christ In Postmodern Philosophy*, Frederiek Depoortere, London, 2008, T&T, p 81.

[104] *The Beginning of All Things*, Hans Kung, Cambridge, UK, 2008, William B. Eerdmans Publishing Company, p 180

[105] There are so many different views from scientists on what *deep reality* is. Here in brief and therefore lacking the subtleties and nuances they might deserve, for those interested, are the different schools of thought about *deep reality* that come out of the particle/wave description controversy, as well as those proposing what might be before the universe was:

a) There is no deep reality, the observer's consciousness creates reality; that reality comes straight out of consciousness. It depends upon the measuring, so it cannot be ascribed to the object independent of the measuring device and the act of measuring. David Mermin tired to express it with the words: "The Moon really isn't there if you don't look at it." But, of course, they never answer what the thing doing all this is, consciousness itself.

b) Reality is created out of both, the observer and the object, but as such reality cannot be made out of objects having innate attributes, it is still conscious-generated. For this school, one's own conscious mind is again the basic reality, and the things in the world 'out there' are not much more than useful constructs built out of one's own past experiences, somehow coded into one's consciousness. The famous Schrodinger's Cat is the colorful and celebrated thought experiment famous or infamous to this school. Of which, Hawking, paraphrasing a German General, said, "When I hear of Schrodinger's Cat, I reach for my gun."

c) Reality is a choice. Because the very act of choosing is always involved in what we measure. In this view, meaning rests on action, which means decisions, which in turn decide the answers. However the criticism of their position is one of who does the choosing if they, as they do, do not invoke consciousness as a prerequisite? In fact, say it must not be.

d) Reality consists of potentiality and actuality both. But what is underlying everything is pure potentiality. So the unmeasured world literally is—and is a world unrealized potential. Yet, it cannot be seen as anything other than a kind of dreamlike mirage waiting to be awakened into actuality. Yet actuality itself is a physical fiction but incomprehensible as such because we could not possibly comprehend what it could possibly be like to live in a world of pure potentiality. One has to wonder then were one does live? Perhaps in Zero's tub and the ontological madness he proposed.

e) There is a universe for every possible observation, each of them equally real, and anything that can happen does happen. This is sort of the opposite of the above; and although not in Zero's tub, it leaves us wandering Esher's stairway, these particular scientist assuring us there are a plethora of other stairs out there we could also wander. But for what purpose they cannot say, just that there is no observer problem here—everything and anything goes.

f) Deep reality exists whether we observe it or not and so there must be a hidden variable, which when known, gives us the single possibility.

g) Quantum objects have real attributes, are real, but the logic of knowing them is just different from that we normally use—a nonstandard type of logic is needed to understand deep reality. But it really offers no help in scaling this impasse.

h)   An ordinary-reality interpretation of quantum reality is possible. Reality is undivided wholeness connected by 'pilot' waves—a pilot wave in effect tells a particle how to move and is undetectable, but real; a quantum object is to composed of a single 'thing'—particle or wave, but both part of reality . . . the wave not a wave of matter!!! . . . in a phenomenon of non-locality. So what exactly is it?

i)   Reality is a wave function traveling both backwards and forward in time. The point is that it is explicitly nonlocal and as such the future is in some way affecting the present and the past, at least in so far as it enforces correlations between quantum events. It involves real entities that are unobserved and superluminal transfers of information. The startling results of the Bell Interconnectedness checks in here. We can't get into the pages upon pages it would take to explain that, but in short, it starts with the puzzling EPR paradox we have already seen and works on to say to say to all the scientists that you can have either locality or objectivity but not both which means you have to sacrifice locality to keep your objective worldview with its hidden variables. Superluminal connections are required. Even so, the Bell himself opted for an objective reality.

j)   The universe is rooted in superstrings out of which comes mass and an explanation of our elusive elemental particle. It starts with a 10 dimension make up that curls in six and leaves us our four dimension and the universe we know, except not as a space of points, but a new vision of space, with vibrating, rotating strings or extensions, very short extensions, where-in bosons and fermions become unified while, at the same time, remaining separate. Fermons make up the material side of the universe, while bosons are responsible for its forces. This has given birth to many string and superstring theories, some even comparing it to a holographic image, or a shadow universe hovering along with our own; reality changing according to which superstring you might fancy.

k)   The universe is rooted in twistors out of which come mass and an explanation of our elusive elemental particle. In fact, the twistors have their own twistor space where everything is reduced to geometry, a space not built out of points at all, but of twisting congruences created out of straight null lines, which are the tracks taken by massless particles which move at the speed of light, in a world of complex dimensions which is the primordial space of the first elementary particles. Mass is secondary to the whole process. Penrose, the initiator of this, uses not the mainstream of particle physics, but the fields of relativity and the mathematics of complex spaces, using complex analysis in math along with cohomology to achieve his abstract world in which quantum theory and relativity meet. Nonlocality turns out to be essential, for in the world of twistor theory the whole idea of points are replaced by nonlocal descriptions, in which a point is really nonlocal in its deeper nature, explained merely as at intersection of twistors which must be perceived from a global perspective. Space-time itself appears to be fundamentally nonlocal. So twistors can be thought of as generalizations of light rays or null lines and are defined by complex numbers, in a helicity or 'spin' of a massless object which can be positive, negative, or zero, and as zero look exactly like rays of light in space-time. However, twistors real home is twistor space. Penrosegive us a map of reality where our familiar space-time may not be the background where the elementary particles play out their lives, but the opposite, where quantum systems define their own space-times.

l) It is all a combination of both twistors and superstrings, with twistors as the starting point (excuse the expression in this case) of superstrings which in turn give us the elementary particle, et cetera.

m) The membrane version is one that states that space may extent into unseen or invisible dimensions, and our world trapped in that. Instantons, alpha vacua, and multidimensional membranes wrap around one another, traveling through blackness and bounce back, transformed, but beyond our perception. What a brane is said to be, is a break in space-time, a border where two different dimensions meet. It seems to be sort of reflections of some inner geometry according to one of its greatest proponents—no not Pythagoras or Plato—Joe Polchinski, who determined through mathematics that branes were a surface to which things attach, and were in this case the fundamental ingredients of the universe. Physics has to answer to nature as we know, so this whole idea of membranes is still only a mathematical construct. But Polchinski believes that branes are real. However, that is faith not science when the shouting stops; and he admits as much: "It is possible that nature doesn't work that way," he told the *LA Times* reporter, K. C. Cole, writing about branes. "But it's so rich with possibilities, if it's not good for this, it's probably good for something else." But even if branes are not real, a man named Carroll (Sean not Lewis) said, "they will have taught us a useful lesson that we should have known all along, which is that we don't have a clue to what's going on." I think that sums it up perfectly.

If this interests you further, you can pursue it in *Paradigms Lost*, John L. Casti, Chapter 7, as well as, *Quantum Theory and Measurement*, J. A. Wheeler and W. Zurek, eds. Princeton, NJ, Princeton Press, 1983; Wheeler's "Beyond the Black Hole" in *Some Strangeness in the Proportion,* H. Woolf, ed, pp 341-375; *The Universe in a Nutshell*, by Stephen Hawking, p 46; *A Brief History of Time*, Stephen Hawking, Bantam Books, 1988, p 174; The Emperor's New Mind, Oxford University Press, Oxford, 1989, p 327.

[106] *Man's Search For Meaning*, Viktor Frankl, Washington Square Press, 1963. p 131

[107] *A Passion for the Impossible*, edited by Mark Dooley, State University of New York Press, New York, 2003. John Caputo uses the notion of obligation, and Edith Wyschogrod the notion of "without whom" on page 303-304.

[108] *Prayers and Tears of Jacques Derrida,* John Caputo, Bloomington, Indiana University Press, 1997, p 333.

[109] I am playing off of what Caputo says about us not knowing who we are. Of course we don't know all about us, but in the factical and fractical of it all, live still gives us a foundation, and not one based on faith. To deny one's self-being is the unforgivable sin, for you then do indeed have nothing to go on, and can never either really love or know love. We—each of us—know 'I am and I can love'—existence and the deepest experience in existence. That is there for us.

[110] *Inferno*, Dante, XXIII, 37-41

[111] *Sonnet* XXIII, Shakespeare, lines 14-15 It is the 400th Anniversary of Shakespeare's Sonnets, which were dedicated to a W. H.—who seems to be The Earl of Southampton, an intimate and seeming lover of the Bard. The recent discovery of the beautiful painting of Shakespeare (done while he was alive) was found in the Earl of Southampton's collection in Ireland and only solidifies the Sonnet connection and now the painting, as well as actual notes to the Earl saying he loved him. Shakespeare was 46 around the time of the painting. It is a much better rendition of the Bard than any other.

[112] *Corinthians*, 13

[113] *Man's Search For Meaning*, Viktor Frankl, Washington Square Press, 1963. pp 58-59; 64

[114] *Sonnet* CXVI, Shakespeare, lines 14-15

[115] *Beyond Good and Evil*, Friedrich Nietzsche, trans. Marianne Cowan, Chicago 1965, A Gateway Edition, p viii

[116] Isaac Bashevis Singer, as quoted by his grandson, Stephen R. Dujack, in an article in *The Los Angeles Times*, April 21.

[117] *The Brothers Karamazov*, Fyodor Dostoyevsky, trans. Constance Garnett, New York 1957 A Signet Classic, pp 292-314

[118] *Coldplay*

[119] *Thus Spoke Zarathustra*, Friedrich Nietzsche, section 2.

[120] *The Tiger,* William Blake

[121] *On Being A Christian*, Hans Kung, trans Edward Quinn, New York, 1984, Image Books, p 429

[122] *God After Darwin*, John F. Haught, Westwiew Press, 2000, p 20

[123] *The Varieties of Religious Experience,* by William James, Collier Books, New York, 1961, p 138

[124] *The Rebel*, Albert Camus, New York 1956, Vintage Books, p 303

[125] *the desperate encounter between our human inquiry and the silence of the universe,* my translation of a sentence from Camus' *The Rebel*; whether it is a correct translation, it says it the way I wish to.

[126] *Les Prix Nobel*, Stockhom 1994, Nobel Foundation

[127] Jackie Gleason

[128] *Beauty*, John O'Donohue, New York, 2004, Perennial, p 212.

[129] *Autobiography*, Bertrand Russell, London 1971, Unwin, p 149.

Stopover at a Cave

[1] This is a segment of an unpublished novel of mine called *Wisdom After The Big Bang*.

Tying the air together

[1] *Stephen Hawking's Universe*, John Boslough, New York, 1989, Avon Books, p 46

[2] *The Fabric Of The Cosmos*, Brian Greene, New York, 2004, Vintage Books, p 393

[3] *The Fabric Of The Cosmos*, Brian Greene, New York, 2004, Vintage Books, p 400

[4] *The Fabric Of The Cosmos*, Brian Greene, New York, 2004, Vintage Books, p 471

[5] *The First Three Minutes: A Modern View of the Origin of the Universe*, Steven Weinberg, New York, 1977, Basic Books, p 154-155

[6] Although these are my own translations of Augustine's phrases, I would highly recommend the following books if one is interested in Augustine.

Both Garry Wills' books are excellent, *Saint Augustine*, a Lipper/Viking Book, 1999; and his *Confessions*, a Penguin Classics, 2006. Also for a wide study of Augustine, *Augustine Through the Ages*, general editors, Allan D Fitzgerald, John C. Cavadini, a Wm, B. Eerdman Publishing, 1999. There is also *Confessions, St. Augustine*, translation by Frank Sheed, Haccet, Indianapolis, 1970.

[7] *Waiting For Godot*, Beckett, Act II, p 58 (Evergreen edition)

[8] *Waiting For Godot*, Beckett, Act II, p 56 (Evergreen edition)

[9] *Waiting For Godot*, Beckett, Act II, p 59 (Evergreen edition)

[10] *Waiting For Godot*, Beckett, Act I, p 16 (Evergreen edition)

[11] *Process & Reality*, A. N. Whitehead, 1960, New York, Cambridge University Press, p 520-521

[12] Belief and belove. In *Wilfred Cantwell Smith, A Reader*, edited by Kenneth Cracknell, "The English Word 'Believe'" Chapter 13, pp 127-137, Smith equates the two in an etymological delving into Old English, *leof, liof, lufu*, as well as Wycliffe's usage of *bilefe* and German *belieben*, stating that, "The word 'believe', then, began its career in early Modern English meaning "to belove", "to regard as life"; then going on to ultimately showing how faith and belief came to mean the same thing in our contemporary usage, which is the opposite of belove. I prefer to stay in the contemporary usage of the words, as well how Kierkegaard uses the word faith, and in turn, Caputo after him, where faith has no evidence for what you are holding, yet you accept it, leap into it, hold it dear even, but still with nothing to go on. For me, love is rooted in reality, so belove and belief are two very different approaches and meanings. If one wants to use *credo* as "I give my heart to," however, I have no quarrel, as long as it is understood in terms of love, and thus rooted in experience, which would still be opposite of believe in our present day understanding of the word; and also faith. Better not to confuse the issue and us belove and forget about belief and faith.

[13] *Meister Eckhart, The Essential Sermons, Commentaries, Treatises, and Defense*, Mahwah, NJ, 1981, Paulist Press; *Sermon 5b*

[14] "*The Case For Tragic Optimism*," a postscript to *Man's Search For Meaning*, V. Frankl, New York 1985, Pocket Books, p 178

[15] *Gita and Mahabharata*, A Mentor Book, New York, 1944, page 27.

[15] *Deuteronomy* 6:5.

[17] *Meister Eckhart, The Essential Sermons, Commentaries, Treatises, and Defense*, Mahwah, NJ, 1981, Paulist Press; *Sermon 16b (DW I, p 271); A Passion for the Impossible*, edited by Mark Dooley, State University of New York Press, New York, 2003, pp 311-312.

18 *Quest*, V. Virom Coppola, Xlibris, 2004, p 187. Nietzsche, *Antichrist* 31, in Werke II, p 1192, in English translation, pp 147-148
19 *Agamemnon*, Aeschylus
20 *Republic*, VII, Plato, 517, a, my translation
21 *Deutschland*, Gerard Manley Hopkins
22 Nietzsche, *Werke und Briefe. Historisch-Kritische Gessamtaausgaabe* V, p 471
(English Translation, Twenty German Poets, ed. Kaufmann, Random House, New York, 1962, p 143)
23 *The Exploding Stage*, Norris Houghton, New York, 1971, A Delta Book p 150
24 *The Rebel*, Albert Camus, New York, 1956, Vintage edition, p 11
25 *The Rebel*, Albert Camus, New York, 1956, Vintage edition, p 32
26 *The Crucified God*, Jurgen Moltmann, Minneapolis, 1993, Fortress Press, p 253
27 *Nietzsche, Werke und Briefe. Historisch-Kritische Gesamtausgabe* II, p 428 (E.T. *Twenty German Poets*, ed, transl and intro by Walter Kaufmann, Random House, p 143
28 *Thus Spoke Zarathustra*, Nietzsche, Baltimore, Maryland, Penguin Books, Book IV, p 267
29 This saying is unsourced in Nietzsche; it is however widely attributed to him, and even Frankl uses.
30 Rex, Cathleen Lewis, Nashville, 2008, Thomas Nelson, pp 230-237
31 *Darkness Visible*, William Styron, New York, 1990, Random House, p 66
32 *Darkness Visible*, William Styron, New York, 1990, Random House, p 81
33 Part I chapter 7, "*Vom Lersen und Schriben*" "*On Reading and Writing*"
34 *The Beginning of All Things*, Hans Kung, Cambridge, UK, 2008, William B. Eerdmans Publishing Company, pp 33-34
35 From an unpublished novel *Mary's Memories,* V. Virom Coppola, 2006.
36 Quoted by Frankl in *Man's Search for Meaning*, New York, 1963, Washington Square Press, p 30
37 *The Odyssey, A Modern Sequel*, Nikos Kazantzakis, New York, 1958, A Touchstone Book
38 *Gerard Manley Hopkins*, Paul Mariani, New York, 2008, Viking, p 414
39 *Gerard Manley Hopkins*, Paul Mariani, New York, 2008, Viking, p 428
40 Nietzsche, *Antichrist* 18, in Werke II, p 1178 (English translation, The Antichrist, New York/Harmondworth, 1968, p 128) and the Kazantzakis

notions from his *The Odyssey: A Modern Sequel*, Nikos Kazantzakis, trans. Kimon Friar, New York, 1958, Simon & Schuster, p xvii

41   *Hymne de l'Univers,* Pierre Teilhard de Chardin, New York, 1961, Harper & Row p 21

42   *Hymne de l'Univers,* Pierre Teilhard de Chardin, New York, 1961, Harper & Row p 33

43   *The Invisible Pyramid,* Loren Eiseley, New York, 1970, Charles Scribner's Sons, in this order, p 47

44   *The Invisible Pyramid,* Loren Eiseley, New York, 1970, Charles Scribner's Sons, in this order, p 47

45   *The Invisible Pyramid,* Loren Eiseley, New York, 1970, Charles Scribner's Sons, in this order, p 48

46   The phrase comes from *The Invisible Pyramid,* Loren Eiseley, New York, 1970, Charles Scribner's Sons, in this order, p 33

47   *The Invisible Pyramid,* Loren Eiseley, New York, 1970, Charles Scribner's Sons, in this order, p 46

48   Etienn Gilson, *Heloise and Abelard*, Ann Arbor Press, p 42. Also, Charlotte Charrier, *Heloise dans l'histoire et dans le legende*, and B. Schmeidler, *Der Breifwechsel Zwischen Abelard und Heloise eine Faschung?* XI, p 1-30

49   *Les Prix Nobel*, Stockholm 1994, Nobel Foundation

50   *The Revelation and the Covenant*, Martin Buber, 1988, Humanity Books, p 48

51   *Eclipse of God*, Martin Buber, New York, 1952, Harper & Brothers p 115

52   *The Serpent and the Rainbow*, Wade Davis, New York, 1985, Warner Books

53   Schopenhauer, *Die Welt als Wille und Vorstellung*, in Werke I, pp. 550-551 (English translation, *The World As Will*, Vol I, p 524)

54   *Rational Mysticism*, John Horgan, Boston, Houghton Mifflin Company, A Mariner Book, p 119

55   *Rational Mysticism*, John Horgan, Boston, Houghton Mifflin Company, A Mariner Book, p 128-129

56   *The End Of Science*, John Horgan, New York, 1997, Broadway Books, p 182

57   *Deut* 31:17-18; 32:20

58   Plato, *Phaedo,* 85c, tr. Harold North Fowler (London: Heinemann, 1914), quoted in Miller, God and Reason (New York: Macmillan, 1972), 233; also quoted by Loren Eiseley in The Unexpected Universe, New York, 1969, A Harvest/HBJ Book, p 21

59   *The New American Bible, Exodus* 3:14; *Qur'an* 50:16

Supermetaphysics

1   *Paradiso*, Dante, Canto XXXII, lines 139—my translation
2   If you are interested in what I have to say on Buddhism, confer my book *Quest*, pp 140-164.
3   *Meister Eckhart, The Essential Sermons, Commentaries, Treatises, and Defense*, Mahwah, NJ, 1981, Paulist Press; *Deutsche Schriften*, Bihlmeyer, Frankfurt, 1961, pp 352-357
4   *Meister Eckhart, The Essential Sermons, Commentaries, Treatises, and Defense*, Mahwah, NJ, 1981, Paulist Press; *blos vergotet.*
5   *Meister Eckhart, The Essential Sermons, Commentaries, Treatises, and Defense*, Mahwah, NJ, 1981, Paulist Press; Koch, *Weiterwirken*, p 139; see M. G. Sargent, "The Transmission by the English Carthusians of Some Late Medieval Spiritual Writings," *Journal of Ecclesiastical History 27*, (1976), pp 225-240
6   *Meister Eckhart, The Essential Sermons, Commentaries, Treatises, and Defense*, Mahwah, NJ, 1981, Paulist Press; B. M. Reichert, ed., Acta capitulorum generalium ordinis praedicatorum 2 (Momumentum ordinis fratrum praedicatorumh istorica 4 1889) p 258
7   *Sermon 83: Renovamini spiritu (E[. 4:23)* in *Meister Eckhart, The Essential Sermons, Commentaries, Treatises, and Defense*, Mahwah, NJ, 1981, Paulist Press, p 207
8   *Sermon 48: Ein meister sprichet: aliu glichiu dinc minnent sich under einander,* in *Meister Eckhart, The Essential Sermons, Commentaries, Treatises, and Defense*, Mahwah, NJ, 1981, Paulist Press, p 198
9   *Book of Causes*, prop 6, Aristotle
10 *Luke* 15:11-32
11 Both de Finance, *Etre et Subjectivite*, p 254, and *The Meaning of Love*, Robert Johann, p 89
12 *The Varieties of Religious Experience*, William James, New York, 1961, Collier Books, p 42

Journey's End

1   *Gilgamesh*, X, iii, Old Babylonian Version
2   *The Man Who Saw Through Time*, Loren Eiseley, New York, 1973, Charles Scribner's Sons, p 116

Index

Amor In Actu

Breinigsville, PA USA
01 July 2010
241009BV00001B/3/P